THE CONFEDERATION GROUP
OF CANADIAN POETS, 1880–1897

$65.00

*D.M.R. Bentley*

# THE CONFEDERATION GROUP
# OF CANADIAN POETS,
# 1880–1897

UNIVERSITY OF TORONTO PRESS
Toronto Buffalo London

© University of Toronto Press Incorporated 2004
Toronto Buffalo London
Printed in Canada

ISBN 0-8020-8739-6

Printed on acid-free paper

**National Library of Canada Cataloguing in Publication**

Bentley, D.M.R.
    The Confederation Group of Canadian poets, 1880–1897/D.M.R. Bentley.

    Includes bibliographical references and index.
    ISBN 0-8020-8739-6

    1. Canadian poetry (English) – 19th century – History and criticism.  I. Title.

PS8151.B45 2004      C811'.409      C2003-904451-3

The photographs reproduced herein are taken from the 1893 edition, with portraits, of *Later Canadian Poems*, edited by J.E. Wetherell, B.A. Toronto: The Copp, Clark Company, Ltd.

This book has been published with the help of a grant from the Canadian Federation for the Humanities and Social Sciences, through the Aid to Scholarly Publications Programme, using funds provided by the Social Sciences and Humanities Research Council of Canada.

University of Toronto Press acknowledges the financial assistance to its publishing program of the Canada Council for the Arts and the Ontario Arts Council.

University of Toronto Press acknowledges the financial support for its publishing activities of the Government of Canada through the Book Publishing Industry Development Program (BPIDP).

*For Suzie*
*and*
*Michael, Simon, and Diana*

# Contents

*Acknowledgments*   ix

*Notes on Dates, Quotations, and Citations*   xi

*Abbreviations*   xiii

INTRODUCTION   3

1 YOUNG CANADA: 1880–1884   24

2 CANADIANISM: 1885–1890   70

3 AESTHETICS: WORKMANSHIP AND VARIETY   111

4 NATURAL ENVIRONMENTS   145

5 THERAPEUTIC NATURE   177

6 SUPERNATURALISM   204

7 INTERNATIONAL AND NATIONAL RECOGNITION: 1889–1895   241

8 DISINTEGRATION   273

## AFTERMATH    291

*Notes*    299

*Works Cited*    363

*Index*    391

# Acknowledgments

The University of Western Ontario and the Social Sciences and Humanities Research Council of Canada have generously supported my research and writing on Canadian poetry for many years. An SSHRC Research Grant enabled me to undertake the research culminating in this book and an SSHRC subvention through the Aid to Scholarly Publications Programme assisted its publication. Western's support has come through the Department of English, the Faculty of Arts, and the Academic Development Fund, as well as through the superb staff of the D.B. Weldon Library and the energetic assistance of students in the Work Study Bursary program. To both institutions I owe a very great debt of gratitude.

I also owe thanks of different kinds and magnitudes to the many friends, colleagues, and graduate students at Western and elsewhere who have helped in a multitude of ways with the creation of this book: Jack Adams, Susan Birkwood, Laurel Boone, Wanda Campbell, Patricia Chalmers, David Clark, Tom Collins, Jim Doyle, Stan Dragland, Len Early, Fred Foy, Michael Gnarowski, Don Hair, Michele Holmgren, Ross Kilpatrick, Gerald Lynch, Elaine McInnis, Ian MacLaren, Nick Mount, Brandy Ryan, Amanda St Jean, Mark Savolis, Dick Stingle, Eleanor Surridge, Brian Trehearne, Tracy Ware, Joe Zezulka, and, especially, my indefatigable research assistant, Steven Artelle, and my endlessly patient editorial assistant, Kat Evans.

Siobhan McMenemy, Frances Mundy, and Ken Lewis of University of Toronto Press have my grateful thanks for their extremely thoughtful and meticulous handling of the manuscript. So too does Lisa Platt of Hothouse Canada for the design of its cover. The anonymous reviewers of the manuscript for the Press and for the ASPP provided me with much perceptive and constructive commentary for which I am also grateful.

My debt to the late Malcolm Ross for over three decades of support and advice is immense. He was looking forward to seeing this book, as I was to what I hoped would be his pleasure in it.

Finally, and as always, my greatest debt of gratitude is to my wife, Susan, and to our three children, Michael, Simon, and Diana. The book's dedication to them is but a feeble response to the ineffable blessing of their love, support, joy, and encouragement.

# Notes on Dates, Quotations, and Citations

To assist readers in obtaining a clear sense of chronological positions and relationships, and in locating poems for further study, the date of a poem's first appearance in a book by its author is given in parentheses after its title. The dates assigned to books are similarly those of first publication. When known and relevant, the birth and death dates of authors are given with the first mention of their name. Unless otherwise indicated, the compositional date(s) of poems are based on information in Desmond Pacey and Graham Adams's edition of Roberts's *Collected Poems*, L.R. Early's 'A Chronology of Lampman's Poems,' John Robert Sorfleet's edition of Carman's *Poems*, Laurel Boone's editions of Campbell's *Selected Poetry and Essays* and 'The Collected Poems of William Wilfred Campbell,' Robert L. McDougall's 'D.C. Scott: The Dating of the Poems' and Leon Slonim's 'A Critical Edition of the Poems of Duncan Campbell Scott,' and Frederick George Scott's notes in his *Collected Poems*.

To avoid making the list of works cited more cumbersome than it has to be, items in newspapers and periodicals that are minimally cited and quoted are identified by date and page in the text itself.

In prose quotations only, ampersands have consistently been rendered as 'and,' contractions have sometimes been expanded for clarity, and punctuation has occasionally been added or removed to avoid stylistic clumsiness.

# Abbreviations

Unpublished materials in Canadian university archives and special collections are cited by an abbreviation of the university's name (thus, DalU = Dalhousie University, McGU = McGill University, QU = Queen's University, SFU = Simon Fraser University, TCU = Trinity College University, UT = University of Toronto, VU = Victoria University, University of Toronto).

The following abbreviations of published works are used in parenthetical citations, footnotes, and notes:

*AC*      *An Annotated Edition of the Correspondence between Archibald Lampman and Edward William Thomson (1890–1898)*. Ed. Helen Lynn. Ottawa: Tecumseh, 1980.

*CL*      Charles G.D. Roberts. *Collected Letters*. Ed. Laurel Boone. Fredericton: Goose Lane, 1989.

*CP*      Charles G.D. Roberts. *Collected Poems*. Ed. Desmond Pacey and Graham Adams. Wolfville, NS: Wombat, 1985.

*CPFGS*      Frederick George Scott. *Collected Poems*. Vancouver: Clarke and Stuart, 1934.

*ER*      Archibald Lampman. *Essays and Reviews*. Ed. D.M.R. Bentley. London: Canadian Poetry Press, 1996.

*L*      Bliss Carman. *Letters*. Ed. H. Pearson Gundy. Kingston and Montreal: McGill-Queen's University Press, 1981.

*MI*      *At the Mermaid Inn: Wilfred Campbell, Archibald Lampman, Duncan Campbell Scott in 'The Globe,' 1892–93*. Ed. Barrie Davies. Literature of Canada: Poetry and Prose in Reprint. Toronto: University of Toronto Press, 1979.

*P*        Archibald Lampman. *Poems.* With a Memoir by Duncan Camp-
           bell Scott. Toronto: Morang, 1900.
*PBC*      Bliss Carman. *Poems.* Arranged by R.H. Hathaway. New York:
           Dodd, Mead, 1931.
*PDCS*     Duncan Campbell Scott. *Poems.* Toronto: McClelland and Stew-
           art, 1926.
*PP*       Bliss Carman. *Pipes of Pan.* Boston: L.C. Page, 1906.
*PWWC*     [William] Wilfred Campbell. *Poems.* Toronto: William Briggs,
           1905.
*SPCP*     Charles G.D. Roberts. *Selected Poetry and Critical Prose.* Ed. W.J.
           Keith. Literature in Canada: Poetry and Prose in Reprint.
           Toronto: University of Toronto Press, 1974.
*SPE*      William Wilfred Campbell. *Selected Poetry and Essays.* Ed. Laurel
           Boone. Waterloo: Wilfrid Laurier University Press, 1987.
*War*      *The War among the Poets: Issues of Plagiarism and Patronage among*
           *the Confederation Poets.* Ed. Alexandra J. Hurst. London: Cana-
           dian Poetry Press, 1994.

THE CONFEDERATION GROUP
OF CANADIAN POETS, 1880–1897

# Introduction

I

In the 27 April 1929 issue of the *McGill Fortnightly Review* (Montreal), F.R. Scott (1899–1985) published his now well-known attack on the Canadian Authors' Association, an organization founded in 1921 to promote the interests of Canadian writers. 'The air is heavy with Canadian topics,' begins the third stanza of 'The Canadian Authors Meet,' 'And Carman, Lampman, Roberts, Campbell, Scott, / Are measured for their faith and philanthropics, / Their zeal for God and King, their earnest thought' (*Collected Poems* 248). In the remainder of the poem, the five Confederation poets named by Scott – Bliss Carman (1861–1929), Archibald Lampman (1861–99), Charles G.D. Roberts (1860–1943), William Wilfred Campbell (1860–1918),[1] and Duncan Campbell Scott (1862–1947) – are associated with the principal objects of Scott's attack, 'new authors' so lacking in the High Modernist virtues of innovation and internationalism that they still aspire 'To paint the native maple, and ... to set the selfsame welkin ringing.' Such an association is not entirely unfair – Carman, Roberts, and Duncan Campbell Scott were themselves prominent members of the Canadian Authors' Association in 1929 – but it rests on a truncated and demeaning approach to Canada's literary and cultural history that simultaneously assimilates the principal Confederation poets to the Romantic-Victorian Revival of the 1920s and reduces them to exemplars of the Modernists' self-serving stereotypes of Victorian and colonial ideas and attitudes.[2] It is the purpose of the essays in this book to cast fresh light on the Confederation poets and their work by revisiting the literary and cultural milieu of late nineteenth-century Canada in which they lived, thought, wrote, and came together as a group whose existence has more frequently been assumed than its characteristics, dynamics, and, indeed, membership have been firmly established and closely examined.

The retrospective term 'Confederation poets' has its origin, not, as is often supposed, in Malcolm Ross's *Poets of the Confederation* (1960), but in the dedication that the group's earliest anthologist, William Douw Lighthall (1857–1954), attached to his *Old Measures: Collected Verse* (1922): 'To the Poets of Confederation, My Friends and Companions.' Nevertheless, it was Ross's selections of Roberts, Carman, Lampman, and Duncan Campbell Scott (not Campbell, note) that provided the first generation of university-trained Canadian literature specialists with what they came to regard as the core canon of post-Confederation and pre-Modern Canadian poetry: poems representative of the four 'Poets of the Confederation' that – and who – could bear study in the unsentimental light of New Criticism. Until Ross's definition and delimitation of a category that, despite occasional protests, still remains intact and functional, the 'Poets of Confederation' or 'Confederation poets' were known under a variety of titles – 'the Canadian school' (Pierce, *Outlook* 71), 'the Systematic School' (Logan and French 105), and, most commonly, 'the 'Sixties Group' or 'the Group of the 'Sixties'[3] – and their numbers usually taken to include several other well-reputed writers who were born in Canada in the early 1860s, including E. Pauline Johnson (1862–1913), Gilbert Parker (1862–1932), and, a presence in the background if not the text of 'The Canadian Authors Meet,' F.R. Scott's father, Frederick George Scott (1861–1944). Arbitrary though they may seem, the criteria of literary stature and date and place of birth that have invariably been used to establish membership of the Confederation group (as it will be called here) do in fact reflect a social and historical reality, for, as Archibald MacMechan (1862–1933) observes in *Head-Waters of Canadian Literature* (1924), 'the writers in [the group were] all children at the time of Confederation, they [were] formed by the institutions then created, they all beg[a]n to produce and to emerge into notice in the same decade. The national impress [was] upon them all; and all w[o]n recognition and even popularity outside their own country' (142). Slightly inaccurate though it is in one detail – the poets so far assembled under the rubric of the Confederation group 'beg[an] to produce and to emerge into notice,' not 'in the same decade,' but between 1880 (Roberts's *Orion, and Other Poems*) and 1895 (Johnson's *The White Wampum*) – MacMechan's account of their formative influences and literary achievements has the great merit of succinctly stating the reasons that, explicitly or implicitly, have undergirded most attempts by literary historians and critics to establish the characteristics and contours of what A.J.M. Smith (1902–80) went so far as to describe in his Introduction to *The Oxford Book of Canadian Verse* (1960) as a 'national school of reflective nature poetry' (xxxiv).

But is MacMechan's account of the commonalities of the Confederation group adequate and is Smith's description of it as a 'school' accurate? Are there other characteristics that unite the group and, given the geographical division of its core members between New Brunswick (and, later, New York) (Roberts and Carman), Ontario (Lampman, Campbell, and Duncan Campbell Scott), and Quebec (George Scott), did they ever cohere to the degree that warrants the term 'school'? More specifically, did they share particular concerns, themes, and techniques? Were all of the poets so far mentioned – Roberts, Carman, Lampman, Campbell, Johnson, Parker, and the two Scotts – equally members of the group? Did the group have a leader? A discernible duration? Yet other members? Some preliminary answers to these questions will emerge later in this Introduction and others will occupy ensuing chapters, but some initial responses to them need to be registered in order to establish a basis for proceeding. First (and as MacMechan, Smith, and others have also observed in different ways) a defining characteristic of the poetry of the Confederation group in the eyes of the poets and their associates is its 'workmanship' (MacMechan 119) or 'technical excellence' (Smith, 'Introduction' xxxiv). It was this quality that supposedly elevated the Confederation group's poems above most earlier and contemporaneous Canadian poetry and, beginning in the late 1880s, provoked a hostile response from Campbell that helped to bring about the group's dissolution in the mid-1890s. Second, the impetus for uniting poets from different regions of Canada around the ideal of workmanship came by example and precept from Roberts, whose departure for New York in December 1897 made fully apparent the disintegration of the group that had become more and more evident in the early-to-mid '90s. And third, a full realization of the critical role played by Roberts in drawing his fellow poets together into what W.J. Keith felicitously calls a 'loose Confederation' (*Canadian Literature* 33) not only permits the recognition that, despite its geographical diversity and lack of a formal manifesto, the group did have a centre, a credo, and a duration, but also sanctions judgments about the degree to which even its core members – Carman, Lampman, Campbell, the two Scotts, and Roberts himself – participated in its activities and program.[4] Once

George Frederick Cameron

William Wilfred Campbell

Bliss Carman

Archibald Lampman

Charles G.D. Roberts

Duncan Campbell Scott

Frederick George Scott

E. Pauline Johnson

the dynamics and commonalities of the group have been established even in this very preliminary fashion, the way is clear to an appreciation of why and how Johnson, Parker, and other writers such as Lighthall[5] who were more or less closely involved with the group can nevertheless be seen as peripheral or tangential to the circle formed by its core members.

In the 1930s, Roberts was occasionally inclined to extend membership of 'the 1860 group' as far as Helena Coleman (1860–1953) and Albert E. Smythe (1861–1947) on the grounds that they were born at the right time,[6] but in the early 1890s when the group was in its heyday he made no bones about either its exclusivity or, to introduce another of its salient characteristics, its maleness. Writing to MacMechan on 30 May 1893, he names himself, Carman, Campbell and 'the two Scotts' as the members of 'our little band' and signs himself 'fraternally yours' (*CL* 173), an expression that he largely reserved for Campbell, Lampman, and Frederick George Scott (see *CL* 91, 93, 105, 111, 168, 175, 188). Carman and Roberts, who, of course, were cousins and close confidants, almost invariably referred to one another as 'Old Man,' though in one letter of 1890 Roberts also refers to Carman as 'mon frère' (*CL* 122).[7] Carman's request to Lampman on 9 February 1891 to 'remember [him] to that Man, Duncan Campbell Scott' (SFU) is exceptional only in the degree to which it emphasizes the maleness that constituted a strong bond among the poets of the Confederation group. Lighthall's description of Roberts as a 'poet, canoeist, and Professor of Literature' in the Introduction to *Songs of the Great Dominion* (1889) (xxiv) provoked the contempt of Campbell (see *MI* 204) and the mirth of A.C. Stewart (1867–1944) (see chapter 8), but it is merely one of countless attempts by the Confederation group and their associates to establish virile youthfulness as a basis for identifying the young poets and the new Dominion of Canada.

In addition to maleness, date of birth, and evidence of workmanship, a principal qualification for membership in Roberts's 'little band' in May 1893 was the successful or imminent publication of at least one volume of poetry: at the time of his writing to MacMechan, Roberts had published *In Divers Tones* (1886) as well as *Orion, and Other Poems* (1880), Campbell, *Snowflakes and Sunbeams* (1888) and *Lake Lyrics and Other Poems* (1889), Lampman, *Among the Millet, and Other Poems* (1888), and Frederick George Scott, *The Soul's Quest and Other Poems* (1888); Duncan Campbell Scott's *The Magic House and Other Poems* (1893) was about to appear, as were Campbell's *The Dread Voyage: Poems* (1893), Carman's

*Low Tide on Grand Pré: A Book of Lyrics* (1893), and Roberts's own *Songs of the Common Day, and Ave: An Ode for the Shelley Centenary* (1893); and, as Roberts almost certainly knew, Frederick George Scott was in the process of deciding whether to publish *My Lattice and Other Poems* (1894) in Canada or the United States.[8] Lampman had been attempting since 1892 to interest an American publisher in the collection of poems that finally appeared in 1896 as *Lyrics of Earth* (see Bentley, 'Introduction,' *Lyrics of Earth (1895)* 7–11). In contrast, the writers peripherally or tangentially associated with the group had yet to establish or consolidate their reputations as poets in 1893: Parker's *A Lover's Diary* did not appear until 1894, Johnson's *The White Wampum* until 1895, and Coleman's *Songs and Sonnets* until 1906; Lighthall's *Thoughts, Moods, and Ideals* had appeared in 1887 and Smythe's *Poems Grave and Gay* in 1891, but neither of them would publish another volume of poems until well into the twentieth century. With hindsight and primarily on the basis of birthdates, Roberts would expand 'the 1860 group' to nearly a dozen, but in 1893, its *annus mirabilis*, his 'little band' was limited to six male poets in their early-to-mid thirties, all of whom had firmly established or confidently impending literary reputations. 'I am sure that there are many who would consider that Carman or Lampman take[s] precedence of me,' wrote Roberts to an unidentified correspondent in that year. 'I am always more than content to be counted the equal of those two. And as for the others, – Campbell and the two Scotts, – they certainly show great possibilities, and any of them may turn out to be a Captain of the whole crowd of us' (quoted in Daniells 403).

Roberts's letter of May 1893 to MacMechan contains two further elements that are of considerable importance in establishing the perimeters and characteristics of the Confederation group with respect to its membership, its temporal duration, and its aesthetic principles. The first of these is Roberts's mention of the 'little anthology for Ontario Schools' that constitutes the first collective appearance in print of his 'little band,' J.E. Wetherell's *Later Canadian Poems* (1893). When proposed in 1892 by Wetherell (1851–1940), an Ontario teacher and editor of textbooks whose other anthologies include *Poems of the Love of Country* (1905) and *Three Centuries of Canadian Stories from John Cabot to John Franklin* (1928), *Later Canadian Poems* was enthusiastically endorsed by Roberts, who appears to have assisted in both its compilation and promotion.[9] 'A volume like it, of purely Canadian poems, would ... be of the greatest value to Canadians,' he told Wetherell on 1 November 1892; 'I shall do my utmost to procure the adoption of the work in the schools of Nova Scotia and New Brunswick' (*CL* 157). Writing to Carman later in the same month and then again on New Year's Eve, Roberts placed less emphasis on the nationalistic aspects of Wetherell's proposed anthology 'for use in High Schools and Colleges over Canada' than on its potential benefits for the 'small band': 'he wants no names in his volume but *yours, Lampman's, Scott's, Campbell's, Pauline Johnson's, and mine. He wants to use half a dozen poems from each of us, save, perhaps, Pauline!* ... It will be good for us all ... He will do it *well*, and give us a good send off ... The Collection will be select; and it will help impress our greatness on the rising generation!!' (*CL* 160, 163–4). This last remark is patently hyperbolic, but it nevertheless reflects Roberts's sense that *Later Canadian Poems* might well be a means of consolidating and furthering the group's reputation in Canada and elsewhere. 'It seems to me the volume ought to attract attention,' Carman told Wetherell on 26 May 1893; 'I hope your publishers will not omit to send a copy to the *Dial* in Chicago, among other American papers' (*L* 52). A month later he reported ecstatically to his friend and fellow expatriate Peter McArthur (1866–1924), who was then the editor of *Truth* (New York), that 'there is a cheap edition [of *Later Canadian Poems*] – for schools!!!' (*L* 54).

As Wetherell's anthology evolved through the winter of 1892–3, it became less 'select' in ways that both pleased and displeased Roberts. Since he appears to have pointed Wetherell towards the work of Frederick George Scott, Roberts was 'glad' at Scott's inclusion (see *CL* 161, 168), but he was horrified by Lampman's suggestion, fully articulated a year earlier in 'Two Canadian Poets: A Lecture' (19 February 1891), 'that *George Frederick Cameron* [1854–85] is the biggest man of us all!' (*CL* 164), and did his best to dissuade Wetherell from including more than a token recognition of Cameron's work in the volume on the grounds that 'he died before he *found himself*' and produced 'no thoroughly wrought whole poem' (*CL* 161, and see 166). Despite Roberts's arguments, however, Cameron is a major presence in *Later Canadian Poems*: the space allotted to his work (20 pages) shares the middle ground with Carman (22) and Frederick George Scott (18) between the lows of Campbell (13) and Duncan Campbell Scott (14) and the highs of Lampman and Roberts (both 27). Not only does Cameron share with the 'little band' the honour of having a portrait photograph in the anthology (see pages 6 and 7) but, as a consequence of the alphabetical ordering of its contributors, his photograph faces the title page. Yet perhaps Roberts's status as the 'biggest man' in *Later Canadian Poems* is signalled by the presence on that title page of the hortatory final stanza of his 'Canada' (1885): '*But thou, my country, dream not thou!/ Wake, and behold how night is done,/ How on thy breast, and o'er thy brow,/ Bursts the uprising sun!*' Nevertheless, the prominent inclusion in the anthology of a dead poet whose work he held in low esteem can only have dampened Roberts's hope that the volume would proclaim to young Canadians especially the dawning of a new day for Canadian poetry.

Probably less dismaying to Roberts than the prominent inclusion of Cameron in *Later Canadian Poems* was the 'supplement' that, as Wetherell observes in his brief Preface, departs from 'the original plan of the book' to 'represent ... within somewhat narrow limits the notable work produced in recent years by some of our women writers.' Consisting of twenty-five pages (two fewer than the number allotted to each of Roberts and Lampman), Wetherell's 'Supplement' contains poems by six women – Johnson (5), Agnes Ethelwyn Wetherald (1857–1940) (4), Isabella Valancy Crawford (1850–87) (2), Susan Frances Harrison (1859–1935) (2), Agnes Maule Machar (1837–1927) (2), and Sara Jeannette Duncan (1861–1922) (1)[10] – that are arranged by theme rather than author, the result being that the female poets appear less as individuals than as members of a supporting chorus. A partial exception to this is Johnson, who dominates the 'Supplement' visually as well as numerically because of the inclusion of a portrait photograph. But, whereas the photographs of the men in the volume show only their head and shoulders, Johnson's extends to below her pelvis and emphasizes the curvaceous body beneath her lace-trimmed dress. With her neat hair, confident smile, and appraising gaze, the Johnson of *Later Canadian Poems* is an embodiment of the turn-of-the-century New Woman – knowing, accomplished, and somewhat masculine, but also a fetchingly feminine object of male desire; in short, an ideal female member of 'the men of the 'sixties' if such were genuinely possible. As, in fact, it almost was: in December 1892, Roberts had wondered to Wetherell whether Johnson had 'enough good work for a volume of poetry,' and when that doubt was dispelled by the publication of *The White Wampum* in 1895, he confidently introduced her to the American poet and editor Richard Watson Gilder (1844–1909) as 'one of the acknowledged leaders of our Canadian group' (*CL* 161, 210). But his description of her to another American poet and editor, Edmund Clarence Stedman (1833–1908), captures the qualities that in every sense engendered her relationships with 'our Canadian group': 'I gave her a[n] [introductory] card to you. Beware, beware, beware! She is charming; and she is a poet!' (*CL* 214).

The second element in Roberts's May 1893 letter to MacMechan that helps to establish the perimeters and characteristics of the Confederation group (and, indeed, curtailed even Johnson's peripheral relationship with it) is a body of references to the fact that the recognition being accorded to them in Canada, England, and the United States was provoking 'jealousy' and 'littleness' on the part of Campbell (*CL* 174–5). The letter refers specifically to the likelihood that the alphabetical order of the male poets in *Later Canadian Poems* stemmed from Campbell's objection to Wetherell's original plan to place Roberts 'at the front of the Collection,' but its more general comments suggest that Roberts had in mind one or more of the increasingly rebarbative attacks on contemporary poets and poetics that Campbell had been publishing since the previous winter in the 'At the Mermaid Inn' column that he shared with Lampman and Duncan Campbell Scott in the Toronto *Globe*. On 3 December 1892, for example, Campbell lambasted Lighthall's *Songs of the Great Dominion*, an anthology in large measure shaped by Roberts, for its 'utter lack of [a] literary standard,' its failure to 'represent ... [or] foreshadow' the 'true Canadian literature,' and its representation of 'Canada ... as a crude colony'; and on 4 February 1893 he used the article 'About Critics and Criticism' by the Canadian expatriate writer W. Blackburn Harte (1867–99) in the February number of the *New England Magazine*[11] as a pretext to inveigh against the 'fraternal system of back-scratching ... and back-biting' that 'runs like a dry rot all through our system of literary toil and ambition' (*MI* 203, 251). Ten days before Roberts's letter to MacMechan, Campbell concluded a column on the vacuous formalism of the poetry in American magazines by observing that in the current literary milieu 'the keen businessman who is literary has usurped the place of the true literary genius who ... thus sinks into a condition of neglected outlawry,' and some two weeks later he expatiated at length on the 'utter lack of imaginative creative ability' in the poetry of the 'cold-blooded professional writers for magazines, who ... turn out any amount of stuff, more from ambition than from a desire to produce what is in them' (*MI* 316, 331, 334). Roberts had every reason to take such remarks personally in 1893: in addition to being a fervent advocate of the 'ideal of finish' or 'polish' in poetry that Campbell roundly deprecates (see also *MI* 188-90), he was also deeply committed to fostering a 'fraternal system' among the Confederation poets and, moreover, heavily engaged both in consolidating his literary reputation and in using his writing to supplement his meager salary as a professor at King's College in Windsor, Nova Scotia. No doubt, overwork, financial problems, and domestic tensions accounted for the physical and mental exhaustion to which Roberts frequently alludes in his letters of the early 1890s (see *CL*),[12] but Campbell's bellicose remarks and attitude can have done nothing to alleviate the unhappiness that appears to have dogged him until well into the summer of 1893 and, indeed, until his departure for the United States in December 1897.

Nor was Roberts alone in feeling the effects of Campbell's attitudes and remarks. As will be seen in chapter 8, the ever more pointed and targeted barbs that became a feature of his contributions to 'At the Mermaid Inn' assisted in the demise of the column that had constituted the most visible sign of the colloquy of the Ottawa chapter of the Confederation fraternity, and in the ensuing two years Campbell's attacks would escalate into what quickly became known as the 'War among the Poets' – the exchange of letters, articles, and even editorials in several Ontario and New Brunswick newspapers that followed his (or a friend's) exposé of the 'fraternal system' of the Confederation poets in the 11 May 1895 issue of *Saturday Night* (Toronto)[13] and his depiction of Carman as 'perhaps the most flagrant imitator' – that is, plagiarist – 'in North America' in the 16 June 1896 issue of the *Sunday World* (Toronto) (*War* 30). Far from being merely a 'tempest in ... [a] teapot,' as Carl F. Klinck claims in *Wilfred Campbell: A Study of Late Provincial Victorianism* (1942) (97), the 'War among the Poets' was the result of deep differences of opinion regarding the means and ends of poetry that from the outset made the Confederation group an unstable fraternity and in the course of time contributed to its disintegration.

Like all but the simplest entropic processes, the disintegration of the Confederation group occurred gradually but in observable stages, such as Carman's departure for New York to assume the editorship of the *Independent* in January 1890, Lampman's analysis of the shortcomings of Roberts's work in his 'Two Canadian Poets' lecture of February 1891, the termination of the 'At the Mermaid Inn' column in July 1893, and the 'War among the Poets' in the spring and summer of 1895. Probably the most critical of these losses of mass and cohesion was the reorientation of Roberts himself to the United States, which seems to have begun in earnest with his 'sick leave' (*CL* 173, 174) in the Washington, DC home of the American poet Richard Hovey (1864–1900) in April and May 1893 and built steadily towards his permanent removal to New York in December 1897. One of many signs of the group's declining energy was the failure of Frederick George Scott's proposal to carry forward the momentum generated by *Later Canadian Poems* in three 'small volume[s]' by Roberts, Lampman, and himself that would be 'uniformly and tastefully' bound and brought out as a 'set, to be sold in case, for

Xmas' (letters to Roberts and Lampman, 24 May 1893).[14] Busy, depressed, and dismayed by Campbell's behaviour as he was, Roberts responded to Scott's proposal with enthusiasm and an eye to its fraternal possibilities: 'the idea that you suggest is a good one ... though I would want to see *Carman* added thereto,' he wrote on June 15; 'those little *triplet* or *quadruplet* affairs seem to sell well at Xmas time. You, L[ampman], and myself; Carman, Duncan C. Scott, and Campbell, – would make two sets of good stuff' (*CL* 174). It is symptomatic of the strengths and weaknesses in the mid-1890s of the group that Roberts had done so much to unify and guide that of the two remaining (or surviving) letters that he wrote to Scott at this time the first, dated 15 December 1894, focuses on elements of *My Lattice and Other Poems* (1894) that seem 'careless and hasty' and the second, dated 30 March 1895, speaks of Roberts's resignation of his professorship at King's College and fulfils Scott's request for a critique of one of his poems with a note written on a train bound for Boston. When the publication of *The White Wampum* in 1895 finally brought Johnson as close as she could come to membership in the Confederation group, the group itself was nearing the final stage of its disintegration, and, moreover, Johnson's flourishing career as a vaudevillian performer of her poems – she 'started her first comprehensive Canadian tour ... towards the end of 1894' (Van Steen 26) – scarcely afforded her time to write poetry, let alone to settle into a literary circle (in fact, her next collection of poems, *Canadian Born*, did not appear until 1903).

This is not to say that the poets of the Confederation group ceased to interact with one another after 1897. Campbell remained on speaking terms with his fellow Ottawa poets but espoused the dying cause of British Imperialism with a didactic fervour that would probably have alienated them even if they had shared his political and racial beliefs. Roberts and Carman resumed the close relationship that had been confined to letters and visits when Carman moved to New York in 1891, and Lampman and Duncan Campbell Scott strengthened the bond of friendship that would only be broken by Lampman's premature death in 1899. Dependent on their writing for a livelihood but free of domestic constraints, provincial attitudes, and nationalistic concerns, Roberts and Carman joined Hovey, the expatriate English poet Richard Le Gallienne (1866–1947), and other apostles of the avant-garde in celebrating the pleasures and mysteries of erotic love and the open road, Roberts in *New York Nocturnes and Other Poems* (1898) and *The Book of the Rose* (1903), and Carman in the four volumes of the *Vagabondia* series (1894–1912) and the five somatic poetic sequences of *Pipes of Pan* (1898–1905). The most accomplished and important book that either of them published after the turn of the century, *Sappho: One Hundred Lyrics* (1903), consists of a sequence of poems by Carman with an Introduction by Roberts. In contrast, Lampman and Scott, both comfortably employed in the civil service in Ottawa, remained wedded to tamer and less flamboyant subjects and themes of recognizably Canadian caste and relevance and with an increasing emphasis on the peoples and landscapes of the North and West that provides the continuity between such late Lampman poems as 'Temagami' and 'The Lake in the Forest' and the so-called 'Indian' poems of Scott's *New World Lyrics and Ballads* (1905) and *The Circle of Affection and Other Pieces in Prose and Verse* (1947). The Christmas cards containing one or two poems by each of them that they sent to family friends until Lampman's death reflect both their conventional lives and their continuing collaboration. Predictably, Frederick George Scott, whose *Unnamed Lake, and Other Poems* (1897) appeared a year after he became a curate in Quebec City and quickly earned him the title of 'the Poet of the Laurentians,' remained closer to the Ottawa poets than to Roberts and Carman. On a trip to Halifax in the summer of 1898 to attend the four-hundredth anniversary of John Cabot's landing in Canada, Lampman spent time both going and returning with Scott. '[H]e wished to be remembered to you,' Lampman told his wife on August 6. 'He is a nice fellow' (SFU). Entropy had taken its toll. Within a year Lampman would be dead, and a year later the century would be over. The remaining members of the group that the Toronto *Globe* had described on 7 October 1893 as 'the bright coterie whose verse ... has given gratifying prominence to the poetic literature of their country' (20) would go on to write and publish many things, but never again with the same sense of shared energy, purpose, and achievement that they had experienced between 1880 and 1897 when, inspired by Roberts and then by one another, they had been 'the Poets of Confederation.'

## II

Like Tennyson's Ulysses (and anyone else for that matter), the poets of the Confederation group were a part of all that they met. Born in provinces that were shaped by the theory that colonies are not 'new societies' but 'old societies in new places' (Wakefield 329),[15] they came to maturity in a semi-autonomous Dominion[16] that the most influential Tory writer of the pre-Confederation period, Thomas Chandler Haliburton (1796–

1865), had figured as a '*bundle of sticks*' needing only 'to be well united' (264)[17] and that the most influential Whig writer of the post-Confederation period, Goldwin Smith (1823–1910), would figure as 'a number of fishing-rods tied together by the ends' and destined for 'union ... with the American Commonwealth' (*Canada and the Canadian Question* 192, 268). '"Eph Wheeler,"' Oliver Murchison informs his family in Duncan's *The Imperialist* (1903), '"he's got twenty-five cents, an' a English six pence, an' a Yankee nickel"' (11). So, too, did the cultural environment – what Pierre Bourdieu calls the *habitus* (*Logic* 54) – in which the Confederation group lived and wrote. Faced with the same three political choices that had confronted Canadians before Confederation and would continue to do so until well into the twentieth century – national independence, allegiance to Britain, and annexation to the United States – all six poets were in different proportions post-colonials, loyal Victorians, and committed North Americans, at different times proudly Canadian, truculent or deferential towards Britain, receptive, attracted, and obedient to American literary culture and the opportunities that it afforded. Both individually and collectively, then, the poets of the Confederation group must be understood as the inhabitants and interpreters of a politically complex and tense environment in which, not for the first or last time in Canadian literature, poetry was a focal point of intense interest as an indicator of the present and future state of the country. It is no exaggeration to say that a major reason for the group's very existence was a viciously circular conviction in the minds of many thinkers of the day that only a distinctive Canadian literature could validate Canada's nationality and that only the full achievement of that nationality could produce a distinctive Canadian literature.

To appreciate the importance attached to Canadian literature in the post-Confederation period, it will be necessary to trace the nationalism of the Confederation group back to its origins in Romantic nationalism (chapter 1). It will also be useful in proceeding to recall that the post-Confederation period was the time of, among other things, the Canada First movement (1868), the Red River Rebellion (1869–70), the National Policy (1879), the North West Rebellion (1885), the Canadian Pacific Railway (1871–85), and 'the Exodus' (or, in today's terminology, 'the brain drain') – a period, in short, of national aspiration, achievement, trauma, and anxiety. Surely, many Canadians thought, poetry was required to celebrate Canada's distinctive landscapes and heroic past, to voice its peoples' feelings, dreams, and aspirations, to give it a proud presence in the literature of the English-speaking world? In the eyes of

Roberts and the man who helped to propel him to national prominence in the early 1880s, Joseph Edmund Collins (1855–92), a grave danger to Canada's national and literary ambitions lay in the all-too-apparent possibility that Canadians would be satisfied by mediocre writing because it dealt with Canadian subjects and themes rather than demand of the country's poets and novelists work of sufficient workmanship and universality to compete with the best contemporary literature in English. So it was that with the mixture of idealism and hucksterism typical of the age that saw Oscar Wilde performing himself on Canadian stages (1882)[18] and Timothy Eaton issuing his first mail-order catalogue (1884), Roberts and Collins set about promoting first Roberts himself, then Lampman, and eventually the other members of the Confederation group as the creators of poems whose excellence could not be disputed because it had been recognized internationally. '[W]e should be sorry to see the transcendent genius of Mr. Roberts cage itself within the bounds even of this ample Dominion,' wrote Collins in the chapter on Canadian 'Thought and Literature' in his 1883 biography of Sir John A. Macdonald; 'he may find ..., as he has found, inspiration' in 'our wondrous forests, and our rushing rivers ... yet if he wish to go beyond, and sing to all quarters of the world a note that posterity will not let die, as he will, for his seems to be the ambition, and his power is supereminent, then shall we gladly let him go, bidding him God speed' (471).

As perhaps a necessary part of the promotional strategy set in motion by Roberts and Collins, the Confederation group all but ignored earlier Canadian writing and largely condescended to its surviving practitioners. Charles Heavysege (1816–76) is entitled to 'a permanent place upon our roll' of writers, argued Roberts in 1883, because his *Saul: A Drama* (1859, 1869) was admired by Hawthorne and praised by the *British North American Review,* but nevertheless his 'intellect ... [was] too little under the discipline of culture' and his work is 'rough-hewn' (*SPCP* 252–3); Charles Sangster (1822–93) is 'a pioneer in our literature, but were he writing now his verse would be of much less account' (*CL* 88); Alexander McLachlan (1818–96) was not worth mentioning. In 1888, when Lighthall mooted the idea of persuading McGill University to give honorary M.A. degrees to Roberts and Sangster, Roberts thanked him for proposing an idea that would 'bring the College into relation with our literary effort,' but added: '... do not think me ungracious if I say that I hardly class Sangster and myself as in the same boat ... It would be better not to class us together' (*CL* 88). In his chapter on Canadian 'Thought and Literature,' Collins had been much harsher:

In nearly every school-book we find something from Mr. Sangster, which is given as a sample of 'good Canadian poetry'; but any of this writer's verse that we have read, and we think that we have seen it all, was not worth a brass farthing. His name only appears here that it may not be confounded with Canadian *poets*. (496)

In the absence of 'Canadian *poets*' worthy of emulation, the Confederation group inevitably looked elsewhere for masters and models upon which to pattern the Canadian poetry of the dawning era.

A year after the First World War drew that era finally to a close, Ezra Pound recalled that the 'true Penelope' of his own North American poetic apprenticeship around the turn of the century was Gustave Flaubert (61). For the Confederation group, coming to poetic maturity as they did more than a generation before the advent of Anglo-American Modernism, the equivalent of Pound's *beau-idéal* was The English Romantic Poet, particularly Keats, Wordsworth, and Percy Bysshe Shelley. '[T]hat most glorious Titan of poets – John Keats!' Roberts exclaimed to an American correspondent in the summer of 1884, and in the fall of the same year: 'the very name of Keats is to me like a breath from the garden of spice' (*CL* 40, 42). 'Keats has always been such a fascination for me and has so permeated my whole mental outfit that I have an idea that he has found a sort of faint reincarnation in me,' wrote Lampman a decade later; 'I am only just now getting quite clear of the spell of that marvellous person; and it has taken ten years to do it' (*AC* 119). 'The distinctive nature of Wordsworth's poetry is something so high, so ennobling, so renovating to the spirit,' wrote Roberts in the interim, 'that it can be regarded as nothing short of a calamity for one to acquire a preconception which will seal him against its influence' (*SPCP* 274). Such statements as these and, more important, the evidence of their poems confirm that, as L.R. Early, Les McLeod, Tracy Ware, and others have long-since demonstrated, much of the poetry of the Confederation group is well described by such terms as 'Canadian Post-Romanticism' (McLeod) and 'Northern Romanticism' (Ware). In fact, it is thanks in no small measure to the extensive and foundational work of Early, McLeod, and Ware[19] that 'the influence of English Romanticism' is fully recognized by Canadian literary scholars and repeatedly registered throughout the present study as an important 'context ... for the appreciation of the achievements of Confederation poetry' (Ware, 'A Generic Approach' 4). Whether adjectivally modified or alone, Romanticism was a matrix from which most poetry written in

Canada during the post-Confederation period drew energy and suste-
nance.

But it must also be borne in mind that the major Romantic poets were
viewed by their Canadian heirs through the filter of Victorian writers
whom they admired with similar fervour. At university and for sometime
afterwards, Lampman was heavily under the influence of Thomas
Carlyle, and during the same and subsequent years his opinions of
Romantic poets were shaped by Carlylean principles, as well as by
such influential studies as John Addington Symonds's *Shelley* (1878)
and Roden Noel's *Life of Byron*.[20] The title of the volume in which Roberts's statement about Wordsworth appears is *Poems of Wordsworth (from
Arnold's Selections)* – that is, from Matthew Arnold's 1879 *Poems of Wordsworth*, the edition that 'largely determined the view of Wordsworth for
many decades' (Culler 574). 'It is not the original Wordsworth that the
Wordsworthians worship, but Arnold's Wordsworth,' groused Campbell
in 1893. 'It is the same with the Shelleyites. They follow some miserable
critic, who ought to have been hanged ere he dared to misinterpret
genius in the face of its own words' (*MI* 252). It was probably under the
influence of Arnold's introductory essay on Keats in T.H. Ward's *The
English Poets: Selections with Critical Introductions* (1880) that Lampman
discovered the poet who would eventually be the subject of the mosaic
of Victorian responses to the poet that he assembled between 1891 and
1893 under the title 'The Character and Poetry of Keats.'[21] And it was
probably through the work of Arnold's successor as Professor of Poetry
at Oxford, John Campbell Shairp, that he refined his understanding of
what both critics called 'poetic interpretation.'[22] 'I should like to say
something about the reading that is occupying my attention at this
time,' Roberts told Lampman in 1882,

> But I won't! I shall only refer to him you speak of, second to no living writer
> in prose or verse, M. Arnold. His prose works, especially *Essays in Criticism*,
> if you are not not already familiar with them, you will find the richest of
> intellectual fruits. That on 'Heine'; on 'Translating Homer'; on 'Maurice
> de Guérin,' with others, are quite incomparable.[23] Above all he is so toler-
> ant, so lucid and unprejudiced, so broad in his grasp and so exquisite in his
> expression. But enough. (CL 30)

'In our own time I think we allow ourselves to be a little too much daz-
zled by ... Tennyson and ... [Robert] Browning' and thus 'we are apt
almost to pass by a poet who in this ... age occupies the clearest and

noblest plane of all[:] ... Matthew Arnold' wrote Lampman ten years later; 'in his genius is that rare combination of philosophy and the poetic impulse in the highest degree ... With a mind blown clear as by the free wind of heaven he surveys the extent of life ... Only the noblest emotions, life, beauty, and thought, possess him' (*MI* 97–8). In Arnold, Roberts and Lampman especially found the *beau-ideal* of The Victorian Poet and Man of Letters,[24] a figure almost as important as a model for their self-fashionings as The Romantic Poet. Their 'Canadian Post-Romanticism' and 'Northern Romanticism' were also, as Klinck recognized in calling his thesis and book on Campbell 'A Study in Late Provincial Victorianism,' a displaced continuation of the supposedly masculine values of intellectual clarity, moral seriousness, disinterested inquiry, and social responsibility for which 'high Victorian' still seems the most adequate term.[25]

Yet even these attempts at literary positioning and labelling are not entirely satisfactory, for there are other strains in the poetry of the Confederation group that militate against an exclusive alignment of their work and attitudes with the continuity of selective admiration that stretches back from the high Victorians to the Romantics. Thanks primarily to their inspirational teacher at Fredericton Collegiate, George Robert Parkin (1846–1922), Roberts and Carman were strongly partial to the poetry of Dante Gabriel Rossetti, Algernon Charles Swinburne, and, later, William Morris, a taste not shared by Lampman, who nevertheless drew heavily on Morris's *News from Nowhere* (1890) for the utopian vision of 'The Land of Pallas' (1900).[26] More congenial to Lampman than the sensual and iconoclastic poetry of the Pre-Raphaelites were the nature writings of the American Transcendentalists, particularly Emerson and his disciple John Burroughs, an author who, as will be seen in chapter 4 of the present study, had a powerful impact on all the members of the Confederation group, with the possible exception of Frederick George Scott. With its debts not only to Burroughs and Shairp, but also to the ideas of the American mind-cure movement and to the greater Romantic odes of Keats and Arnold, Lampman's 'Among the Timothy' (1888) is merely a prominent example of the sorts of creative combinations that resulted from the co-presence in Canada of the elements represented metaphorically by the British and American coins in the pocket of Duncan's Eph Wheeler. It is but one indication of the complexity of what Roberts much later called 'Canadian Poetry in its Relation to the Poetry of England and America' (1933) that, although no American reviewer of *Among the Millet, and Other Poems* registered either surprise or bafflement at Lampman's botanical and ornithological references, an English reviewer was charmed by the 'sketch of ... what Mr. Lampman calls ... "British sparrows"' and confessed to being 'quite ignorant as to what "... Timothy" might be' ('A Canadian Poet' 52, 53). Duncan Campbell Scott would later recall this last remark in arguing that, because Canada has a 'decent, old fashioned climate, which corresponds in all essential points to that which has bronzed the poets of old England,' Canadian poets are simultaneously blessed with the ability to be 'understood' when 'sing[ing] of the season[s] in their old round' and obliged to 'depend for local colour on whatever there is of difference in our manner of looking at the old world with its changeful beauty' (*MI* 9).[27] To be both widely 'understood' and recognizably 'differen[t]': here in only slightly dissimilar terms is the challenge to which the poets of the Confederation group had to rise in their efforts to find favour with readers outside Canada while also fulfilling their role as articulators of a new nation.

Apparently because he was perceived as a thoroughly un-Canadian incarnation of American democracy, Whitman was almost entirely rejected as a model by all members of the Confederation group except Carman, whose residence in the United States dictated that he at least 'live in hope' of being 'open' (*L* 105) to the poet whom Campbell described a few days after his death on 26 March 1892 as 'the voice of [the Republic's] unmentionable reality of thought and existence' (*MI* 51). In contrast to Whitman, Longfellow was unobjectionable but available only as a point of departure and source of resonance for the Confederation group for the obvious reason that in *Evangeline* (1847) and, to a lesser extent, in *Hiawatha* (1855) he had treated of Canadian subjects and landscapes in a manner that had to be transcended not imitated by any Canadian poet aiming for distinctiveness and distinction. A somewhat similar case is Poe, a writer whose highly distinctive subjects and styles in both poetry and prose were so familiar to late nineteenth-century readers on both sides of the border that they could not easily be adapted without incurring a sense of déjà vu or unoriginality – a property that Campbell would discover to his chagrin in the 'War among the Poets' (see chapter 8) and Carman would have posthumously applied to his early poems by James Cappon in *Bliss Carman and the Literary Currents and Influences of His Time* (1930) (see 11–18). The fact that in 1844 Poe accused Longfellow and other American poets of plagiarism and that in 1895 Campbell levelled the same charge at Carman may seem purely coincidental without a recognition that in literary cultures that are dependent on external models, but striving to become independent from them, acrimony between or among writers will almost inevitably call forth an accusation of plagiarism. The case of Adam Kidd (1802–31) in Lower Canada in 1830 is another case in point.[28]

Not even a brief survey of the Confederation group and 'the Literary Currents and Influences of [Their] Time' would be complete without reference to the fact that by the early-to-mid 1890s, Roberts, Carman, and Duncan Campbell Scott were beginning to show evidence of contact with the poems, plays, and essays of Maurice Maeterlinck and other avatars of the *symboliste* aesthetic in their deliberate use of suggestiveness, musicality, and indeterminacy as means of conveying a sense of life's insoluble enigmas and mysteries. In 'the symbolism of today,' wrote Hovey in 1894 of such works as Roberts's recently published 'The Young Ravens That Call upon Him' (1896), 'events, ... personages, ... sentences rather imply than definitely state an esoteric meaning ... [B]ehind every incident, almost behind every phrase, one is aware of a lurking universality, the adumbration of greater things' ('Modern Symbolism' 5). Lampman, Campbell, and Frederick George Scott held themselves aloof from the aesthetic-decadent movement that hosted *symbolisme* before it entered the literary mainstream en route to becoming a major component of Modernism, but the other three members of the group all drank deep of the *symboliste* spring and thus also of the esoteric or occult beliefs with which it was associated. As will be shown in chapter 6, the growth of all the members of the Confederation group away from their orthodox Christian roots towards the forms of 'Nature worship' that Roberts describes in 'Canadian Poetry in Its Relation to the Poetry of England and America' as 'mystical theosophy' and 'Neo-Platonic pantheism' (82) is one of the many ways in which their story is worth telling both for itself and as a reflection of its times.

As intimated several times already in this Introduction, the story of the Confederation group is also worth telling as an instance in Canadian literature of poetic as well as personal interaction and influence. By no means all of the resemblances between and among poems by Roberts, Lampman, Carman, Campbell, and the two Scotts can be ascribed to the sort of cross-fertilization that frequently occurs in groups of writers: some may reflect common influences from writers outside the group, and some may be the result of two or more members of the group hitting independently upon a similar theme, image, trope, or phrase; but others can with some certainty be attributed to the literary influence of one member of the group on another. To give just one example, the well-known resemblance between Roberts's 'The Solitary Woodsman' (1898) and Lampman's 'The Woodcutter's Hut' (1900) might be ascribed to a shared debt to Thoreau and other avatars of Romantic solitude, or to a parallel recognition of the thematic potential of workers attuned to Nature's cycles, or to a combination of these and similar factors. But it may also be attributed at least in part to the influence of one member of the group on another, in this instance, Lampman on Roberts, for, although 'The Woodcutter's Hut' did not appear in a volume by Lampman until 1900, it was written on 29 December 1893 and available in print by December 1894, less than a year before Roberts began offering 'The Solitary Woodsman' to American magazines for publication (see *CL* 211–12). Moreover, it appeared in a prestigious periodical – *Scribner's Magazine* (New York) – that was extremely well known to Roberts, whose 'The Ballad of Crossing the Brook' (1896) had, as a matter of fact, appeared there six months earlier. The indebtedness of Lampman's 'The Favorites of Pan' (1895) to Roberts's 'The Pipes of Pan' (1886) has long been recognized.[29] When 'The Woodcutter's Hut' and 'The Solitary Woodsman' are added to the picture, it shows that inspiration flowed back and forth between the two poets, as no doubt (and as will be seen repeatedly in the forthcoming pages) it did at different times and in different ways between and among other members of the group.

With these large patterns and movements as its backdrop, the present study aims to shed fresh light on the characters, activities, interactions, and writings of the six poets of the Confederation group during the period from 1880 to 1897, when, as argued earlier, they came together as never again around a common set of concerns, values, and aims. Neither an influence study nor a biographical investigation nor a political or sociological analysis, *The Confederation Group of Canadian Poets, 1880–1897* is sometimes all of these things, but it is primarily a literary history of six poets whose work seems to me to be important enough in itself and for Canadian culture to warrant careful contextualization. At heart, it is an expression of a debt of gratitude to two of the poets of whom it treats, Roberts and Lampman, for poems that helped me as an immigrant to Canada and then as a migrant from British Columbia to Nova Scotia and Ontario first to come to terms with and then to feel at home in places with which I had little connection. If there were such a thing as a thank-you book, this would be it.

# CHAPTER ONE

# Young Canada: 1880–1884

## I

'I suppose, from your intimacy with Collins, that you are one of us right through, a Canadian Republican!' enthused Roberts to Lampman in a letter of 23 September 1882. 'We want to get together literary and independent Young Canada, and to spread our doctrines with untiring hands ... I am anxious indeed to get to Toronto ... to put in execution many schemes. I hope under those circumstances the close duet of C[ollins] and I would become an equally inseparable trio, yourself making the third of the triumvirate' (*CL* 29). The Collins to whom Roberts refers in this highly significant letter was Joseph Edmund Collins, and the 'literary and independent Young Canada' whose doctrines he hoped Lampman would help to spread was a Canadian offshoot of the Romantic nationalism that during the earlier part of the century had fuelled nationalistic aspirations throughout Europe and the Americas. Today, Collins is all but unknown to Canadian literary scholars except as the author of a contrived romance risibly entitled *Annette, the Métis Spy: A Heroine of the N.W. Rebellion* (1886), and the impact of Young Ireland on Canada is recognized, if at all, only in the pre-Confederation proselytizing and 'Canadian Ballads' (1858) of Thomas D'Arcy McGee (1825–68).[1] Yet, as intimated by John Coldwell Adams in a paper on 'Roberts, Lampman, and Edmund Collins' at the University of Ottawa's Roberts Symposium in 1983 and echoed by M. Brook Taylor in his entry on Collins in the twelfth volume of the *Dictionary of Canadian Biography* (1990), Collins was one of the most important influences on the formation and early activities of the Confederation group, and, as a brief outline of its history and doctrines will shortly suggest, the Young Ireland movement, a salient antecedent of its literary and political program in the early 1880s.

But first, who was Joseph Edmund Collins and how did he come to be friends with Roberts and Lampman? By Adams's description, 'a chubby, hot-headed Newfoundlander who looked (and sometimes acted) like the stage-comedy version of an Irishman' ('Roberts' 5), Collins was born in Placentia and lived in St John's before moving to Fredericton in 1875 to study law, a course that he soon abandoned to become, briefly, a schoolteacher and then, in October 1878, the editor and publisher of the Fredericton *Star*. It is possible that during his Fredericton years Collins knew Roberts, who was the second cousin of his wife, Gertrude Anna (née) Murphy (Adams 7; Taylor 204),[2] but likely they became close friends in Chatham, New Brunswick, where they both moved in the fall of 1879, Collins to become editor of the Chatham *North Star* and Roberts to become headmaster of the Chatham Grammar School. Certainly, in Roberts's '*camouflaged autobiography*' (*CL* 593), E.M. Pomeroy describes Collins as Roberts's 'most intimate friend in Chatham' and relates that the two men enjoyed 'many canoeing trips together' (37) before Collins departed for Toronto in 1881 to become an editor for the *Globe*. Adams speculates that 'while he was putting the finishing touches on his forthcoming *Orion, and Other Poems*' during this period, Roberts 'turned to Collins for encouragement and advice' ('Roberts' 8), and Taylor goes further, suggesting that 'around campfire and sitting-room Collins pushed Roberts to greater effort as a poet and greater commitment as a nationalist, and ... saw the publication of *Orion, and Other Poems* in the autumn of 1880 as the breakthrough necessary to the creation of a Canadian literature' (204). 'Collins had a message to convey,' observes Taylor, 'namely, the promotion of an independent, even republican, Canada. In particular, he sought by fostering the literary culture of the nation to give the inert political body of confederation a heart and soul of its own; and it was on the educated youth of the country ... that he focused his efforts' (204).

Although these speculations and observations are essentially correct, they beg some crucially important questions about the nature and sources of Collins's literary nationalism and the timing and effects of its impact on Roberts. Of particular significance to the aetiology of the Confederation group is the matter of whether Collins's nationalism was a formative influence on *Orion, and Other Poems* or an interpretative supplement to the volume that fuelled or even initiated the construction of it as the premier poetic production of the new Dominion of Canada. An examination of the extant issues of the newspapers that Collins edited between October 1878 and 26 October 1881 (when he announced to the readers of the Chatham *Star* that he 'no longer h[ad] a responsible editorial connexion' with the paper) lends support to the latter hypothesis by indicating that his literary nationalism came to the fore, if not into being, in the late winter and early spring of 1881 as a consequence of his reading of two essays by Nicholas Flood Davin (1840–1901), the Irish-born journalist, lawyer, politician, and poet whose rise to prominence as a spokesman for Canada had begun eight years earlier with *British versus American Civilization* (1873), the second in the series of National Papers that was inaugurated in 1871 by William Alexander Foster's *Canada First; or, Our New Nationality*. The editorials and columns that Collins published prior to the spring of 1881 reveal him to have been, like Davin, a Liberal Conservative[3] who supported Sir John A. Macdonald's National Policy as 'under all circumstances ... by far the best' bulwark against annexation to the United States and the disintegration of the Dominion through secession (Prospectus, the *North Star* and the *Star*, 4–22 September 1880). They also reveal that prior to the spring of 1881 Collins saw no special connection between his political beliefs and the works of Canadian literature that he occasionally published and reviewed while eclectically catering to his readers' literary needs through such fare as a serialization of Sir Walter Scott's *Ivanhoe*, a reprinting of John Greenleaf Whittier's poem on 'Bayard Taylor,' and a selection of Addison and Steele's letters to the *Spectator*. After the spring of 1881, however, the possibility of a Canadian literature and a recognition of its need for active support became increasingly evident in Collins's writings in the *Star*, particularly in three items: an appreciation of a poem by Roberts, 'Off Pelorus,' which had just been published in *Rose-Belford's Canadian Monthly Magazine and Literary Review* (1879–82)[4] (April 20), a two-part article on a poem by one of Roberts's ex-pupils, Thomas Guthrie Marquis (1864–1936), which had recently won a prize at Queen's College in Kingston (April 30, May 4), and an editorial that supports the proposal of the then governor-general, Lord Lorne, for the establishment of a Canadian Academy of Letters (the Royal Society of Canada) on the grounds that such an institution would eliminate factionalism among Canadian writers and promote excellence in Canadian literature (June 29).

But most significant of all because it is both an early symptom and a clue to the source of this quickening interest in Canadian poetry and its national context is an 'Editorial Gleanings' column of April 2, in which Collins begins by stating that he has 'ordered back numbers of the Canadian *Monthly*' and proceeds to 'make extracts [from them] ...

which may prove of some interest,' including a passage from 'A Love Idyl' ('a gem of its kind') by the Canadian poet and historian Charles Pelham Mulvaney (1835–85)[5] in the October 1880 number and, more important, a short excerpt from a review of *Orion, and Other Poems* in the November 1880 number that announces Roberts's work to be '"true poetry, unmarked by mannerism any more than Shelley is marked by it"' and wonders whether '"such a book as this by Mr. Roberts of New Brunswick [does not] justify us in adjuring good things of the spread of a genuine literary spirit in Canada. Here is a writer whose power and originality it is impossible to deny – here is a book of which any literature might be proud."' 'Highly complimentary words, but no higher than deserved,' remarks Collins: 'Mr. Roberts' poems have found general favor; and those who read them are wishing for more. We hope soon again to hear the sound of his lyre.' It is as if Collins had been suddenly brought to the recognition that Roberts might be not just a strong young poet but a strong young poet of national importance.

The two essays by Davin that appear to have assisted greatly in the quickening of Collins's literary nationalism also appeared in *Rose-Belford's Canadian Monthly Magazine*, though not in back issues. The first, published in March 1881 and entitled 'Great Speeches,' is a discussion of the oratorical skills of Canada's major politicians and clergymen in relation to their English and Irish counterparts, which Collins hails in the March 30 issue of the *Star* as 'the best essay we have ever seen in a Canadian, perhaps in any publication.'[6] Addressed principally to the 'young men' of Canada (270, 285), it begins with a lengthy exordium on Canadian art and literature that stresses the need for Canadians to make their history and landscape their own through the power of 'imagination' and then, after lamenting the Canadian tendency to withhold praise from Canada's writers until they have been endorsed outside the country, proceeds to proclaim Louis-Honoré Fréchette (1839–1908), whose *Les Fleures boreales* (1879) won the prestigious Prix Montyon of the Académie Française in 1880, 'our first national poet' (272). '[H]is imagination ... is steeped in local tints,' writes Davin of Fréchette:

> ... the lakes, the mighty rivers, the snowy landscape, the bright skies of Canada, the blizzard of winter, the rapid vegetation of May, all these are reflected in his song ... The heroes of Canadian history call forth the deepest and most touching notes of his lyre ... In 'Nuit d'Été' – a poem which ... could

hardly be understood by any one not a Canadian – the pictures are all racy of the soil; the vast solitudes, the meteoric sky, the sonorous pines, the young man seeing his sweetheart home, the liberty, the confidence, the long farewell. The national poet is a singer, in whose song we find his time and country. (272)

In Collins's (and, it may safely be assumed, Roberts's) reading of this and other passages in 'Great Speeches' may lie the inciting moment of the Confederation group – the motivating contact with the assumptions and perceptions that would power the Young Canada phase of their development.

If so, then at least part of the impetus for this development can already be traced to the Young Ireland movement, for in describing the imagery of Fréchette's poetry as 'racy of the soil' Davin uses a phrase meaning 'characteristic of a certain country or people' that was 'chiefly used with reference to Ireland' (*OED*) on account of its source in the motto of Young Ireland's short-lived newspaper, the *Nation* (1842–8): 'To create and foster public opinion in Ireland and to make it racy of the soil.' By the early 1890s 'racy of the soil' would be in frequent use as a description of Canadian poetry. In the 23 May 1890 issue of the *Week*, for example, another poet, essayist, and historian of Irish descent, Thomas O'Hagan (1855–1939), began a brief survey of 'Canadian Poets and Poetry' with the bold assertion that 'Canadian poetry is racy of the soil' because 'it has within it the life and national aspirations of our people' (389), and two years later in the 'Brief Literary Notes' section of the February 1892 issue of the *Owl* (Ottawa) the phrase was used to define 'local literature' (307) in the context of the Canadian Authors' Night in Toronto that Fréchette and Lampman had declined to attend.[7] When he expanded his brief survey into a lengthy article in 1895, O'Hagan would deploy 'racy of the soil' in a context that makes all but explicit the parallel between early Victorian Ireland and late Victorian Canada. Whether celebrating Canada's natural scenery, forging ballads from 'the bold adventures and heroic achievements of the early missionary explorer and pioneer,' or 'stirring ... visions and dreams of patriotism and promise' in 'the national breast of "Young Canada,"' he enthused, the 'note of all [Canada's] singers is individual – indigenous. Their songs are racy of the soil, charged with the very life-blood of the people ... One of the chief of this young and promising band of singers is Charles G.D. Roberts' (*Canadian Essays* 11, 14).[8]

The second essay by Davin that had a profound effect on Collins in the spring of 1881 merited not one but two articles in the *Star.* Describing Davin as 'one of the foremost writers in the Dominion,' the first of these articles, published on May 4, expresses Collins's delight that in 'The Future of Canada' he has selected such an important theme and 'spike[d] the guns' of George Anderson, a proponent of Imperial Federation, and William Clarke, a proponent of Annexation.[9] Davin's 'thought is vigorous, and fresh as the flowers of May,' concludes Collins's article; 'there is a ring about every sentence ... that carries the consequential conclusions of the writer, straight home.' The precise nature of those conclusions is spelled out in Collins's second article on 'The Future of Canada,' a piece that begins in the May 7 issue of the *Star* by endorsing Davin's rejection of Imperial Federation as a viable option for Canada and proceeds on May 11 to reiterate the main points of his refutation of the five principal arguments against Canadian Independence, namely (in Collins's slightly modified wording):

1. Canada could not maintain her independence.
2. Canada has not the force and colossal energy of the United States.
3. Canada is stranded among the snow and ice of the North West without the historic culture of Europe, or the heroic aspiration of America.
4. Canada has no literature, no new national types – America has the beginnings of both.
[5.] There is not room for two peoples on the North American Continent. ('The Future of Canada' [May 11])

In responding to these arguments in 'The Future of Canada,' Davin subverts a straightforward reading of his political position by first denying that, in 'contend[ing] that Canada could, if necessary, stand alone,' he is 'advocating Independence' and then going on to canvass the potential advantages and eventual likelihood of Canada becoming an independent republic:

If the time had come to make Canada a Republic, there is nothing to prevent her people accomplishing the task of nation building. Mr. Clarke says we have not the assimilating power of the United States. No colony could have this power to the same extent as an independent country. Were Canada independent to-morrow, we should see immigrants become Canadians with greater rapidity than at present. There are disadvantages as well as advantages in the colonial relation, and one of the disadvantages is that men's ideas and affections continue to revolve around a distant centre, whose inspiring heart-throb they can hardly feel.

...

Canada is content with her present lot, and able and determined, if necessary, to stand alone ...

...

The strongest sentiment at present is for holding on to the British connexion. Until we can stand alone, and perhaps afterwards, we mean to hold on to that.

...

Why should not two peaceful republics, or a republic and a British colony make this continent sacred to peace and concord? (496–7)

Despite the denial with which they are prefaced, these remarks leave the impression that Davin supports the eventual establishment of a Canadian republic, as, indeed, does the conclusion of the essay, where an affirmation of colonial loyalty comes with a scarcely veiled warning to Britain to do well by Canada and a resounding endorsement of the national sentiments and aspirations of Canadians:

England's real interests are to keep up the present connexion or aid her strong child until he can put on the toga. She may again have to face a world in arms, and in that event unless a most imprudent policy is dealt out to Canada, young Canadians in thousands would be ready to traverse every sea to spill their lives for her safety and honour.

'We' should lose nothing, says Mr. Clarke. It has been shown that England would lose. But that is not the question, as Mr. Clarke admits. The question is what are the real interests of Canada. In considering these, the sentiments of Canadians surely cannot be ignored. Those sentiments are not fed by mere considerations of profit and loss. Canada lives for us as England for Englishmen, as France for Frenchmen, as the Fatherland for Germans,

> On no nymph's marble forehead sits
> Proudlier a glad virginity,*

---

* These two lines are from 'A Letter from Newport,' F.W.H. Myers's celebration of the racial and linguistic unity of 'Mother' Britain and her American 'Child' that nevertheless exhorts the latter to '[s]pread ... [her] arms afar,' to roll her 'golden harvest westward,' and to '[a]lly the tropics and the pole' (225–6).

and unless the stars in their courses fight against us; unless the immortals have decreed it otherwise; we mean one day to place her among the foremost nations of the earth. (498)

It is as difficult to doubt that 'The Future of Canada' fanned the embers of the Canadian republicanism that Roberts envisaged Collins sharing with Lampman in September 1882 as it is to avoid the speculation that Collins left Chatham for Toronto in the fall of 1881, not merely for 'considerations of profit and loss,' but also to participate at the intellectual centre of Canada in the push towards full nationhood. It is also difficult to ignore the possibility that Davin's unusual conception of Canada as a 'strong,' male 'child' growing towards the maturity indicated in republican Rome by the wearing of a toga lies in the background of Roberts's depiction of the country in 'Canada' (1885) as a 'Child of Nations, giant-limbed' who, as yet, 'stand'st among the nations ... with unanointed brow' (*CP* 85). Even if the relationship between Davin's and Roberts's descriptions is merely coincidental, it points once again to the masculinist assumptions that permeated the writing and context of the Confederation group.[10] Who more qualified than a young Canadian male to proclaim Canada's right to the *toga virilis* of maturity or – for Davin reverts to the conventional representation of the nation as a female in his final paragraph – to praise the classical beauty and seize the 'proud virginity' of the young country?

Davin's response to the charge that 'Canada has no literature' in 'The Future of Canada' is brief but significant, for in addition to asserting that there is 'plenty of literary talent, both French and English,' in Canada and observing that all North American literature is 'borrowed from Europe, and is European qualified by the influence of a new country' in which 'one man is in all respects the equal of another' (494), he advances two arguments whose implications may have shaped the activities of Collins and Roberts in the early-to-mid 1880s: (1) the argument that a national literature requires a national 'audience' and, therefore, must 'follow ... the birth and growth of a nation';[11] and (2) the argument that Canadian 'schools and universities w[ould], in due time, bear their legitimate fruit' in the form of an indigenous literature (494). To the committed nationalists that Collins and Roberts were in the process of becoming in the spring of 1881, these arguments can only have pointed to two related courses of action: (1) the creation of an audience for Canadian writing that by its very existence would testify to the existence of a Canadian literature and a Canadian nation; and (2) the cultivation in Canadian 'schools and universities' of a generation capable of producing and appreciating the literature of the new nation (494). To an extent, both Collins and Roberts were already working towards these ends in Chatham, Collins with an explanation of the mythological basis of 'Orion' in the 6 October 1880 issue of the *Star* and Roberts in the teaching of literature and composition in the high school. (As Collins notes in 'Honours for a Chatham Boy' in the 30 April 1881 issue of the paper, Marquis's poetic abilities had been 'nurture[d] and develop[ed]' with 'valuable aid ... from his preceptor.')[12] But their concerted effort to generate a national audience and intellectual milieu for Canadian literature would not reach its full force until the winter of 1882–3 when Collins, by then anticipating the publication of his *Life and Times of the Right Honourable Sir John A. Macdonald* (1883), enlisted Lampman's help in promoting Roberts's literary and academic career (more of which in a moment), and Roberts himself, now the headmaster of the York Street School in Fredericton and, no doubt, frustrated by teaching only young children (see *CL* 28), was dreaming of joining Collins and Lampman in Toronto to further their 'schemes' of 'a literary and independent Young Canada.'

Among the numerous essays in 'back numbers of the *Canadian Monthly*' that may have helped to shape the dreams and schemes of the assembling Confederation group, one deserves special consideration because, although neither excerpted nor mentioned by Collins in the *Star*, the rhetoric and imagery of its call to national consciousness seem to have had a deep impact on Roberts. The essay in question is 'The New Canada: Its Resources and Productions' (1875), by Charles Mair (1838–1927), a founding member of Canada First and the author of *Dreamland and Other Poems* (1868). Parts of its rousing final paragraphs could be mistaken for the program of Roberts's nationalistic activities and writings in the 1880s:

This new Dominion ... stands, like a youth upon the threshold of his life, clear-eyed, clear-headed, muscular, and strong. Its course is westward. It has traditions and a history of which it may well be proud; but it has a history to make, a national sentiment to embody, and a national idea to carry out. There was a time when there was no fixed principle or national feeling in Canada ... But that time has passed away. Young Canada has come to the front, and we are now a nation, with a nation's duties to perform, privileges to maintain, and honour to protect. That national sentiment which has yet to defend the 'meteor flag' from the Atlantic to the Pacific, is opening amongst us like a flower. All true men will carefully water the plant; all wise men will assiduously nourish its growth ... Its power and cohesiveness are being felt at last, and already it is binding the scattered communities of British America together in the bonds of a common cause, a common language, a common destiny ... One of its infallible signs is the growth of a national literature. This, to be characteristic, must taste of the wood, and be the genuine product of the national imagination and invention ... This, then, is the light which we must cause to shine before men and before nations; the abstract of our national life and ideas; the concrete feeling and inspiration of this country. (163–4)

In Lampman's 'excited pride' on reading *Orion, and Other Poems* in May 1881, Malcolm Ross sees a reflection of 'the peculiar national spirit of the immediate post-Confederation period' and detects 'an echo at some remove' of '"Canada First"' ('Introduction' x). If the essays of Davin and Mair had anything like the impact on Collins and Roberts that the evidence suggests, Canada First found more than a distant echo in the dreams and schemes of the 'triumvirate' that by November 1882 had formed the nucleus of the Confederation group. As Norah Story wisely observes in her *Oxford Companion to Canadian History and Literature*, Macdonald's National Policy was a dim reminder of the nationalism of Canada First, but its 'real fruit was the flowering of the literary movement of the 1880s that is associated with the names of ... Roberts, ... Carman, ... Campbell, Lampman, and ... Scott' (146).

Exactly when and how Collins became friends with Lampman in Toronto is something of a mystery. Both Adams and Taylor speculate that Collins was the unnamed 'somebody' whom Lampman mentions in his 19 February 1891 lecture on 'Two Canadian Poets' as the source of the copy of *Orion, and Other Poems* that he read, as he recalls, 'one May evening' 'almost ten years ago ... [when] an undergraduate at College' (*ER* 94). 'It seemed to me to be a wonderful thing that such work could be done by a Canadian, by a young man, one of ourselves,' he remembered; 'it was like a voice from some new paradise of art calling to us to be up and doing.' Unless this Archimedean moment took place in May 1882, however (and this seems unlikely, given Lampman's memory that Roberts's book was 'then recently published'), Collins cannot have been the source of Lampman's copy of *Orion, and Other Poems* for he did not move from Chatham to Toronto until October 1881. That the two met over the Winter of 1881–2 accords with Carl Y. Connor's statement that at this time Lampman's academic work 'suffered somewhat' because he assumed responsibility for preparing the November 1881 and March 1882 numbers of *Rouge et Noir* and because 'his mind was full of literary plans due to his association in college with his friend, J[ohn] A[lmon] Ritchie [1863–1935], and in the city with J.E. Collins ... and Charles G.D. Roberts' (53). Drawing on unspecified sources, Connor adds that Lampman, Collins, and Roberts 'sometimes visited Toronto friends, who were greatly entertained by the[ir] animated talk, ... their eager interest in the new poetry, Roberts's plans for Canadian journalism, and arguments about the conflict of science and religion in the days when Darwin and Huxley were so much read and when doubt and skepticism seemed in the very air' (53). None of Roberts's extant letters mentions or intimates that he visited Toronto before paying the brief 'visit to the upper Provinces' in August 1883 that is recorded in the August 25 issue of the *New Brunswick Reporter and Fredericton Advertiser* and moving his family there on September 21 to assume the editorship of the *Week* (*New Brunswick Reporter and Fredericton Advertiser*, 22 September 1883; and see Adams, *Sir Charles God Damn* 30–1).[13]

That Lampman was ideologically predisposed and therefore quickly receptive to the literary and liberatory nationalism of Collins and Roberts is indicated by two articles that he published in *Rouge et Noir* during his middle and final years at Trinity College. In the first of these, a guarded appreciation of *The Revolt of Islam* (1818) published in December 1880, Lampman carefully negotiates the Anglican values of Trinity College to argue that, 'blasphemous infidelity' aside, Shelley's epic poem is 'a magnificent poet's dream' of 'liberat[ion] from all government' that keeps alive the ideals of the French Revolution and confirms the view that Shelley is 'the poet of the future' whose work will be increasingly 'received and admired' as men become 'more liberal' (*ER* 5, 9). In the second, an enthusiastic survey of 'German Patriotic Poetry' published in March 1882, Lampman unabashedly declares his nationalistic sympathies by arguing that, although 'patriotic verse' is 'generally rude and rugged ... [with] little of the finish of art,' it deserves a nation's attention and admiration 'as the passionate expression of the feelings which stirred to the inmost depth its greatest and bravest hearts in the stirring periods of ... national history – the embodiment in mighty music of the faith and the glory of its forefathers' (*ER* 28). So caught up in the spirit of Romantic nationalism was Lampman by the summer of 1882 that, as he told Ritchie with a hint of embarrassment in a letter of July 24, 'From writing an essay in commendation of German patriotic poetry, I have proceeded to deeper depravity and written an addition to that patriotic poetry myself – entitled '"The Last Sortie"' (quoted in Connor 57). Set during the Franco-Prussian War (1870–1), which finally fulfilled 'the vision of a United Germany' that, in Lampman's view, was 'the central dream of [German] ballad music' (*ER* 30), 'The Last Sortie' was admired by Roberts in his letter of 23 September 1882 for its 'fine swing and lilt' (*CL* 30) and published in *Rouge et Noir* some two months later, where it languished until 1983, when L.R. Early reprinted it in 'Twenty-Five Fugitive Poems by Archibald Lampman.'[14] Omitted though it was from Lampman's own collections of his poems, 'The Last Sortie' is both an accomplished poem and a testament to the Romantic nationalism that bonded him to Collins and Roberts in 1882.

There is further evidence of the closeness of the 'triumvirate' of Collins, Roberts, and Lampman in 1882 in the fact that Collins was staying with Lampman in Orangeville when Roberts wrote to him on September 23[15] and that part of Roberts's letter is devoted to the advantages for a young literary nationalist of the teaching position that Lampman was apparently already thinking of abandoning in order to move to British Columbia:

> Collins said that you have a Classical Mastership[16] ... which may be much less of a strain than the Principalship of a large school [such as York Street] ... As for Br[itish] Columbia, I should be sorry to see you, even for a very short time, remove yourself so far from the centres of Canadian life and thought ... As for your profession, our profession, it has th[e] advantage ... that, once thoroughly acquired, [it] might be more compatible with literary efforts; – you do not require to devote 3 or 4 of your young and vigorous years wholly to special training before you can make your living thereby. Collins appears to be able to make a living wholly by his pen ... but most of the rest of us of the literary guild must make literature only our staff ... as yet. We may by strenuous effort soon succeed in spreading the literary and national spirit in Canada so as to make literature an entirely self supporting profession for us. This should be one of our aims; and speed the day that sees it accomplished. (*CL* 29)

With an audience for Canadian literature would come support for Canadian writers. In the meantime, teaching in a small school beyond the elementary level could serve the threefold purpose of providing income, time for writing, and access to young minds. By the fall of 1882, Young Canada had in place both a coherent ideology and a practical plan of action, albeit one whose third component – classroom teaching – was already proving so unsatisfactory to Lampman that, as confirmed by the appearance of his name on October 25 as a candidate for the impending round of Civil Service examinations (*Ottawa Citizen* 2), he was beginning to look for more congenial alternatives.

Given the cogency and aggressiveness of the triumvirate's 'schemes' by the fall of 1882, it is scarcely surprising that a conspiratorial and even militant note can sometimes be heard in Roberts's letters of late 1882 and early 1883. In his letter of September 23, he imagines Collins and Lampman drinking 'rye' (the liquor of choice, surely, for a Canadian nationalist) and making 'seditious utterances,' and in the two letters that he wrote on 12 December 1882 and 30 March 1883 to Carman, who was then studying at the University of Edinburgh, avuncular advice mingles with a sense of impending action:

> I am counting confidently on your *doing something* for Canada, with the rest of us, that small body who are pinning their faith on the near approaching awakening of Canada, in politics, art, song, intellectual effort generally. I feel it in [my] bones or in the air, or by virtue of my office as '*sacer vates*' so to speak, that within a very few years there is going to be lots for us to do in Canada and the very best of us young men will be wanted to do it. Do what? We'll see when the time comes; let us meanwhile be ready. (*CL* 32–3)

> I am ... studying every spare moment, at the political questions of the day, particularly in the matter of Independence, to which I am devoted heart and soul, and to which a large party of the best and most energetic men of Canada are rapidly gathering themselves. You will be one of us when we get you back here again! ... A national feeling is awakening, quietly but surely ... I am mainly occupied now in gathering my forces; soon I'll begin to scribble and proselytize to the fullest extent of my power. I have already converted several opponents in Fredericton. (*CL* 34)

Implicitly present in these letters and explicitly stated in Lampman's essay on 'German Patriotic Poetry' is a belief in the necessary involvement of poets in a national 'awakening' that is generally evocative of such more-or-less radical Romantic and Victorian poets as Shelley, Byron, Swinburne, and Morris but more specifically reminiscent of the doctrines and activities of the movement that Roberts's description of his 'party' as 'literary and independent Young Canada' may have been intended to invoke: Young Ireland.

## II

By the time of Roberts's writing to Lampman in September 1882, the so-called Irish Land War, which began in earnest in 1879, brought Charles Stewart Parnell to the United States seeking support for his Home Rule Party in 1880, and, needless to say, continued long after Gladstone's Land Act of 1881, had for several years generated a high level of journalistic interest in Ireland throughout Canada, especially in such areas as northeastern New Brunswick where a sizeable fraction of the population was of Irish origin. In a reflection also of Collins's background and sympathies, the Chatham *Star* reported continually on Irish affairs throughout 1880–1, with a bias always towards the 'true and patriotic' struggle for 'emancipation and self-government' (8 January 1881).[17] Parnell's activities and speeches were reported in detail as, in September 1881, were the visit to Ireland and 'Letter on the Land Bill' of Sir Charles Gavan Duffy, a principal founder of Young Ireland and the author of an authoritative account of its origins and ideas that may well have been known to Collins and Roberts by 1882, *Young Ireland: A Fragment of Irish History, 1840–1850* (1880, 1881, 1884, 1896). As described by Duffy, the 'cardinal purpose' of the 'little band' (quoted in Collins, 'Sir Charles Duffy') that sowed the seeds of Parnell's agitations was to achieve Ireland's independence from Britain through a 'repeal or ... dissol[ution] of the Union' and its preliminary aim was to awaken or revive Irish 'self-reliance and self-respect' through the publication in the *Nation* of materials related to their country's heroic history, current condition, and national ambitions (298, 152). 'Nationality is the ... first great object,' trumpeted the newspaper's Prospectus, 'a Nationality of the spirit as well as the letter – a Nationality which may come to be stamped upon our manners, our literature, and our deeds ... a Nationality which would be recognized by the world, and sanctified by wisdom, virtue, and prudence' (quoted in Duffy 80).

To achieve their immediate and ultimate goals, the strategists of Young Ireland harnessed the power not only of journalism, but also of literature and, particularly, poetry. Variations and translations of the 'national ballads' 'sung among the people' 'probably produced the most marvellous results,' recalls Duffy, but almost as effective were 'historical ballads of singular vigour' by 'young poets' such as Clarence Mangan and Richard D'Alton Williams that made 'the great men and great achievements of their race familiar to the people' (164–5). Writing in 1870 in the *New Dominion Monthly* (Montreal), the Canadian poet who later became the literary editor of the *Montreal Gazette* (1879) and a correspondent of Roberts, John Reade (1837–1919), would regard the story of Young Ireland and the *Nation* as 'too well known to require telling' in detail, but he would nevertheless quote one of the movement's famous precepts ('"Give me the making of a nation's ballads and I care not who makes its lands"') and dwell at length on its conception of 'literature [as] ... [a] strong ... engine of patriotic effort' and 'ballads [as] a leading medium for the dissemination of national feeling' (14–16). Almost certainly with his eye more on Canada than on Ireland, Reade opines that 'it is in countries that nature or destiny has made grand and pensive, or where destiny has been kind and destiny cruel, that the spirit of song has ever loved to build her sanctuary' (16).

Of course, the most visible conduit of these ideas and strategies to Canada was the very man who provided Reade with the subject of his article: Thomas D'Arcy McGee, who joined the staff of the *Nation* in 1846 and, after helping to plan an abortive Irish rebellion in 1847–8, moved to the United States and, in 1857, to Montreal (Davis 79; Neatby 490–1). Within a year of arriving in Canada East, McGee was using the pages of his newspaper, the *New Era* (1857–8), to argue for the 'Protection of Canadian Literature' on the grounds that 'Every country, every nationality, every people, must create and foster a National Literature, if it is their wish to preserve a distinct individuality from other nations.' 'Literature is the vital atmosphere of nationality,' he asserted in the 10 June 1857 issue of  the newspaper: 'No literature, no national life – this is an irreversible law ... Come! let us construct a national literature for Canada, neither British nor French nor Yankeeish, but the offspring of the soil, borrowing lessons from all, but asserting its own title throughout all.' A year later, he added example to precept in his *Canadian Ballads, and Occasional Verses* (1858), a volume dedicated to Duffy 'In Memory of Old Times' and issued simultaneously by publishers in Montreal (John Lovell) and Toronto (W.C.F. Caverhill). In addition to ballads on Sebastian Cabot, Jacques Cartier, Henry Hudson, the War of 1812, the launch of the *Griffin* ('the first sailing vessel that ... navigated the great lakes' [60]), and other 'great men and great achievements,' the volume contains extensive historical notes on the ballads and a Preface presenting them 'to the younger generation of Canadians' in the belief 'that we shall one day be a great northern nation, and develope [*sic*] within ourselves the best fruit of nationality, a new and lasting literature' (n.pag.).[18] It is a testament to the impact of Young Ireland on Canadian thinking about the nature and importance of 'National Literature' during the period surrounding Confederation that the title page of Henry J. Morgan's *Bibliotheca Canadensis; or, A Manual of Canadian Literature* (1867) carries a quotation from McGee, and its 'Introductory Remarks' includes a call to 'every patriotic subject' of the 'new northern nation' to support the literary efforts of 'the younger men' who were in the process of creating a literature reflective of Canada's 'New Nationality' and its 'bright hopes ... for national greatness' and 'an independent position' (viii). McGee's fervent appeal in 'The Mental Outfit of the New Dominion' (1867) to 'the educated young men of Canada,' especially 'those who venture upon authorship,' to assist in establishing their country's 'mental self-reliance' by 'doing something in their own right on their own soil' (1, 6–7) was quoted repeatedly in books, articles, and addresses during the decade following Confederation and almost certainly proved inspirational to many Canadian writers, not least those associated with the Canada First movement. In *Canada First; or, Our New Nationality; an Address* (1871), by William Alexander Foster (1840–88), one of the founders of Canada First, McGee's call for 'self-reliance' becomes a summons to a 'higher national life' and McGee himself a martyr to the new Dominion (31–6). In 'Canadian Materials for History, Poetry, and Romance' (1871), by John George Bourinot (1837–1902), the future author of *The Intellectual Development of the Canadian People* (1881) and *Our Intellectual Strength and Weakness* (1893), the same call provides the climax for a survey of Canada's literary achievements and potential (203–4). In *The Irishman in Canada* (1877), Davin quotes Foster's tribute to McGee and refers to McGee's association with the *Nation* (4n, 649). '[A]t the dawn of Confederation,' 'Thomas D'Arcy McGee said ... that the existence of a recognised literary class will, by-and-by be felt as a State and social necessity,' asserted Frank Yeigh (1861–1935) on 14 January 1889 at the first of several Canadian Literature Evenings held in Toronto and Ottawa (see chapter 7). 'Has that time not arrived?' (*Globe*, 15 January 1889, 3).

As important as Young Ireland may have been as an antecedent of the program and aspirations of 'literary and independent Young Canada,' it was by no means the ultimate origin or only manifestation of the association between nationality and literature that motivated the Confederation group in the early-to-mid 1880s. Although its politics were ultra-conservative rather than liberal or radical, the Young England movement, from which the generational name Young Ireland seems to have been derived (see Duffy 291 and Davis 56–7) may also lie in the background of Young Canada, if only through Roberts's knowledge of the life and work of the most politically and literarily accomplished of its founders, Benjamin Disraeli. Marquis recalls Roberts working on 'Disraeli's latest novel,' *Endymion* (1880), at Chatham in 1880, 'studying ... the ... construction and character delineation' (quoted in Pomeroy 36) of a work that, like the earlier trilogy of novels in which Disraeli also embedded his Young England ideas and associates (*Coningsby* [1844], *Sybil* [1845], and *Tancred* [1847]), places 'fiction (and/or history)' (Faber 255) at the service of political analysis and advocacy. Both before and after Disraeli's death on 19 April 1881, the editorials and columns of the *Star* make frequent references to his life and work. Davin compares him at length to Macdonald in 'Great Speeches' (4) and elevates him to heroic status in the *Earl of Beaconsfield, with Disraeli Anecdotes Never Before Published* (1876).[19] It is thus as difficult to discount Young England as a presence in the background of the Confederation group as it is to distinguish whatever impact it may have had on their literary nationalism from that of Young Ireland.

One reason for this is that Young England, Young Ireland, and Young Canada are all offshoots of a Romantic nationalism whose roots, as Lampman seems to have come close to recognizing, lie in such German theorists of nationality as Johann Gottfried Herder and Friedrich von Schlegel, who argued that literature, especially poetry, is an essential ingredient of national consciousness and cohesion.[20] To Herder in *Ideen zur Philosophie de Geschichte der Menscheit* (1774–91), which was translated in 1800 as *Outlines of a Philosophy of the History of Man*, 'the songs of a people [Volkslieder] are the best testimonies of their peculiar feelings, propensities, and modes of viewing things,' and collections of 'tales and songs' such as the 'northern *Edda*' a manifestation of 'the spirit of the people' and, therefore, a 'national treasure' (216, 481, 552).[21] To Schlegel in *Geschichte der Alten und Neuen Literatur*, which was translated in 1818 as *Lectures on the History of Literature, Ancient and Modern*,

> there is nothing so necessary ... to the whole intellectual existence of a nation, as the plentiful store of those national recollections and associations ... which it forms the great object of the poetical art to perpetuate and adorn. ... [W]hen a people are exalted in their feelings and ennobled in their own estimation, by the consciousness ... that they have a *national poetry* ... we are willing to acknowledge that their pride is reasonable, and they are raised in our eyes by the same circumstances which gave them elevation in their own. (9)

To Duffy in the Preface to *The Ballad Poetry of Ireland* (1845), which may have gone to as many as forty editions by 1880 (see Duffy 666), the example of the 'intellectual revolution commenced' by 'the world-famous German ballads' of Goethe and others gave reason to hope that modern Irish 'ballads also will herald the happy coming of a native literature' (quoted in Holmgren 166). If McGee was one of the conduits through which these ideas came into late nineteenth-century Canada, another, who may himself have been influenced by McGee (see Ballstadt 87), was the Edward Hartley Dewart (1828–1903) of *Selections from Canadian Poets* (1864). 'A national literature is an essential element in the formation of national character,' wrote Dewart in the 'Introductory Essay on Canadian Poetry' in his anthology; 'it is not merely the record of a country's mental progress: it is the expression of its mental life, the bond of national unity, and the guide of national energy' (ix). Perhaps Roberts had Dewart's resonant and ringing assertions in mind when he wrote in his address 'The Beginnings of a Canadian Literature,' which he delivered at the University of New Brunswick on 28 June 1883, that 'the literature of a nation' is not only the best indicator of its 'mental growth and progress,' but also the reflection of its 'inmost heart ... the revelation of [its] present and future character' and the mould that shapes its 'future character' (*SPCP* 243–4).

The pattern of diffusion and adaptation that these quotations represent explains the near-ubiquity in late nineteenth-century Canada of the Herderian conception of literature and (to reiterate) especially poetry as, in Dewart's words once more, 'the subtle but powerful cement' of a nation (ix). As proved time and again by the materials discussed by Carl Berger in *The Sense of Power: Studies in the Ideas of Canadian Imperialism, 1867–1914* (1970) and S.M. Beckow in 'From the Watch-Towers of Patriotism: Theories of Literary Growth in Canada, 1864–1914' (1973), the relationship between Canadian literature (or the absence of it) and Canada's national aspirations (or colonial status) was a topic of continual and heated discussion between Confederation and the First World War, nowhere less disinterestedly than in the group who, of course, had most to gain from the growth of national consciousness that was held sometimes to be the cause and sometimes the consequence of literary achievement – the country's creative writers and literary critics. Nor were discussions and theories about the relationship between literary and national development and progress confined to Canada during this period. Surveying the achievements of Canadian and Australian literature in the Introduction to *A Victorian Anthology, 1837–1895* (1896), a book that, ironically, presented Roberts to the English-speaking world as 'an influential leader of [a] new and promising group of [Canadian] writers' (702) on the eve of the Confederation group's disintegration, Edmund Clarence Stedman found 'one noteworthy trait of colonial poetry ... [to be] the frequency with which it takes the ballad form' (xiv). 'By some law akin to that which makes balladry ... the natural song of primitive man, of the epic youth of a race or nation,' theorizes Stedman, 'so its form and spirit appear to characterize the verse of a people not primitive, though the colonial pioneers of life and literature in a new land.' If one source of impetus for 'literary and independent Young Canada' was German Romanticism by way of Young Ireland and Young England, another was a literary atmosphere redolent with pronouncements about the functions and characteristics of poetry 'in a new land.'

## III

It is impossible to be certain but plausible to speculate that one consequence of Davin's coronation of Fréchette as Canada's 'national poet' in his 'Great Speeches' essay of March 1881 was a conscious decision on the part of Collins and Roberts to make *Orion, and Other Poems* the basis for claiming a similar status for its author, at least in English Canada. Not least because of the disparity in their ages and accomplishments (in the spring of 1881, Roberts was barely twenty-one; Fréchette was over forty and the author of numerous books), such a hypothesis may seem far-fetched, but it gains credibility in the light of the reviewing history of *Orion, and Other Poems* and the promotional activities of Collins. As initially reviewed in New Brunswick in the Fredericton *Capital* (5 October 1880), the Chatham *Star* (October 6), and the *Miramichi Advance* (November 4), Roberts's book was heralded primarily as a personal and regional achievement even by Collins (for, although anonymous, the review in the *Star* is at least partly by him):[22] 'there is fidelity to the facts and a felicity of expression in ... descriptive passages [in 'Orion'] which give promise of a high degree of excellence' (*Capital*); 'the very description of [Orion's] garb and mien is enough to give our young poet a life-long reputation' (*Star*); 'a good thing has come out of the New Brunswick Nazareth' (*Advance*).[23] But already in the decidedly mixed review in the *Capital*,[24] there is a gesture towards higher goals and a larger forum that must have been in the minds of Collins and Roberts when they read Davin on Fréchette as 'our national poet':

[Mr Roberts] has read his books with good results. Now let him read men, nature, his country and his own heart, and he can accomplish very much indeed. Canada has no Canadian poet. It has a score or more of men and women, who, keeping into the old grooves, give us verses upon verses; but no one, no English-speaking one, at any rate, seems to have drawn any inspiration from the legends, the history of Canada, or the unutterable grandeur of its scenery. If we were to advise Mr. Roberts, we would suggest that a year or two in the great west, amid the vast prairies and mountains would fill his memory with scenes and store his mind with thoughts and facts which would prove of great value to him. A writer who derives his knowledge from the hills and valleys of New Brunswick, and yet can write the ... description of sunset [in *Orion*] ought to take the very foremost rank if he studied nature under her grandest aspects.

Less avuncular but, because of its location, an even more compelling invitation to Roberts to seek national stature is the review of *Orion, and Other Poems* in the November 1880 number of *Rose-Belford's Canadian Monthly Magazine,* from which, as seen earlier, Collins would draw excerpts in April 1881 to demonstrate that the volume had found 'general favour' and was regarded as both highly original and an auspicious sign for 'the spread of a genuine literary spirit in Canada.' Neither naïve nor lacking in ambition, Collins and Roberts must have realized that for the tide generated by *Orion, and Other Poems* to take them unto fortune they would have to do everything in their power to assist in the spreading of 'genuine literary spirit' and Roberts's literary reputation in Canada.

As editor of the *Star* and, beginning in the winter of 1881–2, city editor of the *Globe*, Collins could do little in print either to further the schemes of Young Canada or to promote Roberts's work and career in the national forum. But when his chance came in the form of a commission from the Rose Publishing Company (as Rose-Belford became in 1882) to write a book that was certain to achieve national attention, he did not waste it. His *Life and Times of the Right Honourable Sir John A. Macdonald* concludes with an unequivocal endorsement of 'Canadian Independence' as the only option that 'will satisfy the manly, yearning spirit of our young Canadians' and a stirring call to all Canadians 'to bestir ourselves, to organize, and to tire not nor rest until our Colonialism shall have become a thing of the past, and our Canada stand robust, and pure, and manly, and intelligent among the nations of the earth' (497–8). Moreover, these ringing national sentiments come at the end of a sixty-two* page chapter on Canadian 'Thought and Literature,' in which more than fifteen pages are given over to celebrating Roberts as 'beyond any comparison, our greatest Canadian poet' (465). For reasons that will become apparent in due course, Collins's hopes for Canadian literature and independence are muted to the point of despair in the second political biography that he wrote for Rose's Canadian National Series, *Canada under the Administration of Lord Lorne* (1884), yet even there *Orion, and Other Poems* is 'conspicuously superior to any in our literature' and Roberts 'displays a strong original power, and an almost entirely new and individual method of treatment' (355, 356).

Nor did Collins restrict his promotion of Roberts and his work to his political biographies. No doubt with Lampman's assistance, he availed himself of the *Rouge et Noir* in February 1883 to publish an anonymous review of *Orion, and Other Poems* that elevates Roberts to 'the same seat with Mat[t]hew Arnold,' registers a 'thrill of pride ... because he is of ourselves – a Canadian' (a statement later echoed by Lampman in 'Two Canadian Poets'), and audaciously suggests that he should be appointed to a professorship at Trinity College: 'the pity is that we have not Roberts ... here, in the great centre of the Dominion, and as it ought to be the literary centre, we want him. Might it be too much to hope that our College authorities would some day ... set apart to him a chair in English literature in our College? He would draw all our aspiring young men around him there' (12, 13). The same suggestion in almost exactly the same words, but with the inclusion of University College as an alternative venue for 'this adorning star of native talent, this example of Canadian possibility' (479–80), concludes Collins's encomium to Roberts in

---

* Collins ends both the chapter and the biography with the two concluding stanzas of 'Perinde ac Cadaver' (1871), a Blakean diatribe by Algernon Charles Swinburne in which a corpse-like England is exhorted by Liberty to awaken from her materialistic slumber and once again champion the values that inspired Oliver Cromwell and John Milton. '"Freeman he is not, but slave, / Who stands not out on my side ...,"' Collins quotes Liberty as saying,

> 'Time shall tread on his name
> That was written for honour of old,
> Who hath taken in change for fame
> Dust, and silver, and shame,
> Ashes, and iron, and gold.' (Swinburne 1:878)

'Perinde ac Cadaver' was first pubished in *Songs before Sunrise*, a volume in which Swinburne voices his support for Italian independence and his loathing of political oppression.

*Life and Times of the Right Honourable Sir John A. Macdonald.*[25] Its absence from *Canada under the Administration of Lord Lorne* may be explained by Collins's success during 1882–3 in securing for Roberts the founding editorship of the *Week* (1883–96), the 'Independent Journal of Literature, Politics, and Criticism' that began publication in December 1883 with the support of one of the most respected and articulate men in Canadian journalism, the English-born man of letters Goldwin Smith. By early November 1883, Roberts was well placed to 'scribble and prose-lytize' on behalf of Canadian Independence 'in the great centre of the Dominion' and in a periodical that was supported, he assured Fréchette in a letter of November 8, by 'abundant capital' (*CL* 36).

To judge by a lost Lampman letter of 22 August 1882 that Connor summarizes in *Archibald Lampman: Canadian Poet of Nature* (1929), Collins was friendly enough with Smith in the summer of that year to dine with him in his baronial Toronto home (the Grange) and to participate in his plans for the creation of a new 'literary monthly' (Connor 59). This being so, then Collins was very likely the architect of the agreement whereby Roberts, by his own description in his letter of 10 March 1883 to Carman, published 'a lot of stuff' anonymously (*CL* 34) in the April, July, and October 1883 numbers of the second series of Smith's periodical, the *Bystander,* which began publication in January of the same year with an editorial statement of commitment to policies that 'promise to bring wealth, happiness and the virtues which follow in their train to the homes of the Canadian people' and to the principle of replacing the 'dependency' of 'the Colonies' on 'the Mother Country' with 'mutual citizenship' so that Britain may be 'the mother of free nations' (Goldwin Smith, Editorial 1). Among the 'stuff' that Roberts published in the *Bystander* in 1883 are an article on 'The Change in Government in N[ew] Brunswick,' in which he reiterates his claim that 'there is a quiet, but rapid and steady growth of feeling in favour of Independence' in the Province (94); an article on 'Imperial Relations,' in which he critiques proposals for 'Imperial Federation' and 'Diplomatic Independence' (195–96); and two notes on 'Canadian Literature,' in which, among other things, he praises Collins's biography of Macdonald (twice), laments the fate of Canada's 'national aspirations' following Confederation, and argues that, 'if it were ... recorded or capable of being recorded,' 'the history of the Pioneer' would 'furnish [Canadians] with a religion of gratitude' ([October] 329).[26] Since it is likely that Collins also contributed to the *Bystander* (and, certainly, saw his biography announced and advertised in its April and July numbers), both men must have been well pleased by the fall of 1883 not only with their own achievements and prospects, but also with the progress that they had made in promulgating their vision of Canadian Independence.[27]

The best was yet to come, however, for the months following Roberts's removal to Toronto to assume the editorship of the *Week* late in September 1883 were to prove the zenith of Young Canada. After 'a delay at the publishing house' (Rose in Toronto), *Life and Times of the Right Honourable Sir John A. Macdonald* came off the press in the fall and created a stir in political and literary circles.* True to an announcement in the October number of the *Bystander*, the first issue of the *Week* appeared on December 6 and quickly became a lively forum for 'Politics, News, [and] Literature.' By Christmas, Roberts, his wife, and their son were well established in a rented house, where they were soon joined by the Collinses (Pomeroy 49). Neither Collins nor Roberts wasted time in availing themselves of the *Week* as a sure and powerful outlet for their writing and ideas: 'International Copyright,' Collins's trenchantly ironic analysis of the implications for Canadian authors of the 'honour of being [in] a Colony of Great Britain' (5),[28] appeared in the first issue, and 'Westmoreland [later 'Tantramar'] Revisited,' Roberts's vividly realized description of a Canadian locale that is rich in history and suffused with affection, in the third issue. Nor were Lampman and Carman ignored. Lampman's 'The Monition' (later 'The Coming of Winter'), a strangely erotic treatment of the arrival of winter that anticipates Isabella Valancy Crawford's handling of the same theme in *Malcolm's Katie* (1884),[29] appeared in the first issue, and Carman's 'La Belle Canadienne,' a warmly appreciative depiction of a French-Canadian woman that helped to convince Roberts that his cousin possessed 'the true flame' (*CL* 37), in the fourth. As yet imperceptibly to outsiders, the Confederation group had begun to make its mark with well-crafted celebrations of their country's landscapes, seasons, and peoples.

There is appropriateness to the fact that 'The Monition' appeared on

---

* Several months prior to the appearance of Collins's biography, Roberts gave its 'first seven chapters' a rave review in the 19 March 1883 issue of the Saint John *Daily Telegraph*, predicting that it would 'step at once into the front rank of our literature' and find 'an audience far beyond the borders of Canada, as one of the most brilliant biographies of the day.' In the 'Review of Literature, Science and Art' in *The Dominion Annual Register and Review for… 1883* (1884), Roberts quotes the passage from which these fulsome statements are taken with the comment that 'the volume of Mr. Collins' was 'thus spoken of in the columns of the St. John *Telegraph*' (207).

the same page and after 'International Copyright' in the first issue of the *Week* for since 1882 Collins had been Lampman's almost constant mentor, first in Toronto and Orangeville and then, after Lampman took up his position with the Post Office Department in January 1883, in Ottawa. During the Christmas period preceding Lampman's removal to Ottawa, the pair had 'many long communings ... over past writings and future plans,' and during the ensuing winter, when Collins was in Ottawa researching and writing *Canada under the Administration of Lord Lorne*, they 'smoked and talked and walked together, busy with number-less schemes' (Connor 65, 76). Collins was very likely responsible for an article in the 16 January 1883 issue of the Toronto *World* that notes Lampman's appointment to the Post Office Department in Ottawa, characterizes him as 'one of Canada's rising literateurs,' and expresses the hope that 'the leisure afforded him in his new sphere will give him sufficient time for the pursuit of ... literary labours' that, when added to the 'established merit of Roberts, Fréchette and other young Canadi-ans,' will result in a substantial 'Canadian literature' (1; and see the *Citi-zen* [Ottawa], 17 January 1883, 1). No doubt because Lampman was in a new job and a strange city in the early months of 1883, he relied heavily on Collins for advice and encouragement at that time, sending him 'two winter poems'[30] for comment in January, showing him 'six chapters of a full-blown novel' a few weeks later (quoted in Connor 66, 76), and, in return, writing the advance review of Collins's biography of Macdonald that appeared in the 30 June 1883 issue of the *Canadian Illustrated News* (Montreal) and 'contributing descriptions of scenery' to *Canada under the Administration of Lord Lorne* (Connor 72). 'We must work, John, and keep our pens perpetually to paper,' Lampman urged Ritchie (who was still at college, and achieving some poetic success)[31] early in 1884, 'and with old Joseph Edmund to egg us on we shall surely do something' (quoted in Connor 76).

The enthusiastic comments on the 'Thought and Literature' chapter of *Life and Times of the Right Honourable Sir John A. Macdonald* with which Lampman concludes his highly laudatory review leave no room for doubt that the 'something' he envisaged doing was consistent with Col-lins's views on Canadian literature and Independence:

A great part of the chapter is devoted to glowing and masterly examination of the works of the two first of Canadian singers, Roberts and Fréchette, in his unbounded admiration of whom we entirely agree. In this chapter will be found what charms us most in the whole work, the author's perfect and loving patriotism – patriotism, as we understand it, devoted wholly to Canada no longer as a child in leading strings, but as the apportioned home of a people who have accumulated a peculiar feeling and character of their own, who are in truth rapidly becoming one of the distinct upon earth, self-dependent, jealous of their manhood. (*ER* 45)

Little wonder that Lampman's 'numberless schemes' in 1883–4 included the project that eventually became *The Story of an Affinity* (which, however, was not written until 1892–4): 'a strictly Canadian poem, local in incident and spirit, but cosmopolitan in form and manner. It is a hard thing to get at. I have been dreaming, however, of locating some simple story in the Niagara district, among the old farmsteads – something in accordance with the quiet toilsome life there – maybe dated forty or fifty years back in rougher times – making it sober and realistic, so to speak, in the metre of [Longfellow's] *Evangeline* but more like Goethe's *Hermann and Dorothea* or, nearer still, to the translations from a Swedish poet, [Johan Ludwig] Runeberg, who wrote lovely things about the peasants of Finland' (quoted in Connor 78).

When Lampman wrote this in the 'summer' of 1884 (Connor 77), his schemes and dreams had already been dealt a severe blow by the events that began to unfold earlier that year. In January and February, he and Carman each published two more poems in the *Week*, but late in February their ready access to the journal that seemed set to catapult them to prominence in Canada was suddenly curtailed by Roberts's resignation as its editor. 'It is necessary for me to be what I seem,' Roberts told Carman in a letter of February 28. 'I could have got on comfortably ... by being a stalking horse for G[oldwin] S[mith], but not otherwise ... Poetry is going to be discounted with the *Week*, so I send back y[our] poems, which I had intended to use soon. They are the real thing ... and I am more pleased than I can tell you at the genius you are developing' (*CL* 38–9). In her usual capacity as a vehicle for Roberts's own views, Pomeroy provides the reasons for his resignation:

> The insurmountable difficulty lay ... in the wide divergence of views held by the Owner and the Editor. Goldwin Smith ... was an embittered Englishman and an obstinate promulgator of the doctrine that the ultimate destiny of Canada lay in annexation to the United States. Roberts ... belonged at the time to the little band of ardent Independents, and the idea of Annexation was abhorrent to him. Goldwin Smith, not unnaturally, wished to use the columns of the *Week* in advocacy of his pet theory. Roberts was adamant in

his refusal to permit such propaganda so long as he remained Editor. It was an impossible situation. Consequently, at the end of February, Goldwin Smith released his Editor and paid him the balance of a year's salary. (51)

In a way, the most surprising aspect of the relationship between Smith and Roberts is that it developed and endured to the extent that it did. Smith had been a committed and outspoken proponent of Annexation since at least 1877,[32] and neither Roberts nor Collins made any secret of their sympathy for Canadian Independence in their contributions to the *Bystander.* Perhaps, as Roberts and Pomeroy imply, Smith saw Canadian independence as an intermediate and necessary stage in Canada's transition from dependence on Britain to union with the United States and merely exploited the energy and enthusiasm of Roberts and Collins to this end. Or, less cynically, perhaps he drew from that same energy and enthusiasm the impetus to revive the dream of Canadian nationhood that he had shared with the Canada First movement after his arrival in Toronto in 1871 (see Berger 74). Whatever the case, Smith certainly opened the second series of the *Bystander* to independentist construal not only in his initial editorial on 'mutual citizenship,' but also in a vigorous salute to Canada First. 'What are our National Policy and Commercial autonomy but tributes to "Canada First"?' he asked in the opening number of the journal:

'We will govern our own country. We will put on the taxes ourselves, we will do so, and we do not desire England, Ireland, or Scotland to tell us we are fools ...' Such is now the language of the Conservative Prime Minister. Not many years ago he would have been accused of seeking the dismemberment of the Empire, and perhaps, by the more hysterical Imperialists, of wanting to bring about a civil war. When 'Canada First' came into existence, the very utterance of the name Canadian nation was denounced as treason. Who denounces it as treason now? ('Third Parties')

There can be little, if any, doubt that Smith was an Annexationist in the early 1880s, but passages such as this gesture towards Canadian nationalism in a way that makes Roberts's involvement and then disillusionment with the *Week* and its 'owner' perfectly understandable. After all, had not Collins been convinced or deluded while writing his biography of Macdonald that Smith was a *'genius'* whose arrival in Canada 'marked the beginning of a new era in national aspiration and literary ambition' and whose 'teaching' was still exercising a positive influence on the 'young country' in the 'formative period of [its] national character' (458, 455, 462)?

Whether Smith was temporarily inclined towards Canadian Independence in 1882–3 or merely an 'embittered Englishman' and a committed Annexationist who used his young 'Editor' as a 'stalking horse,' the golden handshake of 'the balance of a year's salary' that he gave Roberts enabled him to conclude his letter to Carman of February 28 with the boast that he was now 'going to depend entirely on [his] pen' and 'had lots of work, with sure pay, cut out for [him]' (*CL* 39). Pomeroy is doubtless correct in suggesting that Roberts's admission to Carman on August 23 that he has been 'both busy and bothered' (*CL* 41) indicates that 'his pen was not making as much money as he hoped, as much, indeed, as was necessary for the head of a family' (Pomeroy 52). Nevertheless, he was able to muster enough money late in the summer to visit New York, where his reception by such well-known American literary men as Thomas Bailey Aldrich (1836–1907) and Richard Watson Gilder must have built upon a sense of disappointment over the fate of Young Canada to result in his decision, as he informed another American writer, Charles Leonard Moore (1854–1923), in a letter of September 20, to 'break ... up housekeeping [in Toronto] with the intention of going to live in New York' (*CL* 42). Nor was this merely a pipe dream, for according to late October 1883 issues of newspapers in New Brunswick, Roberts was 'tendered the position of associate editor of the *Manhattan*,' the New York magazine in which he would subsequently publish 'The Sower' (1886).[33] Perhaps it was this offer that occasioned 'The Poet Is Bidden to Manhattan Island' (1886), a mock-pastoral that both begins and ends on a serious note:

> Dear Poet, quit your shady lanes
>   And come where more than lanes are shady.
> Leave Phyllis to the rustic swains
>   And sing some Knickerbocker lady.
> O hither haste, and here devise
>   Divine *ballades* before unuttered
> Your poet's eyes *must* recognize
>   The side on which your bread is buttered!
> ...
> Your heart, dear Poet, surely yields;
>   And soon you'll leave your uplands flowery,

Forsaking fresh and bowery fields,
    For 'pastures new' – upon the Bowery!
You've piped at home, where none could pay,
    Till now, I trust, your wits are riper.
Make no delay, but come this way,
    And pipe for them that pay the piper! (*CP* 81, 82)

The initial reason for what would ultimately prove to be merely a lengthy deferral of Roberts's 'intention ... to live in New York' was the emergence of another possibility – a position in the civil service in Ottawa – that might well have recaptured and even increased the momentum of Young Canada by allowing him to remain in Ontario and to further his association with Lampman. 'If New York fails me I shall pass the Civil Service Exams, and try for a good post,' he told Carman while visiting Ottawa in October 1884 after moving his family from Toronto to Fredericton:

> They think of establishing a *Government Printing Bureau* next winter, and [Sir Leonard] Tilley [the New Brunswick Father of Confederation who was then Macdonald's finance minister] questioned me closely as to my qualifications thereon. That is the sort of work for you and me. Short hours, easy work, lots of vitality left for creation ... What if we could both get here? Would not music flow from our pens till the world stood still to listen? Think it over. (*CL* 44)

As certainly as Roberts's perception of the advantages for a writer of a position in the civil service was shaped by Lampman and his new friend and fellow civil servant Duncan Campbell Scott, whom Roberts apparently met for the first time during this visit (Pomeroy 53), his positive response to Ottawa was a result of the fêting that he describes to Carman in a letter of October 25: 'I am being delightfully entertained. Have been given two small parties, drives, symposiums, etc., and in fact am being made such a lion of that I expect the roar of the beast will soon resound throughout the nation' (*CL* 44). Ottawa 'has both lovely and rugged surroundings,' he added in a letter to Carman on 28 November 1884; 'It is characteristic and peculiar. And the air is sympathetic towards literature' (*CL* 45). New York beckoned, but the dream of Young Canada was still alive.

In the event, however, Roberts did not join Lampman and Scott in the civil service in Ottawa, but returned to Fredericton, where he lived in his parents' house with his growing family (a second son was born in October 1884 and a daughter in September 1886) and continued his attempt to earn his living by his pen. If not with Roberts's resignation from the *Week* in February 1884 then with his return to Fredericton in December of that year, the Young Canada phase of the development of the Confederation group was all but over, leaving those whom it had deeply touched aimless and dispirited as regards the future of Canadian poetry. In a letter of 28 November 1884, Roberts confessed to Carman that he had 'been in a very slough of despond' and was 'not yet quite out of the dismal region' (*CL* 45). In a letter to Ritchie that Connor dates merely to the 'summer' of 1884, Lampman describes himself as being 'in the barren wilderness' psychologically and creatively, and in a letter of 29 January 1885 to another friend, May McKeggie, he gives a similar account of his condition: 'I have been very dull and out of spirits – oppressed with innumerable things – debts; ill success in everything, in capacity to write and want of any hope of succeeding in it if I do' (TCU). Since Roberts, too, complains of pecuniary embarrassment ('I have not fifteen cents. And I have had to write to the Father-in-law for money' [*CL* 45]), there can be no doubt that one cause of the two writers' depression was financial, but this merely throws into relief the extent to which the collapse of the dream of 'literary and independent Young Canada' into the reality of 'poetry ... discounted with the *Week*' adversely affected the material as much as the psychological and creative condition of the Confederation group. Between February 1884 and the end of the year, Roberts wrote and published only a handful of poems and essays, whose titles and subjects – 'To the Memory of Sidney Lanier,' 'The Slave Woman,' 'In Notre Dame,' 'Reporting in New York,' 'Notes on Some of the Younger American Poets,' 'Edgar Fawcett' – reflect his temporary disengagement from national issues.'[34] During the same period, Lampman attempted to alleviate his financial and psychological distress by writing two fairy tales, 'Hans Fingerhut's Frog-lesson' and 'The Fairy Fountain,' a sequence of sonnets to his future wife, Maud Playter ('The Growth of Love'), and such poems as 'April' (May 1884) and 'In October' (October 1883–October 1884) that reveal the increasing facility in therapeutic nature poetry that would soon produce 'Among the Timothy' (August 1885), 'Heat' (July 1887), and other masterpieces (see chapter 5). Less affected by the collapse of Young Canada than either Roberts or Lampman because he was in Edinburgh until August 1883, Carman returned to pursue his desultory career as a student, teacher, surveyor, and writer in Fredericton until the death of his mother in February 1886 gave him just enough emotional and financial freedom to move to the United States in September of that year. Roberts's 'Birch and Paddle' (1886), which is dedicated '*To Bliss Carman*' and was almost certainly written during his sojourn in New Brunswick (see *CL* 48), testifies to the closeness of the two poets at that time and to the awakening perception of the natural world as a therapeutic refuge from 'care ... task and toil' (*CP* 96).

As for Collins, after the publication of *Canada under the Administration of Lord Lorne* in 1884, he 'tir[ed] of ... political biographies' (M. Brook Taylor 205) and turned his hand primarily to the money-making historical romances for which he is infamous in Canadian literary studies: *The Story of a Greenland Girl* (1885), *The Story of Louis Riel: The Rebel Chief* (1886), *The Four Canadian Highwaymen; or, The Robbers of Markham Swamp* (1886), and, of course, *Annette, the Métis Spy* (1886). His remarks on 'English-Canadian Literature' in the 28 August 1884 issue of the *Week* offer a glimpse of his attitude in the wake of the collapse of Young Canada:

> There is no Australian Literature, no Heligoland Literature, no Rock-of-Gibraltar Literature: neither is there a Canadian Literature. A number of books have been written by English-speaking colonists here, but the majority of them have the tone of the kitchen of empire ... I suppose that, in a sort of way, with respect to flavour and local colour, we would soon have a Canadian literature if Canada were a nation in the harmony of her provinces as well as in name. We are not now united, except by legislative cords that cut into the flesh of one another, for we are all pulling in different ways: so that if we did speak of a literature we would be obliged to divide the term and say, 'a New Brunswick Literature,' 'a Nova Scotia Literature,' 'a British Columbia Literature.' (614)

Towards the end of the essay, Collins briefly praises several poets and, predictably, bestows special praise on Roberts ('his note is original, virile, and manly. His range is wide, and his work full of sensuousness and colour, and the music of happy as well as skilful word arrangement' [615]), but his overall assessment of contemporary Canadian poetry is devastatingly negative:

> In these days nearly every sentimentalist writes verse; and he not only writes poor verse, but he gives himself airs, adopting the affectations and the attitudes of some gymnast writers of the modern school. About a thousand silly young men in this country repeat the following line [adapted from Swin-

burne's 'In Memory of Barry Cornwall' (1: 366)] till they grow drunken and inspired:

'And his heart grew sad, that was glad, for his sweet song's sake,'

and, inspired, they go away and endeavour to write in the same strain. (615)

Since Lampman is not mentioned in 'English-Canadian Literature' and therefore not exempted from Collins's charges, he would have had every reason to regard them as both a criticism and a challenge – a criticism of such callow and imitative poems as 'A Fantasy' and 'Three Flower Petals' in earlier issues of the *Week* and a challenge to move on to more 'original, virile, and manly' efforts.

With the completion of the Young Canada phase of the Confederation group in 1884, Collins ceased to be a major force in its development and direction. After the publication of the last of his historical romances in 1886, he moved to New York and, as the editor of a new weekly journal entitled the *Epoch*, continued to promote Roberts by placing *In Divers Tones* (1886), which is dedicated to him, in the company of volumes by such well-known British and American poets as Swinburne and James Russell Lowell (11 February 1887) and by giving it an eloquent and laudatory review as one of the 'best [books] that of late years have been added to English poetic literature' (1 April 1887) (quoted in Adams, 'Roberts' 12). In a number of the Halifax *Critic* commemorating the twentieth anniversary of Confederation (June 1887), Collins surveyed the poetic events of the previous years with a detachment that belies his close involvement with them, asserting the existence of a Canadian 'people' who came of their own accord to recognize *Orion, and Other Poems* as the 'rival' of Fréchette's work and attributing the extravagant claims made on behalf of *In Divers Tones* in the *Epoch* to 'one of the leading literary papers in New York' (1, 2). Soon Collins was to become a pitiful shadow of his loyal, inspiring, and crafty self, however, for 'whether as a cause or a consequence' of his disappointments and desultoriness, 'he turned to drink, undermining both his health and his marriage' (M. Brook Taylor 205) and taxing to the limits the friendship and hospitality of Roberts at Windsor and Carman in New York (see Adams, 'Roberts' 13). On 23 February 1892, at the age of thirty-seven, he died in a New York hospital. 'In Mr Collins there was a genuine streak of genius,' recalled Lampman in his 'At the Mermaid Inn' column on 19 March 1892:

He had an exceedingly rare faculty of appreciation as regards the true and the good in literature, and especially in poetry ... His genuine delight in fine literary work and his boundless enthusiasm for it were a source of refreshment and help to all who were much in his company ...

There are two or three – perhaps more – young writers, whose names are now well known in the Dominion, who remember Collins with an especial feeling of tenderness, gratitude, and almost of reverence. To his helpful enthusiasm, his kindly praise, his eager excitement, they owe the courage and self-confidence which enabled them to take the first daring step in the difficult and unpromising path of literature. Collins was almost the literary father of some of the young men who are now winning fame among us. There are only a few people who know what Joseph Edmund Collins has done in this way for our literature, and perhaps all that he has done will never be known. (*MI* 40)

If Collins's sad fate was partly an after-effect of the failure of the Young Canada phase of the Confederation group, Lampman's appreciation of his 'genius' and importance is its belated epilogue: all that Collins did as 'almost the literary father' of Roberts, Lampman, and perhaps Carman will never be known, but between 1880 and 1884 it was clearly a very great deal.

Looking back in the 12 June 1884 issue of the *Week* on the years in which the hopes of Young Canada reached their zenith and nadir, one of the most dedicated promoters and practitioners of Canadian writing in the post-Confederation period, Graeme Mercer Adam (1839–1912), saw a 'literary interregnum' in which the malaise evident in Britain and the United States had been exacerbated in Canada by a variety of factors, including a preoccupation with 'newspapers' and 'business' that was causing 'even the professional classes ... to ... los[e] their poetic sensibilities and becom[e] indifferent to the claims of culture' (439). 'In Canada,' continued Adam, the effects of what would come to be called modernity, were being compounded by other factors, specifically,

the ebbing of our national spirit, a growing intellectual callousness, and a deadening of interest in the things that make for the nation's higher life. Native literature, with nothing to encourage it, is fast losing the power to arrest attention and is perceptibly dying of inanition ... But for denominational pride our universities would be in danger of becoming extinct. Journalism of a certain kind flourishes, but the newspaper, as an engine of culture and a vehicle of independent critical thought, can hardly be said to

exist ... [Canada's] colonial status, and the anomalies of the literary copyright law, which surrender the native book-markets to the American publisher, are further serious obstacles to literary progress. (439)[35]

This is indeed 'a severe indictment of the country's intellectual status,'
but, as Adam gently reminds his readers, it stems from 'a quarter of a century's observation of the facts, and ... [from] close contact with those who
have long striven to make of the desert a watered plain.' Like Kent's final
speech in *King Lear*, it speaks with an authority borne of direct experience of events too sad to allow for much optimism about the future.

Although Adam would probably not have included Collins and Roberts among those who had 'long striven' to create a native literature,
their interests and their careers coincided with his in ways that would
seem uncanny if they were not a reflection of the movements and personalities that gave Canadian literary culture its shape in the years surrounding Young Canada. To judge by its content and location, Adam's
'Outline of Canadian Literature' in Henry Winthrow's *History of Canada*
(1876) provided Collins with a model for the 'Thought and Literature'
chapter in *Life and Times of the Right Honourable Sir John A. Macdonald*. To
judge by the dedication of *Canada under the Administration of Lord Lorne*
to Adam in gratitude for 'Indispensable Help when I Was Entering the
Calling of Literature' and as 'Testimony to His Untiring Zeal in Striving
to Forward the Cause of Our Wretched Canadian Literature,' he had
used the various positions that he held in the late 1870s and early 1880s
– editor of the *Canadian Monthly Magazine* and *Rose-Belford's Canadian
Monthly Magazine* from 1872 to 1882, literary assistant to Smith and business manager of the *Bystander* between 1880 and 1883 – to assist Collins
and Roberts in their forays into the literary and journalistic worlds of
Toronto. Older and perhaps more tenaciously patriotic than they, but
no less susceptible to the vicissitudes of the Canadian 'national spirit' in
the post-Confederation period, Adam would soon enact a pattern that
Collins and Roberts would reveal to be typical of diehard literary nationalists who sought to earn or augment their income by the pen in Canada
in the 1880s and 1890s: first popular and patriotic history (Adam's *The
Canadian North-West: Its History and Its Troubles* was published in 1885);[36]
then historical or sentimental romance set in Canada (his collaboration
with Agnes Ethelwyn Wetherald, *An Algonquin Maiden: A Romance of the
Early Days of Upper Canada*, appeared in 1887); and, finally, after shifts
that mimic with almost comical precision the economic and ideological
forces at work in the period (a *Handbook of Commercial Union* in 1888 and

*Toronto, Old and New* in 1891), emigration to the United States (1892). It is a sign of the times in which Young Canada burned and sputtered that surrounding 'An Interregnum in Literature' in the May and June 1884 issues of the *Week* are articles that discuss the arguments, counter-arguments, and reasons for a phenomenon that had been the cause of intense debate in Canadian and American newspapers since before the beginning of the decade: the 'Emigration of the Young Men of Canada to the United States.'[37] Ironically, the one member of the Confederation group who had expressed a desire to go south would wait more than a dozen years to do so. In the meantime, he would enact the return that is both celebrated and refused in the poem that stands as the finest achievement of Young Canada.

## IV

In both the popular and the strict senses of the term, 'Tantramar Revisited' – or 'Westmoreland Revisited' as it was called in the third number of the *Week* – has come to be regarded as a masterpiece. Anthologized dozens of times during and after Roberts's lifetime, it has received more critical attention than any other of his works, the reason being that it has seemed to critics to stand out among his early poems both for its 'originality in tone and treatment' and in being a 'true whole' (Cappon, *Charles G.D. Roberts* 18, 20) that possesses the organic, cohesive, 'definite and satisfying structure' (Pacey, *Ten Canadian Poets* 48) that was valued by both post-Romantic and 'New' critics. Under scrutiny from various perspectives and in varying degrees of intensity by W.J. Keith, D.G. Jones, William Strong, David Jackel, and others, 'Tantramar Revisited' has come to be seen as somewhat less 'original,' 'whole,' and 'satisfying' than it was judged by earlier critics, but the consensus nevertheless remains that it is a remarkably accomplished and affective poem that, in Keith's words, shows the poet 'at the height of his power' ('Introduction' xxi). In the volume devoted to the Confederation poets in the *Canadian Writers and Their Works* series (1983), 'Tantramar Revisited' is described by George Woodcock as Roberts's 'famous masterpiece' (19) and by Fred Cogswell as one of his 'two greatest poems' ('Charles G.D. Roberts' 223) (the other being 'The Iceberg' [1934]).

Whatever else it may or may not be, 'Tantramar Revisited' is the beneficiary both formalistically and conceptually of 'The Pipes of Pan,' the poem that, on the authority of Pomeroy (and, hence, Roberts himself), Desmond Pacey placed immediately before it in the chronological arrangement of the 1985 *Collected Poems*. Written in the summer of 1883 (see Pomeroy 48) when Young Canada was nearing the zenith that would come with Roberts's brief tenure as editor of the *Week*, 'The Pipes of Pan' is composed of alternating lines of dactyllic hexameter and pentameter, a classical form that is perfectly suited to its theme of the migration of the music and spirit of Pan from ancient Greece to North America. After being tossed into the river Penëus in the Arcadian valley of Tempe, runs the narrative of the poem, the fragments of a set of Pan's 'outworn pipes' were 'wind-blown ... Over the whole green earth and globe of sea ... to secret spots' where the god thus 'comes ... in his workings' though not 'in a visible form' (*CP* 77). Any 'mortal' finding such a 'secret spot,' be it a 'glade' in London's Kensington Gardens, where Arnold had contrived to be 'breathed upon by the rural Pan' (*Poems* 256) in *Empedocles on Etna, and Other Poems*, or a 'shad[y] covert' on the Bay of Fundy in New Brunswick, can set Pan's pipes 'to their lips' and acquire the god's 'charm-struck / Passion for woods and the wild, the solitude of the hills' (*CP* 78).

In its fitting use of the classical form that Roberts would later call 'Ovidian elegiac metre' (*Selected Poems* vii) to transplant the spirit of a figure from classical mythology to the Canadian environment, 'The Pipes of Pan' achieves two ends: (1) it naturalizes – indeed, nationalizes – Roberts's earlier and highly esteemed poems on themes from Greek mythology ('Memnon,' 'Orion,' and 'Actaeon') by making an Arcadia spirit a potent and inspiring presence in Acadia; and (2) it affirms the suitability of classical themes and forms as vehicles for the treatment of Canadian landscapes and concerns, a 'fit' that he had already exploited in the sapphics and choriambics of 'Miriam' (1880) and the 'Ovidian elegiac metre' of 'A Breathing Time' (1892)[38] and would soon put to masterful use in 'Tantramar Revisited.'[39] With 'The Pipes of Pan' and its formalistic and thematic cognates, Roberts effectively resolved for himself and the Confederation group the dichotomy between classical and Canadian sources of inspiration, technique, and theme. It is scarcely surprising, then, that in 'To the Singers of Minas' (1893) John Frederic Herbin, a Nova Scotian poet of Acadian descent, would depict Roberts as a resurrected Hellenic artist who has transformed 'green-walled Acadie into a later Greece' and the 'broad green plain of ... Tantramar' into 'the Tempe of [his] ancient time' (*The Marshlands* 51). As Sandra Djwa has observed ('Lampman's Fleeting Vision' 132), 'The Pipes of Pan' had a particular impact on Lampman, whose 'The Favorites of Pan' (1895), written in May 1892, gives the Greek god an Ontario presence by associating the 'murmur of [his] pipes' with the piping of frogs (133), a sound regarded by the enormously influential American nature writer John Burroughs as the herald of Spring in North America (see chapter 4). With 'The Pipes of Pan' and even more obviously with 'Tantramar Revisited,' it became possible to conceive of 'a strictly Canadian poem' – as Lampman did in the summer of 1884 – as 'local in incident and spirit, but cosmopolitan in form and manner.'

Strong evidence that at the time of writing 'The Pipes of Pan' and 'Tantramar Revisited' Roberts was vexed by the question of whether a poet could be both classical and Canadian is provided by the Alumni Oration on 'The Beginnings of a Canadian Literature' that he delivered at the University of New Brunswick on 28 June 1883. Probably with an eye on the possibility of being appointed to a professorship at the university, Roberts is at pains in the opening portion of his address to impress upon his listeners the importance of Canadian universities as 'centres' of the 'nation's intellectual life' and vanguards of its 'intellectual and literary progress' (*SPCP* 245). In the interests of 'national feeling' and the 'national spirit,' he argues, Canadian universities should especially encourage and reward literary achievement because literature is an index of a nation's cultural and social advancement that 'in its widest sense is ... the fruition of thought, and contains not only nourishment for present mental wants, but also the perfected seed whence new thought shall spring in the future' (*SPCP* 248, 244). By affirming a 'vital connection with the soil' and contributing to the 'vivid realization' of the nation's achievements and aspirations, 'universities in Canada' would become genuinely 'Canadian universities' (*SPCP* 247). With these nationalistic sentiments as his exordium (the classical term is entirely appropriate in this context), Roberts turns to survey the 'two parallel streams' of existing Canadian literature, finding in French Canada, particularly in the poetry of Fréchette, 'a literature ... [that is] in a high degree polished and artistic, [and] imbued with unmistakable Canadian flavour' (*SPCP* 248–9), and in English Canada a plethora of writers of uneven quality and a few, including Smith, Davin, and Collins, who are worthy of high praise.* Only in his final paragraph and then only by

---

* Smith has 'identified himself with Canada to Canada's incalculable benefit'; Davin is 'widely known for important works of a semi-historical character, and for essays on various literary and popular subjects'; and Collins's *Life and Times of ... Macdonald ...* is of 'great intrinsic importance, and ... in its department the most brilliant production of our prose literature' (*SPCP* 257).

implication does Roberts address the relationship between his own poetry and the Canadian literature that requires the 'sympathy and guidance' of Canadian universities, but when he does so his remarks are of very considerable interest and importance.

Turning by way of epilogue to the 'perpetual injunction to our verse-writers to choose Canadian themes only' (*SPCP* 258),[40] Roberts proceeds to address the opposition between native and cosmopolitan in current literary debate,[41] first by arguing that the option of founding 'a *new* literature' is no more open to Canadians than to Americans because both are heirs to 'the whole heritage of English Song,' then by averring that 'the domain of English letters knows no boundaries of Canadian Dominion, of American Commonwealth, nor yet of British Empire,' and, finally, by asserting that, even so, poetry written in Canada by a Canadian cannot fail to bear traces of its origins if its author possesses the requisite originality and creativity:

> Of course the tone of a work, the quality of the handling, must be influenced by the surroundings and local sympathies of the workman, in so far as he is a truly original and creative workman and not a mere copyist. To the assimilativeness and flexibility of genius it is as impossible that its works should lack the special flavour of race and clime, as that honey from Himettus should fail to smell of the thymy slopes. By all means let our singers preserve to the sweetness which they gather a fragrance distinctive of its origin. It is true we have much poetical wealth unappropriated in our broad and magnificent landscapes, in our seasons that alternate so swiftly between gorgeousness and gloom, in the stirring episodes scattered so abundantly throughout parts of our early history; but let us not think we are prohibited from drawing a portion of our material from lands where now the very dust is man. (*SPCP* 258–9)

Fundamental to Roberts's attempt to abolish 'Canadian themes' as the prerequisite for Canadian literature is his subordination of the issue of subject matter to the stylistic and creative norms of workmanship and originality that he and Collins would repeatedly use to argue that international standards rather than Canadian content are the only valid criteria for assessing the merits of any work written in Canada or by a Canadian. But, keenly aware as he was in the summer of 1883 that his claim to fame in Canadian literature and his hope for an appointment in a Canadian university rested to that point on a volume of poetry entitled *Orion, and Other Poems*, Roberts also argues that a 'workman' of 'genius'

(such as himself) will *inevitably* produce work that is *both* international in stature *and* Canadian in 'flavour.' That he does so by alluding to the famous honey from the mountain (Hymettus) overlooking Athens and employing an apian metaphor derived from Seneca's Epistle LXXIV ('On Gathering Ideas') is a deft (and perhaps somewhat mischievous)* touch with which to bring to a close an argument for a literature that draws at least as much on cosmopolitan as native sources.

Of Collins's complete agreement with the principles articulated in 'The Beginnings of a Canadian Literature' and practised in 'The Pipes of Pan' and 'Tantramar Revisited' there can be no doubt. In the opening chapter of *Canada under the Administration of Lord Lorne*, he opens a footnote in order to give a lengthy excerpt from 'Tantramar Revisited' (37n), and in a later chapter on the 'Literature of the Period [and] the Royal Society' he returns, as already seen, to heap praise upon 'the most conspicuously superior [book] in our literature':

> [*Orion, and Other Poems*] belonged to the new school of verse writers, and it stood out as an original, strong and commanding creation. There was nowhere heard the small local voice of provincialism; but there was given the note, unbounded by geography, that appeals to the sentiment in man which is not begotten of locality. Yet have these verses the flavour of their birthplace, the impulse of our lakes and hills, and the perfume of our clover fields; but it is the quality without the filters of locality, a flavour that gives an additional charm to this song as the honey of Hymettus is made more delicious – to use a phrase of Mr. Roberts' own – by the 'smell of the thyme slopes.' It has been the custom to judge the Canadian writer either according to no standard at all, or ... against some native predecessor; but no such method will suffice for ... Mr. Roberts ... We must take him into the court where are found our other masters of English song, and among those there we must assign to him a place on the front benches. (355)

'[B]ut ... Yet ... but ...': Collins's awkward twists and turns of logic and syntax point up the success with which Roberts had dealt with the same contentious issues in the summer of 1883. The merit of Collins's approach,

---

* The point that Seneca draws from the parallel between the creation of honey by bees and a writer's creative use of sources is the reverse of Roberts's: 'we should so blend ... several flavours into one delicious compound that, even though it betrays its origin, yet it nevertheless is clearly a different thing from that whence it came' ('ut etiam si apparuerit, unde sumptum sit, aliud tamen esse quam unde sumptum est, appareat') (1: 278–9).

however, is that it makes unequivocally clear the insistence of both men on international standards, cosmopolitan themes, and the inevitable and intrinsic rather than merely elective or thematic nature of the Canadianness of Canadian literature.

The enabling combination of the international and the local, the classical and the Canadian, that constitutes the cosmopolitan nationalism of Roberts and Collins informs every aspect of 'Tantramar Revisited.' Not only is the poem cast in 'Ovidian elegiac metre,' but it is also a Romantic return poem in the tradition of Wordsworth's 'Tintern Abbey' and a Victorian sea meditation in the manner of Swinburne's 'Evening on the Broads' whose roots ultimately lie in eighteenth-century topographical poetry. Yet at the same time it is a 'Canadian idyll' (Cappon, *Charles G.D. Roberts* 18), a detailed and vivid portrayal of a unique and historical Canadian landscape as seen through 'the fervent, loving eyes'[42] of a native son. The first few lines of the poem quickly and insistently establish its lineage and identify its peer group by echoing both Wordsworth and Swinburne* and by inviting the reader to recognize in the amalgamation of elements from these two writers in an adapted classical form the mark of an 'original and creative workman, and not a mere copyist':

Summers and summers have come, and gone with the flight of the swallow;
Sunshine and thunder have been, storm, and winter, and frost;

---

* A few lines from the beginning of 'Lines Composed a Few Miles above Tintern Abbey, on Revisiting the Banks of the Wye during a Tour, July 13, 1798' and 'Hesperia' will serve to establish the echoic aspect of the opening of Roberts's poem:

Five years have past; five summers, with the length
Of five long winters! and again I hear
These waters, rolling from their mountain-springs
With a soft inland murmur ... (Wordsworth 2:259)

Out of the golden remote wild west where the sea without shore is,
    Full of the sunset, and sad, if at all, with the fulness of joy,
As a wind sets in with the autumn that blows from the region of stories,
    Blows with a perfume of songs and of memories beloved from a boy ... (Swinburne 1:173)

The resemblance between these passages and the opening lines of 'Tantramar Revisited' consists of similarities of tone, mood, diction, and, in the case of Swinburne, rhythm, for as Keith observes, 'the dominant rhythm' of Roberts's poem as a whole 'bears a rough but none the less palpable resemblance ... to the rolling rhetorical periods of "Hesperia"' ('Charles G.D. Roberts and the Poetic Tradition' 58).

Many and many a sorrow has all but died from remembrance,
Many a dream of joy fall'n in the shadow of pain
Hands of chance and change have marred, or moulded, or broken,
Busy with spirit or flesh, all I most have adored;
Even the bosom of Earth is strewn with heavier shadows, –
Only in these green hills, aslant to the sea, no change! ( *CP* 78)

The movement from the general (or cosmopolitan) to the particular (or local) that is signalled in the last two lines of this passage gains momentum in the remainder of the poem's opening verse paragraph, but the description of the landscape 'aslant to the sea' still remains so generalized that it could refer to any number of picturesque sites[43] in Canada, Britain, and elsewhere:

Here where the road that has climbed from the inland valleys and wood-
    lands,
Dips from the hill-tops down, straight to the base of the hills, –
Here, from my vantage-point, I can see the scattering houses,
Stained with time, set warm in orchards, meadows, and wheat,
Dotting the broad bright slopes outspread to southward and eastward,
Wind-swept all day long, blown by the south-east wind.

The reference to 'scattering houses, / Stained with time, set warm in orchards, meadows, and wheat' at the centre of this passage bespeaks the presence in the landscape of a long-established agricultural community and, in so doing, heralds the poem's imminent shift towards historical, communal, regional, and national concerns.

That shift is accomplished in the ensuing verse paragraph through references to landscape forms and place names that, in combination, proclaim the uniqueness of the area being described and (to borrow the terms of Henri Lefebvre's *The Production of Space*) demand that it be understood both as a physical place and as a 'script' of past 'associations and connections' (37):

Skirting the sunbright uplands stretches a riband of meadow,
Shorn of the labouring grass, bulwarked well from the sea,
Fenced on its seaward border with clay dykes from the turbid
Surge and flow of the tides vexing the Westmoreland marshes, –
Yonder, toward the left, lie broad the Westmoreland marshes, –
Miles on miles they extend, level, and grassy, and dim,

Clear from the long red sweep of flats to the sky in the distance,
Save for the outlying heights, green-rampired Cumberland Point;
Miles on miles outrolled, and the river-channels divide them, –
Miles on miles of green, barred by the hurtling gusts,
Miles on miles beyond the tawny bay is Minudie. (*CP* 78–9)

The landscape forms and place names mentioned in this passage establish that it is a description of the area extending from Roberts's 'vantage-
point' at or near his childhood home at Westcock, New Brunswick, across
the dykelands and tidal marshes at the head of Cumberland Basin on the
Bay of Fundy towards the village of Minudie, Nova Scotia – the area surrounding and including what were and are commonly known as the
Tantramar Marshes.[44]

Since Roberts spent most of the first fourteen years of his life (1860–
74) at Westcock, there is no question that the area surveyed in 'Tantramar Revisited' had for him the strong personal 'associations and connections' that lie at the emotional core of the poem. But by virtue of his
intimate and extensive knowledge of the Tantramar region, Roberts also
knew it to be rich with historical and political resonances. Built by the
Acadians and augmented by the British, the 'clay dykes' that protect the
'meadows' from the 'turbid / Surge and flow of the tides' are both a poignant 'symbol of a people who, though exiled, were to return to
become an important segment of the population of Atlantic Canada'
(William B. Hamilton 140) and a physical manifestation of the constructive achievements and potential of French and English Canadians.
Named Fort Beauséjour when it was built by the French in the early
1750s, renamed Fort Cumberland when it was captured by the British in
1755, and strengthened in the expectation of attack during the American Revolution and the War of 1812, the fortress that is tactfully placed
under erasure with the reference to 'green-rampired Cumberland
Point' is a reminder of past French-English hostilities and animosities
that are best ignored except as evidence of their absence and as back-
drops for historical romances (such as Roberts's own 'The Rawdon's
Luck' in the 18 July 1883 number of the *Continent* [Philadelphia]).
Begun as 'the Acadian settlement of Menoudie' (a name 'traceable to
the Mi'Kuaq *Munoode*, "a sack or bag"'), the village of Minudie in Nova
Scotia adjoins the 'large Marsh on ... Cumberland Basin [that] ... was
called by the French *les champs élysées* and is still known locally as the
"Elysian Fields"' (Hamilton 362–3). Situated on the border between
New Brunswick and Nova Scotia, renowned for the prosperity of their

agricultural and fishing industries, and home to a mixed French and English population, the Westmoreland or Tantramar Marshes could themselves be construed as a microcosm of Canada's rich and diverse past and present.

In fact, this is almost exactly how the area is presented in the essay on Nova Scotia by R. Murray and A. Simpson that follows Roberts's contribution on New Brunswick in *Picturesque Canada; the Country As It Was and Is* (1882–4),[45] the lavishly illustrated introduction to Canada's 'scenery ... history and ... people' that was intended by its editor, George Monro Grant (1835–1902), 'not only [to] make [Canadians] better known to [them]selves and to strangers, but also [to] stimulate national sentiment and contribute to the rightful development of the nation' (1:i):

> Following the Cumberland Basin, we come into the region of rich marshland, dikes, great herds of cattle, vast expanse of meadow dotted here and there with hamlets and villages. The dike-lands of Nova Scotia cover nearly 40, 000 acres, and additions are made from year to year. The largest share of these fertile acres is under the spectator's eye as he gazes over the Tantramar Marsh, an inexhaustible mine of wealth to the agriculturists around. Here are visible a few vestiges of the war-period – Fort Lawrence and Fort Cumberland, the scenes of the last struggles between nationalities which now dwell together in peace under the folds of the British and Canadian flags. The passions of 1755 are as obsolete as these forts and ... old rusty cannon ... From its hillside [the town of Amherst, NS] looks abroad on as fair a rural scene as Canada anywhere presents – marshes, meadows, orchards, sloping uplands, dark belts of forest. (2:835)

The absence of any mention of the Westmoreland or Tantramar Marshes in Roberts's essay on New Brunswick in *Picturesque Canada* raises the possibility that this passage helped him to recognize their potential as a condenser of 'national sentiment' and perhaps even prompted him to change the title of his poem from 'Westmoreland Revisited' to 'Tantramar Revisited' prior to its appearance in *In Divers Tones* in 1886.[46]

In the remainder of the poem, the emphasis becomes increasingly personal and the tone recuperative as Roberts alternates between observation of the landscape as it is and memories of it as it was in an elegiac celebration of the human and animal life that it supports: 'Now at this season' – that is, late summer or early fall (the hills 'aslant to the sea' are 'green' but the 'riband of meadow' below is 'Shorn of the labouring grass') – the 'fishing boats [lie] dry on the flats,' the fishing 'reels are empty and idle,' the nets 'hang from the rafters / Over the fresh-stowed hay in upland barns,' and 'fathoms of drift-net' no longer 'uploom ... sombrely over the land,' but this present 'stillness' serves as a prompt to memories of times past when 'the net-reels' were 'Wound with beaded nets, dripping and dark from the sea' and each reel 'groaned' with 'men at the windlass' as 'the net, / Surging in ponderous lengths, uprose and coiled in its station' (*CP* 79).[47]

After quoting extensively from these observations and recollections, Cappon comments that Roberts may have 'lavished the resources of his style a little too freely on [his] description' of the nets and reels because 'its luxuriance is rather overpowering' (*Charles G.D. Roberts* 20). The description to which Cappon refers is certainly abundant, but it need not seem excessively so if account is taken of the personal basis of the poem (Roberts would tell Lorne Pierce in 1927 that as a boy at Westcock he 'used to go out occasionally with the fishermen' and 'knew their lives intimately' ['Interview' 64]) and, more important, its political motivation. As Roberts well knew from his stint in Chatham and his work on *Picturesque Canada,* in the early 1880s New Brunswick was in the throes of a severe economic depression and population exodus as a consequence of the collapse of its timber and ship building industries. In the 1860s and early 1870, when Roberts was growing up there, 'Westcock was a shipbuilding centre, wooden ships [that is]' ('Interview' 64), and in November 1878 the Marquis of Lorne and Princess Louise were 'surprised ... to see ... men employed building ... sea-going schooners of heavy draught' in 'their back yards' on the Tantramar Marshes (Collins, *Canada* 35). By the early 1880s, however, the shipbuilding industry was in steep decline in the area, leaving agriculture and fishing as the mainstays of its economy. Both the absence of references to shipbuilding and the abundance of references to fishing and, less conspicuously, agriculture in 'Tantramar Revisited' reflect Roberts's commitment to fostering 'national sentiment' in Canada by emphasizing the country's achievements and prospects. Writing of the lower reaches of the Saint John River in *Picturesque Canada,* he asks, 'What shall be said of the fertility of soil which often yields two crops in one season – in the spring a crop of *fish,* a liberal crop; and later an equally bountiful gift of grain or roots or hay?' Later, in the same essay, he remarks that the 'exportation of fish packed in ice is a growing industry' in Chatham (2: 761, 785). Among many other things, 'Tantramar Revisited' says that New Brunswick possesses all the natural and human resources necessary to be a vital component of Canada.

Numerous critics have puzzled over the fact that in the final verse paragraph of 'Tantramar Revisited' Roberts decides to remain on his 'vantage-point' in the hills rather than descend to the marshes that have so vividly awakened his memories:

> Yet, as I sit and watch, this present peace of the landscape, –
> Stranded boats, these reels empty and idle, the hush,
> One grey hawk slow-wheeling above yon cluster of haystacks, –
> More than the old-time stir, the stillness welcomes me home.
> Ah, the old-time stir, how once it stung me with rapture, –
> Old-time sweetness, the winds freighted with honey and salt!
> Yet will I stay my steps and not go down to the marshland, –
> Muse and recall far off, rather remember than see, –
> Lest on too close sight I miss the darling illusion,
> Spy at their task even here the hands of chance and change. (*CP* 79)

Gathering up images and phrases from earlier in the poem to announce and achieve closure, Roberts ends 'Tantramar Revisited' on a note of denial that smacks of escapism: fully aware from both observation and knowledge that 'the hands of chance and change' are at work in his boyhood landscape, he prefers to retain the delusion that this is not so rather than risk the confirmation that it is. More than a cherished falsity is protected at the end of 'Tantramar Revisited,' however, for the distance that sustains 'illusion' and the 'stillness' that succeeds a stirring experience are also among the principal prerequisites of abstract thinking, reconstructive remembrance, and idealistic poetry. To 'Muse and recall far off' and in peace is to recollect in tranquility, to create the conditions identified by Wordsworth with poetic composition, to establish the stance from which 'Tantramar Revisited' and poems like it can be written – the stance, that is, of the cosmopolitan nationalist who is so positioned in and above his provincial environment that he can not only draw on his personal experience of its elements for poetic material, but also, and more important, craft that material into the substance of high art. In the terms of the epilogue of 'The Beginnings of a Canadian Literature,' 'Tantramar Revisited' shows that Roberts was well able and quite willing in the months preceding his departure for Toronto to assume the editorship of the *Week* to 'appropriate' the 'poetic wealth' of Canada's 'broad and magnificent landscapes,' changing 'seasons,' and 'early history' for his own personal and political purposes.[48] But in its affirmation of elevation both as a state and as an act, a stance and an end, the masterpiece of

Roberts's Young Canada period also exemplifies the hierarchy that he and Collins sought to express in the figure of the 'honey from Himettus': the best Canadian poets are those whose work not only, and inevitably, 'preserves to [its] sweetness ... a fragrance distinctive of its origin' but also, and crucially, transcends its coloniality by sounding a 'note, unbounded by geography, that appeals to the sentiment in man which is not begotten of locality':

> Ah, the old-time stir, how once it stung me with rapture, –
> Old-time sweetness, the winds freighted with honey and salt!
> Yet will I stay my steps and not go down to the marshland ...

Thanks in part to the vigour with which Roberts waged the battle against provincialism and localism in the early 1880s, the continuity between his ideas and those of the Young Ireland movement does not become fully apparent in his public pronouncements until several years later when, revitalized by the 'Canadianism' to be examined in the next chapter and perhaps stimulated by the statements of O'Hagan and others that were quoted earlier, he reminted the slogan 'racy of the soil' and rethought his preference for cosmopolitanism over patriotism. 'It is patriotic and altogether seemly that we should expect Canadian literature to savour of the soil from which it springs,' he wrote in the May 1892 instalment of the 'Modern Instances' column that he published in *Dominion Illustrated* (Montreal) between February and August of that year:

> [This] demand is nothing more than a demand for sincerity and sympathy. It means that we desire our literature to be genuine and original, not artificial and imitative. It is not desirable, as some would have it to be, that Canadian literature should concern itself exclusively with scenes and themes Canadian; yet this is the interpretation sure to be put upon the demand, both by the advocates of a narrow localism, who read into it much more than it is intended to claim, and those on the other hand who affect so cosmopolitan a breadth of view as to be superior to the emotions of patriotism. It is an ignorant folly that would restrict a writer to his own surroundings in his choice of scene or theme. It is an emasculated folly that fancies patriotism obsolete, or reckons on dispensing with the native spirit. Of the two follies the latter is the more urbane, but the former is the more easily condoned, being the nearer akin to wisdom. (251)

'[S]avour of the soil' or 'native savour' (each term is repeated three times in the course of the column) is now more than an inevitable quality of the best poetry: it is definitive of poetic excellence because it stems from a 'sincer[e],' 'sympath[etic],' and 'authentic' relationship between the poet and 'soil and clime, landscape, legend and human example' of his native land:

> He may restrict himself rigidly to native themes, and attain supreme excellence; but the native savour is not dependent upon the autochthonous [or indigenous] character of the theme. On the other hand, supreme excellence is hardly to be obtained, however broad one be in choice of subject, if the finished work be found wanting in this native savour ... To bring the point home, our writers may take subjects from Canadian story, and scenes from Canadian landscape, yet miss, for reasons inherent in themselves, the savour of the soil, which is the salt to keep one's product from decay. Others, again, may concern themselves little about the birthplace of their theme, yet breathe in every line the flavour of Canadian field ... Wheresover their imaginations wander, they carry with them the savour of the soil. (251–2)

'[R]acy of the soil' had found a Canadian habitation and name.

# CHAPTER TWO

# Canadianism: 1885–1890

## I

As the debacle of the *Week* receded into memory over the winter of 1884–5, Roberts's health and spirits began to revive, and he soon returned, strengthened and incensed by experience, to the task of proselytizing on behalf of Canadian Independence. A measure of the intensity of his commitment to the cause at this time can be gained from an article on Goldwin Smith that he published on 11 July 1885 in the 'Authors at Home' series in the New York *Critic*. 'The Canadian Nationalists, with whom [Smith] is believed to be in sympathy,' he writes with pungent irony, 'owe him both gratitude and a grudge':

> He has made plain to us our right to our doctrines, and the rightness of our doctrines; he has made ridiculous those who would cry 'Treason' after us. But we would wish that he would suffer us to indulge a little youthful enthusiasm, as would become a people unquestionably young; and also that he would refrain from showing us quite so vividly and persistently all the lions in our path ... His words go far to weaken our faith in the ultimate consolidation of Canada; he tends to retard our perfect fusion, and is inclined to unduly exalt Ontario at the expense of her sister Provinces. All these things trouble us, as increasing the possibility of success for a movement just now being actively stirred in England, and toward which Goldwin Smith's attitude has ever been one of uncompromising antagonism – that is, the movement toward Imperial Federation. ('Authors' 14)

Within three years, Roberts would find himself supporting Imperial Federation as a bulwark against Annexation, but in 1885 he is convinced that 'the vital germ' of 'Canadian Nationalism' that was planted by Canada First 'has sprung up from border to border of the land, till now it has a thousand centres [and] is clothed in a thousand shapes': the dream of Young Canada had gone the way of the Round Table, but in Roberts at least its ideals and goals were a long way from extinction.[1]

By the time that he publicly settled the score with Goldwin Smith in the *Critic*,[2] Roberts had composed at least one of the 'patriotic poems' that 'crystallized' his 'intense love for Canada,' his 'devotion to the theory of Independence,' and his determination 'to arouse his apathetic country[men] to a realization of the greatness of their ... country' (Pomeroy 67). According to Elsie Pomeroy (68), 'Canada' (1886) was both written and privately published for 'personal circulation' (*CP* 414) in January 1885 and followed 'within a few months' by 'Collect for Dominion Day' (1886) and 'An Ode for the Canadian Confederacy' (1886), the other two poems that, with 'Canadians Are We (A Toast for Dominion Day)' (1889), constitute an explicit poetic statement of the Canadian nationalism that undergirds his literary activities in the late 1880s. 'Canada' is 'a lyric with a purpose,' he told the American poet and essayist Charles Leonard Moore in a letter of 16 June 1885: 'I am a devoted Canadian independent' (*CL* 48).

Patriotic poetry is now so far out of fashion that 'Canada' has for most critical and pedagogical purposes disappeared from Canadian literature. Anthologies designed for classroom use rarely include any of Roberts's nationalistic poems (an exception is Carole Gerson and Gwendolyn Davies' *Canadian Poetry: From the Beginnings through the First World War* [1994], which includes 'An Ode for the Canadian Confederacy'), and David Jackel is almost alone among critics in making a concerted effort to appreciate pieces that even he sees as amalgams of 'bombast ... triteness,' and 'empty rhetoric' in which 'exhortation usually takes the place of content, and what content there is is often puzzling and perplexing' ('The National Voice' 45–6). Yet, to judge by the number of times that it was reprinted, excerpted, anthologized, and praised in the 1880s and '90s (see *CP* 414), 'Canada' was one of the best-known and most admired poems by any Canadian poet. It was certainly held in very high esteem by the literary editor of the *Montreal Gazette*, John Reade,[3] who wrote in the *Dominion Annual Register and Review for ... 1886* (1887) that 'Professor Roberts has done honour to himself and to Canada by two fine poems – both of a markedly patriotic strain – "Canada" and the "Collect for Dominion Day." The former, beginning with the line: "O child of nations, giant-limbed" is full of force and the strong hopefulness of youth, enamoured of freedom and confident of winning in the battle of life' (211). 'It also,' he adds, 'voices the aspirations of young Canada for independence.' In *Problems of Greater Britain* (1890) it is the only English-Canadian poem mentioned by Sir Charles Wentworth Dilke, who quotes its first four stanzas and affirms that it 'has much political interest' (74), and in 'Canadian Poets and Poetry' (1895) Thomas O'Hagan, though he quotes 'An Ode for the Canadian Confederacy,' proclaims 'Canada' 'the best patriotic poem ... that has yet been produced in this country' (15).

When it was privately printed in January 1885, 'Canada' began with a stanza that is indeed 'puzzling and perplexing,'* but in its first public appearance in the Toronto *Globe* on 4 January 1886 and in all subsequent printings, the poem opens with the apostrophe and personification quoted by Reade and moves smoothly into the series of questions and exclamations that conclude with the aspirational exhortation of the fourth stanza:

O Child of Nations, giant-limbed
   Who stand'st among the nations now
Unheeded, unadored, unhymned,
   With unanointed brow,

How long the ignoble sloth, how long
   The trust in greatness not thine own?
Surely the lion's brood is strong
   To front the world alone!

How long the indolence, ere thou dare
   Achieve thy destiny, seize thy fame, –
Ere our proud eyes behold thee bear
   A nation's franchise, nation's name?

The Saxon force, the Celtic fire,
   These are thy manhood's heritage!
Why rest with babes and slaves? Seek higher
   The place of race and age. (*CP* 85)

---

* O Thou whose young hands grasp the keys
  To open half a continent,
  The waves of those confining seas
  On two worlds' shores are turbulent! (*CP* 413)

The most striking feature of these lines is their insistent personification of Canada as male rather than female: 'giant-limbed,' leoninely powerful, and possessed of 'manhood's heritage,' Canada is a fully grown 'Child of Nations' whose 'ignoble sloth' and lamentable 'ignorance' are the only barriers to its achievement and celebration of full independence. From Roberts's confidently masculinist perspective, the time has long since come for young, mature, and male Canada to cease being dependent on Mother Britain and, more specifically, the 'Mother of Nations' (Roberts's term for Queen Victoria in a poem written for her Golden Jubilee in 1887) (*CP* 112).[4] More than many of its original readers may have realized, 'Canada' came from the pen of both a republican and a nationalist.

It is consistent with the masculinist assumptions of the opening stanzas of 'Canada' as well as with their biblical rhetoric ('unanointed,' 'sloth,' 'How long ...?') that in 'Collect for Dominion Day' Roberts expresses his desire to see Canada's 'scant' and fractious inhabitants fused into a unified and 'mighty state' in the form of a prayer to the 'Father of nations ... to whom all nations kneel' (*CP* 89). By contrast, the language of 'An Ode for the Canadian Confederacy' is less biblical than sexual ('This North whose heart of fire / Yet knows not its desire'), and the sex of the 'Child of Nations' is changed in the final lines to female:

> Shall not our love this rough, sweet land make sure,
> > Her bounds preserve inviolate, though we die?
> > > O strong hearts of the North,
> > > Let flame your loyalty forth,
> > And put the craven and base to an open shame,
> > Till earth shall know the Child of Nations by her name! (*CP* 90)

Perhaps it was the Riel Rebellion of March to May 1885, a national trauma to which Roberts refers somewhat cryptically in 'Collect for Dominion Day' as 'blood late shed to purge the common shame' (*CP* 89), that led him to reconceive Canada as a virginal female in need of male protection. No less as the beneficiary of male power in 'An Ode for the Canadian Confederacy' than as its embodiment in 'Canada' is Roberts's 'Child of Nations' a reflection of the masculinism that never lies very far from the centre of his thinking and his activities.

In the central portion of 'Canada,' Roberts gives substance to his assertion that the 'Child of Nations' has reached maturity first by pointing to Canada's global presence as a maritime nation and then by invoking a series of great men and heroic events from the country's past. Like the references to 'Saxon force,' 'Celtic fire,' and other racial stereotypes in the poem's opening stanzas, the 'blood-red' flags and smoking funnels of Roberts's description of Canadian ships are period aspects of the poem that have grated on later sensibilities:

> I see on every wind unfurled
>   The flag that bears the Maple Wreath;
> Thy swift keels furrow round the world
>   Its blood-red folds beneath;
>
> Thy swift keels cleave the furthest seas;
>   Thy white sails swell with alien gales;
> To stream on each remotest breeze
>   The black smoke of thy pipes exhales.
>
> O Falterer, let thy past convince
>   Thy future, – all the growth, the gain
> The fame since Cartier knew thee, since
>   Thy shores beheld Champlain!
>
> Montcalm and Wolfe! Wolfe and Montcalm!
>   Quebec, thy storied citadel
> Attest in burning song and psalm
>   How here thy heroes fell!
>
> O Thou that bor'st the battle brunt
>   At Queenston and at Lundy's Lane, –
> On whose scant ranks but iron front
>   The battle broke in vain! –
>
> Whose was the danger, whose the day,
>   From whose triumphant throats the cheers
> At Chrysler's Farm, at Chateauguay,
>   Storming like clarion-burst our ears? (*CP* 85–6)

The twofold purpose of Roberts's historical survey is to awaken national sentiment and to emphasize the contributions of both the French and the English to the creation and preservation of Canada. References to Cartier and Champlain evoke the exploration and settlement of New

France in the 'Brave Old Days' (as George Monro Grant calls the first instalment of his influential essay on 'The Dominion of Canada' in the May to August 1880 numbers of *Scribner's Monthly*), and mention of the 'storied citadel' above Quebec City recalls Britain's efforts until well into the nineteenth century to fortify Canada against American attack. Pivotal to these developments, of course, was the Battle of the Plains of Abraham, the subject of the most resonant and deceptively simple line in the poem: 'Montcalm and Wolfe! Wolfe and Montcalm!' With its chiasmic reversal and then reiteration of the order in which the names of the opposing generals usually appear, the line bestows priority on Montcalm and generates associations that would have been especially vivid at the time of the poem's writing and publication in 1885–6. By then, a joint monument to Wolfe and Montcalm had stood in Quebec City since 1828 and supplied the inspiration for numerous literary and artistic works, including a stanza beginning 'WOLFE and MONTCALM!' in *The St. Lawrence and the Saguenay* (1856), by Charles Sangster, and, more recently, an illustration in the Quebec segment of *Picturesque Canada* (1: 46), and in 1884 the American historian Francis Parkman (1823–93) concluded his epical narrative of the struggle between France and England in North America with the two volumes of *Montcalm and Wolfe*. What Roberts says of the monument to Wolfe and Montcalm in *A History of Canada* (1897) applies equally well to the stanza in which they appear in his poem: it stands as 'a fit emblem of the union of the two races who fought that day together for the mastery of Canada' (159).

As richly significant in a slightly different but closely related way are the references in the two ensuing stanzas to battles of the War of 1812. To a republican nationalist such as Roberts was in the mid-1880s, the British and Canadian victories on the Niagara Peninsula and in the St Lawrence Valley in 1812 and 1813 did not bespeak 'Canada's preference for the British connection and devotion to the British throne' as they did to heirs of the Loyalist tradition and proponents of imperial federation like William Kirby (1817–1906) and George Taylor Denison (1839–1925) (see Berger 89–99); rather, the battles of Queenston Heights and Lundy's Lane represented the heroism of the English-Canadian militia in defence of their homeland, and the battles of Chrysler's Farm and Chateauguay the willingness of the French Canadians to fight side by side with their English countrymen to preserve their homeland from annexation to the United States. '[T]heir loyalty is unswervingly directed upon this Canada which is now their fatherland – our fatherland,' Roberts had written of the French Canadians in 'The Beginnings of a Canadian Literature'; 'that their patriotism is no lip-service, no cold-blooded expedience, let Chateauguay and Chrysler's Farm attest' (*SPCP* 249). Nowhere more than in such remarks and in the historical stanzas of 'Canada' is it apparent that Roberts's 'Child of Nations' is the offspring of a fantasy of union out of conflict and his narrative of its past an hallucination of racial reconciliation that deploys an invented tradition[5] to displace the harsh realities of Canada's past and present.

In the final four stanzas of the poem, Roberts envisages a Canada in which all the country's 'sons' whether at home or abroad are eager candidates for a national awakening, the sole exceptions being the Canadians who died during the Nile expedition to relieve General Charles George Gordon at Khartoum in 1884–5:

On soft Pacific slopes, – beside
    Strange floods that northward rave and fall, –
Where chafes Acadia's chainless tide –
    Thy sons await thy call.

They wait; but some in exile, some
    With strangers housed, in strange lands, –
And some Canadian lips are dumb
    Beneath Egyptian sands.

O mystic Nile! Thy secret yields
    Before us; thy most ancient dreams
Are mixed with far Canadian fields
    And murmur of Canadian streams.

But thou, my country, dream not thou!
    Wake, and behold how night is done,
How on thy breast, and o'er thy brow,
    Bursts the uprising sun! (*CP* 86)

Appearing for the first time and twice repeated in these stanzas, the word 'Canadian' lends climactic and incantatory force to Roberts's extraordinary suggestion that the burial of some of their countrymen beside the Nile has allowed Canadians to gain access to the occult ('mystic') knowledge associated with ancient Egypt. This markedly unorthodox idea is abandoned in the final stanza, however, as the poem reverts to biblical rhetoric with echoes of Isaiah's call to Jerusalem to awake (Isaiah 51.9 and 52.2) and St Paul's call to the Ephesians to arise from the sleep of unenlightenment (Ephesians 5.14). 'Canada' thus ends much as it began, by drawing on the Judeo-Christian tradition of exhortation to urge Canadians to national consciousness and action.

It was an exhortation that apparently had immediate appeal in a Canada vexed not only by the events and aftermath of the Riel Rebellion, but also by a depressed economy and the resulting exodus of young people Roberts's 'exile[s] .../ With strangers housed' – to the United States, Australia, and elsewhere. 'My "Canada" ... has gone the rounds of the Canadian press very thoroughly,' he observed on 22 January 1886, 'and [it] is still being fought over by the editors' (*CL* 56). Although spoken by a disciple, T.G. Marquis's suggestion in 1893 that 'Roberts might be considered the Corphaeus [that is, the leader of the chorus] of the Independence movement in Canada' is neither infelicitous nor inaccurate, and, while Marquis doubtless errs on the side of generosity in proclaiming 'Canada,' 'Collect for Dominion Day,' and 'An Ode for the Canadian Confederacy' 'full of the fire that makes a nation,' his analysis of their place in the poet's oeuvre and the conditions that have worked both for and against their canonization is perceptive and astute:

> If, in his Tantramar poems, he has succeeded in portraying his native land with truthful eye and loving heart, in his patriotic poems he has caught the spirit of liberty and freedom that burned so gloriously in the heart of Shelley; and he has struck a stronger chord of patriotism than any other Canadian. But his power in this direction will not be recognized until others have been filled with something of the same spirit – till the sons of Canada are determined that earth shall know the "Child of Nations" by her name. And the day is not far distant. (Marquis 575)

It is no more fortuitous that the Roberts selections in A.J.M. Smith's *Book of Canadian Poetry* (1943) and Ralph Gustafson's *Penguin Book of Canadian Verse* (1957) begin with 'Canada' than it is that the poem is now conspicuous by its absence from most anthologies of Canadian literature: as Marquis was not able to predict, Canadians have proved as capable of being emptied as well as filled by the spirit of nationalism – a fact that has frequently made anything beyond a forensic appreciation of such poems as 'Canada' all but impossible.

As enthusiastic as was their reception by his contemporaries, Roberts's patriotic poems did nothing to alleviate the pecuniary embarrassment that compelled him and his family to live with his parents in Fredericton for several months during 1884–5. But early in 1885 financial relief came in sight in the form of the newly created professorship in English and French literature at King's College, Windsor, which was formally announced at the College's spring convocation. '[E]ver since [my] appointment I have been working hard to freshen up my French,' he told Moore in a letter of September 7 from Quebec City; 'here to ... [the] most picturesque and romantic and inspiring of New World cities, I have betaken myself to be compelled to talk French' (*CL* 51). With his removal to Windsor soon after his return from Quebec later that month, Roberts entered the ten-year period that he came to regard as 'perhaps [the] most fruitful' of his creative career (Pomeroy 66). Between 1885 and 1890, French would prove as important to his nationalistic project as to his professorial duties.

## II

It is in the nature of nationalism that it attempts to subsume the local and the regional to the larger purposes of national unity and national aspiration. This is evident in 'Canada' in the treatment of 'soft Pacific slopes' and 'Acadia's chainless tide' as merely the longitudinal limits of the country whose 'sons' await nationalistic awakening and, contrary to what its title might lead a reader to expect, it is also evident in the lecture 'The Outlook for Literature: Acadia's Field for Poetry, History, and Romance,' which Roberts delivered at Windsor on 14 December 1885 and published in the New Year's Day 1886 supplement of the *Halifax Morning Herald*. The lecture begins with an unequivocal statement of Roberts's conviction that 'the future of literature in Nova Scotia ... must be the future of literature in Canada':

> We must forget to ask of a work whether it is Nova Scotian or British Colum-
> bian, of Ontario or of New Brunswick, until we have inquired if it be broadly
> and truly Canadian. It is the future of Canadian nationality with which every
> son of Canada is most concerned; and our literature will be false to its trust,
> will fail of that very service for which young nations have ever relied upon
> their literature, if it does not show itself the nurse of all patriotic enthusi-
> asms, and the bane of provincial jealousies. (*SPCP* 260)

With this as his overriding premise, Roberts proceeds in 'The Outlook for Literature' with his 'consideration of the part likely to be played by Nova Scotian talent in the making of [Canada's] national literature' by first offering some general suggestions about the quality of that talent and the characteristics of the literature that will emanate from it.

At the heart of Roberts's ensuing claim that Nova Scotia's contribution to Canada's national literature will be of the 'higher and more imaginative' variety is the assumption, reminiscent of the epilogue of 'The Beginnings of a Canadian Literature,' that the most exalted and creative writing occurs in places that are rich in human history and tradition. '[T]o a greater degree than any province save Quebec,' he asserts, Nova Scotia has a 'wealth of tradition, variety of surrounding, and a soil well tempered by human influences, – a soil that has been cradle and grave to a now fair number of generations. This last means much, for a raw soil seems rarely to flower into imaginative work' (*SPCP* 260–1). Nor in Roberts's view does 'inspiring material' for Nova Scotia's writers lie merely in their 'past, and in [their] hopes for the future': such 'aspects of the present' as 'the lives of [the province's] fishing populations ... lumber camps, and drives' also furnish 'picturesque and striking material' for literature (*SPCP* 261).[6] That Roberts did indeed regard such material as national rather than regional in nature is confirmed by his remark to William Douw Lighthall in September 1888 that he is working on 'a lyric narrative of Tantramar fisher-folk's lives' and at the same time planning 'more Canadian *Nationalistic* and *aspirational* work' along the lines of 'An Ode for the Canadian Confederacy,' which Lighthall had admired (*CL* 87, and see 82).

Supplementing the notion of (cultivated) soil as a stimulus to (imaginative) writing in 'The Outlook for Literature' is a form of environmental determinism derived, in all likelihood, from 'Scenery and the Mind,' the introductory essay in *The Home Book of the Picturesque; or, American Scenery, Art, and Literature* (1852), by the collection's editor, C.L. Magoon. An influential American heir of the environmental determinism of Montesquieu and Herder, Magoon argues that a nation's scenery and weather exercise a formative influence on the mind or character of its people and, hence, on their art and literature. Thus the 'grand natural scenery' of countries such as the United States 'tends permanently to affect the character of those cradled in its bosom' and to dispose them towards 'patriotism the most firm and eloquence the most thrilling,' and the American disposition towards freedom and adventure is the result of such scenic and meteorological features of their environment as 'elastic' air and 'granite highlands' (25). 'In our landscape,' asserts Roberts,

> earth and sea and sky conspire to make an imaginative people. These stern coasts, now thundered against by Atlantic storms, now wrapped in noiseless fogs, these overwhelming tides, these vast channels emptied of their

streams, these weird reaches of flat and marsh and dike, should create a habit of openness to nature, and by contrast put a reproach upon the commonplace and the gross. Our climate with its swift extremes is eager and waking, and we should expect a sort of dry sparkle in our page, with a transparent and tonic quality in our thought. If environment is anything, our work can hardly be tame. (*CP* 261)

Roberts's final sentence may indicate a degree of scepticism about the influence of environment on literature, and if it were not itself an instance of the 'dry sparkle' that it describes, his 'tonic' water metaphor might be regarded as facetious, but such ideas were taken very seriously indeed in late nineteenth-century Canada. To cite just one cognate example: in 'Two Canadian Poets: A Lecture' (1891), Lampman also draws upon *The Home Book of the Picturesque*, specifically on Washington Irving's essay on the Catskill Mountains region of the American Northeast, to argue that, since 'we know that climatic and scenic conditions have much to do with the moulding of national character,' a Canadian race and literature can be expected to manifest qualities that reflect both the 'diversity' of the country's scenery and the combination of 'pitiless severity' and 'guttering splendour' of its winters (*ER* 93). As will be seen in chapters 5 and 6, the medicinal and therapeutic properties of Canadian landscapes and climates towards which Roberts gestures with the word 'tonic' were a central component of Lampman's poetry in the mid-to-late 1880s and, like climatic determinism, would loom similarly large in the work of Campbell, Carman, Duncan Campbell Scott, and Roberts himself in the 1890s.

When he turns to survey Nova Scotian 'history and tradition' in the remainder of 'The Outlook for Literature,' Roberts subdivides his material into three parts: 'Indian legend,' 'the story of the French,' and the 'noble themes' provided by 'our own ancestors,' specifically the Loyalists. Both in diction and in tone, Roberts's remarks on 'Indian legend' as a source of literary inspiration recall his comments on the same topic in the *Dominion Annual Register and Review ... for 1883,** but with the sig-

---

* 'A ... demand on behalf of American critics [for a distinctively and exclusively American literature] called forth interminable epics and romances celebrating the sometimes imaginary virtues and not always agreeable peculiarities of the Red Indian. These certainly smacked of the soil ... and were as a rule received quite rapturously. For the most part they have ... been relegated to the vast but half-forgotten catalogue of the injuries which the unfortunate Indian has been compelled to endure at the hands of his white oppressor. In America the cry has died away, self-convicted of its own inutility' ('Literature' 206).

nificant difference that they are not framed by a Collinsian attack on 'th[e] perpetual injunction to our verse-writers to choose Canadian themes only' (*SPCP* 258):

> There is continual demand for the working of this field, and continual surprise that it should be so long unharvested. Both the demand and the surprise are as old as literature in North America, and are likely to grow much older before being satisfied. The legends are, some of them, wildly poetic and vigorous in conception; and they are easily attainable, both from the lips of their hereditary possessors and from such books as [Charles G.] Leland's admirable 'Legends of the Algonquin Indians' [that is, *The Algonquin Legends of New England* (1884)]. But the stuff seems almost unavailable for purposes of pure literature. The Indian has left a curse in his bequest, and the prize turns worthless in our grasp. The host of American poems and romances with the Indian for inspiration form, [Longfellow's] 'Hiawatha' being [only partially] excepted, a museum of lamentable failures. They are the crowning insult to a decaying race ... Only indirectly, by association and suggestion, is Indian legend likely ... to exert marked influence upon our creative literature. (*SPCP* 261–3)

More than a little condescendingly, Roberts concludes by suggesting that 'there is room to do invaluable work in the collection and comparative study of Indian folk-lore and kindred matter, for the results of which there is now a ready appreciation.'

Although Roberts's remarks on 'Indian legend' in 'The Outlook for Literature' reflect his attitude up to the time of writing, they contain no foreshadowing of the poetic levies on 'Indian folk-lore and kindred matter' that he would make during the next two years. In the essay on New Brunswick in *Picturesque Canada*, the 'quaint fable' of the disappearance of the Algonquin hero 'Clote Scaurp' (Glooscap) is characterized as 'the Melicite "Passing of Arthur",' credited with possessing 'the wild, impressive beauty of Celtic legend,' and embedded in a conversation with a 'trusty' but superstitious guide (Frank Solas), which suggests that it was 'heard from the lips' of one of its 'hereditary possessors' (3: 780) when, in fact, it was taken almost verbatim either from the travel guide that apparently furnished Roberts with the plan for his essay, M.F. Sweetser's *The Maritime Provinces: A Handbook for Travellers* (1875), or from another book that was almost certainly known to both Roberts and Sweetser, Arthur Hamilton Gordon's *Wilderness Journeys in New Brunswick in 1862–63* (1864).[7] By 1886 Roberts had changed his views about the suitability of 'Indian folk-lore and kindred matter' as an 'influence upon ... creative literature' for in *In Divers Tones* there are not one but two substantial poems based on Melicite and Micmac legends: 'The Departing of Clote Scarp' and 'The Quelling of the Moose.' Neither poem is among Roberts's best, but 'The Departing of Clote Scarp,' an epyllion that predictably owes almost as much to Tennyson's 'The Passing of Arthur' (1870) as it does to Gordon's and Sweetser's versions of the legend of Glooscap's departure, soon achieved prominence as a national poem in Lighthall's *Songs of the Great Dominion* (1889) and *Canadian Poems and Lays* (1893).

Unlike 'Indian legend,' 'the story of the French in Nova Scotia' is embraced by Roberts in 'The Outlook for Literature' as a rich source of literary inspiration both because it 'reads less like history than romance,' and because it combines 'pathos' and 'remote[ness]' in a manner that 'admits full poetic treatment' (*SPCP* 262). Contributing to the literary potential of Acadian material, Roberts suggests, is the fact that it 'has already proved itself adapted to exquisite treatment' in Longfellow's *Evangeline* (1847). On the twin premises that 'most of the greater power of our literature, and of all literature, has been wrought upon subjects familiarized by previous handling' and that 'all great themes show a certain inexhaustibility, and admit of being more than once or twice splendidly treated,' Roberts argues that

> Longfellow's handling of Acadian story has simply glorified the theme for later singers. Every dike and ancient rampart, and surviving Acadian name, and little rock-rimmed haven, from the wind-rippled shifting sepulchre of Sable Island to the sunny levels of Chignecto, should be a breeding ground for poem, and history, and romance. It would be hard to imagine a region more fascinating to the thought, more suffused with the glamour of a splendid, imperishable past half veiled in mystery than is the Island of Cape Breton. (*SPCP* 263)

To the extent that many of the details mentioned here evoke either 'Tantramar Revisited' or 'Echoes from Old Acadia' (the series of prose sketches, including one entitled 'French Gardens, Sable Island' that Roberts published in the *Current* [Chicago] during the winter of 1884–5 and may still have been thinking of expanding into a book [see *CL* 55]),[8] Roberts's argument is self-serving – as, indeed, is his metaphorical use of the field metaphor of his title in relation to his literary precursors: 'Leland has left behind some very good gleaning [that is, unharvested material], owing to the wideness of the field which he has occupied' and, vis-à-vis Longfellow, 'he ... who breaks a new field' 'has the hardest task ... but his successors as a rule reap the richest harvest' (*SPCP* 262, 263). The implication is clear: as the new owner-workers of the Acadian field pioneered by Longfellow in *Evangeline*, Nova Scotia's genuinely imaginative writers – Roberts and, in due course, Carman – are well set to reap an abundance of what Pierre Bourdieu calls 'cultural capital' – poems, histories, and romances from which they could derive prestige and income (see Bourdieu, 'Production' 262; and Bentley, *Mnemographia* 1:303–5). It is no exaggeration to say that many of the most remunerative works that Roberts 'harvest[ed]' in the 1890s, including no fewer than four novels set in French Acadia and a guidebook, the *Land of Evangeline and the Gateways Thither* (1895), were 'harvest[ed]' from the field that he began to expropriate from Longfellow in 'Tantramar Revisited' and proclaimed a 'breeding ground' for imaginative Canadian writing in 'The Outlook for Literature.'

In turning finally and briefly to the Loyalists as sources of literary subjects, Roberts finds that the remoteness that permits Acadian material to be treated poetically is absent: 'our ancestors have left us noble themes' but 'perhaps these are matters scarcely yet remote enough to take the highest treatment' (*SPCP* 263). Until that time comes, the preservation of dying traditions in local histories is an honourable and valuable undertaking because, though such histories require no 'great literary skill' and cannot be counted 'among the highest' literary achievements, they nevertheless constitute 'a secure investment in the future' because they are the works 'upon which after-workers in the field shall find themselves of necessity dependent' (*SPCP* 264).[9] More than Roberts's earlier uses of the field metaphor in the essay, this last statement demands that literary activity be regarded as analogous to agricultural work and capital investment as a source of national wealth. According to the *King's College Record*, it was not until the fall of 1886 that Roberts supplemented Millicent Garrett Fawcett's *Political Economy for Beginners* (1884) with Simon Newcomb's *Principles of Political Economy* (1886) and parts of Adam Smith's *Wealth of Nations* (1776) on the English curriculum at the College,[10] but 'The Outlook for Literature' suggests that in the winter of 1885–6 he had inferred a connection between national literature and national wealth that makes the earlier reference to Bourdieu's theory of cultural capital less anachronistic than it might first have appeared. In Roberts's concluding expression of 'confidence that the Nova Scotian element in that Canadian literature which our hearts are set upon building will not fail of being important and of rare quality' can be discerned a recognition that the literary wealth of the Canadian nation as a whole depends on the wealth of its component regions, which, in turn consist of local communities and individual workers. It is no great leap from Smith's view that those most motivated to 'cultivat[e] ... and adorn' their land are small landowners 'who know every part of [their] little territory' and 'view ... it with all the affection which property ... naturally inspires' (1:419) to Roberts's appeal to Nova Scotians to compile 'those minute and loving records of particular localities' (*SPCP* 263) upon which the future wealth of Canadian literature will depend.

It is not fortuitous that the first poem that can be said with certainty to have been composed in the immediate aftermath of 'The Outlook for Literature' is a superb sonnet that, as Desmond Pacey and W.J. Keith observe, 'belongs to the category of rural life' (Pacey, *Creative Writing* 44) or 'rural description' (Keith, 'Introduction' xxi). Dated 7 April 1886 (*CP* 421), 'The Potato Harvest' fulfils the mandate of Roberts's lecture in two ways: (1) by finding 'picturesque and striking material in some aspects of the present' life and scenery of Nova Scotia; and (2) by treating a theme that Longfellow had 'glorified ... for later singers' in *Evangeline* – namely, 'the advent of autumn' and the onset of evening on an Acadian farm:

> Now recommenced the reign of rest and affection and stillness.
> Day with its burden and heat had departed, and twilight descending
> Brought back the evening star to the sky, and the herds to the homestead.
> Pawing the ground they came, and resting their necks on each other,
> And with their nostrils distended inhaling the freshess of evening.
> Foremost, bearing the bell, Evangeline's beautiful heifer ...
> ...
> Late, with the rising moon, returned the wains from the marshes,
> Laden with briny hay, that filled the air with odour. (110)

While the subject and the diction ('household,' 'wain') of 'The Potato Harvest' gain resonance from Longfellow's handling of the season when 'Harvests were gathered in,' the poem's 'quiet, casual tone and ... unobtrusive plainness of statement' (Pacey, *Creative Writing* 45) are a decided departure from *Evangeline*, as is its use of the Petrarchan sonnet form as a frame for the picturesque scene, which, as Pacey remarks, Roberts observes with a 'painter's eye':[11]

A high bare field, brown from the plough, and borne
  Aslant from the sunset; amber wastes of sky
  Washing the ridge; a clamour of crows that fly
In from the wide flats where the spent tides mourn
To yon their rocking roosts in pines wind-torn;
  A line of grey snake-fence that zigzags by
  A pond and cattle; from the homestead nigh
The long deep summonings of the supper horn.

Black on the ridge, against that lonely flush,
  A cart, and stoop-necked oxen; ranged beside
  Some barrels; and the day-worn harvest-folk,
Here emptying their baskets, jar the hush
  With hollow thunders. Down the dusk hillside
  Lumbers the wain; and day fades out like smoke. (*CP* 91)

Whereas Longfellow's autumn scene is bathed in the romantic light of 'the evening star' and 'the rising moon' and animated by Evangeline's 'beautiful' and emblematic 'heifer,' Roberts's depiction of rural life in Acadia is starkly unromantic: the sky is an 'amber waste,' the oxen are 'stoop-necked,' the sounds are raucous and ominous, the 'harvest-folk' are 'day-worn,' and the commodity that they are harvesting is the unglamorous potato. It is 'sunset,' the tides are 'spent,' and the day is transient as 'smoke.' 'A grey snake-fence' – an object that Roberts may have regarded as typically Acadian or Canadian[12] – 'zigzags' untidily through a landscape of 'pond' and 'cattle' from which the day fades with no more significance than 'smoke.'

In 'The Potato Harvest,' Roberts demonstrates that 'subjects familiarized by previous handling' do indeed 'admit of being more than once or twice splendidly treated,' but he also displays his awareness that the poet who would 'reap the richest harvests' from the field broken by Longfellow in *Evangeline* must cultivate a very different and less romantic crop – potatoes gathered in baskets in the light of common day rather than 'wains ... / Laden with briny hay' in the light of 'the rising moon.' The 'pieces descriptive of Canadian scenes' are 'better' than the 'patriotic poems' in *In Divers Tones*, commented William Morton Payne in the May 1887 number of the *Dial*; 'their expression is carefully thought out, and their local color is decided ... "The Potato Harvest" is a good example ..., and a fine piece of poetic realism' ('Recent Poetry' 17). By August 1887, Roberts was already 'planning [the] series of sonnets of "The Common Day"' that constitute the bulk of his *Songs of the Common Day* (1893) (the allusion in the book's title, of course, is to Wordsworth's 'Intimations' ode),[13] but between the contemplation and the publication of his sonnet series he began to align himself with a political movement that provided a convenient aegis for both his nationalism and his cosmopolitanism: Imperial Federation.

Before following Roberts into the Federationist phase of his political and poetic development, cognizance needs to be taken of the fact that during the mid-1880s both Lampman and Carman, the latter certainly under Roberts's influence and the former perhaps also so, wrote poems that accord with the nationalistic program set out in 'The Outlook for Literature' and fulfilled in *In Divers Tones*. Written in June 1886, Lampman's 'Between the Rapids' (1888) takes the form of a monologue by a voyageur as he passes the 'fair green fields' of home en route to the *pays d'en haut* (*P* 36). Powerfully evocative of the landscape and culture of the St Lawrence River valley, it resonates with echoes of 'Tantramar Revisited' and Thomas Moore's 'Canadian Boat-Song' (1806), as well as with poems whose links are with France rather than French Canada.* It was the distinctively Canadian subject matter of 'Between the Rapids' that made it a particular favourite of British reviewers of *Among the Millet, and Other Poems* and a source of great envy to Roberts when, in 1889, his 'Canadianism' had achieved its full momentum (see *CL* 111 and chapter 7). Less favoured by reviewers but probably more influenced by Roberts is Lampman's 'The Loons' (1888), a sonnet written, very likely, in May or June 1887 that draws on the same sources in Algonquin legend as 'The Departing of Clote Scarp' (and perhaps on the poem itself, which was published the previous year in *In Divers Tones*) to portray the birds of its title as once 'happy' in Glooscap's friendship but now, 'many hundred years' since 'at last he took his unseen way,' condemned to 'search and wander querulously, / Crying ... / With weird entreaties, and in agony /

---

* The voyageur's 'Ah, well I question, for as five years go, / How many blessings fall, and how much woe' (*P* 36) recalls Roberts's poem (and, thence, Wordsworth's 'Tintern Abbey') and, as argued elsewhere, both the setting and the cadences of 'Between the Rapids' are reminiscent of Moore's 'Canadian Boat-Song' (see Bentley, 'Near the Rapids' 366). 'And where is Jacques, and where is Virginie' (*P* 37) echoes several lines and the refrain of Dante Gabriel Rossetti's translation of François Villon's 'The Ballad of Dead Ladies' (1870) ('Where's Hipparchia, and where is Thais ... where are the snows of yester-year' [*Works* 541]), and 'Heaven gleams and then is gone' (*P* 38) echoes the description of the lighthouse in the opening lines of Matthew Arnold's 'Dover Beach' (1867) ('on the French coast the light / Gleams and is gone' [240]).

With awful laughter pierc[ing] the lonely night' (*P* 119). Not until the late 1890s in 'The Lake in the Forest' (1900), a greater Romantic lyric addressed to 'Manitou' (*P* 313), and in 'At the Long Sault: May, 1660' (1943), an unfinished epyllion about the French-Canadian hero Dollard des Ormeaux (or Daulac), did Lampman refer more than tangentially in his poems either to Canadian history or to Native mythology.

Although there is little surviving evidence of Carman's political views and creative activities between 1885 and 1887, one of the poems that he wrote and published at that time is strongly indicative of his acquiescence in Roberts's nationalistic program. Dated 'June 1886' and published in the October 1886 issue of the *Kings's College Record*, 'Low Tide on Avon' is an early version of 'Low Tide on Grand Pré' (1893) that was apparently written in the summer of 1886 when Carman was staying with Roberts in Windsor and imbibing the spirit that had produced 'The Outlook for Literature.' Whereas the final version of 'Low Tide on Grand Pré' focuses entirely on a transcendental experience that is shared by the speaker and his unnamed lover, 'Low Tide on Avon' contains an interpolated tale in which the sun that 'lingers,' 'yet ... not for us, ' in both versions of the poem does 'stay,' but – and this is the most startling difference between the two versions – for the spirit of Evangeline, whose physical absence is mourned by the Avon River of her native Acadia:

A grievous stream that to and fro,
　　Athrough the fields of Acadie,
Goes wandering, as if to know
　　Why one beloved face should be
　　So long from home and Acadie!

And every year in June for him
　　There comes a dream – Evangeline,
As on that day her loss made dim!
　　Through all the years that intervene
　　His deathless love Evangeline!

At evening fall in midsummer,
　　Just when the radiant fleurs-de-lis
From trammel of winter and the stir
　　Of breathing Death one hour are free,
　　She comes with radiant fleurs-de-lis!

Above the ageless hills there breaks,
   Over their purple bloom of pine
And blue ravines, in crimson flakes,
   Her light whose hands are come to twine
   Shadow of rose and shade of pine.

And all the land makes glad her coming,
   If only once in a year of time,
The Underking's strong hands o'ercoming,
   She moves one night through a dream sublime,
   In beauty still untouched of time. (quoted in Vincent 134, 136)

A compound of Persephone,* the Blessed Damozel, and the *genius loci* of Acadia, the Evangeline of 'Low Tide on Avon' is also a solar heroine whose annual return coincides not only, as Thomas Vincent has suggested, with the 'summer solstice' (131), but also with the feast day of St John the Baptist, a focus for patriotic celebrations among French Canadians in the Maritimes as well as Quebec since the early nineteenth century. With her 'radiant fleurs-de-lis,' her 'hands ... come to twine / Shadow of rose and shade of pine,' and her association with both 'Avon' and 'Acadie,' Carman's Evangeline is, in short, the ever-resurgent and unifying spirit of Canada, the fantasized essence of the 'deep, horizontal comradeship' of which 'imagined communities' are compounded (Benedict Anderson 16).

## III

'I read with great pleasure your speech at the Imperial Federation meeting,' Roberts told George Taylor Denison on 7 May 1888. 'I am supporting the movement now, down here, quietly, being turned from my *Independence* line by the necessity of all loyal Canadians to unite against the Annexationists. Imp[erial] Fed[eration] will satisfy me! God speed to you!' (*CL* 73). This was Roberts's response to a widely publicized speech

---

* A beautiful maiden goddess condemned to spend every winter with Hades ('The Underking'), Persephone (Kore, Proserpine) was permitted to return to the upper world every spring – hence, her association with rebirth rituals of various kinds (see chapter 6; and Bentley, 'Threefold in Wonder,' 31–2 and 49–55, for Carman's use of the Eleusinian Mysteries, to which the cult of Persephone was believed to have given rise, in *Sappho: One Hundred Lyrics* [1903] and elsewhere).

of 24 March 1888 in which Denison proposed 'the establishment of a branch of the Imperial Federation League' in Toronto for the twofold purpose of furthering 'the objects of the League'[14] and strengthening 'the ties which bind Canada to the Mother Land' (*Speeches* 5). As Denison makes almost libellously evident in his speech, his proposal was motivated by 'the movement for Commercial Union' with the United States, a reaction to Macdonald's National Policy that was led by 'a traitor in New York' (the expatriate Canadian entrepreneur Erastus Wiman [1834–1904]) and supported by 'the evil designs' of other traitors closer to home, including Goldwin Smith and Graeme Mercer Adam (who, it may be recalled, published a *Handbook of Commercial Union* in 1888). Imperial Federation, Denison and his fellow Imperialists were convinced, would both 'consolidate the Empire and give the Canadian people greater influence among the nations of the world': '... it would be [no] more than fifty years before Canada, with her vast resources and constantly increasing population, would have as much interest [that is, advantage and influence] in the Federated Empire as the Mother Country herself' (6).

Arrayed with Denison against the severance of 'the ties ... b[inding] the Canadian people to the Mother Land' and 'the destruction of the national life of the country' (5) that they saw as the consequences of commercial union were George Monro Grant and George Robert Parkin, the former Roberts's editor in connection with *Picturesque Canada* and the latter his and Carman's teacher at the Fredericton Collegiate Grammar School in the early-to-mid 1870s. In 1883, Roberts had characterized Parkin as 'almost alone' in his Imperialism and pronounced '[h]is party ... dead' (*CL* 34);[15] and in March 1887 he had looked forward with relish to 'the *clashing* of opinion' between articles on Canada's political future by himself and Parkin (*CL* 63) in a forthcoming issue of the *Century*,[16] but by the spring of 1888 his views were undergoing a shift that began in pragmatism and moved towards endorsement. 'As to Canada's destiny, though primarily an Independent, I have Federation sympathies [and] [a]m intensely anti-annexationist,' he told Lighthall on 2 June 1888; 'Federation on *certain lines* would suit me thoroughly. But Canadian autonomy would have to be absolutely secured. England should be simply *Primus inter pares* [First among equals]' (*CL* 82). 'Parkin I won't tackle, – certainly not at present,' he told Gilder some six weeks later; 'I want to strengthen his hands against Annexation ... Imp[erial] Fed[eration] is just now making the best stand against it, so I'll help Imp[erial] Fed[eration]. Federalists and Independents need to join their forces just now in Canada' (*CL* 86). When Parkin's article 'The Reorganization of the British Empire' eventually appeared in December 1888, Roberts gave it his almost unmitigated approval:

> Mr. Parkin advocates with great force and persuasiveness the scheme of Imperial Federation, and advocates from a patriotic Canadian standpoint. Canadians who regard Independence as the more natural destiny of their country have no quarrel with such Federationists as Mr. Parkin, who would tolerate no scheme of Federation that did not leave to Canada the same degree of independence as it should retain for England. All true Nationalists, whether they look toward an absolute independence or such independence as would be possible in a federal union of equals, may join hands in eternal antagonism to the ignoble alternative of annexation. ('The World of Books,' *Progress* [Saint John], [8 December 1888])

Four years later in an excoriating review of Smith's *Canada and the Canadian Question* (1891), Roberts would expound the 'visionary' nature of Imperial Federation while still mooting the possibility that Canada 'might prefer to develop her great resources along the lines of national independence' ('The Future of Canada' 386), but eventually even that residual echo of his earlier thinking would fall silent.

By the end of 1888, Imperial Federation thus inflected by Independence was little short of a war cry in Roberts's immediate circle. 'In a late letter ... you said you believed that in five years we would have to fight for Canada!' he told Denison on December 29. 'I read that passage to my dear friend, ... Bliss Carman, who is an ardent Federationist. It inspired him, and he wrote a stirring little lyric ["Clarion"] thereupon, – which I will get and send you. *Windsor* is no place for a Branch of the [Imperial Federation] League, – the people are *fat and indifferent*' (*CL* 100).[17] '[T]he project of Imperial Federation appeals to a broad and higher patriotism, and fits more logically upon our career than independence,' runs the climactic paragraph of *A History of Canada* (1897):

> Indeed, it gives a fuller meaning to our whole past, – to our birth from the disruption of 1776, – to our almost miraculous preservation from seizure by the United States while we were yet but a handful of scattered settlements, – to our struggle for unity, – to our daring and splendid expansion, – and to the cost at which we have secured it ... It is possible to conceive of a form of Imperial Federation which would so guard the autonomy of each federating nation and so strictly limit the powers of the central government as to satisfy even those who desire absolute independence ... Imperial Federation

would admit to us full practical manhood without the dishonour of annexation, or the risk of the ingratitude of independence. (445–6)

As Roberts's concluding metaphor implies, Imperial Federation would allow the 'Child of Nations, giant-limbed' not merely to grasp 'manhood's heritage,' but to do so without either incurring the displeasure of the Mother Country or suffering the disgrace of a union with a United States which, for the metaphor to hold, must be envisaged as a less than suitable female (or, just conceivably, male) partner: better the hope of equality with a grateful parent than the demeaning bed of a disreputable mate.

Although less important surely than the arguments and example of Denison, Grant, and, especially Parkin,[18] an influence on Roberts's developing sympathy for Imperial Federation in the mid-to-late 1880s may well have been Charles Mair's *Tecumseh: A Drama* (1886), a work later described by Mair himself as 'one of the literary sources of Canadian Imperial sentiment' (quoted in Berger 65). A founding member of Canada First who had himself made the journey from Independence to 'the vastly nobler conception' of Imperial Federation ('The New Canada' 161; and see Berger 65), Mair drew heavily on the 'opinions and advice' of Grant and Denison in the writing of *Tecumseh*, a manuscript of which was apparently admired by Roberts when it was shown to him by Denison in February 1883 (Shrive 78, 82). So closely involved with its composition was Denison especially that Mair went so far as to describe *Tecumseh* to him not merely as '"our play"' but as '"more yours than mine"' (quoted in Shrive 103) – apportionings that could well apply to Isaac Brock's rousing reply to an unpatriotic settler in the fourth act:

You have no faith! Then take a creed from me!
For I believe in Britain's Empire, and
In Canada, its true and loyal son,
Who yet shall rise to greatness, and shall stand
At England's shoulder helping her to guard
True liberty throughout a faithless world.
Here is a creed for arsenals and camps,
For hearts and heads that seek their country's good;
So go at once, and meditate on it! (72–3)

In large part because of Denison's efforts in promoting it (see Shrive 103–6), *Tecumseh* 'probably attracted more attention than any previous English work which ha[d] made its appearance in Canada' (Reade, 'Literature' 210–1) and garnered glowing reviews in the *Week* (W.D. Le Sueur), the *Varsity* (Toronto) (G. Mercer Adam), and in countless newspapers across the country. (Typically, the *Morning Chronicle* [Quebec] hailed it as a lesson in 'true patriotism' and the *British Whig* [Kingston] as a work 'for all Canadian royalists – in fact, for all Canadians' [quoted in Shrive 99].) Writing to Mair on 10 March 1886, Roberts pronounced him a 'brother craftsman' and showered *Tecumseh* with his most generous praise: 'I ... confess ... that I have hitherto considered my own poetry the best yet done in Canada. But *Tecumseh* is better. It is by far the finest thing Canadian Literature has produced ... As a Canadian and your friend, I am simply delighted with pride over *Tecumseh*, – and shall certainly spare no effort to do something myself that shall equal it' (*CL* 58).

In 'The Poetic Outlook in Canada,' a 'survey' of 'those acres [of Canadian intellectual effort] ... from which we are to expect a poetic harvest' that appeared a little over a year later in the June 1887 number of the *Critic* (Halifax), Roberts tempers his enthusiasm for *Tecumseh* with the Collinsian reservation that the drama betrays 'a certain provincialism of tone and a lack of sympathy with modern mental attitudes,' but overall he has high praise for both the work and its author: '... its excellences ... [are] deeply significant for us who are watching for the new light within our borders ... [H]is atmosphere and coloring [are] unmistakably Canadian; his patriotism full-blooded and fervid. His utterance is such as fits the lips of a son of this land of splendid heritage and heroic stock; it is forceful, straight-forward, and virile' (10). The 'new light within our borders' would begin to shine brightly for Roberts in November 1888 when he started to use the term 'Canadianism' (*CL* 96, 98, 101) to describe a 'love of Canada'[19] that accepted Imperial Federation as the best available bulwark against Annexation and conceived Canadian literature as a potent means of fostering 'Canadian possibilities and aspirations' (*CL* 90).

It is perhaps an indication of Roberts's reconciliation to the idea of the British Empire as the context for Canadian national and literary aspiration that in 1887 he wrote to Ernest Rhys, an editor with the English publishing house Walter Scott, to enquire whether the firm would consider doing a Canadian equivalent of an Australian anthology – *Australian Ballads and Rhymes* (1888) – that was then in progress under the editorship of Douglas Sladen.[20] In April 1888, such a volume was duly commissioned from Roberts, but on May 23 he received a letter from Lighthall informing him that another Walter Scott editor, William

Sharp,* had commissioned Lighthall to do a similar anthology. Explaining that he was already editing an anthology for Walter Scott – *Poems of Wildlife* (1888) ('a thoroughly cosmopolitan volume, though it contains Canadian poems,' including two excerpts from *Tecumseh*) – Roberts offered to resign the Canadian anthology in favour of Lighthall, adding that it would give him 'the greatest pleasure ... to be ... whatever assistance ... in the way of suggestions and so forth' that Lighthall might permit (*CL* 77). If Lighthall agrees, Roberts concludes, he will sing his praises to Rhys and Sharp and suggest to them that the anthology 'should aim to show *the best* as well as the most Canadian of our poetry.' As he put it some six weeks later when suggesting which of his own poems might be included in the anthology, 'I should like my own poetry to [be] represented ... chiefly by such work as "The Tantramar Revisited," ... "Canada," ... and a series of "Sonnets of the Common Day" which I am working at ... [b]ut I would like my work on more *general* sub-

---

* A Scottish-born man of letters who published his creative work under the pseudonym 'Fiona Macleod,' Sharp was among the influential men in Britain and the United States whom Robert cultivated for promotional purposes. '[H]e is ... the strongest and most genuinely inspired' of England's 'younger singers,' he wrote of Sharp's *Romantic Ballads and Poems of Phantasy* in the 12 January 1889 issue of *Progress;* 'his verse has not, for the most part, as captivating a melody as that of Mr. [Edmund] Gosse, but his genius seems to me more vital, more stimulating, more exuberant, and of a larger mould' (16). By the late summer of the same year, Sharp was in New Brunswick staying with Roberts, and in September *Progress* happily reported the presence of poems by Roberts and Lampman in Sharp's anthology of *American Sonnets* (21 September 1889, 6). 'I found it very greatly helpful to know him as intimately as possible ... He is one of the very foremost literary men of London of this generation,' wrote Carman of Sharp during his stay at Kingscroft. 'We get on very well together, and he thinks some of my work pretty good' (*L* 30, and see *CL* 111–12). Carman's prescience would pay off, for as Muriel Miller observes, 'in February 1890, an almost unprecedented thing for an unknown writer was to happen to him. An unsolicited offer to publish a book of his poems came to him – ostensibly through Sharp – from the London publisher, David Nutt [who would eventually publish the English edition of *Low Tide on Grand Pré*]' (64). On 21 October 1893 and 6 January 1894, the *Academy* (London) carried measured but overwhelmingly favourable reviews by Sharp of *Songs of the Common Day* and *Low Tide on Grand Pré*, each of which included extravagant praise of both poets (see chapter 7). Carman subsequently repaid the favours in 'Mr. Sharp's Poems,' a lengthly review article in the 15 September 1894 number of the *Chap-Book* (Chicago) that hails Sharp's *Vistas* as 'one of the freshest inspirations in contemporary letters' (223). Just how far Roberts was prepared to go to procure the help of influential men of letters is indicated by the postscript in an 15 April–23 May 1888 letter to Edmund Clarence Stedman: 'I have been rather hard struck by [Matthew] Arnold's death. After you, he is one, of the greatest men of the day, who most influenced my aims and motives. He had also been very warm and generous to me' (*CL* 75).

jects not to go *entirely* unrepresented' (*CL* 84). Clearly, cosmopolitanism was still very much a presence in Roberts's thought as he assumed his role as informal editorial adviser to Lighthall in the creation of the first anthology to include works by all members of the Confederation group: *Songs of the Great Dominion: Voices from the Forests and Waters, the Settlements and Cities of Canada* (1889). Despite Roberts's cosmopolitan pleadings, Lighthall selected and arranged the contents of his anthology on the principle that it should be 'Canadian in tone throughout' (*CL* 87). Thus Roberts is represented by 'Canada,' 'Collect for Dominion Day,' 'Frogs,' 'To Winter,' 'Burnt Lands,' 'Birch and Paddle,' 'The Tantramar Revisited,' and 'The Departing of Clote Scarpe,' and the volume is divided into sections under such headings as 'The New Nationality,' 'The Indian,' 'Places,' and 'The Spirit of Canadian History.'

But Lighthall, though quite deaf to Roberts's requests for the inclusion of a sample of his cosmopolitan (classical) work, and very probably a major influence on his new-found 'Canadianism,' was by no means a narrow nationalist. Three years before embarking on *Songs of the Great Dominion*, he published a handbill entitled *Adjustable Federation* (1885), in which he argues for a balance between 'national independence' and imperial interdependence that would leave 'the peoples of the Empire' 'all free yet bind ... each to the rest wherever a bond would give strength or advantage' and, more important, 'teach ... [them] to know one another ... [and] prepar[e] the way ... for the coming alliance of English-speaking nations and for that certain final constitution "The Federation of the World."'* Every aspect of *Songs of the Great Dominion* is consistent with this vision: in Lighthall's Introduction, Canada is characterized as the 'Eldest Daughter of the Empire, ... the Empire's completest type,' and 'a voice ... in the Empire of today' (xi, xxiii); the opening section of the anthology is devoted to 'The Imperial Spirit' and contains poems entitled 'Hastings' (Reade), 'Advance of the Empire' (Mary Barry Smith), 'Canada to England' (anonymous), 'Empire First' (John Lesperance), and 'The Canadians on the Nile' (William Wye Smith);[21] and the volume as a whole is dedicated 'To that Sublime Cause, the Union of Mankind, which the British Peoples, if They Are True to Themselves and Courageous in the Future as They Have Been in the Past, Will Take to Be the Reason of Existence of Their Empire; and to the Glory of Those Peoples in the Service of Man.' Published the year before and the year after *Songs of the Great Dominion*, Lighthall's *Sketch of*

---

* The phrase that Lighthall quotes is, of course, from 'Locksley Hall,' where Tennyson looks into the future and sees a 'Federation of the world ... lapt in universal law' (696).

*the New Utilitarianism* (1888) and *Spiritualized Happiness-Theory; or, New Utilitarianism* (1890) indicate that the roots of his philosophy and the anthology into which it blossomed lay in his addition of a form of evolutionary idealism – a belief that a Mysterious Power is causing all life to progress upwards towards a condition of spiritualized happiness – to the neo-Kantian social liberalism of Thomas Hill Green, particularly Green's *Prolegomena to Ethics* (1883) and his *Lectures on the Principles of Political Obligation* (1886) (and see Lighthall, *The Young Seigneur* 191–3). Since Roberts told Lighthall on 6 October 1888 that he was about to 'read, mark ... learn ... and inwardly digest' *Sketch of the New Utilitarianism*, he may have had it in mind two weeks later when, in replying to recent letters from Lighthall to Carman and himself, he wrote, 'yea, indeed, let us who are true Canadians ever strengthen each others' hands and unite to keep pure our ideals. The difficulty I feel is to keep sane and dignified in my tone when I speak of Canada. The name thrills me, and I have difficulty in keeping foolish tears out of my eyes when I am talking to my classes of Canadian possibilities and aspirations. But I keep myself under bit and bridle, fearing mere sentimentality' (*CL* 89, 90). In any event, there can be little doubt that Lighthall did play a major part not only in stoking the fires of Roberts's 'Canadianism' at this time, but also in directing it towards supervening ethical and idealistic goals.[22]

As a resident of Montreal since the 1870s (when he moved there from his native Hamilton), Lighthall knew better than Roberts the threat posed to a racially and linguistically based conception of national and imperial unity by non-English-speaking peoples such as the French Canadians. Before assuming the editorship of *Songs of the Great Dominion*, he had risen to the challenge of engendering a sense of national if not post-national community in Canada in *The Young Seigneur; or, Nation-Making* (1888), a historical romance with the dual aim, according to its Preface, of 'mak[ing] the atmosphere of French Canada understood by those who speak English' and of '*map[ping] out a future for the Canadian nation*, which has been hitherto drifting without any plan' (iii). A direct descendant of *The Golden Dog (Le Chien d'Or: A Legend of Quebec)* (1877), the historical romance by the arch-Loyalist and Imperialist William Kirby,[23] *The Young Seigneur* has as its hero a youthful and aristocratic politician of French and English descent with the bilingual name of Chamilly Haviland,[24] who spends much of the work explaining to an Ontario member of Parliament named Chrysler his plans for the 'cultivation of the national spirit' and the creation of an 'Ideal Canada' that, unlike 'Plato's ... Republic, Bacon['s] ... New Atlantis, [and] More['s] Utopia,' will become a reality if Canadians 'boldly aim' to make it so

(193, 11). Although Haviland's plans are thwarted by corrupt politicians and he himself meets an untimely death, he fulfils his purpose of giving a local habitation and a fictional name to the idealistic social liberalism that Lighthall proposes in the Introduction to *Songs of the Great Dominion* as Canada's answer to the question of whether the British Empire will last: 'IT WILL, IF IT SETS BEFORE IT A DEFINITE IDEAL THAT MEN WILL SUFFER AND DIE FOR; and such an Ideal – worthy of long and patient endeavour – may be found in broad-minded advance towards the voluntary Federation of Mankind' (xxiii). It was in the same spirit that Lighthall included 'a bow to the French' (xxxvi) in *Songs of the Great Dominion* in the form of Appendices on 'The Old Chansons of the French Province' and 'Leading Modern French-Canadian Poets' – a gesture that, given the magnitude of the challenge that it attempts to address, can only be described as bibliographically too little, too late.

*The Young Seigneur* has survived shifts in literary and ideological fashion even less successfully than 'Canada,' but Roberts, predictably, 'delight[ed] in the earnest spirit' of the novel (*CL* 88) and set about promoting it and Lighthall with almost Denisonian fervour. His younger brother Goodridge (1860–92) ('a most enthusiastic Canadian' [*CL* 95]) was enlisted to write a review for the *King's College Record* but assigned the task back to Roberts, who eventually gave Lighthall, his work, and himself extravagant and pseudonymous praise in the November 1889 issue of the magazine.* In November and December 1888, Roberts gave a talk on *The Young Seigneur* to the Haliburton Society, a club founded at King's College in 1884 to encourage the study of Canadian literature,[25] used it as the pretext for proposing Lighthall for membership of the Society, and, on the evening of his election, 'read a lot' of it to an enthu-

---

* '[Y]ou are the only one of our singers whom my brother reserved for *me* to write about [in his column on "The Canadian Poets" in the *King's College Record*],' Roberts told Lighthall in a letter of 21 November 1888, 'so send him ... *bare facts*, and I'll do the rest, under a *nom de plume*!' (*CL* 96–7). Signed Stanley F.W. Symonds, the piece on Lighthall in 'The Canadian Poets' series begins by conceding the existence of a 'Mutual Admiration Society' in Canada that is 'continually load[ing]' 'petty and commonplace poets (?) ... with eulogy' but quickly exempts both Lighthall and Roberts himself from the phenomenon and then proceeds to give a brief account of Lighthall's life and work that celebrates his 'patriotism and national pride,' to quote poems and passages from his *Thoughts, Moods and Ideals: Crimes of Leisure* (1887), and to summarize the purposes and ideals of *The Young Seigneur* – namely '"to map out a future for the Canadian nation"' based on the four principles of 'Industry, Economy, Progress and [Moral] Seriousness' (14–16). If Roberts did indeed write the piece, he took great care to disguise the fact stylistically as well as through the use of a pseudonym, for it has none of the verve of his other critical essays.

siastic group of 'students, ... Professors, [and] town men' (*CL* 92, 96, 98). '[P]ure Canadianism,' he rhapsodized to Lighthall on December 23, 'and it took hold beautifully' (*CL* 98).

It was for a more public forum, however, that Roberts reserved what may have been his most lavish 'expression of ... admiration' for *The Young Seigneur* (*CL* 90). Making the novel the focus of the 3 November 1888 instalment of the literary column that he had been writing since May for the Saint John *Progress,* he hails it as a manifestation of an 'awakening' and 'thrilling' 'national and patriotic motive.' Imbued with the 'ideal ... of a united Canada working on distinctive lines to the highest and purest national development,' it is 'a work of deep significance' in which 'the life observed is always that of the two races in contact,' and its author's fervent 'Canadianism ... embraces not only our race and its aspirations, but ... our splendid landscape as well.' To conclude the review, Roberts quotes at length from two passages in the chapter entitled 'The Ideal State,' where Haviland 'outline[s] his national ideals,' a heady concoction of social liberalism, muscular Christianity, and national socialism aimed at the creation of 'the Ideal Physical Man' who will be equipped by 'True Education' to see and do 'The National Work': 'we must never stop short ... until ... every Canadian is the strongest and most beautiful man that can be thought,' explains Haviland in the first passage, with insouciant disregard for approximately half of Canada's population. 'Let him have a scheme of facts that will give him an idea of the ALL ... We must be One People'; 'Canada must be Perfectly Independent'; 'there must be No Proletariate'; and

> the nation must work all together as a whole. The public plan must be clearly disseminated, and especially the aim "To do pre-eminently well our portion of the improvement of the world." Consecrated by our ideal also we must seek to draw together, and foster a national distinctiveness. Canada must mean to us the Sacred Country, and our young men learn to weigh truly the value of such living against foreign advantages ... [L]et us make to ourselves proper customs and peculiarities ... Let the man who was a hero – Daulac, Brock, the twelve who sortied at Lacolle Mill;[26] our deathless three hundred at Chateauguay, – never ... be forgotten ...
>
> Think ... of a country that lives ... on the deepest and highest principle of the seen and the unseen ... [errors corrected]

It is a measure of the resonance that such ideas had for Roberts in the fall of 1888 that at the climax of his introductory remarks on *The Young Seigneur* he proclaims the novel 'a veritable "Book of Gold" for all Young Canada' and 'declare[s] with pride' that 'Young Canada ... is a term which now embraces most of Canada's older and wiser sons.'

To judge by the literary projects that Roberts had planned in December 1888, *The Young Seigneur,* together with *Tecumseh, The Golden Dog,* and Kirby's similarly inflected *Canadian Idylls* (1884), blazed the trail for the creative path that he would follow for the next four years: 'yea, truly, I have a long Canadian work or two in course of devising,' he told Lighthall in his letter of December 23: 'a Quebec – *Bigot,*[27] – work, perhaps in dramatic form, frankly connected with Kirby's book; a series of Canadian idylls; and a narrative poem of Acadian life and story – very unlike *Evangeline* in conception – to be called '"Beauséjour"' (*CL* 99). None of these ambitious projects came to fruition in quite the way envisaged by Roberts, but elements of each are clearly discernible in his major literary undertakings of 1888–90: the 'Quebec ... work' in *The Canadians of Old* (1890), his translation of the French-Canadian historical romance *Les Anciens Canadiens* (1863), by Philippe-Joseph Aubert de Gaspé (1786–1871);[28] the 'series of Canadian idylls' in 'How the Mohawks Set Out for Medoctec' and 'The Keepers of the Pass,'* the balladic treat-

---

* Both poems are preceded by prose explanations that serve the twofold purpose of informing the reader about the historical events upon which they are based, and inviting them to be read as exemplary tales of (Canadian) heroism in the face of enormous odds, the lesson taken by Roberts in 'Canada' from the battles of the War of 1812:

  When the invading Mohawks captured the outlying Melicite village of Madawaska, they spared two squaws to guide them downstream to the main Melicite town of Medoctec, below Grand Falls. The squaws steered themselves and their captors over the Falls. (*CP* 114)

  When the Iroquois were moving in overwhelming force to obliterate the infant town of Montreal, Adam Daulac and a small band of comrades, binding themselves by oath not to return alive, went forth to meet the enemy in a distant pass between the Ottawa River and the hills. There they died to a man, but not till they had slain so many of the savages that the invading force was shattered and compelled to withdraw. (*CP* 117)

  In a letter of 4 March 1887 to Gilder, Roberts claims that 'How the Mohawks Set Out for Medoctec' 'narrates a true story still told by the Melicite Indians of the river St. John, who rejoice over the heroism of their squaws to this day. But for these two women, there is little doubt but that the whole Melicite tribe would have been annihilated by their ancient enemies the Mohawks' (*CL* 64; and see Bentley, 'Charles G.D. Roberts's Use of "Indian Legend" in Four Poems of the Eighteen Eighties and 'Nineties'). Based directly or indirectly on the highly romanticized account of the expedition of Adam Dollard des Ormeaux (Daulac) (1635–60) in Parkman's *The Old Régime in Canada* (1874) (73–82), Roberts's treatment of what had come to be called 'the Canadian Themopylae' in 'The Keepers of the Pass' may have supplied part of the inspiration for Lampman's projected treatment of the same theme in 'At the Long Sault: May, 1660.'

ments of Native and French-Canadian heroism that he had already published in periodicals by the end of 1888 and would place together in *Songs of the Common Day*,[29] and 'The Raid from Beauséjour' in the 'long boys' romance of Acadian life' (*CL* 112) that appeared first in the February-May 1892 number of the *Dominion Illustrated Monthly* and subsequently in *The Raid from Beauséjour, and How the Carter Boys Lifted the Mortgage: Two Stories of Acadie* (1894) and as *The Young Acadian; or, The Raid from Beauséjour* (1907).

Arguably, the most important and accomplished of these 'Canadian *[n]ationalistic and aspirational* work[s]' (*CL* 87) is *The Canadians of Old* (or *Cameron of Lochiel* as it became in 1905), for Roberts's translation, though published in New York, represents his most extended attempt to address what he calls in his brief Introduction to the novel the 'series of problems' residing in the 'dual character of the Canadian people and ... Canadian literature' ([5]). 'We, of English speech, turn naturally to French-Canadian literature for knowledge of the French-Canadian people,' he continues in his Introduction, and de Gaspe's 'historical romance ... gathers up and preserves in lasting form the songs and legends, the characteristic customs, the phases of thought and feeling, the very local and personal aroma of a rapidly changing civilization' ([5–6]). In addition to providing a window onto French Canada past and present, the intended goal of *The Canadians of Old* was to 'throw ... a strong side-light upon the motives and aspirations of the [French-Canadian] race' in the hope that 'a close knowledge' would lead to the conclusion 'that perhaps the extreme of Quebec nationalism is but the froth on the surface of a not unworthy determination to keep intact the speech and institutions of French Canada' ([6]). The perception of French Canada embedded in Roberts's Introduction and translation is inevitably much more complex than this statement suggests, but its fundamental point has stood the test of time and shows a high degree of sympathy for the desire to protect and perpetuate Quebec 'civilization' that *Les Anciens Canadiens* comes close to suggesting (and herein perhaps lies part of its appeal for some English-Canadian readers) was always a lost cause. (The novel's French-Canadian protagonist, Jules d'Haberville, marries an English woman, but their child is named Archie, and Jules's sister, Blanche, refuses to marry its Scottish protagonist, Cameron of Lochiel, and so dies childless.)

As Roberts strove in the late 1880s and early 1890s to create a Canadian consciousness that would transcend the racial, linguistic, and regional forces that, in Collins's words, were 'pulling in different ways' against national unity ('English-Canadian Literature'), he also sought to remove himself once again from the periphery to the centre of the country. Numerous letters written to various supporters and confidants between January 1888[30] and June 1889 indicate that during this period, and always with emphasis on his Canadianism, he applied in rapid succession for professorships in political science at the University of Toronto, English literature at Toronto again[31] and also at Queen's, and that when these options came to nought (Queen's appointed James Cappon [1885–1939] to its Chair of English in 1888, and Toronto, William John Alexander [1855–1944] to the parallel position at University College in 1889), he submitted and withdrew an application for the Chair vacated by Alexander at Dalhousie University (see *CL* 69–108). No doubt for pecuniary as well as careeristic reasons, Roberts devoted a good deal of his time in the late 1880s to critical writing and extramural lecturing. A study of 'Pastoral Elegies' appeared in the *New Princeton Review* in May 1888 and eventually furnished the Introduction to the edition of Shelley's *Alastor and Adonais* (1902) that he already had in contemplation in 1888–9 (see *CL* 90, 107), when he was also planning 'a manual for teachers of English literature' – an expansion, very likely, of the article on 'The Teaching of English Literature' that he published in the *Christian Union* in April 1888. As his hopes for an academic position faded in the spring of 1889, Roberts began to concentrate his energies elsewhere, visiting Boston and New York to find publishers and make connections in late April and early May and accepting an invitation from the recently founded Society of Canadian Literature and the Montreal Society for Historical Studies to deliver a lecture in Montreal on 'The Literary Life in Canada' (*CL* 102, 107, 109) in mid-May.[32] In early February of the following year, he delivered lectures in Quebec and Lennoxville and in early April in 'New Glasgow, Amherst, Antigonish, Moncton, etc. etc.' (*CL* 114, 118). Roberts's hopes for a professorship had faded, but not his need to supplement his fixed and meagre salary of '$1,000 a year,' a sum that he represented to at least two correspondents as insufficient to meet his needs (*CL* 70).

To the extent that Roberts's financial problems and professorial ambitions were among his abiding concerns during the late 1880s, they cannot plausibly be separated from the Canadianism that made him a fervent promoter of Canadian writers and writing in the fall of 1888: as rose the tide of national sentiment and Canadian literature, so rose the professional and financial prospects of the author of 'Canada.' This is not to suggest that Roberts's Canadianism was merely opportunistic or self-serving, however, for there can be no doubt whatsoever that his feelings for Canada were genuine, intense, and motivating. In keeping with his view that one of 'the purposes ... served by the teaching of English' should be the creation of 'a capacity for wise patriotism' ('The Teaching of English' 14), he was 'talking to his class of Canadian possibilities and aspirations' in October 1888, and some two months later he considered his 'thorough-going Canadianism' as one of his prime qualifications for a Chair of English (*CL* 90, 101). As president of the Haliburton Society (1885–96), he was 'talk[ing] Canadianism all the time to the members' in November of the same year (*CL* 96) while also arranging for the Society to publish, with an Introduction by himself, *Haliburton: The Man and the Writer* (1889), by the Nova Scotia legislative librarian Frances Blake Crofton (1841–1912). On reading Lighthall's 'Canada Not Last' (1887) in November 1888, he was 'filled with envy,' and in December of the same year 'The Battle of Chateauguay,' a paper by the same author, filled him with 'patriotic stirrings innumerable' (*CL* 97, 102).

Most telling of all is the marked turn towards Canadianism in 'The World of Books' column that, as noted earlier, Roberts published in the Saint John *Progress*: from the inception of the column on 5 May 1888 until September 15 of the same year, all of the books reviewed or discussed were by American authors, but on and after September 15 the number of Canadian books and authors selected for review or mention rose dramatically.[33] The turning point came on September 15 with a review of four books of Canadian poetry – *Lyrics on Freedom, Love and Death* (1887), by George Frederick Cameron, *Poems and Translations* (1887), by Mary Morgan (c. 1856–?), *Fleur de Lys and Other Poems* (1887), by Arthur Weir (1864–1902), and *De Roberval, a Drama; also The Emigration of the Fairies, and The Triumph of Constancy, a Romaunt* (1888), by John Hunter-Duvar (1830–99) – a review that Roberts interrupts to remark on 'the sense of encouragement it has brought [him]' and to expatiate on the current state of the nation:

It is impossible to overlook the vast advance which has been made, within the last dozen years, by Canadian thought. In all Canadian literary effort there is manifest a gain in culture, in breadth, in insight, in facility. In other words, we are ripening. At the same time, with the escape from provincialism of diction, form and method, there is an increased feeling for local coloring and for native themes. We are getting more self-reliant. We are beginning to work more in our own way, and at the same time to apply to our work the tests of cosmopolitan standards. Even a beginning of this sort is of deep significance. Such a beginning is rarely made till a people begins also to realize itself a nation.

Roberts has small praise for Weir's work, finds Morgan's poems weak on 'Canadian flavour' but strong in 'culture and cosmopolitanism,' proclaims Cameron's 'noble achievement' a 'help ... toward the establishment of ... national self confidence,' and couples Hunter-Duvar's *De Roberval* with Mair's *Tecumseh* as 'two noble dramas, on purely Canadian themes, and set in purely Canadian surroundings and atmosphere,' that 'should be in the hands of all Canadians who love good literature and love their country.' Under the aegis of Canadianism, all the tensions and misgivings surrounding the aetiology and character of Canadian literature over which Collins and Roberts had fretted and theorized earlier in the decade achieved an equilibrium born of confident equipoise: in December 1888, Roberts would lament to Lighthall the 'lack in Canada [of] a definite standard of beauty' to bring to bear on Canadian poetry (*CL* 98), but his review of 15 September indicates that his Canadianism had given him the conviction both to formulate and to apply such a standard.

At least as significant as the 'appreciation' of *The Young Seigneur* that appeared in the 3 November 1888 instalment of 'The World of Books' are the reviews of Lampman's *Among the Millet, and Other Poems* (1888) and Campbell's *Snowflakes and Sunbeams* (1888) in the 26 January and 9 March 1889 instalments of the column. Characteristically, Roberts begins both reviews by referring to the recent 'awakening of intellectual life' ('*Among the Millet*') and 'literary spirit ... in Canada' ('W.W. Campbell's Poems'), and in the former he revisits the agricultural metaphor of 'The Outlook for Literature' to suggest that Lampman's book is a fulfilment of premonitions of 'an approaching harvest for these acres which so long we have been tilling almost in vain.' Equally characteristically, he finds much to praise in the work of both poets: Lampman possesses the 'Protean quality ... indicate[d] by the term genius' and 'in power of lyric description ... [Campbell] must occupy a very distinctive place in the narrow front rank of Canadian singers.' But neither review is as effusive as Roberts's 'appreciation' of *The Young Seigneur* or even his endorsement of *De Roberval*; rather, the tone of both is subdued, considered, almost headmasterly. Each poet is discussed in terms of his influences (Lampman has 'affinities' with Keats, Emerson, and Swinburne; Campbell with Keats, Poe, and Swinburne); each is situated in relation to an audience (Lampman's name is 'already deeply significant' in Canada because his poems have appeared in magazines and circulated 'among Canadian men-of-letters ... in manuscript'; Campbell, 'like others of our stronger and more original writers, ... is finding it necessary to win recognition at home by first securing it abroad'); and each is made aware that his 'first fruits' are both imperfect and promising (Lampman's poems have 'comparatively few defects, and these are unimportant' but nevertheless worth mentioning; '*naivete*,' 'diffuseness,' 'over-elaboration,' a lack of 'humour'; Campbell's 'little collection' is 'limit[ed] ... as to range and subject' and 'does not contain verse of quite the same high excellence as that which [he] has recently given us in certain of the American periodicals'). The overall impression created by the two reviews is of an older, wiser, and more experienced poet dispensing advice and encouragement. Here is Roberts providing a context for Lampman's work:

> To one who is watching with fervent solicitude the awakening of intellectual life in Canada, the past year has been one of profound congratulation ... The indications here in Canada are, it seems to me, far more favorable than those to the south of us. The note among our rising writers is one of more passion, more purpose, more seriousness and import than that sounded by the younger Americans. It is a note akin rather to that which our neighbours heard when the voices of [William Cullen] Bryant [1794–1878] and [Edgar Allan] Poe [1809–49], of [Henry Wadsworth] Longfellow [1807–82], [Oliver Wendell] Holmes [1804–94] and [Ralph Waldo] Emerson [1803–82] captured their ears. With us in Canada, though we may appear to trifle a little with ballades and villanelles and triolets, there is a strenuous undercurrent almost always to be detected. The apparent trifling is but the striving after an unimpeachable technique; the underlying motive is one of deep seriousness and impassioned expectancy.

In '*Among the Millet*' and 'W.W. Campbell's Poems,' Roberts unobtrusively establishes himself as the sage overseer and solicitous advocate of the poets who are in the process of creating the golden age of Canadian poetry, a role that he had begun to assume in private several months earlier.[34]

On the evidence of his *Collected Letters*, Roberts started to correspond with Campbell during or a little before October 1888 (probably as a result of his involvement in the preparation of *Songs of the Great Dominion*)[35] and resumed his correspondence with Lampman in the following month. In a letter of October 31 that appears to be a response to an initial letter from Campbell, he carefully establishes a professional and a personal relationship with the poet, sympathetically enquiring after his physical well-being ('alas for the toothache. Are you quit of [it] yet?'), confidentially involving him in his professorial ambitions ('*entre nous*, I have my eye on the new chair of English ... [at] Toronto University. Have you a pull on anyone of importance there?'), and flatteringly acknowledging and reciprocating his compliments ('it is only the generous praise of a fellow craftsman that is *really* worth having'; 'I read with exceeding pleasure all the poems you sent me, – some of them have a truly magnificent power') (*CL* 91). With a combination of discernment, flattery, and assistance that may have confirmed or even generated Campbell's decision to make his second book a collection of *Lake Lyrics and Other Poems* (1889), Roberts pronounces him at his 'very best' in his '"Lake" work' and encourages his hopes for wider exposure by telling him that he has already sent his poems to the English editor Alfred Henry Miles, presumably for inclusion in *The Poets and the Poetry of the Century* (1892–7), and relaying a request from Sladen for material for *Younger American Poets, 1830–1890* (1891). In due course, Miles's ten-volume anthology would appear with three poems by Roberts but none by Campbell, and Sladen's would include an Appendix of 'Younger Canadian Poets' attributed to Goodridge Roberts but partly edited by Sladen himself that foregoes strict alphabetical order to begin with four poems by Campbell, three of which are *Lake Lyrics* ('Keziah,' 'A Lake Memory,' and 'Manitou').[36] (Because Sladen was 'acquainted too late with the unusual merit of Duncan Campbell Scott' [li], his work does not appear in 'Younger Canadian Poets.' All the other members of the Confederation group are well represented, however, and each is specifically signalized by Sladen in his Introduction 'To the Reader' [l–li].)[37] Nor did Roberts ignore national venues in his promotion and encouragement of Campbell: the 'Literary Notes' column in the 12 January 1889 issue of the *Dominion Illustrated* records that the editor has a letter from Roberts with 'the welcome news that the author of "Snowflakes and Sunbeams" is rector of St. Stephen N.B.,' together with a critical appraisal that apparently had an effect: Campbell, writes the editor, quoting Roberts, '"is very strong in a sort of impassioned lyric description, and his *winter* verse is of our very best in that line." We shall now take occasion to have another look at his little ... pamphlet' (see also *CL* 99).

No doubt because he had known Lampman for several years and very likely because he admired his poetry more than Campbell's, Roberts greeted the news of the imminent publication of *Among the Millet, and*

*Other Poems* with truly Denisonian zeal. 'Let us "boom" it!' he exclaimed in a letter of 16 November 1888:

> I will myself review it for *Progress* ... I will get it reviewed in the St. John *Globe*, St. John *Telegraph*, Halifax *Herald*, Halifax *Chronicle*, Halifax *Critic*. The *King's College Record* (under my brother's editorship) will handle you enthusiastically ... I will see personally to the reviews in the ... *Globe* and ... *Telegraph*, placing ... copies in suitable hands for the purpose. I will write to the ... *Herald*, *Chronicle*, and *Critic*, telling them ... to handle [the book] with the respect and admiration due to so important a contribution to our literature. ( *CL* 93)

And so on with the names of reviewers, booksellers, and 'sympathetic' poets throughout the Maritimes. When Lampman's book arrived in December, Roberts was 'in the midst of exams,' but he 'read it nearly all' and took a few moments to give it unstinting praise and to suggest further plans for its promotion:

> I ... am filled with enthusiastic delight and pride. It seems to me one of the finest first vol[ume]s ever issued by a poet. The genius of it is utterly beyond question. Among the poets across the line there are none of the like age to compare at all with you and Carman. We will make this a glorious epoch in our country's history, I do from the bottom of my soul believe. Your sonnets are exquisite, your lyrics not less admirable. Shall particularize later on, – and in public shall speak with no uncertain note. Carman is staying with me, and has been parading up and down the room raving on your verses. Send him a copy (to Fredericton, N.B.) and he will give it a long and glowing review in the Boston *Advertiser*! Shall place all copies you wish me to. Shall write to a N[ew] Y[ork] critic of you at once. ( *CL* 97)

The letter concludes with the address of Andrew Lang, the influential British man of letters, an offer to exchange photographs, and a request for Lampman's assistance with Roberts's bid for the Chair of English at Toronto. The fact that on 28 December 1888 Carman wrote to thank Lampman for sending him a copy of *Among the Millet, and Other Poems* and to express his desire 'to say a few words about the book in the *Daily Advertiser* of Boston' (SFU)[38] is but one indication of the two poets' willing cooperation in Roberts's promotional schemes.

If there is one poem that fully expresses the spirit of Canadianism that infuses Roberts's letters and reviews of 1888–9 it is 'Autochthon' (1893), which was published as a broadsheet for private circulation in December 1888 and then introduced to wider readerships in the February 1890 number of the *University Quarterly Review* (Toronto) and the 12 April 1890 issue of *Progress*. (Surely not fortuitously, in the *University Quarterly Review*, it is the lead item and it is followed by 'The National Sentiment in Canada,' by John George Bourinot, which quotes with approval 'An Ode for the Canadian Confederacy' [23]: the stock of nationalism was high, and Roberts was reaping the dividends.) Invoking through its title[39] the ancient Athenians' claim that their ancestors actually sprang from the soil that they inhabited, 'Autochthon' is a monologue spoken by 'the spirit' of life, a ubiquitous driving force that at first seems to be a manifestation with different embodiments of the 'something ... / Whose dwelling is the light of setting suns, / And the round ocean and the living air, / And the blue sky, and in the mind of man' in Wordsworth's 'Tintern Abbey' (2: 262): 'I am the spirit astir / To swell the grain ... I am the life that thrills / In branch and bloom ... I am the infinite gleam of eyes that keep / The post of [earth's] repose ... I flash in the prismy fire that dances o'er / The dew's ephemeral ball,' and so on (*CP* 122–3). In its final two stanzas, however, 'Autochthon' swerves away from Wordsworthian spiritism (or animism) to link the life force with the national spirit:

> I am the voice of the wind
>   And wave and tree,
> Of stern desires and blind,
>   Of strength to be;
> I am the cry by night
>   At point of dawn,
> The summoning bugle from the unseen height,
>   In cloud and doubt withdrawn.
>
> I am the strife that shapes
>   The stature of man,
> The pang no hero escapes,
>   The blessing, the ban;
> I am the hammer that moulds
>   The sion of our race,
> The omen of God in our blood that a people beholds
>   The foreknowledge veiled in our face. (*CP* 123)

Little wonder that Roberts was keen to see 'Autochthon' reprinted in J.E. Wetherell's *Later Canadian Poems* (see *CL* 161): it is his quintessential statement after 'Canada' of his belief in the Canadian nation as a spiritual entity energized by the life force itself.[40]

Taken together, the letters and reviews that Roberts wrote during the winter of 1888–9 reveal that he was the centripetal force that brought the Confederation group together and inspired its members with a sense of common cause. Merely one more instance of this are his comments on Campbell's unsuccessful bid for the parish of Windsor: 'I have talked you up much ... Be sure, if there is a thread to catch, I will catch it, and unravel it in your interest. What a delightful little *Academe* we could have here! By the way, would you care to join our *Haliburton Society*? ... 'T would ... enlarge your constituency, and add to you ardent admirers' (*CL* 99). As 1888 became 1889, only the two Scotts remained outside the circle, but they were not to remain so for long. In his letter of November 16 to Lampman, Roberts expresses sympathy for an overworked Duncan Campbell Scott, and in a letter of the following November he indicates his continuing concern and hopes: 'my greetings to Scott! I am watching him with great interest. What next from him?' (*CL* 111). In the midst of his flurry of activity over Campbell and Lampman, Roberts received a copy of *The Soul's Quest and Other Poems* (1888) from Frederick George Scott and responded in a letter of January 15 with characteristic enthusiasm and plans: 'this verse does great honour to our young literature – to the advancement of which my energies are most fervently devoted. I have made a note of the volume for ... [the Saint John *Progress*] ... I shall also put the poems in the hands of my brother, Goodridge Bliss Roberts, who edits the *King's College Record*. He is preparing a series of biographical and critical studies of Canadian authors ... Let me congratulate you warmly on your success' (*CL* 103).

A little over two weeks earlier, Frederick George Scott had been publicly congratulated on his 'success' by Lighthall in a review of *The Soul's Quest and Other Poems* in the 28 December 1888 issue of the *Week*. Writing as 'Wilfrid Chateauclair,' Lighthall concedes that 'Scott ... has not outgrown close imitation of the measures and themes of Tennyson' but suggests that 'he is in many a passage equal to some of the deeper phases of his master, and one cannot read him carefully without feeling that he may have, decidedly, a future' (56–7). Quoting 'Time' as a fine example of 'realistic imagination,' praising 'Justin' and 'Evolution' for their philosophical earnestness, and excerpting 'The Soul's Quest' itself to illustrate Scott's capacity for originality, Lighthall draws his review to a close on a nationalistic note by commending the 'broad liberal expression' of 'Catholicism' and the 'Indian wail' of 'Wahonomin,' and quoting the third stanza of 'In Memoriam,' his tribute to 'Those Killed in the Canadian North-West [in] 1885' (57). But by far the most significant aspect of Lighthall's review of *The Soul's Quest and Other Poems* lies in the reaching towards a definition of Confederation poetry and a delineation of the Confederation group with which it begins:

> A Canadian literature, promising to be fine, conscious and powerful, is budding and blossoming, book after book, writer after writer. The nature of it shows that it is the result of Confederation. Its generation is that which has grown up under the influences of the united country. One of its peculiarities – which has causes in the nature of the opportunities permitted by our social life at present – is that its form, for the time being, is a verse literature. We have seen issued this year, and last, and the year before, the works of several singers such as have never previously been equalled among us, except possibly in three or four instances. Roberts's *In Divers Tones*, Mair's *Tecumseh*, the late Miss Crawford's wonderful *Old Spookses' Pass*, and, lately, Bliss Carman's rich verse, and the *Snowflakes and Sunbeams* of William Wilfred Campbell, easily recur as examples ... Every Canadian would be the better for adding them to his library and studying them ...
>
> Such are some observations suggested by parts of ... *The Soul's Quest and Other Poems* ... (56)

With the elimination of the two writers who do not satisfy Lighthall's generational criterion (Mair was born in 1838, Isabella Valancy Crawford in 1850) and the addition of Lampman and Duncan Campbell Scott, the Confederation group is here identified, defined, and celebrated as the begetter of a new and promising Canadian literature.

On 10 August 1889 'The World of Books' column in *Progress* contained a brief biographical sketch of Frederick George Scott that proclaimed *A Soul's Quest and Other Poems* 'an acquisition to Canadian poetry' and discerned 'a newness and strength about [Scott's] work that must make all Canadians eager for more like it, although work "like it" will come from few pens – some half-dozen easily named.'[41] By the end of the year, poems by both of the Scotts had appeared in *Progress* (Frederick George's 'Aestheticism' on September 26 and Duncan Campbell's 'Song' ['I have done ...'] on October 12), as had a review of *Lake Lyrics and Other Poems* that begins with another tentative definition of the Confederation group solely in terms of their dates of birth:

The men who are now foremost in Canadian letters were born between 1860 and '62. The New York *Critic* [on October 5] speaks of the quartette of Canadians of increasing literary fame, and it is a remarkable fact that two of this quartette [Roberts and Campbell] were born in '60 and two in '61 [Carman and Lampman]. And Mr. Weir [1864–1902], author of *Fleurs de Lys* [1887], and Rev. F.G. Scott, author of *A Soul's Quest, and Other Poems*, were born in '64 [and] '61 respectively. (19 October 1889, 6)

In all respects now but one – the presence of Weir rather than Duncan Campbell Scott – the 'we' of '[w]e will make this a glorious epoch in our Country's history' had been assembled.

It is a measure of how far Roberts travelled in the six years following the dark winter of 1884–5 that in the May 1891 number of *Canada* (Benton, New Brunswick), a short-lived magazine founded that year to capitalize on the nationalism of the day, he could again argue fervently in 'Literature and Politics'[42] for a 'connection' between literature and nationality that is mutually beneficial in direct proportion to its closeness:

> The literature of a people, if genuinely a national product, is of necessity shaped by the national character. It is the effect, not the cause, of the national character. In its turn, however, when once set in motion with the nation's force behind it, it exerts an almost incalculable influence upon the directon of the nation's aims, upon the mode in which the national character takes expression. This it continues to do, so long as its connection with the springs of national life is full and vital. The ideal, surely, of a national literature, is that it shall be the most perfect expression in written words of the best of the nation's thought and feeling. The ideal of a national politics, speaking broadly, is that it shall be the most effective expression in act and deed of the best of the national thought and aspiration. (51)

In support of his argument, Roberts cites several examples of historical periods in which 'national literature and ... national politics [went] ... hand in hand' to mutual benefit, including Elizabethan England, seventeenth-century France, and contemporary Germany ('no more the work of Bismarck than of Goethe, Schiller, Fichte, Arndt') and Italy ('the rallying cry of "Italia Irredenta" was a cry of poets and patriots') (51–2). No mention of Canada is made in 'Literature and Politics,' but readers who had followed the trajectory of Roberts's aesthetic beliefs and practices, which will be examined in chapter 3, would have had no difficulty in recognizing the personal element in his statement that in periods when 'national literature' and 'national politics' become 'estranged,' 'literature makes alliance with dilettantism' and becomes 'generally characterized by cleverness rather than by large impulse and strenuous purpose' – or, indeed, by his statement that, 'whether they will it or no,' 'the writers of a nation are ... to a great extent the teachers of a nation' (51, 52).

# CHAPTER THREE

# Aesthetics: Workmanship and Variety

I know that [Roberts] lacks tenderness, variety, elasticity and that he never approaches the nobler altitudes of feeling; yet that early work of his has a special and mysterious charm for me – and it is indeed excellent, of an astonishing gift in workmanship ...

– *Lampman, 'Two Canadian Poets: A Lecture' (1891)*

Mr. Carman ... tells us that the poems [in *Low Tide on Grand Pré* (1893)] ... have been selected with reference to their similarity in tone. Probably he is right in adopting this principle ... At any rate, this has been done, and with great success.

...

With [*The Magic House and Other Poems* (1893) by] Mr. [Duncan Campbell] Scott we enter ... upon a volume of greater variety and of different interest.

– *'Recent Poetry,' Week 11 (22 Dec. 1893): 86*

## I

As has already been glimpsed at several points in the preceding pages, the aesthetic that Roberts promoted both within and outside the Confederation group during its coalescence in the 1880s was centred on his notion of craftsmanship or workmanship. Both explicitly in 'The Beginnings of a Canadian Literature' (1883) and implicitly in his critiques of the work of Carman, Lampman, and other members of the group, Roberts took the position that the choice of a Canadian subject or theme was neither a necessary nor a sufficient condition for the creation of a good

Canadian poem. What was crucial, in his view, was that poems by Canadian writers should be the technical equals of the best poetry being produced in France, Britain, and the United States. Subject and theme were irrelevant, he argued in 'The Beginnings of a Canadian Literature' (see chapter 1), because a poem by a Canadian would inevitably bear the traces of its Canadian origins so long as its author is 'a truly original and creative workman and not a mere copyist' (*SPCP* 258). In tandem with his avowed cosmopolitanism, Roberts's emphasis on workmanship not only encouraged the other members of the Confederation group to hone the tools and skills of their vocation, but, by helping to free them from the 'narrow provincialism' of the demand for 'a literature that shall be distinctively and narrowly Canadian ... both [in] subject and treatment' (Roberts, 'Literature' 206), it also encouraged them to write poems on a greater variety of topics and in a greater variety of forms than might otherwise have been the case. Thus it was that by the early 1890s most of the members of the Confederation group exhibited a twofold aesthetic of workmanship and variety that helped to dictate both the contents and the forms of their work and, ironically, provided a basis for the aesthetic disagreement that eventually helped to tear them apart.

## II

The aesthetic of workmanship that Roberts diffused through the Confederation group in the 1880s derived from several sources, some – most prominently Keats[1] – exemplary and others critical. Most notable in the latter category were the critical essays of Edmund Gosse, particularly 'A Plea for Certain Exotic Forms of French Verse' (1877), where the influential English man of letters predicates his celebration of 'the six most important of the poetic creations of old France' with a moral-aesthetic paean to the poet as artificer:

> To make immortal art out of transient feeling, to give the impression of a finite mind infinite expression, to chisel material beauty out of passing thoughts and emotions, – this is the labour of the poet; and it is on account of this conscious artifice and exercise of constructive power that he properly takes his place beside the sculptor and the painter ... If, therefore, as we must, we regard poetry as one of the fine arts, it need not surprise us to have to dismiss the purely spontaneous and untutored expression of it as of little else than historical interest. In the present age the warblings of poetic improvisation cannot expect more attention than the equally artless impromptus of an untaught musical talent. (53)

Citing Swinburne, Morris, and the Rossettis as examples of a healthy flight from blank verse to fixed forms, Gosse proceeds to discuss the sonnet as an instance of the 'increasing variety and richness of rhyme, elasticity of verse, ... strength of form,' and 'workmanship' of contemporary English poetry. 'In the present generation we write sonnets on the pure Petrarchan model ... in spite of or because of its very difficulties':

> That the rhymes of the octett [*sic*] must be two instead of four ... encourages us to brilliant effort. We acknowledge that the severity of the plan and the rich and copious recurrence of the rhyme serve the double end of repelling the incompetent workman and stimulating the competent. This being so, why should we not proceed to the cultivation of other fixed forms of verse, which flourished in the earliest days of modern poetic literature, and of which the sonnet, if the finest, is at least but one? (56)

Of the impact on the Confederation group of Gosse's program and the literary developments that it at once celebrated and extended there can be no doubt. By far the most common form in the oeuvres of Roberts and Lampman in the 1880s and early 1890s is the Petrarchan sonnet, and, despite a growing aversion to fixed forms, Campbell wrote dozens of sonnets, all but a few Petrarchan.[2] The 'model sonnet' that Duncan Campbell Scott describes in his earliest extant letter, dated 19 September 1889, is Petrarchan (indeed, Scott's letter is veritably Gossean in its insistence that 'one can[not] be too strict about ... form ... [W]e would have better sonnets – that is, finer thoughts better expressed – if the rules were adhered to').[3] Almost all of Frederick George Scott's numerous sonnets, even his 'Shakespeare' (1888), are Petrarchan, as in structure and grammar are the many irregular and unrhymed sonnets that Carman wrote after the turn of the century.[4] It was during the years of the group's formation, however, that Roberts, Lampman, and Carman were most infatuated with the 'six ... poetic creations of old France' championed by Gosse – 'the *rondel,* the *rondeau,* the *triolet,* the *villanelle,* the *ballade,* and the *chant royal*' (56–7).

The obvious bridge between the aesthetic crystallized by Gosse and the aesthetic practices of the members of the Confederation group was *Orion, and Other Poems.* In 'Two Canadian Poets: A Lecture' (1891), Lampman would famously recall that what most impressed him about Roberts's work when he first encountered it in May 1881 was the 'Tennyson-like richness and strange, earth-loving Greekish flavour' of 'Orion' itself (*ER* 95). But this enthusiastic account of the volume's content and impact needs to be supplemented by Roberts's own considered assessment of its literary qualities and its seminal role in the aetiology of the Confederation group in 'Canadian Poetry in Its Relation to the Poetry of England and America' (1933):

> All the verses it contains were written between the ages of sixteen and nineteen, – most of them before I was eighteen. They are the work of practically a schoolboy, drunk with the music of Keats, Shelley, Tennyson and Swinburne. They are distinctly 'prentic work, distinctly derivative, and without significance except for their careful craftsmanship and for the fact that they dared deliberately to steer their frail craft out upon world waters, – certain of these youthful efforts appearing in the pages of the chief English and American magazines. But the only importance attaching to the little book lay in the fact that it started Lampman writing poetry and was the decisive factor in determining Carman to make poetry his career. (80–1)

To Roberts, then, the 'importance' of *Orion, and Other Poems* lay in its impact on Lampman and Carman and its 'significance' in its 'craftsmanship' and cosmopolitanism. What is not evident even from Roberts's very astute remarks is that much of the craftsmanship, cosmopolitanism, and, hence, impact of *Orion, and Other Poems* must be attributed to its formal elements: following the Tennysonian blank verse and Swinburnian hexameters of 'Orion' are poems in a striking variety of forms, including a series of four ballades, a series of three rondeaux, two Keatsian odes, two Petrarchan sonnets, and individual poems in several classical and English meters and stanza forms (for example, tail-rhyme, *Troilus* and Spenserian stanzas, and sapphics, choriambics, and alcaics).[5] Both in its formalistic virtuosity and in its thematic variety, *Orion, and Other Poems* set the standard for volumes published by the Confederation group in the ensuing decade and more.

Roberts was not content to lead merely by example, however. In 'The Beginnings of a Canadian Literature,' he not only gave a clear statement of his belief in workmanship as the *sine qua non* of worthwhile Canadian poetry, but also brought his aesthetic standards to bear on the poetry of French and English Canada, judging the former 'polished and artistic, imbued with unmistakeable Canadian flavour, yet not servilely provincial in its themes,' and the latter by turns 'rough-hewn' (Heavysege), 'uneven' (Hunter-Duvar), and lacking in 'range of subject' (Kate MacLean) (*SPCP* 249, 252, 253). The commitment to careful and consistent workmanship that lies behind all these judgments is also evident in Roberts's comments on the work of Lampman and Carman before and during his months as editor of the *Week* in late 1883 and early 1884. On September 23, two of Lampman's poems ('The Last Sortie' and probably 'Derelict') are praised for exhibiting 'the pulse of humanity' but criticized for 'an evidency of haste, and too little of determined perplexing and polishing' (*CL* 30). On 31 December 1883, two of Carman's rondeaux are mentioned as having been received at the editorial offices of the *Week*, 'but not yet ... read closely,' and on 11 January 1884 they are rejected for publication because 'not quite even in merit throughout' (*CL* 38). Roberts's letters of the late fall and early winter of 1884 reveal that, although he followed Carman's lead in writing triolets and rondels at that time,[6] this did not prevent him from critiquing his cousin's efforts in both forms. 'The triolet is matchless,' he told Carman on November 27; just as

> that on the Ball Programme is one of the most perfect light triolets in the language, so this I believe to be the only really and wholly effective serious triolet. As a severe-eyed critic I have no fault to find with it. I long to get at the work of talking about such work publicly. The rondel is unquestionably beautiful, but not perfect. It has such a lyric lift and ring that one is carried over the obscurity ... But the obscurity exists, and herein lies one of your chief dangers ... Try and say what must be said, rather than be content with what ... may be said. Try and give the impression that nothing else could be said just there; this will give your work the quality of inevitableness, which ... when predominant in a poet's work, writes after his name more unmistakably than anything else can, the word Master. (*CL* 46)

In addition to revealing an astute and penetrating critical intelligence (Carman's tendency to content himself with less than 'what must be said' could indeed be identified as the chief weakness of his work), Roberts's letters to Lampman and Carman confirm his leadership of the emerging Confederation group in matters of form and technique as well as ideas and politics.

Of special note in Roberts's letter to Carman is his recourse to what he terms 'the quality of inevitableness,' a criterion that he would explain in a letter to Frederick George Scott over two years later: '*everything* [in a poem] must be made to look as if the difficulty of the form had *nothing* to do with it! Every word must be *inevitable*' (*CL* 198). Even when thus explained, 'inevitableness' is difficult to define precisely, though it is clearly related to the dictum that art should conceal artifice. In practice, it seems to have meant that poets should avoid being seen to have chosen a particular word or rhyme to fulfil the requirements of their chosen form and metre. A result of both facility and craftsmanship, talent and revision, its absence would be manifested in excrescent words, awkward rhythms, and clumsy rhymes, any one of which could detract from the effect of a lyric. Writing to the American poet Charles Leonard Moore on 16 June 1885, Roberts judges Oscar Wilde's 'general output of lyrics [to be] not of a very high quality' because 'only here and there does one come across a lyric which contains the inevitableness which will make it live' (*CL* 49), and it may be inferred that when he praised the 'lyrics' of *Among the Millet, and Other Poems* as 'admirable' and the 'sonnets' as 'exquisite' in a letter to Lampman of 18 December 1888 (*CL* 97), he did so because he recognized in them the 'inevitableness' that he had earlier demanded of Carman and would later demand of Frederick George Scott (and, very likely, other members of the Confederation group).

To some extent, the longing to express his views publicly that Roberts confided to Carman on 28 November 1884 had already been fulfilled in two articles that were published after his departure from the *Week*, 'Notes on Some Younger American Poets' (24 April 1884) and 'Edgar Fawcett' (26 June 1884). Neither of these articles so much as mentions a Canadian poet or poem, but they are of considerable interest on two counts: as reflections of Roberts's aesthetic views and as indications of his thinking on the nature of schools of poetry. Evidently intended as the first of a series of articles on 'the younger school' of American poets – that is, Fawcett (1847–1904), Joachim Miller (1841?–1913), Sidney Lanier (1842–81), Richard Watson Gilder, and others – 'Notes on Some of the Younger American Poets' begins with two observations and a question: (1) 'the acknowledged chiefs of American song for the most part have fallen, or have laid down their pens'; and (2) 'they have formed no "schools"' and gathered no 'following[s] of pronounced disciples' (328). What accounts for this? Roberts's full answer does not come until the article on Fawcett, but it is implicit in his argument in 'Notes on Some of the Younger American Poets' that of all 'the acknowledged Chiefs of American Song' – Poe, Emerson, Longfellow, Whitman, and Oliver Wendell Holmes – only one, Holmes, is likely to generate 'a following of disciples,' the reason being that no future practitioner of the type of poetry upon which Holmes left the indelible 'impress of his genius' can possibly 'afford to neglect his instruction' (328). That Holmes's forte was '"society verse"' or '*vers de société*,' a type of poetry whose 'characteristics ... are elegance, decorum, moderation, neatness of expression, perfection of form, and coolness of sentiment and tone,'[7] only serves to increase the likelihood that Roberts saw in him a partial parallel with himself as a technical exemplar and mentor for a new school of poets. Since Roberts had begun to develop 'a warm friendship' with Holmes after the American poet responded enthusiastically to *Orion, and Other Poems* (Pomeroy 38–9), there is also a likelihood that he regarded himself as something of a disciple.[8] Certainly, a number of Roberts's poems of the early and mid-1880s, including 'La Belle Trombon-iste' (1885) and 'The Marvellous Work' (1886), suggest that he may have taken instruction from Holmes's work both in the light vein of such pieces as 'Dorothy Q.' and 'the purely serious vein' of 'The Chambered Nautilus' and 'The Living Temple' (see Roberts, 'Notes' 328).

After a brief recapitulation of the argument of 'Notes on Some of the Younger American Poets,' Roberts delivers himself in the preamble to 'Edgar Fawcett' of an aesthetic statement that, with the substitution of Lampman and Carman for Edmund Clarence Stedman and Thomas Bailey Aldrich, could easily be an expression of his view of the state of contemporary Canadian poetry:

> It is undeniable that in certain of the most distinguished of American poets exists a marked deficiency in the sense of form, in symmetry of construc-tion, and in finish ... Stedman and Aldrich have hardly a living superior in matters of pure technique, in the essentially artistic qualifications of a poet. But these stand out as exceptions. Sometimes it looks as if the idea were of supreme importance, and to be developed at all hazard, while the medium of expression is handled with a trace of impatience or contempt. In the mi-nor poets much more than this is apparent. One feels too often that their reverence for their art is scanty, that they have a disdain for careful and de-voted labour, perhaps no perception whatever of the need of recasting, of polishing, of perfecting. An idea, an emotion, an incident, or a romance is forced into ill-fitting garments of crudely-constructed verse. (471)

Against this dismaying backdrop stands Fawcett, 'a young poet ... who is essentially an artist, reverencing deeply his art, and master of all its tech-nicalities' – a poet possessed of 'the artist's intolerance of slovenly work-manship, ... an unerring sense of proportion' and 'symmetry of design,' and a capacity to combine 'exquisite compactness' with freedom from 'obscurity' (472). Roberts would soon come to see the limitations of Fawcett's work,[9] but in the early 1880s he evidently regarded him as a poet worthy of emulation as well as 'earnest regard.' In fact, the model for 'The Sower,' the Petrarchan sonnet inspired by the painting of the same name by Jean-François Millet that Roberts first published in the July 1884 number of the *Manhattan* (New York), is clearly Fawcett's Petrarchan sonnet entitled 'Sleep / (For a Picture),' which Roberts discusses admiringly in 'Edgar Fawcett' and proclaims superior even to Dante Gabriel Rossetti's 'For a Venetian Pastoral' (472), which 'is surely the most perfect sonnet-music in the language' (437).[10] The fact that the letter of 12 December 1882, in which Roberts assumes the role of '*sacer vates*' (inspired bard) to conjur for Carman 'the near approaching awakening of Canada, in politics, art, song, [and] intellectual effort generally,' refers to a letter in which Fawcett has 'hail[ed] [him] as a leader of the choir' (*CL* 33) suggests that the American also played a part in solidifying Roberts's sense of himself as the leader of an emerging school of Canadian poets.

Largely as a result of Roberts's personal example and critical efforts, the association of the Confederation group with careful workmanship was firmly established in Canadian literary circles by the late 1880s. Thus Agnes Maule Machar ('Fidelis') praised Lampman's 'high degree of general artistic excellence and careful technique' (251) in a review of *Among the Millet, and Other Poems* in the 22 March 1889 issue of the *Week*, and Lilly E.F. Barry, writing of the same poet in the same periodical on 10 April 1891, emphasized 'the high state of finish which characterizes all ... [his] compositions' (300). For his part, Lampman had no doubt about the Archimedean moment of the aesthetic of workmanship. '[B]efore the appearance of *Orion* [, *and Other Poems*],' he wrote in 'Two Canadian Poets: A Lecture, 'all the verse writing published in Canada ... was of a more or less barbarous character. The drama of *Saul* by Charles Heavysege and some of Heavysege's sonnets are about the only exceptions, which can be made to this statement ... [George Frederick] Cameron, although a poet of greater spontaneity,* a more passionate force,

---

* A sense of what was meant by this term can be gained from the following passage in 'Canadian Literature' by the Canadian journalist, historian, and poet Theodore Arnold Haultain (1857–1941) in the first number of the *Lake Magazine* (Toronto) (August 1892): 'spontaneity is the first of all the tests to be applied to anything calling itself by the name of art. If a poem or a painting, a sonata or a statue, if anything in the realm of art is not spontaneous, it is as sounding brass or a tinkling bell. If it is not the outcome of real and intense internal feeling, craving expression and careless of everything but its own instinctive adherence to truth of matter and beauty of form – in a word inspired – it is not art' (19). From this and other occurrences of the term, it is very clear that 'spontaneity' as popularly conceived is a quality likely to be stifled by the careful formalism advocated by Roberts.

and a much higher range of feeling, than ... Roberts does not equal him in perfection of style. He neither aimed at, nor attained the same artistic excellence of workmanship' (*ER* 95). Nearly a quarter of a century later, Roberts's long-time friend and admirer John Daniel Logan (1869–1929) would cement and summarize the association of the Confederation group with workmanship in *Highways of Canadian Literature (1924)*: *Orion, and Other Poems* was the source of 'the First Renaissance in Canadian Literature' because it evinced 'a certain ... *artistic finish* in [its] craftsmanship' that had not been present 'in previous books of verse by native-born Canadians ... With the publication of his *Orion*, Roberts sounded the death knell of slovenly or indifferent technique in Canadian poetry. Working with him, and largely under the influence of his ideal of technical finish in verse, were Lampman, Carman, Campbell, Pauline Johnson, Duncan Campbell Scott, Frederick George Scott, and others. They all cared supremely for fine technique in poetry' (107).

Of course, the commitment of the Confederation group to '*artistic finish*' was neither as unanimous, straightforward, nor enduring as Logan suggests and, indeed, knew, for at the very inception of their correspondence in June 1888 he and Roberts had agreed that in its most rarefied form, the 'passion' for French forms, the contemporary devotion to 'fine technique' had exhausted itself in 'satiety and weariness' (*CL* 83). As Roberts's curiously post-coital comments indicate, he was neither alone in his feeling of formal exhaustion nor bereft of reasons for experiencing it personally. In their responses to his *In Divers Tones* volume of 1886, friends and reviewers alike had taken him to task for emphasizing form at the expense of other qualities. 'It is not in the dilettante rondeau of compliment, but in the treatment of themes which call forth the creative and reflective forces of his genius, that Prof. Roberts will win his way to wider recognition as a poet,' wrote the reviewer for the Chatham *World* (2 April 1887). 'He has ... fallen into the sin of the nineteenth-century, a fondness for formal verse such as the Ballade and Rondeau,' observed T.G. Marquis in the 26 July 1888 issue of the *Week*; 'the paucity of rhyme in the English Language is a sufficiently onerous chain to the muse without making artificial ones. In such styles of verse the sense must often give way to the rhyme' (559). Nevertheless, added Marquis, 'in the sonnet Professor Roberts is a master, and several of his will compare with the very best in the English language.'

That Roberts took such criticisms to heart is evident both from his subsequent formal choices (after 1886 he wrote and published many sonnets but no rondeaux) and from several comments in his letters and reviews of the late 1880s. '[Y]our criticism ... is just,' he told Lighthall on 30 September 1888; 'I have long felt ... the need of my work to free itself from a certain scholasticism of subject ... Of old, I worshipped nothing but beauty ... That phase I have outgrown' (*CL* 87). 'The note among our rising writers is one of more passion, more purpose, more serious-ness and import than that sounded by the younger Americans,' he wrote in a portion of his 26 January 1889 review of *Among the Millet, and Other Poems* that is worth quoting again in this context:

> With us in Canada, though we may appear to trifle a little with ballades and villanelles and triolets, there is a strenuous undercurrent almost always to be detected. The apparent trifling is but the striving after an unimpeach-able technique; the underlying motive is one of deep seriousness and im-passioned expectancy.

In line with the Canadianism that he saw exemplified in the work of Lighthall and Lampman, Roberts was in the process in 1889 of aban-doning the culs-de-sac of formalism into which his quest for workman-ship had drawn him and rededicating that workmanship to the Canadian subjects and themes that he had once regarded as inessential. The sense of freedom and renewal in 'The Waking Earth' (1893), a son-net first published in the *Independent* on 23 May 1889, could well be aes-thetic as well as seasonal and sexual (see chapter 4).

The evidence of Roberts having outgrown the doctrinaire formalism 'phase' that had enamoured him of classical and French forms did not fully appear until the publication in 1893 of *Songs of the Common Day, and Ave: An Ode for the Shelley Centenary*. In the meantime, reactions against formalism proliferated and intensified both outside and within the Con-federation group. 'From faithful critics on all sides the cry has been going up of late years that poetry was too much given over to the wor-ship of form,'[11] wrote Roberts in 'The World of Books' column in *Progress* on 12 October 1889:

> The cry is one of needed warning and cannot be too pertinaciously reiter-ated. In a vast deal of contemporary work one feels that the initial impulse has come less from a need of giving utterance to some vivid emotion or high idea than from an idle itch for experimenting in bizarre verse-forms. I am keenly alive to the fact that this experimenting in verse-forms has its val-ue. It gives faculty, it opens one's eyes to the defects of his technique, it helps one to realize how flexible our language may become; but, like all ex-

perimenting, it is perilous by reason of its fascinations. And often it happens that the writer who at first thought only of how he might best achieve a fine poem, gradually lowers his aim to the accomplishment of a delicate piece of verbal filagree that can be ticketed Rondeau, or Ballade, and judged as such mainly.

Roberts exempts the sonnet from opprobrium, but a little over two weeks later in the *Week* Edward Burrough Brownlow ('Sarepta') (1857–95) made no such concession: 'artificial forms of verse have been resuscitated from Provençal graves to serve as winding-sheets for much wasted genius,' he lamented, 'and the history and analysis of all physical and psychical nature is temporarily preserved in an interminable multitude of sonnets, for which kind of composition a veritable epidemic has long set in and shows no sign of abatement' ('The Sonnet. – VIII' 760). As Collins put it in a letter of 27 August 1891 to Lampman, 'there is a reaction against mere form.'[12]

Several months before Collins's letter, Lampman had participated vigorously in the 'reaction against mere form' in 'Two Canadian Poets,' the lecture on Cameron and Roberts that he delivered to the Ottawa Literary and Scientific Society on 19 February 1891. Although best-known as a celebration of Lampman's momentous first encounter with *Orion, and Other Poems* in May 1881, the lecture is more centrally concerned with establishing a moral-aesthetic contrast between Roberts's 'perfection of style' and Cameron's 'greater spontaneity' that makes Cameron the more admirable of the two poets:

> In Mr. Roberts' work, notwithstanding the great ability that has gone to the making of it, there is often a certain weightiness and deliberateness of phrase, which suggests too strongly the hand of the careful workman, and robs it of the fullest effect of spontaneity ... In Mr. Cameron's work ... we come into contact with ... a man who dwells among genuine thoughts and genuine feelings, and speaks a language full of spontaneity, force and dignity. (*ER* 107–8)

As admirable as they are in many ways, including their 'workmanship' (96), Lampman suggests, too many of Roberts's poems have 'a scholarly character'; he has 'not sufficient ease and flow to work well in complicated stanzas'; 'occasionally [his] work is spoiled by an effect of strain and elaborate effort'; his sonnets are 'unevenly successful,' and his patriotic poems are 'clever, but heavy, pompous and more of the tongue

[than] the heart' (96, 101, 102, 105, 107). In contrast, Cameron's work is 'penetrating, elastic,* and full of high sound,' 'simple, manly and bracing,' 'sincere' and 'genuinely poetic' (108, 113, 114). A year or two earlier,[13] Lampman had ended a lecture on 'Style' by quoting some 'unsurpassably fine' lines from 'Tantramar Revisited' (90). In 'Two Canadian Poets: A Lecture,' a passage from the same poem is quoted to illustrate Roberts's 'keen sympathy with nature and his strenuous and scholarly gift of expression,' and the lecture concludes with a reading of two of Cameron's poems, one of which, 'The Week vs. Wendell Phillips,' was occasioned by 'a virulent attack' on the American orator and reformer that 'appeared in ... the *Week* directly after the announcement of his death' on 2 February 1884 (Cameron, *Lyrics* 184n) – that is, during Roberts's editorship.[14]

An examination of the full consequences of the rift between and among Lampman, Roberts, and other members of the Confederation group that was becoming evident in 1891 must await a later chapter, but the point can be made here that the animosity evident in 'Two Canadian Poets: A Lecture' extends even to the American poet whose workmanship Roberts had effusively praised in the *Week* some six years earlier. In the 'artifice of phrase' that they employ 'to convey ... the rank warm luxurian[ce]' of the Greek landscape, observes Lampman of a passage in 'The Pipes of Pan,' 'some of the ... lines are in a slight degree over done, [and] remind ... one in that respect of the American poet Edgar Fawcett, who is very fond of reaching natural effects by artifices of this kind' (*ER* 100–1). As the 'reaction against mere form' grew in the early 1890s, Lampman would again use Fawcett as the target of his attacks on bloodless formalism, this time in his contributions to the 'At the Mermaid Inn' column: 'the cleverest sonnets we have are those of Mr. Edgar Fawcett. They are the cleverest, the strongest, the most ingenious, and the least-touching' (17 September 1892); 'his talent [is] brilliant, ingenious, productive, but artificial, overstrained, and devoid of tenderness' (20 May 1893) (152, 316). Lampman's few comments on Roberts in 'At the Mermaid Inn' either damn his work with faint praise

---

* A sense of the meaning of this term can be gained from a passage in another article in the *Lake Magazine*, 'The Canadian Oliver Goldsmith,' by the Maritime teacher and literary journalist W.G. MacFarlane (18?–?): 'the ... rhyming couplet ... is ... a fine medium of expression; it has such an easy pleasant swing and its elasticity permits the swelling heart to give utterance to its feelings freely' (December 1892, 287). As was the case with 'spontaneity,' 'elasticity' was popularly conceived as a quality likely to be stifled by adherence to a too-rigid poetic form.

or couch praise in stringent reservations: 'Chas. G.D. Roberts has written at least one sonnet of a high order, "Reckoning," and several others of marked and individual excellence'; 'Canadian Streams' in the 1892 number of the *Dominion Illustrated* (Montreal) is 'one of Professor Roberts's patriotic outbursts' that contains 'many lines ... [that] are very grand ... in a way ... yet ... seem to come shouldering up with a conscious and premeditated effort';[15] and 'Ave' reveals 'our master workman in verse' to be a member of the idolatrous 'cult' of 'Shelley worshippers' who has nevertheless produced a poem of impressive 'beauty' and 'fervour' that contains numerous examples of 'his vivid and luxurious delight in splendid landscape and the richness of his gift as a word painter' (a term which, as will be seen in a moment, cannot be construed as an unalloyed compliment) (153, 193, 239).

While Lampman's critiques of formalism and its practitioners remained fairly constant in tenor and tone from 1891 to 1893 (and beyond), Campbell's hostility to 'artificial poetry' (as he termed it) and to his fellow Canadian poets escalated to fever pitch in his contributions to 'At the Mermaid Inn' in the course of 1892 and 1893. On 28 May and 1 October 1892, two American poets, James Whitecomb Riley and Thomas Bailey Aldrich, are by turns heartily complimented and gently rebuked, the former for managing to remain 'sincere and natural' 'in these days, when there is so much artificial verse-making,' and the latter for allowing himself to become 'too much the artist ... to be a great popular poet to the people, who require a stronger heart-touch than his artistic repression will allow' (80–2, 160).[16] On November 12 of the same year, the 'fad' for 'finish' and 'polish' in poetry has become, for Campbell, inimical to creativity and contrary to nature:

The greatest genius, and the one that bids most for immortality, is the genius that is the most uneven in flight and finish. Nature requires contrast, and the greatest and strongest poetry is that which at times is rugged and bold. To spend years polishing down a man's thoughts and visions into a certain glittering monotony is just as though nature would level her hills and fill up her valleys into an immense plain ... [V]erse ... should be as near nature as possible. (*MI* 189)

A premonition of what the following years would bring from Campbell's pen came on 10 December 1892 with his contention that what Canada needs most 'at the present stage of [its] literary development ... [is] frankness of opinion and proper, unbiased judgement ... [L]iterary critics and journals [must] take the trouble to thoroughly study our literature and examine into its real merits ... [for] [t]o judge our poets as patriotic poets or human poets or nature poets or poet artists, or as disciples of this or that school, is both unnatural and absurd' (209).

Having thus established at least to his own satisfaction that his prejudices accorded with the laws of nature and reason, Campbell proceeded in his 'At the Mermaid Inn' columns of 1893 to identify violations and to prosecute their perpetrators: in the plethora of recent sonnets only 'half a dozen ... [are] true poems,' and these are 'not found among the delicate word artists who have wrought so hard in that direction' (March 18); in its review of contemporary American poetry in its tenth anniversary issue, the *New York World* is right in recognizing an absence of 'great truth' and an 'abundance' of 'over-perfect style' in the fad for old French forms (May 20); the inheritors of Tennyson's tendency to 'polish and over-refine' his poetry are a host of 'college graduates ... [who] can turn out any amount of the kind of gentle, sensitive verses with a sort of delicate finish that the magazines of today seem to require' (June 17); the term 'quality' has become 'a sort of apology for the kind of pseudo-poetry that is marking these times, and which, in the absence of real poetic imagination and creative ability, has taken to pensive musings and landscape painting in words' (July 1) (278, 315–16, 331, 333, 341). Since Campbell's accusatory finger points more and more in these passages towards Roberts and Lampman (both of whom were, of course, 'college graduates' and adept at 'landscape painting in words'), they must have suspected that their poems in particular were the target of the two parodies that appeared over the name 'John Pensive Bangs' in the column of July 1 (the anniversary of Confederation). Both of these, the first, entitled 'At Even' and contemptuously introduced as 'of course ... a sonnet,' and the second, entitled 'Pitching Hay' and similarly dismissed as the product of 'no lofty thoughts or wide knowledge of nature and man,' echo the poems of Roberts and Lampman in setting and phraseology as well as in form and theme,* and several other aspects of

---

* For example, 'the sombre fields' of the first line of 'At Even' recalls both the 'sombre lands' of Lampman's 'In October' (1888) (*P* 22) and the 'sombre slope' of Roberts's 'The Furrow' (1893) (*CP* 130), and the 'solitary hobbling toad' of 'Pitching Hay' parodies the references to frogs in the sonnets of both poets. 'Now I must rack my wits / To find a rhyme, while all the landscape reels' in 'At Even' similarly evokes the opening line of Lampman's 'Heat' (1888) ('From plains that reel to southward' [*P* 12]), and Campbell's concluding list of sonnet titles ('"Raking Chips",' '"The Lonely Clam",' ... '"Hoeing Potatoes"' and so on) seems aimed at the sonnet series of Roberts's *Songs of the Common Day* (1893).

the satire suggest that Campbell's 'verse-maker' is at least in part an amalgam of the two: 'Bangs' has been to college, he has 'read Matthew Arnold,' and he has garnered the extravagant praise of a critic who commends 'At Even' for being 'Millet-like in its terse realism' – a reference very likely to both 'The Sower' and *Among the Millet, and Other Poems* (341–2).[17] It is difficult to doubt that the termination of 'At the Mermaid Inn' with the 1 July 1893 column was not a consequence at least in part of Campbell's increasingly rebarbative and finally satirical attitude to his fellow poets.

Although Roberts's insistence on workmanship as the overriding criterion for Canadian poetry resulted in tensions and disagreements that contributed to the disintegration of the Confederation group in the mid-1890s, it also helped to sharpen the technical skills of the group's members and, at least as important, to direct their attention to form and its implications. Among Lampman's contributions to the 'At the Mermaid Inn' column in 1892 is a piece that turns on an imaginary conversation with a 'sonneteer' who 'takes a sort of inhuman delight in torturing [the poet] with sonnets of his own composition on all sorts of flippant and improper subjects' (87). On being treated to readings of two sonnets that confirm his 'abhorrence ... [of] persons ... who profane and misapply the sonnet' – the first a trivial account of falling asleep and the second a starkly realistic description of the ugly side of urban life – the poet censures the sonneteer in the first instance for failing to find a '"form ... less ridiculously inapplicable to the smallness and homeliness of [his] subject"' and in the second for '"violat[ing] every law of moral dignity and literary decency"' (88, 89). Clearly evident in these humorous remarks is a serious moral-aesthetic whose roots lie in the classical theory of decorum: the sonnet is more 'suitable' (Lampman's word) to some themes and subjects than to others – a rule of propriety that the fictitious 'sonneteer' chooses to flout in order to offend the poet's sense of seemliness and decency. That the 'sonneteer' ends the encounter by breaking into 'a roar of coarse and offensive laughter,' 'filliping' the 'pellets' into which he has 'crushed ... his papers ... into [the poet's] face,' and 'str[iding] rudely out of the room' (89) is a dramatic reflection of Lampman's belief as expressed in his essay on 'Style' (circa 1890) and elsewhere that literary style and personal conduct are directly related.[18]

Although the themes and subjects 'suitable' for treatment in the sonnet are not specified by Lampman in 'At the Mermaid Inn,' it is plausible to infer from his own formal practices that he regarded the form as

appropriate only for serious and elevating materials, be these meditations on external nature, examinations of profound emotions, or statements of moral and philosophical principles (categories of which 'In
November,' 'An Old Lesson from the Fields,' and 'The Truth' in the
sonnet section of *Among the Millet, and Other Poems* are representative
examples). Only the poem entitled 'The Dog,' with which *Among the Millet* closes, might appear to be a violation of Lampman's 'law of moral
dignity and literary decency' in its use of the Petrarchan sonnet form to
describe the 'small ... and homel[y] ... subject' of throwing 'balls' for an
insouciantly ugly dog (*P* 121); however, the exclamation with which
'The Dog' opens ('"Grotesque!"') and the reflexivity of some of its
phrasing ('queer feet / Planted irregularly,' 'we ... defied him / With ...
loose criticism') indicate that it is an exercise in incongruity that aims to
extract humour by treating a comically ugly subject in a serious form,
which is itself rendered comical (and thus appropriate) by ridiculous
rhymes ('him' for all the *a* rhymes in the octave, 'pigs' and 'legs' for one
of the rhymes in the sestet).

Perhaps because he was also classically trained, Roberts evidently
shared Lampman's acute sense of formal decorum. None of the sonnets
in the 'Songs of the Common Day' series or elsewhere violates the rules
implied by Lampman's statements; and his practice vis-à-vis the ballade,
rondeau, triolet, and other forms confirm his awareness of their appropriateness for some but not other subjects and tones. Moreover, Roberts
appears to have recognized from the outset that the Petrarchan sonnet
was a suitable form for what Campbell derisively calls 'landscape paint-
ings in words' – 'terse[ly] realistic' depictions of picturesque rural and
architectural scenes for which the rectangular outlines of the sonnet
provide the equivalent of a picture frame.[19] Evidence for this perceived
homology begins to accumulate with the two Petrarchan sonnets in
*Orion, and Other Poems*, 'Iterumne?' and 'At Pozzuoli,' both of which
depict classical landscapes and themes, the latter, as Ross S. Kilpatrick
has shown, partly inspired by an illustration of 'the temple of Jupiter
Serapis at Pozzuoli' near Naples in James Dana's *Manual of Geology*.[20] A
clutch of sonnets of the early 1880s such as 'To Fredericton in May-time'
(1881) and 'In September' (1881) signal a growing recognition of the
suitability of the Petrarchan sonnet to picturesque Canadian scenes, but
it is with 'The Sower,' which was probably written early in 1884, that
Roberts begins fully to exploit the potential of the form's octave/sestet
configuration as a vehicle for descriptions that move from background
to foreground, general to particular, objective to subjective. A juxtaposi-

tion of 'The Sower' and 'The Furrow' (1893) from the 'Songs of the Common Day' series will serve to illustrate Roberts's use of the sonnet form to reinforce such shifts, as well as to establish the picturesque lineage and qualities of the sonnets that Roberts described in July 1888 as his 'Canadian pictures':

### THE SOWER

A brown, sad-coloured hillside, where the soil
   Fresh from the frequent harrow, deep and fine,
   Lies bare; no break in the remote sky-line,
Save where a flock of pigeons streams aloft,
Startled from feed in some low-lying croft,
   Or far-off spires with yellow of sunset shine;
   And here the Sower, unwittingly divine,
Exerts the silent forethought of his toil.

Alone he treads the glebe, his measured stride
   Dumb in the yielding soil; and though small joy
   Dwell in his heavy face, as spreads the blind
Pale grain from his dispensing palm aside,
   This plodding churl grows great in his employ; –
   God-like, he makes provision for mankind.

### THE FURROW

How sombre slope these acres to the sea
   And to the breaking sun! The sun-rise deeps
   Of rose and crocus, whence the far dawn leaps,
Gild but with scorn their grey monotony.
The glebe rests patient for its joy to be.
   Past the salt field-foot many a dim wing sweeps;
   And down the field a first slow furrow creeps,
Pledge of near harvests to the unverdured lea.

With clank of harness tramps the serious team.
   With sea air thrills their nostrils. Some wise crows
   Feed confidently behind the ploughman's feet.
In the early chill the clods fresh cloven steam,
   And down its griding path the keen share goes.
   So, from a scar, best flowers the future's sweet.

Although 'The Furrow' is more secular (and sexual) than 'The Sower,'[21] its descent from the earlier poem is as apparent as the achieved consonance in both pieces of picturesque description and the Petrarchan sonnet form. As has been argued elsewhere,[22] a similar consonance between form and content is discernible in 'Tantramar Revisited,' where the alternating lines of dactyllic hexameter and pentameter accord with the scenery being described not only in their 'out rolled' horizontality (*CP* 78), but also, as an early critic pointed out, in the ebb and flow movement captured by Coleridge's well-known distich on and in the form: 'In the hexameter rises the fountain's silvery column; / In the pentameter aye falling steadily back.'[23]

Campbell's hostility to fixed forms and technical polish was in part a reflection of the widespread 'reaction against mere form' that Collins mentioned to Lampman in August 1891 and in part a manifestation of a profound distrust of convention and artifice that arose from his Wordsworthian belief that 'simplicity and directness of manner' – 'direct, simple naturalness' – 'are essential to the highest art' (*PWWC* v). Not fortuitously, the 'At the Mermaid Inn' column of 17 June 1893, in which Campbell roundly condemns what he sees as the Tennysonian tradition of 'polish and over-refine[ment],' concludes with a paean to Wordsworth, as a poet of 'simple, grand emotion' who 'is not and never could be a minute scenic artist, such as the descriptive sonnet writers we have today' (334) (a statement that, of course, ignores the existence of Wordsworth's many descriptive sonnets). In the late 1880s, however, Campbell was probably flattered by Roberts's comment that in *Snowflakes and Sunbeams* (1888) he 'shows the instincts of the craftsman imbued with right reverence for his craft,' and, as suggested in the previous chapter, he may even have been encouraged to make his second volume a collection of *Lake Lyrics, and Other Poems* (1889) by Roberts's suggestion that the 'promise' of his early work was already being fulfilled in the 'lyric splendor of "The Winter Lakes" and "A Lake Memory,"' which had recently appeared in 'American periodicals' ('The World of Books,' *Progress,* 9 March 1889, 6). 'No other Canadian poet ... has so rendered the spirit and form of our winter scenes, – unless, perhaps, Mr. Lampman in one or two instances,' wrote Roberts; 'the sublime landscapes of the Great Lakes, Mr. Campbell has pre-empted as his own peculiar field; and he is likely to hold sway there without a rival, by reason of the Swinburnian resonance and the breadth of his rhythmic phrases, combined with his deep and subtle insight into external nature in her most impressive aspects.'

The astuteness of Roberts's remarks on the aptness of Campbell's 'br[oad] rhythmic phrases' to the 'sublime landscapes of the Great Lakes' is immediately apparent in the opening stanzas of 'The Winter Lakes,' where the choice of anapestic pentameter with frequent anacrusis and catalexis and alternating feminine and masculine rhymes provides a brilliant formal reflection of the immense, monotonous, and outstretching vistas that they describe:

Out in a world of death far to the northward lying,
    Under the sun and the moon, under the dusk and the day;
Under the glimmer of stars and the purple sunsets dying,
    Wan and waste and white, stretch the great lakes away.

Never a bud of spring, never a laugh of summer,
    Never a dream of love, never a song of bird;
But only the silence and white, the shores that grow chiller and dumber,
    Wherever the ice winds sob, and the grief of winter are heard.

Crags that are black and wet out of the grey lake looming,
    Under the sunset's flush and the pallid, faint glimmer of dawn;
Shadowy, ghost-like shores, where midnight surfs are booming
    Thunders of wintry woe over the spaces wan. (*PWWC* 345–6)

The last line of the first stanza of 'The Winter Lakes' is especially effective in its use of alliteration, rhythmic variations, and long vowel sounds to emphasize the empty monotony of the vista and to replicate the centrifugal movement of the eye towards the horizon: 'Wan and waste and white, stretch the great lakes away.' Although one of its remaining stanzas is flawed – shorn of 'the quality of inevitableness' – by a syntactical awkwardness that stems from the need for a word to rhyme with 'thunder' ('Moons that glimmer above, waters that lie white under ...'), the poem as a whole is very successful in using patterns of repetition, references to death and mourning, and tropes derived from the Gothic tradition ('Lands ... like spectres,' 'Shadowy shapes ... haunting the spaces white,' 'Lonely hidden bays ... haunted by shadowy shores') to present the Great Lakes as an immense space whose effect on the viewer is by turns awe-inspiring and terrifying, astounding and discomforting – in a word, sublime.

As much as anything else, it may have been Campbell's preference for the sublime over the picturesque that lay behind his hostility to fixed forms, for surely the corollary of a temperamental preference for the grand and expansive in external nature and human emotion must be a rejection of the small and the circumscribed, whether it be in the realm of landscape, feeling, or poetic form. Even in defending the sonnet, had not Wordsworth likened it to a 'convent's narrow room,' a 'scanty plot of ground,' a 'prison,' and a 'cell' (3: 1)? Again not fortuitously, Campbell's political movement in the 1890s from the fervent nationalism of such poems as 'National Thanksgiving Chant' (1891)[24] and 'Ode to Canada' (1896) to the outspoken imperialism of 'England' (1897), 'Sebastian Cabot' (1897), 'Victoria' (1901), 'Crowning of Empire' (1901), 'The Discoverers' (1904), and numerous other poems of the post–Confederation group period is reflected in his choice of increasingly open, infinitely expansive, and traditionally English forms such as blank verse that correspond both to the 'vast spaces' of the British Empire and to the 'vaster dream' of 'Subduing all with iron titan will' ('Rhodes,' *SPE* 90–1). (Campbell would give fullest poetic bent to his Imperialism in *Sagas of Vaster Britain: Poems of the Race, the Empire, and the Divinity of Man* [1914], the very title of which echoes the concept of 'Greater Britain' articulated by Sir J.R. Seeley in *The Expansion of England* [1883, 1895], a work that probably lies centrally in the background of the development in his political thinking in the 1890s.) When Campbell turned to the sonnet as a vehicle for brief celebrations of the 'national dream' and the 'vaster Britain' in the years around the turn of the century, his preference was predictably for variations of the Shakespearean or English version of the form, as in 'Our Heritage':

Not all the fire of Burns, the mind of Scott,
   The stern and holy human zeal of Knox,
   Nor that wise lore which human life unlocks
Of magic Shakespeare, Bacon's subtlest thought,
Nor Milton's lofty line sublimely wrought,
   Not gentle Wordsworth 'mid his fields and flocks,
   Nor mystic Coleridge of the wizard locks,
Hath power to raise us to our loftiest lot:

But that rare quality, that national dream,
   That lies behind this genius at its core,
   Which gave it vision, utterance; evermore,
It will be with us, as those stars that gleam,
   Eternal, hid behind the lights of day,
   A people's best, that may not pass away. (*SPE* 80–1)

When this was first published as a pamphlet in Ottawa in 1902, it was entitled 'Our Heritage. Sublimity.' In a variation of the Shakespearean sonnet form by the poet who, as Roberts had correctly surmised in 1889, would always be associated with 'the sublime landscapes of the Great Lakes,' the combination of national and imperial sentiment that characterized Canadian Imperialism found one of its most fitting forms of expression.

Neither as temperamentally and ideologically disposed as Campbell and Carman to open spaces and forms nor as morally and politically committed to non-coercive form or order as Lampman and Frederick George Scott,[25] Duncan Campbell Scott would prove to be the most formalistically experimental member of the Confederation group. 'You could find plenty to say about metre [in my work] and I have invented not a few new stanzas,' he told Pelham Edgar in 1905. 'Give me some credit for logic as applied to aesthetics for I declare that I value brain-power at the bottom of everything' (*Some Letters* n.pag.). Wisely standing to one side of the aesthetic and personal controversies into which Campbell drew the other members of the group, Scott never wavered from a dedication to form that might have resulted in aestheticism if it had not been grounded in a perception of technique as functional and supportive rather than arbitrary and decorative. Objectionable though they may now be as depictions of Native peoples, 'Watkwenies' (1898) and 'The Onondaga Madonna' (1898) employ the Petrarchan sonnet with a keenly ironical sense of its association with idealized women, and 'The Forsaken' (1905), 'On the Way to the Mission' (1905), 'At Gull Lake: August, 1810' (1935), and 'A Scene at Lake Manitou' (1935) juxtapose various loosened and stanzaic verse patterns with a superb sense of their relative effectiveness as vehicles for kinetic, static, and pictorial subject matter. As much if not more than Roberts, Duncan Campbell Scott understood the value of poetic form as a means by which a poet can exercise writerly discipline and enhance readerly pleasure to achieve what E.K. Brown called 'a mixture of restraint and intensity ... [that] grasps at one and will not let go' (122) – a poetry that, at its best, involves and satisfies the reader both emotionally and intellectually.

As for Roberts himself, it is not a little ironical that he had to wait until after his departure for the United States in February 1897 had sounded the death knell of the Confederation group to receive his highest compliment for achieving the workmanship that he had laboured so hard, and so often thanklessly, to emphasize and to exemplify. 'There is in him a sense of artistic finish,' wrote the reviewer of *The Book of the*

*Native* (1896) in the 18 March 1897 issue of the *Nation* (New York) – '"the perfection and precision of the instantaneous line",' in Ruskin's phrase – without which genius leaves its work still undone' (207). Whether entirely justified or not, this judgment must have greatly heartened Roberts after the previous years' assaults on his aesthetic principles and practices. Perhaps it even encouraged him in the pursuit of 'artistic finish' and formal subtlety that, as demonstrated elsewhere,[26] is very much in evidence in the volume that he published a year after moving to the United States, *New York Nocturnes and Other Poems* (1898).

## III

'I never consciously set to work to make a book of a certain type of poems ... And I have tried to avoid collecting one kind of poem in one book. I prefer variety. I have opposed Carman in this.'[27] Embedded in these statements by Roberts to Lorne Pierce in June 1927 are references to the second aesthetic principle shared by members of the Confederation group and to the one member of the group who rejected that principle. Almost needless to say, neither 'variety' as a principle for the construction of a collection of poems nor the rejection of it in favour of a uniformity of form and/or theme originated with Roberts or Carman: Virgil, Horace, Tibullus, Propertius, and Ovid are merely the best known of the Augustan poets who 'took cognizance of variety' (*varietas*) in organizing their collections either to 'parade ... [their] virtuosity' or to satisfy their readers' demands for 'diversity' (William S. Anderson 44–9), and both the aesthetic of variety and the motives for its exercise were still very much alive in the late nineteeth century, particularly among classically trained poets and readers such as Roberts and Lampman – indeed, Kilpatrick has compellingly argued 'that Roberts' chief model for his arrangement of the poems in *Orion* was the *Odes* of Horace' (xix). By the same token, the use of numerous techniques such as 'structural symmetries,' 'thematic and imagistic metaphors among the poems,' and 'some pattern of serial arrangement' (for example, a seasonal or narrative progression) can be traced at least as far back as the Alexandrian poet Callimachus (Fraistat 5–6) and was also very much alive in the late nineteenth century, particularly among poets like Carman who looked to the Pre-Raphaelites for their poetic models. It is not without intriguing geopolitical implications that the issue of variety versus uniformity was a cause of both agreement and discussion in the Confederation group: in the organization of books, as in the choice of forms and the depiction of landscapes, aesthetics may be closer to politics than they initially appear.

Except for an honorific comment on 'the variety of Mr. Fawcett's power' in his June 1884 essay in the *Week* (472), Roberts's published criticism and extant letters of the 1880s and early 1890s make no explicit mention of the principle that nevertheless lies centrally in the background of many of his literary judgments during this period and, more important, came increasingly to dictate the content and arrangement of his collections at this time. A preference for variety over uniformity is clearly evident, for example, in Roberts's comments on *Among the Millet, and Other Poems* and *Snowflakes and Sunbeams* in the 26 January and 9 March 1889 issues of *Progress*. Lampman's 'verse ... possess[es] the essential, but Protean, quality which we indicate by the term genius,' but 'Campbell's note is not yet one of any great range.' To the extent that this last remark was intended to be constructive as well as critical, it was probably shaped at least in part by the critical response to Roberts's own début volume, for, while *Orion, and Other Poems* was repeatedly heralded as a breakthrough and warmly endorsed in the November 1880 number of *Canadian Monthly* as a manifestation of his 'varied and vivid powers' (553), it was also faulted for its bookish artistry and narrowness of theme. 'Now let him read men, nature, his country and his own heart, and he can accomplish very much indeed,' counselled one reviewer, and another: 'now that our author is no longer at college, but a man among men, it is to be presumed that he will ... marry his muse to more modern and interesting themes' (*Capital* [Fredericton], 5 October 1880; *Miramichi Advance* [Chatham], 4 November 1880).

That Roberts also took these criticisms to heart is evident in the very title of his second volume. Taken from Tennyson's *In Memoriam* (1: 2), where it alludes to Goethe's mastery of 'many different styles' (*Poems* 864n), *In Divers Tones* calls attention to the variety of mood and manner encompassed by the collection, which includes patriotic poems (such as 'Collect for Dominion Day' and 'Canada'), landscape sonnets (such as 'The Potato Harvest' and 'The Sower'), classical pieces (such as 'Actaeon' and 'The Pipes of Pan'), as well as a greater Romantic lyric ('Tantramar Revisited'), two poems on Native themes ('The Quelling of the Moose' and 'The Departing of Clote Scarp'), several pieces of *vers de société* (for example, 'The Poet Is Bidden to Manhattan Island'), a couple of ballades, a translation of a poem by Louis-Honoré Fréchette, and (note the appropriateness of the French form) a rondeau in his honour. '[A]s compared with *Orion, and Other Poems*, *In Divers Tones* reveals a broadening of the author's interest in the living world,' wrote John Reade of the volume when it eventually appeared after much delay in April 1887 (see *CL* 61–5); 'as the title implies, the book is the offspring of many moods, and it is addressed to many minds' (15 April 1887). Thanks primarily to *In Divers Tones*, the perception of Roberts's poetry as narrow in theme and finical in technique was replaced in the late 1880s and early 1890s with the view that he was a poet of multifaceted talent whose gifts are especially evident in his 'patriotic poems,' his 'classical pieces,' and his 'sonnets of farm life' (Sladen, quoted in 'The World of Books,' *Progress*, 23 November 1889). In the November 1891 number of *Dominion Illustrated*, W.G. MacFarlane would write of 'patriotic verse and ... Canadian nature poems' as the 'two sides of [Roberts's] genius ... that make him a Canadian poet' and a third 'variety of his poems' that had to be reckoned with – 'those after Greek models' (494). By the early 1890s, then, Roberts had apparently overcome his reputation as a narrow and scholarly poet and come to be seen instead as a man of quite broad interests who had produced excellent poems in no less than three modes.

This was not sufficient for Lampman, however, for in 'Two Canadian Poets' Roberts is faulted not only for his sacrifice of 'spontaneity' on the altar of 'workman[ship],' but also for his lack of breadth and diversity. True, 'his poems are written upon many various subjects, and either of his books might appear on a cursory glance to be somewhat remarkable for variety,' says Lampman, but in fact 'only three or four really different notes are struck, and all the poems are found to be attuned to these' (*ER* 107). (In contrast, Cameron of course has 'all the fervour, the breadth and energy of thought, the sensitive humanity that Professor Roberts lacks' [108].) In thus faulting Roberts, Lampman was merely bringing to bear on a fellow member of the Confederation group the aesthetic principle that he had articulated five years earlier in the preamble of 'The Modern School of Poetry in England' (1886):

> ... it seems to me that in endeavouring to reach approximately the worth of a living poet, there are two qualities to be especially looked for ... These are variety or versatility, and geniality. The work of all the greatest poets has been very varied, and it has been very genial. Looking with a wide and hearty and sympathetic eye upon all life, they have touched innumerable notes, and have absorbed themselves readily into every phase of its humour or pathos. (*ER* 59)

When judged in the light of the interlocking (and Coleridgean) criteria of 'versatility' and 'geniality,' no member of the 'Modern School of Poetry in England' – that is, the Pre-Raphaelites – passes muster: Rossetti 'had not the large mobile heart, that can throw itself into every variety of life ... He is confined in art and has no variety of flavour'; Swinburne's 'vocabulary is not large, his range of imagery is astonishingly narrow,' and 'he has certain set images ... which perpetually recur ... with the effect of monotony in every thing he has written'; and Morris's long poems are all characterized by 'universal monotony and want of hearty life' (*ER* 63, 64, 67). Of all the Romantic and Victorian poets whom Lampman canvasses in his literary essays and lectures, only Tennyson and Keats (especially the latter) come close to meeting the criteria of 'variety' and 'geniality,' which in 'Poetic Interpretation' (circa 1892) become salient attributes of 'the perfect poet,' a figure who 'would have no set style' but, rather, 'a different one for everything he should write, a manner exactly suited to the subject' (*ER* 127). To Lampman, Keats is 'the most perfect' of nineteenth-century poets because, unlike Wordsworth (his closest contender among the Romantics), 'he was governed by no theory and by no usurping line of thought and feeling. He was beyond all other men disposed to surrender himself completely to the impression of everything with which his brain or his senses came into contact' (*ER* 128).

While Lampman's preference for 'variety' doubtless stemmed in part from his classical training, it also reflects other components of his intellectual make-up, including Coleridge's attribution of the multifariousness of Shakespeare's characters to his universal mind (see *ER* 264, 322), Arnold's association of unrelieved 'mental stress' with 'morbid[ity]' of mind and 'monotonous[ness]' of expression (*Complete Prose* 1: 2–3), and, of course, Keats's conceptions of 'negative capability' and the 'chameleon poet' (see *ER* 322–3, 331). As the annotations to Lampman's *Essays and Reviews* amply attest, these and similar ideas were common in the work of John Campbell Shairp, W. J. Courthope, and other conservative critics to whom Lampman was heavily indebted for his aesthetic opinions and literary judgments (see *ER* xx–xxiii and 244f). But perhaps there was a specific source of Lampman's tenacious adherence to the principle of variety not only in his critical writings but also, and, more important, in his arrangement of two of his three published books of poetry, *Among the Millet, and Other Poems* and *Alcyone* (1899): a lengthy and anonymous review of Philip Bourke Marston's *Wind-Voices* (1883) that appeared in the April 1884 number of the *Manhattan*, the New York magazine on which, as will be recalled from chapter 1, Roberts was offered the position of associate editor in October of the same year. Heralding *Wind-Voices* as 'a noticeable event in the history of Victorian poetry,' the *Manhattan* goes on to praise the volume for fulfilling the promise of 'strength' and 'variety' that had been awakened by his first book (*Song-Tide* [1871]) but frustrated by his second (*All in All* [1874]). *Wind-Voices* is 'more varied in kind than any recent volume we can recall,' enthuses the reviewer; 'ballads are here, full of strength and vigor – narrative poems, rich in beauty and description – lyrics, as musical as any singer has given us. In some poems ... we perceive a dramatic quality ... [L]ovely poems in which ... flowers have found their souls make a special feature of the book, and, finally, there are some eighty sonnets ... In short, this volume of poems [is] full ... of variety ... beauty and subtlety, and no one who really loves what is best in poetry should leave it unread' (396–7).[28] Of Lampman's familiarity with this review there is only circumstantial evidence in the form of the presence in the same number of the *Manhattan* of two items that appear to have made a forceful and lasting impact on him: Arnold's essay on 'Literature and Science,' which, among other things, enunciates the theory of 'the four powers' that provides the basis for the educational program of the protagonist of *The Story of an Affinity*;[29] and an essay on the American painter Jasper Francis Cropsey, by William Henry Forman, in which Lampman probably encountered the quotation from Washington Irving's 'The Catskill Mountains' in *The Home Book of the Picturesque* that, as seen in chapter 2 and discussed further in chapter 4, furnished the conception of environmental determinism expounded in 'Two Canadian Poets.'[30]

As much as Lampman's comments on the effect of 'climatic and scenic conditions ... [on] the moulding of national character' and literature resemble those of Irving, they also differ in one important respect: whereas Irving places primary emphasis on the 'sublimity and beauty' of the climate and scenery of the Northeastern States and calls attention to 'the sublime melancholy of ... autumn' (quoted in Forman 374), Lampman places his emphasis on aspects of the Canadian environment that accord with the aesthetic principle of variety and its corollaries ('elasticity,' 'spontaneity') by which he finds Roberts wanting:

... we [in Canada] have the utmost diversity of scenery, a country exhibiting every variety of beauty and grandeur. A Canadian race, we imagine, might combine the energy, the seriousness, the perseverence of the Scandinavians with something of the gayety, the elasticity, the quickness of spirit of the south. If these qualities could be united in a literature, the result would indeed be something novel and wonderful. (*ER* 93)

From this it follows in the logic of environmental determinism that 'diversity' or 'variety' will be a definitive characteristic of authentic Canadian literature, that if Cameron's poetry manifests these qualities more than Roberts's, it is a better reflection of Canada, and so on.

Since *Among the Millet, and Other Poems* was published nearly three years before Lampman delivered his 'Two Canadian Poets' lecture in front of the Ottawa Literary and Scientific Society on 19 February 1891, the presence in the book of a great variety of styles and subjects is less likely to be a programmatic reflection of the ideas that he later adapted from Irving than merely a reflection of the preference for diversity over monotony that he had earlier expressed in 'The Modern School of Poetry in England.' In retrospect, however, the variousness of a book that included all the species of poetry identified by Marston's reviewer as well as two ballades and a sonnet sequence ('The Frogs') may well have seemed to Lampman to be an anticipation of the literature that might one day emerge from the action of the Canadian environment on the Canadian character. In this light, the programmatic variety of the *Alcyone* volume, which consists of poems in an almost irreducible diversity of modes and moods interspersed at varying intervals by sonnets inspired by Canadian nature, can be construed as a reflection not just of an aesthetic principle but of the diversity that Lampman regarded as distinctive of Canada.

The fact that both *Among the Millet, and Other Poems* and *Alcyone* were privately funded and printed meant that Lampman did not have to contend in either case with the demands of a publisher for commercially viable material. Such was not the case with the two or more collections in which he attempted to interest American publishers in the decade between the publication of *Among the Millet, and Other Poems* and his decision in the winter of 1897–8 to 'get [*Alcyone*] printed and bound in Edinburgh,' with the 'name [of an Ottawa firm] on the title page as publishers' (*AC* 195, and see 199). Precisely why only *Lyrics of Earth* (1895 [1896]) found its way into print in the 1890s is difficult to determine, but a plausible speculation is that the other collections assembled by Lampman were either too heterogeneous or too monomorphic to win acceptance in a poetry market that was already glutted with books of both types.[31] Certainly, the collection that he assembled in the fall of 1892 under the title 'Pictures and Meditations' failed to find a publisher (see *AC* 49, 52), as did the 'Century of Sonnets' that he assembled a year later (see *AC* 125, 129, 138, 143). Thanks to Edward William Thomson's 'better idea of constructing a book' for the American market, *Lyrics of Earth* took shape in the summer of 1895 as a sequence of lyrics of varying lengths organized around the seasonal cycle and conveying the sense of a spiritual journey (*AC* 144, and see 141, 143, 149, 153), in which form (and, no doubt, with Thomson's friendly assistance) it was accepted by the Boston publishing house of Copeland and Day. However, Thomson's skill at 'composing and naming a book' was of no avail in the case of 'A Century of Sonnets': in October 1895, Lampman responded to his friend's suggestion that the sonnets be subdivided into sections with a proposal to put 'the love sonnets ... almost at the front' of the sequence, to remove 'ten of the descriptive sonnets and mix the rest in with the general ones ... to make a variegated collection of 90' under the Petrarchan and Rossettian title of 'Sonnets of Life and Death,' but in March of the next year he abandoned this scheme, telling Thomson that 'in deference to commercial opinion' he had decided to 'split up the volume' and include twelve of the 'nature sonnets' in *Alcyone* 'to make a variety' (*AC* 158, 166). When Copeland and Day, prompted by poor sales of *Lyrics of Earth*, informed Lampman in the fall of 1897 that they would not honour their agreement to publish a second collection of his poems, the last remnant of his willingness 'to shape [his] books with a ... view to the taste of publishers' disappeared (*AC* 176, and see 192–5). If *Alcyone* 'contains "a good deal of admirable, and some very noble work" ... [as] you say ... and the publisher won't have it,' he had told Thomson on 30 August 1896, 'then it is the worse for the publishers. Moreover if it is as you say it will be read someday and by those who know' (*AC* 176).

Because he had lived in the United States since September 1886 and worked since Frebruary 1890 as literary editor of the *Independent* (New York), Carman was even more qualified than Thomson to gauge the disposition of American publishers and readers. He was also deeply aware through his reading of Poe and Whitman as well as Rossetti and Swinburne of the theory and practice of the long poem as lyric sequence, a genre in which variety and uniformity co-exist in a relationship analogous to that between the parts and the whole of an extended musical composition. Indeed, it was in precisely such terms that Carman presented his début volume, *Low Tide on Grand Pré: A Book of Lyrics* (1893):

The poems in this volume have been collected with reference to their similarity of tone. They are variations on a single theme, more or less aptly suggested by the title, Low Tide on Grand Pré. It seemed better to bring together between the same covers only those pieces of work which happened to be in the same key rather than to publish a larger book of more uncertain aim. (*Low Tide on Grand Pré*, n.pag.)

Together, this prefatory note and the explanatory title of *Low Tide on Grand Pré: A Book of Lyrics* indicate not only that Carman was aware of the full meaning of the term 'lyric,' but also that he conceived of the 'book' as an ensemble based on the principle of harmonic 'variation ... on a ... theme' rather than as a miscellany devoted to the display of diversity and virtuosity. It is consistent with Carman's understanding of the lyric and the book as such that he oversaw every aspect of the creation of *Low Tide on Grand Pré* from the selection of the typeface to the choice of colour for the covers[32] and that only rarely in his creative career did he resort to the 'and Other Poems' formula of *Orion, and Other Poems* and *Among the Millet, and Other Poems* for the title of a book. 'The thin volumes of verse occasionally put forth by Mr. Bliss Carman have a unity not often found in such collections,' William Morton Payne would observe in the 'Recent American Poetry' column in the *Dial* (Chicago) on 1 September 1898; 'each volume is a careful selection from a considerable mass of material, and brings together pieces of the same class' (133).

*Low Tide on Grand Pré: A Book of Lyrics* comprises only twenty-five poems, but, as Odell Shepard observes in a vocabulary that nicely captures the literary sensibility to which Carman appealed, 'it contains half a dozen pieces of pure verbal witchery which were made for no conceivable reason in the world except for love of beautiful sound ... [I]n this carefully winnowed and delicately harmonized collection, it was made evident that America had a new poet who could both sing and say, who combined a finished craftsmanship with unmistakable power' (34, 36). Reviews in the United States, England, and Canada were 'ruinous in [their] praise' (*L* 108),[33] and the book sold so well that, after the New York publisher of the first edition (Charles L. Webster) went bankrupt in 1894, it was quickly published in a second and slightly enlarged edition by the new and aggressive Chicago publishing house of Stone and Kimball (see *L* 63). By the end of 1894, Stone and Kimball had twice reprinted the book, first in a 'limited (50-copy) edition' and then in a full run (*L* 67, 91). '[I]t sells right away,' Carman told Hovey on 1 March

1895 (*L* 91). Just how successful *Low Tide on Grand Pré* was can be gleaned from the fact that, while only 270 of the 500 copies of *Lyrics of the Earth* printed by Copeland and Day ever left their premises, Carman's book went to a third edition in 1895 and was subsequently reprinted five times by two other American publishers (Lamson, Wolffe and Company and Small, Maynard and Company).[34] Little wonder that Lampman complained to Thomson on 4 December 1897 that 'the books [Copeland and Day] publish are not really published, only printed and bound' (*AC* 193).

Despite its critical and commercial success, *Low Tide on Grand Pré* did not entirely satisfy Roberts. 'This collection, being made up of poems exclusively in the minor key, leaves unrepresented one side of Mr. Carman's genius, – a side which is of particular importance in these dilettante days,' he complained in the 15 June 1894 number of the *Chap-Book* (Boston) (which Carman was by then editing); nowhere in it is heard the 'joyous major note, masculine and full-throated,' of 'certain [of Carman's] poems in the periodicals' ('Mr. Bliss Carman's Poems' 54). Echoing the advice that he had given to his cousin a decade earlier, Roberts credits him with a distinctiveness that derives from his 'mastery of the inevitable phrase, the unforgettable cadence,' and his 'combination of verbal simplicity and an extreme complexity of suggestion and intention,' the latter a quality that points towards the diagnosis of Carman's 'weaknesses' with which the review draws to a conclusion:

> His structure is often defective, – he is not always careful in regard to the architectonics of verse. Many of his poems are built as waywardly as a dream, and one sometimes feels that parts of one poem might as easily fit into the framework of another. He has a tendency to repeat his effects; and while his poems are sharply differentiated from those of other poets, they are not always well differentiated from each other. There is also, at times, a curious and bewildering intricacy of thought which may justly be called obscurity; but this is a fault which Mr. Carman is rapidly eliminating from his work. (57)

'[S]tructure ... architectonics ... framework': the disparity between these schematic terms and Carman's musical analogy is an index of the aesthetic gulf that had perhaps always separated the two poets. The fact that in 1894 Roberts was repeating the advice of a decade earlier against diffuseness and obscurity should have alerted him to the error of believing that Carman was 'rapidly' mending his ways. No more could the poet whose 'single' and recurring 'theme' had its origins in the ebb and flow of the tides across the space between land and sea construct poems that are 'sharply differentiated ... from each other' than could he rest content in the confines of poetic forms. Carman's major work of the 1880s was 'Corydon,' a pastoral elegy on Matthew Arnold, but it was never finished. The lyrical sequence on which he was working when he died, *Sanctuary* (1929), consists of sonnets, but they are unrhymed. The *Vagabondia* volumes that consolidated and advanced his reputation in the 1890s celebrate the pleasures of the open road in loosened verse. To the extent that there are homologies between Imperialism and sublimity and between variety and Canadian nationalism, Carman's 'free-trade Tory[ism]' (*L* 349) and, indeed, his residence in the United States were the corollaries of the sequences of individual yet interdependent lyrics that poured from him in the wake of *Low Tide on Grand Pré*.

## IV

As good an example as any of the distinctive qualities of Carman's best poetry and of the careful workmanship upon which it surely rests is the title poem of his first volume. Cast, appropriately, in the stanza form of Song 9 of Sir Philip Sidney's *Astrophil and Stella* ($ababb_4$), 'Low Tide on Grand Pré' announces the theme and establishes the key for the lyrics that follow. In the first three stanzas, repeated words, rhymes, syllables, and vowel sounds combine to create a euphony whose almost hypnotic effect reinforces the dream-like quality of the description (notice, for example, the repetition of 'un' in stanza 1, the recurrence of 'dream' and 'stream' both within and at the ends of lines in stanzas 2 and 3, and the frequency of long vowel sounds in all three stanzas):

> The *sun* goes down, and over all
>   These barren reaches by the tide
> Such *un*elusive glories fall,
>   I almost *dream* they yet will abide
>   *Un*til the coming of the tide.
>
> And yet I know that not for us,
>   By any ecstasy of *dream*,
> He lingers to keep luminous
>   A little while the grievous *stream*,
>   Which frets, *un*comforted of *dream* –

> A grievous *stream*, that to and fro
>   Athrough the fields of Acadie
> Goes wandering, as if to know
>   Why one beloved face should be
>   So long from home and Acadie. (*PBC* 3; emphasis added)

Also noticeable in these lines is the interstanzaic fluidity provided by the 'And' and the dash that begin and end the second stanza. In conjunction with the verbal and phonetic repetitions that similarly traverse stanza breaks, the effect of this fluidity is to minimize the 'interruption of continuity' that J.J. Sylvester, a Victorian poetic theorist whose work was well known in Carman's circle in the early 1890s, regarded as 'the one irremissible sin of lyric composition' because it disrupts the process through which 'the hearer [is brought] into emotional sympathy with the composer' (32). That such ideas were very much in Carman's mind during the period preceding the publication of *Low Tide on Grand Pré* is confirmed by 'The Technic of Rhyme,' the third of four articles on poetics that Richard Hovey published in the *Independent* between August 1891 and September 1894, where Carman is credited with proposing 'colliteration' as an alternative to 'syzygy,' the term used by Sylvester in *The Laws of Verse* (1870) and adopted by Sidney Lanier in *The Science of English Verse* (1880) to describe 'repetitions that fall indiscriminately on accented and unaccented [syllables] in sufficient number to give unity to a passage by subtly filling the ear with the insistence of a dominant tone color' (3).

In the ensuing six stanzas of 'Low Tide on Grand Pré' a question reminiscent of Dante Gabriel Rossetti's speculations about pre- and post-existence in 'Sudden Light' (1870)* initiates a sequence of reminiscences that culminate in a moment of intense spiritual awareness. Although each of the stanzas is end-stopped, verbal and phonetic repetitions once again work to overcome discontinuity. Notice particularly the way in which in the following stanzas the repetition of 'sun' both as word and syllable serves a twofold purpose: it extends the harmonic 'theme' introduced by the 'sun' of the poem's opening line, and it prepares the way for the aural and metaphysical 'variation' of 'subtler,' a word bril-

---

* 'I have been here before, / But when or where I cannot tell ... You have been mine before, – / How long ago I may not know ... Has this been thus before?' (*Works* 200). As Campbell would point out in June 1895 in 'Poetry and Piracy,' several other phrases and lines in Carman's poem are reminiscent of Rossetti (see *War* 32 and chapter 8).

liantly chosen to indicate that, although prompted by the physical effects of a sunset and figured in the 'unelusive glories' of sunlight, the memory conjured by the poem derives its intensity and significance from a type of illumination that is elusive, numinous, and transcendental[35] – tied to a particular place, person, and experience but in its essence beyond full comprehension and description. This is the reason for the slight awkwardness in the first line of the fourth of these stanzas, where 'that' is not a conjuction but a demonstrative pronoun pointing towards a transcendental signified:

> Was it a year or lives ago,
>     We took the grasses in our hands,
> And caught the summer flying low
>     Over the waving meadow lands,
>     And held it there between our hands?
>
> The while the river at our feet –
>     A drowsy inland meadow stream –
> At set of sun the after-heat
>     Made running gold, and in the gleam
>     We freed our birch upon the stream.
>
> There down along the elms at dusk
>     We lifted dripping blade to drift,
> Through twilight scented fine like musk,
>     Where night and gloom awhile uplift,
>     Nor sunder soul and soul adrift.
>
> And that we took into our hands
>     Spirit of life or subtler thing –
> Breathed on us there, and loosed the bands
>     Of death, and taught us, whispering,
>     The secret of some wonder-thing.
>
> Then all your face grew light, and seemed
>     To hold the shadow of the sun;
> The evening faltered, and I deemed
>     That time was ripe, and years had done
>     Their wheeling underneath the sun.

So all desire and all regret,
  And fear and memory, were naught;
One to remember or forget
  The keen delight our hands had caught;
  Morrow and yesterday were naught. (*PBC* 3–4)

Like the word 'something' in Wordsworth's description of the universal spirit in 'Tintern Abbey,' the phrase 'some wonder-thing' is as precise as any description of such an apprehension can be, though, of course, it is vulnerable to Roberts's charges of 'obscurity' and 'extreme complexity of suggestion and intention.'

The final stanza of 'Low Tide on Grand Pré' is a poignant expression of the sadness that accompanies a (Keatsian) return from the memory of a timeless moment to the reality of a present in which the operation of time is all too apparent because visible in the movement of the tide:

The night has fallen, and the tide ...
  Now and again comes drifting home,
Across the aching barrens wide,
  A sigh like driven wind or foam:
  In grief the flood is bursting home. (*PBC* 4)

The insistent attribution of human qualities to the seascape in this stanza makes absolutely clear that in all its phases the poem is a reflection of states of experience rather than, as Roberts might have preferred in the early 1890s, a realistic description of a scene followed by a meditative response to it. For all its moody fluidity, however, 'Low Tide on Grand Pré' is a superb example of the workmanship that Roberts so deeply valued and ardently promoted: the syntactical echo of the poem's opening line ('The sun goes down, and over all ...') in the opening line of its final stanza ('The night has fallen, and the tide ...'), the repetition with variations of 'barren reaches' and 'aching barrens' in its first and final stanzas, the fulfilment in the 'bursting home' of the 'flood' of the anticipated 'coming of the tide' – all of these patterns work in concert to bring 'Low Tide on Grand Pré' to a close whose seeming inevitableness must have satisfied even Roberts that Carman was a master of his craft.

# CHAPTER FOUR

# Natural Environments

These stern coasts ... should create a habit of openness to nature, and by contrast put a reproach upon the commonplace and the gross. Our climate with its swift extremes is eager and waking, and we should expect a sort of dry sparkle in our page, with a transparent and tonic quality in our thought. If environment is anything, our work can hardly prove tame.

– *Roberts, 'The Outlook for Literature' (1886)*

We know that climate and scenic conditions have much to do with the moulding of national character. In the climate of this country we have the pitiless serenity of Sweden with the sunshine and the sky of the north of Italy, a combination not found in the same degree anywhere else in the world ... A Canadian race, we imagine, might combine the energy, the seriousness, the perseverance of the Scandinavians with something of the gaiety, the elasticity, the quickness of spirit of the south. If these qualities could be united in a literature, the result would indeed be something novel and wonderful.

– *Lampman, 'Two Canadian Poets: A Lecture' (1891)*

When Roberts and Lampman suggested that the scenery, climate, and atmospheric qualities of Canada might one day give rise to a Canadian national character and, hence, to a distinctive Canadian literature, they were not merely echoing statements made about New England by Washington Irving (see chapter 2) but, like Irving himself, articulating a concept of environmental determinism whose roots lay in Locke's theory of mental development and Herder's theory of national identity. Since 'our imagination nourishes itself' 'upon the impressions which our senses gather in during childhood,' 'it takes the colour that it feeds on' runs Roberts's version of Locke in 'The Savour of the Soil' (1892); thus, 'individuality is much the product of the soil upon which it took shape,' and, by Herderian extension, nationality is an inevitable component of any writer's work no matter what its 'themes and scenes': 'wheresoever the ... imaginations [of writers] wander, they carry with them the savour of the soil' (252). As the enormously influential French literary historian Hippolyte Adolphus Taine put it in his essay on 'Art in Greece' (1869; trans. 1875), which was very likely known to Roberts if not Lampman, 'a people always receives an impression from the country it occupies': 'countless circumstances of soil and climate combine' to form the 'mental mould' of a people, and, from that mould, 'all ideas' and artistic creations 'issue in relief' (362, 387).

In one or more of many articulations, such theories and assumptions lie in the background of R.G. Haliburton's *The Men of the North and Their Place in History* (1869), William A. Foster's *Canada First; or, Our New Nationality* (1871), William H. Hingston's *The Climate of Canada and Its Relations to Life and Health* (1884), and numerous other iterations of the environment > mentality > art thesis, including, of course, the many claims of Canadian heirs of Young Ireland that Canadian poetry will be or has become 'racy of the soil.' 'Those who expect to see "A new Athens rising near the pole"' in Canada 'will find themselves extremely disappointed,' Arabella Fermor had asserted in *The History of Emily Montague* (1769); 'genius will never mount high, where the faculties of the mind are benumbed half the year... [and] the cold ... brings on a sort of stupefaction' (Brooke 130).[1] On the contrary, wrote Thomas D'Arcy McGee as the Confederation period was dawning, Canada's geographical position is 'favourable' to the production of a 'National Literature': 'northern latitudes like ours have ever been famed for the strength, variety and beauty of their literature,' and Canadian writing 'must assume the gorgeous coloring and gloomy grandeur of the forest ... Its lyrics must possess the ringing cadence of the waterfall, and its epics be as solemn and beautiful as our great rivers' ('Protection'). If Iceland is anything to go on, suggested Hingston, Canada's literary future was assured, for had not the learned Lord Dufferin, the new Dominion's third governor general (1872–8), observed that '"devoting the long leisure of their winter nights to intellectual occupations"' had enabled '"the Icelandic settlers ... [to become] the first of any European nation to create for themselves a native literature"' (quoted in Hingston 108n)? 'It is undeniable ... that the natural as well as the social environment has much to do with the development or repression of the "shaping power of the imagination",' asserted an anonymous writer in the 27 May 1889 issue of the *Globe.* Thus, 'distance from the sights and sounds of the grand old ocean and the primeval forest, the absence from the horizon of cloud-capped mountain or frowning cliff, ... have their insensible, but very real and powerful, effect in dulling the poetic fancy,' and 'one might pretty safely predict that the Rockies and the Selkirks, with their towering peaks, frowning precipices and awful gorges, must, at no distant day, call into being a distinct race of Western poets' ('The Decay of Imagination').

It is tempting but too easy to argue that the line of transmission thus briefly sketched means that the Confederation group inhabited an intellectual as well as a physical environment sealed by the American border. The debts of Roberts and Lampman to Irving militate against such an exclusionary argument, as does a large body of evidence indicating that in turning towards the natural environment for materials that were recognizably original because local or indigenous and, therefore, outside the existing repertoire of English Romantic and Victorian poetry, the Canadian poets were largely guided by American nature writers. Nor is this surprising, for, as the easy adaptation of Irving's statements by Roberts and Lampman clearly indicates, the northeastern states, the Maritime provinces, and the southeastern portions of central Canada have a great deal in common in terms of their scenery, climate, atmosphere, flora, and fauna. Indeed, the chief guide for the Confederation group among American nature writers of the late nineteenth century, John Burroughs, repeatedly sanctions such commonalities in 'Nature and the Poets,' the very essay in his *Pepacton* collection of 1881 that, as it happens, Roberts added to the English syllabus at King's College in 1886 ('The Work of the English Department'): for example, Burroughs pronounces 'our common blue violet ... the only species ... found abundantly everywhere in the North' and, in a discussion of Edmund Clarence Stedman's 'Snow-Bound,' observes that 'it is characteristic of our Northern and New England fields that they are 'edged with green' in spring long before the emerald tint has entirely overspread them' because 'along the fences, especially along the stone walls ... the land is fatter ... from the deep snows and other causes [and because] the fence absorbs the heat, ... shelters the ground from the wind, and [hence] the sward quickly responds to the touch of the spring sun' (7:102). 'April seems to come a little sooner, and to be a little more luxuriant in southern New England than it used to be in New Brunswick,' Carman told the Toronto journalist and photographer Melvin Ormond Hammond

(1876–1936) in a letter of 23 April 1910, 'but her traits are very little changed':

> The frogs pipe, the maples and wild cherries break in bloom, the golden-wing calls from the hardwood ridges, the blood-root is white along the roadsides, and the red-shouldered blackbird flutes on his rustic whistle, just as they did in the golden age beside the St. John. Trilliums, too, and anemones, and spring-beauties, and dog-toothed violets, and other ravishing children of the woods, all lovely as of old ... (*L* 174)[2]

It is no mere coincidence but a synchronicity born both of environmental similarities and of Burroughs's influence on the Confederation group that explains why a great many of the flora and fauna of New England that he describes in 'Nature and the Poets' as 'rich materials ... that have yet hardly been touched' in American poetry (7:109) also appear in the work of the Confederation group (to give but a partial list to supplement Carman's: the mullein, the golden-rod, the hepatica, the white and yellow violet, the kingbird, the bobolink, the vireo, the cat-bird, the phoebe-bird, and the oven-bird [7:84–110]). Little wonder that in his 'At the Mermaid Inn' column for 9 July 1892 Lampman observes that, 'according to Burroughs,' 'the hermit[-thrush] ... [is] the finest of our songsters' or that a week later in the same forum Campbell asserts that 'for those who love nature and nature's studies Burroughs is a never-dying friend' (110–11). Among the Confederation poets, as among their contemporaries in the United States, Burroughs's 'prestige' was apparently as great in the 1880s and 1890s as that of Emerson and Whitman, two writers to whom his own 'love [of] nature and nature's studies' was, of course, deeply indebted (Westbrook 50).

As obviously an heir to the environmental determinism of Herder, Taine, and, especially, the Montesquieu of *De l'Esprit des lois* (1748) as well as to the aggressively American Romanticism of Emerson and Whitman, Burroughs was convinced that the origins of national characteristics and differences lie in climate. '[N]o doubt many of the differences between the English stock at home and its offshoot in our country are traceable to this source,' he argues in *Winter Sunshine* (1875): 'because the English climate is temperate, the English are a sweet and mellow people' whose life and literature are characterized by such qualities as 'reverence ... [and] homeliness'; in contrast, Americans and their literary productions are given to 'finical, self-complacent smartness' and 'forward[ness]' because the 'American climate has a much keener edge' 'both of frost and fire' that 'sharpens the wit ... favors an irregular, nervous energy ... [and] goads us day and night' (2: 174–5, 148–9, 156). Especially formative of the (North) American character in Burroughs's analysis are seasonal extremes and the rapidity of seasonal changes, particularly in the 'initiative month' of April in the continent's more northerly regions (6: 107, 93). '[I]s there anything like an April morning?' he asks in his essay on 'April' in *Birds and Poets, with Other Papers* (1877), a first edition of which was owned by Lampman:[3]

> One hardly knows what the sentiment of it is, but it is something very delicious. It is youth and hope. It is a new earth and a new sky. How the air transmits sounds, and what an awakening, prophetic character all sounds have! ... The great sun appears to have been refurbished, and there is something in his first glance above the eastern hills, and the way his eyebeams dart right and left and smite the rugged mountains with gold, that quickens the pulse and inspires the heart. (6: 97–8)

'Does not the return of the year, the sudden and golden dawn of our summers, come to us with an energy of exhilaration quite unknown to the people of southern latitudes?' asks Lampman in his 'At the Mermaid Inn' column of 9 April 1892; 'with us the coming of spring is the signal for a physical and intellectual revolution and revival, a new birth of buoyant and unconquerable energy rendering us capable of undreamed-of labours and immense undertakings' (51–2). In 'April in the Hills' (1895), the first version of which was written three days before the column (Early, 'Chronology' 86), Lampman sees the rejuvenation of the year merely as a source of personal, spiritual awakening ('I rise / With lifted brow and upward eyes. / I bathe my spirit in blue skies, / And taste the springs of life' [*P* 128]), but in 'At the Mermaid Inn' he uses it as a point of departure for a series of observations about the formative effects of climate on character that echo those in 'Two Canadian Poets' and also intimate, in their emphasis on seasonal extremes and changes, the presence of Burroughs as well as Irving in Lampman's 'meteorological determinism' (Westbrook 94):

> Our summer heats are keen and wholesome, and neither depress nor enervate. Autumn with its refreshment of splendid colours and its tonic days comes before we have lost anything of the vital impulse, and carries us on with renewed energy into the depth of that trying season which is our severest test. Yet even through the winter months, bitter but bracing, labour

is a moral necessity, and we continue to present it with strenuous energy, if not with actual joy. In Canada with the snows and frozen months of Stockholm and St. Petersburg we combine the long days, the blue sky, and the splendid sunshine of the north of Italy. There has never been any other nation on earth so situated, and we cannot but suppose that our people will in the future develop an unusual buoyancy and novel energy of character. (52)

There may also be Canadian sources for Lampman's 'meteorological determinism,' but its very evident origins in the work of Irving and Burroughs (whose 1875 collection, it will be recalled, is entitled *Winter Sunshine*) render it a curiously American – specifically New England – expression of the effect of climate on Canada's national character.

Both in *Birds and Poets, with Other Papers* and in *Pepacton*, Burroughs repeatedly draws attention to a creature whose 'prophetic ... sounds' he regards as a uniquely (North) American sign of the arrival of spring:

Among April sounds there is none more welcome or suggestive to me than the voice of the little frogs piping in the marshes. No bird-note can surpass it as a spring token; and as it is not mentioned, to my knowledge, by the poets and writers of other lands, I am ready to believe it is characteristic of our season ... Generally the note is very feeble at first ..., and only one voice will be heard, some prophet bolder than all the rest ... Soon, however, ... say toward the last of the month, there is a shrill musical uproar, as the sun is setting, in every marsh and bog in the land ... There is a Southern species, heard when you have reached the Potomac, whose note is ... harsh and crackling ... The call of the Northern species is far more musical. (6:96–7)[4]

What a chorus goes up from our ponds and marshes in spring! The like of it cannot be heard anywhere else under the sun. In Europe it would certainly have made an impression upon the literature. An attentive ear will detect first one variety, then another, each occupying the stage from three or four days to a week. The latter part of April, when the little peeping frogs – *hylodes* – are in full chorus, one comes upon places, in ... drives or walks late in the day, where the air fairly palpitates with sound; from every little marshy hollow and spring run there rises an impenetrable maze or cloud of shrill musical voices. After the peepers, the next frog to appear is the clucking frog ... (7:144)

In the first of these passages (from *Birds and Poets, with Other Papers*) may be the textual origins not only of the 'trill and trill' of the 'Tremulous sweet voices' that 'flute-like, answer ... / One to another' 'From the pale-weeded shallows' in Lampman's 'April' (1888), but also of the 'piping' that emanates from 'whispering river meads / And watery marshes' 'when spring [is] in her glee' ('Frogs' 1888) and, like the singing of Keats's nightingale, enables the speaker of the sonnet sequence briefly to escape the temporal world to 'lands where beauty hath no rest ... and the sun / But ever half-way sunken toward the west' (*P* 7–8). In the second (from *Pepacton*), perhaps in conjunction with Lampman's poems,[5] may be the textual origins of 'When Milking-Time Is Done' and 'Frogs,' two sonnets in the spring portion of Roberts's *Songs of the Common Day* (1893) in which frogs figure as 'cool-fluting ministers of dream' whose 'myriad ... mellow pipes' when heard at 'sunset' 'Make shrill the slow brook's borders,' render 'all the air ... tremulous,' and bring therapeutic 'release' to 'tired ears' (*CP* 117, 121). If so, then credit must go once again to an American writer for alerting Lampman and Roberts to the presence in their natural environment of a creature whose sound, though not unique to Canada, is nevertheless characteristic of the central and eastern Canadian spring.[6]

A further aspect of Burroughs's writings that may well have helped to awaken Roberts and Lampman to the characteristics and effects of the natural environment is his notion that in the seasonal cycle in northerly regions both spring and fall are sites of fierce conflict between winter and summer, and, thus, April has an inverse counterpart in November, as, less starkly, does May in October. 'In the fall, the battles of the spring are fought over again,' he suggests in the essay entitled 'Autumn Tides' in *Winter Sunshine*.

There is the same advance and retreat ... between the contending forces, that was witnessed in April and May ... Both seasons have their equinoxes, both their filmy, hazy air, their ruddy forest tints, their cold rains, their drenching fogs, their mystic moons; both have the same solar light and warmth, the same rays of sun; yet, after all, how different the feelings which they inspire! One is the morning, the other the evening; one is youth, the other is age ... It is rarely that an artist succeeds in painting unmistakably the difference between sunrise and sunset; and it is equally a trial of ... skill to put upon canvas the difference between early spring and late fall, ... between April and November ... The spring is the morning sunlight, clear and determined; the autumn, the afternoon rays, pensive, lessening, golden. (2: 98–9, 102–3)

While this passage raises some echoes in the spring and fall sonnets of *Songs of the Common Day*, particularly in 'The Flight of the Geese' (1893), where the sounds of the lightless night is 'filled' with 'April forecast' and April remembered (*CP* 129), its resonances in Lampman's work are both numerous and rich, probably because, in conjunction with similar passages in Burroughs's work, it lent seasonal substance to the spring/morning/youth and fall/evening/old age quadrants of the cyclical system that, as argued elsewhere,[7] lends structure to his entire poetic oeuvre.

Among the many Lampman poems that appear to bear the imprint of Burroughs's thinking about spring and fall are 'Winter Hues Recalled' (1888) and 'Indian Summer' (1899): in the first, an evocation of a Wordsworthian 'spot ... of time' that also owes much to the early books of *The Prelude*,[8] the 'radiant day' recollected in tranquility occurred in February rather than April, but it is nevertheless the scene of a resonantly Burroughsian 'struggle / 'Twixt sun and frost' in which, 'with advancing spears, / the glittering golden vanguard of the spring / Holds the broad winter's yet unbroken rear / In long-closed wavering contest'; in the second, a sonnet in which the season is figured as an 'old gray' man with 'misty head' who is lost in 'a golden dream of youth,' the fall is similarly the scene of a battle, this time with victory going to 'the polar armies [that] overflowed / The darkening barriers of the hills' and 'The north-wind ringing with a thousand spears' (*P* 28, 225).

Such parallels and contrasts are a recurring feature of the seasonal poems in *Among the Millet* and *Alcyone*, as are atmospheric descriptions that may be responses to Burroughs's call for accurate and nuanced renditions not only of diurnal and seasonal phenomena, but also of the differences of appearance and emotion engendered by such phenomena. In 'April' in *Among the Millet*, for example, 'The creamy sun at even scatters down / A golden-green mist across the murmuring town,' and in the contrasting poem immediately following, 'An October Sunset,' 'the thin cloudflakes seem to lean / With their sad sunward faces aureoled / And longing lips set downward ...' (*P* 4, 6). A similar attention to detail and effect is observable in the seasonal sonnets in *Alcyone*: as 'The air seethes upward with a steamy shiver' towards a sky 'as pearly blue as summer,' the speaker of 'In March' can 'almost forget that winter ever was'; as he looks out over 'dusking fields and meadows shining pale / With moon-topped dandelions' during a summer sunset in 'Evening,' his thoughts grow by turns 'dark' and bright; and as the unbroken 'gray sky' sheds 'No ... light on any field' in 'The Autumn Waste,' 'Life, hopes, and human things seem wrapped away, / ... in one long decay' (*P* 179, 198–9, 228–9). Lampman's powers of observation and description and his cyclical and dialectical habits of mind were not acquired from Burroughs, but they were almost certainly encouraged and consolidated by such essays as 'April,' as very likely was his sense of Canada's natural environment as a rich source of fresh material for poetic treatment.

That Lampman's sense of the significance as well as the richness of the subject matter available to him in his natural environment was quickened by Burroughs is a conclusion that follows almost inevitably from a reading off the seven collections of nature essays that the American writer published in the 1870s, 1880s, and 1890s (the four not already mentioned are *Wake-Robin* [1871], *Locusts and Wild Honey* [1879],[9] *Fresh Fields* [1884], and *Riverby* [1894]). Both as fresh subjects for poetry and as prophetic harbingers, Lampman's frogs are creatures of Burroughs's writings as well as of the Canadian spring. Similarly, several details of 'Heat' and 'Among the Timothy' surely gain significance and precision as seasonal markers and sensory experiences from Burroughs's observations apropos the 'poetry of midsummer harvesting' in *Birds and Poets, with Other Papers* on the harmonies and correspondences among the sounds and textures of that time of year:

> The characteristic sounds of midsummer are the sharp, whirring crescendo of the cicada or harvest fly, and the rasping, stridulous notes of the nocturnal insects ... [T]he grass and the grain at this season have become hard. The timothy stalk is like a file; the rye straw is glazed with flint; the grasshoppers snap sharply as they fly up in front of you; the bird-songs have ceased; the ground crackles under foot; the eye of the day is brassy and merciless; and in harmony with all these things is the rattle of the mower and hay-tedder ... (6:54–5)

– and also, according to Lampman's poems, 'the crackling rustle of ... pitch-forked hay' and the 'idly clacking wheels' of 'a hay-cart' (*P* 16, 12). When seen against the backdrop of Burroughs's description of the predominantly 'sharp' sounds and textures of midsummer, such elements of 'Heat' as 'the cool gloom of the bridge' and the 'thin revolving tune'[10] of the 'thrush' take on added significance as indications of the mental equipoise that begins fully to emerge in the final stanza of the poem with the speaker's statement that 'Yet to [him] not this or that / Is always sharp or always sweet' (*P* 12–13).

Of Lampman's three volumes of poetry the most Burroughsian in both structure and subject matter is obviously *Lyrics of Earth*. Arranged with E.W. Thomson's help around the cycle of the seasons, the volume begins with the arrival of spring ('Godspeed to the Snow') and would have ended, if a printer's error had not necessitated the placement of 'The Sun Cup' in the final position, with a celebration of the anticipated pleasures of memory that is disrupted by 'a vision ... / Of the labouring world' (*P* 171–2 ['Winter-Store']). All but a few of its poems are thus bracketed by pieces devoted to the sights, sounds, and psychological effects of the period between April and November and, correspondingly, morning and evening, youth and old age, classical times and the present day.[11] No doubt, many if not most of the details and responses registered in *Lyrics of Earth* are the result of direct observation, but this does not deny Burroughs a role either in directing Lampman's attention to certain phenomena or in supplying him some of his materials (or both). In 'April in the Hills,' for instance, several of the birds mentioned are given special status in *Birds and Poets, with Other Papers* as an early manifestation of the arrival of spring: 'April's bird with me is the robin,' declares Burroughs;[12] no American poet has yet written of 'the first swallow that comes twittering up the southern valley'; and none has described the 'first note of [the bluebird] in early spring, – a note that may be called the violet of sound, and as welcome to the ear, heard above the cold damp earth, as is its floral type to the eye a few weeks later' (6:75, 36). Lampman also mentions the shore lark, which Burroughs describes as a 'bird ... of the far north,' and, in discerning 'tenderness' in the vesper-sparrow's song in 'The Return of the Year' (1895), may have had in mind the American writer's characterization of it as all 'peace and gentleness' (6:16, 86). When Lampman wrote of 'waken[ing] with the waking earth' and 'match[ing] the bluebird in mirth' in the final stanza of 'April in the Hills,' perhaps he was remembering both a personal experience in April 1895 and Burroughs's observation in his first collection of nature essays (*Wake-Robin* [1871]) that the bluebird is 'the first bit of color that cheers our northern landscape' and his assertion in the same place that bluebirds 'warble more confidently ... gleefully' and 'cheerily' after 'threat of snow is completely past' (1:190, 3). Perhaps Lampman was also remembering actual sounds of midsummer as well as Burroughs' description of them when in July 1889 he wrote in 'Comfort of the Fields' (1895) of 'the jolted wains, / The thresher's humming,' 'The locust's rattle,' and 'The prattling cricket's intermittent cry' as a 'feast of summer sounds' (*P* 149). Perhaps the 'spectral happiness,' the 'nameless and unnatural cheer' and 'pleasure secret and austere,' that comes to the speaker in the 'thin light' and 'chill air' of 'In November' (1895) is the product both of a personal experience in November 1889 and of Burroughs's remark in *Winter Sunshine* that 'our Northern November day is like spring water ... There is chill in it and an exhilaration also' (2: 111). Such speculative possibilities could be multiplied many times over, but surely the essential point is now clear: Lampman's descriptions of natural phenomena and their effects resemble those of Burroughs both because their environments had much in common and because Burroughs's descriptions helped to determine what he saw and how he responded. In naturalistic observation as in landscape aesthetics, the eye largely sees the phenomena that it has been conditioned to see, and any description that ensues is necessarily the outcome of a textual as well as an actual experience: art imitates both art and life.

Carl Y. Connor's impression that Lampman 'wanted every man to be a John Burroughs or a Bradford Torrey [1843–1912], or, better still, a loafer with an open heart and a perceptive eye' (148) has the twofold merit of recognizing Burroughs's importance to him and of acknowledging another American literary naturalist whom he greatly admired. 'Mr. Torrey is an ornithologist of the heart,' 'a poet-naturalist ... of the class of writers to which Thoreau and ... Burroughs belong,' Lampman asserts in his 'At the Mermaid Inn' column of 23 February 1892 by way of recommending Torrey's *A Rambler's Lease* (1889) as the 'next best thing to a morning's walk in the woods or along some country lane' (12–13). A little over a year later, in his column of 25 February 1893, he goes further: 'although not yet as well known as either [Thoreau or Burroughs],' Torrey is 'a finer and more suggestive thinker than Burroughs, and a more pleasing, if a less brilliant one, than Thoreau ... [He] is not only a most minute and patient observer, after the persistent modern manner, of the habits of plants and birds, but also a literary artist ... a poet-philosopher ... and a humorist of th[e] tenderly reflective sort ...' whose essays, particularly 'In Praise of the Weymouth Pine' in *The Footpath Way* (1892), 'introduce ... his readers to inexhaustible sources of innocent and pleasurable activities, put ... them upon the watch for innumerable delightful suggestions, and prepare ... them for a world of tender and humanizing influences' (265–6). 'It is a kind of writing that I take to instinctively,' Lampman had said of Torrey's

*A Rambler's Lease* in a letter to Thomson on 9 December 1891; 'Burroughs is the same kind of worker and his books are charming' (*AC* 27).

On the basis of the resonances between two of Lampman's poems and the lengthy excerpt from Torrey's essay on the Weymouth pine that he quotes in his 'At the Mermaid Inn' column of 25 February 1893, there is a distinct possibility that the relationship between the two writers involved a degree of reciprocal influence and reinforcement. A 'priest of the true religion' of Nature that stands silent in the 'cathedral' or 'temple' of the forest until the 'heavenly influence' of the wind inspires its innumerable leaves to 'utter ... things ... deeper than words' (quoted 266), Torrey's Weymouth pine has resonances in Lampman's earlier as well as later work: it anticipates the 'priestly pines' whose 'murmur' and 'pensive power' calm and inspire the speaker of 'In the Pine Groves' (1900), a pair of sonnets written in or about August 1892, and it recalls 'the pines / Like tall slim priests of storm' and the 'sad trees ... [that] murmur incoherently' among the 'wind-heaped traceries' of fall in 'In October' (1888) (*P* 267–8, 21). The Lampman-Thomson correspondence confirms that by the summer of 1891 Torrey knew and admired Lampman's poetry and that, through Thomson, the two writers met in Boston later that year (see *AC* 9, 41, 51), and the editor of the correspondence, Helen Lynn, has done a valuable service by noting that among the things that they had in common was a keen 'interest in ornithology' (10). A member of the Audubon Society since 13 June 1887,[13] Lampman evidently regarded Torrey's accounts of birding as one of the most 'charming and helpful' aspects of his books and probably drew inspiration from their emphasis on the 'family operations and moral qualities' of birds (*MI* 265)[14] for such poems as 'To the Warbling Vireo' (1900), 'Nesting Time' (1900), and 'The Robin' (1976), all of which were written in the 1890s. For his part, Torrey probably used his position as an editor of the *Youth's Companion* from 1886 to 1901 to ensure that the magazine provided a steady outlet for Lampman's poems – twenty-six in all between November 1891 and April 1899, including the three ornithological pieces just mentioned.

The fact that 'On the Companionship with Nature' (1900) was written in June 1892 and published in the *Youth's Companion* on December 1 of the same year places the sonnet that Connor and many others have regarded as the 'best sum[mary] of Lampman's attitude to Nature' in its 'soothing, enspiriting, instructing and ennobling' aspects (163) very much in the context of his admiration of Burroughs and Torrey as well as in the broader context of his, and their, indebtedness to Wordsworth, Emerson, and the Romantic tradition in general:

> Let us be much with Nature; not as they
> That labour without seeing, that employ
> Her unloved forces, blindly without joy;
> Nor those whose hands and crude delights obey
> The old brute passion to hunt down and slay;
> But rather as children of one common birth,
> Discerning in each natural fruit of earth
> Kinship and bond with this diviner clay.
> Let us be with her wholly at all hours,
> With the fond lover's zest, who is content
> If his ear hears, and if his eye but sees;
> So shall we grow like her in mould and bent,
> Our bodies stately as her blessèd trees,
> Our thoughts as sweet and sumptuous as her flowers. (*P* 258–9)

It is not beyond the bounds of possibility that a model for Lampman's 'fond lovers' of nature was 'the class of writers' in which, four months earlier, he had placed Thoreau, Burroughs, and, above all, Torrey, a 'poet-naturalist' 'intent upon the everyday life of the woods and fields,' 'an ornithologist of the heart ... who never carries a gun, never kills a bird,' but, rather, 'watches with a happy and affectionate interest [Nature's] multiform activities and intelligences, its little dramas and episodes, and records them in a style full of amusement and sympathy. Like a gentle poet and philosopher as he is, Mr. Torrey ... bring[s] ... perpetual charmed surprise to anyone who is himself a lover of the wild wood and its gentle inhabitants' (*MI* 12–13).

Although Roberts never gave explicit expression to his admiration of Burroughs, his addition of the 'Nature and the Poets' essay in *Pepacton* to the English syllabus at King's College in 1886 bespeaks an intimate knowledge of at least some of the work of the American naturalist during the period between May 1886 and September 1892, when he composed the majority of the 'realistic sonnets' and lyrics that became *Songs of the Common Day* (*CL* 78). (On 31 May 1887 he sent 'The Cow Pasture' to Edmund Clarence Stedman for an opinion, and on 12 March 1891 he told Carman that he had sent the manuscript of the book to Longman [see *CL* 66, 130].) Among the poems from this period that bear the clear imprint of Burroughs are two, 'The Waking Earth' (first published in the *Independent* on 23 May 1889) and 'The Furrow' (first published in the *Century Magazine* in April 1890), which appear among the spring sonnets in *Songs of the Common Day*. With its 'shining haze,' its 'bird-notes thin,' and its ecstatic celebration of returning life and light ('Death is over and done. / The glad earth wakes; the glad light breaks; the days / Grow round, grow radiant. Praise for the new life!' [*CP* 120]), the octave of 'The Waking Earth' echoes several passages in Burroughs, none more clearly than the description of spring in 'Notes by the Way' in *Pepacton*:

> A few days ago, Winter had not perceptibly relaxed his hold; then suddenly he began to soften a little, and a warm haze to creep up from the south ... Next day the sun seemed to have drawn immensely nearer; his beams were full of power; and we said, 'Behold the first spring morning! And, as if to make the prophecy complete, there is the note of a bluebird, and it is not yet nine o'clock'... [N]ow the sky is full of radiant warmth, and the air of a half-articulate murmur and awakening. How still the morning is! (7: 152–3)

A similar debt is evident in the sestet, though this time to a passage in 'April' in *Birds and Poets, with Other Papers*. The 'type' of April in 'our northern climate' is 'the first spear of grass,' enthuses Burroughs:

> The senses – sight, hearing, smell – are as hungry for [April's] delicate and almost spiritual tokens as the cattle are for the first bite of its fields ... [T]he full translucent streams, the waxing and warming sun, – how these things and others like them are noted by the eager eye and ear! ... Then its odors! ... The perfume of the bursting sod, ... of the fresh furrows ... The west wind the other day came fraught with a perfume that was to the sense of smell what a wild and delicate strain of music is to the ear. It was almost trans-cendental ... I imagined it came ... from beyond the horizon, the accumulated breath of innumerable farms and budding forests ... I know well the odors of May and June ... but they are not so ineffable and immaterial and so stimulating to the sense as the incense of April. (6:93–4)[15]

'What potent wizardry the wise earth wields, / To conjure with a perfume!' echoes Roberts:

> From bare fields
> The sense drinks in breath of furrow and sod

And lo, the bound of days and distance yields;
    And featherless the soul is flown abroad,
    Lord of desire and beauty, like a god! (*CP* 120)

It is difficult to believe that Roberts wrote these lines without the passage from Burroughs either in front of him or at the back of his mind.

This is not to suggest that the sonnets of *Songs of the Common Day* are merely verse adaptations of passages from *Pepacton* and *Birds and Poets, with Other Papers*. On the contrary, and as 'The Furrow' can economically illustrate, Roberts's poems augment as well as adapt Burroughs's descriptions and, moreover, stamp them with a very different set of preoccupations and concerns. In 'April,' Burroughs characterizes the month in which he is 'born again into new delight and new surprises' as 'the month of the new furrow' and envisages the 'brightened mould-board' of a 'plow ... upon [a] hill' 'flash[ing] in the sun' as 'line upon line the turf is reversed, until there stands out of the neutral landscape a ruddy square visible for miles, or until the breasts of the broad hills glow like to breasts of ... robins' (6: 93, 105). In 'The Furrow,' Roberts similarly depicts the 'grey monotony' of a 'sombre slope' and 'unverdured lea' being transformed by the 'first slow furrow' of a 'keen [plough] share' (*CP* 130), but there the similarity ends: Roberts's 'slope' is by 'the sea'; at its foot there is a 'salt field' (a salt marsh flooded by tides); and the soil or 'field' that 'rests patient for its joy to be' is a 'glebe' (a piece of land attached to a parish church).[16] There are also 'many a dim wing sweep[ing]' over the sea, 'Some wise crows / Feeding confidently behind the ploughman's feet,' and, in the final lines, a description of the sights and sounds of a spring ploughing that is remarkable for its combination of realistic detail and sexual suggestiveness: 'In the early chill the clods fresh cloven steam, / And down its griding path the keen share goes. / So, from a scar, best flowers the future's sweet' (*CP* 130). Whereas Burroughs negates the sexual aspect of the 'breasts of the broad hills' by likening them to 'the breasts ... of robins,' Roberts uses several words – 'cloven' (split, with a suggestion of woman as 'the cloven sex'), 'griding' (piercing, with a grating sound), 'scar,' and 'sweet' – that metaphorically evoke sexual initiation as the necessary prelude to future pleasure as well as fecundity. 'The Furrow' may have drawn impetus from a Burroughs essay, but it also garners energy from elsewhere to burn like several other sonnets in the *Songs of Common Day* series with a diaphanous combination of local detail and sexual innuendo.[17]

Much the same can be said of 'The Hermit-Thrush' (1893), a poem 'reminiscential' (*CL* 154) of Carman's 'Marjorie Darrow' (more of which in due course) and thus both directly and indirectly influenced by Burroughs. Written in the summer of 1892 (a holograph manuscript at Queen's University is dated 'August 23, 1892') and included in the 'Poems' section of *Songs of the Common Day*, 'The Hermit-Thrush' resembles Carman's poem in being constructed around an italicized chorus based on Burroughs's 'verbal paraphrase' of the 'evening hymn' of the hermit thrush (Westbrook 19) in *Wake-Robin*: '"O spheral, spheral!" [it] seems to say,' writes Burroughs; '"O holy, holy! O clear away, clear away! O clear up, clear up!"' (1:60). In Roberts's rendition, this becomes:

> Oh, clear in the sphere of the air,
>    Clear, clear, tender and far,
> Our aspiration of prayer
>    Unto eve's clear star! (*CP* 143–4)[18]

For Burroughs, the 'pure and serene' 'contralto' of the hermit thrush is more suggestive than any other 'sound in nature' of 'religious beatitude' (1: 47). But for Roberts the 'divine ... psalm' that emanates at 'sunset' from the 'call' of the 'cloistral ecstatic ... In the cool green aisles of the leaves' (*CP* 143) prefigures heavenly happiness of a very different kind: singing at nightfall '*unto eve's clear star*' – that is, Venus – the hermit thrush voices '*our aspiration of prayer*' for sexual fulfilment from a 'cell' that is also a 'shrine of a power' – the power of erotic love – 'by whose spell / Who so hears aspires and believes!':

> O hermit of evening! thine hour
>    Is the sacrament of desire,
> When love hath a heavenlier flower,
>    And passion a holier fire! (*CP* 143)

Technically, rhetorically, and thematically reminiscent of Dante Gabriel Rossetti's use of an antiphonal chorus and Christian terminology in the service of erotic love in 'Troy Town' and 'Eden Bower,' 'The Hermit-Thrush' was written when Roberts was sexually involved with Maud Clark ('the Queen of Bohemia') and the as of yet unidentified Mrs Robertson (see *CL* 152). Both in form and substance, it uses Burroughs merely as a point of departure for the journey into the realm of sanctified erotic love that he would more fully chart in *A Sister for Evangeline*:

*Being the Story of Yvonne de Lamourie* (1898), *New York Nocturnes and Other Poems* (1898), and *The Book of the Rose* (1903).

On the evidence of Roberts's poems of the late 1880s and early 1890s, it is apparent that, however much his 'interpretation of nature'[19] differed from Burroughs's, he heeded the naturalist's call in 'Nature and the Poets' and 'Notes by the Way' for poets to attend to 'the accuracy of the details of their pictures' of Nature, to be 'accurate when they particularize,' to stick 'close ... to fact,' and, in short, to know their natural history (7: 79, 86, 167). Not only the 'realistic sonnets' and poems of *Songs of the Common Day* or, indeed, *The Book of the Native* (1896), but also the animal stories in both *Earth's Enigmas: A Book of Animal and Nature Life* (1896) and *The Kindred of the Wild: A Book of Animal Life* (1902) attest to the extent to which Roberts answered Burroughs's call to (North) American writers to give scrupulously accurate expression to their distinctive environment(s). It is especially ironical, then, that the one brush with Burroughs for which the Confederation group remains known is the 'Nature Fakir' controversy that was ignited by his article entitled 'Real and Sham Natural History' in the March 1903 issue of *Atlantic Monthly* and briefly singed Roberts four years later when 'On the Night Trail' in *The Haunters of the Silences: A Book of Animal Life* (1907) was criticized by President Theodore Roosevelt as a 'fairy tale' 'so utterly ridiculous' in its depiction of 'the wolf and the lynx' that anyone familiar with them 'loses patience' (quoted in Edward B. Clark 774). In defending himself against Roosevelt's charge, Roberts argued that there were 'two separate and distinct schools of nature students' in the United States, those believing with Burroughs and the President that 'the action of animals is governed purely by instinct' and those like himself and Jack London (1876–1916) who 'believe that animals are activated by something distinctly akin to reason' (quoted in Pomeroy 179). 'I do not say that I have not made mistakes,' he concluded; 'I have made several, but neither John Burroughs nor the President has so far detected them and I am not going to reveal them myself.' Differ though he did in many ways from Burroughs, Roberts was also in one crucial respect – fidelity to Nature – his disciple.

But of all the members of the Confederation group the one who probably felt Burroughs's influence most profoundly and enduringly was Carman. Certainly, there can be no doubt of Carman's admiration and appetite for the American naturalist's works. Reviewing the Scottish pocket edition of *Winter Sunshine* in the May 1885 issue of the *University Monthly* (Fredericton), he reveals that he has also read *Wake-Robin* and

*Fresh Fields*, expresses admiration for Burroughs's 'keen-eyed,' 'healthy and exact' observations on the differences between English and American national character, and lavishes special praise on his style, proclaiming 'Autumn Tides,' 'The Apple,' and 'The Exhilaration of the Road' 'exquisite prose idylls' that possess a 'literary' merit absent from Thoreau's *Walden* (123). Almost thirty years later, in a letter of 25 January 1914, he would evoke Burroughs's famed dedication to accuracy in naturalistic observation to reprove the American poet William Griffith (1876–1936) for a confusion in the second stanza of his 'Canticle': 'do you mean [that the characters in the poem] are praying for the spring to stay until autumn? Or am I to gather that the partridge drums in Spring? I am sure that he would love to drum for you at any season, but I doubt if John Burroughs would allow him to. How about it?' (*L* 206).[20] In the years prior to the First World War, Burroughs was at least as strong an influence on Carman as Thoreau and almost as formative an influence on him (as on Burroughs himself) as Emerson.

By a coincidence that would not have escaped Carman's notice, he was born in the same renovative and portentous spring month as Burroughs. 'April is my natal month, and I am born again into new delight and new surprises at each return of it,' enthuses the American naturalist in 'April.' 'Its name has an indescribable charm to me. Its two syllables are like the calls of the first birds, – like that of the phoebe-bird, or of the meadowlark. Its very snows are fertilizing ...' (6:94). Carman also felt a special affinity with his 'natal month,' which, as he repeatedly states in the essays collected in *The Kinship of Nature* (1904), brings 'the renewal of the ancient rapture of earth,' 'the old Aprilian triumph' (95, 64). In 'The Vernal Ides' in the same collection, he borrows a phrase from Emerson[21] but takes a leaf from Burroughs in affirming the formative influence of 'the vernal ides' on 'the northern imagination': 'long inheritance of April happiness has given us that peculiar malady we call spring fever; has given us, too, a special spiritual sympathy or wonder in the reviving year. This truly religious sense has made itself widely felt in the racial expression, in the arts of poetry and painting,' of northern peoples (66). Perhaps taking his cue from Burroughs's essay on 'Spring Poems' in *Birds and Poets, with Other Papers* but focusing specifically on English responses to April, Carman refers admiringly to the opening lines of the *Canterbury Tales* and quotes Robert Browning's 'Home Thoughts from Abroad' and Rudyard Kipling's 'In Springtime' as examples of what Burroughs calls 'spring songs' or 'vernal poems' (6: 109, 112). But for his characteristic modesty, Carman might have mentioned or quoted his own 'Spring Song' in *Songs from Vagabondia* (1894), a poem whose rollicking stanzas contain many touches reminiscent of Burroughs, not least its catalogue of migrant birds 'Making northward with the spring' and its celebration of the 'Shrilling pipe or fluting whistle' of the 'frog and tree-toad' (10–11). Such touches can be found in most of Carman's later spring poems, from the 'frogs in silver chorus' and the 'first robin at his vespers / Calling far, serene and clear' in 'April Weather' (1898) (*PP* 17–18) to the 'high pealing strain' of the 'rainbird' and the 'trilling note / Of the tree frog' in *April Airs: A Book of New England Lyrics* (1916) (12, 15). Little wonder that in *Our Friend John Burroughs*, Clara Barrus summarizes Burroughs's emotive attitude to April in the (in)famous chorus of 'Spring Song': 'Make me over, mother April, / When the sap begins to stir!' (Barrus 1: 256; *Songs from Vagabondia* 10–13).

In both 'April' and, more interestingly, in 'Spring Poems,' Burroughs makes the point that spring is not solely a time of rapturous awakening: '... they are not all jubilant chords that this season awakens. Occasionally there is an undertone of vague longing and sadness, akin to that which one experiences in autumn. Hope for a moment assumes the attitude of memory and stands with reverted look. The haze ... awakens pensive thoughts' (6:108). The bitter-sweet mood that Burroughs here attributes to April can be found greatly amplified in another of the essays in *The Kinship of Nature*, a meditation on 'Easter Eve' in which Carman presents the Christian celebration of 'the immortal fancy of an imperishable life' both as a 'great spring festival' of 'renewal' (93–9), and as a time of tension between jubilation and sadness:

> ... what memories return with the April winds! The breath of approaching life sifts through the trees and grasses, the sound of running water stirs in the wild places, the birds make songs as they fly, there is everywhere the renewal of the ancient rapture of earth; yet in the twilight one remembers all those glad experiences which are to be repeated no more, and the faces of unreturning companions. So ... if Easter is the gladdest of days, the eve of Easter is the saddest. (95–6) [22]

As indebted as these sentiments seem to be to Burroughs's observation that April's sights, sounds, and scents are 'delicate and almost spiritual tokens' that have the power to 'make ... [one] both glad and sad' (6: 93), they go further than Burroughs ever did[23] in recognizing the 'spiritual' and, indeed, religious aspects of spring by relating the season's natural and emotional characteristics not only to the Christian festival of death and resurrection, but also to the 'lovely and encouraging natural religion' of ancient Greece that finds intimations of immortality in 'the returning forces of the grain and the sun and the vital air' (94–9). Carman's appreciation and understanding of the characteristics and effects of April were doubtless enriched by Burroughs, but his conception of 'the old Aprilian triumph' as a comforting reminder of the certitudes of 'fine and ancient' 'natural religion' in 'Easter Eve,' 'The Vernal Ides,' and other works written around the turn of the century such as 'Saint Valentine' (1904), 'The March Hare's Madness' (1904), and, as argued elsewhere, *Sappho: One Hundred Lyrics* (1903)[24] derives from other sources, most notably Karl Otfried Müller's discussion of the emergence of the Eleusinian and Orphic mysteries from myths connected with the seasonal 'disappearance and reappearance of vegetable life' in his *History of the Literature of Ancient Greece* (trans. 1858).[25]

A further aspect of Burroughs's work that seems to have appealed to Carman is his conviction that, while April is the month of renewal and inspiration, it is not necessarily a month conducive to artistic creativity. 'In the spring, one vegetates; his thoughts turn to sap; another activity seizes him,' Burroughs suggests in 'Autumn Tides'; 'for my part, I find all literary work irksome from April to August; my sympathies run in other channels ... As fall approaches, the currents mount to the head again. But my thoughts do not ripen well till after there has been a frost ... A man's thinking, I take it ... wants plenty of oxygen in the air' (2:103). In 'Touches of Nature' in *Birds and Poets, with Other Papers*, he puts the matter more succinctly: '... when the sap begins to mount in the trees, and the spring languour comes, does not one grow restless indoors? ... [T]he spring ... makes one's intellectual light grow dim. Why should not a man sympathise with the seasons and the moods and the phases of nature? ... [W]hat his great mother feels affects him also' (6:56). As the striking similarity between this and the chorus of 'Spring Song' attests, Carman fully agreed; indeed, his petition for animal vitality and the 'indolence' to enjoy it at the close of 'Spring Song' also echoes Burroughs (see *Songs from Vagabondia* 13), as do his musings in 'The Vernal Ides' on whether spring is 'truly a time favourable to artistic creation':

> If there are seasons of the mind, its April should be a month of starting and growth, of extended horizons, renewed vigour, fresh inspirations. But the month of fruitage is September or October, and the achievements of art

are ripened to perfection in the Indian Summer of the soul. It is not under the immediate stress of a great emotion that a great work is produced; most often it is the result of ... a long, silent cogitation, when the mind sits in autumnal luxury thinking of itself. (67–8)

More obviously for Carman than for Burroughs, the relationship between artistic creativity and the seasonal cycle is an environmentally inflected variation of Wordsworth's belief that poetry is the product, not of 'powerful feelings' per se, but of 'emotion recollected in tranquility.'[26] In 'The Vernal Ides,' as in 'Easter Eve,' Burroughs's thinking on April is the stem upon which Carman grafted ideas from other sources, the result being a discursive hybrid of American and English elements that many commentators on Canada's cultural identity would consider typically if not quintessentially Canadian.

It is a measure of the impact on Carman of Burroughs's complex and suggestive conception of April that it provided a large component of his 'most ambitious work' of the 1880s (Gundy 25), the pastoral elegy on the death of Matthew Arnold on 15 April 1888 that he entitled 'Corydon' and intended to publish in 'a limited edition of seventy-five copies ... at [his] own expense' (*L* 26). According to available evidence, the elegy was to be divided into three parts, 'Death in April,' 'Midsummer Land,' and 'Autumn Guard,' 'each preceded and followed by a lyric interlude'[27] and each provided with an epigraph from another pastoral elegy.[28] Probably because the third part of 'Corydon,' the enigmatically titled 'Autumn Guard,' was never finished (see *L* 26, 28, 32), the scheme never came to fruition;[29] however, the first part, 'Death in April,' was published in the April 1889 number of *Atlantic Monthly*, the second, as 'Corydon: An Elegy' in the March 1890 number of the *Universal Review* (London), and three of its lyric interludes entitled 'Stir,' 'Ad Vesperum,' and 'E Tenebris' survive, the first in the 25 January 1889 issue of the *Critic* (Halifax) and the other two after 'April in the Hills' in the portion of the projected book that Carman had privately printed in Fredericton in 1888.

On the basis of the existing portions of 'Corydon' there is no doubt that Burroughs lies centrally in its background. Cast in a stanza form appropriately reminiscent of Arnold's 'Thyrsis' and structured by the three components of the traditional pastoral elegy – loss ('Death in April'), mourning ('Corydon: An Elegy'), and consolation (intimated in the final stanza of 'Corydon: An Elegy')[30] – it relies heavily on Burroughs's conception of April as a pivotal month in northern climates and for northern peoples, figuring 'Mother England' in the aftermath of

Arnold's death as a 'Northland wan' in the process of being 'freshen[ed] once more' by 'Midspring,' and April herself as a sad 'child of remembrance [and] mother of regret' who is nevertheless the glad parent:

> ... of all dappled hours,
>   Restorer of lost days, for whom we long;
> Bringer of seed time, of all the flowers and birds;
>   Sower of plenty, of the buds and showers;
> Exalter of dumb hearts to brink of song;
>   Revealer of blind Winter's runic words! ('Death in April' 458, 461)

Several passages in both 'Death in April' and 'Corydon: An Elegy' permit the inference that the consolation that Carman intended to provide in the third part of the poem involved a combination of Burroughs and 'natural religion' in which April's ability 'evermore [to] redeem / The world from bitter death' ('Death in April' 460) would have been assimilated to a syncretic mixture of Christian and 'ancient' ideas of immortality: in one stanza near the end of 'Corydon: An Elegy,' 'Death holds a smile most like foreknowledge of life' that 'victors' must 'Await ... since God wrought / Strength out of calm and reverence out of joy'; and, in another, a 'gold-mouthed veery [thrush] answering / His brother pilgrim' is described as the 'Chrysostom of silence and repose' and enlisted as 'as essoiner ... unto Death' on behalf of those who, like 'Orpheus ... Corydon,' and the bird itself 'go as the wind wandereth' (435, 436).[31] Perhaps it was Burroughs's comment in *Wake-Robin* on the 'sweetness and wildness' of its 'soft, mellow' song 'when heard in the warm twilight of a June day in our deep northern forests' (1: 25, 141) that recommended the veery to Carman as a messenger of the living in the court of Death.

Nor is this at all far-fetched, for not only is 'Corydon: An Elegy' set in 'High June ... with sun / As only this far North can know' (425), but the poem's three extant interludes are also indebted specifically to Burroughs's writings on birds and birdsong. In 'Stir,' which was to be 'the introductory lyric of the first part,' the sound of birds 'In Northward flight' is a sign of the arrival of 'golden April' when 'The sap goes upward with morning / And death is a dream' (*Critic* [Halifax], 25 January 1889, 3); and in both 'Ad Vesperum' and 'E Tenebris,' which were perhaps intended to follow 'Death in April' and precede 'Midsummer Land,' the song of a thrush at twilight is conceived as a 'cool rush' that will 'rebrim / The world' with 'calm,' and at dawn as a 'wild wood charm' that heralds the 'sheer / Blue morning.'[32] Although the reference to the 'gold-mouthed veery' in 'Corydon: An Elegy' suggests that Carman had that species of thrush in mind as the source of the song in 'Ad Vesperum' and 'E Tenebris,' the association of the song with a peace born of eschatological hope assimilates the two interludes to Burroughs's hugely influential conception of the hermit thrush's song as 'the voice of ... calm, sweet serenity' and the 'deep, solemn joy that only the finest souls may know' (1:47). It may even be that the idea of using thrush song as a leitmotif in 'Corydon' came from 'When Lilacs Last in the Dooryard Bloom'd' (1865–6) by way of Burroughs's observation in *Birds and Poets, with Other Papers* that Whitman's 'threnody is blent of three chords, the blossoming lilac, the evening star, and the hermit thrush, the latter playing the most part throughout the composition' (6: 37).[33] Burroughs could be describing the elegies of both Whitman and Carman when he writes that 'it is the exalting and spiritual utterance of the "solitary singer" that calms the poet' in the face of death.

The poem in which Carman most successfully combines Burroughsian elements with 'natural religion' is 'Resurgam,' written on 15 April 1908 (Sorfleet 167) and first published in *The Rough Rider and Other Poems* (1909). Echoing 'Easter Eve,' 'Resurgam' begins by folding the Christian festival of death and resurrection into the spring process of renewal and rebirth, first by juxtaposing the two events and then by attaching religious associations to natural phenomena: 'Lo, now comes the April pageant / And the Easter of the year. / Now the tulip lifts her chalice, / And the hyacinth his spear ... Child of immortal vision / What hast thou to do with fear?' (*PBC* 220–1). There then follows a Burroughsian catalogue of spring sights, sounds, and scents – 'the migrant wings com[ing] northward,' the 'full brimming river margins,' the smoke of 'brush fires' – whose effect on humans ranges from the merely physical ('the blood beats in the vein') to the intuitively spiritual:

Through the faint green mist of springtime,
Dreaming glad-eyed lovers go,
Touched with such immortal madness
Not a thing they care to know
More than those who caught life's secret
Countless centuries ago. (*PBC* 222)

Like the 'Dreaming glad-eyed lovers' of this stanza, the 'priests and holy women' who celebrate Christ's 'death and resurrection' 'With ...

incense, chant and prayer' later in the poem are for Carman a 'new fulfilment' of the same Aprilian intimations of immortality that inspired
ancient Egyptian worshippers of Osiris to 'Put ... on ... green attire ... to
greet the fire / Of the vernal sun' and inspired the ancient Greek adepts
of Adonis to sing

> Linus songs of joy and sorrow
> For the coming back of spring, –
> Sorrow for the wintry death
> Of each irrevocable thing,
> Joy for all the pangs of beauty
> The returning year could bring.

'[C]ould bring': in 'Resurgam,' as in 'Easter Eve,' Carman tempers affirmation with uncertainty, urging his readers to direct the energy of the
'spring renascence' to humanitarian and spiritual ends ('Take thy part
in the redemption / Of thy kind from bonds of earth ... Share the life ...
eternal' of the great artists and mystics who made themselves 'Lords of
time' [223]), and he concludes the poem, like the essay, with a question:

> Still remains the peradventure,
> Soul pursues an orbit here
> Like those unreturning comets
> Sweeping on a vast career,
> By an infinite directrix
> Focussed to a finite sphere, –
> Nurtured in an earthly April,
> In what realm to appear? (224)

A similar combination of credulity and uncertainty characterizes the
lame conclusion that Carman attached to the poem entitled 'Easter Eve'
(1916) when he published it in *Later Poems* (1921):[34] 'I share the life eternal with the April buds and the evening star. / The slim new moon is my
sister now, the rain, my brother; the wind my friend. / Is it not well with
these forever? Can the soul of man fare ill in the end?' (*Poems* 226). Since
the parallel between 'the old Aprilian triumph' in northern climates and
the persistence of the human soul after death is at best tenuous, Carman's later involvement with Spiritualism and Theosophy[35] was perhaps
the inevitable outcome of the connection between Burroughsian deter-

minism and natural religion that he first attempted to forge in the late 1880s. In any case, Carman's spiritualized April is the most elaborate product of the influence of Burroughs on the Confederation group.

Although the two Scotts were largely exempt from that influence, there are some indications that directly or indirectly they, too, felt the impact of Burroughs's nature writings. Predisposed by his faith and profession to look through Nature to 'Nature's God' (39), Frederick George Scott nevertheless treats birdsong on occasion as a source of human significance and restorative power ('The Poets of the Woods' [1934]), and in one instance ('In the Winter Woods' [1906]) goes so far as to express a sense of kinship with the 'Grim old trees' of a windswept forest:

> Something in my inmost thinking
> Tells me I am one with you
> For a subtle bond is linking
> Nature's offspring through and through,
> And your spirit like a flood
> Stirs the pulses of my blood. (*CPFGS* 6)

Much more attributable to Burroughs's influence than this or any other passage in Frederick George Scott's poems are portions of the numerous treatments of seasonal phenomena and birdsong that are scattered throughout the work of Duncan Campbell Scott. Three of the poems anthologized in *Later Canadian Poets* and reprinted in *The Magic House and Other Poems* – 'The End of the Day,' 'The Fifteenth of April,' and 'September' – bear the unmistakable imprint of Burroughs, the first in its characterization of the 'hermit thrush' as a 'timorous eremite,' the second in its catalogue of the sights and 'sounds' of April, and the third in its parallel catalogue of the sights and sounds of September (*PDCS* 238, 282–3, 85). Much the same can be said of several other poems in both *The Magic House* and *Labor and the Angel* (most notably in the latter's 'March,' 'In May,' and 'Rain and the Robin'), and Burroughs remains a discernible influence in Scott's seasonal and ornithological poems for several years after the turn of the century.

Even in his early work, however, Scott, like the other members of the Confederation group, combined material drawn from Burroughs with distinctly un-Burroughsian elements to produce poems marked by individuality as well as indebtedness. Reflecting an interest in the relationship between seasonal and astronomical phenomena that may have originated with James Thomson's *The Seasons*, Scott frequently intersperses naturalistic observations with references to stars and planets; for example, 'the vesper sparrow' sings 'under Venus' in 'The Fifteenth of April,' 'Orion lies outrolled' as the 'slopes ... slowly grow ... gold' in 'September,' and in 'March' a 'driver' returning from a sugarbush sees 'the sinking Pleiads bend and blow' like 'a silver ship' surmounted by the 'rosy banner' of 'frail aurora' (*PDCS* 282, 85, 138). While these and similar examples show Scott supplementing Burroughs with astronomy, others show him departing from the American naturalist in his interpretations and renditions of birds and their songs. One case in point is Scott's reading of the hermit thrush's song in 'The End of the Day,' not as a suggestion of 'serene religious beatitude ... [that] seems to say "O holy, holy! O clear away ..."' (1:47), but as an expression of

> ... risen tears and pain,
> As if the one he loved was far away:
> 'Alas! another day – '
> 'And now Good Night, Good Night,'
> 'Good Night.' (*PDCS* 238)

Another is his interpretation of the wood peewee in the poem of that title in *New World Lyrics and Ballads* (1905), where, taking as his point of departure Burroughs's comment that the 'common or wood peewee excites the most pleasant emotions, both on account of its ... exquisite mossy nest' and its 'plaintive,' 'pensive, and almost pathetic note' (1: 210, 49; and see 1:50 and 6:28–31), he offers his own fanciful reading of the song of the bird that 'builds his nest in the greening trees' in 'Springtime' as a 'pensive note' full of grief and longing that nevertheless emanates from a 'heart ... filled' with 'joyance ... / And not with brooding sadness':

> If he might utter as he willed
>   His strain would mount in gladness;
> It meaneth joy in simple trust,
>   Though pensively it rings;
>
> Not as he would but as he must
>   He sings. (*PDCS* 139)

At least as much as any other member of the Confederation group,

Scott would evidently have agreed with Burroughs that 'the bird [is] the original type and teacher of the poet' (6:2).

One of the most Burroughsian poems by a member of the Confederation group, Carman's 'Marjorie Darrow' was also one of the most controversial Canadian poems of the 1890s. First published in the *Independent* on 1 September 1892, it consists of nine four-line stanzas narrating the unhappy love affair of the young woman of its title[36] and nine six-line choruses, each of which is a variation of Burroughs's rendition of the song of the hermit thrush as '"O spheral, spheral! ... O holy, holy! O clear away, clear away! O clear up, clear up!"' (1: 47). Thus, when Marjorie Darrow is introduced as a woman of 'twenty year / With the perfect cheek of cream and tan' (1), the 'thrushes' song' is rendered as '*Clear, clear. / Dawn in the dew! / Reap, reap! / Gold in the dawn. / Clear ...,*' and when she is as yet unaffected by love, as '*Sphere, sphere, / Sphere of the dawn, / Sphere of the dawn in the dew, / Leap, leap! / Fold in the dew, sphere, / Spheral, sphere!*' Such variations continue as the poem's unfortunate protagonist moves through the stages of passion ('Marjorie Darrow's heart was hot'), fulfilment ('Marjorie Darrow's arms were lithe'), and abandonment ('Marjorie Darrow's eyes were wet') towards the death implied by the final stanzas and choruses:

Marjorie Darrow loved too well
  But if death walked in the garden there
The blood-red poppies held their peace,
  Nodding as if unaware.

  *Fear, Fear,*
  *Under the dawn!*
  *Under the cold of the dew;*
  *Sleep, Sleep!*
  *Far in the dawn*
  *Fear no fear!*

Then sleep crept into the bones of the wind,
  With always his one more field to roam;
And like a hunter out of the hills
  The scarlet sun went home.

*Sheer, sheer;*
*Sheer in the blue*
*Far in the sweep of the blue,*
*Deep, deep!*
*Gone, thou art gone,*
*Dear ...*

Almost as evident as the presence of Burroughs in 'Marjorie Darrow' are the presences of Whitman and the Pre-Raphaelites, Whitman in echoes not only of 'When Lilacs Last in the Dooryard Bloom'd,' but also of the tale and song of the bereaved mockingbird in 'Out of the Cradle Endlessly Rocking' (a 'treatment of the bird' that Burroughs considered 'quite unmatched in [American] literature' and quoted at length in *Wake-Robin* [9–12]), and the Pre-Raphaelites in the emblematic use of 'blood-red poppies' in the first of the two stanzas quoted above, in the allusion earlier in the poem to an unhappy love story of the distant past ('There lurked the story, proud and sad, / That braced the battle gear of war / When the young world was sad'), and in the deployment after each narrative stanza of a repetitive but varied chorus (see, for example, Rossetti's 'Troy Town' and Morris's 'The Wind'). Once again, Carman's ability to combine elements from British and American sources is striking if not culturally typical.

Some two weeks after the appearance of 'Marjorie Darrow' in the *Independent,* the September 16 issue of the *Week* contained an editorial paragraph on the poem that began by expressing pride in the recent success of 'young Canadian bards' in placing their work in 'leading American journal[s] or magazine[s]' but then proceeded to confess failure after numerous attempts to wrestle 'some clear conception of the meaning' of 'some fugitive poem or sonnet' and to quote two stanzas of Carman's poem under the question *'What do the italicised words and phrases mean?'* (660). A second editorial paragraph followed in the September 30 issue of the *Week,* accompanied by a full text of the poem and a letter signed 'E.' that parodies the poem's choruses and characterizes them as 'Rot, sweet rot!' (699). In the intervening and following days, the controversy spread to the daily newspapers and prompted numerous interventions, most notably in 'At the Mermaid Inn' columns by Duncan Campbell Scott (September 24) and Lampman (October 1), a lengthy article on 'Onomatopoeia and Mr. Bliss Carman' by J.A.T. Lloyd (*Week,* October 7), a brief response to Lloyd's article by 'W.' (G.W. Wicksteed)[37] (*Week,* October 21), a further editorial paragraph in the *Week* containing a defence of the poem against the charge of obscurity from 'an admirer and personal friend of Mr. Carman' (October 14), and, finally, a letter from 'Pastor Felix' (Arthur John Lockhart) disclosing his identity as the author of that defence and quoting a letter from Carman himself on various aspects of the poem, including the function of the choruses as a 'suggestive ... sort of accompaniment' to the narrative and the relationship between Marjorie Darrow and her lover: 'the tragedy of [her] life was not [his] death ... but the death of his love for her ... She yielded [to him] *because* [her arms] were lithe and the pulse of the ancient race of the earth was too strong in her to be restrained. Marjory did no sin. She was deceived – the old sad story' (793).

Now the controversy surrounding 'Marjorie Darrow' is revelatory in two important respects. First, it shows the decided preference of what 'E.' calls 'ordinary readers' in Canada for easily intelligible poetry that exhibits 'at least a surface of common sense.' 'The story [of "Marjorie Darrow"] is obscure, in as much as the general reader is obliged to study it out,' commented the *Week* in its second editorial; 'worse still, we doubt if the average reader, unaided, can be sure, even after careful study, that he understands it just as the poet meant it. This is the radical defect in much of [Robert] Browning's poetry' (30 September 1892, 159–60). '[W]hat are we to say of this spirit of conscious, I had almost said *cunning*, vagueness which we see so much of in modern versification?' asks Lloyd after again invoking Browning as a prime offender and before alluding to Arnold in defence of the preferences of the '"anonymous multitude"': 'have we no right to protest against this, to ask, if not for "sweetness," at any rate for "light"?' As revelatory of the likes and dislikes of the 'ordinary,' 'general,' or 'average' Canadian reader as these remarks is the *Week*'s tactful selection in its third editorial of Carman's recently published and plainly allegorical 'The Night Express' (1895)[38] as a more acceptable poem than 'Marjorie Darrow' for the twofold reason that it is 'in a large measure free from the fault of obscurity' and that it is 'one of the most graphic bits of objective verse we have seen for some time' (14 October 1892, 724). Evidently, the cognitive and aesthetic preference of the majority of Canadian readers in the early 1890s was for poems of a descriptive and realistic cast whose meaning is relatively accessible and enlightening. This conservative predilection for poetry in the high Romantic-Victorian tradition over poetry in the emerging *symboliste*-Modernist line does much to explain not only the relative unpopularity of Carman's poetry in Canada during the 1890s, but also the quick acceptance of Lampman's less obscure, more realistic poetry by contemporary Canadian readers and the otherwise surprising failure of any Canadian newspaper or periodical to reprint Duncan

Campbell Scott's *symboliste* tour de force, 'The Piper of Arll,' from *Truth* (New York), where it appeared on 14 December 1895. That Roberts was in the process of meeting the demand of Canadian readers for realistic and accessible poetry at the time of the 'Marjorie Darrow' controversy needs no additional emphasis here (see chapters 2 and 3), but the point can be made that his comments to Carman about 'Marjorie Darrow' and 'The Night Express' in letters of September 26 and November 7 reflect both his hard-won aesthetic shrewdness and his constructive concern for his cousin's literary advancement:

> As for 'Marjorie Darrow,' it's *damn fine*, – but don't do it again! It is the sort of thing that, done once supremely well, as you have done ..., is *enchanting*. But more in a similar line would seem like mannerism, and weaken the effect of this. I wonder if I make my feeling clear in the matter![39]

> I tell you ... 'The Night Express' is a *hit!* It gets hold of all sorts and conditions of men. [James] De Mille read it at the Haliburton [Society] the other night, with great effect. It is quite the best thing our language has produced on the steam-engine! And the *next* best thing is also by a Canadian – Lampman's 'At the Railway Station.' (*CL* 154, 158)[40]

The second respect in which the 'Marjorie Darrow' controversy is revelatory is as a reflection of the state of the Confederation group and its supporters in the fall of 1892 – that is, at the time when public perception of them as a group was nearing its zenith. Most revealing in this regard is the speed with which first Duncan Campbell Scott and then Lampman came to Carman's defence in 'At the Mermaid Inn,' using the column less to justify the poem *per se* than to celebrate the achievements of its author as a triumph over the impediments faced by Canadian writers: 'our country furnishes for ... literary m[e]n absolutely no chance of living by [their] art,' but it should at least extend to them the honour of 'criticism [that is] genial but not flattering, just but not envious' (Scott); 'in this country,' 'few ... care' to 'interest themselves in young contemporary writers,' and 'still fewer ... have any notion of ... [Carman's] immense promise [and] immense accomplishment ... because he is confronted by the same obstacle that stands in the way of every new writer of obstinate originality – the impenetrable stupidity, th[e] invariable short sightedness of publishers' (Lampman) (*MI* 154, 159). Admitting that he has read only the two stanzas of 'Marjorie Darrow' that were published in the September 16 issue of the *Week* and calling upon the paper to publish the poem in its entirety, Scott nevertheless opines that it 'must contain some story, lyrically hinted at, after Mr. Carman's manner' and asserts that, since 'poetry is an art by which impressions are conveyed as well as ideas,' its choruses must be judged on the basis of their success or lack of success in 'convey[ing] an impression of the [thrushes'] song' (155). Counting himself among 'those few personal friends of Mr. Carman ... who have been especially favoured with an opportunity to judge his work,' Lampman pronounces him a Romantic genius whose poetry is imbued with the spirit of Canada:

> With great imaginative power and a most uncommon gift of musical versification, he has discovered and taken up a quite new poetic standpoint. His poems are suffused with a new and peculiar and most beautiful imaginative spirit, a spirit which is that of our own northern land, developed in the atmosphere of the Norse,[41] with tinges of Indian legend. Many people will complain of his obscurity, and he is often – very often – obscure, because he does not aim at conveying clearly-cut images and ideas, but prefers, in obedience to a powerful impulse of his own mind, to steep his reader's imagination in splendid moods through the agency of magnificent metrical effects and a vast and mysterious imagery. Whether obscure or not, for the true lover of poetry there is one presence that covers a multitude of faults – the presence of beauty ..., and Mr. Carman's work is exquisitely beautiful. (159–60)

Somewhat concealed by the gesture towards universality and abstraction with which this passage concludes is its generative assumption that a Canadian poet of Carman's 'power' and skill is a medium through which the spirit of Canada is made manifest to receptive readers in a content and form whose qualities – newness, vastness, mysteriousness, and, indeed, obscurity – are those of the northland(s) from which it emanates. As Lampman put it in 'Two Canadian Poets: A Lecture,' 'we know that climatic and scenic conditions have much to do with the moulding of national character' and, hence, literature.

The third and final way in which the 'Marjorie Darrow' controversy is revealing returns the discussion to Burroughs but now in the context of Canadian readers' responses to the poem's indebtedness to various writers and works. Two things are remarkable about these: (1) their infrequency: neither Scott nor Lampman treats the poem as other than entirely original; Lockhart merely states that 'Burroughs uses the phrase "O spheral, sphere" to express the liquid bell of the hermit thrush' (*Week*, 14 October 1892, 724); and only Wicksteed offers 'the first lines of the pretty nursery song ["See-saw, Margery Daw ..."]' as the possible 'prototype' of the poem (*Week,* 21 October 1892, 747);[42] and (2) their geniality: none of the commentators apparently perceived the poem's indebtednesses as a fault. The conclusion to be drawn from these responses can only be that in the fall of 1892 the few readers who cared to comment publicly on Canadian poetry accepted both the need for 'criticism [that is] genial not flattering' and the nature of Canadian poems as the products of an 'imaginative power' whose compositional procedure involved a high degree of borrowing and adaptation. Nearly seventy years later, in his Introduction to *The Oxford Book of Canadian Verse* (1960), A.J.M. Smith would coin the term 'eclectic detachment' to describe the 'one advantage' of the Canadian poet's 'separateness and semi-isolation from modernity':

> He can draw upon French, British, and American sources in language and literary convention; at the same time he enjoys a measure of detachment that enables him to select and adapt what is relevant and useful. This gives to contemporary Canadian poetry in either language a distinctive quality – its eclectic detachment. This can be, and has been, a defect of timidity and mediocrity; but it can also be ... a virtue of intelligence and discrimination. (li)

In the fall of 1892, Carman's Canadian readers and fellow Confederation poets were inclined by their conviction that a distinctive and accomplished Canadian literature was desirable and imminent to give him full credit for originality, but one voice – Campbell's – was conspicuous by its absence from the genial chorus, and when it was heard its charge was not 'timidity' or 'mediocrity' but plagiarism.

# CHAPTER FIVE

# Therapeutic Nature

In 1881, four years after he had been commissioned to design a public park for Mount Royal in Montreal, the American landscape architect Frederick Law Olmsted (1822–1903), who was then as now most famous for his role in the creation of Central Park in New York City, published a monograph in which he laid out the principles underlying his proposal for Mount Royal. 'Beside and above' the 'inducement which the enjoyment of it presents to change of mental occupation, exercise, and air-taking,' runs a key passage in *Mount Royal, Montreal* (1881),

> charming natural scenery ... acts in a more directly remedial way to enable men to better resist the harmful influences of ordinary town life, and recover what they lose from them. It is thus, in medical phrase, a prophylactic and therapeutic agent of vital value; there is not one in the apothecaries' shops as important to the health and strength or to the earning and tax-paying capacities of a large city. And to the mass of the people it is practically available only through such means as are provided by parks. (22)

'We can apply the term [charm] ... to scenery,' Olmsted continues,

> because of a common experience that certain scenery has a tendency to lift us out of our habitual condition into one which, were the influence upon us stronger and the moods and frames of mind toward which it carried us more distinctly defined, we should recognize as poetic. Let us say that for the time being the charm of natural scenery tends to make us poets. There is a sensibility to poetic inspiration in every man of us, and its utter suppression means a sadly morbid condition. Poets, we may not be, but a little lifted out of our ordinary prose we may be often to our advantage. (22)

The conception of 'natural scenery' as a 'therapeutic agent' that is so confidently articulated in these and other passages in *Mount Royal, Montreal* was not original to Olmsted, though he was one of its most renowned avatars: as Gail Thain Parker, Donald Meyer, T.J. Jackson Lears, and other cultural historians have compellingly demonstrated and thoroughly documented,[1] American culture in the decades following the trauma of the Civil War (1861–5) was increasingly infatuated with mind-cure theories of the sort advanced by Olmsted – so much so, in fact, that Lears writes of the period between 1880 and 1920 as characterized by a 'therapeutic world view' (xvi). It is scarcely surprising, then, that almost from the outset Nature was conceived as therapeutic by the poets of the Confederation group or that much of their work from the mid-1880s onwards turns on the therapeutic effects of natural scenery.

Given the acute unhappiness that Lampman appears to have experienced as a consequence of his departure from Trinity College in 1882, his removal to Ottawa in 1883, and his disappointment over the fate of *Young Canada* in 1884, it is equally unsurprising that of all the poets in the Confederation group he was the first to produce work distinctly based on a therapeutic conception of Nature. A further reason for this was the fact that, after he began to court his future wife, Maud Playter, in 1884, Lampman was in close contact with her father, Dr Edward Playter (1834/5–1909), a physician, journal editor, and health reformer who had moved his practice from Toronto to Ottawa in 1882 in order to lobby for the creation of a federal body 'to regulate matters such as sanitation, quarantine, and food adulteration' (Bator). As Roberts puts it in his 'Review of Literature, Science and Art' in *The Dominion Annual Register and Review for ... 1883*, 'efforts have been made towards the establishment of a Dominion Sanitary Health Association with the head office in Ottawa, and Government has the matter under consideration. Prominent in this laudable project is Dr. Playter, of Ottawa, who in his periodical, the *Sanitary Journal*, has been untiring in his exertions for the promotion of the public health' (212). The suspicion from this passage that Roberts's interests were beginning to overlap with Playter's is confirmed by the first issue of the magazine into which the *Sanitary Journal* mutated in November 1885: among the contributors to *Man: A Canadian Home Magazine* devoted to *Literature and Popular-Science, Public and Individual Hygiene, [and] Social and Domestic Economy* are Collins, Lampman, and, of course, Roberts himself.[2]

Neither Roberts's contribution to the first number of *Man* – a reprinting of 'Out of Pompeii' from *Later Poems* (1881) – nor Collins's – a bio-

graphical sketch of Sir William Dawson (1820–99) under the pseudonym 'Gamma' – reflects in any way the therapeutic theories of the mind-
cure movement, but the same cannot confidently be said of Lampman's
offering. Very likely written during the period of unhappiness that followed his move to Ottawa and certainly finished by the summer of 1884
(when it was rejected for publication by *St. Nicholas: A Monthly Magazine
for Boys and Girls* [New York]) (see Dentley, 'Introduction,' *Fairy Tales*
x–xi), 'Hans Fingerhut's Frog-Lesson: A Fairy Tale' concerns a poet
whose frustrated desire for 'unlimited good living, sympathy, and, above
all, praise' causes him to become angry at the world, to pervert his art,
and to revert to the trade of tailor, in which he had been apprenticed
(*Fairy Tales* 4). So extreme is his anger that 'little children [are] afraid to
pass his door,' 'his cutting and sewing' produce 'shapeless work,' he
resorts to 'scrawling satires on the gates of all whom the people hon-
ored,' and he determines finally to 'pass away out of the town ... never to
return' (4). When he does so, the sights and sounds of wild and rural
Nature ('the blue sky and the fresh green earth, the song of birds, the
piping of the crickets and grasshoppers, the wind in the trees and the
clink of the cow-bell') at first merely exacerbate his anger ('he cursed
the heavens and the earth and all happy and beautiful things in them');
however, thanks to the stern tutelage of an elf who turns him into a frog
so that he can once again, as in his days as a poet, correctly 'interpret
the song of the stream,' he does come to understand the meaning and
message of Nature (4–5). Once Hans has fully understood and internal-
ized the lesson of the stream song – namely, that 'everything in the
world' can be 'perfectly happy and peaceful' if it has 'something great
and noble to strive towards' (10) – he is able to return to town without
anger, to resume his work as a tailor, and, most important, to compose
songs that are socially acceptable and beneficial:

> So Hans came to the town, and the noise and stir of the streets were be-
> come quite pleasant to him. He no longer walked with his usual defiant
> stride, downcast face and scowling brow. The portly figures and round fac-
> es of the busy burghers, and the well-filled purses at their girdles no longer
> made him fierce and envious ...
>
> All that day, and many days, he sat in his stall and sewed and stitched ...
> and sang so many glad, beautiful songs ... that the little children ... came
> and gathered round him ... with delight and wonder in their eyes ... The
> fame of his singing spread, and the halls of the great were opened to him
> again. But from that day the great songs that he made were nothing like his

former ones. There was never anything bitter and complaining in them. They were all sweet and beautiful and wise. (11)

Not only does contact with Nature 'act in a ... directly remedial way' on Lampman's autobiographical protagonist, but it also 'lifts [him] out of [his] habitual condition into one which ... we should recognize as poetic.' It is almost as if Olmsted's remarks supplied Lampman with the inspiration for his fairy tale.

While *Mount Royal, Montreal* cannot be said with certainty to have been known to Lampman, Roberts, and Collins, there is a strong likelihood on account of their association with Playter and *Man* that all three of them were familiar with 'Busy People,' an article in the mainstream of the mind-cure movement by James MacDonald Oxley (1835–1907), a Nova Scotia–born lawyer who had been resident in Ottawa since 1882 (when he became legal advisor to the Department of Marine and Fisheries) and would soon embark on a successful career as a writer of fiction for boys (his *Up among the Ice Floes* would appear in 1889). (As a matter of fact, when Roberts visited Ottawa in October 1884 he was 'a guest of Mr. Oxley, of the Marine Department' [*Ottawa Daily Citizen*, 23 October 1884, 3].) Published in the second number of *Man* (December 1885), Oxley's article begins by suggesting that the contemporary 'hatred of inaction' and 'stress' upon hard work can exact high social and psychological costs:

The man that is over-busy ... by no means makes the best of life, even though substantial success may crown his eager efforts. He is always engrossed in his work, – carries it about with him everywhere, – cannot fix his thoughts upon anything else, and consequently can never take any proper relaxation or enjoyment. His brain is always brimming with plans and projects, dollars and cents. In the street he hardly finds time to exchange friendly nods with his acquaintances; at home, his burdensome business blinds him to its simple joys and comforts; abroad, his mind is too occupied with dry-goods or discounts, lumber or grain to appreciate the beauties of nature or art. (55)

Conceding that 'there is a vast deal of nonsense said and written about over-worked brains nowadays' and avowing that his intention is not to 'plead ... the cause of the idler,' Oxley advocates a 'golden mean' consisting of 'the happy blending of hard work' with what he calls 'wise idleness' – that is, 'quietly absorbing something through the eye or ear that for the time at least drowns the petty businesses and worries of life as the incoming tide silently engulfs the pebbles on the beach' (56). 'My busy friends,' he concludes, 'possess your souls in patience,' and make the time 'to spend in quiet culture of mind and heart' (56–7).

If not 'Busy People' then a text (or conversation) very like it may well have provided the program for several of Lampman's poems of the late 1880s that extol the psychological benefits of 'quietly absorbing something through the eye and ear that for a time    drowns the petty businesses and worries of life.' The closing lines of two much anthologized poems are cases in point. 'The Frogs' (written in May 1887) and 'Heat' (written in July 1887) both describe in their different ways the state of mental and physical well-being that comes through attentive surrender to the sights and sounds of the natural world, in the former, the 'voices high and strange' of the frogs and, in the latter, the many sharply observed details of plants, animals, and rural life. In 'The Frogs,' the natural world serves as a tranquillizer and in 'Heat' as a tonic, but in both cases the result is a negation of the 'petty businesses and worries of life':

Morning and noon and midnight exquisitely,
    Rapt with your voices, this alone we knew,
Cities might change and fall, and men might die,
     Secure were we, content to dream with you
     That change and pain are shadows faint and fleet,
    And dreams are real, and life is only sweet.

And yet to me not this or that
Is always sharp or always sweet;
In the sloped shadow of my hat
    I lean at rest, and drain the heat;
Nay more, I think some blessèd power
    Hath brought me wandering idly here:
In the full furnace of this hour
    My thoughts grow keen and clear. (*P* 10)

That 'The Frogs' is followed in *Among the Millet, and Other Poems* by the grimly realistic vision of 'An Impression,'* and 'Heat' by the fully

---

* Whereas time seems to stand still in 'The Frogs' ('moments are as aeons, and the sun / But ever sunken half-way toward the west'), in 'An Impression' 'the city time-bells [that] call / Far off in hollow towers ... Count out the old dead hours' and prompt the speaker to envision 'the haggard dreadfulness / Of dim old age and death' (*P* 7, 10).

achieved revitalization of 'Among the Timothy,' indicates that the escapism of the former requires chastening and that the clairvoyance of the latter requires amplification. Sharply individuated and various as they are, the therapeutic nature poems of Lampman's first volume constitute an ensemble whose underlying pattern of restorative excursion and necessary return is made increasingly explicit in the three poems with which the volume begins: 'To My Wife,' where the poet chivalrically represents his work as 'hours' of 'musing time' that he is now 'bring[ing] ... back again' to his 'Belovèd'; 'Among the Millet,' where his statement that he 'could' lie all day watching clouds in the sky as they were envisaged by poets 'in time of old' indicates that he will not do this; and 'April,' where 'the long sweetness of an April day' spent absorbing the sights and sounds of Nature results, not in somnolent solipsism, but in humanitarian action:

Ah, I have wandered with unwearied feet
...
　　　　　　　　　　　　... and quite forgot
The shallow toil, the strife against the grain,
Near souls, that hear us call, but answer not,
The loneliness, perplexity and pain,
And high thoughts cankered with an earthly stain;
And then, the long draught emptied to the lees,
I turn me homeward in slow-pacing ease,

Clearing the cedar shadows and the thin
Mist of gray gnats that cloud the river shore,
Sweet even choruses, that dance and spin
Soft tangles in the sunset; and once more
The city smites me with its dissonant roar.
To its hot heart I pass, untroubled yet,
Fed with calm hope, without desire or fret.

So to the year's first altar step I bring
Gifts of meek song, and make my spirit free
With the blind working of unanxious spring,
Careless with her, whether the days that flee
Pale drouth or golden-fruited plenty see,
So that we toil, brothers, without distress
In calm-eyed peace and godlike blamelessness. (P 1, 5–6)

Almost needless to say, the cycle of excursion and return in which the reader of the therapeutic poems of *Among the Millet* participates vicariously requires perpetual repetition, for no sooner has the urban, work-a-day world been re-entered than the restorative influence of Nature begins again to be required: the speaker and the reader of 'April' are 'untroubled *yet*' by the 'dissonant roar' of the city, but their charmed state is as temporary as the assaults on it are continual.

The fact that both 'April' and 'Among the Timothy' were written before the publication of 'Busy People,' the former in May 1884 and the latter in August 1885, means that whatever impact Oxley's essay might have had on 'The Frogs' and 'Heat' the sources of Lampman's two most extended poetic treatments of therapeutic Nature and the psychological malaise for which it was deemed a cure must lie elsewhere. It is quite possible, for example, that the origin of the 'dissonant roar' of the city in 'April' lies directly or indirectly in *American Nervousness, Its Causes and Consequences: A Supplement to Nervous Exhaustion (Neurasthenia)* (1881), where the influential mind-cure theorist George Miller Beard (1839–83) argues that urban noise is among the many aspects of 'modern civilization' that cause the psychosomatic symptoms of what he calls 'Americanitis' (98–9).[3] It is also quite possible that Beard's book, or some other equally popular work such as *Wear and Tear; or, Hints for the Overworked* (1871) by the inventor of the rest-cure, S. Weir Mitchell (1829–1914),[4] lies in the background of Lampman's now well-known statement to Hamlin Garland (1860–1940) on 25 April 1889 that his 'design for instance in "Among the Timothy" was not in the first place to describe a landscape, but to describe the effect of a few hours spent among the summer fields on a mind in a troubled and despondent condition' (quoted in Doyle, 'Archibald Lampman' 40). Nor should the search for works that might have shaped Lampman's conception of Nature as a mental restorative be confined to the American mind-cure movement, for as Olmsted remarks of the testaments to the charm of natural scenery by Wordsworth, Emerson, James Russell Lowell and other writers that serve as epigraphs in *Mount Royal, Montreal* such 'ideas ... have long had considerable currency' ('Preface,' n.pag.). That Lampman was apparently an enthusiastic reader of Arnold by the time he entered into correspondence with Roberts in September 1882 (see *CP* 30) merely points to another of many channels through which ideas that are given a more medical cast by Mitchell, Beard, Olmsted, and countless others could have reached the two poets by the early 1880s, namely, Arnold's conception of the poet as 'Physician of the iron age' in 'Memorial Verses'

(1852), and as the creator of 'varied anodynes' for the 'strange disease of modern life, / With its sick hurry, its divided aims, / Its heads o'ertaxed, its palsied hearts ...' in 'The Scholar-Gipsy' (1853) (*Poems* 227, 342). It may not be fortuitous that an echo of these last lines can be heard at precisely the moment in 'Among the Timothy' when the speaker makes a conscious decision to release his mind from its ordinary preoccupations into the natural world: 'Ah! I will set no more my overtasked brain / To barren search and toil that beareth nought ... But let it go, as one that hath no skill, / To take what shape it will ...' (*P* 14–15).[5]

More than any other writer, with the possible exception of Emerson, it was the Wordsworth whose 'healing power' Arnold extols in 'Memorial Verses' (*Poems* 229)[6] who exemplified for the late nineteenth century the therapeutic properties of natural scenery and nature poetry. The first of Olmsted's epigraphs in *Mount Royal, Montreal* comes from 'Tintern Abbey,' and Wordsworth is the poet whom he chooses to illustrate his contention that 'the charm of natural scenery tends to make us poets.' Moreover, to make his case Olmsted quotes extensively from *On the Poetic Interpretation of Nature* (1877), by John Campbell Shairp, a critic whose work appears to have had a major impact on Lampman beginning with the writing of 'The Modern School of Poetry in England' early in 1885 and to lie centrally in the background of his later essays 'Style' and 'Poetic Interpretation' (see *ER* 244–52, 260–73, and 302–15). As Arnoldian as Arnold himself was 'Wordsworthian' (*Complete Prose* 9: 55), Shairp concludes his chapter 'Wordsworth as an Interpreter of Nature' with an account of the poet's own experience of the curative power of Nature that could well have provided the program for 'Among the Timothy' and, indeed, 'Heat' either in the original or in Olmsted's quotations. After returning from France in the wake of the Reign of Terror and Britain's declaration of war, argues Shairp, Wordsworth was 'wandering around about aimless and dejected' until his sister Dorothy 'saw and understood his mental malady' and

> took him once more to lonely and beautiful places, till Nature again found access to him ...
>
> But there was not a restoration only ... She opened his eyes to perceive in Nature minute lovelinesses formerly unnoticed, his heart to feel sympathies and tendernesses for human things hitherto uncared for ... He felt once again, like the breath of spring, visitings of the imaginative power come to him ... (*On Poetic Interpretation* 257)

In Shairp's analysis, this 'sanative process' resulted for Wordsworth in a new sympathy for 'the laboring poor' and a mature understanding of Nature as an entity possessed of a 'life' or 'spirit' that 'spoke through visible things to his spirit' and had certain 'qualities inherent in it':

> Calmness, which stilled and refreshed man;
>
> Sublimity, which raised him to noble and majestic thoughts;
>
> Tenderness, which, while stirring in the largest and loftiest things, condescends to the lowest, with the humblest worm and lowest weed as much as in the greatest movements of the elements and of the stars. (257)

'Above all' and finally, says Shairp, Wordsworth now saw 'Nature ... to be the shape and image of right reason, reason in the highest sense, embodied and made visible in order, in stability, in conformity to eternal law' and now 'discovered that in order to attain the highest and truest vision of Nature, the soul of man must not be altogether passive, but must act along with and in unison with Nature, must send from itself abroad an emanation, which, meeting with natural objects, produces something better than either the soul itself or Nature by herself could generate' (259, 261).

With due allowances for selection and adaptation, 'Among the Timothy' can easily be read as a poetic treatment of Shairp's 'sanative process' and its salutary results:

> *Stanzas 1–3* ('aimless ... dejected ... mental malady'): '[W]eary of the drifting hours, / The echoing city towers, / The blind gray streets, the jingle of the throng ... And weary most of song,' the speaker has betaken himself to the countryside 'seeking some comfort for [his] aching mood' (*P* 14). There he seats himself beside a 'stump' among 'dead daisies' and 'swathes' of grass that a mower has recently cut into a 'circle clean and gray' (all metaphors, of course, for the morbid condition produced by the work-a-day world of 'gray streets') and ponders the fact that the 'high moods ... that sometimes made [his] heart a heaven ... Begirt with shapes of beauty and the power / Of dreams that moved ... With changing breaths of rhyme' have 'all gone [as] lifeless' as 'dead' 'leaves' (*P* 13–14).
>
> *Stanzas 4–6* ('minute lovelinesses ... sympathies and tendernesses ... visitings of the imaginative power'): After projecting his mind into the natural world 'to take what shape it will' and imagining it assuming various animate forms (an ant, a spider, a bee), the speaker observes the effect of 'little breezes' in the 'rocking grass,' noticing particularly that they seem to

'teas[e] the slender blossoms' and 'scarcely heed the daisies that, endowed / With stems so short they cannot see, ... stare / Like children in a crowd' (14–15). He also observes the 'glimmering leaves' of a 'pale poplar' that 'beat / Together like innumerable small hands' when the breeze blows and, when it is still, 'Hang wan and silver-gray; / Like sleepy maenads ... / Half-wakened by a prowling beast' – a cluster of figures that represent an imagination as yet only semi-restored and thus capable only of producing fanciful similes.

*Stanzas 7–9* ('imaginative power ... calmness ... the soul not ... altogether passive but ... act[ing] along with and in unison with Nature ... the shape and image of right reason ... order ... stability ... eternal law'): With his imagination now capable of metaphors ('The dry cicada plies his wiry bow / In long-spun cadence, thin and dusty sere; / ... the small grasshoppers' din / Spreads soft and silvery thin'), the speaker recognizes the presence of a harmony between and among Nature and human beings whose labour is in time with nature's rhythms ('The crickets creak ... And ever and anon a murmur steals / Into mine ears of toil that moves alway, / The crackling rustle of the pitch-forked hay / And lazy jerk of wheels') (*P* 16–17). The final two stanzas of the poem represent 'the highest and truest vision of Nature' that flows from the restored imagination when it is 'not altogether passive' but 'send[ing] from itself abroad an emanation,' 'act[ing] along with and in unison with Nature' to produce what Wordsworth himself describes in 'Tintern Abbey' as something 'half create[d]' and half 'perceive[d]' (2: 262):

As so I lie and feel the soft hours wane,
    To wind and sun and peaceful sound laid bare,
That aching dim discomfort of the brain
    Fades off unseen, and shadowy-footed care
Into some hidden corner creeps at last
    To slumber deep and fast;
And gliding on, quite fashioned to forget,
    From dream to dream I bid my spirit pass
Out into the pale green ever-swaying grass
    To brood, but no more fret.

And hour by hour among all shapes that grow
    Of purple mints and daisies gemmed with gold
In sweet unrest my visions come and go;
    I feel and hear and with quiet eyes behold;

And hour by hour, the ever-journeying sun,
   In gold and shadow spun,
Into mine eyes and blood, and through the dim
   Green glimmering forest of the grass shines down,
Till flower and blade, and every cranny brown,
   And I are soaked with him. (*P* 16)

These stanzas anticipate 'Heat' both in conveying a sense of perceived
and achieved 'right reason' and in suggesting that exposure to the light
and heat of the sun can simultaneously relax the body and reinvigorate
the mind, a notion that may derive from the traditional practice of
removing invalids to warm climates (a therapy that would certainly have
been known to Lampman, if only because it was applied to Keats in a
final, desperate attempt to slow the progress of his tuberculosis).[7] 'I ...
always lay down [*Among the Millet, and Other Poems*] with an inward and
heartily sincere blessing for the person who can give such exquisite pleasure as one derives from we'll say the last five verses of "Among the Timothy",' Isabella Voorhis told Lampman on 13 December 1891; '[the
poems] expressing your perceptions of Nature ... are very invigorating
to one. They are things which just *do one good* cooped up in the mael-
strom of a place [that is, New York] with nothing but brick walls[,] elevated trains and impure air outside the house' (SFU).
   Lampman's heliotherapeutic poems and their underlying Wordsworthian patterns are very much a presence in two of Campbell's most successful Nature poems of the early 1890s, 'In the Strength of the Morning'
and 'An August Reverie,' both of which were first published in *The Dread
Voyage* (1893). In the former, the speaker wanders 'in fields knee-deep
in grass' and 'by the shade of woods' with results that enable him to go
'Back ... to the world ... / Filled with the glory of earth's light ... To battle
with [his] fate':

   My heart grows great and lonely ...
With the large wisdom of the woods,
Full of the morning's haunted moods.

The world grows faint and far away,
   As morning grows a dream at noon;
Here the great silences do pray,
   With spread arms in a voiceless swoon:
The fields gleam out and far away

Across the hum and hush of day.

I breathe life's airs and feel my heart
  Leap into being, like a brook
That from a mountain crag doth start,
  And falls in snowy thunders shook:
So all earth's glories in my heart
Surge outward, nature's counterpart. (*SPE* 50)

In the latter, a similar sense of kinship with Nature, this time stemming from the speaker's special affection for such commonplace plants as the 'daisy' and 'thistle,' yields a happiness based on an acceptance of the mutability of all living things and an apprehension of the existence of a realm beyond the material world: 'Knowing no love but of the wind and sun' and 'still all nature's when their life is done,' 'common weeds' are both 'a part of all the haze-filled hours, / The happy, happy world all drenched in light' and a prompt to 'Thought, that is the greatness of his earth, / And man's inmost being,' to 'find ... heavens where the senses may not go' (*SPE* 56).[8]

In his 'At the Mermaid Inn' column for 16 July 1892, Campbell provides an account of the therapeutic effects of Nature that could double as a gloss on 'Heat,' 'Among the Timothy,' 'In the Strength of the Morning,' and 'An August Reverie':

Now in the midsummer heats, when the roar and the discord of cities become unbearable, and hard thought and reading are almost an impossibility, the spirit of life, if it calls at all, beckons to us ... from the far-off hill countries or breezy shores. Under the open sky is the suitable place for summer existence whenever it can drop for a space the fetters of toil. The country ways and shady lanes, the clover-scented meadows melodious with song of birds   ... call us with their drowsy suggestions and somnolent sounds. Happy is the man who can throw off his age and responsibility with his office clothes and city cares, and hie him to the shores of some rushing river or some pebbly lake, and dream or ruminate as best may please him, and let the winds of heaven and the glad sunlight drench him, body and soul, and blow out all the sickly fancies from heart and brain. The far summer hazes, the far summer sounds, that quiet tired nerves and revive jaded energies, are better than all the elixirs discovered by man. (*MI* 111)

A valuable 'companion' to 'nature's draughts and nature's voices,' continues Campbell, is a book 'that will charm and soothe, rather than worry and excite,' a function fulfilled by such 'charming' works as Washington Irving's *Book of the Hudson* (1849), the sketches of John Burroughs, and 'the remarkable tales' of 'the great [Norwegian] poet and novelist of the north,' Bjørnstjerne Bjørnson (1832–1910), in whose 'pages [the reader] will find the strength of the hills, the beauty of the skies and waters, and the freshness and hope of the morning' (*MI* 111–12). Although Campbell regards books 'that will charm and soothe' as a supplement to rather than a substitute for the therapeutic effects of Nature, he nevertheless provides a rationale for the medicinal book that is more explicit than anything found in *Among the Millet, and Other Poems* and well in advance of similar notions advanced by Roberts and Carman.

Scattered through Roberts's poetry and critical prose from the mid-1880s onwards are several indications that he was increasingly intrigued by current theories of the therapeutic value of Nature and nature writing. At the conclusion of 'The Pipes of Pan' (1886), written in 1883, contact with the departed Greek god's discarded syrinx merely causes 'mortals' to 'fly the heedless throngs and traffic of cities' and to 'Haunt mossed caverns, and wells bubbling ice-cool' where 'their souls / Gather a magical gleam of the secret of life' (*CP* 78), but in the Introduction to *Poems of Wild Life* (1888), written in 1888, 'modern verse' inspired by the wilderness affords 'a measure of escape from the artificial to the natural' that 'our dilettante-ridden society is in need of' (ix, xiv). By 1892, in 'Wordsworth's Poetry,' his introduction to J.E. Wetherell's *Poems of Wordsworth (from Arnold's Selections)* (1892), Wordsworth is 'the surest guide we have to those regions of luminous calm which this breathless age so needs for its soul's health' (*SPCP* 274), and by 1902, in 'Introductory: The Animal Story,' his introduction to *The Kindred of the Wild*, the animal story not only 'frees us for a little from the world of shop-worn utilities and from the mean temement of self,' but also offers 'the ... gift of refreshment and renewal' (29). Very likely the greatly increased awareness of therapeutic theory evinced by these last two quotations stemmed in part from Roberts's own experience during 1890–1 with what Dr Beard would have had no difficulty in diagnosing as neurasthenia. 'Please forgive me [for my long silence],' Roberts begged William Morton Payne in a letter of 8 August 1891, 'your last letter came when I was away in the wilds, with birch and paddle, trying to recuperate. As I was utterly used up, very nervous and miserable in every way, I went quite out of reach of all work ... [F]or the last twelve month[s] I have been dull and depressed (with a sort of nervous prostration,[9] the after effect of *Grippe*) ... My pen has been too weary for anything but *necessary* undertakings ... Thank you for being interested in my poor guide-book, written in the midst of great depression' (*CL* 134).[10]

The guide-book to which this letter refers is *The Canadian Guide-Book: The Tourist's and Sportsman's Guide to Eastern Canada and Newfoundland* (1891), which Roberts co-authored with William Ernest Ingersoll, an American naturalist, travel writer and editor of the *Cosmopolitan* (New York), who in 1889 had travelled across Canada researching a series of articles for his magazine (and, according to a story in the 23 January 1889 issue of the *Globe*, 'looking for clever Canadian writers [to] ... tell him' more about the country than he had learned some years earlier as a writer for the Canadian Pacific Railway [4]). Modelled on 'the famous Baedeker Handbooks,' it draws heavily on *Picturesque Canada* but tempers the nationalism of Grant's compilation with various accommodating gestures towards the American tourists for whom it was primarily intended,[11] including references to Longfellow's *Evangeline* and assurances that the climate of the Maritimes and the St Lawrence region is 'not unlike that of New England' (2, 254). The relationship of *The Canadian Guide-Book* to earlier and later touristic literature and the presence in it of several of Roberts's own poems (including 'The Departing of Gluskâp' [1886] and, under the title of 'Menagwes,' 'The Vengeance of Gluskâp' [1896]) are but two of several aspects of the book that call for further study. What is of special interest here is the inviting reference in the book's Introduction to the 'invigorating climate' of Canada and the complementary assertion in the advertisement for the Windsor and Annapolis Railway in its final pages that 'Health-seekers' who avail themselves of the 'Splendid Steamships Running in Connection to and from Boston and St. John, N.B.' to travel on the railway's '"Land of Evangeline" Route' will find themselves "in one of the best climates on the footstool, where the air is the only medicine required to keep you fresh as paint." Such claims for the salubrity of the Maritime and Canadian climates are, of course, ubiquitous in pre- and post-Confederation writing,[12] but the terminology and targeting of the Windsor and Annapolis Railway's advertisement has particular relevance in the present context because, according to Beard, 'nervous exhaustion' or 'American nervousness' (255) was especially prevalent in 'the Northern and Eastern States' and in the 'brain-working household[s]' of 'the better classes of ... larger cities' (23, 24). Whether by chance or design, Roberts's *Canadian Guide-Book* was an invitation to well-heeled neurasthenics in such cities as Boston and New York to enjoy the therapeutic benefits of a trip to Canada's maritime provinces.

The question of chance or design does not arise in relation to the tourist guide that Roberts wrote for the Dominion Atlantic Railway[13] in the winter of 1894–5 (see *CL* 188–91) and published in time for the 1895 high season. On the inside cover of *The Land of Evangeline and the Gateways Thither* (1895), an advertisement for the DAR proclaims 'EVANGELINE'S LAND ... the wonderland of artists, the sportman's paradise, [and] the healthiest spot on the footstool' – a thrice-blessed destination for people who 'have a care for [their] pocket, health and time ... love scenery, variety and comfort ... [and] want to see the land that poets, romancists and artists have made their own.' In the opening paragraphs of his Introduction, Roberts continues in the same vein and with his eye very much on urban and upper-echelon Americans: 'the tourist ... escaping to the cool atmosphere [of Nova Scotia] from the tropic fervors of Washington Street or Broadway' will find much to enjoy in landscapes rich in 'the heritage of a romantic and mysterious past' and bathed in the 'transfiguring glow' of Longfellow's 'imaginings' (1). Of special therapeutic value for Americans suffering from the physical and psychological consequences of the monotony, cacophony, and pollution of New York and other Northeastern cities is natural scenery that is by turns stimulating and relaxing ('austere grandeur alternates with softest loveliness, ... the wilding piquancy of untrained Nature with the rich peacefulness of well-tilled farms'). More beneficial yet for such people is Nova Scotia's 'good air': 'tonic and temperate, guiltless of malaria, ignorant of hay-fever, friendly to work, to play, to sleep, to appetite,' 'it touches to content the o'er-wrought nerves, and fills with healing breath the troubled lungs' (2).[14] As the words 'good,' 'guiltless,' and 'ignorant' in this description suggest, Nova Scotia is more than merely a salubrious destination for neurasthenic Americans; in *The Land of Evangeline and the Gateways Thither*, it is an earthly paradise within easy reach of the debilitating pandemoniums of the 'Northern and Eastern States' on the steamers and trains of the Dominion Atlantic Railway. Fifteen years later, in *The Beauty, History, Romance and Mystery of the Canadian Lake Region* (1910), Campbell would construct the northern Great Lakes in much the same paradisal and therapeutic terms as 'an Eden' where 'the very air is full of a vigor and life-giving essence, and the nights [are] cool, dry and restful, with brooding repose for jaded nerve and care-wracked brain. Here man can, if he sanely chooses, renew his life for a season, and forget that he is a serf or a hireling' (20–3). It is no exaggeration to say that in these and countless statements like them lie the impetus for the cottagization of the shores of eastern and central Canada's ocean and lakes.

While Campbell predictably connects his Ontario Eden with the imperialist ethos in *The Canadian Lake Region* by envisaging the northern Great Lakes as 'an effective barrier' that 'shut[s] Ontario off from the communities to the south and west' (30),[15] Roberts almost as predictably represents Nova Scotia as a paradise for artists and writers by emphasizing its abundant and fresh subject matter, and the perceptual as well as the psychological qualities of its air:

> ... here is material rich and unwrought waiting for [the writer's] pen – landscape, legend, and tradition; and in the wholesome air thought runs clear and the brain is capable ... [T]he great tides, the wide marshes, the vast red gaping channels supply subjects [for the artist] which are new both in line and colour; and the moisture in the bland air gives 'atmosphere' to soften all harsh edges. (2)

That these remarks were aimed at a particular social and regional audience is clear from a letter that Roberts wrote on 15 July 1893 to Lorin Ellis Baker asking him as president of the Yarmouth (Nova Scotia) Steamship Company ('the pioneer tourist line in Nova Scotia' [Woodworth 115]) to 'extend ... the courtesy of a pass, both *ways, – and ... special attention on the journey*' to 'Mrs. Henrietta Russell, of New York, the famous Delsartian teacher, [who] expects to come on a camping expedition to Windsor ... with a small party of friends and pupils' (*CL* 176). 'All Mrs. Russell's movements will be attentively chronicled in Boston and NY papers,' he adds, 'and she has a very wide influence among society and travelling classes in America ... It is my own persuasion that is bringing her and her party this way; but it will be easy to secure *her* influence in the future, toward inducing tourists of her class to visit this part of the world.' The Henrietta Russell to whom Roberts refers here was, of course, the close companion and future wife of Carman's boon companion and future collaborator Richard Hovey, and the 'camping expedition' to which he refers, the second of two camps in the grounds of his house at Windsor in the summers of 1892 and 1893 that brought a whiff of Bohemia and a scent of scandal to the staid High Anglican atmosphere of King's College. Since John Coldwell Adams has already described in some detail the goings-on at Kingscroft during 1892–3 (see *Sir Charles God Damn* 43–9), it is sufficient for present purposes merely to mention that in 1892 Russell had given birth to an illegitimate child by Hovey and that in the early 1890s Roberts was having affairs with at least two women, including his family's live-in governess, Maude Clark, whom he styled 'the "Queen of Bohemia"' (*CL* 137) after the title character of a best-selling novel of the day.[16] The significant point about all this is that by 1892–3 Roberts, Carman, and Hovey were none-too-discreetly practising the philosophy of sensual freedom as a cure for the mental and physical ills of modern society that would soon find poetic expression in such works as *Songs of Vagabondia* (1894) and *New York Nocturnes and Other Poems* (1898). In and around the tent village at Kingscroft in the summers of 1892 and 1893, the 'good air' of Nova Scotia apparently proved very friendly indeed 'to play, to sleep, [and] to appetite.'

There can be almost as little doubt that Henrietta Russell was the immediate inspiration for the philosophy of mind-body-spirit harmonization to which Roberts, Hovey, and Carman began to subscribe in the early 1890s as there is that the ultimate source of their 'unitrinian' beliefs was the work of the French dramatical aesthetician François Delsarte (1811–71) as practised in New York by the innovative American dramatist Steele MacKaye (1842–94) and introduced to a wider reading audience by numerous books and articles, most notably Genevieve Stebbins's much reprinted *Delsarte System of Dramatic Expression* (1886).[17] Adams speculates that Roberts first met Russell in April 1893 when, suffering again from a combination of 'influenza and overwork' (48), he joined Carman and Hovey for what amounted to a rest cure at Hovey's parents' house in Washington, DC (see *CL* 168). By that time, he was probably almost as familiar as Hovey and Carman with Russell's major contribution to Delsartean and therapeutic literature: the collection of essays entitled *Yawning,* which she published in New York in 1891 as number 1 in 'The Delsarte Series.' An exposition of Delsarte's conception of human beings as compounds of 'three distinguishable natures' ('a nature that must think, a nature that must feel emotions, and a nature that must have sensations'), *Yawning* engagingly proposes the activity to which its title refers as paradigmatic of the 'three orders of motion' – '*succession, opposition,* and *parallelism,*' – that must be involved in any system of exercise ('gymnastic') if it is to develop and harmonize the 'physical,' 'mental,' and 'moral or emotional' components of the 'human trinity' (15, 41–2, 45). Without such unitrinian development and balanced harmonization, argues Russell, each of the three components of human nature may 'degenerat[e] into its ultimate form, that of the physical being – debauchery, that of the moral – bigotry, and that of the mental – madness':

> A mind over-stimulated and worked to the exclusion of physical or mental activity, ends either in insanity or in nervous prostration. Physical activity, deprived of moral impulse, thoughtful plan, or ambition, degenerates into some form of decay. The sole sway of the emotional nature ends no better, producing bigotry in religion, sentimentalism in life, and hysteria in trouble. You might as well expect the half to make the whole, as thought, emotion, or sensation alone to make a man. (46–9)

'We are a brain-weary and emotion-weary generation,' asserts Russell; 'let us develop our muscles! ... Let us try to come at the laws of the mind and soul through the laws of the body' (58, 67–8). In the 21 November 1891 issue of the *Dominion Illustrated*, Annie Crawford (18?–?) would summarize the Delsarte System as 'a revelation to ... nerve-bound persons who, with well-developed muscles, keep such tension upon them when not in use that vital force is uselessly squandered. It teaches how to conserve vital energy; how to avoid wasteful nerve tension; so that the student works better, rests better, and also, by the physical exercise of certain nerves, gains more brilliancy and activity of mind' (485).

The immediate outcome of Roberts's renovating stay in Washington in the spring of 1893 was 'The Ballad of Crossing the Brook' (1896), a lyric that reflects his new-found buoyancy both in its rollicking ballad metre and in its light-hearted theme. (While 'a-Maying in the morn' a 'simple country lad' carries 'a dainty maid' with 'elfin eyes' across a stream [*CP* 180], as Roberts in fact had while staying with the Hoveys [see Pomeroy 88–9 and Adams, *Sir Charles God Damn* 48].) Less directly but almost as certainly the outcome of Roberts's recovery of 1893–4 are the three lyrics dealing singly and collectively with physical, mental, and moral (or emotional) rebirth that he published with a keen sense of their seasonal appropriateness in spring issues of various American magazines: 'Resurrection' (*Harper's Weekly*, March 1894), which likens the 'emerge[nce] to light' of human souls after death to the regeneration of 'daffodil, lily, crocus' and other flowers in the spring; 'The Quest of the Arbutus' (*Century Magazine*, April 1894), which proclaims a kinship between the 'eager blood' that the speaker feels in his veins in April and 'The swelling sap that thrill[s] the wood,' but laments the absence of a female companion to share the moment; and 'Renewal' (*New Outlook*, May 1894), which petitions the 'Mother of the leaves and rain' for a return to child-like 'joyous[ness],' 'grave simplicity,' 'dream and vision,' and 'fellowship with wonder' (*CP* 175–6). More explicit than any or all of these three poems in its celebration of the therapeutic properties of Nature is 'Kinship' (*Harper's Magazine*, August 1894), a lyric that antici- pates Roberts's introduction to *Kindred of the Wild* in its affirmation of a 'companionship of earth' and also proclaims its Delsartean origins in its insistence on the mental, emotional, and, ultimately, spiritual as well as the physical components of 'the faithful healing' that Mother Nature offers her 'hurt' children:

> Take me, Mother, – in compassion
>    All thy hurt ones fain to heal.
>
> Back to wisdom take me, Mother;
>    Comfort me with kindred hands;
> Tell me tales of the world's forgetting
>    Till my spirit understands. (*CP* 142)

The emphasis in these and ensuing lines of 'Kinship' is on mind and spirit, but earlier in the poem there are references to the physi- cal aspects of both human and non-human Nature ('Childlike fin- gers, childlike eyes,' 'the candour of the sod,' 'the twine of questing tree-root, / The expectancy of leaves,' and so on). Russell must have been pleased by her success as a mediator of Delsarte's theories.

She can only have been more so when contemplating the work of Hovey and Carman, who by the end of 1894 had drawn upon her inter- pretation of Delsarte to develop an elaborate and essentially therapeutic approach to poetry whereby every element of language corresponds to either the mental, the physical, or the emotional (moral, spiritual) com- ponent of human nature. For example, in 'Delsarte and Poetry,' pub- lished in the 27 August 1891 issue of the *Independent* (New York), Hovey argues of 'metrical feet' that 'troche[e]s ... are emotional,' 'the English pseudo-anapest ... [is] physical,' and 'the iambus ... is mental' (3–4), and in 'The Technic of Poetry,' published in the 7 April 1892 issue of the same magazine, he quotes Russell to argue that 'the Delsartean princi- ples of parallelism, opposition and succession' have similar linguistic manifestations, 'parallelism' ('mentality') in regular metre and end- stopped lines, 'opposition' ('sensation or passion') in irregular metre and run-on lines, and 'succession' ('emotion,' morality, spirituality) in 'all modulation of vowels and consonants' (9–10; and Russell, 15, 149).

'In the most beautiful versification, all three modes' are used together because, as Hovey explains in the last article in the series, 'The Elements of Poetic Technic' (*Independent*, 27 September and 4 October 1894),

> All art, said [Delsarte] has for its final object to express man, and through expression to develop the qualities expressed. It is essential in man to have three natures, physical, mental and moral. Subtract any one of these, and the result would no longer be human. These three are entirely distinct, and cannot be confused with one another. The activity of the first is life and sensation, of the second thought, of the third love or its opposite. The aim of the first is strength, of the second truth, of the third goodness. The reward of the first is pleasure, of the second wisdom, of the third freedom. Yet these three activities inhere in one and the same indivisible personality; these three aims, strength, goodness and truth, are but phases of the one divine beauty; and these three rewards, pleasure, wisdom and freedom, shall in the perfect man become one happiness. (5; and see Russell 45)

To write a unitrinian poem is both to express and to encourage the holistic perfection that betokens a happy and healthy person.

Given the finical nature of the Delsartean 'technic' advanced by Hovey and Carman, it is almost a miracle that they were able to write any poetry at all, let alone the three *Vagabondia* volumes that they co-authored between 1894 and Hovey's untimely death in February 1900. But to what extent, if any, are the poems in *Songs from Vagabondia* (1894), *More Songs from Vagabondia* (1896), and *Last Songs from Vagabondia* (1900) obedient to the poetic laid out in Hovey's essays of 1891–4? A full answer to this question would require pages of close analysis that the quality of many of the *Vagabondia* poems does not justify, but a short answer with brief illustrations is both possible and necessary. Even a few lines of the poem that opens *Songs from Vagabondia* in the 'irregular ... reckless,' and 'rollicking' manner that William Morton Payne, reviewing the volume in the 1 February 1895 number of the *Dial*, found both unpleasing and inartistic (84),[18] indicate that 'the English pseudo-anapestic' is being consciously used by Hovey to suggest the value of unrestrained physical activity as a counterbalance to the mind-numbing conformity of a work-a-day world that denies its denizens the freedom

... to be oddities,
Not mere commodities,
Stupid and salable

Wholly available
Ranged upon shelves;
Each with his puny form
In the same uniform,
Cramped and disabled;
We are not labelled
We are ourselves.  (2)

It can easily be imagined that Hovey regarded the combination of 'parallelism' (end-stopped lines), 'opposition' (run-on lines), and 'succession' ('modulation of vowels and consonants') in this passage as a technical simulacrum of the mind-body-emotion triad that unitrinianism sought to harmonize. Much the same can be imagined of passages such as the following from 'Down the Songo,' where the second line calls attention to regularities, irregularities, and absences of rhyme (*aab-cddde*) that may well have been intended to communicate a sense of unitrinian harmony, as, indeed, may the passage's varying line lengths and rhythms (notice particularly the contrast and shift between the long, iambic [mental] opening lines and the short, trochaic [emotional] final line):

The rhythmic drowsiness keeps time
To hazy subtleties of rhyme
That seem to slip
Through the lulled soul to seek the sleepy shore.
The idle clouds go floating by;
Above us sky; beneath us sky;
The sun shines on us as we lie
Floating. (18)

To the very extent that this passage recalls 'Heat' and 'Among the Timothy,' it indicates that the therapeutic theory of rest or idleness in natural surroundings as a cure for mental or nervous stress is as much a presence in the *Vagabondia* volumes as in *Among the Millet, and Other Poems*.

Nor should the strong evidence be overlooked that Lampman's work was one of the channels through which a therapeutic understanding of Nature came to Hovey and, especially, Carman. As seen in chapter 2, *Among the Millet, and Other Poems* was greatly admired by Carman – so much so in fact that, as he graciously conceded in response to Campbell's accusation of plagiarism in 1895 (see chapter 8), a process of 'subconscious appropriation' had allowed the line 'With small innumerable sound' from 'Mr. Lampman's beautiful poem "Heat"' to find its way 'wholesale' into 'The Eavesdropper' (1893), a 'blunder' that he had corrected in the second edition of *Low Tide on Grand Pré* (see *War* 35, 91–2). Moreover, in a letter to Lampman on 25 January 1892, Carman writes of 'Comfort of the Fields,' which is arguably the most explicitly therapeutic nature poem in *Lyrics of Earth*,*

> that to me it comes with tender, enduring, and most intimate solace; taking on itself the office of hands that are no longer near to soothe in calm. It is a very sweet and wise thing and has fallen on my heart with abundance of relief beyond the requital of words. May the dear wood-gods give you tenfold reward ... for this gentle service rendered to an unworthy fellow vagrant. (SFU)

Not only do these heart-felt remarks testify to the taste for therapeutic Nature poetry in the Confederation group, but they also indicate the degree to which such poetry could actually work as a substitute for the sort of physical and mental comfort traditionally supplied by a parent, lover, or clergyman. A ministering poem might not completely take the place of a ministering angel, but it could be a very efficacious surrogate.

For none of the poets of the Confederation group was this more true

---

* In the opening stanza of 'Comfort of the Fields,' Lampman suggests that, for him, the best 'remedy for easement after grief, / When the rude world has used thee with despite' is

> to break forth, to drop the chain,
> And grasp the freedom of this pleasant earth,
> To roam in idleness and sober mirth,
> Through summer airs and summer lands, and drain
> The comfort of wide fields into tired eyes. (*P* 148)

After four stanzas describing the sights and sounds encountered during a Nature ramble, the poem concludes:

> Thus, with a smile as golden as the dawn,
> And cool fair fingers radiantly divine,
> The mighty mother brings us in her hand,
> For all tired eyes and foreheads pinched and wan
> Her restful cup, her beaker of bright wine:
> Drink, and be filled, and ye shall understand! (*P* 150)

than for Carman. Both in content and context, his contributions to the *Vagabondia* volumes tirelessly celebrate Nature, wine, women, song, camaraderie, and the open road as antidotes to the 'Cramped and disabled' life of the work-a-day world, with the power to restore a healthful balance among the mental, physical, and spiritual components of human nature. Like 'charming natural scenery' in Olmsted's formulation of the therapeutic world-view, the bundle of elements that Carman and Hovey subsumed under the term 'vagabondia' were conceived as an 'inducement ... to change of occupation, exercise, and air taking' and as 'therapeutic agent[s] of vital value' not merely to the health of overworked urban Americans, but also to the economic well-being of the 'large cit[ies]' and, indeed, the country as a whole. The first two *Vagabondia* volumes evince a rhythm of excursion and return whose typical beneficiary Carman would later describe as the 'American whose orbit lies between Wall Street and the park' (*Poetry of Life* 107) or, more likely, a country retreat: *Songs from Vagabondia* begins with 'Vagabondia' ('Then up and away / Till the break of day ...' [4]) and ends with 'Comrades' ('Comrades, gird your swords to-night, / For the battle is with the dawn' [54]); and *More Songs from Vagabondia* begins with 'Jongleurs' ('Lay down your ledgers, your picks and your shovels ... writs and attachments ... Comments and scholia, / [World's melancholia]' [2]) and ends with 'At the End of Day' ('Give a cheer! / For our joy shall not give way. / Here's in the teeth of to-morrow / To the glory of to-day!' [72]). Because *Last Songs from Vagabondia* was published in the wake of Hovey's untimely death on 4 February 1900, it begins with a series of bleak and elegiac poems before reprising the usual pattern of excursion and return with 'Holiday' ('Out of the weltering city, / Out of the blaring streets ... Farewell despondency, fear ... And thou, frail spirit in me ... Behold, thy brothers the elms ...' [22]) and 'The Adventurers' ('Soldiers of Fortune, we unfurl / The banners of forlorn hope, / Leaving the city smoke to curl, / O'er dingy roofs where puppets mope ... And the great wind that bore us here / Will drive our galleys home again' [79]). Almost needless to say, Carman was fully aware of the Odyssean pattern undergirding all three *Vagabondia* volumes: 'on ... Monday there are carnations in the button-holes of Wall Street,' he would write *in The Kinship of Nature* (1903), and 'every hansom on the avenue is freighted with the destruction of another Troy' (54).

To appreciate why therapeutic ideas and techniques increased rather than diminished in importance for Carman in the period preceding and following the publication of *Last Songs from Vagabondia,* two factors need to be taken into account. The first of these is Hovey's death, for this on top of financial and other problems precipitated Carman into 'a slump of nervous dyspepsia,' an 'abyss of nervous "goneness",' so severe that it necessitated a rest-cure in a sanatorium 'in the pines' in Thomasville, Georgia, in March and April 1900 (*L* 127–30). The second is the impact on his life of Mary Perry King, a student of Russell's ideas and methods, with whom be began an affair early in 1897 and, later in the same year (and with the assistance of her accommodating doctor-husband), started a Delsartean school for women that ran until 1904, alternating between a 'beautiful hous[e]' in New York and a secluded cottage in the Catskill Mountains northwest of the city (Carman, 'Apostle' 583). (The school collapsed in 1904 because King herself had a nervous breakdown and then moved for over a year to Japan to join her sick and temporarily aggrieved husband. After they returned in 1906, the Kings purchased a house in the residential town and summer resort of New Canaan, Connecticut, where, with Carman's help, they opened the Unitrinian School of Personal Harmonizing in 1910.) In their different but closely related ways, Carman's 'nervous dyspepsia' of 1900 and his close relationship with the Kings in the years surrounding it can only have expanded his understanding of therapeutic theory and deepened his conviction of the value of mind-body-spirit harmonization. Whatever portion of Carman's thinking remained untouched by Delsartean therapeutics prior to about 1898 did not remain so for long after 1900. As demonstrated in detail elsewhere (see Bentley, 'Carman and Mind Cure'), the three collections of essays entitled *The Kinship of Nature* (1903), *The Friendship of Art* (1904), and *The Poetry of Life* (1905), which Carman assembled from weekly columns that he had published in the Boston *Evening Transcript* between 1896 and 1903, are knit together by unitrinianism as, of course, are the works that he wrote in collaboration with King: *The Making of Personality* (1908), *Daughters of Dawn: A Lyrical Pageant or Series of Historical Scenes for Presentation with Music and Dancing* (1913), *Earth Deities and Other Rhythmic Masques* (1914), and *The Man of the Marne and Other Poems* (1918). It is probably no exaggeration to say that all the major new volumes of poetry that Carman published between 1900 and the First World War are not only permeated with unitrinianism but were also intended to 'medicine the mind' (*Kinship* 58) in one or other of the two ways described in *The Making of Personality*: as 'sedatives' 'to induce rest and invite sleep in uneasy brains' by providing 'solace and peace' or, conversely, as 'tonics' to 'cheer ... our waking hours, when the spirit is unstrung and the mind unattuned,' by providing 'a brave, courageous thought or a happy inspired fancy' (239–40). Only one volume of this period, *The Rough Rider, and Other Poems* (1909), can be said to qualify fully as a 'tonic' (it is named for the volunteer cavalry regiment that Theodore Roosevelt raised during the Spanish-American War of 1898 and dedicated to the president, who was also an advocate of masculine strenuousness as a cure for what was widely seen as the creeping effeminacy of American life),[19] but several volumes can readily be described as 'sedatives,' most notably, *Sappho: One Hundred Lyrics* (1903)[20] and the five collections of 1898–1905 that became *Pipes of Pan* (1906), a compendium that when sampled in all but small quantities reveals both the success and the danger of a soporific aesthetic.

At first glance, Duncan Campbell Scott seems to have been untouched by the therapeutic theories and concerns that so engaged other members of the Confederation group at different times and in varying degrees in the 1880s, 1890s, and, in Carman's case, well beyond. None of the poems in either of Scott's two first volumes, *The Magic House and Other Poems* (1893) and *Labor and the Angel* (1898), contains any explicit gesture towards mind-cure, and neither do any of his contributions to 'At the Mermaid Inn.' Evidence of Scott's guarded participation in the mind-cure movement can be found, however, in the second of the two poems that preface the short stories collected in *In the Village of Viger* (1896), which figures the reader's entry into the fictional world of a French-Canadian village on the outskirts of a noisy and expanding city as the equivalent of a therapeutic excursion into Nature:

> Whoever has from toil and stress
> Put into ports of idleness,
> And watched the gleaming thistledown
> Wheel in the soft air lazily blown ...
>
> ...
>
> Might find perchance the wandering fire,
> Around St. Joseph's sparkling spire;
> And wearied with the fume of strife,
> The complex joys and ills of life,
>
> Might for an hour his worry staunch,
> In pleasant Viger by the Blanche. ([vi])

It seems likely that when he wrote the first four lines of this prefatory poem, Scott had in mind Lampman's testaments to the healing power of 'idleness' in 'Heat' and 'Among the Timothy.'

Since the wheel of the discussion has come almost full circle in returning to Lampman, the last word on the therapeutic aspect of the work of the Confederation group may go to him in the opening and closing stanzas of 'An Invitation to the Woods,' an amusing treatment of the curative effect of immersion in the natural world that he wrote in September 1897 during his second-to-last camping holiday in the wilderness and published in the *Youth's Companion* less than eight months before his death (see *AC* 190–2):

> Are you broken with the din
>   Of the street?
> Are you sickened of your thin
>   Hands and feet?
> Are you bowed and bended double
> With a weight of care and trouble,
>   Are you spectral with a skin
>   Like a sheet?
>
> Take your body and your soul
>   To the woods,
> To the tonic and control
>   Of its moods,
> Where the forest gleams and quivers,
> Where the only roads are rivers,
>   And the trunk-line bears the whole
>   Of your goods.
> ...
> You shall waken blithe and bold
>   As a cork
> From a bed that is not sold
>   In New York,
> You shall thrive and grow no thinner
>   On a chunk of bread for dinner,
> With a jack-knife and a cold
>   Piece of pork.
> Oh! the triumph of the hound!
>   Oh! the joy,

When the rapid spins you round
   Like a toy!
When you race with birch and paddle,
And the stern-sheet for a saddle,
   You shall feel yourself as sound
   As a boy.
(quoted in Early, 'Twenty-Five Fugitive Poems' 65–7)

The temptation to dismiss this as parody is strong and perhaps justified, but Lampman's account of the circumstances of its composition in a letter to Thomson on 1 October 1897 suggests that it cannot be so easily classified: 'we ... portaged into a little ... brown-watered lake – deep, silent, surrounded by unbroken woods, seldom visited by anyone. There we camped and stayed, and fed upon partridges and black bass, and grew fat – so fat and comfortable did I grow that I became inspired with ... doggerel. Duncan was also much benefited, and took on a healthier hue' (*AC* 191).

# CHAPTER SIX

# Supernaturalism

One of the most striking characteristics of the Confederation poets as a group is their shared roots in the Anglican tradition. Frederick George Scott was educated at Bishop's College in Lennoxville, Quebec, and King's College in London, England, ordained a priest in the Church of England in 1886, and through most of the period of the group's effective existence, served as a curate or rector in parishes in Drummondville and Quebec City. Between 1882 and 1891, Campbell was a theology student, first at Wycliffe College, Toronto, and then at the Episcopal Theological School in Cambridge, Massachusetts, a deacon and priest in West Claremont, New Hampshire (1885–7), and the rector of Anglican churches in St Stephen, New Brunswick (1888–90), and Southampton (near Wiarton), Ontario (1890–1). The fathers of both Roberts and Lampman, George Goodridge Roberts and Archibald Lampman, Senior, were Anglican ministers and members of the Society for the Propagation of the Gospel, and each poet dedicated a volume of poetry to his father (*Orion, and Other Poems* and *Alcyone*). Being of Loyalist stock, Carman's family had both political and doctrinal reasons for its commitment to the Church of England (Shepard 4–5); his uncle, Donald Bliss, was the rector of the Anglican church at Mount Whatley, New Brunswick; and his first piece of verse, written in 1875, was an 'Easter Hymn' (Sorfleet, 'Introduction,' *Poems* 14). Only Duncan Campbell Scott had no connection with Anglicanism, but his father, William Scott, was a Methodist minister of the moderate rather than Calvinist persuasion whose position was therefore close doctrinally to the Church of England.[1] More than many other Canadians during the post-Confederation period, then, the poets of the Confederation group were born and raised in environments in which Christianity in its Anglican and moderate forms was a continual and formative presence.

   Of the importance of the religious component of the poets' upbring-
ing for the development of their social and aesthetic values there can be
little, if any, doubt. Both the Anglican and the Methodist Churches in
Canada were strongly committed to the communal and educational as
well as the spiritual welfare of their charges, and both conceived of
themselves as having important roles to play in developing Canadian
nationhood and culture. 'I owe the emotion that I felt for the confederation of Canada to my father,' Roberts recalled in 1927 ('Interview,' 64),
and in Pomeroy's biography he remembers his father expressing the
hope that his '"son [would] grow up to play his full part"' in '"the building of th[e] young nation"' (10). (To the extent that Roberts went on to
lead the Confederation group, his father's hope was fulfilled by not one
son but six.) By grace of having fathers who were ministers, Roberts,
Lampman, and Duncan Campbell Scott grew up in households where
writing was an integral part of work and life; indeed, Lampman's father
was himself a poet,[2] and Scott's was the author of several works of non-
fictional prose.[3] With respect to the poetry of Roberts, Carman, and
Roberts's younger brother Theodore Goodridge Roberts (1877–1953)
and cousin Francis Sherman (1871–1926), Malcolm Ross has convinc-
ingly argued in 'A Strange Aesthetic Ferment' that a portion of its
emphasis on 'beauty, art and nature' derives from the High Church
movement that came to Fredericton with its first Anglican Bishop, John
Medley (1804–92), two decades before Confederation and bequeathed
to the young writers who grew up in Canon Roberts's rectory an abiding
'sense of the kinship of beauty and holiness' (19, 17). Both Lampman
and Frederick George Scott also came into contact with the controversial doctrines and aesthetic innovations of Anglo-Catholicism, Lampman at Trinity College, where the provost, the Reverend George
Whitaker (1811–82), was a 'High Church clergyman of the old school'
(quoted in Reed 85),* and Scott at the Ritualistic Church of St John the
Evangelist in Montreal and then in England, where his Catholic lean-
ings were such that in 1883 he arranged for an audience with Cardinal
Newman (see Thomas Adams 161 and Djwa, *The Politics of the Imagina-*

---

* '[N]either Whitaker not his pupils remotely approached the extremes of many Tractar-
  ians in England' (Headon 916), but Trinity College was repeatedly the target of 'charges of ritualism and Roman teaching' during his provostship (1851–81) (see also Reed
  14–66). Moreover, shortly after Whitaker's death and Lampman's graduation in 1882,
  the College built a chapel in the Gothic style favoured by the High Church movement
  and established chairs in the names of two of its prime movers, John Keble and E.B.
  Pusey, both of whom had supported an earlier appeal to increase the College's en-
  dowment (see Reed 71, 88–9).

*tion* 16–18). At the very least, it can be said that Anglican and Methodist Christianity was, in Pierre Bourdieu's terms, an 'active presence' that 'deposited in each [member of the Confederation group] ... schemes of perception, thought and action' (*Logic* 54) that would continue to influence in one way or another their ways of seeing, thinking, and acting.

At the core of this legacy was, of course, a belief in the existence of a transcendent reality centred in a Deity who is immanent in but distinguished from the material world of 'chance and change' (a phrase in Roberts's 'Tantramar Revisited' [*CP* 79] that, surely not fortuitously, echoes one of the prayers that are said after the Offertory in the Anglican Book of Common Prayer). It was to the service of that Deity that Frederick George Scott was able to devote himself both as a priest and as a poet. 'Thy glory alone, O God, be the end of all that I say,' runs the final poem in *The Soul's Quest and Other Poems*; 'Let it shine in every deed, let it kindle the prayers that I pray; / Let it burn in my innermost soul, till the shadow of self pass away, / And the light of Thy Glory, O God, be unveiled in the dawning of day' (123). Scott's Anglo-Catholic sympathies led to some difficulties with his bishop and parishioners in a province where Anglican fears of 'Popery' were exacerbated by its looming presence (see Djwa, *The Politics of the Imagination* 16–22), but he was uniquely fortunate among the poets of the Confederation group in being able to sustain his faith through and beyond a period in which Christian beliefs were subjected to almost continuous and frequently compromising interrogation. Before the poets were born, the Higher Criticism had undermined the credibility of the Bible as an expression of literal truth, evolutionary theory had exploded Christian conceptions of the origins of humanity, and Schopenhaurian pessimism had elevated the will to the position of metaphysical dominance upon which Nietzsche would build in *The Birth of Tragedy* (1871) and other iconoclastic and disconcerting texts. By 1869, the 'melancholy, long, withdrawing roar' of 'the Sea of Faith' that Arnold had heard on 'Dover Beach' (1867) (*Poems* 242) had left behind the word 'agnostic' (a coinage of the science writer T.H. Huxley), and in 1880 the *Spectator* (London) would suggest that 'agnosticism' was in most cases merely a synonym for 'atheism' (*OED*).

But the *Spectator* was wrong, for what was left for many late Victorians on both sides of the Atlantic after their Christian beliefs had been compromised or destroyed was an abiding orientation towards the transcendent and an ineluctable yearning for religious experience.[4] Argus-like, that yearning looked in many directions, two of which are critically important to the Confederation group: (1) mythology and folklore as

understood by Max Müller, John Fiske, and other comparative mythographers as the basis and explanation for the metaphors upon which all religions are founded; and (2) occult and Oriental religious systems as expounded by Helen Blavatsky, William Butler Yeats, and other participants in the Theosophical and Spiritualist movements as alternatives or supplements to traditional Christianity. In both of these directions lay new and exciting prospects for the poets: if aligned with the former, they could exploit myth and folklore to reach beyond what Fiske called the 'prosaic and coldly rational temper' of the modern mind to 'the mental haunts of primeval humanity' (16); if aligned with the latter, they could use techniques of suggestion to create a transrational 'subconscious art' (Carman, *Kinship of Nature* 147) aimed at conveying a sense of life's deep and insoluble mysteries.

Given Campbell's conception of 'the great poet [as] he of the great heart, strong intellect, and wide and deep knowledge, who ... reaches out and down into all the recesses of the human heart with a natural instinct that knows and feels what other men often take a lifetime to dream' (*Week*, 16 March 1894, 368), it is scarcely surprising that he was especially receptive to the alignment of poetry with myth. When he resigned as rector of the Anglican church in Southampton in May 1891 to take up a temporary position in the Department of Railways and Canals in Ottawa, the reason given was 'ill-health' (*Saturday Night*, 27 June 1891, 5), but there can be little doubt that doctrinal problems and perhaps even religious uncertainty also contributed to the decision. As indicated by the 'Invocation to the Lakes' in *Lake Lyrics and Other Poems*, the 'philosophy of life and basis for religion' that in earlier years had been nurtured by 'the ... multitudinous murmurs, ... sublime distances, ... infinite vastness ... and over-arching skies'[5] of Lake Huron was heavily indebted to Wordsworth but innocent of the pantheism of such poems as 'Tintern Abbey':

> I love thee, lakes, and all thy glorious world,
>   Blue, wrinkled, mist-encircled 'neath the sky.
> ...
> From sky and wave I drink thy nectared draught,
>   From jewelled brim that stars of heaven span:
> When, lo, 'tis lore of God my heart hath quaffed,
>   And sympathy for man. (*Lake Lyrics* 51–2)

Elsewhere in the volume, '*the jewels of nature / Are set in the light of God's smile*' (10), 'forests ... kneel ... in the dreamiest haze / That God sends down in the summer' (23), and Nature is a 'cathedral' with 'great vaulted arches' where 'God's glad weather / Haze wrap[s] heaven, wave and shore' (30–1). Only fleetingly in the few poems derived from Native legends and in the 'Sun-god' that 'Mark[s] the seasons with track of flame' (40) is there even a hint in *Lake Lyrics and Other Poems* of religious heterodoxy in the making.

Less than a year after his resignation, however, Campbell had sufficiently espoused the iconoclastic theories that he found in Fiske's *Myth and Myth-Makers: Old Tales and Superstitions Interpreted by Comparative Mythology* (1872) to publish a passage of startling insensitivity in the 27 February 1892 instalment of his 'At the Mermaid Inn' column:

> It may not be generally known that much of the so-called history of the past is pure mythology. Much of the early part of the Old Testament, such as the stories of the Garden of Eden, The Flood, the Serpent, The Story of Jonah, have all been proved to belong to the class of literature called mythic. The story of the Cross itself is one of the most remarkable myths in the history of humanity connected with the old phallic worship of some of our remote ancestors ... Probably the greatest stumbling-block to real knowledge of the past is the false religious prejudice which is hampering modern society to a large extent in countries like Canada; but even this is rapidly passing away in the more cultured localities. It is a poor and tottering religion that has to be bolstered up by ignorance. (*MI* 25–6)

After proclaiming 'mythology ... a beautiful and instructive study' and directing 'beginners' to Fiske's book, Campbell concludes his column with the promise that he 'will have more to say on the subject later on' (26).

It was not to be. On February 29, the *Globe* stated its regret that Campbell had been 'allowed to make ... remarks on religious matters of which [it] hasten[ed] to express [its] strongest disapproval' (4), and on March 5 the poet 'heartily' apologized for causing offence, lamely claiming that his column was 'hurriedly' written and 'necessarily compressed,' and clumsily attempted to explain away its description of 'the story of the cross as mythical':

> I had not the slightest allusion to the history of early Christianity or the death of Christ. What I meant was the story or history of the cross as a symbol of religious worship, as found in ancient native religions, such as Mayan, Babylonian, Egyptian, Aztec, and other ancient religious systems in

connection with their mythic origins as deduced by Max Müller and other distinguished authorities ... I would say farther, that I had not the slightest idea of an attack on Christianity ... (*MI* 30)[6]

Choosing his words very carefully, Campbell also asserts his 'reverence for the sacred and hallowed in the universe' and refers his readers to his 'principal writings' for proof that he 'believe[s] with Tennyson: "Let knowledge grow from more to more / But more of reverence in us dwell"' (30–31). The letter concludes with a request that 'the "Rev." be omitted from future references' to himself since he has 'voluntarily renounced that title, not from any disrespect for [his] former calling, but from the simple wish to be regarded as a layman' (30–1) – a layman disposed, the letter makes clear, to a religion that is natural rather than revealed, progressive rather than static, and centred, not on the Christian God, but (and notice the circularity of the logic here) on an attitude of 'reverence' for all that is worthy of being revered.

To judge by the poems that he wrote in the early 1890s and published in *The Dread Voyage: Poems* (1893), Campbell's abandonment of orthodox Christianity resulted initially in extremes of feeling that were almost manic (or bi-polar) in intensity. On the one hand, poems such as 'The Dread Voyage' itself offer a tragic vision of human destiny by which 'Hearts wherein no hope may waken ... Chartless, anchorless, forsaken, / Drift ... to the dark' as a consequence of 'some race-doom unforgiven' (*SPE* 45). On the other, poems such as 'In the Strength of the Morning' enact a comic narrative of spiritual enlightenment through communion with Nature and a resulting renewal of purposeful activity:

Out here across the wind-blown land,
     Where all is great and glad and new,
I feel my spirit's wings expand
     Like eagle's under heaven's blue:
Great with the strength of sea and land
I grasp life's problem's in my hand.

Back downward to the world I go,
     Filled with the glory of earth's light;
No demon dread can overthrow,
     No dreams of evil e'er affright:
To battle with my fate I go,
Across the days of strife and woe. (*SPE* 51)

Not until 'the autumn of 1894' or perhaps later,[7] when he urged his compatriots to 'take up the burden of empire' (*SPE* 57) in 'The Lazarus of Empire' (1899), did Campbell find the secular religion that his desire for belief apparently required. Thereafter, he became a typical Canadian imperialist in his reconciliation of 'a vehement Canadianism with an equally vehement imperialism' (Boone, *SPE* 4) and of necessity gave at least rhetorical paramountcy to the Kiplingesque God of country and empire in dozens of poems that are often remarkable and frequently under-appreciated for their verbal energy, their historical imagination, and the sheer force of their commitment to the belief that, thanks in great measure to the British Empire, humanity as a whole is becoming ever more civilized and spiritualized. In *The Sense of Power: Studies in the Ideas of Canadian Imperialism, 1867–1914*, Carl Berger very rightly dubs Campbell 'the unofficial poet laureate of Canadian imperialism' (192).

After the turn of the century, the search beyond the borders of orthodox Christianity for purposive answers to the riddle of humanity's origin, progress, and destiny that had taken Campbell first to mythology and then to imperialism brought him to the idiosyncratic combination of the two with ideas drawn from archaeology, ethnography, and theosophy that he called 'The Tragedy of Man.' Conceived as a refutation of the 'Darwinian Theory of Evolution,' Campbell's twenty-two-chapter treatise and the poems that stem from it ('The Tragedy of Man,' 'Immortality,' and 'The Divine Origin')[8] propose that 'man in his higher representation on this earth' is 'the result of a fusion, at some remote period, of a mysterious race of beings' 'from without the planet' or at least connected to 'the outside universe' with 'a lower, autochthonous, or purely earth race, who were possibly evolved from the lower creation' and, on the basis of this, constructs a metanarrative of human spiritual evolution in which Christianity and evolutionary theory combine to supplement each other's deficiencies. Thus, the Fall as recounted in Genesis is not a 'mere myth' but a 'cardinal truth' about the 'degradation of man' that constitutes 'the first great tragedy' and holds 'the secret of the origin and destiny of man'; their belief in 'this doctrine,' in the existence of God and in the divinity of Christ, has made 'great races such as the British ... the greatest of peoples' and placed them 'in the very forefront of modern civilization and culture'; and 'all [God's] paths lie upward and outward and the destiny of the man and the race of today still possess all of the primal divine possibilities of emancipation and achievement' (*SPE*, 188–95). 'It is a remarkable fact,' Campbell adds, 'that all of the greatest human literature is a part of

antiquity and quite out of touch with all that is modern ... The language
of poetry, called inspired, is no doubt but a harkening back to the common speech of the Gods' (194, 196).

In the poems to which the lucubrations of 'The Tragedy of Man' gave
rise there is a predictable amount of versified prose ('Legends and
myths, so called / By the modern, material ken') and wishful thinking
('I voice again the immortal, / I say anew the divine'), but, occasionally,
as in the resonantly Miltonic and oddly Swinburnian opening lines of
the lyric of the same title, they achieve a bardic sonority appropriate to
the high seriousness of their themes:

Long, long ago;
  Ere these material days;
Ere man learned o'er much for the golden glow
  Of Love's divine amaze;
Ere faith was slain; there came to this sad earth
  A high, immortal being of source divine,
And mingling with the upward climbing life,
  Like crystal water in some fevered wine,
Wakened in one red blood mysterious strife,
    Knowledge of good and ill, and that sad birth
    Of splendour and woe for all who yearn and pine.

And this is why,
  Down in the craving, remorseful human heart
There doth remain a dream that will not die
  An unassuagèd hunger, that o'er the smart
Of sorrow and shame and travail, clamours eterne
For some high goal, some vision of being superne
  Life doth not grant, earth doth not satisfy.

This is the secret of the heart of man
  And his sad tragedy; his godlike powers;
His summer of vastness, and the wintry ban
  Of all his greatness high which deity dowers ... (*SPE* 130)

It is a testament to the cross-fertilization that occurred among the poets
of the Confederation group decades before this poem was written that
between its echoes of Milton and Swinburne can be heard reminiscences of the cadences and diction of Roberts's 'The Pipes of Pan' and

Lampman's 'Winter-Store.'* In marked contrast to Yeats during the same period, Campbell sought no new style as a vehicle for his heterodox ideas but quite deliberately cast them in the idioms of bygone ages. The reader who is counselled to 'hold in ... heart / A great and invincible hope ... That the earth is God's' and the soul is immortal in 'Immortality' (*SPE* 131) is addressed as 'you of the hungry heart,' a phrase taken from Tennyson's 'Ulysses.' To the end, Campbell remained both stylistically and metaphysically a late Victorian provincial.

When Roberts observed in 1933 that one of the 'consideration[s] which give unity to ... Canadian poetry' of the period inaugurated by *Orion, and Other Poems* is a broadly 'religious ... attitude toward this life and the future,' he was obviously thinking very generally of a large number of poets; but when he specified in the same lecture that 'a sort of mystical theosophy [and] a Neo-Platonic pantheism or Nature worship' were 'among the religious creed[s]' espoused by Canadian poets during the post-Confederation period he probably had in mind Carman, himself, and one or two others ('Canadian Poetry' 82). That both poets did indeed give credence and expression to ideas of the sort mentioned by Roberts became evident at several points in previous chapters: Roberts's 'Canada' (1886), it was observed, contains a reference to the 'secret' of the 'mystic Nile,' and his 'Autochthon' (1893) is spoken by a 'spirit' that is pantheistically present throughout Nature (chapter 2); and Carman's writing in both poetry and prose from as early as 1889 onwards draws heavily on American Transcendentalism (chapter 3) and contains numerous and increasingly explicit gestures towards the 'natural religion of ancient Greece,' the Eleusinian mysteries, and other occult beliefs that were ultimately subsumed by his Delsartean or unitrinian theory of mind-body-spirit harmonization (chapters 5 and 6). Surveying

---

* Compare the central lines of Campbell's opening stanza with Roberts's description of the goat god's playing by the river Penēus in ancient Greece: 'Hither comes Pan, to this pregnant earthy spot, when his piping / Flags; and ... / Fits new reeds to his mouth with the weird earth-melody in them, / alive with a life able to mix with the god's' (*CP* 77); and the central lines of his second stanza with Lampman's description of the subversion of his intention to 'feed on memory' in 'Winter-Store': 'across the windy night / Comes ... a vision sad and high / Of the labouring world [that] ... Pricks my soul with sudden stare ... A something I cannot control, / A nameless hunger of the soul' (*P* 171–3). The final lines of Campbell's opening verse paragraph echo *Paradise Lost* 1:1–3 ('Of Man's First Disobedience, and the Fruit / Of that Forbidden Tree, whose mortal taste / Brought Death into the World, and all our woe ...'), and the paragraph as a whole recalls the second section of Swinburne's *Atalanta in Calydon* ('Before the beginning of years, / There came to the making of man / Time, with a gift of tears; / Grief, with a glass that ran ...' [2:258]).

the Canadian poets of his generation in 1933, Roberts saw a cohort of 'incorrigible and unrepentant idealists' who 'are all fundamentally antagonistic to everything that savours of materialism, and even of such high and stoical pessimism as that of Matthew Arnold' ('Canadian Poetry' 82). Yet both he and Carman were at one time as Arnoldian as they were Anglican. When did this change and why?

Neither Roberts nor Carman seems to have undergone a dramatic shift in religious orientation comparable to Campbell's resignation from the clergy, but there is a good deal of evidence that the two men were in spiritual transition in the late 1880s and early 1890s, and that the first half of 1892 was something of a turning point for both of them. Charting Roberts's poetic and spiritual progress largely from his own perspective in the late 1930s and early 1940s, Elsie Pomeroy maintains that, despite the gradual shift in his work from 'classical themes' to 'descriptive and interpretative' (or 'landscape') poetry, and thence 'to poems of philosophy and mysticism,' 'he had always been, fundamentally, the mystic' (115); however, in his account of his stay with Roberts and Carman at Windsor in the summer of 1889 in *On the Cars and Off* (1895), Douglas Sladen states that at that time Roberts was 'not mystical like ... Carman' (6), a perception borne out by the fact that, with the exception of 'Autochthon,' which was first published in December 1889 (and, in any case, puts mysticism at the service of nationalism), all of the explicitly 'mystical' (that is, pantheistic) poems to which Pomeroy subsequently refers – 'Origins' (1896), 'Kinship' (1896), and 'The Unsleeping'[9] – were apparently written and certainly first published in the early-to-mid-1890s (see *CP* 178, 181, 186). To judge by the revisions of 1886–7 that tranformed the nationalistic-cum-mystical 'Low Tide on Avon' (see chapter 2) into the purely mystical 'Low Tide on Grand Pré' (see chapter 3), Carman's 'mystically-oriented idealis[m]' intensified in the late 1880s, probably, as J.R. Sorfleet has compellingly argued, under the impact of Josiah Royce's 'systematic "proof"' in *The Religious Aspect of Philosophy* (1885) that '"the world is divine and full of life."'[10] To judge also by the poems that he wrote and published in the early 1890s, most notably 'A Pagan's Prayer' (December 1891)[11] and 'Spring Song' ('Make me over, mother April ...') (December 1893), Carman's pantheism further intensified in the early 1890s when, among other things, both he and Roberts became close friends with Richard Hovey and the three 'high Anglican pagans' (the term is Carman's [quoted in Miller 110]) hatched plans for what became *Songs from Vagabondia* (1894).

The late winter and early spring of 1892 were a time of great emotional and spiritual turbulence for both Roberts and Carman. Early in the year, they were despondent because of overwork (see *CL* 142–3 and *L* 45–6), and each was casting about for new possibilities: 'I would run straight to N[ew] Y[ork] if it could at all be done,' Roberts told Carman on February 27, and on April 6: 'I have been for a long time miserable' (*CL* 143, 145). 'I tell you three years at this desk [on the *Independent*] will make me a finished and complete pagan,' Carman told one correspondent on April 16, and to another he confided on May 26 that he had 'been in the dolefuls lately,' would be 'leav[ing] the *Independent* soon,' and had 'several good things in prospect' (quoted in Miller 81, *L* 46). Moreover, both were deeply shaken by the death of Roberts's younger brother, Goodridge Bliss Roberts, on February 4 and 'to a certain extent grieved' (*CL* 142) by the death on February 23 of their sometime mentor, Joseph Edmund Collins. Earlier in the year, Carman had made a trip to Boston that evidently proved fruitless as regards new prospects but highly fruitful in other ways. 'Do ... write me fully of those new and heavier views of life which thou hast so rashly picked up in Boston,' Roberts begged his cousin on February 27; 'I am disturbed till I know more' (*CL* 143).

The exact nature of the 'new and heavier views of life' that Carman acquired in Boston may never be known with absolute certainty, but the work of Stephen Maxfield Parrish, T.J. Jackson Lears, and others allows for some very accurate guesses to be offered. Led by the poet Louise Imogen Guiney (1861–1920) and the publisher Frederick Holland Day (18?–1932), Boston's artistic and intellectual circles of the early 1890s were undergoing a renaissance driven by a confluence of Transcendentalism and *fin-de-siècle* aestheticism that simultaneously stripped Transcendentalism of its Puritan component and provided aestheticism with a spiritual dimension. The result, which Lears labels 'anti-modernism,' was indeed a constellation of 'new and heavier views of life' – a stylish rejection of materialism in the idealistic spirit of Emerson and Thoreau, two writers for whom Carman, of course, already had a profound admiration (see especially note 35 in Chapter 3). By January 1892, the Boston renaissance had a vehicle in the *Mahogany Tree*, a short-lived periodical 'devoted solely to the "fine arts,"' opposed to 'all Philistinism, even the Philistinism of advertisements and the hope of making money,' and committed to 'the deeper side of American life.'[12] In April, the *Mahogany Tree* was joined by another short-lived periodical, the *Knight Errant*, whose aims were very similar but more inflected, as its title indicates, by the medievalism of the Rossettian branch of Pre-Raphaelitism and by the reformist goals of the Arts and Crafts Movement.[13] Of Carman's familiarity with the Boston circles whose ideas these periodicals represented there can be no doubt whatsoever. He had known and corresponded with Guiney since his time at Harvard during 1886-8, and on 15 January 1892 he wrote to Day to thank him for the loan of his copy of Yeats's *The Wanderings of Oisin, and Other Poems* (1889, 1892) (*L* 17, 43). Tellingly, the letter to Day also comments on the Blakean quality of two of Yeats's poems, 'Girl's Song' and 'Ephemera,' and expresses apprehension on the basis of 'something Miss Guiney said' that in their forthcoming edition of Blake's works Yeats and Edwin J. Ellis would 'try ... to patch out a scheme of philosophy for [the poet].' It is not at all beyond the bounds of possibility that the 'new and heavier views of life' that Carman acquired in Boston early in 1892 included elements of Theosophy, Rosicruceanism, Neoplatonism, and other heterodox 'scheme[s] of philosophy' that by that time had attracted the interest of Yeats and other occultists on both sides of the Atlantic.

Whether or not as a result of Carman's Bostonian ideas, the summer of 1892 was pivotal for both him and Roberts. Back in New York as editor of *Current Literature*, Carman was apparently inspired by a statement in an 'Old English Statute' pertaining to 'Vagabonds and Vagrants' – 'Such as wake on the night and sleep on the day, and haunt customable taverns and alehouses and roust about, and no man wot whence they come, nor whither they go' (*PBC* 338) – to write the first of the *Vagabondia* poems, a ballad that at one point invokes and then undercuts the Christian account of creation ('In the beginning God made man / Out of the wandering dust, men say') and at its conclusion advances a playfully vague conception of God and heaven:

There is a tavern, I have heard,
   Not far, and frugal, kept by One
Who knows the children of the Word,
   And welcomes each when day is done.

Some say the house is lonely set
   In Northern night, and snowdrifts keep
The silent door; the hearth is cold:
   And all my fellows gone to sleep ...

Had I my will! I hear the sea
   Thunder a welcome on the shore;

> I know where lies the hostelry
>   And who should open me the door! (*Independent*, 8 December 1892, 1; *PBC*
> 34)

Around the time that 'The Vagabonds' was written, Carman and Roberts visited one another in Windsor and New York, and in September Hovey (who some two years earlier had abandoned his theological studies and plans to enter the Episcopalian priesthood) came to stay with Roberts at Kingscroft. The result for Roberts was a burst of creative activity that produced several short poems, eighty lines of 'Ave! (an Ode for the Shelley Centenary, 1892)' and an ambitious plan for 'a long lyrical drama ... after the type of Shelley's *Prometheus Unbound*' but centred, like Rossetti's 'Eden Bower,' on Lilith, the mythical first wife of Adam (*CL* 154–5). 'Do you know of, or can you hear of, any Adamic literature that might add to my knowledge of the Witch Wife, "not a drop of whose blood was human"?' he asked Carman (quoting Rossetti's poem) after Hovey's departure; 'if thou canst, pick up ... an *unexpurgated* translation of the *Talmud*, and also a copy of [Sabine] Baring-Gould's *Legends of the Patriarch Prophets*' (*CL* 155).[14] Roberts's Lilith drama was never completed, but its proposed subject is an index of his awakened interest in heterodox religious ideas.

During the ensuing two years, in which (see chapter 5) Roberts spent several weeks with Hovey's family in Washington, DC and hosted summer camps at Kingscroft, his published poetry showed little evidence of his movement away from Anglicanism. In 'Ave!' the atheistic Shelley is said to have followed the same 'star' as Dante and seen 'the living God / And worshipped ..., beholding Him the same / Adored on earth as Love' (*CP* 148, 151).[15] At the conclusion of 'Whitewaters,' a ballad that was published in the 14 December 1893 issue of the *Independent*, a 'father, mother, [and] child' fall asleep 'where no storm breaks, nor terror stirs / The peace of God' (*CP* 159). And in the poem with which Roberts elected to close the series of sonnets in *Songs of Common Day, and Ave* (1893), he aligns himself with the tenets of Christian Natural Theology in his assumption that the (God-given) powers of human observation and reason can move from 'the things that are made' to an apprehension of 'invisible things' and 'even [the Creator's] power and Godhead' (Romans 1.20):[16]

> In the wide awe and wisdom of the night
>   I saw the round world rolling on its way,

Beyond significance of depth and height
  Beyond the interchange of dark and day
I marked the march to which is set no pause,
  And that stupendous orbit, round whose rim
The great sphere sweeps, obedient unto laws
  That utter the eternal thoughts of Him.
I compassed time, outstripped the starry speed,
  And in my still soul apprehended space,
Till, weighing laws which these but blindly heed,
  At last I came before Him face to face, –
And knew the universe of no such span
As the august infinitude of Man. (*CP* 133)

With its allusion to 1 Corinthians 13.12 ('For now we see through a glass darkly; but then face to face') and its echo of *Paradise Lost* 7: 166–8 ('bid the Deep / Within appointed bounds be Heav'n and Earth ... because I [God] am who fill / Infinitude'), 'In the wide awe and wisdom of the night ...' is to most appearances exactly the sort of poem that was expected of a professor at an Anglican college and a leading light in Canadian poetry. (In fact, the sonnet was reprinted in both the *King's College Record* and in *Later Canadian Poems.*) [17] Nevertheless, the indeterminacy of 'Him' in the octave and its association through capitalization with 'Man' in the sestet allow for a less straightforward reading towards which Carman pointed in January 1895 when he quoted the sonnet as evidence that, although 'without superstition of any sort, [Roberts] is yet imbued with the ancient worship of Nature' and that 'the quiet of a northern pantheism pervades all his deeper work' ('Mr. Charles G.D. Roberts' 165). Not until he resigned from King's College and departed for the United States was Roberts free to express openly the heterodox religious beliefs that he had by then been harbouring for several years. [18]

While marking time in Fredericton between his resignation and his departure, Roberts considered using 'A Pagan Prayer-Book,' a phrase coined by Carman, as the title of a new collection of poems (*CL* 209), but chose instead *The Book of the Native* (1896) for a volume whose pantheism is again carefully concealed by the terminology of Christian worship and devotion. Framed by a dedication that ends with the author's 'spirit [lifted] close' to his dead brother 'In memory and prayer' by the 'strength,' 'faith,' and 'calm' of the natural world, and by 'A Child's Prayer at Evening,' which begins with a Latin translation of the lines 'Father, who keepest / The stars in Thy care' (*CP* 143, 204), *The Book of the Native* contains most of the poems of unitrinian regeneration/resurrection that Roberts wrote while recuperating with the Hoveys in Washington early in 1893, but it also contains many pieces in which heterodox and agnostic inclinations are redirected along lines that do not contradict a Christian interpretation. In 'Origins,' for example, the human soul is ultimately borne away from the natural world of 'The enigmatic Will,' genetic predeterminism, and natural instinct 'past the bourne of space / To the unaverted Face'; in 'An April Adoration' the sights and sounds of spring are figured as 'a liturgy of prayer' and 'a psalm of praise' that rise 'to God,' who, in the concluding stanza, 'Hear[s] the adoration song of Earth'; and in 'Earth's Complines' the decidedly pantheistic experience of being privy to a conversation among the blooms of 'tall white lilies' in a twilit garden leads initially to a sense that 'The spirits of earth' are 'Serving among the lilies, / In an ecstasy of prayer,' then to a feeling of the 'kinship' of the human 'soul' to 'the soul of trees ... / ... white, eternal seas – / ... flickering bats and night-moths,' and, finally, to a recognition that what has been seen is 'The image of God's face' in 'the deep of [the] heart' (*CL* 186–7, 188–9, 196–7). Roberts's own recent poetry cannot have been entirely absent from his mind in 1897 when in 'The Poetry of Nature' he forthrightly identified 'the pantheistic proposition' and its inevitable corollary, 'the unity of man and God,' as an increasingly prominent feature of 'the nature-poetry of the last fifty years' and unabashedly concluded that 'whosoever follows the inexplicable lure of beauty in colour, form, sound, perfume, or any other manifestation, – reaching out to it as perhaps a message from some unfathomable past, or a premonition of the future – knows that the mystic signal beckons nowhere more imperiously than from the heights of nature-poetry' (*SPCP* 280–1).

It is characteristic of Roberts that 'the inexplicable lure of beauty' that he followed during his New York years belonged primarily to women. There is a 'love that should be, not a pastime, but a prayer, not an episode, but an eternity ... Few, indeed, are they who are born to endure the light of its uncovered face; but all have heard the dim tradition of it ... [I]n silence was plighted that great troth which shall last, it is my faith, through other lives than this' (7, 280): these and other statements like them in the first novel that Roberts published after his removal, *A Sister to Evangeline: Being the Story of Yvonne de Lamourie* (1898), are very much in the 'same spirit ... [as] the love-poems in ... *New York Nocturnes*, which were written during the same period' and published as a poetic sequence with 'Other Poems' in the same year

(Pomeroy 152). A series of linked poems with a metaphysical narrative like *Songs of the Common Day* before it and *The Book of the Rose* (1903) after it, 'New York Nocturnes' resembles the poems in the latter volume in presenting erotic love not only as, in the words of 'The Poetry of Nature' again, 'a message from some unfathomable past [and] a premonition of the future,' but also as a place of intersection and reconciliation between the sacred and the profane, the earthly and the heavenly, the human and the divine. With an audacity learned from Rossetti, Morris, and Swinburne, Roberts celebrates love and the beloved in 'New York Nocturnes' and *The Book of the Rose* in sanctifying terminology drawn from Christian ritual and devotion and, even more audaciously, from the narrative of Christ's passion, death, and resurrection. 'Half passion and half prayer' in diction and tone, both sequences conflate Nature and God into the apotheosized beloved (the capital *S* she of the climactic 'Nocturne of Consecration' in 'New York Nocturnes') whose kiss is a 'mystical perfection' that presages 'another joy' in 'other worlds' beyond 'fate,' 'time,' and 'change' (*CP* 239–40).[19] It is scarcely surprising that the puritanical Desmond Pacey found in *New York Nocturnes* and *The Book of the Rose* mainly the 'perfervid and artificial' products of 'a mind which has turned in upon itself without the moral strength to make a real "confession of it all"' ('Introduction' xxiii). For better or for worse, Roberts had liberated himself from King's College, the Maritimes, his marriage, and his religion.

Since Carman was largely free of such constraints throughout the 1890s, he had little need to dissemble his heterodox views and themes. Indeed, from almost the moment he moved to the United States in September 1886 to study with Royce at Harvard, he began the spiritual odyssey that would take him in the course of his life through an astounding variety of religious experiences and systems, from the forthright Transcendentalism of 'Low Tide on Grand Pré' to the equally forthright Theosophy of 'Shamballah' (1925).[20] In the early-to-mid-1890s, Carman's restless spirituality combined with two other factors – his exposure in 1892 to the heterodox ideas of Yeats and others, and his affection for a young American woman named Jessie Kappeler, whom he met later the same year while staying with the Hoveys in Washington – to attract him to the Platonic and Neoplatonic idea that love and beauty can provide intimations of immortality and glimpses of eternal realities. Thus in *Songs of the Sea Children*, a sequence of love poems inspired by Kappeler but not published until 1903, the speaker 'Feels immortality begin / As [the beloved's] long kisses surge and climb,' proclaims 'Her body ... the only gate / Of Paradise' and her 'kiss' more 'wonderful' than that of 'Lilith in the garden,' and wonders whether, in her, the 'sumptuous night' has brought to him, a 'Lover of beauty,' 'The Rose of Beauty of all time' (*PP* 63, 117, 158). Arranged to reflect the cycle of the seasons, *Songs of the Sea Children* concludes by paying the beloved what for Carman may have been the supreme compliment: 'In the new birth of all things bright and fair' that is spring, she is 'very April, glory, light, and air, / And joy and ardour ... !' (*PP* 179).

It is an indication of the connections and affinities that Carman had developed with Boston circles by the mid-1890s that when he had his second volume of poems ready for publication in 1894 he offered it to two publishing houses in the city, first to Frederick Holland Day's new firm of Copeland and Day (1893–9), who refused it because it contained illustrations by Thomas Meteyard and they had decided 'not [to publish] illustrated poetry' (*L* 101), and then to Lamson, Wolffe and Company (1895–9), who shared some of the same interests and personnel as Copeland and Day (see Kraus 22). Announced by its subtitle as 'A Book of the Unseen,' *Behind the Arras* (1895) is a programmatic application of Hovey's definition of 'modern symbolism' in the introduction to his 1894 translation of the *Plays* of Maurice Maeterlinck as a literary mode characterized by evocative suggestion rather than explicit statement:

> It by no means ... involves a complete and consistent allegory. Its events, its personages, its sentences rather imply than definitely state an esoteric meaning. The story, whether romantic ... or realistic ..., lives for itself and produces no impression of being a masquerade of moralities; but behind every incident, almost every phrase, one is aware of a lurking universality, the adumbration of greater things. One is given an impression of the thing symbolized rather than a formulation. ('Modern Symbolism' 5)*

---

\* With no reference to any personal knowledge of the three men, Hovey names Carman, Roberts, and Gilbert Parker the foremost practitioners of symbolism in North America, citing Parker's 'The Stone' in *Pierre and His People* (1892) and Roberts's 'The Young Ravens That Call upon Him' in the May 1894 number of *Lippincott's Monthly Magazine* (Philadelphia) as prime instances of a type of 'symbolism [that is] suggestive rather than cut-and-dried' (6). '[I]t promises well for the literature that is to be,' adds Hovey, 'that the strongest of the young writers of today have a tendency to myth-making' that reveals itself in their adherence to this modern 'symbolic principle' (7, 8). While not all readers of 'Modern Symbolism and Maurice Maeterlinck' were fooled by Hovey's insouciance ('it will ... strike the better critical sense ... as a plate of delectable sweetmeats rather recklessly offered to two or three of Mr. Hovey's young Canadian friends for

The purpose of the symbolism in *Behind the Arras* is to direct the reader towards 'Unseen' spiritual realities whose indeterminacy places them beyond the reach of straightforward allegory and ordinary reason. 'There are dimensions still, / Beyond thought's reach, though not beyond love's will, / For soul to fill' declares the speaker of the volume's title poem, and in its most ambitious piece, the meditation of a musician on his violin entitled 'Beyond the Gamut' in reference to the 'full range of notes which a voice or [musical] instrument is capable of producing' (*OED*), there are several statements to similar effect: '... thought cannot far without the symbol!'; 'Soul may pass out where all color ends'; 'I, at my wits' end, may still develop / Unknown senses in life's larger room'; 'every sense's impulse / Is a means the master soul employs ... Joys of earth are journey-aids to heaven, / Garb of the new sainthood sane and whole. / Earth one habitat of spirit merely ...' (*PBC* 73, 98, 100–1). Throughout the volume, houses and their components (rooms, windows, doors) and various means of artistic expression (tapestry, painting, and, especially, music) are figuratively used to suggest the way in which the world that is accessible to the senses provides, in Hovey's phrase, 'an adumbration of greater things.'

Although *Behind the Arras* was faulted by William Morton Payne in the *Dial* (Chicago) for a 'lack ... [of] finish and lucidity' (16 February 1896, 116), it was greeted with predictable enthusiasm and comprehension by the avant-garde Boston periodical *Poet-Lore*, which commented particularly on 'the illusive and yet fascinating suggestiveness of the symbolism' of 'Behind the Arras' itself and provided a description of the poem's effects and purposes that could have been written by Carman himself:

After reading the poem one feels as if emerging from some mystic realm, where, by means of ethereal symbols, the mind has caught glimpses of the

---

which they will be expected to make due return' wrote the reviewer for the *Independent* on 18 April 1895 [18]), his essay doubtless played a major part in cementing the connection between Carman and *symbolisme* that culminated in 1896 in his being anointed 'The American High Priest of Symbolism' by the *New York World* (see Miller 154–5). For a detailed discussion of the *symboliste* aspects of the short stories of Parker and Roberts and their possible sources in Maeterlinck's plays (more of which in due course in the present chapter) see Bentley, '"The Thing Is Found to Be Symbolic."' In the Prefatory Note to the 1903 edition of *Earth's Enigmas: A Book of Animal and Nature Life* (1896), Roberts states that 'most of the stories in th[e] collection attempt to present one or another of those problems of life or nature to which, as it appears to many of us, there is no adequate solution within sight' ([5]).

vanishing-points of thought, yet it is all so simply, even reticently done. And the drift of it? mayhap the climbing of the spirit to even higher regions of beauty through the growth of will and love!

...

Bliss Carman's [poetry] ... is pervaded by the peculiar aroma of his own individual genius. He amplifies ... thought into a complete expression of what we take to be his own individual philosophy, briefly stated, – the development of the soul by means of the senses, the first annihilation of evil, and the perfect fruition of love. (*Poet-Lore* 8.2 [1896] 95–7)[21]

Apparently neither Payne nor the *Poet-Lore* reviewer was troubled by aspects of *Behind the Arras* that flow from a combination of its philosophical consistency and technical uniformity: repetition and predictability. Most readers can absorb in small doses poems in which the analogical matrix determines that God, or the 'One,' or the 'Overword' be figured as a weaver ('Behind the Arras'), a musician ('Beyond the Gamut'), a juggler ('The Juggler'), a train driver ('The Night Express'), a jester, or 'The Final Critic' ('In the Wings'), and some will even be able to accept the fact that only after eighty-four four-line stanzas of 'The Lodger' does the narrator reveal that the lodger 'gives his name / As Spiritus' (*PBC* 79, 80, 112, 96), but many will tire quickly of being asked over and over again to participate in poetic treasure hunts in which the clues are too obvious and the treasure too easily guessed. With *Behind the Arras*, Carman, unfortunately, moved further along the path that led from the harmonic unity of *Low Tide on Grand Pré* to the soporific uniformity of the *Pipes of Pan* series.

Some three months after the appearance of his second book in January 1896, Carman travelled to England and France for the purposes of having a holiday and meeting writers whose work he admired. In London, he met, among others, the English godfather of *symbolisme* Arthur Symons, and the 'dark Celtic velvet inspired mystic eloquent refined W.B. Y[eats] himself, the William Blake of this smaller generation,' but missed the American novelist and journalist Harold Frederic and the English man of letters Edmund Gosse (*L* 109–10). In Paris, he frequented the haunts of the *symbolistes* but struggled with his poor French, and found himself 'passed everywhere for a "young American writer"' (*L* 110). Even before he left, however, Carman had become disenchanted with the modish truculence and world-weariness of both the American and the European branches of the decadent movement,[22] and, after a sojourn with Roberts and Hovey in Nova Scotia during which they prepared *More Songs from Vagabondia* for publication, he was able to tell Guiney that 'all those *Yellow* and *Chap-Books* and *Savoys* and *Philistines* are capable of egregious bad taste and offensiveness' and only tolerable 'because they are willing to dare' (*L* 111–12). Less than three months after he wrote this on 15 October 1896, Carman returned from Boston to New York in preparation for Roberts's arrival, a reunion that resulted in a brief period of flamboyant bohemianism in which the two cousins, Hovey, and the English expatriate writer Richard Le Gallienne were dubbed by a New York newspaper 'The Angora School of Poets' because of their long and unkempt hair (see Miller 165). But by far the most momentous event for Carman in the early months of 1897 was the personal involvement with Mary Perry King that would lead in the ensuing years to a revitalization and intensification of his commitment to the Delsartean or unitrinian theory of mind-body-spirit harmonization that, as seen in the previous chapter, Carman first encountered in 1893 through Henrietta Russell, who had also been King's teacher.

In *Bliss Carman* (1923), a book that Carman himself held in high regard (see *Letters to Margaret Lawrence* 104), Odell Shepard sums up King's version of unitrinianism as an 'effort to close the breach made by an Orientalized Christianity between body and spirit and to reveal the truth which the Greeks so well knew, that body, mind, and spirit are to be raised to their highest powers not separately ... but together' (128). As a key component of 'personal harmonizing,' 'physical culture, to Bliss Carman,' Shepard asserts, 'is actually and really an article of religion, on a par with faith and good works. There is no milder way of expressing his belief without falsifying it' (128–9). In unitrinianism, then, Carman found a long-lasting resolution to the spiritual questionings and questings that had occupied him for the better part of a decade, an all-inclusive system of thought and action that allowed him to envisage and contribute to the melioration of individual human beings and, hence, humanity as a whole. When Margaret Lawrence was planning an article on him in 1928, Carman told her that 'the one prose book [she] need[ed] most' was *The Making of Personality* (1908), adding: 'it has all the philosophy up to that time and until a very few years ago ...' (104).

At first glance, the differences between Carman and Lampman with respect to religious matters seem so to outweigh their semblance as to beggar comparison. Whereas Carman seems almost from the beginning to have been a restless and adventurous thinker, Lampman appears to have been cautious and conventional, carefully skirting the radicalism and atheism of Shelley's *The Revolt of Islam* while at university[23] and at the same time and for several years later wholeheartedly accepting the Carlylean gospel of hard work and simple faith as the best remedy for the ills of modern society and modern individuals.[24] The pieces assembled in *Among the Millet, and Other Poems* are deliberately diverse in genre and subject matter, and the volume as a whole gives priority to therapeutic Nature poems and prominence to classically inspired themes (at thirteen pages, 'An Athenian Reverie' is the longest poem that Lampman published during his life-time). Yet several of the volume's narrative poems – 'The Three Pilgrims,' 'Easter Eve,' 'The Organist,' and 'The Monk' – treat of Christian subjects and themes. Moreover, in 'The Martyrs' (1888) Lampman expresses not only admiration for those whose undoubting faith enabled them to make their supreme sacrifice and nostalgia for 'Those sterner days, when all men yearned to ... [the] / White souls whose beauty made their world divine,' but also a seemingly sincere belief in the enduring value of their example:

> ... still across life's tangled storms we see,
>    Following the cross, your pale procession led,
>       One hope, one end, all others sacrificed,
> Self-abnegation, love, humility,
>    Your faces shining toward the bended head,
>       The wounded hands and patient feet of Christ. (*P* 115)

Believing that 'poetry ... which ranges itself on the side of passion against eternal law is a disturbing influence to human progress and is therefore of no real value to us,' Lampman found little to admire in the work of Byron and the Pre-Raphaelites,[25] twitted Roberts for the 'pitiless egotism' and 'brawny passion' of two of his love poems, and found inspiration for his final essay, 'Happiness,' in a passage in Arnold's *Last Essays on Church and Religion* (1877) where obedience to '"the higher self, or reason, or whatever it is to be called"' is held to be the source of '"happiness and life"' and obedience to the '"lower [self]"' of '"sense, appetite, [and] desire"' the source of '"death and misery"' (*ER* 120, 107, 361). If during the mid-1890s Lampman had an extramarital relationship with his co-worker Kate Wadell, it must have been either Platonic (in the popular meaning of the term) or tinged with a sense of guilt that seems to have been largely unknown to Carman and Roberts.

Nevertheless, there are aspects of Lampman's thought and writing that hint at an uneasy relationship, not with the values and ideals of

Christianity, but with the rituals and attitudes of the Church and its ministers. In the opening stanza of 'In October' (1888), 'pines / Like tall slim priests of storm, stand up and bar / The low long strip of dolorous red that lines / The under west' as if presiding over 'masses' in which 'pain-crazed lips ... move and murmur incoherently' (P 21), and in the central section of *The Story of an Affinity* (written during 1892–4), Christian ritual and piety are depicted in an even less flattering light as part of the protagonist's education in the ways of the world:

> He sat in the great churches and amid
> The grandeur of their silken ceremonies
> Heard the vaults thunder with the solemn chants
> And sacred hymns immeasurably sad,
> Wherein the universal human heart   .
> Had voiced the quietude of its vast despair,
> And all the awful weariness of life.
> He heard the pastor with an impassioned tongue
> Preach the great love and brotherhood of man
> While round him, silent in the velvet stalls,
> The rich and proud, the masters of the world,
> Sat moveless as the ever-living gods,
> While all that worldly thunder rolled and rang
> About their heads and pitiless ears in vain. (2:331–44)

That this passage is an expression of Lampman's own feelings is clear from a letter of 2 November 1897 in which he explains to Thomson his reasons for going to church only 'about three times a year':

> It always depresses me ... In those prayers and terrible hymns of our service we are in the presence of all the suffering of the world since the beginning of time. We have entered the temple of sorrow and are prostrate at the feet of the very God of affliction ... It is the secret of the success of Christianity. As long as there is suffering on the earth, the pathetic figure of Christ will stand. In the old days when men were children there were worshipers of light and joy. Apollo and Aphrodite and Dionysos were enough for them; but the world has grown old now ... It is sad, and moody and full of despair and it cleaves to Christ, its natural refuge. (AC 194)

As these last two quotations make abundantly clear, disgust with the opulence of church furnishings, the depressing effect of religious music, the social ineffectiveness of Christian teaching, and the uncaring hypocrisy of wealthy congregations had no small part to play in the sharp swerve towards socialism and Hellenism that becomes evident in Lampman's poems of the early 1890s – in 'To a Millionaire' (October 1891), his indictment of wealth amid poverty, in 'Xenophanes' (December 1891), his affirmation of the Greek philosopher's relevance to the modern condition, in 'Favorites of Pan' (May 1892), his account of how frog song became a vehicle for Pan's liberating music as the classical gods were being routed by 'hostile hymns and conquering faiths' (*P* 132), and in 'The Land of Pallas' (circa August 1891–February 1896), his utopian vision of a society untainted by, among other things, social class and organized religion.

There seems to have been a twofold reason for this swerve: exposure to new friends and exposure to new ideas. On 3 April 1890 Lampman travelled to Montreal to spend the Easter weekend with Lighthall, and in May and August the two men again spent time together ('Letters of Lampman' 71–4), no doubt discussing the current state of Canadian literature and the 'Spiritualized Happiness–Theory; or, New Utilitarianism' that Lighthall presented in a lecture before the Farmington School of Philosophy in June of the same year. Taking as its point of departure the social liberalism of Thomas Hill Green, Lighthall's argument that a 'Mystical Power' which connects the 'mental' and 'mechanical' aspects of the human brain 'govern[s] *everything* for progress towards happiness' and 'ethics' and his alignment of this evolutionary process with 'Christian aspiration' and the 'Christian Ethic' (11, 18, 21) may well have struck an answering chord in Lampman; certainly, several of the poems that he wrote in May 1890 and following months – 'The Better Day,' for example, and 'The Sweetness of Life' – display the keen interest in the sources of human happiness and the alleviation of human suffering that frames the seasonal poems of *Lyrics of Earth* and underlies the utopian vision of 'The Land of Pallas,' a poem that Lighthall 'always thought was [Lampman's] ideal of a future Canada.'[26] For his part, Lighthall may have drawn some inspiration from Lampman for his own vision of the country's future in *Canada, a Modern Nation* (1904) as a haven of 'order, peace and happiness to hundreds of millions' (7).

If so, then Lighthall's advocacy of the public ownership of land in *Canada* suggests that as early as 1890 he might have been especially interested in his friend's socialist views. Gleaned in part from John Macoun (1831–1920), Archibald Campbell (18?–?), and other members of his Ottawa circle (see Connor 84) and in part from another new friend, Hamlin Garland (see *ER* 353), Lampman's socialism appears to have been clarified into the vision of 'The Land of Pallas' by his reading of two works, *Fabian Essays in Socialism* (1889) and *News from Nowhere* (1890, 1891), the former an enormously influential collection by Sidney Webb, George Bernard Shaw, and others that advocates a gradual and peaceful evolution towards socialism and the latter a more imaginatively engrossing socialist fantasy by William Morris in which the narrator is granted a dream vision of an ideal future society and wakes inspired to work for its realization in the grimy present.[27] Since 'The Land of Pallas' was not begun until August 1891, it is possible that Lampman encountered one or other or both *Fabian Essays in Socialism* and *News from Nowhere* during the three weeks that he spent in Boston with yet another new friend, Thomson, in late August and early September of that year. In any case, Lampman's Boston excursion was a stirring and horizon-opening event for him: he visited 'Walden Pond ... and the graves of Emerson, Thoreau and Hawthorne'; he made numerous literary contacts and 'set in train' the possibility of a teaching appointment at 'Cornell or some other university'; and he returned to Ottawa deeply conscious of how 'ill-read' he was and resolved to 'clothe ... [him]self in severity' by reading George Henry Lewes's *The History of Philosophy from Thrale to Comte* (1871),[28] a work saturated with the belief that, having reached what Auguste Comte termed the 'positive' stage of its development, modern society required a new social order to replace Christianity. (In fact, Comte's proposal for a 'new Religion of Humanity' was already familiar to Lampman in an essay entitled 'Leon Gambetta: A Positivist Discourse' [1883] by his influential English disciple Frederic Harrison, that Lampman had quarried for a piece in the July 1883 issue of *Rouge et Noir* [see *ER* 233–4].)[29]

It is tempting to argue from Lampman's likely familiarity with Lighthall's 'Spiritualized Happiness-Theory,' his deepening engagement with various types of socialism, and his at least passing familiarity with posivitism and its Religion of Humanity that all the necessary strands of his thought are now in place to account for the evolutionary and melioristic idealism that characterizes much of the poetry he wrote between 1890 and his death. For this to be nearer the reality, however, two more strands need to be added: Transcendentalism and Theosophy. Of these, the first needs no elaboration: initially through Carlyle and Wordsworth and then through Thoreau, Emerson, Burroughs, and other American writers, Lampman was almost continually exposed to literary expressions of the foundational tenets of Transcendentalism, which include, of course, a belief in the imminence of God in Nature, a conviction that beauty, truth, and goodness emanate from the Over-Soul and provide the individual soul access to it, and a correlative certainty that such access can be achieved without the aid of organized religion or other mechanisms external to the individual. That Lampman knew and understood the work of the transcendentalists whose graves he visited in Boston in 1891 there can be no question at all. 'Emerson's sympathy for nature ... is a sympathy of force, a cosmic sympathy,' he wrote in his 'At the Mermaid Inn' column on 22 April 1893; 'he is drawn to nature because in the energies of his own soul he is aware of a kinship to the forces of nature, and feels with an elemental joy as if it were a part of himself the eternal movement of life' (*MI* 298). With its obvious debts to Wordsworth's 'Intimations' ode, particularly in its nostalgia for 'the power to see / The threads that bind us to the All, / God or the Immensity,' and its equally obvious reliance on the transcendentalist faith in the ability of the individual who 'knows the great and fair' to 'Become ... / One with earth and one with man, / One ... with the planets and the stars' (*P* 166, 167), the opening section of 'Winter-Store' (circa January 1892)[30] merely displays its literary and philosophical roots more clearly than other Lampman poems of the 1890s (and, indeed, earlier).

Somewhat more difficult to identify are the theosophical components of Lampman's thought and work. Founded in New York in 1875 for the purpose of seeking 'esoteric truth ... [through] occult research' (Bruce F. Campbell 28), the Theosophical Society had as its threefold purpose: '"1. To form a nucleus of the Universal Brotherhood of humanity without distinction of race, creed, sex, caste, or color. 2. To encourage the study of Comparative Religion, Philosophy, and Science. 3. To investigate the unexplained laws of nature and the powers latent in man"' (quoted in Kuhn 113). Among its principal tenets were a belief in the transmigration of souls and a denial of the existence of a personal god, and among its defining characteristics, a reliance on elaborate systems of cosmology and psychology and on recondite terminology, much of it drawn from Buddhism and Hinduism. Three such terms with brief definitions appear among notes made by Lampman during 1898–9:

Mir-ham-oya – final complete self-consciousness.
Manvantara  – the great process of expansion and contraction, the day of Brahma.
Pralaya    – the period of concentration, the night of Brahma.[31]

Another much used theosophical term, 'astral plane' (meaning the

level of existence occupied by the 'astral' or spiritual double of the natural body) appears in a somewhat despondent letter that Lampman
wrote to Thomson on 22 November 1893: 'I wish there were some place
in the "Astral Plane" or other-where, in which our spirits might smoke
etherial pipes, and talk over ... plaguy matters' (AC 102). Jocular as it is,
Lampman's reference to the 'astral plane' indicates not only that he
was familiar by the fall of 1893 with at least one theosophical notion,
but also that his familiarity was shared with at least one of his close
friends. None of the Lampman-Thomson letters gives any indication of
precisely when or how they acquired what knowledge they had of Theosophy, but the three terms and definitions that Lampman recorded in
his later notes suggest that by 1898–9 he had access to one or more
handbooks of Theosophy, such as the *Working Glossary for the Use of Students of Theosophical Literature* (1890), which went to a third edition in
1892.[32]

Lampman's familiarity with theosophical terms and concepts would
be of no more than passing interest if it were not for the fact that it
occurs around the time in which, as he told Thomson in a letter of
5 March 1894, he was 'passing through some spiritual revolution' that
was giving him 'unusual agonies' (AC 107). As the same letter indicates,
an immediate product of this 'spiritual revolution' is 'Peccavi, Domine'
(1899), a poem that Lampman had composed on 20 February 1894 as
an 'act of self-relief' and would subsequently revise in accordance with
Thomson's observations, in a letter of March 6, that its conception of
God was 'inconsistent':

> I assail the concluding lines of the fourth verse. Here's a God with feet, on
> a Judgement seat – a Jahwe – to whom you make the conventional submis-
> sion of hands between feet and dust upon your head ... But there's no Jah-
> we elsewhere in the poem. The God is the Great Spirit of the universe
> passionless and kind in whose eternal rhyme the stars, mists and the aeons
> roll ... and the impersonal Spirit – inconceivable as embodied – all your
> picture being non-Jewish – your God the conception of a wider intelligence
> ... I would say that a striking and excellent effect could be had [in the
> fourth verse] by changing the second quatrain in such a wise as to make
> the poet in the attitude (to a not-Jahwe Deity) that a modern man would
> naturally assume to the non-Jehovah, God. (AC 109–10)

Even as revised, 'Peccavi, Domine' is not entirely free of Judeo-Christian
elements (it ends in an attitude of 'utter dumb humility'), but as three

of its stanzas make abundantly evident, its 'God' is indeed 'the Great Spirit of the Universe':

> O Power to whom this earthly clime
>   Is but an atom in the whole,
> O Poet-heart of Space and Time,
>   O Maker and immortal Soul,
> Within whose glowing rings are bound,
>   Out of whose sleepless heart had birth
> The cloudy blue, the starry round,
>   And this small miracle of earth:
>
> Who liv'st in every living thing,
>   And all things are thy script and chart,
> Who rid'st upon the eagle's wing,
>   And yearnest in the human heart;
> O Riddle with a single clue,
>   Love, deathless, protean, secure,
> The ever old the ever new,
>   O Energy, serene and pure.
> ...
> I stand upon thy mountain-heads,
>   And gaze until mine eyes are dim;
> The golden morning glows and spreads;
>   The hoary vapours break and swim.
> I see thy blossoming fields, divine,
>   Thy shining clouds, thy blessèd trees –
> And then that broken soul of mine –
>   How much less beautiful than thee! (*P* 219–20)

Given the heterodox component of the context from which these stanzas emerged, it is tempting to speculate that 'The golden morning' that discloses the 'blossoming fields, divine, / Th[e] shining clouds, th[e] blessèd trees' is an allusion to the Order of the Golden Dawn, one of the occult groups with which Yeats was involved in the 1890s. Be this as it may, 'Peccavi, Domine' indicates that by early 1894 Lampman had moved well away from orthodox Christianity and, encouraged by Thomson, was prepared to move even further.

Among the poems collected in *Alcyone* (1899) and *Poems* (1900) that further testify to the direction taken by Lampman during and after his 'spiritual revolution' (or, surely better, evolution) of the early 1890s

'The Clearer Self ' (written in January 1894) stands out for its associa-tion of the 'Soul' with an 'Energy serene and pure' that is climbing towards 'some height ... / Of unimagined grace and power' and for its petition to the 'Master Spirit of the World' for the capacity 'to know, to seek, to find ... The clearer self, the grander me!' (P 199–200). So, too, do 'A Vision of Twilight' (written in September 1895), an account of an ideal city of dream inhabited by people who have lived in 'a thousand worlds of old' and are learned in 'the secret ways of thought,' and 'The Largest Life' (written in August 1894, December 1896, and January 1897), a sequence of three sonnets culminating in the assertion that a life properly lived is one in which the individual spirit is so aligned with 'The tide of sovereign truth' that perpetually flows towards ultimate 'beauty' that 'the great light be[comes] clearer' and 'the great soul ... stronger' (P 197, 198, 301). In 'The Land of Pallas,' a 'priestless worship of the all-wise mother' has replaced organized religion; in 'Alcyone' itself (written in November 1893) the 'great and beaming star' for which the poem is named[33] can inspire 'Man [to] ... Seek ... for the spirit unconfined / In the clear abyss of mind'; and in 'The Lake in the Forest' (written circa September 1897) the Ojibway 'Manitou' is described as the 'Spirit of the earth' and experienced as a 'living presence, face to face' (P 208, 178, 313). Nevertheless, the longest poem in *Alcyone*, 'Vivia Perpetua' (written in December 1894), is an account of the conversion and martyrdom of St Perpetua and her companions by a narrator who contemplates his own death in the conviction that 'the other blessèd ones / Await [him] at the opening gates of heaven,' and its two most achingly personal poems, the elegies entitled 'White Pansies' and 'We Too Shall Weep,' which Lampman wrote shortly after the death of his infant son on 4 August 1894, envisage death as a peaceful and 'dream-less' sleep that 'changeth not, nor knoweth end' (P 242, 227–8).[34] Lampman may have gone through a 'spiritual revolution' or evolution in the final decade of his life, but the varieties of religious experience in the last volume that he prepared for publication attest as eloquently as its miscellaneous genres and subjects to his enduring commitment to the principle of variety.

Of all the members of the Confederation group, Duncan Campbell Scott was the most reticent about his religious views and, hence, poses the greatest challenge to a spiritual biographer. As close as he came to commenting explicitly on his religious beliefs is in a letter of 26 Novem-ber 1946 to E.K. Brown, where he responds to Brown's labelling of him as a 'Presbyterian' with a statement that begins as clarification and ends in vagueness:

> I was born into the Methodist Connection when the adherents were called
> Wesleyan Methodists and were close to the reverend founder of the sect;
> they seem to have forgotten him in their Union [with Presbyterians and
> Congregationalists in 1925 to form the United Church of Canada] and I
> have forgotten them all having wandered far away and am lost in a wilder-
> ness, but I have a strong Faith of my own, [and as] you see I spell faith with
> a capital. (Quoted in McDougall, *The Poet and the Critic* 180–1)

Only to the extent that they testify to Scott's movement away from Methodism towards an unspecified personal faith are these remarks useful to
the present discussion, for not only were they written nearly fifty years
after the disintegration of the Confederation group, but they also post-
date by fifteen years his marriage in 1931 to Elise Aylen (1904–72), a
woman whose theosophical beliefs had found expression in *Roses of
Shadow* (1930) and whose quest for '"the Truth in the world of the Lie"'
took her after Scott's death to the feet and bed of an Indian swami
(McDougall, *Totems*, 195–202). The question that must be faced here,
then, is whether Scott's religious wandering began in the days of the
Confederation group and, if so, under what circumstance, in what direction, and with what literary consequence?

The best evidence for an affirmative answer to the first of these questions resides in the short stories of *In the Village of Viger*, which, when
viewed chronologically on the basis of their publication in newspapers
and periodicals between 1887 and 1893, reveal the increasing emphasis
on supernatural themes that is also evident in the collection itself. All of
the *Viger* stories that were published in *Scribner's Magazine* in October
1887 and March 1891 – 'The Desjardins,' 'Josephine Labrosse,' 'The Little Milliner,' and 'The Wooing of Monsieur Cuerrier' – depict a world of
realistic psychological and material causes and effects, but those published in the same magazine in October 1893 – 'The Bobolink,' 'The
Pedler,' and 'Sedan' – contain events and characters that have supernatural elements. (In 'The Little Milliner,' for instance, such evidences of
encroaching modernity as 'the reflections of thousands of gas-lamps' in
the night sky are recorded in precise detail, but in 'Sedan' the protagonist, Paul Latulipe, knows without being told that the French have been
defeated in the battle of 1870 for which the story is named [3, 37–8].)
Two other stories in the collection – 'The Tragedy of the Seigniory' and
'Paul Farlotte' – also participate in the movement from realism to supernaturalism: in the former, which was first published in April 1892 in the
Boston fiction magazine *Two Tales*, the protagonist, Louis Bois, is 'as

superstitious as an old wife' and gradually comes to believe that a dog is a human 'spirit in canine form'; and in the latter, which was not published prior to its appearance in the *Viger* collection, the protagonist, Paul Farlotte, is frequently 'greeted with visions of things that had been, or that would be, and s[ees] figures where, for other eyes, hung only impalpable air' (59, 81). In fact, his 'vision' of his mother's death in France is the climax both of the short story that bears his name and of the collection as a whole:

> He saw a garden much like his own, flooded with the clear sunlight, [and] in the shade of an arbor an old woman in white cap was leaning back in a wheeled chair, her eyes were closed, she seemed asleep. A young woman was seated beside her holding her hand. Suddenly the old woman smiled a childish smile, as if she was pleased. 'Paul,' she murmured, 'Paul, Paul.' A moment later her companion started up with a cry; but she did not move, she was silent and tranquil. Then the young woman fell on her knees and wept, hiding her face. But the aged face was inexpressibly calm in the shadows, with the smile lingering upon it, fixed by the deeper sleep in which she had fallen.
>
> ...
>
> Later in the day he told Marie that his mother had died that morning, and she wondered how he knew. (89)

It would be folly, of course, to credit Scott with the supernatural capacities and convictions of his fictional characters, but the chronology of the stories in *In the Village of Viger* does indicate that in the early 1890s he had become more than passingly interested in what in today's parlance would be described as paranormal phenomena.

A similar augmentation of realism by supernaturalism is discernible in the poems that Scott published in periodicals in the late 1880s and early 1890s, though here the transition occurs a little earlier, with the publication in the June 1890 number of *Scribner's* of the lyrical anti-narrative that would furnish the title of *The Magic House and Other Poems* (1893). With its isolated and brooding female persona and its indeterminate but evocatively medieval setting, 'The Magic House' 'hark[s] back to the Pre-Raphaelite mood as much *fin-de-siècle* poetry did,' observes Brown in *On Canadian Poetry*: '... the woman in the magic house is a sister of the Blessed Damozel and of the Lady of Shallot'; like the other 'dream-pieces' in Scott's first volume, it 'introduce[s] one to a nightmare world, in which not only are logical relations suspended as they are in symbolist verse, in much of Carman's early work to take a Canadian example, but the relation even between images is extremely loose, exactly as in vivid dreams' (124, 123). Astute as they are, Brown's observations leave the *symboliste* and supernatural aspects of Scott's 'dream-pieces' unconnected when, in fact (and as Alan Mercier has shown at length in *Les Sources ésoteriques de la poésie symboliste [1870–1914]*), they are intimately connected and, indeed, interdependent: in *The Magic House and Other Poems*, as in *Behind the Arras*, *symboliste* suggestiveness is used to imply 'an esoteric meaning.'

This is especially true of one poem in Scott's first collection that Brown does not mention, 'The Sleeper,' which was first published in the *Independent* on 15 June 1893 but, curiously, omitted from *The Poems of Duncan Campbell Scott* (1926):

Touched with some divine repose
   Isabel has fallen asleep,
Like the perfume from the rose
   In and out her breathings creep.

Dewy are her rosy palms,
   In her cheeks the blushes flit,
And a dream her spirit calms
   With the pleasant thought of it.

All the rounded heavens show
   Like the concave of a pearl,
Stars amid the opal glow
   Little fronds of flame unfurl.

Then upfloats a planet strange,
   Not the moon that mortals know,
With a magic mountain range
   Cones and craters white as snow.

Something different yet the same,
   Rain by rainbows glorified,
Roses lit with lambent flame –
   'Tis the maid moon's other side.

When the sleeper floats from sleep
   She will smile the vision o'er,

See the veinèd valleys deep,
  No one ever saw before.

Yet the moon is not betrayed,
  (Ah, the subtle Isabel!)
She's a maiden and a maid
  Maiden secrets will not tell. (27)

With its identification of Isabel with the flower whose mystical resonances Yeats was contemporaneously invoking in *The Rose* (1893), its
evocation of a planet rich in Platonic and occult ('magic')[35] as well as
amatory significance, and its refusal to reveal secrets and resolve enigmas, 'The Sleeper' has been described by a critic who was extremely well
informed about such matters, A.J.M. Smith,[36] as an exercise in 'arcane
knowledge' ('Poetry' 109). That the poem contains both esoteric and
erotic elements is, of course, entirely consistent with the mystical and
poetic traditions with which it is aligned (and, indeed, with one of the
poems that it loudly echoes: Rossetti's 'Rose Mary').
  The question of precisely how and when Scott acquired his knowledge
of *symbolisme* is difficult to answer, but his contributions to 'At the Mermaid Inn' during 1892–3 provide some broad clues and specific leads.
Far more interested than either Campbell or Lampman in contemporary
English and European literature, Scott devotes two columns to analysing
plays by Ibsen (13 February and 12 November 1892), provides a poetic
rendition of a portion of the posthumously published and extremely voguish journal of the Swiss critic Henri-Frédérick Amiel (1821–81)
(30 July 1892), interrupts a discussion of Flaubert's letters to quote Pater
on music as the art towards which all other arts should aspire (4 February
1893), and, generally, peppers his contributions with thoughts about new
publications by such writers as Morris and George Meredith. Given these
interests, it seems more than likely that in the 1890s Scott became
acquainted with the drama and perhaps the poetry of Maurice Maeterlinck, the Belgian *symboliste* whose *Plays* Hovey would publish in translation in 1895 and who, as Lampman observes in his 'At the Mermaid Inn'
column of 12 March 1892, 'was suddenly and enthusiastically hailed a
short time [earlier] by the literary press of Paris as "The Belgian Shakespeare"' (*MI* 34). 'This young writer is the author of a volume of poems
[*Serres chaudes* (1889)], ... a tragedy [*La Princesse Maleine* (1890)], and two
short plays [*L'Intruse* and *Les Aveugles* (1890)],' 'one of which [*L'Intruse*]
has just been translated and brought out in London, but ... with only limited success' (34–5). If Scott did indeed know Maeterlinck's work, then

this might account for the presence in two of the short stories that he first published in October 1893 – 'The Bobolink' and 'The Pedler' – not only of the evocative suggestiveness that is typical of *symboliste* poetry and drama, but also of central characters who are both blind and mysterious – the 'little blind daughter' whose questions often leave her father 'mystified' in the former and the 'green spectacle[d]' *fou* who seems 'clothed with power' to the people of Viger in the latter (51, 74–5). It would also lend stature to Bernard Muddiman's observation that 'The Sea by the Wood' and 'The Wood by the Sea,' both of which were composed in April 1900 and included in Scott's *New World Lyrics and Ballads* volume of 1905, are 'almost like the early poems of Maeterlinck' in their 'strange ethereal music,' their 'vague and bizarre' quality (38).

Of course, the most extended, impressive, and anthologized poetic product of the *symboliste* aesthetic that Scott probably absorbed from several sources during the 1890s is 'The Piper of Arll.' First published in *Truth* (New York) on 14 December 1895 and first collected in *Labor and the Angel* (1898), the 'delicate phantasy ... about the sea and singing and a romantic end' whose 'longing ... wistfulness, and ... images' made a 'deep impression' on John Masefield (1878–1967) when he read it in New York in 1895 (UT and quoted in Brown 123–4), Scott's dream-like and enigmatic narrative is everything that a *symboliste* poem should be: centred on a musician whose harmonious existence with Nature is temporarily shattered by the appearance, in response to his playing, of the mysterious ship in which he is eventually 'Empearled within the purple heart / Of the great sea' at a spot 'unmarked of any chart' (*PDCS* 40), it answers fully to Hovey's contention that 'modern symbolism' 'by no means ... involves a complete and constant allegory. Its events, its personages, its sentences rather imply than definitely state an esoteric meaning ... [B]ehind every incident, almost every phrase, one is aware of a lurking universality, the adumbration of greater things.' As true as this is, however, the overall impression left by 'The Piper of Arll' is less one of spiritual or even artistic profundity suggestively presented than of *symboliste* motifs and techniques brilliantly deployed for decorative purposes. Here is its concluding description of 'The piper and the dreamy crew' of the ship in the 'unrecorded deeps' of the 'great sea':

> Their eyes are ruby in the green
> Long shaft of sun that spreads and rays,
> And upward with a wizard sheen
> A fan of sea-light leaps and plays.

Tendrils of or and azure creep,
And globes of amber light are rolled,
And in the gloaming of the deep
Their eyes are starry pits of gold.

And sometimes in the liquid night
The hull is changed, a solid gem,
That glows with a soft stormy light,
The lost prince of a diadem.

And at the keel a vine is quick,
That spreads its bines and works and weaves
O'er all the timbers veining thick
A plentitude of silver leaves. (*PDCS* 40)

The best word to describe these stanzas is exquisite: 'wizard' is nicely evocative of the supernatural, 'starry pits' is engagingly suggestive in its confounding of expectations, 'The lost prince of a diadem' is a clever use of a metaphor within a metaphor to multiply resonances rather than to clarify significance, but, overall, the stanzas have at least as much in common with an art nouveau lampshade as with a serious *symboliste* poem. It may not be entirely fortuitous that the magazine in which it was first published, *Truth*, was primarily an organ of light entertainment that frequently featured 'social satire' and '"spicy"' pictorials (Mott 4: 84).*

To the very extent that it is a brilliant and self-contained exercise in the *symboliste* manner, 'The Piper of Arll' stands to one side of the path that took Scott from the interest in supernatural phenomena displayed by several of his poems and short stories of the early 1890s to the engagement with the philosophical and spiritual questions raised by

---

* The decorative effect of 'The Piper of Arll' is enhanced in *Truth* by the illustrations with which it is surrounded and over which it is printed. Given that place of publication can be an important factor in establishing the context and purpose of a work (see Bentley, *The Gay]Grey Moose* 187–200), it should be observed that both *In the Village of Viger* and Scott's *Labor and the Angel* volume of 1898 were published by Copeland and Day, as was a second edition of *The Magic House and Other Poems* in 1895. It is quite possible that Scott met Copeland and Day when he visited Boston in April 1894 (see *AC* 116), though the formality of his letters of 1895 and 1896 to them (*QU*) are not indicative of friendship. Scott's first wife, Belle Warner Botsford (18?–1929), was a Bostonian whom he met in Ottawa.

life's mysteries that becomes increasingly evident in his work around and after the turn of the century and achieves its fullest expression in the profound meditative works of *Lundy's Lane and Other Poems* (1916) and *The Green Cloister* (1935): 'Meditation at Perugia' (1916), 'Lines Written in Memory of Edmund Morris' (1916), 'The Height of Land' (1916), 'Reality' (1935), 'Compline' (1935), and 'Chiostro Verde' (1935). That Maeterlinck was one of Scott's principal guides on his spiritual journey is confirmed by a letter of 18 June 1904 to Pelham Edgar in which he draws a contrast between Yeats, whom he regards as having become 'cryptic and unreadable' in his use of 'symbols and allusions,' and the Belgian writer:

> Think of Maeterlinck and reflect how much more important is his work for the mystical side of life ... He is endeavouring to awaken the wonder-element in a modern way, constantly expressing the almost unknowable things which we all feel. His is the work of the modern Mystic and he does not require a fund of Irish legends to set imagination aglow. (VU; *More Letters* 23–4)

Gary Geddes assumes that these remarks refer to Maeterlinck's poetry (172), but it is more likely that they refer to his plays and to *Le Trésor des humbles*, an extraordinarily influential collection of essays that was published in 1896, translated a year later by Alfred Sutro, and reprinted numerous times in the years preceding the First World War.[37] If Scott knew Sutro's translation, which seems highly likely, he would have known as well that in its Introduction, A.B. Walkley aligns Maeterlinck with the Plotinian branch of Neoplatonism that also lies centrally in the background of Transcendentalism and Theosophy:

> Plotinus ... enlarged the boundance of art by discovering in the idea of beauty an inward and spiritual grace not to be found in the 'Platonic idea.' That too, is what M. Maeterlinck is striving for ... His cardinal doctrine will, I conjecture, be something like this ... The mystery of life is what makes life worth living ... He is penetrated by the feeling of mystery in all human creatures, whose every act is regulated by far-off influences and obscurely rooted in things unexplained. Mystery is in us and around us. Of reality we can only now and then get the merest glimpse ... We grope among the shadows towards the unknown ... In silence is our only chance of knowing one another. And 'mystic truths have over ordinary truths, a strange privilege; they can neither age nor die.' (x–xii)

In characterizing Maeterlinck's thought, Walkley draws a quotation from another of his works that might also have been known to Scott, *L'Ornament des noces spirituelles du Ruysbroeck L'Admirable* (1891), that uncannily suggests the affinities between *The Treasure of the Humble* and the poems in which he explores his own conviction that 'mystery' lies 'at the root of everything' and within the reach of human understanding (VU; *More Letters* 28): 'we are here ... on the borderland of human thought and far across the Arctic circle of the spirit' (viii). 'Here is peace,' Scott would write in November 1915 on the height of land between Hudson Bay and Lake Superior, 'and again'

> That Something comes by flashes
> Deeper than peace, – a spell
> Golden and inappellable
> That gives the inarticulate part
> Of our strange being one moment of release
> That seems more native than the touch of time,
> And we must answer in chime:
> Though yet no man may tell
> The secret of that spell
> Golden and inappellable. (*PDCS* 47–8)

'Though *yet* no man may tell / The *secret* of that *spell*': in these lines, and in Scott's speculation later in the poem that at some future time humans will achieve an understanding of life's mysteries that will make even Christianity seem 'uncouth' (*PDCS* 50), lies the combination of evolutionary optimism and questing heterodoxy that in one form or another appears in the work of every member of the Confederation group except Frederick George Scott, and which could well be described as 'a strong Faith, ... with a capital' *F.*

It would be a mistake to conclude this chapter without regretting that the primary focus of the study of which it is a part on the years between 1880 and 1897 has rendered anything like a complete examination of subsequent developments in the religious and spiritual components of the thought and work of the members of the Confederation group all but impossible. It would also be a mistake to attempt to remedy this necessary but regrettable shortcoming at this point with a series of broad and sweeping generalizations. Let the chapter conclude, then, with the hope that its manifest shortcomings will be remedied by future scholarship and that, in the meantime, they can be somewhat alleviated by recourse to existing studies of Campbell, Roberts, Carman, Duncan Campbell Scott, and, indeed, Lampman and Frederick George Scott that reach beyond what has been possible here.

# CHAPTER SEVEN

# International and National Recognition: 1889–1895

Mr. Lampman has been lauded in London; professor Roberts is accounted among the 'Victorian Poets'; Mr. Campbell is recognized in New York. What more do we want? That they should be recognized in Canada? Surely a continental recognition will more speedily bring about this, than would colonial recognition bring about the other.

— *Theodore Arnold Haultain, 'A "Canadian Literature"' (1892)*

In 1880, Roberts's *Orion, and Other Poems* was heralded in Canada as the harbinger of a new epoch in Canadian literature, not merely because it was a precociously accomplished volume of poetry, but also, and as important, because it contained poems that had already appeared in the pages of *Scribner's Monthly* (New York). '"Memnon" and "Drowsihood," are familiar to the reader of *Scribner,*' wrote the reviewer in the November 1880 number of *Rose-Belford's Canadian Monthly and National Review* (Toronto); 'does not the publication of such a book as this ... justify us in arguing good things of the spread of a genuine literary spirit in Canada? Here is a writer whose power and originality it is impossible to deny – here is a book of which any literature might be proud' (553). To the extent that it reflects the insecurity and deference of an emerging culture, the dependence of national upon international recognition in the reception of Roberts's first volume is entirely predictable as well as predictably typical of responses to the Confederation poets both individually and as a group during the period of their rise to prominence: following the trajectory initiated by Roberts and reinforced by his admirers,[1] international preceded national recognition for each member of the group, bringing with it first for Lampman and then for Campbell loud calls for the federal government to support Canadian poets of international stature and, almost certainly, fuelling the desire of all six poets (and doubtless others) for the international recognition upon which national fame and financial reward so clearly depended.

Since the trajectory of Roberts's reputation after the publication of *Orion, and Other Poems* has already been plotted (see chapter 1), the discussion is free to concentrate fully on the period from 1889 to 1895, which marked the apogee of the poets' national fame during the post-Confederation period and, arguably, lent them the cultural capital from which at different times and in varying degrees they continued to draw dividends and earn interest throughout their lives. As seen in the final pages of chapter 2, the winter of 1888–9 witnessed the partial success of Roberts's efforts to consolidate and promote the work of the Confederation group as the long-awaited answer to the call for an accomplished and distinctive Canadian literature. Just how partial was that success can be gauged from the fact that at the first public event to celebrate the 'budding and blossoming' of Canadian literature that Lighthall identified in his 28 December 1888 review of *The Soul's Quest and Other Poems*, the 'Canadian Literature Evening' that took place under the auspices of the Toronto Young Men's Liberal Club on 14 January 1889, the only member of the Confederation group to be so much as mentioned in the speeches was Roberts, and even he was not among the authors whose work was recited (an honour extended only to Charles Mair, Edward Hartley Dewart, Charles Sangster, George F. Cameron, Alexander McLachlan, William Albert Sherwood [1859–1919], Joseph Henry Hilts [1819–1903], Canniff Haight [1825–1901], and Helen M. Johnson [18?–?]). Despite the observation of the evening's chairman, John Stephen Willison (1856–1927), that 'Canadian writers are beginning to find their way into the best magazines of the Continent' (quoted in 'Native Literature'), the poets who had conspicuously made such inroads were all but ignored by the event's organizer, Frank Yeigh (1861–1935),[2] in favour of older writers whose poems on the War of 1812 (Mair), Niagara Falls (Dewart), the Huron martyrs (Sherwood), and other blatantly Canadian topics would provide the desired stimulus to 'national sentiment' ('Native Literature').[3] That this decision did not satisfy all tastes can be inferred from an editorial in the 15 January 1889 issue of the *Globe* that characterizes the 'Canadian Literature Evening' as a 'loud' testament to the 'patriotism' of the Young Liberals and to 'the general good sense of their criticisms' but cautions that 'nothing but evil can ensue from indiscriminate and rapturous applause of verses, stories, or essays on the mere ground of their production by inhabitants of this country' ('Canadian Literature'). 'It is evident, from the meeting last night and from many other indications of like import, that a Canadian writer who shall accomplish work worthy to be ranked high in any department of English literature will be hailed with much pride and enthusiasm by his fellow-citizens,' continues the editorial; 'the value of such demonstrations ... is in the evidence they afford that the people of our country crave for it a distinguished literature.'[4]

Three days before the appearance of this editorial, the evidence of accomplishment that was apparently required to generate the 'pride and enthusiasm' of a Canadian writer's 'fellow-citizens' had begun to materialize for Lampman in the form of a highly laudatory review of *Among the Millet, and Other Poems* in the *Spectator* (London). Proclaiming the volume 'full ... of the influence of Canadian scenery and of classical culture,' the review finds that none of its contents 'demonstrat[e] true genius' and discerns in some of its sonnets such reprehensible 'modern' characteristics as a 'tendency to exaggerate the force of the lowest element in the imaginative life' but more than balances these and similar reservations with generous and abundant praise: the volume 'arrests the reader's attention at once'; 'there is so much in it of truth, simplicity, vivacity, and ... passion, that it is very pleasant and sometimes even impressive reading, from beginning to end'; 'Mr. Lampman has a true eye and a true sense of humour'; he 'can write verse in which there is a true "lyrical cry"'; he is a poet of 'thorough culture' (52–3). The other notable feature of the *Spectator* review is its singling out of a masterpiece for particular praise and extensive quotation, for this common enough reviewing practice would prove critical to the perception in Canada that a Canadian poet had indeed 'accomplish[ed] work worthy to be ranked high in ... English literature.' In Lampman's case, 'Among the Timothy' and 'Winter Hues Recalled' are given special notice in the *Spectator* for the 'almost Wordsworthian ... genuineness of their passionate delight in the beauty of the summer and winter scenery of Canada,' but the highest accolade goes to '"Between the Rapids," a Canadian boatsman's eclogue, which has somehow a flavour in it of [Arthur Hugh] Clough's exquisite poem on the Swiss girl who is driving her cows home through a storm, while musing on her distant lover [that is, "Ite Donum Saturae Venit Hesperus" (1862)]' (53). After such praise, followed by five stanzas of confirmatory quotation, what doubt could there be of Lampman's accomplishment and worthiness? The *Globe* certainly saw none: on 25 January 1889 it carried a lengthly excerpt from the review under the statement 'the London *Spectator,* one of the first literary authorities in England, heartily praises "Among the Millet, and Other Poems," by Archibald Lampman, Ottawa.'

Nor did the *Spectator* review go unnoticed by Agnes Maule Machar ('Fidelis'), whose review of Lampman's volume in the 22 March 1889 issue of the *Week* is clearly a Canadian poet's response to the English reviewer. Conceding that 'in either Britain or the United States [*Among the Millet, and Other Poems*] would justly be considered the work of a true poet' and resolving (perhaps with an eye also on the *Globe* editorial of January 15) to provide 'discriminating criticism' and 'honour ... justly due' rather than 'extravagant laudation,' Machar proceeds to take issue with several of the *Spectator*'s judgments without explicitly indicating that she is doing so: 'The Dog' (which the *Spectator* sees as the expression of 'by no means [an] ambitious theme' but quotes in its entirety as 'evidence of [Lampman's] true eye and ... true sense of humour' [52]) is 'an instance of an insufficient theme' that is 'hardly worthy of a sonnet' (251, 252); 'What Do Poets Want with Gold?' (which the *Spectator* also quotes in its entirety but as an example of Lampman in 'idealistic mood' and with the caveat that Goethe would not have agreed with the view that 'Poets speak of passion best / When their dreams are undistressed') is 'one of the strongest lyrics' in the volume that nevertheless contains two lines – 'The sweetest songs are sung / Ere the inner heart is stung' – about which 'we feel inclined to put in a query'; and 'Among the Timothy,' 'Winter,' and 'Winter Hues Recalled' (two of which, it will be remembered, the *Spectator* sees as 'almost Wordsworthian in the genuineness of their passionate delight in the ... scenery of Canada') are lacking 'something which would have given the description a greater value' and, thus, are 'like a noble portico which leads nowhither.' On one poem, however, Machar was in complete agreement with the *Spectator* review: '"Between the Rapids" is altogether delightful,' and worthy, if not of extensive quotation, then of discussion 'in detail because it is a good example of the tenderness, sweetness, susceptibility to natural influences, delicacy of description and musical diction that are characteristic of Mr. Lampman's best work' (252).

Less than a month after Machar's review came resounding confirmation that, as she put it, Lampman's poems are 'not of the class that can be dismissed in a word as "meritorious verse," but are worthy of ... careful appreciative study ... [by] many readers *in* Canada and *out* of it' (252). Writing in the April number of *Harper's New Monthly Magazine* (New York), one of America's most highly regarded men of letters, William Dean Howells (1837–1920), declared himself 'in some haste to speak' of a poet 'toward whom [he] feel[s] something of the high and sacred self-satisfaction of discoverer'[5] and proceeded to lavish praise on *Among the Millet, and Other Poems*:

> Mr. Lampman has always ... the right word on his lips ... [S]ome things with him are thought out in regions ... very wise and noble ... [This] is a book which the reader worthy of it will like to turn to again and again ... [I]t is mainly descriptive; but descriptive after a new fashion, most delicately pictorial and subtly thoughtful, with a high courage for the unhackneyed features and aspects of the great life around us ... [E]very page ... has some charm of phrase, some exquisite divination of beauty, some happily suggested truth. It is no part of our business to guess his future; but if he shall do no more than he has already done, we believe that his fame can only await the knowledge of work very uncommon in any time. (821–3)

Howells quotes 'The Truth,' two sonnets from 'The Frogs,' and, climactically, 'Heat,' placing in italics several lines of the last poem that 'seem ... blest with uncommon fortune of touch where all is excellently good' (822).

It is a mark not only of the reach and impact of Howells's review but also of the effectiveness of the supportive network that Roberts had assiduously constructed for the Confederation group that in a lengthy review of *Among the Millet, and Other Poems* in the 23 November 1889 number of the *Academy* (London), William Sharp echoes Howells by quoting 'Heat' in its entirety as 'one of [Mr Lampman's] most characteristic poems' and uses his review as a forum for promoting Roberts and Carman as well as Lampman:

> ... it is significant that three of the ablest younger poets in either Canada or America are also the latest comers – one an Upper Canadian, one a New Brunswicker, and one a Nova Scotian. The eldest of these is Charles G.D. Roberts, a poet of exceptional promise; one, moreover, whose work is already remarkable, particularly his most recent studies in what, for lack of better phrase, may be termed the higher realism. Mr. Lampman comes next, with his noteworthy volume Among the Millet. Mr. Bliss Carman, whose work has not yet been collected in book-form, is in some respects the most individual artist of the three, though his longer poems occasionally suffer from a baleful obscurity. (334)

Sharp faults Lampman for occasionally using 'unfortunate words' and 'obvious conventionalities,' but he echoes Howells in lavishing praise on his sonnets and, especially, on his treatment of external nature:

'... whenever he has to deal with nature Mr. Lampman is unmistakably the poet. A vividly realistic touch greatly heightens the effect he seeks to produce ... [His] book is full of colour' (334–5). It was no small compliment to Lampman that Sharp chose to review *Among the Millet, and Other Poems* in tandem with Fréchette's *La Légende d'un peuple* (1887), 'a really noteworthy book' by 'the foremost living French-Canadian poet,' which he nevertheless faults for similar flaws of diction and sentiment (335).

Although Howells's praise created ripples on both sides of the border and the Atlantic in the months immediately after its appearance,[6] its full impact was not felt in Canada until the spring of the following year when the 'Dean of American letters' (as he was punningly known) came once again and now even more forcefully to Lampman's aid by naming him as one of the ten North American poets who have 'finally g[iven] us a splendid and unsurpassed literature' and secured 'a place in the British classics' with 'work ... as distinguished and as distinctive in promise as that of almost any group of the past' (646).[7] In the same issue of the *Globe* in which these fulsome judgments were reported, an editorial that is now known to have been written (or at least framed) by Edward William Thomson (who may have also penned the newspaper's 15 January 1889 editorial on the 'Canadian Literature Evening') quotes liberally from Howells's 'true praises of a true poet' as the basis for a call to Sir John A. Macdonald to recognize 'the literary distinction which Lampman has modestly achieved' by transferring him from his 'very ill-paid and laborious position in the Postoffice Department in Ottawa' to one of the 'places in the Federal Civil Service ... which somebody of high character must fill and to which fair salaries are attached' ('Concerning Archibald Lampman'). 'Sir John Macdonald is not all that we would wish in things political,' concludes Thomson, but

> he is well able to understand that Mr. Lampman is not merely a glory to his countrymen, but that his work is of material value to Canada as raising the country's literary repute abroad. We hope the Premier will read 'Among the Millet,' if he has not done so already, inform himself of what the first critics of England and America have said of Mr. Lampman's work, and then proceed as a British Prime Minister would in such circumstances.

Between citing Howells and hectoring Macdonald, Thomson claims that in his own review of *Among the Millet, and Other Poems* in the 10 August 1889 issue of the *Globe* he had placed Lampman 'first among all the younger English poets of the time, those of England and the States

being alike included in the reckoning.' What Thomson's review actually claims, however, is that Lampman is 'not only greatest among Canadian poets, but one whom any nation might be proud to own,' and its overall emphasis on his 'deliberate choice of ordinary every-day words,' his 'simple and noble expression of the greatest spiritual truths,' and the 'scientific' precision of his descriptions of the natural world strongly suggests that Howells's first review (and very likely, the review in the *Spectator*) helped to shape its estimation of Lampman's qualities and stature.

Whatever the genealogy of Thomson's editorial, it had two remarkable progeny: the close and sustaining friendship that began some two weeks later when Lampman wrote to Thomson thanking him for an intervention that he hoped would 'have some effect upon [his] chances for promotion' in the Post Office Department (*AC* 1); and the brief but telling exchange that occurred in the House of Commons on April 28 when John Augustus Barron (1850–1936), the son of Frederick William Barron, whose 'prize pupil' Lampman had been some twenty years earlier at Gore's Landing (see Connor 22–4), turned a debate on additions to the parliamentary library into a discussion of Thomson's suggestion that the poet be assigned to an 'easy' or 'soft' position in the civil service. 'I think the time has come when some recognition should be made of ... Mr. Lampman, whose literary attainments have been recognized among the very foremost literary people in the United States,' urged Barron, 'and I hope ... the hon. the First Minister is able to place Mr. Lampman in some position where he will be able to develop that wonderful literary talent given to him, not only to his own advantage but to the advantage of Canada ... so that the world may see that we recognise talent, as is done in other countries' (*Official Report* 30: 4071). Although Barron's suggestion received no response, it elicited a testament to the quality of Lampman's poetry from Nicholas Flood Davin and an endorsement of the importance of 'national sentiment' from Wilfrid Laurier. Lampman is a 'genuine poet,' 'he has a genuine note of his own,' and he should be 'encourage[d] in the interests of Canada, because ... the life-blood of a people is its literature,' asserted Davin, to which Laurier replied that, though he was not 'prepared to say ... that literature is the life-blood of the people,' he would admit 'that there are no people without literature' and that there could be no 'better mode of promoting a national sentiment [in Canada] than by fostering, as much as possible, native literature and native talent' (30: 4073). 'If such volumes [as Lampman's] were purchased for exchange and circulation in foreign libraries,' he added, 'they could not but have the effect of recommending Canada, and of showing that we are a civilized nation.' After a few further remarks by Laurier on the desirability of 'national sentiment,' the discussion returned to the matter of books for the Library of Parliament. Lampman was not assigned to an 'easy' or 'soft' position in the civil service, and *Among the Millet, and Other Poems* was not 'purchased for exchange and circulation in foreign libraries.'

In September 1890, Lampman's reputation in both Canada and the United States was given a further boost by an article from the pen of Walter Blackburn Harte, an English-born writer who was then working as a reporter for the Toronto *Mail* after serving his journalistic apprenticeship in Montreal from 1887 to September 1889 and before moving to New York in March 1891 to join the staff of the New York *Tribune* (see Doyle, *Fin de Siècle* 19–34). A manifestation of Harte's plan 'to establish himself as an interpreter of Canada to the United States' and 'to promote Canadian culture internationally' (Doyle 30, 33), 'Some Canadian Writers of To-day' in the September 1890 number of the *New England Magazine* is a survey of contemporary English-Canadian writers that makes no effort to conceal either its author's liberal beliefs or his cosmopolitan nationalism: 'the [Canadian] people are slowly working out their own destiny,' Harte asserts, 'and that destiny will certainly involve the annihilation of the last relics of the Old World fetishisms which have been engrafted upon our national life under the British domination ... As the independence of the Canadian people increases, a literature is developing which promises some day to be worthy of the inspiration of our Canadian forests, lakes, rivers, and mountains, and of that full measure of manhood which God intended as a free gift to all men' ('Some Canadian Writers' 22). That Harte's thinking was very much the product of the debates about the aesthetics and politics of Canadian literature that had surfaced time and again in the pages of the country's newspapers and magazines during the previous decade is as evident in these general statements as it is in his more specific comments about Canadian literature:

> It is an indisputable fact that we are on the eve of a great natural crisis in Canada; and an intellectual revolution, which will mark an epoch in our literary history, is already at hand. As is usual in the initial stages of every literature, there are more poets and clever versifiers than writers of good prose in Canada, but the contemporary poets of Canada have placed a wide gulf between them and the preceding generation. Their work has

more technical finish; it shows more signs of culture, and is above all imbued, as the London Athenaeum said recently in a critique of an anthology of Canadian song [i.e., *Songs of the Great Dominion*], with 'the exhilaration that comes in a brilliant climate to men who are by day possessing themselves of nature's secrets and her wealth.' The preponderance of poetry in Canadian literature is very significant. The poets are the precursors of a national upheaval. (22–3)

After reading this passage, it can come as no surprise that when he was living in Montreal, Harte moved in the same circles as Lighthall and that later in the essay he describes Lighthall as 'a man with a future before him in literature, if he does not allow his ambitions in this direction to be swamped by his occupations as a hard-working lawyer' (39).

As he read the introductory remarks to 'Some Canadian Writers of To-day,' Roberts must have felt confident that he would loom large in Harte's pantheon of epoch-making Canadian poets. If so, he would have been sadly mistaken, for when Harte turns to poets after paying due respect to Goldwin Smith and Sir Daniel Wilson (1816–92), he names Lampman, Campbell, Duncan Campbell Scott, and William Patrick McKenzie (1861–1942)[8] as 'the chief exponents' of the 'new school of poetry being formed in Canada' and proclaims Lampman, 'who a short time since received such generous recognition at the hands of Mr. W.D. Howells in *Harper's Magazine*,' 'the sweetest and strongest of this little group of singers ... Mr. Howells ranked him among the strongest singers of America. I venture to assert that there is no living poet in either hemisphere who can present such pictures of natural scenery and natural phenomena as Lampman. In England since Wordsworth there has been no poet equal him in painting the common life of the country' (29–31). Perhaps remembering Thomson's review of *Among the Millet, and Other Poems*, Harte describes the members of the new school as 'apostles of scientific poetry' who 'observe natural phenomena with the careful eyes of a botanist, the knowledge of a woodsman, and the love and awe of a pagan' (29). Both Lampman and Campbell 'occupy a unique position in the world of letters,' he adds, because their poetry combines 'a minute fidelity to nature' with a 'loving appreciation of the multitude of God's daily blessings' and, in so doing, fulfils John Campbell Shairp's prophecy in *On Poetic Interpretation of Nature* that '"part of the work of future poets of nature"' will be '"to write on the universal ideas of science, through the emotions which they excite"' (29–30). As for Roberts, he is merely 'a disciple of Swinburne and Tennyson, and his work is chastened by the influence of Longfellow. He is the senior of Lampman and Campbell, and has a talent for word-painting, but his colors are too lavishly employed' (31). From Roberts's perspective, insult must have been added to injury by the fact that Lampman's portrait precedes and dwarfs his own in the article and by the fact that the article is supplemented by only two poems, 'Lake Huron' (1889), by Campbell, and 'An Invocation' (1888), by Lampman.

Nor would Roberts's self-esteem have been bolstered by the climactic treatment accorded Carman on the final page of 'Some Canadian Writers of To-day':

> Entirely different from Lampman and Campbell ... in his method and style is Bliss Carman, one of the most promising of the bright band of intellectual workers hailing from Nova Scotia. One of the first things which attracts the attention of the critical reader is the wonderful phrasing which runs through all his work. He possesses a faculty of immediately kindling the imagination ... and calling up with a few striking words a whole series of pictures – vivid or shadowy and mystic, according to the dominant mood. His style is quite peculiar to himself. There is no evidence of the influence of any other writer in a line of his poetry. His work is more purely lyrical than that of any other American poet; indeed, the London Academy in a recent review places him in the first rank of contemporary lyrical writers.[9] He never forgets the high character of his calling, and his work is saturated with ... ideality ... The spiritual touch is always there. His language is invariably melodious, but it contains no suggestion of effeminacy or a straining after effect. A rugged strength underlies it all. (40)

It is a mark of the cohesiveness of the Confederation group in the fall of 1890 that Roberts, though hurt and perplexed by the slight to himself in 'Some Canadian Writers of To-day,' nevertheless applauded Harte for writing 'admirably' and 'with ... true insight' of Carman and Lampman (*CL* 124); and Carman and Lampman, though doubtless pleased and encouraged by the attention accorded to them, nevertheless deplored Harte's scanting of Roberts. Harte 'has seriously marred the judicial character of his dicta by one omission,' wrote Carman in the 'Literary Notes' column of the 11 September 1890 issue of the *Independent*:

> The foremost poet of Canada, in reputation as well as in achievements and power, is Mr. Charles G.D. Roberts. If there was one person in Canadian letters whose work could not possibly be skipped, it was he ... It should be dis-

tinctly borne in mind that all the younger Canadians ... are only following Roberts's larger footsteps; and that the spirit of patriotism and poetry within them owes its first stir of life to the stalwart manliness which achieved success in 'Orion,' while they were yet all boys together. (19)

'[Y]ou will like to know that I perfectly agree with what you say' in 'reference to [the] article in the September ... *New England Magazine*,' Lampman told Carman on October 29; 'I do not imagine that any one who has been conversant with literary matters in this country for any length of time questions Roberts's position, among us' (quoted in Greig 1: 11). Not surprisingly, the Saint John *Progress* came to Roberts's rescue, first, on November 1, with a lengthy column by Arthur John Lockhart ('Pastor Felix') regretting Harte's elevation of Lampman, lamenting his failure to accord Roberts the same 'warmth and amplitude' as the other poets, and decrying the tendency in Canadian criticism to fault writers for 'their too great reflectiveness of earlier masters' such as 'Swinburne, Tennyson, and Longfellow' (4);[10] and then, on November 15, by reprinting Carman's defence of Roberts in the *Independent*. As the members of the Confederation group looked back on 1890, some had more reason than others to be pleased by the year's events, but none could have doubted that individually and as a group they were becoming better known and more highly admired both nationally and internationally.

For a few weeks early in 1891, the year looked as if it might become an *annus mirabilis* for Duncan Campbell Scott. The December 1890 number of *Scribner's Magazine* contained 'The Reed-Player' (1893), a poignantly lyrical evocation of the power and mystery of music that was quickly praised in the December 4 issue of the *Independent* not merely as 'the best poem of the month,' but as the best poem to appear in an American periodical during the entire year (23).[11] By early February, Scott's poem had been reprinted in the *Week* (December 26) and the Ottawa *Evening Journal* (January 2) and excerpted in *Progress* (January 24); and the *Independent*'s accolade had been quoted in both the *Journal* (January 16) and, from there, in *Progress* (February 7). (Since Carman probably wrote or at least prompted the notice in the *Independent*, it is scarcely surprising that when Scott published 'The Reed-Player' in *The Magic House and Other Poems*, he dedicated it 'To B.C.,' an addition carried forward to William Archer's *Poets of the Younger Generation* [1902], where it is the only poem by him, then dropped from his collected *Poems* [1926].) The year 1891 was not to be Scott's *annus mirabilis*, however, but Campbell's.

Despite the publication of his 'Canadian Folk Song' in the January 1885 number of *Atlantic Monthly* and the publication of *Snowflakes and Sunbeams* in November 1888, Campbell had not begun to make much of a name for himself either in the United States or in Canada until 1889, when the appearance of *Lake Lyrics and Other Poems* in August, preceded and followed by the publication in the *Century* (New York), the *Youth's Companion* (Boston), the *Independent* (New York), and other periodicals of such poems as 'The Winter Lakes,' 'Vapor and Blue,' 'How One Winter Came to the Lake Region,' 'In the Winter Woods (in the Lake Region),' and 'December in the Lake Region' ('December') prompted 'a New York critic' to dub him 'the "Poet of the Lakes"' (Harte, 'Some Canadian Writers' 31).[12] 'Canada is beginning to be heard through a group of poets whose charming verses have found hearty welcome to the pages of our magazine,' ran a review of *Lake Lyrics and Other Poems* in the 24 October 1889 issue of the *Independent*, 'we are glad to see these *Lake Lyrics* in more permanent form. Mr. Campbell is a hearty, earnest, straightforward singer ... He sings the lakes and landscapes, the air and the life of his country to such effect that one gets a refreshing breath of the province' (27–8). 'There is a considerable power in the Rev. William Wilfred Campbell's ... really brilliant [sketches] of the great Canadian Lakes,' enthused a review of the same volume in the 8 March 1890 number of the *Academy*, 'Mr. Campbell has a genuine passion for his lakes, and in his verse they become wonderfully significant' (305). 'The *Atlantic* [*Monthly*] for December is a strong number,' observed *Saturday Night* on 6 December 1890, 'and William Wilfred Campbell [has] an excellent poem on "Pan the Fallen" [1893]' (7). But fame and fortune did not come fully to Campbell until 'The Mother' (1893), the Poesque rendition of a macabre German superstition that he first published in the April 1891 number of *Harper's Monthly Magazine*, received the fulsome praise of T.H. Sudduth in the April 5 issue of the Chicago *Inter-Ocean*.[13] 'This one little poem by William Wilfred Campbell ... touches a finer chord in the heart than was dreamt of in the poetry of Homer,' wrote Sudduth; it is 'the nearest approach to a great poem which has cropped out in current literature for many a long day' and a 'complete and priceless' 'gem' that belongs 'in th[e] same category' as such poems as Milton's 'Ode on the Morning of Christ's Nativity,' Shelley's 'To a Skylark,' and Longfellow's 'A Psalm of Life.' Within days, 'The Mother' was reprinted in the *Globe* (April 25) and countless other periodicals and newspapers on both sides of the border, as to a lesser extent were Sudduth's rapturous comments (see, for example, 'A Canadian Poet' in the

April 25 issue of the *Globe* and an editorial note in the same day's *Grip* [Toronto]).[14] Also on April 25, an editorial in *Saturday Night* by Hector W. Charlesworth (1872–1945) entitled 'Canada's Greatest Poet' credited Campbell with saving the country from the humiliation caused by Harte's imputation that 'our greatest poets [are] but word-photographers' and asserted that, 'with the exception of ... Whittier, Lowell and Holmes,' [he] is the greatest living American poet in the broad and only true sense of the word' (6). On June 12, the *Week* published a letter from Thomas O'Hagan reiterating the 'great merit' of 'The Mother' (446), and on July 2, the *Globe* announced that on the coming Saturday it would begin publication of 'Maguire's Nan,' a story that would supplement in fiction the 'continental reputation' that 'Campbell ha[d] already won ... as a poet' ('A New Story' 1).

In view of what happened after Lampman was perceived to have won a similar reputation, the ensuing treatment of Campbell is entirely predictable. Perhaps acting on the basis of an article in the 29 August 1891 issue of the *Globe*, which, after alluding to the international successes of Lampman, Scott, and Campbell and referring to Campbell's recent appointment as a temporary clerk in the Department of Railways and Canals in Ottawa, suggested that 'Canadians will not complain if the Government [were to] deal generously with this young singer' ('Canadian Writers' 5), Alexander McNeill (1842–1932) rose in the House of Commons on September 28 to urge Campbell's appointment as superintendent of the Library of Parliament, a position that would permit him 'to follow out the bent of his genius' (*Official Report* 54–5: 6264). In making his case, McNeill (who was the member for Bruce North, Ontario, where Campbell had been rector of St Paul's Church, Southampton, between the fall of 1890 and his move to Ottawa) quoted extensively not only from Sudduth's article, but also from a follow-up piece in 'a San Francisco paper' hailing Campbell as 'a new star in the world of poetry' and 'The Mother' 'a work of literary genius.'[15] 'Mr. Goldwin Smith,' he added, 'speaks in the highest terms of Mr. Campbell's work.' With Laurier's enthusiastic support, McNeill's suggestion came to the Senate on 18 May 1892 but was rejected on various grounds, including the possibility that 'an admirable poet ... might make a very inferior clerk in the Library' (*Debates* 237).[16] There the matter ended, despite a further article in the *Globe* of May 31 arguing that 'if a place cannot be found for [Campbell] in the library ..., the Ministers might look elsewhere' ('The Case of Mr. W.W. Campbell' 4). If the *Globe*'s urgings were not instrumental, then they were surely very helpful in securing the position of clerk in the Department of the Secretary of State that Campbell assumed on 1 August 1892 and occupied until his promotion to the position of clerk in the Archives on 26 August 1908.[17]

While Campbell was being propelled towards a sinecure during 1891–2, he and other members of the Confederation group were also achieving ever greater prominence both within and outside Canada: Roberts and Carman were each given articles to themselves in a series on 'New Brunswick Authorship' by W.G. MacFarlane in the October and November 1891 issues of the *Dominion Illustrated*. Frederick George Scott's novel *Alton Hazlewood: A Memoir, by his Friend* (1892) was published in New York and, though panned by the *Athenaeum* for everything but its 'high moral purpose' (3 June 1893, 697), welcomed by the *Week* for 'the remarkable personality' of its central character and 'the charm of ... [its] style' (29 January 1892, 139). Lampman was described as one of 'the most promising of the younger poets in the English language' in an article by 'J.G.T.' under the heading 'Amerikanishe Litteratur' in the 1891–2 number of *Anglia: Zeitschrift für Englishe Philologie,* and *Among the Millet, and Other Poems* was belatedly and very positively reviewed in the 28 May 1892 number of the *Halifax Herald.*[18] Roberts, Lampman, Campbell, and both Scotts were prominent presences in the *Week*, the *Globe*, and other periodicals and newspapers, and their poems, particularly those that had received international accolades, were continually reprinted in such local collocations as Helen E. Merrill's *Picturesque Prince Edward County* (Picton, 1892) and Mrs John Cameron and Agnes Ethelwyn Wetherald's *Wives and Daughters* (London, Ontario, 1890–2). As the 1892 Christmas season drew to a close, Lampman was once again proposed for appointment to 'one of the leisurely places in the civil service,'[19] and Frederick George Scott published the poem that in time would grace him with at least a modicum of the recognition that 'The Mother' had brought Campbell. 'Singularly fine – strong, imaginative, and highly original – that "Samson"!' Roberts enthused to Scott when his 'Samson' was first published in the 6 January 1893 issue of the *Week*: 'one of the best poems we have produced, decidedly' (*CL* 168). A 'mighty and compelling lyric,' he added of the poem on March 25, and on June 15: 'I *adore* "Samson." That is a *great* lyric – I use the word deliberately and as a critic' (*CL* 169, 174). Others agreed: after the appearance of 'Samson' in *My Lattice and Other Poems*, a review in the 2 March 1895 issue of the *Speaker* (London) proclaimed it 'splendid,' beyond criticism, and 'probably the best American poem for many years' (249; and see O'Hagan, 'Canadian Poets' 793), a judgment immediately repeated in a 'cable dispatch' to the *Globe* and loudly trumpeted there, first as a news item (March 4) and then in the introductory note to a reprinting of the poem in its entirety (March 9). For his part, Scott was so 'exhilarated' by the reception of 'Samson' that he wrote 'A Song of Triumph' (1900), a Whitmanesque celebration of the creative energy that culminated in 'the production of man ... whose home is in the bosom of God' (*CPFGS* 197). For Scott more than for other members of the Confederation group, fame was merely one of God's mysterious ways of working out His plan.

Ten days after the publication of 'Samson' in the Epiphany 1893 issue of the *Week*, the *Globe* announced the tentative program for a second 'Canadian Literature Evening' organized by the Young Men's Liberal Club and to be held that evening (January 16) at the Art Gallery of the Ontario Society of Artists. Whereas the Confederation group had been conspicuous by its absence at the first such evening two years earlier, now those of them who had recently achieved international recognition were to be very much part of the proceedings: Campbell and Duncan Campbell Scott would attend in person, and a letter from Lampman would be read to a predicted 'capacity' crowd (20). 'We had the satisfaction of having with us Canada's greatest poet, Mr. William Wilfred Campbell ..., and Canada's greatest and most representative poetess, Miss. E. Pauline Johnson,' *Saturday Night* reported on January 23. 'Mr. Duncan Campbell Scott read a weird sketch entitled "Veronica" ... [I]t would have been a treat to hear him recite "The Reed-Player" or one of his other poems' (7). According to *Saturday Night* and to the fuller of the two reports on the event in the January 18 issue of the *Globe*, Pauline Johnson was 'the pleasantest contribution to the evening' and the only poet to 'receive ... the honor of ... [a] recall by the audience' (5). ('Her poetry has a sweetness, force and finish, to which was added the interest her "Cry from an Indian Wife" received on account of her descent,' wrote the reporter; 'it was like the voice of the nations who once possessed this country, who have wasted away before our civilization, speaking through this cultured, gifted, soft-voiced descendant.') Nevertheless, the same report describes Campbell's reading of 'The Mother,' which it quotes in full, as 'one of the pleasantest of the evening,' observes that 'there is a fine finish and a sparkle to Mr. Scott's verses,' credits Lampman with being 'one of America's sweetest and strongest singers,' and quotes the 'chairman of the evening,' Frank Yeigh, on the role of such events in promoting 'Canadian nationality' and Canadian literature both at home and 'abroad.' With an eye on Carman's permanent removal to New York in 1890 and

Lampman's rumoured appointment to a professorship at Cornell University, Yeigh observed that, 'while we can rejoice in the fact that our Canadian poets have captured the American magazines, [he] hoped [that] the American editors would not capture our poets' and that 'one of the trio of Ottawa poets [would not] soon join the exodus.'[20] The briefer of the two reports on the second 'Canadian Literature Evening' in the *Globe* scarcely deviates from the newspaper's usual emphasis on international recognition: stressing the dangers of 'insist[ing] that a thing is literature because it is Canadian' and mentioning Johnson only in passing, it remarks that the complaint of neglect is 'not heard from such men as Campbell, Lampman and Scott, who have access to the best magazines of the United States and have won notice in the old world' (4). Although neither report mentions Roberts, his presence can be discerned in the tacit acceptance in both of cosmopolitan standards of workmanship and judgment.

The two major literary events of February 1892 in Toronto – the commencement on February 6 of the 'At the Mermaid Inn' column in the *Globe* and the recital on February 19 that marked the beginning of Johnson's career as a stage performer – were each in their different ways the products of the 'Canadian Literature Evening' of January 16, the former in its capitalization on the existence of an 'Ottawa trio of poets' and the latter in its capitalization on 'the favorable impression' made by Johnson (*Globe*, 20 February 1892, 20). Nor should the prominence attained by the Confederation group be overlooked as a factor in the launching of Johnson's solo career: in announcements for her February 19 recital, she was touted in similar terms as they had recently been as 'the recipient of much praise from high-class English and American journals' and her claim to attention supported by a statement from Roberts that characterizes her as 'the aboriginal voice of Canada by blood as well as by taste and the special breed of [her] gifts' (*Globe*, 18 February 1892, 8). Johnson was never a part of the Confederation group, however, and her apartness was only emphasized by her decision in the fall of 1892 to wear 'the costume of an Indian maiden' when reciting her poems on Native themes (*Globe*, 28 November 1892, 80), an innovation inspired, perhaps, by the 'native costume' of 'the Turkish poetess, Nigjar Hanym' (see the *Globe*, 20 October 1891, 15) or the 'native garb' of the Kaffir troupe that performed in Toronto on 18 February 1892 (see the *Globe* of that date, 80). By the time Johnson appeared in the women poets' 'Supplement' in J.E. Wetherell's *Later Canadian Poems* in May 1893, she was on the verge of achieving international recognition of the sort to which no member of the Confederation group ever aspired or could possibly emulate: as the attractive female enactor of the pathos of a race that was supposedly becoming 'little more than a memory' (Pearson 34).[21]

Not least, but not only, because of the existence of the 'At the Mermaid Inn' column, the months from February 1892 to 1 July 1893 (when the column was discontinued) can be seen as a period of fruition and harvest for the Confederation group, a period in which – to continue the agricultural analogy that was so dear to Roberts in the early 1880s – the work of sowing and growing was long past and the signs of the fall and winter that will be placed on view in chapter 8 were becoming increasingly abundant. Work by all six poets continued to appear regularly in periodicals in Canada and 'abroad,' as did effusive appreciations of their achievements: on 18 June 1892, for example, the *Globe* reprinted 'The Mother' for a third time, now with a lengthy article lamenting that Campbell's 'genius' was more appreciated outside than inside Canada (3), and on 18 March 1893 the same newspaper noted that the March number of the *Californian Illustrated Magazine* (San Francisco) contained Lampman's 'Sirius' (1900) and that the February number of the *Cosmopolitan* (New York) contained poems by both Campbell ('Dusk' [1893]) and Lampman ('After Mist in Winter' [1900]) (8). With the publication in December 1892 of Roberts's *Ave: An Ode for the Centenary of the Birth of Percy Bysshe Shelley, August 4, 1792* came further lustre for the group and confirmation of his leadership. 'The Canadian reading public are not likely to meet with anything more interesting than [this] new publication by Professor Charles G.D. Roberts, our master workman in verse,' wrote Lampman in 'At the Mermaid Inn' on 21 January 1893; 'the beauty and fervour of ... "Ave," and the sonorous pomp of its versification, can hardly fail to possess [the reader's] imagination' (239). On March 9, the reviewer for the *Independent* (perhaps Carman)[22] proclaimed the poem 'a clear, calm, strong, well-sustained piece of verbal art work flushed with a fine and free imagination' and compared its 'workmanship' to that of Keats's 'Ode to a Nightingale,' declaring that 'if he has not quite clipped the golden flower of Keats's supreme rapture-song' 'the Canadian poet has not sunk below the line of distinguished success' (16). When Roberts's ode was reprinted in 1893 with *Songs of the Common Day*, his old pupil, T.G. Marquis, judged it his 'strongest and most original work' and predicted that 'critics will probably place this masterpiece alongside of the best work of the kind that has been done in English since *Adonais*; and this not only on account of its artistic qualities, but for its intensity and depth of thought' (*Week*, 22 September 1893, 1023). Within a month, Sharp would do almost exactly that, declaring 'Ave' 'the most noteworthy poem in *Songs of the Common Day*' and a 'noble ode ... [in which] Mr. Roberts measures himself with the chiefs in lyrical mastery' (535). Roberts had not published a recognized masterpiece since the early 1880s, but in 'Ave' he had a poem to rival or surpass 'The Mother' and, as his letters after its publication amply attest, he was determined to capitalize on its excellence: immediately after its appearance, he had asked Carman to 'review it ... somewhere' and to arrange for Gilbert Parker to do so in England, and a few days later he had commissioned an American clipping service to send him up to '*one hundred*' reviews so that he could see 'whatever may be said of ... ["Ave"] in the United States and Canada' (*CL* 163, 165). The time of sowing and growing was past, but the work of fertilizing and cultivation was continuing.

Without question, the most significant event in the first half of 1893 for the Confederation group as a whole was the publication in May of *Later Canadian Poems*.[23] Very well received on both sides of the border (it does not appear to have been reviewed in Britain), Wetherell's anthology received its most substantive Canadian review in the 7 July 1893 issue of the *Week*, where the Ottawa historian and literary scholar Samuel Edward Dawson (1833–1916), whose 1882 *Study with Critical and Explanatory Notes of Alfred Tennyson's Poem 'The Princess'* lent his views special authority, gave all but its title-page extremely high praise, eloquently judging it

a pleasant book to read, and then to send to some friend of the 'exodus' who, in a far-off country may dream of the dip of paddles in the swift-flowing streams of his native north-land, or long for the leafy shade of the maples, and the soft, dry seats under the pines; for the poems ... [it] contains are redolent of the spirit and feeling of our own Canada, from the lakes to the ocean ... [W]e can tender this little volume to our brothers and sisters of the English tongue in distant lands, with more satisfaction than any other of the collections that have fallen into our hands. It is not an aggregation of poems selected solely because they were written by Canadians, but there is an evenness of literary workmanship throughout the collection, which shows that we have writers who are justly claiming recognition in English literature, solely because of their literary skill and inherent poetic power. (756–7)

In the body of his review, Dawson makes no mention of Cameron and merely bows courteously in the direction of Johnson, Machar, and the other 'ladies' in Wetherell's 'Supplement,' but devotes a paragraph each to Campbell, Carman, Roberts, and the two Scotts and three paragraphs to Lampman, who, he suggests, 'has, of all our poets, perhaps, the greatest power of expression, as well as the most correct ear' (756). Roberts may well have been dismayed by the prominence accorded to Lampman in Dawson's review, but he must surely have been consoled by its emphasis on 'workmanship' and by Dawson's comment that he (Roberts) does 'rise ... to the front rank of our poetical writers' 'when he is under the influence of his own Acadian home, paddling on the rivers of New Brunswick, or by the marsh-lands of Tantramar' (757).

The other significant event in the first half of 1893 for the Confederation group as a whole was the publication in the April 1 issue of the *Globe* of 'Young Canadian Writers from an American Standpoint,' a very substantial and laudatory article by Edward William Bok (1863–1930), the editor of the newly founded *Ladies' Home Journal* (Philadelphia). Drawing heavily but not explicitly on Harte's 'Some Canadian Writers of To-day,' Bok affirms the existence of a 'growing school of young Canadian writers' whose work 'takes the form, for the most part, of poetry' that 'springs out of the emotions arising' from 'know[ing] nature thoroughly, minutely, scientifically' (17). 'Especially is this true of Archibald Lampman and William Wilfred Campbell, two names so often met in American magazines,' writes Bok, but it is also true of Duncan Campbell Scott, another 'devoted student ... of Wordsworth,' who shares Lampman's 'simplicity ... gentle optimism,' and 'deep love of nature.' Siding with Carman on the question of leadership, Bok describes Roberts as 'the acknowledged leader of the Canadian school of writers' and presents the two cousins as paragons of masculinity, 'Carman tall, broad shouldered, flaxen-haired, [with] strong, smooth-shaven features gravely set, and only relieved by the eyeglasses that he invariably wears,' and Roberts 'a man of activity and physical strength, ... a crack oarsman and footballist' who 'plays in the rush line of the college football team and leads his pupils in the rough and tumble scrimmage with as much enthusiasm as in the class room.' Evidently Bok had personal knowledge of Carman and Roberts, and apparently he was drawn to them physically as well as politically.[24] There is no evidence that Frederick George Scott was dismayed by Bok's neglect, but the appearance in the June 3 issue of the *Globe* of a lengthy article rehearsing Campbell's accolades,[25] and anticipating the confirmation of his high stature with the imminent publication of *The Dread Voyage,* strongly suggests by its detailed biographical elements that Campbell was displeased by the relatively brief space accorded to him in 'Young Canadian Writers from an American Standpoint.' The signs of approaching fall and winter were becoming more apparent.

For the most part, however, 1893 was a summer of content for the Confederation group. *The Dread Voyage: Poems* duly appeared in August, *Songs of the Common Day, and Ave: An Ode for the Shelley Centenary* in September,[26] *Low Tide on Grand Pré: A Book of Lyrics* in November,[27] and *The Magic House and Other Poems* in December.[28] In July, Lampman's 'The City of the End of Things' was accepted for publication in the *Atlantic Monthly* (see *AC* 88) and in December, Frederick George Scott's *My Lattice and Other Poems* was accepted for publication early in the following year. On March 9, the *Independent* had seen the audacious daring of 'Ave' as evidence of Roberts's 'divine right' to 'challenge comparison on the highest plane' (17), and on December 7 the same magazine named Carman 'easily one of the best among young American poets' (17). On October 7, the *Globe* observed with satisfaction that 'the splendid work by Campbell, Roberts, Lampman, and others of the bright coterie whose verse appears in the current magazines and in their printed volumes, has given gratifying prominence to the poetic literature of their country, and is creating a demand that publisher and author alike are pleased to note' (20). Quoting the New York *World* on Canada's 'rare crop of poets' and expressing the persistent fear that 'the American public are better acquainted with the work of our poets than are Canadians,' the *Globe* called readers' attention to an advertisement in the same issue by the Methodist Book and Publishing House in Toronto that lists *Among the Millet, In Divers Tones, Songs of the Common Day and Ave, Lake Lyrics,* and *The Dread Voyage* as the first five of nine volumes by 'our Native Poets, whose verse is attracting more than national or even continental attention' (18).[29] 'These, with some fifteen other books of verse by different authors, make up a very respectable showing of native poetic literature,' declared the advertisement. 'Come and Make Their Acquaintance.' The 'bright coterie' had arrived.

During the remainder of 1893, throughout 1894, and well into 1895, the fêting of the group continued, but with increasingly loud intimations of the storm to come. In December 1893 and January 1894, Lampman, Carman, Campbell, and Roberts were prominently featured in a series of articles on 'Our Canadian Poets' by Thomas Conant (1842–

1905) in the *Globe*.[30] On 6 January 1894, Sharp used a review of *Low Tide on Grand Pré* in the *Academy* to declare Carman and Roberts 'the finest poetic voices heard as yet in the Dominion' and to assert that 'it would be difficult to select work surpassing theirs from the mass of verse of high quality produced by the younger American writers' (7). A little over a month later, an evening of 'Native Literature and Song' at Victoria College, Toronto included a recital by Johnson, an address on 'Canadian Literature' by Lewis Emerson Horning (1858–1928),[31] and readings of poems by Lampman, Campbell, and possibly Roberts (see the *Globe* 9 and 10 February 1894). In December 1894, the Harvard professor of economic history, William James Ashley (1860–1927), declared that 'the best poets now living in America were the Canadian poets' and named Carman, Roberts and 'perchance Lampman' (*CL* 189). On 16 March 1895, a lengthy review by 'S' of 'Some New Books' in the *Globe* asserted that 'Lampman's *Among the Millet*, Roberts's *Songs of the Common Day*, Scott's *The Magic House* and Carman's *Low Tide on Grand Pré* are, without exaggeration, events of the greatest importance in the development of [Canadian] literature' and pronounced '*My Lattice* ... quite up to the average Canadian poetry of the close of the century' (10). And in May 1895, the annual meeting of the Royal Society of Canada in Ottawa included a 'novel feature': 'An Evening with Canadian Poets,' in which Lampman, Campbell, Carman, and both Scotts were among those who 'read ... selections' of their own poems (*Globe*, 18 May 1895, 10).[32] No doubt partly because of the presence of Johnson, 'at least a thousand persons' attended the event,[33] which was preceded by an address on Canadian poetry by Professor William Clark (1829–1912)[34] and followed by some remarks by the governor-general, the Earl of Aberdeen (*Globe*, 25 May 1895, 9). On the same day, May 17, Lampman was elected a fellow of the Royal Society, an honour that had been accorded to Roberts in 1890 and to Campbell in 1894 (and would come to Duncan Campbell Scott in 1899 and to Frederick George Scott in 1900). Roberts's absence from the 'Evening with Canadian Poets' was probably due to overwork, coupled with the fact that in March he had resigned his professorship at King's College 'effect[ive] in June' and in May was enthusiastically entertaining the hope of being appointed to 'one of the best Chairs at *Yale*!' (*CL* 196, 199). Indeed, on May 4, the *Globe* treated Roberts's removal to the United States as a *fait accompli* and wondered whether it was yet 'another instance of that deplorable truth that a prophet has no honor in his own country' (14). More than a hint of winter was in the air.

There were other hints, too: on balance, most of the many reviews of books by the Confederation group that appeared in American, British, and Canadian periodicals and newspapers between the summer of 1893 and the spring of 1895 were positive and laudatory, but some were sharply critical and even negative. '[I]t is impossible to avoid wishing occasionally that the author could give us a little more of the brighter and sunnier side of his genius,' observed the *Globe* of *The Dread Voyage* on 19 August 1893. '"In Autumn" and "Autumn" contain a good many thoughts in common, and not a few lines in which the language also is repeated' (6). 'Two qualities that are lacking in these poems are strength and dignity,' complained the same newspaper of *Low Tide on Grand Pré* on 10 March 1894. '[A] certain incoherency of expression arouses in the reader dissatisfaction' (6). *Songs of the Common Day* and *The Magic House* were less harshly treated, but neither remained entirely unscathed. The 'distinctively lyrical poems' are, 'generally speaking, weaker' than the sonnets in Roberts's volume, observed Marquis in the 22 September 1893 number of the *Week*: 'the rhythm and thought are lacking in originality, and often fall into the commonplace' (1023). 'There are ... inequalities in style and expression here and there to which one might object,' wrote 'Pharos' (Laura Bradshaw Durand [1865–1925]) of Scott's volume in the 3 March 1894 issue of the *Globe*; '"In the Country Churchyard" ... is strong and moving in its first eight stanzas, but after this point it falls off.' These and similar remarks are neither unfair nor overstated, but after the extraordinarily extravagant accolades of the previous years, they may well have suggested to the Confederation group and its advocates that Canada was a mean-spirited sow bent on consuming its most promising farrow.

If such an apprehension existed, it would have been confirmed by the review of *My Lattice and Other Poems* that appeared in the *Globe* on 24 November 1894. Drawing a distinction between the 'true poet' whose 'thought is ... alive and vigorous' and the accomplished versifier with a 'facility for jingling words together,' the reviewer proceeds to quote John George Bourinot's contention in *Our Intellectual Strength and Weakness: A Short Historical and Critical Review of Literature, Art and Education in Canada* (1893) that no Canadian poet has yet produced 'a book of poems which can touch the sympathies and live on the lips of the world like those of [John Greenleaf] Whittier and Longfellow' and to cite Scott's volume as an example of this 'inadequacy of power' (12).[35] 'The sympathetic reader is quick to feel the beauty of two or three of the short poems and the weaknesses of the longer and more ambitious attempts to crystallise feeling,' continues the review, but 'the "ground-tone of conventionality" is seldom surmounted' and 'the narrative poems ..., [lacking] power, do not quicken the interest and leave one unimpressed.' Overworked and 'worried' by financial problems though he was, Roberts took the time on December 15 to reassure Scott that, 'whatever [his] defects, "lack of power" is not one of them' (*CL* 187, 188) Characteristically, Roberts then offers Scott some constructive criticism ('I think your execution is sometimes careless and hasty,' but 'the essentials – strength, imagination, music, and individuality – your work seems to me to possess')[36] and some strategic assistance and advice for generating countervailing reviews of *My Lattice and Other Poems*:

> I will write to Gilder [the editor of the *Century*] about your book at once, telling him that you are going to send him a copy. Howells I don't know at all. Better send to him direct, with a letter. They say he is a kind and helpful chap. Better send a copy to Edmund Clarence Stedman, also with a letter. He is generous, warm-hearted, a sympathetic critic, – and he appreciates the approbation of a younger man.
>
> Carman is not connected with the Independent now, and is not likely to see the book unless you send it to him ... He might find it in his way to review it for you. I would do so, with more than pleasure; but I am simply driven to death with overwork and worry. (*CL* 188)[37]

Roberts's letter of 15 December 1894 not only exemplifies his continuing leadership of the Confederation group, but also reveals his unflagging resourcefulness as a manipulator of the reception of the group's books. In the process, it also indicates that there was more than a grain of truth to Campbell's scarcely veiled charge in the 20 April 1895 number of *Saturday Night* that other members of the Confederation group had engaged in the practice of 'log-rolling' – that is, 'band[ing] together for the purposes of mutual admiration, and carry[ing] out their compact by booming one another in the several papers to which they have literary access' (*War* 5). Among the seeds that yielded international and national recognition were the dragon's teeth from which the 'War among the Poets' would shortly spring.

Looking back at the poems that did so much to raise the Confederation group to international and national prominence in the early 1890s – 'Between the Rapids,' 'The Mother,' 'The Reed-Player,' and 'Samson' – it can be seen that they all have three qualities more-or-less in common:

masterful technique, dramatic appeal, and evocative power. With regard
to the first of these commonalities, little needs to be added here to the
discussion of workmanship in chapter 3, except that the technical mastery displayed in all four poems fulfils Roberts's aesthetic stricture that
'everything [in a poem] must be made to look as if the difficulty of the
form had *nothing* to do with it ... Every word must be *inevitable*' (*CL* 198),
and, by so doing, preclude the sort of negative criticism that was levelled
at other poems in the *Globe* and elsewhere. In elaborating on his own
reservations about Frederick George Scott's work on 15 December
1894, Roberts remarked:

> Even in the otherwise well-wrought 'In Via Mortis' you have one line with a
> whole additional foot in it – a hexameter line when the rest are penta-
> meters –; and it does not look as if you did it on purpose – that is, in the ef-
> fort to emphasize a special effect. Here and there you leave out the article,
> as a concession to the metre – which is surely slip-shod; and here and there
> a line seems to me forced and unnatural. (*CL* 188)

Neither Roberts nor any other critic expressed similar reservations
about 'Samson' or, indeed, 'Between the Rapids,' 'The Mother,' and
'The Reed-Player.' 'Mr. Scott's ... muse staggers somewhat' in 'Dion,'
wrote the reviewer in the *Speaker*, but 'in ... "Samson" ... one forgets to
criticise' (2 March 1895, 249).

A further reason for this critical forgetfulness lies in the effectiveness
of all four poems in securing the reader's or audience's quick induction
into their setting and full acceptance of their assumptions. Late nineteenth-century American, British, and Canadian readers wishing to be
transported from the everyday world of home and work into a remote
and exotic realm would have found the opening stanzas of 'Between the
Rapids' highly conducive to such an escape:

> The point is turned; the twilight shadow fills
>     The wheeling stream, the soft receding shore,
> And on our ears from deep among the hills
>     Breaks now the rapid's sudden quickening roar.
> Ah, yet the same, or have they changed their face,
>     The fair green fields, and can it still be seen,
> The white log cottage near the mountain's base,
>     So bright and quiet, so home-like and serene.

Ah, well I question, for as five years ago,
How many blessings fall, and how much woe.

Aye, there they are, nor have they changed their cheer,
    The fields, the hut, the leafy mountain brows;
Across the lonely dusk again I hear
    The loitering bells, the lowing of the cows,
The bleat of many sheep, the stilly rush
    Of the low whispering river, and through all,
Soft human tongues that break the deepening hush
    With faint-heard song or desultory call:
O comrades hold, the longest reach is past;
The stream runs swift, and we are flying fast. (*P* 36–7)

Thanks in no small measure to Lampman's skilful handling of locative phrases ('The point is turned,' 'near the mountain's base,' 'Aye, there they are') readers of 'Between the Rapids' can easily imagine the sights and sounds of the river and shore and, by so doing, assume the perspective of the returning traveller, who, in the third stanza, reveals himself to be a Canadian voyageur. That 'the mood of the *voyageur* is quite real' (Machar 252) is also, for a reader well versed in poetry, partly the result of Lampman's incorporation into the poem's opening and subsequent stanzas of echoes of some of the most affectively nostalgic poems in the Romantic-Victorian tradition – 'Tintern Abbey' ('Five years have past ...' [Wordsworth 2: 259]), Thomas Moore's 'Canadian Boat Song' ('The Rapids are near and the daylight past' [124–5]), and, with 'Where is Jacques, and where is Virginie?' in the fourth stanza, Dante Gabriel Rossetti's translation of François Villon's 'Ballad of Dead Ladies' ('Where's Hipparchia, and where is Thais ... where are the snows of yester-year?' [541]). Almost needless to say, none of these techniques and effects would have been diminished for Canadian readers by the recognition that 'Between the Rapids' recalls 'Tantramar Revisited,' another Romantic return poem in which the speaker ultimately refuses the option of re-entering a familiar landscape.

Given the technical polish, exotic setting, and evocative resonance of Lampman's dramatic lyric, it scarcely comes as a surprise that an inductive and evocative process similar to that of 'Between the Rapids' can be discerned in the opening stanzas of 'The Mother,' which are preceded by a headnote explaining that the poem was inspired by 'the following passage in Tyler's Animism:[38] "The pathetic German superstition that the dead mother's coming back in the night to suckle the baby she has left on earth may be known by the hollow pressed down in the bed where she lay'":

It was April, blossoming Spring,
They buried me when the birds did sing;

Earth, in clammy wedging earth,
They banked my bed with a black, damp girth.

Under the damp and under the mould,
I kenned my breasts were clammy and cold.

Out from the red beams, slanting and bright,
I kenned my cheeks were sunken and white.

I was a dream, and the world was a dream,
And yet I kenned all things that seem.

I was a dream, and the world was a dream,
But you cannot bury a red sunbeam. (*SPE* 36–7)

In 'Between the Rapids,' the repetition of words and syllables within stanzas and in rhyme words plays a subtly hypnotic role in conducting the reader into the poem, but in Campbell's lines repetition is more obviously used as an inductive device: conditioned by the epigraph to accept the poem's remote setting and supernatural premise, the reader readily accedes to the proposition that the speaker is a ghost whose medium of self-presentation is archaic and balladic. The second and third couplets are remarkable for the way in which they use repetition both to establish the reality of the mother's grave and to transport the reader into her sensibility. Notice especially in these couplets the compelling repetition of 'earth,' 'clammy,' and 'damp,' the inductive movement from sight to touch in 'black, damp earth,' and the adjectival use of the word 'wedging' to convey a sense of the constriction of the grave.

Drawing on the perception of the Scottish poet, critic, and folklorist Andrew Lang that the rationalist empiricism of the Victorian era awoke in men and women a compensatory desire to experience '"the stirring of ancient dread in their veins,"' T.J. Jackson Lears sees the popularity of folktale and fantasy around the turn of the century as a manifestation of a 'longing for intense feeling' that found its outlet in both the erotic and the macabre, as well as in combinations of the two (172–3). This would certainly explain not only the enormous popularity of Campbell's poem, but also the fact that, as Lawrence J. Burpee (1873–1946) pointed out in 1900,[39] the version of the poem that was countless times reprinted and recited during the previous decade contains two lines – 'I was a bride in my sickness sore, / I was a bride nine months and more' – that come perilously close to attributing immorality as well as immortality to the mother who first experiences her breasts as 'clammy and cold,' then 'fe[els] [her] breasts swell under [her] shroud,' and, finally, 'nestle[s] [her baby] to [her] throbbing breasts' (*SPE* 36–8). In 'The Mother,' Edgar Allan Poe's notion that the most poignant subject for poetry is a beautiful and dying young woman is given an exotically supernatural twist that is itself Poeian – and with crowd-pleasing results.[40]

In Frederick George Scott's 'Samson,' the process of inducting the reader into the setting and mind of the speaker is immediate and uncomplicated:

> Plunged in night, I sit alone,
> Eyeless, on the dungeon stone,
> Naked, shaggy and unkempt,
> Dreaming dreams no soul hath dreamt. (*CPFGS* 14)

'Eyeless': the word simultaneously signals that the poem is being spoken by Samson after he has been captured and blinded by the Philistines (Judges 16. 21) and alludes to his opening speech in Milton's *Samson Agonistes* ('Eyeless in *Gaza* ...' [41]), a gesture that both acknowledges a debt and exploits a resonance. In the three ensuing stanzas, Scott supplies further details of Samson's physical and psychological setting to secure the reader's imaginative participation in what is to come, which is an elaboration of the hero's prayer to God to 'strengthen' him again so that he 'may be at once avenged of the Philistines for [his] two eyes' (Judges 16. 28). With his defiant characterization of himself to God as the product of a 'faulty architect' who nevertheless possesses a 'tameless will,' Scott's Samson appears to be descended less from the biblical hero than from the Romantic Prometheus, a suspicion confirmed by the poet's comment that 'the inner meaning [of "Samson"] is revolt against the law of heredity' and by his admission with regard to another piece in

*My Lattice and Other Poems*, 'The Frenzy of Prometheus,' that 'the myth of Prometheus ... always appealed to [him]' (*CPFGS* 15, 16, 178, 179). The petition for empathy, strength, deliverance, and a hero's death with which 'Samson' concludes is hymn-like in both theme and technique:

> Israel's God, come down and see
> All my fierce captivity,
> Let thy sinews feel my pains,
> With thy fingers lift my chains.
>
> Then, with thunder loud and wild,
> Comfort thou thy rebel child,
> And with lightning split in twain
> Loveless heart and sightless brain.
>
> Give me splendour in my death –
> Not the sickening dungeon breath,
> Creeping down my blood like slime,
> Till it wastes me in my prime.
>
> Give me back for one blind hour,
> Half my former rage and power,
> And some giant crisis send,
> Meet to prove a hero's end.
>
> Then, O God, Thy mercy show –
> Crush him in the overthrow
> At whose life they scorn and point
> By its greatness out of joint. (*CPFGS* 16)

One may not entirely 'forget ... to criticise' 'Samson' (the final stanza is especially awkward, but may have been theologically necessary: 'mercy,' after all, is the defining quality of the Christian God), but its appeal to an audience nurtured in the ideal of self-sacrificing heroism that Scott himself would enact as a senior chaplain in the Canadian army during the First World War can easily be imagined. 'One seemed to be constantly in the midst of events and heroes of olden times,' Scott would write of his immersion in Edward Gibbon's *Decline and Fall of the Roman Empire* at the time when he wrote 'Samson.' 'I have often thought it was

a kind of premonition of my experience, years after, in the Great War'
(*CPFGS* 179).

Whereas 'Between the Rapids,' 'The Mother,' and 'Samson' are all
acts of ventriloquism in which the poet assumes the character and voice
of an imaginary or mythical character, 'The Reed-Player' appears to be a
personal statement in Duncan Campbell Scott's own voice. It resembles
the other three poems, however, in being a narrative lyric that relies initially on a combination of affective phrasing and descriptive detail to
carry the reader with the speaker into a realm outside the everyday
world of home and hearth.[41] It is quite possible that Burroughs's selection of 'the booming of the bittern' as an illustration of his argument in
*Birds and Poets, with Other Papers* that, to 'susceptible characters, the
music of nature is not confined to sweet sounds' (6: 4) lies behind the
'bittern's cry' of Scott's second stanza:[42]

By a dim shore where water darkening
  Took the last light of spring,
I went beyond the tumult, hearkening
  For some diviner thing.

Where the bats flew from the black elms like leaves,
  Over the ebon pool
Brooded the bittern's cry, as one that grieves
  Lands ancient, bountiful.

I saw the fireflies shine below the wood,
  Above the shallows dank,
As Uriel from some great altitude,
  The planets rank on rank. (*PDCS* 261)

With the scene of the speaker's quest for aural evidence of 'some
diviner thing' thus established as a natural place where intimations of
'ancient' lands and cosmic patterns are possible, the speaker describes
the effects of the 'cadence' emanating from a reed-player whose identity
remains as mysterious as the meaning of his 'message.' Is he merely a
rustic musician or could he be Pan playing his syrinx? Whoever he is, his
'cadence' has a magical ability akin to that of the poem itself to sur-
round the listener with beauty and to awaken a sense of life's insoluble
mystery:

And now unseen along the shrouded mead
  One went under the hill;
He blew a cadence on his hollow reed,
  That trembled and was still.

It seemed as if a line of amber fire
  Had shot the gathered dusk,
As if had blown a wind from ancient Tyre
  Laden with myrrh and musk

He gave his luring note amid the fern;
  Its enigmatic fall
Haunted the hollow dusk with golden turn
  And argent interval.

I could not know the message that he bore,
  The springs of life from me
Hidden; his incommunicable lore
  As much a mystery.

And as I followed far the magic player
  He passed the maple wood,
And when I passed the stars had risen there,
  And there was solitude. (*PDCS* 261–2)

Unlike the Pied Piper, whose 'luring note' leads the innocent to their destruction, the 'unseen' reed-player and the poet lead the listener to a 'solitude' that sits on the cusp between the Romantic withdrawal into Nature that enables communion with self and cosmos and a Modern sense of human aloneness in a universe whose meaning can never be known. Five years after 'The Reed-Player' catapulted him to fame in the winter of 1890–1, Scott capitalized on key components of its success in the more fully realized and mysterious events of 'The Piper of Arll' (1898), and ten years later, in the midst of the First World War, he set his most extended meditation on the 'hidden' and 'incommunicable' secrets of existence, 'The Height of Land,' on the geographical cusp between Lake Superior and Hudson Bay. It is difficult to doubt that 'The Reed-Player' and its positive reception was a critical stage on Scott's journey towards the masterpieces upon which his reputation still to a considerable extent rests.

Of all the poems that brought the Confederation group to international and national prominence in the early 1890s, 'The Reed-Player' is the most interesting for what it also reveals about the group's dynamics. Dedicated, as remarked earlier, 'To B.C.' in *The Magic House and Other Poems* (56), it was at least partially inspired by Carman's 'The Reed-Player,' a Petrarchan sonnet published in the 1 March 1889 number of the *Week*, where it is described as having been written 'On the Flyleaf of Mr. Lampman's New Book of Poems' (198). Moreover, Carman's sonnet, which figures Lampman himself as a 'brother' to 'the loon and whippoorwill' who has 'notched a river reed from the blue limpid shallow-bars' of a 'Northern lake' and 'blown / The surge and whisper of the heart spring,' may well have drawn inspiration, as Maia Bhojwani has suggested, from Lampman's 'notion of the poet as a child of Pan' ('Northern Pantheism' 34) in 'The Poets' (1888) and 'Favorites of Pan,' poems which in their turn (and as suggested in chapter 1) probably owe debts to Roberts's 'The Pipes of Pan' (1886). Nor was Campbell excluded from this interconnecting chain of influence, for his depiction of Pan in 'Pan the Fallen' (1893) as a 'grotesque shape,' 'Part man, but mostly brute,' whose heart is nevertheless 'god-like' and whose gaze is directed towards 'some far heaven / Whence a soul had fallen down' (*SPE* 41) probably derives at least in part from Lampman's description of the 'Children of Pan' in 'The Poets' as 'Half brutish, half divine, but all of earth, / Half-way 'twixt hell and heaven, [and] near to man' (*P* 114). If it was Frederick George Scott's Christian faith and priestly vocation that prevented him from participating in the conflation of classical myth, Canadian nature, and poetic identity in the figure of Pan that occurs in the work of the other members of the Confederation group, this would once again confirm the supposition that in some respects he was precluded from fully sharing the group's interests and emphases.[43] When Campbell compared Lampman in 'Bereavement of the Fields' (1900) to 'some rare Pan of those old Grecian days, / Here in our hour of deeper stress reborn' and asserts that 'His inward ear heard ever that satyr horn / From Nature's lips reverberate night and morn' (*SPE* 67), he could also have been describing Roberts, Carman, Duncan Campbell Scott, and, of course, himself in the days before the 'War among the Poets' shattered forever the unity that the group had experienced in the late 1880s and early 1890s.

That the Confederation group was recognized outside and within Canada for more than the poems that gave them near-celebrity status scarcely needs to be said. Carman's 'The Yule Guest' (1897) was honoured with a lavishly illustrated six-page spread in the December number of the *Cosmopolitan* and designated as essential reading for 'every Canadian who finds pride in the progress of a son of the soil' in the December 10 issue of *Saturday Night* (15; and see *Saturday Night*, 24 December 1892, 15). Shortly before its publication in the March 1894 number of the prestigious *Atlantic Monthly*, Thomson told Lampman that '"The City of the End of Things" will do you good, I'm sure, and the *Atlantic* too' (*AC* 105), and immediately after its appearance Joseph Edgar Chamberlin wrote in the *Boston Evening Transcript* that 'the poem will not be popular' in Chicago because of its depiction of the grim future of just such a city but 'in Boston it ought to be' because 'we are not so near to dwelling in this City of the End of Things as we might be' (quoted in *AC* 111). 'Assuredly Lampman is conquering another province,' added Thomson a few days later (*AC* 109).[44] No more than 'The City of the End of Things' did Duncan Campbell Scott's 'The Piper of Arll' 'conquer ... another province' of literature, but, as subsequent publishers and introducers of his work frequently reminded readers, it captured the imagination of a future British poet laureate or, in Masefield's own words in a much-quoted letter to Scott of 12 November 1905, 'impressed me deeply, and set me on fire' (*UT*).[45] Apparently, Roberts's 'A Nocturne of Consecration' had a similar effect on the American poet Richard Henry Stoddard (1825–1903), who told the editor of the *Independent* after its publication there on 2 December 1897 that it was 'the greatest love poem in the language since Spenser's "Epithalamium"' (quoted in Pomeroy 152). In 1902, Campbell's 'An Empire's Greeting' was 'sung before Queen Alexandra' (*SPE* 4), and in 1915 Frederick George Scott's 'Requiescant' was published in the London *Times* (*CPFGS* 193). From the mid-1890s to the early 1920s, Carman was a highly influential presence in American literature whose work had a well-documented impact on Pound, Robert Frost, Wallace Stevens, and Edwin Arlington Robinson.[46] '[H]e was widely read on both sides of the Atlantic,' writes David Perkins of Carman in *A History of Modern Poetry: From the 1890s to the High Modernist Mode*, 'his standing was such that he was asked to edit *The Oxford Book of American Verse* (1927)' (114). Changes in literary taste eclipsed the poets of the Confederation group outside as well as inside Canada, but for a time their stars shone more brightly than those of almost any Canadian writers either before or since.

# CHAPTER EIGHT

# Disintegration

A number of literary men, some of whom have no connection with the
Royal Society [of Canada], have asked the Honorary Secretary to direct ...
attention ... to the advisability of having published in the [Society's] 'Transactions' a short critical review of those Canadian books which have appeared in the course of the year and are deserving of encouragement ...
The object would be to stimulate literary taste by that judicious criticism
which is rarely seen in the Canadian press. As things are now, we see either
the indiscriminate eulogy of zealous friends or the wholesale advertising of
publishers who appear to have literary editors in their employ, whose special duty is to insert notices in the press ... Newspaper notices ... consequently ... rank as so many advertisements.

> – Proceedings and Transactions of the Royal
> Society of Canada for the Year 1894 *(1895)*.

In the May 1895 number of *Munsey's Magazine* (New York), an American
journalist named Joseph Dana Miller published 'The Singers of Canada,' an essay combining portrait photographs, biographical information, critical estimates, and copious quotations of poetry into a mosaic
purporting to represent 'the achievements and the prospects of the
northern school to which Carman, Roberts, Lampman, and Campbell
belong' (*War* 10). Superficial though it necessarily is, Miller's survey of
'the northern school' contains explicit and implicit judgments and
rankings of the Confederation group that could scarcely have posed
more of a threat to its already fragile civility if they had been intended to
do so. 'Chief of the group of new Canadian singers ... stands Bliss Carman,' proclaims Miller; 'he is the Canadian Tennyson ... Mr. Howells
ranks Lampman with the strongest of American singers. His knowledge

of nature is something more than intellectual – it is affinitive ... Roberts, the Longfellow of Canada,' is 'not a mere intellect' like Matthew Arnold. Duncan Campbell Scott 'has the magic which fits words and phrases to his subject with a felicity that is not surpassed ... in the work of his associates ... What could be better than the opening stanza of [Frederick George] Scott's "In Via Mortis" ... ?' (*War* 12–13). And what of Campbell? '[H]is fame in Canada is perhaps as wide as that of Lampman or Roberts,' but he 'is a rhetorician rather than a poet,' a writer who has 'caught ... a sympathetic knowledge of a certain aspect of nature, [but] without the joyousness of Lampman, the exhilarant music of Carman, or the subtlety of [Duncan Campbell] Scott ... "The Dread Voyage" is a poem which Poe might have written' (*War* 22–3). The article contains portrait photographs of Carman, Lampman, Roberts, Pauline Johnson, the two Scotts, and the Ottawa poet John Henry Brown (1859–1949) (whose *Poems: Lyrical and Dramatic* was published in 1892), but none of Campbell. Unwittingly, Miller had created the incident that would give rise to the 'War among the Poets.'

A response to 'The Singers of Canada' was not long in coming. On 11 May 1895, *Saturday Night* (Toronto) carried an anonymous article either by someone sympathetic to Campbell or by Campbell himself that decries the absence of a photograph of him in Miller's article, deflates its author's fulsome judgments of other poets by subjecting them to caustic irony, and declares that

> the Canadian poets given the foremost place ... [in the piece] have conspicuously failed to catch the ear of the Canadian people ... Carman writes for poets, critics, and the attachés of magazine offices. Lampman is described as a pastoral poet, yet who, outside the ranks of those ... engaged in the manufacture of magazines, can recognize him as such ... [And] Roberts ... has failed to reach the ears of any but our scholars ... With all our poets ... Canada is left en-hungered for poetry, for they nearly all write in the elephantine language of the encyclopaedia on themes to which our primal population has no access ... Poets are supposed to be the singers of a people. (*War* 28–9)

The battle lines had been drawn: on the one side lay the scholarly practitioners of poetry intended for the producers and readers of magazines and supported by a mutual admiration society of fellow poets and critics; on the other, Campbell, a singer of the people, whose 'great poem, "The Mother,"' is not even mentioned by Miller (*War* 26).

Almost certainly it was Miller's identification of the resemblance between Campbell's work and Poe's that provoked the next salvo in the 'War among the Poets,'[1] 'Poetry and Piracy,' an attack on Carman as 'perhaps the most flagrant imitator on this continent,' which appeared in the Toronto *Sunday World* on 16 June 1895 (*War* 30). Subtitled 'A Canadian Poet's Predatory Instincts' and signed 'By Another Canadian Poet' (a mask that Campbell was quickly forced to cast aside), 'Poetry and Piracy' takes as its point of departure Miller's assertion that the poets of the Confederation group are not 'mere echoes' but original voices, and it proceeds to juxtapose quotations from Carman's poems with quotations from poems by Dante Gabriel Rossetti, Robert Louis Stevenson, Rudyard Kipling, Walt Whitman, and several other British and American poets in order to demonstrate that 'Carman is merely an echo, and a poor one at that':

> Without any dramatic power, any human lyrical quality, or any originality of thought or feeling, he has gone from poet to poet and has stolen, in as far as he is capable, the ground work in style and rhythm of his vague lyrics, which even were they original would be decidedly imperfect, owing to vagueness, constant repetition of phrases, which tire, especially when introduced with a grave lack of taste into poems needing a totally different phraseology. Instead of being the most original of our poets Carman is by all odds the most imitative and the most barren of idea and treatment of what he imitates. (*War* 42)

Almost needless to say, some of the passages that Campbell juxtaposes are indeed indicative of indebtedness on Carman's part; for example, the line 'So all desire and all regret ...' in 'Low Tide on Grand Pré' could well derive from lines in Rossetti's 'Insomnia' ('And with regret ...') and 'The One Hope' ('When vain desire at last and vain regret ...'), and, as observed in chapter 4, the chorus of 'Marjorie Darrow' certainly echoes the rendition of birdsong in Whitman's 'Out of the Cradle Endlessly Rocking' (which, in turn, echoes Burroughs) (*War* 31–2, 41; Rossetti, *Works* 234, 108). Several of the juxtaposed passages resemble one another only very slightly, however, and the overall impression left by 'Poetry and Piracy' is well expressed in an editorial entitled 'The Attack on Bliss Carman' in the June 19 issue of the *Globe*: '... the ... charge against Mr. Carman ... [is] far-fetched and strained. It would be possible on similar lines to carry successfully an indictment of plagiarism against any living writer ... Anyone with leisure could find instances ad infinitum where Arnold has used language identical with other writers of English. Carman cannot be expected to invent a new vocabulary for his work' (*War* 45, 46).

In the ensuing weeks, the fracas quickly spread to the Ottawa *Journal*, the Saint John *Telegraph*, and other Canadian newspapers (see *War* 47–90) and soon elicited letters of defence from three of Carman's friends and admirers, Albert E. Smythe, a writer whom Roberts would later include in the Confederation group (see Introduction), Peter McArthur, the editor of *Truth* (New York), who had already accepted poems by Carman and would accept Duncan Campbell Scott's 'The Piper of Arll' (see chapter 6),[2] and George M. Acklom (1870–19?), a teacher at the Collegiate School in Windsor, Nova Scotia, to whom, as will be seen in a moment, Roberts had entrusted the task of coming to Carman's aid. (All three letters, and most of the other material discussed here, are reprinted in Alexander J. Hurst's very useful *War among the Poets: Issues of Plagiarism and Patronage among the Confederation Poets*; see 58–61, 66–74, 93–9.) Rounding out the chorus were two letters in the *Sunday World* (June 23, July 7) from Miller, the first a defence of both Carman and himself, and the second an assault on Campbell that the newspaper entitled 'A Few Final Words' and expected to bring the controversy to an end (*War* 62–3, 83–6).

It did not, for on July 2 Campbell had availed himself of the pages of the *Globe* to initiate a new phase of the battle with an accusation that, in the words of an editorial in the same newspaper on the following day, 'open[ed] up appalling vistas of acrimonious controversy' (4): Miller's article, he announced, was but one manifestation of a conspiracy among Carman, Roberts, and Lampman to promote themselves at his expense. More specifically, Campbell's letter of July 2 refers darkly to laudatory articles on each other's work by Carman and Roberts in the previous year's *Chap-Book*,[3] to Carman's repeated nomination of Roberts, Lampman, and Duncan Campbell Scott as 'the three men who have lent lustre to Canadian poetry,'[4] and to the 'cooking up of [Miller's] article in the interests of some of the men included – ... that some of these men either altered the final full proof or that it was done for them' (5). 'Fancy writers of any standing cooking up a proof in this way,' concludes Campbell, 'but fancy these men reading all of this balderdash about themselves and even trying to improve upon it at the expense of a fellow-writer ... I must here express my supreme contempt for the men that act in such a manner and the conditions which allow such men to flourish.' 'Mr. Carman and Mr. Campbell belong to a circle of writers of whom Canada has every reason to be proud,' observed the *Globe* in a further attempt to contain the hostilities; 'we take pleasure in drawing attention to the merits of their work: we like to hear the muses sing, but it is a fearsome thing to us to behold Melpomene tearing out handfuls of Euterpe's hair' (4).

Within a week, the bellicose behaviour of the Muse of Tragedy towards the Muse of the Flute had provoked responses that reveal much about the internal dynamics and public presence of the Confederation group. On July 5, the *Globe* published a letter by the Ottawa lawyer and writer Charles Morse (1860–1945)[5] that characterizes Campbell's letter of July 2 as an 'hysterical screed' and 'frenzied onslaught' 'carried ... to the verge of silliness' by 'the colossal egotism' of its author (3), a counter-attack whose effect was registered by Lampman in a letter to Campbell that provides a unique window unto Campbell's state, Morse's motivation, and Lampman's attitude to the events of the previous weeks:

My dear Campbell

Duncan has told me this morning that some person, probably bent on mischief, had informed you that Mr. Morse was preparing a further article against you. I met Mrs. Morse on the street and asked her whether this was the case. She said no, as far as she knew. I told her that if her husband had any such intention it would be a very wise thing to drop it, and the lady promised me on Morse's behalf that if there was any such idea in his mind it would not be carried into effect. So there is no likelihood of your being called upon for battle in that direction.

At the same time I may say that I do not blame Morse in the least for his attack upon you. Mrs. Morse is a cousin of Carman, and blood, you know, is thicker than water. There is never anything to be gained by getting up a row. Let each of us silently possess his own soul, and develop whatever is brightest and best in it, and give the product to the world, when we can, and as we can, after processing it to the fairest shape possible. There is little enough true work being done, and it is a shame that those who have a portion of the gift to do it should waste their time and vitality in confounded foolishness as you have just been doing, if you will pardon my speaking with great plainness.

Yours very sincerely,
A Lampman[6]

The revelation that Morse's wife was Carman's cousin can only have reinforced Campbell's conviction that he was the victim of a conspiracy, but perhaps Lampman's Carlylean advice (and allusion to Luke 21. 19) and his concluding admonition served to dissuade his colleague from further action, at least temporarily, for the next salvo from Campbell's pen did not appear in the *Globe* until over a month later, on August 10.

In the interim, Carman had responded to Campbell's attacks with a letter of his own that appeared in the same newspaper on July 13 under the title 'The War among the Poets.' In a tone that is almost seraphic in its elevation and calmness, Carman's letter confronts and defuses each of Campbell's charges in turn – his 'alleged plagiarism' by 'leav[ing] others to decide as they please,' his supposed collusion in the writing of Miller's article by asserting that 'it was prepared entirely without [his] assistance,' and his manifest preference for the work of Roberts, Lampman, and Duncan Campbell Scott over Campbell's by stating without apology that he 'like[s] their poetry and believe[s] in it' (*War* 91–2).

Of greater import than these aspects of the letter, however, are two components of it that bear on the relationships between and among Carman and the other members of the Confederation group with whom he found himself bracketed by Campbell: his concession that, as Campbell had charged in 'Poetry and Piracy,' a line from Lampman's 'Heat' – 'With small innumerable sound' – had indeed found its way verbatim into his own 'Eavesdropper' (1893);[7] and his admission that, although one of the group, Roberts, was 'his oldest friend,' 'another' (Lampman) he had 'never seen' and 'the third' (Scott) he had 'only met once' (*War* 91, 92). Together the two facts – (1) that, in his own words, Carman 'read and admired' a Lampman poem so much that he assimilated a line of it by 'subconscious appropriation' (*War* 91) and (2) that, in July 1895, over a decade after Roberts began the process of drawing Carman and Lampman together to form the nucleus of the Confederation group, the two men had yet to meet – speak volumes about the roles played by shared interests *and* geographical separation in the group's dynamic. Distance prevented all but the Ottawa members of the group from interacting regularly with one another, but it may also have increased the attentiveness of Carman and Roberts to their colleagues' poems *per se*, and vice versa: absence may have bred contempt in Campbell, but, in Carman, Lampman, and Scott, it seems to have bred admiration and affection. When thanking Carman for a copy of 'Pulvis et Umbra' (1893) on 29 October 1890, Lampman judged it his most fully achieved poem to date, adding that some of its 'lines have been forcing themselves upon my memory for the past day or two so persistently that I have had to postpone work of my own that I had in hand – and it is a strong thing to say of a piece of writing, – that it confronts the reader with another individuality in a manner so forcible and attractive, as for a while to shake him from his own' (quoted in Greig 1: 1). Several times in 1891, Carman had invited Lampman to visit him in New York; on November 14 of that year, he thanked him warmly for a picture of 'you and D.C.S. together'; and a few months later, in accepting 'The Poet's Song' for publication in the 12 April 1892 number of the *Independent*, he remarked that it has 'a lot of very large and fine things in it' and 'as a whole ... gives a fellow a fine start of blood' (SFU). On 5 November 1895, Scott, styling himself 'Your sincere friend,' thanked Carman for a copy of 'At Michaelmas' (1896), a 'beautiful poem [that he has] ... read many times with growing pleasure' (QU). Carman's 'sweet-nature' would become almost legendary (see Colum vi), and there can be little doubt that it was greatly responsible for the camaraderie that existed between him, Scott, and Lampman during and after the glory days of the Confederation group.

Campbell's third and perhaps most devastating salvo in the 'War among the Poets' was aimed not just at Carman and Miller but also at Francis Lillie Pollock (1876–19?),[8] the author of a letter in the July 20 issue of the *Globe* that had attempted to arrive at a balanced assessment of the work of Carman, Roberts, and Campbell but, in doing so, had judged Campbell's recently published *Mordred and Hildebrand: A Book of Tragedies* (1895) 'an unmitigated failure' because of 'an apparently wilful debasement of the material, of the *dramatis personae*, and a slovenly use of language' (10). Under the title 'The Poet Campbell on the War Path,' Campbell's letter in the August 10 issue of the *Globe* quotes personal letters from Carman, Miller, and Pollock to demonstrate the duplicity of all three men: 'each ... publicly condemn[ed] my work in the severest manner; each ... privately apologize[d] to me' (*War* 119). Since none of the three disputed the veracity of the apologies quoted by Campbell, they can be assumed to be accurate, if only as attempts to deflect his anger: '"... as to [the] omission of yourself [in the 1890 article in the *Independent*],[9] what does it matter? You have written your work. It is beautiful. That is enough"' (Carman); '"You are mistaken in supposing that what I might say or what anyone might say ... could really injure you"' (Miller); '"I must ... confess that I haven't read [*Mordred* and *Hildebrand*]. For the basis of my remarks on them, ... I depended partly on the review in the *Globe* and partly on the letter of a "friend" who has, or says he has, seen them ... I now believe that the *Globe* is rather "down" on you in the present troublesome time ... I ... can only ask you to pardon me"' (Pollock) (*War* 117, 118, 119). (The review to which Pollock refers appeared in *the Globe* on July 6. Judging Campbell's poetry lacking in lyricism and increasingly 'repellent' in its sombreness, it is especially harsh in its judgment of *Mordred*: '... its defects are so many that we shrink from naming them. To generalize, it is exceedingly artificial, the plot and development are repulsive, the characters unnatural, the language, to use a mild term, unfitting,' and – this obviously in response to Campbell's charge of plagiarism against Carman – it contains 'some ... lines dangerously reminiscent of Tennyson' [21].)[10] In an editorial in the same issue as Campbell's letter, the *Globe* suggested that 'the "battle of the poets"' had now 'ceased to be either amusing or instructive' and 'ought to come to an end' (9), but again this was not to be because, with his letter of August 10, Campbell unleashed a weapon that had been in his arsenal since before the controversy began – namely, the explosive charge of 'log-rolling' or 'mutual puffing in literary productions' (*OED*).

Imported from Britain and given currency in North American critical discourse by an editorial in the 28 February 1895 number of the *Nation* (New York),[11] 'log-rolling' is the subject of an article entitled 'American Literary Conditions' that Campbell had published in *Saturday Night* on April 20, but not until August 10 did he bring it to bear, not merely on Carman, Miller, and Pollock, but also on Roberts, Lampman, and Duncan Campbell Scott, all of whom, he now averred, 'have been either working in with the log-rollers or accepting as reliable criticism worthy of notice the miserable cooked up self-advertisements which they or some of their friends have foisted on the public' (*War* 120). Given the evidence presented by Campbell, this was a powerful charge, and, not surprisingly, it rekindled the interest of the Toronto *World* in the controversy that it had helped to ignite some two months earlier. Indeed, on August 18 and 19, the *World* threw itself squarely behind Campbell, proclaiming him 'the first of our poets,' printing and reprinting a lengthy article by him under the banner 'Campbell Returns to the Attack. He Discusses Literary Log-Rolling,' and declaring itself long aware of the efforts of a 'coterie of Canadian poets ... to boom themselves and to cry down those of whom they are jealous, or whom they feared' (*War* 133–4). 'Mr. Campbell appears to us to have altogether the best of the argument with his rivals,' opined the *World* on August 19; 'he possesses what is often rare in poets – a large measure of logic – states his case in clear terms, gives his reason, and makes good his conclusions' (*War* 134). On August 18 and 19, the *World* also printed and reprinted Campbell's 'The Log-Rollers; or *Chap-Book* Poets Their Own Reviewers,' one of several satirical poems and squibs that were generated in whole or in part by the 'War among the Poets' (three others being 'A Deserving Canadian Poet,' an attack on Campbell by 'Bavius MacFlecknoe' in the July 20 issue of the *Globe* [10], 'Bards of the Boiler-Plate,' an attack on Carman, Roberts, and their supporters by Charles Gordon Rogers [18?–19?][12] in the July 21 issue of the *Sunday World*, and 'Here lies little Willie deep down in the grumps ...,' another attack on Campbell, this time by Carman in the August 1 number of the *Chap-Book* [225–6]).[13]

Nor was the *World* the only publication to side with Campbell. Remaining true to its assessment of him as 'the greatest Canadian poet' and reminding readers of its own reservations about 'the clique that sets itself up as the Literary Supreme Court of Canada,' *Saturday Night* had cautiously aligned itself with Campbell on 20 April 1895 (1), and on August 17 it named Miller and Pollock 'the first casualties of a campaign that promises many casualties' but might have the salutary effect of 'disclos[ing] the real status of the contestants – showing whether they were really poets or really critics, or were merely made to seem such through a careful system of inter-friendly traffic' (1). 'What evidence is there that we have a real poet in Canada?' asked the magazine:

> So tinged with suspicion is the whole system of poet-manufacture, that before we respect William Dean Howells' verdict in regard to Mr. Lampman we feel called upon to ask if the two gentlemen had met before ... [Howells'] eulogistic remark was made. In regard to the praise which certain English papers have bestowed upon Messrs. Carman and Roberts, we feel like asking how much Mr. Douglas Sladen, who fished with them in New Brunswick, had to do with it. So much influence does personal magnetism exert in criticism that we are disposed to wish that we could trace out the Chicago editor who passed so high a eulogium upon Mr. Campbell's best poem, 'The Mother,' so that we could get at the impulse that moved him to testify ... [T]he whole system whereby raw specimens of humanity are turned into ethereal poets and their twaddle hailed as divine, is so well organized and has so little to do with genius that we are apt to accept nothing in good faith.

'Poetry is no longer the vehicle of the highest expression, for ... the poets are sitting in a row ... admiring each other's proficiency in "weaving nothing into naught,"' the magazine added on September 28 (quoting a satirical squib by Campbell); 'where are we to find in the product of our Canadian poets anything to correspond with Mr. E.W. Thomson's

*Old Man Savarin, and Other Stories* [1895]? Nowhere' (5). Clearly, the 'War among the Poets' was doing the Confederation group no good at all in the competition between poetry and fiction for readers' attention that was becoming as evident in Canada as it was in the United States in the mid-1890s. ('"The taste for poetry is becoming a lost accomplishment,"' one American periodical would observe in 1898, and another: '"the preponderance of fiction ... is the most salient feature in the literary history of our times"' [quoted in Mott 4:120, 111].)

In the months following Campbell's third and final attack on Carman, Roberts, and their supporters there were at least two public attempts to reconcile the warring parties: the reprinting in the August 24 issue of the *Globe* (13) of the positive review of Campbell's *Snowflakes and Sunbeams* that Roberts had published in the Saint John *Progress* in March 1889; and the publication in the October 18 number of the *Week* of an article by William Clark that uses Thomas O'Hagan's essay 'Canadian Poets and Poetry' (1895) as the pretext for emphasizing the achievements of all six members of the Confederation group, especially Campbell (1110).[14] As Christmas approached, even *Saturday Night* experienced a surge of good will: 'whilst I think that some of our poets over-rate themselves,' wrote its 'Books and Authors' columnist on December 21, 'yet at this softening season of the year I am prepared to admit that much good verse has been written by "the Canadian school of poets," and to suggest that the time is appropriate for the purchase of a few volumes of native verse' (14). During the weeks before Christmas, *Saturday Night* and other publications carried an advertisement for 'Holiday Books' by the Toronto publisher William Briggs listing five volumes by 'Canadian Poets,' John Wilson Bengough's *Motley: Verses Grave and Gay* (1895), Frederick George Scott's *My Lattice and Other Poems*, Roberts's *Songs of the Common Day*, Carman's *Behind the Arras*, and Agnes Ethelwyn Wetherald's 'just issued' *The House of Trees and Other Poems* (1895). On 4 January 1896, the writer of the 'Books and Authors' column observed that in the January number of the *Bookman* (New York) 'some of our Canadian singers are again to the front. Portraits are given of Archibald Lampman, Duncan Campbell Scott, E. Pauline Johnson and Ethelwyn Wetherald. A poem, "When the Birds Fly Home" [1923], by William Wilfred Campbell is also given and the "Canadian group" appreciatively spoken of editorially' (5).

Despite the efforts of the peacemakers and rehabilitators, however, the 'War among the Poets' had taken a heavy toll on the public perception as well as on the internal cohesiveness of the Confederation group.

No doubt, it contributed significantly to the decline of interest in poetry in general and the group's work in particular that was already becoming apparent before and became increasingly so in its aftermath. Apart from Campbell's ill-fated *Mordred and Hildebrand,* no volumes of poetry by members of the group were published in 1895, and when they did appear in 1896 there was little of the eager anticipation or enthusiastic response of earlier years. Neither *The Book of the Native* (Roberts) nor *Lyrics of Earth* (Lampman) nor *More Songs from Vagabondia* (Carman and Hovey) was reviewed in the *Week* – a reflection also, perhaps, of the growing preference for fiction over poetry, for in 1896 the same periodical did publish reviews of Duncan Campbell Scott's *In the Village of Viger* and Roberts's *Earth's Enigmas* and *Around the Campfire.* Worse, what attention the Confederation group did attract in Canada in 1896 was often biased towards the negative by memories of the recent controversy. Here, for example, is Gordon Waldron (18?–?) in 'Canadian Poetry: A Criticism,' published in the December 1896 number of the *Canadian Magazine* (Toronto), a periodical that since its inception in 1893 had 'made it a special policy to publish Canadian writers' (Gordon Roper 269):

A ... study of later [that is, recent] publications discloses the fact that poetic inspiration [in Canada] runs fairly in the narrow channels made by a small coterie of writers, the chief among whom are Campbell, Carman, Lampman and Roberts. These poets, having won the ear of a generous and patriotic, though uncritical press, have been raised to an imposing authority, which restrains all originality and all determined devotion to poetry as a fine art. (101)

Judged by its 'appeal to human interest' and its 'effect ... upon readers of refined feeling,' the 'Canadian poetry of the day fails,' asserts Waldron:

Campbell, Carman, Lampman and Roberts can hardly be said by the most generous to have written anything of lasting merit ... They are not without virtues, and it may be fairly said that they are all men of great talent. They have mastered the mechanics of versification. They have music and flowing rhythm. They have great elevation of diction, and their patriotic zeal well befits the honourable enterprise in which they are engaged. Action they scarcely attempt, [however, and] ... their works are singularly barren of ideas of universal human interest ... (102, 103)

After several paragraphs of sharply unsympathetic criticism in which each of the four poets and some of their most celebrated poems, including, 'Ave' and 'The Mother,' are analysed and found wanting, Waldron concludes that 'Canadian poetry is devoid of life and interest,' adding: 'it is not enough that [Canadian poets] find a ready market for their writings to fill up the vacant page-spaces of magazines, or even that their art is the affectation or fad of a literary coterie. If they would succeed they must reach the feelings and imaginations of their readers, as the great writers of the past have done' (107, 108).

More inclusive and flamboyant in its critique of the once 'bright' but now tarnished 'coterie' and their associates is the Popean satire of 'Scribblers in the Service of Folly' that Alexander Charles Stewart had published earlier in 1896 as a pamphlet with the somewhat misleading title *The Poetical Review: A Brief Notice of Canadian Poets and Poetry*.[15] To all intents and purposes a 'memorial' of the 'War among the Poets,' Stewart's poem is prefaced by a statement of its six 'objectives':

> FIRST – To show that the interest in Canadian Poetry is not (as some of our scribblers complain) dead, but on the contrary, very much alive.
>
> SECOND – To prove to the self-elected synod of rhymers that their doctrine is a crude and fallacious superstition believed in by no one save themselves.
>
> THIRD – To inform the said synod that the world fails to weep when its august head, Mr. Roberts, succumbs to poetical hysterics at the sight of a pumpkin, which, if calmly considered, can in nowise be asserted even by a Professor, to 'Rival the Unrisen Sun.'
>
> FOURTH – To notify all and sundry of that honorable body that this country utterly refuses to endorse nonsense, even should the writers thereof carry into effect, the harassing threat, to leave their native land unless the people will read their rubbish.
>
> FIFTH – That no amount of newspaper controversy can make their productions sell.
>
> SIXTH AND LAST – That Poets and Poetry have not sunk as yet to that commercial basis above which rhymers have never risen. (70)

Using the second edition of Lighthall's *Songs of the Great Dominion, Canadian Poems and Songs* (1892),[16] as a pretext, Stewart lambastes each member of the Confederation group in turn – Roberts as the perpetrator of 'tantramarian nonsense,' Carman as a participant in log-rolling, Campbell as a pedlar of 'mimicked Tennysonian rant,' Lampman as a dozy observer of 'midsummer,' Duncan Campbell Scott as a composer of 'specious phrase,' and Frederick George Scott as a vendor of 'mutilated verse' that 'he alone sh[ould] read' (74–83).[17] Stewart has some kind words for Carman ('thy rising strain / Shows power, thy cousin's never shall attain') and Lampman (he 'shall outgrow his present rhyme, / And soar to stellar heights, alone sublime'), but he reserves his bouquets  for Isabella Valancy Crawford, Thomas D'Arcy McGee, Alexander McLachlan, Pauline Johnson, and a few others whose poems satisfy his criteria of 'Simplicity and truth' (76, 83, 88). Characterizing himself as unencumbered by the 'Government salaries' that 'prevent' 'nearly all our bards ... [from] speaking' (he was a 'tunnel and bridge contractor at Fort William, Ontario' [Wallace]), Stewart concludes the *Poetical Review* by enjoining Canadian poets to forsake their 'mists and frogs, / Lakes, loons ... *Injuns* and Acadian bogs,' to 'Leave Southern critics to their native songs,' and to content themselves instead with winning their 'native land's applause' by 'Toil[ing] for her glory and support[ing] her laws' (69, 89). Ironically, it was only those members of the Confederation group who had secure salaries, government or otherwise, who could afford to take Stewart's advice. The resignation from King's College of the poet whom Stewart envisages as the occupant of a 'triumphal car' drawn by 'harnessed bards' had become effective in June 1895, and in February 1897 he moved to New York as an editor of the *Illustrated American* and in hopes of securing a professorship at an American university.

Of all the allies of the Confederation group, none remained more publicly sympathetic to their cause in the aftermath of the 'War among the Poets' than O'Hagan. While increasing attention was being paid by Canadian magazines and newspapers to the fiction of Thomson, Parker, and others and to the poetry of writers outside the group, O'Hagan found an excuse for their fall from favour in their failure to produce fashionable dialect verse. The final stanza of his 'The Plaint of Poets Unemployed (TO BE SUNG BY BLISS CARMAN, CHARLES G.D. ROBERTS, DUNCAN CAMPBELL SCOTT, ARCHIBALD LAMPMAN, WILLIAM W. CAMPBELL AND THE OTHERS)' in the 10 July 1897 issue of *Saturday Night* (7) may err in its identification of the reason for the Confederation group's fall from grace, but it does sound an elegiac note that seems appropriate to its subject:

But O, ye gods and goddesses, that have been well disposed to us,
  (To us poor, proud Parnassians) in the good old days that were,

Behold with ruth and pity, how the public purse is closed to us
Because we write good English verse, with neither brogue nor burr.

In *Wilfred Campbell*, Carl F. Klinck dismisses the 'War among the Poets' as a 'tempest in ... [a] teapot' (97), but in *The War among the Poets*, Alexandra J. Hurst describes it as 'a significant episode in Canadian literary history' that is 'curiously revelatory of the social, cultural, and political milieu of late-Victorian Canada' (xi). Arguably, it was and is both of these things and also something more and less significant – namely, the most visible sign of the disintegration of the Confederation group by internal fissures that for more than a decade had all but disappeared from sight owing, in no small measure, to Roberts's remarkable success (1) in unifying its six members under the banner of workmanship and cosmopolitanism and (2) in using influential periodicals, newspapers, and writers on both sides of the border and the Atlantic to promote them as icons of the distinctive literature that the new Dominion of Canada was expected to produce. Not surprisingly, two letters that Roberts wrote to Carman during the initial stages of the 'War' confirm that even as he was making plans to leave Canada he was at work polishing the image of the Confederation group and mitigating the effect of Campbell's dissension. 'I *revised* that *Munsey* article a lot! When they sent it to me it was an awful mess of mistakes,' he told Carman on 9 May 1895, and on July 11: 'what a screeching jackass W.W.C. has made of himself, – and how nicely McArthur settles him! I'd have done it but only knew of it all the other day. However, I set *Acklom*, who has leisure and a most eviscerating pen, upon the idiot; and we have got off a neat letter to the Toronto *Globe*! No one is hurt but Campbell by all this thing! What a pewking ass he is!' (*CL* 202, 205). Within weeks, the manipulation of the press and the critics that had helped to bring the Confederation group to international prominence would be laid bare with a vengeance that had been smouldering almost undetected for years, and, contrary to Roberts's assertion, every member of the group would be hurt by the revelation.

Like many actual wars, the 'War among the Poets' was preceded by skirmishes that revealed the polarization of its contending 'thought styles' (Douglas xii) and 'political cultures' (Schwarz and Thompson 61). On 4 February 1893, in what may be taken as the first clear indication of his emerging hostility, Campbell drew upon the article 'About Critics and Criticism' by Walter Blackburn Harte, in that month's number of the *New England Magazine* to characterize himself as someone who had 'persistently refuse[d] to enter into [the] fraternal system of back-scratching ... and back-biting' that 'runs like a dry rot all through [the North American] system of literary toil and ambition' and 'lurks in [the] corners of some of our best critical journals, ... haunts the doors of great city editors, [and] worms its way into great publishing houses' (*MI* 251).[18] In May and June of the same year he again made American literary culture the subject of 'At the Mermaid Inn' columns, now to fault contemporary poetry for an absence of 'great subject matter' and 'true literary genius' and for an 'overplus' of 'dainty conceits ... delicately spun lyrics, and ... purely descriptive' verse (*MI* 314–16, 331–4). And, of course, on July 1, he commandeered the column for the satirical attack on the 'Millet-like ... realism' of 'John Pensive Bangs' and the scornful dismissal of artistic '"correctness"' and '"finish"' that helped to draw the collaborative effort to a close. Eight months later, in the 16 March 1894 issue of the *Week*, he returned to the offensive in a letter solicited by Lewis Emerson Horning 'on the present state and outlook for the future of [Canadian] literature' (*Week*, 9 March 1894, 344), this time using terms that loudly anticipate his articles and letters of the following year:

> We have several clever men who have made their names as magazine writ-ers, but just what impression their work is having on the national life is hard to discover ... In fact, it has become quite fashionable among certain literary cliques to rather scorn the work of a man who has the power of im-pressing the public ... But this power ... is to my mind the true test that marks out the real poet from the mere clever versifier ... [the] word artist ... the carv[er] of magazine cameos ... polished sonnets and delicate lyrics ... True genius ... is shamed out of the public notice by the glittering finish and the clever sneer of the magazine verse-maker ... and his friend, the newspaper critic, who worships the little tin-art god ... My ideal of the great poet is he of the great heart, strong intellect, and wide and deep knowl-edge, who with an exquisite sympathy towards all the tragedy and beauty of existence, reaches out and down into all the recesses of the human heart with a natural instinct that knows and feels what other men often take a lifetime to learn. (*Week*, 16 March 1894, 368–9)

In this letter, the battle-lines are drawn in a way that any student of eigh-teenth- and nineteenth-century aesthetics will immediately recognize as an iteration of the opposition between the idea of the poet as maker (*poiein*) and the poet as sage (*vates*). To the extent that Roberts's insistence on *both* poetic workmanship *and* universal themes had helped to define the Confederation group during the previous decade, the opposition between technique and genuineness that Campbell and, to a lesser extent, Lampman (see chapter 3) began to articulate in the early 1890s heralded the group's disintegration, not just by indicating the existence of personal animosity within it, but also by undermining its foundational aesthetic principles.

Almost inevitably, any examination of the aetiology of the 'War among the Poets' must sooner or later confront the question of what motivated Campbell to embark on the course of action that led to the escalating conflicts of 1893–5. Was he driven by 'jealousy,' as Roberts and Archibald MacMechan seem to have suspected as early as May 1893 (see *CL* 173)? If so, was his jealousy caused, as Acklom (and Roberts) suggested in May 1895, by 'the wounding of an inordinate self-esteem' or, worse, by a 'hypochondriacal mania, which ... sometimes leads its victim to imagine that he is being unjustly persecuted by his friends' (*War* 98)? None of these possibilities is discounted by the description of Campbell's behaviour and condition in a letter of 6 May 1895 by Lampman to Thomson:

> Campbell has actually got it into his head (and firmly rooted there) that I – I mind you – am engaged with Roberts and Carman in an underhand intrigue to destroy his reputation. On two occasions he has even accused me of this by broad hints to my face, and both times I lost my temper and flared up – a thing very rare in me – and talked to him pretty roughly. He harbours infinite wrath and bitterness against me. Campbell is a monomaniac on the subject of his reputation. His state of mind in regard to such matters amounts absolutely to madness. (AC 139)

The knowledge that Campbell was obsessively and perhaps paranoically protective of his reputation does more than explain his reaction to Miller's article: it points to a possible starting point for his 'monomania' in events that occurred early in 1892 and, in one way, brings the present study full circle.

In January of that year, the same 'Editor's Study' column in *Harper's Monthly Magazine* that in April 1889 and March 1890 had done so much to boost Lampman's international and national reputation contained a short review of *Lake Lyrics and Other Poems* in which Howells, while discerning 'traits of imaginative thoughtfulness and ... a freshness of fancy' in Campbell's work, faulted him for 'a want of carefulness of technique' and 'blemishes ... in his workmanship' (316). Even in passages of his best poem, 'Lazarus,' that 'stir and kindle the mind and move the heart,' says Howells, 'the teeth are set on edge by the elision of the definite article.' Less than a month after the appearance of Howells's review, the Saint John *Progress* published an anonymous letter that used the newspaper's comments on Walter Blackburn Harte's 'Canadian Journalists and Journalism' (December 1891) as the pretext for a diatribe that reads like a rehearsal for Campbell's interventions in the latter stages of the 'War among the Poets.' Claiming for its author the authority of someone who has 'been in a position to know and hear a good deal of the methods and doings of a certain class of small literary folk who, by means of such mouthpieces as Mr. Harte, are constantly proclaiming themselves – to each other mostly – in American and English literary periodicals,' the letter proceeds to describe the offenders and their activities in terms that could easily apply to Carman and Roberts, the former in his capacity as assistant literary editor of the *Independent* from 1890 to 1892 and the latter as a crony of Richard Watson Gilder, the editor of the *Century* from 1881 to 1909:

> They travel mainly on the friendly criticism of each other in periodicals to which they may have access, either as contributors or as 'associate' editors. For the most part their work, especially their verse, has no market value and has generally been published in high quarters like Century and Harper's only through a personal 'pull'... These are the men that received the greatest share of attention from Mr. Harte [in 'Some Canadian Writers of To-day']. Mr. Harte ... wrote a request to every Canadian poet or writer he knew, and requested each one to write out a short account of his life and work ... Such articles as [his] are disgraceful and probably you are aware even more than I of the extent to which fictitious reputations are being built up out of nothing. (*Progress*, 20 February 1892, 4)

To substantiate these allegations, the author of the letter gives three examples drawn from first-hand experience: 'a representative Canadian literary man' who, despite being 'loudly proclaimed as such' and 'occasionally publishing [poems] ... in high quarters,' had his 'new volume of poems' rejected by Harper Brothers of New York because, 'they stated, [it] was not up to standard' (perhaps Campbell); 'well-known Canadian poet ... with whom everyone is acquainted, who has never (until recently) published except "for private circulation only" at his own expense, and circulated among his friends and acquaintances' (probably Carman); and 'a Canadian who was ... editor of the *Epoch*' at the time of Harte's request and whose 'well-known' 'work on Canadian literature and history' is not mentioned in 'Some Canadian Writers of To-day' because he declined to supply 'a short account of his life and work' (almost certainly Joseph Edmund Collins). The letter concludes by casting aspersions on 'a certain "Dr"' who may have got his 'LL.D. in exchange for an F.R.S.C.'[19] and by affirming its author's privileged position and moral intent: 'I have seen the inside workings of the clique and I am personally acquainted with a number whom I am sorry to say belong to it, and I could tell you much more. I have long been wishing that some one would undertake a crusade for the sake of simple justice to men who really have earned reputations but who scratch the back of no one.'

So strongly does this letter anticipate Campbell's charges of log-rolling and, indeed, his preliminary foray against 'back-scratching ... and back-biting' in the 4 February 1893 instalment of 'At the Mermaid Inn' that his authorship of it seems beyond doubt. But, as a letter of 27 February 1892 from Roberts to Carman reveals, two members of the 'clique' at which it was aimed knew better:

> I was profoundly surprised, and to a certain extent grieved, by the news of poor Collins' death. I remembered the old regard, – which had not, however, been really the same for years, though up to a year and a half ago I had not acknowledged the fact to myself. My profound distrust of him had absolutely killed my affection for him. It is the Collins of years ago that I shall try to remember. Yes, I saw that unhappy letter in Progress, and instantly detected C's hand in it. Whom was he hitting at? (*CL* 142)

If the disintegration of the Confederation group is to be assigned a starting point, none could be either more plausible or more appropriate than 'that unhappy letter in *Progress*' by the man who had done so much to bring the group into existence and to raise it to prominence. Thanks in no small measure to Joseph Edmund Collins, the end of the Confederation group was nascent in its beginning.

# Aftermath

Although the poets of the Confederation group continued to interact with one another after the 'War among the Poets' and after Roberts's removal to New York, they did so more and more as subgroups and then as dispersed individuals than as a 'set of men'[1] whose work displayed similar characteristics and goals. For almost a decade in the 1880s and 1890s, six poets of 'the same generation' – 'four friends,' a 'close ... associate,' and one who 'st[ood] somewhat apart' – (Smith, 'Introduction' 21) – had together provided proof that a body of poetry written by Canadians could be distinctive and accomplished enough to be a worthy expression of national identity. This was no mean feat, and credit for achieving it must go principally to Roberts, who not only published the volume of poetry that prepared the ground for the group, but also, with Collins's help, assembled its members, beginning with Lampman and Carman, and proceeding to Campbell and the two Scotts. Such sobriquets as 'the father of Canadian poetry' have long been out of fashion, but if anyone is deserving of that title surely it is Charles G.D. Roberts.

After the death of Lampman in 1899 and the departure of Roberts from New York to Europe in 1907, the Confederation group very obviously became what it had been in the process of becoming since the 'War among the Poets': several increasingly individualistic writers whose philosophical orientations and professional activities were taking their work in very different directions. Between 1897 and 1914, Roberts's principal foci were syncretic love poetry and the realistic-symbolic animal story;[2] Carman's, the expression in poetry and non-fictional prose of unitrinian therapeutics and esoteric philosophies;[3] Campbell's, the glorification in prose and verse of Canada as a component of 'Vaster Britain;'[4] Duncan Campbell Scott's the preservation of Lampman's poetic legacy and the articulation of spirituality through 'Indian' subjects and northern landscapes;[5] and Frederick George Scott's, the writing of meditative, admonitory, and inspirational poems and sermons in the orthodox Anglican tradition. When the First World War once again provided the members of the erstwhile group with a common cause, each responded in a characteristic and different way: Roberts, by enlisting in the British Army; Carman, by working with the Vigilantes to bring the United States into the conflict,[6] Campbell, by helping to recruit and train soldiers to serve the Imperial cause; Duncan Campbell Scott, by ensuring the smooth running of the Department of Indian Affairs and the Royal Society of Canada; and Frederick George Scott, by enlisting in the Canadian army and serving as senior chaplain to the First Canadian Division. All five poets also put their pens at the service of the war effort, but only a couple of the results – Duncan Campbell Scott's 'To a Canadian Aviator Who Died for His Country in France' (1916) and Frederick George Scott's 'Requiescant' (1915) – rise to their difficult task with any more than a modicum of distinctiveness or distinction.

There is a curious and even uncanny appropriateness to the fact that Campbell died of pneumonia brought on by exhaustion on New Year's Day, 1918, for the war was both the end of one era and the beginning of another. 'How strange the stars have grown; / The presage of extinction glows on their crests / And they are beautied with impermanence,' Duncan Campbell Scott had written in November 1915 in 'The Height of Land' (1916);[7] 'A lemming stirs the fern and in the mosses / Eft-minded things feel the air change, and dawn, / Tolls out from the dark belfries of the spruces' (*PDCS* 50). In a letter of 5 April 1917, Carman had articulated his sense of an ending and a beginning more directly and with great prescience:

> Perhaps when the war is over, and we begin to arrange our ideals of life on a new basis, we shall have some fine poetry again. But I feel that when that time arrives, only new men, young men, or those who have taken part in the struggle will be entitled to take part in the new parliament of art. The Victorian days belong to history. I believe the new days will be better, but I doubt if any of the men who came to maturity before the great war will be able to find the new key, the new mode, the new tune. (*L* 244)

More than either Carman or Frederick George Scott, Roberts and Duncan Campbell Scott would attempt to find 'the new key, the new mode, the new tune,' but only in the broadest sense of the term can even the experimental pieces in Roberts's *The Iceberg and Other Poems* (1934) or Scott's *The Green Cloister: Later Poems* (1935) be described as Modern.[8] On the eve of the Second World War, Frederick George Scott's son F.R. Scott spoke for much of the generation that had been born around and after the turn of the century when he asked 'how shall I hear old music' in 'an hour / Of new beginnings, concepts warring for power, / Decay of systems' when 'the tissue of art is torn / With overtures of an era being born'? (87).

Of course, there were many people in the decades following the First World War who preferred 'old music' to 'the new tune,' 'Low Tide on Grand Pré' to *The Waste Land,* 'The Group of the 'Sixties' to '"The Men of 1914"' (Lewis 9). The war had greatly increased Canada's stature as a nation, winning it a seat at the Versailles treaty negotiations and on the League of Nations and creating a wave of Canadian nationalism reminiscent of the post-Confederation period. In the ensuing decade, the combination of nationalism and anti-modernity[9] that F.R. Scott would satirize in 'The Canadian Authors Meet' led to the lionization first of Carman and then of Roberts: between 1921 and his death in 1929, Carman undertook several reading and lecture tours in central, western, and eastern Canada, and in 1925 Roberts returned from Europe to undertake a similar tour of Ontario and the West, the success of which persuaded him to embark on a further tour of the Maritimes and to settle permanently in Toronto, where he died in 1943.[10] Such honours as the Royal Society of Canada's Lorne Pierce Medal were showered on both poets (Roberts in 1926, Carman in 1928), as well as on Duncan Campbell Scott (1927), who had been elected president of the Society in 1922. (To F.R. Scott's mirth and his own embarrassment there was even an attempt to dub Carman the unofficial poet laureate of Canada.) In addition, both Roberts and Carman were the subjects of substantial critical monographs in the 1920s and early 1930s, most notably Odell Shepard's *Bliss Carman* (1923), James Cappon's *Charles G.D. Roberts and the Influence of His Time* (1925), Rufus H. Hathaway's 'The Poetry of Bliss Carman' (1925), A.M. Stephen's 'The Poetry of Charles G.D. Roberts' (1929), and Cappon's *Bliss Carman and the Literary Currents and Influences of His Time* (1930).[11] In short, both popular and critical acclaim came to Roberts and Carman on a scale for which their reception some thirty years earlier provides the only antecedent in Canadian literary history.

As this second wave of adulation buoyed the two poets to new heights at least in Canada, there was also a brief renewal of the close personal and creative relationship that they had enjoyed during and for sometime after the days of the Confederation group. In 1920, Carman had visited Roberts in England, and in 1925 the cousins were again reunited at the Canadian Chautauqua on Lake Muskoka (Pomeroy 255, 282–3). The title poem of Roberts's first substantial collection of poetry since 1919,[12] *The Vagrant of Time* (1927), harks back to earlier attitudes and collaborations in its vagabondish themes and figures (indeed, its opening stanza dates from 1908), as in very different ways do 'Spring Breaks in Foam,' 'In the Night Watches,' and most of the other poems in the volume. Two of Carman's finest late poems – the scantily rhymed sonnet 'Wild Geese' (1929) and the heavily rhymed ballad 'Sweetheart of the Sea' (1929) – hark even further back, the former to Roberts's 'The Flight of the Geese' (1893) and Campbell's 'Indian Summer' (1881), and the latter, as John Robert Sorfleet observes in his 1976 selection of Carman's *Poems*, 'to the moment of mystical insight commemorated in '"Low Tide on Grand Pré"' (169). Elsie Pomeroy's comment that on Lake Muskoka the two poets 'were able to indulge freely in their old pastime of canoeing which, almost fifty years before, had inspired Roberts to write to his cousin the poem "Birch and Paddle" [1886]' (282–3) nicely captures the cultural and personal mood of their renewed relationship: creative collaboration had once been an exhilarating, even vertiginous, adventure; now it was rooted in rheumy nostalgia.

Although not as spectacularly as Roberts and Carman, the other members of the Confederation group, both living and dead, were also raised to prominence by the nationalistic anti-modernity of the interwar years. Campbell's *Poetical Works* was published in 1923, Duncan Campbell Scott's compendious *Poems* in 1926, and Frederick George Scott's *Collected Poems* in 1934. (Roberts's *Poems* had appeared in 1907 and a *Selected Poems* would appear in 1936. Carman's *Ballads and Lyrics* appeared in 1923 and his *Poems* in 1931.) Lampman's *Poems* (1900) were reprinted several times between the wars; Norman Guthrie's *The Poetry of Archibald Lampman* (1927) and Carl Y. Connor's *Archibald Lampman: Canadian Poet of Nature* (1929) were published in and shortly after the Diamond Jubilee of Confederation; and in 1931 the Canadian Authors' Association unveiled a memorial cairn near Lampman's birthplace in Morpeth, Ontario. 'Because of him,' said Arthur Stringer (1874–1950) to the large crowd that attended the unveiling of the cairn, 'every bloodroot that blooms in early spring, every maple that reddens with autumn, every sheaf of grain that stands golden amid its stubble, every orchard and millet-field, every stream and valley and woodland has more beauty and meaning for us. Because of what he has given us, every sunrise and sunset is brought closer and made more poignant and memorable to us' (8). No doubt there were many who would have made similar comments about the other five poets of the Confederation group. Certainly, Carman's death on 8 June 1929 was followed by an outpouring of grief that included a national memorial service in Fredericton Cathedral and the erection in the same city of a granite memorial that was unveiled on 18 October 1930 by the premier of New Brunswick, J.B.M. Baxter.[13] Almost needless to say, the names of all the members of the Confederation group figure prominently in *The Literary Map of Canada*, which William Arthur Deacon (1890–1977) produced in 1936 – the same year as the Modernist anthology *New Provinces* – to assist in the task of educating Canadians about their national literature (see Deacon 178–9).

Soon after he returned to Canada in 1925, Roberts had 'renewed his friendship' with the two Scotts (Pomeroy 277), and he and Duncan Campbell Scott were honoured guests at the unveiling of the Lampman Memorial Cairn, but otherwise there appears to have been little contact between or among the three members of the Confederation group who survived into the 1930s and 1940s. Very likely, the 'howling success' (*CL* 328) of Roberts and Carman as reciters and speakers, together with their reputations as womanizers, caused both Scotts to distance themselves from their former confrères and, moreover, contributed to the antipathy towards the two cousins and their work that began to pervade academic circles before the Second World War. 'Our literary history must be rewritten, and some of the landmarks removed,' E.K. Brown (1905–51) told Duncan Campbell Scott in 1943: 'Carman and Roberts will no longer do as landmarks. I think that A.L., and you and Ned Pratt *will* do, and that you three must be the main landmarks' (McDougall, ed., *The Poet and Critic* 70). A few months later, these remarks would receive influential expression in Brown's *On Canadian Poetry* (1943), which contains separate chapters on each of Lampman, Duncan Campbell Scott, and E.J. Pratt (1883–1964) but only slight and frequently slighting commentaries on the work of Roberts and Carman. A few months later still, Duncan Campbell Scott would respond to the linking of Carman and himself in a letter from John Masefield by commenting dryly to Brown that he was 'not overcome by the association ... As you know, Bliss and I were not ploughing and sowing together' (111). As for Campbell and Frederick George Scott, the former is mentioned only in passing and the latter not at all in *On Canadian Poetry,* and both receive short shrift in the Scott-Brown correspondence: in discussing Carl F.

Klinck's *Wilfred Campbell* (1943), Scott characterizes Campbell as a man who had 'much good in hi[m]' but 'develope[d] into a Snob,' and in surveying the reviews of *On Canadian Poetry,* Brown responded to a comment that Duncan Campbell Scott's 'verse is often sentimental' by wondering whether he had been confused with 'the Archdeacon????' (56, 98).

As the Modernist and New Critical sensibility reflected in Brown's horror of sentimentality came increasingly to dominate Canadian literary studies after the Second World War, the stock of Lampman and Duncan Campbell Scott continued to rise and that of Roberts, Carman, Campbell, and Frederick George Scott to fall. In Desmond Pacey's *Creative Writing in Canada* (1952, 1961), for example, Lampman and Duncan Campbell Scott receive the lion's share of sympathetic critical attention, as they do also in Roy Daniells's chapters on post-Confederation poetry in the *Literary History of Canada* (1965, 1973).[14] In the University of Ottawa's annual symposium series on Canadian writers, reassessments of Frederick Philip Grove (1973) and A.M. Klein (1974) were followed by reassessments of Lampman (1975) and, after E.J. Pratt (1976) and Isabella Valancy Crawford (1977), Duncan Campbell Scott (1979). Roberts was not considered until 1983 and Carman until 1989. Of the six members of the Confederation group, only Lampman so far has been accorded the honour of a commemorative postage stamp (in 1989).[15] Of course, these and the subsequent critical fortunes of the poets of the Confederation group and of the group as a whole are the result, not just of Modernism and New Criticism, but of changes in the preferences of both academic readers and the general public that have resulted from a variety of factors, not least the success of feminism, the decline in the teaching of Canadian poetry and history in schools, and the emergence of such ideological methodologies as poststructuralism and postcolonialism that Stan Dragland, for example, has brought to bear so fruitfully in *Floating Voice: Duncan Campbell Scott and the Literature of Treaty 9* (1994). Assuming that interest in Canadian poetry continues, it appears likely that both individually and collectively the poets of the Confederation group will continue to move in and out of relative favour in response to shifting social and critical patterns and needs.

It seems appropriate that this study should end on a personal note with a brief statement of the reasons for my own long, continuing, and by no means dispassionate interest in the poets and poetry of the Confederation group. The first of these, as I wrote in the Introduction, is indebtedness to two of the poets for helping me to feel at home in Canada. The second is an extension of the first into the realm of belief: the conviction that poems are an essential part of the soil from which our roots are formed, that in them are nourished the fine filaments that bind us in love to our portion of the earth. The third is more banal and may even seem bathetic, but it lies just as close to the heart of this study. It is the belief that beautiful, moving, and intelligent things are worth preserving and cherishing.

# Notes

## Introduction

1 Laurel Boone has established that Campbell was born in 1860, 'probably in Farmsville, Canada West (now Athens, Ontario),' rather than 1858, in Berlin (now Kitchener), as previously believed by scholars, or 1861, as indicated by his tombstone and stated by his daughter, Faith L. Malloch (see *SPE* xi, 2, 11n4 and Malloch 1). Boone's analysis is supported by statements made about Campbell during his lifetime (see chapter 2 of the present study).

2 For a discussion of the characteristics of the Canadian manifestations of Anglo-American Modernism and their impact on Canadian poetry and Canadian literary studies, see Bentley, *The Gay]Grey Moose*, 251–72.

3 In J.D. Logan and Donald G. French's *Highways of Canadian Literature: A Synoptic Introduction to the Literary History of Canada (English) from 1760 to 1924* (1924; 1928), the group is described as 'The Systematic School' on account of its 'conscious' adoption of a 'throroughly Canadian' 'literary career' (106) and deemed to include, in addition to Roberts, Carman, Lampman, Campbell, Johnson, Parker, and the two Scotts, Charles William Gordon (Ralph Connor) (1860–1937) and Margaret Marshall Saunders (1861–1947). In a subsequent chapter, Logan and French discuss Agnes Ethelwyn Wetherald (1857–1940), Jean Blewett (1862–1934), Francis Sherman (1871–1926), Albert E.S. Smythe (1861–1947), Susan Frances Harrison ('Seranus') (1859–1935), Arthur Stringer (1874–1950), Peter McArthur (1866–1924), and Isabel Ecclestone Mackay (1875–1928) as the 'minor' poets of the 'Systematic Period' (219).

4 The approach of the present study thus contradicts W.H. New's view in his necessarily brief account of the Confederation poets in *A History of Canadian Literature* (1989) that 'they constitute a "group" more for the purposes of lit-

erary classification than for any shared cause, though they were all shaded by the late-Victorian Romanticism of Tennyson and the American transcendentalists' (118).

5 '[T]ho' he was born in 1857,' 'Lighthall *belongs* in th[e] [1860 group],' Roberts told Howard Angus Kennedy on 27 May 1933, adding that he was not sure about 'the French *members*, if any ... They were, I think, much older or else much younger. [William Henry] Drummond was born in 1854' (*CL* 449). As also revealed by the next note, by the 1930s, perhaps partly as a result of the currency of the term 'Group of the 'Sixties,' date of birth had for Roberts eclipsed common characteristics and personal interaction as definitive of the 'group' of which he had long been the acknowledged leader.

6 After listing Carman, Lampman, Campbell, Parker, Johnson, and the two Scotts as 'the men and women of the 1860 group (1860–61–and 62)' in his letter to Kennedy, Roberts adds 'also Helena Coleman and Albert E. Smythe' (*CL* 449). By date and place of birth (1860, Newcastle, Ontario), Coleman could be said to belong to 'the 1860' group, but as a female who did not publish a volume of poems, *Songs and Sonnets*, until 1906, she could not be and was not a member of the Confederation group as it is being defined here. Smythe, too, was born in the right time-frame, but in Ireland, and he did not settle in Toronto until 1889; however, he was male, and his first collection, *Poems Grave and Gay*, was published in 1891. Although he wrote an article in support of Carman during the 'War among the Poets' of 1895 (see *War* 58–61 and chapter 8), he does not appear to have been a close friend of any member of the Confederation group until after the publication of his second collection, *The Garden of the Sun* (1923), which has an Introduction by George Russell ('A.E.').

7 Both MacMechan and Frederick George Scott are addressed by Roberts as 'confrère' (see *CL* 162, 169), a term also used by Logan and French in relation to the 'Systematic School' of 'Roberts and his *confrères*' (219).

8 This is the implication of the letter of 1 April 1893, in which Roberts tells Scott the pros and cons of publishing in Canada and the United States (see *CL* 170). By 1893, Roberts and Carman had also published various privately printed broadsheets, and Campbell and Frederick George Scott had issued privately printed booklets, most notably Campbell's *Poems!* (circa 1880) and Scott's *Justin and Other Poems* (1885).

9 In a letter of 18 March 1930, Roberts writes that 'of all our many Canadian Anthologies I feel that [Mr Wetherell's] is the choicest, the most unerring in its perception of essential poetry' (*CL* 392) but, unfortunately, does not give the name of the particular anthology to which he is referring.

10 It is possible that the inclusion of these women poets in *Later Canadian Poems* was suggested to Wetherell by Campbell, who uses an article by Duncan as the pretext for a column in 'At the Mermaid Inn' on 22 October 1892, in which he observes that 'Canada has many very able writers among her women' and mentions 'the well-known names' of Machar, Harrison, Wetherald, and Johnson (*MI* 177).

11 The article is reprinted as 'About Critics and Criticism: With Other Matters Incidental and Irrelevant' in Harte's *Meditations in Motley* (1894), 105–52.

12 On 8 August 1891, for example, Roberts told a correspondent that he had been 'dull and oppressed (with a sort of nervous prostration ...)' for 'the last twelve months,' and on 19 March and 6 April 1892 he confirmed to Carman that he was 'not overwell yet bodily and mentally' (*CL* 134, 144–5; and see 153, 173, and 183).

13 The article's objection (see *War* 26) to the absence of a portrait photograph of Campbell in Joseph Dana Miller's 'The Singers of Canada' (1895), the piece that prompted the 'War among the Poets,' leaves no doubt of the significance attached to the presence or absence of portraits in publications by or about the Confederation group and their associates (see *War* 26).

14 Scott's letter to Roberts, to which Roberts responded on 15 June 1893 (see *CL* 174), does not appear to have survived, but his copy of it to Lampman is among the Lampman Papers at Simon Fraser University, where it is accompanied by a covering letter in which Scott expresses a desire to meet his fellow poet and extends a warm invitation to him 'to come and spend a few days' in Drummondville: 'I could take you for some pretty drives up the St. Francis [River] ... We are only 60 miles away from Montreal and have a tolerable train service. Can you come next month or the month after? Dominion day-tide?' (SFU).

15 Edward Gibbon Wakefield and his ideas lie centrally in the background of Lord Durham's *Report on the Affairs of British North America* (1839), which, of course, provided early impetus for Confederation.

16 As Frank Birbalsingh observes, Canada was in many respects a 'colonial nation' until well into the twentieth century (3) (and, arguably, beyond) and, as Sarah M. Corse observes, the burgeoning nationalism of the post-Confederation period was 'defined as much by [Canada's] imperial context and connections as by its Canadianness' (50). Carl Berger's *The Sense of Power: Studies in the Ideas of Canadian Imperialism, 1867–1914* (1970) remains essential reading on the relationship between nationalism and imperialism in Canada.

17 For the origins and some of the reach of this metaphor, see Bentley, *Mnemographia Canadensis,* 1: 291.

18 In a letter of 16 June 1885, Roberts claims Wilde as a 'good friend' and asserts that 'when he was in Canada we spent several evenings, or more properly, nights together,' a claim that Laurel Boone wisely disputes in her notes to the letter: 'Roberts's one visit with ... Wilde in October 1882, and the one letter that he may have received from Wilde seem to be the extent of their acquaintance' (*CL* 49, 50). The Canadian leg of Wilde's North American tour is discussed with appropriate wit by Kevin O'Brien in *Oscar Wilde in Canada: An Apostle for the Arts*.

19 See especially Early's 'Lampman and Romantic Poetry,' *Archibald Lampman*, and 'Roberts As Critic,' McLeod's 'Canadian Post-Romanticism: The Context of Late Nineteenth-Century Canadian Poetry,' and Ware's 'A Generic Approach to Confederation Romanticism' and numerous articles on individual poets and poems.

20 For evidence of Carlyle's presence in Lampman's early work, see the Editorial Notes in his *Essays and Reviews* 205–7, 220–1, and especially 232–44 (the notes to his essay on the French politician Léon Gambetta) and the Introduction to his *Fairy Tales*, especially xii–xiii and xvi–xxi. For the impact of the studies of Symonds, Noel, and other Victorian critics and scholars on Lampman's essays on Shelley and Byron, see *Essays and Reviews*, 200–5 and 291–301.

21 The dismaying indebtedness of Lampman's monograph to Richard Monckton Milnes's *Life, Letters, and Literary Remains of John Keats* (1848, rev. ed. 1867), Sidney Colvin's *Keats* (1887, 1889), and other works is chronicled in the Explanatory Notes in *Essays and Reviews*, 318–49.

22 This term and its cognates are frequently used by Arnold in his discussion of poets and poetry and are usually subdivided along the lines of the following explanation of the 'interpretative power' in 'Maurice de Guérin': 'poetry interprets in two ways; it interprets by expressing with magical felicity the physiognomy and movement of the outward world, and it interprets by expressing, with inspired conviction, the ideas and laws of the inward world of man's moral and spiritual nature. In other words, poetry is interpretative by having *natural magic* in it, and by having *moral profundity*' (*Complete Prose* 3: 33). In 'Roberts As Critic,' L.R. Early observes that Roberts often 'invokes ... the presence or absence of "interpretative power"' in his reviews, and notes that Carman quotes Arnold's explanation of the term in 'Maurice de Guérin' in 'Mr. Charles G.D. Roberts,' an essay published in the 15 January 1895 number of the *Chap-Book* (see Early 177–8). Lampman's debts to Shairp's *On Poetic Interpretation of Nature* (1877) and *Aspects of Poetry, Being Lectures Delivered at Oxford* (1881) are demonstrated and discussed in the Editorial Notes in his *Essays and Reviews*, 244–73 and 302–15 (see also chapter 6).

23 In the Editorial Notes in her fine edition of Duncan Campbell Scott's *Addresses, Essays, and Reviews,* Leslie Ritchie observes that Arnold's 'Heinrich Heine' not only contains many of the same quotations from the German writer's work as Scott's earliest extant piece of critical writing, the essay 'The Character and World of Heinrich Heine,' which he probably delivered to the Ottawa Literary and Scientific Society in the early 1890s, but also furnished Scott with 'some of [his] remarks' (2: 520–1).

24 In the Introduction to his edition of Lampman's *Selected Poetry,* Michael Gnarowski suspects that the Canadian poet 'tried to model his own activities on those of the great English man of letters [ – that is, Arnold]' (27).

25 Victorian construals and construction of masculinity and maleness have been the subject of numerous studies in recent years. See, for example, J.A. Mangan and James Malvin, eds, *Manliness and Morality* (1987); David D. Gilmore, *Manhood in the Making* (1990); and James Eli Adams, *Dandies and Desert Saints* (1995).

26 See Bentley, 'William Morris and the Poets of the Confederation,' 32–3 and 36–9. During six months as a 'non-Collegiate student' at Oxford during 1873–4, Parkin heard John Ruskin's 'first lecture [as Slade Professor] on art,' worked on the 'too-famous road at Hinksey' (Willison 30), and apparently became an enthusiastic admirer of the Pre-Raphaelites. In 'To My Teacher and Friend George Robert Parkin' in *The Kinship of Nature* (1903), Carman recalls 'those hours in the classroom, when the *Aeneid* was often interrupted by the *Idylls of the King* or "The Blessed Damozel," and William Morris or Arnold or Mr. Swinburne's latest lyric came to us between the lines of Horace' (vii). See also Roberts's letters of 25 October and 28 November 1884, where he enthusiastically directs Carman to 'The Wind,' 'The Gilliflower of Gold,' and 'Concerning Geffray Teste Noire' in Morris's *The Defense of Guenevere, and Other Poems* (*CL* 44, 47).

27 Scott's remarks are a response to an unnamed Australian poet who 'has turned the season topsy-turvy to let us know how a poet must feel in the Antipodes' (*MI* 8).

28 See Appendix A of the Canadian Poetry Press edition of Kidd's *The Huron Chief,* 109–19

29 See Djwa, 'Lampman's Fleeting Vision,' 142; and Bentley; *The Gay]Grey Moose,* 236–46.

## 1. Young Canada: 1880–1884

1 The most extensive examinations of the literary aspects of McGee's connection with Young Ireland are in two University of Western Ontario

theses, by Kathleen M. O'Donnell (1956) and Michele J. Holmgren (1997), 139–209.

2 According to a notice in the 27 July 1880 issue of the *Star* (Fredericton), the marriage took place in Fredericton on July 23. Less than a week later, on July 29, Collins announced that forthwith the *Star* would cease publication in Fredericton and move 'to where it can draw more nutrition.' Probably the most illuminating account of Collins's life and character is a document generated by his divorce and apparently unknown to either of his biographers. Entitled 'Repenting at Leisure' and published in the 14 September 1889 issue of the Saint John *Progress*, it depicts Collins in his Fredericton days as a character more in keeping with the American West than the Canadian East: '[He] was a newspaper man and a good one at that. He never failed to make a story interesting, but his great fault was a spirit of exaggeration that he never attempted to, or, at least, did not, restrain. He was thoroughly fearless and no man knew when the *Evening Star* came out whether he would figure in its columns as a pillar of the church and a good Christian, or a forger, a wife-beater, or anything else that was bad. Collins' fearlessness was his strong point, but he usually lacked the facts. He was never sure when he loitered on his evening stroll whether some insulted pugilistic citizen would not take into his head to measure him on the sidewalk and decorate his countenance with the latest mixture of black and blue. Horse whips he cared nothing for, and, to do him justice, he was quite indifferent to knuckles. The *Star* sold better the next night for the fracas of the previous evening and the editor was tough. Wearying, however, of repeated assaults, Collins bought a six-shooter, which he located in his pants pocket, and one day when Mr. Sullivan's brawny fists became acquainted with his physiognomy, Mr. Collins prevented a recurrence of the assault by looking calmly into the eyes of Mr. Sullivan over the sight of his shooting iron. This suspended hostilities for a time, but the fracas was continued later in the police court, where Collins charged Sullivan with assault, and Sullivan laid information against him for carrying firearms. The magistrate found an opportunity to add to the revenue of the department of justice from both parties.' The article also notes that when he met his future wife, the Fredericton 'gossips had ... given Collins to another girl' and that 'the present Mrs. Collins had not the full and free permission of her legal guardians to further enthrall the susceptible journalist.' 'Mrs. Collins was a Protestant and Collins a Catholic,' it continues, 'but what mattered that when they loved each other! She rejected the faith of her ancestors and joined the church of her lover ... and one dark night the pair ... were made man and wife in St. Dunstan's chapel ... Society was shocked ... Social ostracism did not trouble the young couple and Col-

lins continued to say what he pleased and take the results ... [A] short time later he left Fredericton, having failed to make the *Star* a financial success ... He went to Chatham and after a rather uneventful career on a paper there – the *North Star* – proceeded to upper Canada. Mrs. Collins accompanied him. Perhaps his greatest hit was his *Life of Sir John A. Macdonald* ... After a varied career in Toronto, he resolved to ... [move to] New York. He went there, and for some time was editor of that bright weekly, the *Epoch.* He had almost absolute control of this promising paper, and it would have been well had he had the entire control. The owner, however, interfered one day with the editorial management and Collins, with his usual hot-headedness, stepped down and out. Since then, it is said, he has had an offer to go to the antipodes to do some literary work ...'

3  Of course, Liberal-Conservative was the name given by John A. Macdonald to the coalition of Tories and moderate reformers that came into being in 1854 and was renamed the Progressive Conservative party in 1942. Although Collins was more Liberal than Tory, in the Prospectus for the *North Star* and the *Star,* he pledges the paper's 'support [to] the liberal conservative party.' '[O]ne of the founders of the Toronto Young Men's Liberal-Conservative Association' in 1876 (Thompson 248), Davin was a committed Liberal-Conservative who put his considerable rhetorical skills at Macdonald's service. It is possible that Collins and Davin knew one another in Toronto after Collins moved there in the fall of 1881 and before Davin moved to Regina in the fall of 1882.

4  *Rose-Belford's Canadian Monthly Magazine and Literary Review* was the successor (sometimes called the second series) of the *Canadian Monthly and National Review* (1872–8), which was also edited by Graeme Mercer Adam (1839–1912).

5  The fact that Mulvaney, like Davin, was born in Ireland renders almost inevitable the observation that Collins's Irish background and interests were a factor in his attraction to the work of both men. Writing to John Reade on 17 January 1880, Roberts expresses 'the highest admiration' for Mulvaney's poetry, with the reservation that 'some of his best poems are *dubious* in subject' (*CL* 26). A frequent contributor to the *Canadian Monthly Magazine,* Mulvaney collaborated with Amos Henry Chandler (1837–80) to produce *Lyrics, Songs and Sonnets* (1880). In his survey of the year's literary productions in *The Dominion Annual Register and Review for ... 1884* (1885), Collins describes Davin's *Eos* (1884, 1889) as 'a very brilliant poem by ... [a] most vivacious writer' and singles out Mulvaney's *Toronto Past and Present* (1884) as 'the most noteworthy' of the books of 'civic literature and history' published in connection with the 'Semi-centennial Celebration' in Toronto (169, 168).

6 Collins rightly remarks that 'the pith' of 'Great Speeches' is 'that Canadian
   orators use too many words in expressing what they have to say' and proceeds to summarize its main arguments, mentioning specifically Davin's
   emphasis on the 'literary flavour' of Macdonald's speeches and repeating a
   quotation from the principal orator of the Young Ireland movement, Daniel
   O'Connell, that '"a good speech is a good thing, but the verdict is *the* thing."'
   McGee is also mentioned in 'Great Speeches' as an orator whose speeches
   had 'the flavour of literary culture' (273), and his argument in 'Protection
   for Canadian Literature' (1858) that Canada's 'National Literature' must
   'assume' or 'possess' the qualities of the 'forest,' 'waterfall,' and 'great rivers'
   of the country may lie in the background of Davin's remarks on the Canadianness of Fréchette's poetry. According to Hector Charlesworth (1872–
   1945) in *More Candid Chronicles* (1928), 23–4, McGee's 'great public success'
   in Canada was probably the principal reason for Davin's decision to remain
   in Canada in 1872 (he had been sent by the *Pall Mall Gazette* [London] to
   write a series of articles on the annexation controversy of that day). For a succinct account of Davin's backgroud and early years in Canada, see Charles
   Beverley Koester, 61–5.
7 Organized by Frank Yeigh (1861–1935) in support of the Young Men's Liberal Club of Toronto, this event took place in that city on 16 January 1892. It
   is discussed in chapter 7 in the context of the literary and political milieu of
   the early 1890s.
8 Either Davin's remarks on Fréchette or McGee's projections regarding a
   'National Literature' (see note 6, above) or both doubtless lie(s) in the background of the catalogue of qualities to be expected in the work of 'our Canadian Longfellow, our Canadian Tennyson, or our Canadian Browning' with
   which O'Hagan concludes his essay: 'something of the sublimity of our
   mountains, the azure of our Canadian skies, the light and glow of our Northern star – something of the sweep and dash of our mighty rivers, the music
   and murmur of our blossoming prairies, the honest manhood of our marts
   and farms, the strong virtues of our homes and firesides, the tenderness of
   our mother's prayers, the sweetness and purity of our maidens' hearts!'
   (*Canadian Essays* 53). And, it is tempting to add, the cloying richness of
   Canadian butter tarts.
9 Anderson's 'The Future of the Canadian Dominion' and Clarke's 'The
   Future of the Canadian Dominion' were published in the September and
   November 1880 numbers of the *Contemporary Review* (London) (38: 396–411;
   38: 805–26).
10 Another precedent for Roberts's description of Canada as a 'Child of
    Nations, giant-limbed' is the following passage from 'Dominion Day, 1879'

by the Kingston poet Agnes Maule Machar ('Fidelis'), which was first published in the July 1879 number of the *Canadian Monthly*. Notice, however, that Machar's Canada is conventionally female:

> Through the young giant's mighty limbs, that stretch from sea to sea,
> There runs a throb of conscious life – of waking energy:
> From Nova Scotia's misty coast to far Columbia's shore
> She wakes, – a band of scattered homes and colonies no more,
> But a young nation, with her life full beating in her breast,
> And noble future in her eyes – the Britain of the West. (Lighthall, ed.,
> *Songs of the Great Dominion* 16)

Canada is similarly conceived as female in 'Dominion Day' by John Reade (1837–1919), the literary editor of the Montreal *Gazette* from 1879 until his death, who sent Roberts a copy of the volume in which it was published, *The Prophecy of Merlin and Other Poems* (1870), in the winter of 1879–80 and elicited a warm but restrained response from the younger poet (see *CL* 26):

> ... to-day [Canada] breathes what to her is the first of a nation's breath,
> As she lies 'neath the gaze of the sun, as a bride, or a child new-born,
> Lies with fair motionless limbs in the beautiful semblance of death, –
> Yet awakes with the joy of a bird that awakes with the whisper of morn.
> (132)

Roberts's conception of Canada as male rather than female may derive in part from Mair, who conceives of Canada in 'The New Canada: Its Resources and Productions' (1875) as possessing an atmosphere of crystal, a climate suited above all others to develop the broad shoulder, the tense muscle and the clear brain, and which will build up the most herculean and robust nation on earth' (164). It may also owe a debt to Davin and, through Davin, to William Dean Howells (of whom more later), for Davin's *Eros: An Epic of the Dawn and Other Poems* (1889) contains a piece entitled 'Young Canada' dated 'April, 1878,' which begins with an epigraph from Howells's *Their Wedding Journey* (1872) describing Canada as 'the hulking young giant beyond St. Lawrence and the Lakes' and proceeds to depict the country as a 'youthful giant, golden-haired, / With fearless forehead ... [and] manhood's thoughts' (133).

11 Collins also quotes Davin's comparison between national and male maturation: 'to find fault with a new country for not having a literature, is as reasonable as trouncing a boy for not growing a mustache' (495).

12 The orotund statement that Marquis's 'Nausicaa' 'shows, beside the fire of the muse, much of the *ars poetica* – a culture that has been in the direction of

Mr. Marquis' sympathies; and creditable to the Pierian fount, whose measures Mr. Roberts supplied' contains an allusion to Pope's *Essay on Criticism* that recalls Davin's observation regarding the 'flavour of literary culture' in the speeches of McGee and Joseph Howe that 'the ideal oratory will always come, as it were, from a vessel which has often been filled at Pierian founts – will betray a nature saturated with the thoughts and language of the great teachers of the world' (273). It also suggests that Roberts may have had a hand in the writing of Marquis's poem.

13 Nor do Roberts's recollections of the period help matters. In his 1927 interview with Lorne Pierce, he responded to the question of 'what interesting ... people' he met in Toronto when he moved there to edit the *Week* in September 1883 with the reply 'I met Lampman. He was a student at Trinity then. I published some of his poems in the *Week* ... I saw a great deal of him ... ' ('Interview' 70). In her 1943 biography of Roberts, Pomeroy, always the faithful recorder of his version of events, states that 'shortly after his arrival [in Toronto], Collins introduced Lampman to [him]' and 'the two poets at once became great friends' (49). Two facts cast doubt on this scenario: first, Lampman graduated from Trinity College in 1882; and second (and more important), he moved permanently to Ottawa in January 1883: he was thus neither 'a student at Trinity' nor a resident of Toronto when Roberts claimed to have met and 'bec[o]me great friends' with him in the fall and winter of 1883. Probably the most likely explanation of how and when Roberts and Lampman met is that they were introduced by Collins during a visit by Lampman to Toronto, perhaps during his Christmas vacation in 1883 and, hence, that Roberts was simply mistaken in thinking that Lampman was a student at the time. But the possibility remains that Connor's sources and Roberts himself were correct in recalling that the friendship began when Lampman was still a student. If so, then Collins, Roberts, and Lampman may have met either (1) during the spring or summer of 1881 (when Collins might have been seeking a position in Toronto and Roberts, according to the May 11 issue of the *Star*, was away from Chatham between May 12 and the end of the summer holidays because of 'weakness of [the] eyes ... brought about by ardent study and too much reading'); or (2) during the winter vacation of 1881–2 (after Collins had moved to Toronto in October and before Roberts left Chatham on January 27 [*Miramichi Advance*, 2 February 1882] to assume the headmastership of the York Street School in Fredericton on February 1); or – and most likely – (3) during the summer of 1882 (when Roberts was free of teaching and administrative duties and Lampman was still in Toronto prior to assuming the position as an assistant master at the Orangeville High School, which he occupied from September to December). If, as

seems likely, Roberts's remark in his one surviving letter of 1881 (October 29) that he has 'not yet heard anything from the Perth Board' (*CL* 27) refers to the Board of Education in Perth County, Ontario, then it would seem that at the time of Collins's departure for Toronto (October 26) he was already contemplating a move to central Canada. By the spring of 1883, Roberts had an additional reason for wanting to leave New Brunswick: as a result of an incident that took place on April 2, he was 'arraigned in the [Fredericton] police court ... [on April 4] on a charge of assault and battery upon [a pupil of York Street School named] Willie Hayes' and, after a two-day trial that garnered interest throughout the province, found 'guilty of the offense as charged' and given a 'nominal fine' of one dollar (Saint John *Telegraph*, 5 and 11 April 1883). On May 2, the *New Brunswick Reporter and Fredericton Advertiser* noted that Roberts had been 'granted leave of absence' and, as of May 1, replaced as principal of York Street School 'for the summer term.' As John Coldwell Adams observes, the New Brunswick 'Board of Education supported Roberts by amending its regulations to make ... clear that [a] principal's authority would be upheld in such circumstances,' but 'the incident may have been the last straw needed to convince him' to seek other employment (*Sir Charles God Damn* 30).

14 As Early points out, the title of 'The Last Sortie' comes from L.P. Brockett's description of the Battle of Buzenval (19 January 1871) in *The Year of Battles; or, The Franco-German War of 1870–71* (1871), 354–5: 'on the 19th of January General Trochu led another and the last sortie against the Germans. His force at this time engaged was 100,000 men ... Notwithstanding the formidable army of French troops, the attack was very feebly sustained, and in the evening Montrefont was retaken by the Germans' (quoted in Early, 'Twenty-Five Fugitive Poems' 67).

15 Roberts's letter begins, 'As you have Collins with you ...' (*CL* 28).

16 In a letter of 9 September 1882, Lampman states that he 'teach[es] Latin, Greek, English Literature, History and German' – an indication that, though he seems to have relied primarily on translations for his knowledge of German patriotic poetry and its contexts (see *ER* 215–22), he had some acquaintance with the language, probably through his mother. Lampman was of German descent on both sides of his family (see Connor 13–17).

17 Much of the coverage of Ireland in the *Star* is sceptical of official versions of events, and in an editorial of 6 April 1881 Collins writes that, 'though we have not been able to give as much space to the great agitation going on in Ireland as we would like to have given, yet we have endeavoured to give our readers as much reliable information on the subject as possible.' Throughout the spring and summer of 1881, the *Star* reprinted 'A Tour through Ire-

land' from the Montreal *Witness*, and on September 3 and 14 it contained items on Duffy's visit to Ireland and a transcript of his letter on the Land Bill, which, among other things, expresses regret that his 'little band' had been unsuccessful in achieving a repeal of the Act of Union in the 1840s. In *Life and Times of the Right Honourable Sir John A. Macdonald*, Collins describes 'the struggles of the great O'Connell for a repeal of the Union' (101) as being one of the three momentous occurrences of the 1840s (the other two being Tractarianism and the repeal of the Corn Law). Nowhere does Collins mention Duffy's *Young Ireland*, but the likelihood is strong that he knew the work and made it known to Roberts.

18 McGee also asserts in his Preface that, 'of all the forms of patriotism, a wise, public-spirited patriotism in literature, is not the least admirable' and cites Homer, Thomas Moore, Sir Walter Scott, and Pierre-Jean de Béranger as evidence that 'Patriotism has been the passion of the noblest succession of sweet singers the world ever saw' (n.pag.).

19 In *The Earl of Beaconsfield*, Davin also refers to Disraeli's use of 'political novels' to further his 'political position' and observes that 'in 1848 he was in his element amid cries of young France, young Germany, young Italy and young England' (34, 27). It is in the final sentence of *Sybil* that Disraeli famously declares that 'the Youth of a Nation are the trustees of Posterity' (431).

20 See Patrick O'Neill's *Ireland and Germany: A Study in Literary Relations* (100–5) for a discussion of the presence of German Romanticism in Young Ireland.

21 In 'German Patriotic Poetry,' Lampman observes that 'the Germans have a larger stock of [patriotic] ballads perhaps than any other nation in the world – fine bursts of patriotism, that paint in clearest colours the affectionate character as well as the romantic history of that brave people' (*ER* 28).

22 A synopsis of the Orion myth at the centre of the review is signed 'ED, STAR.' That Collins is also the author of the surrounding material is indicated by its witty introductory paragraph and by the recurrence of quotations and phrases from it in his discussion of Roberts in *Life and Times of the Right Honourable Sir John A. Macdonald* and in the review of *Orion, and Other Poems* in *Rouge et Noir.*

23 The allusion is to John 1.46: 'Nathanael said unto [Philip], Can there any good thing come out of Nazareth? Philip saith unto him, Come and see [Jesus].'

24 In 'Notes from the Capital' in the 9 October 1880 issue of the *Star,* the negative comments of 'the critics in the *Capital*' are attributed to jealousy: 'you know the *Capital*, beside having a local Latin man, has also a poet on its staff. Now this poet is not very successful himself, and the only publication that will take his verses is the paper he gathers items for; and that paper only

takes his effusions in homeopathic quantities ... so we can easily understand his carping at the success of another.'

25  In addition to containing quotations and phrases that appear both in the *Star* review of *Orion, and Other Poems* and in Collins's biography of Macdonald, the review in *Rouge et Noir* notes in passing that 'Orion' is set on 'Chios – the ... island that was shattered but two years ago by an earthquake' (12). In the 13 April 1881 issue of the *Star*, an article on the Chios earthquake concludes with a reminder to readers that this is the island on which 'Orion' is set and a quotation from the poem.

26  Roberts may have written other articles in the second series of the *Bystander*, such as a piece on 'Mr. Romanes and Evolution,' which discusses the 'complex instincts of animals' and the relationship of Darwinian theory to the Christian understanding of creation (139), but only the four pieces mentioned above can be attributed to him with certainty on the basis of internal evidence alone. This is so of 'Imperial Relations' because the two figures whose views it discusses, Sir Alexander Galt (1817–93) ('Imperial Federation') and James David Edgar (1841–99) ('Diplomatic Independence'), are also mentioned in Roberts's letter of 10 March 1883 to Carman: 'I suppose you got to hear Galt's Edinburgh address on the subject [of Imperialism] ... Little sympathy here for the doctrine! I have a pamphlet, lately written by J.D. Edgar M.P. of Toronto, and published by the Reform Association, advocating most ably the question of *Commercial Independence*' (*CL* 34). In 1883, Galt published his 'Edinburgh address' in *The Relations of the Colonies to the Empire: Present and Future* (and also *The Future of the Dominion of Canada*), and Edgar published the address that he delivered on January 26 of that year to the Reform Association of Toronto as *The Commercial Independence of Canada*. Edgar later published a novel, *The White Canoe: A Legend of the Ottawa* (1885) and a volume of poetry, *This Canada of Ours, and Other Poems* (1893). In 1887–8 he was successful in convincing Liberal policy-makers that 'unrestricted reciprocity' with the United States was more desirable than 'commercial union' because it would not 'deprive Canada of her separate identity' (Stevens 292).

27  There is no indication in Lampman's extant letters that he read any numbers of the second series of the *Bystander*. It is worth noting, however, that the interest in Léon Gambetta that is reflected in the lengthy Carlylean essay on the French statesman that he published in the July 1883 issue of *Rouge et Noir* was shared by Goldwin Smith, who published pieces on Gambetta in both the first (1880) and the second series of the *Bystander* (April 1883). This would scarcely be remarkable if it were not for the fact that in both 1880 and 1883 Smith argues that 'the closest prototype of Gambetta' in French politics

was 'Mirabeau ... [who] died just as the leadership of the Revolution had come definitively into his hands, and he was about to be tried as the constructor of a new order of things' ('The Ascendancy of Gambetta' 377) and that 'what Mirabeau was to the first Revolution, Gambetta was to the second' ('Consequences of the Death of Gambetta' 131). Lampman's 'Gambetta' resembles Smith's 'Consequences of the Death of Gambetta' not only in expounding at length on the parallels between Gambetta and Mirabeau but also by referring by way of introduction to the response of Positivists to Gambetta's death (see 'Consequences' 130 and *ER* 46); indeed, in 'Positivism and Gambetta,' which is also in the April 1881 number of the *Bystander*, Smith again anticipates Lampman by referring specifically to the English Positivist Frederic Harrison.

28  While arguing that, because all literature written in the English language belongs to 'a great republic of English letters,' it should be covered by 'one common law,' Collins does not abandon his Canadian literary nationalism in 'International Copyright' but, rather, advances it through irony, as, for example, in his comment that the fining of a Canadian publisher for producing 'a new edition' of a book whose '"manner" of make [in England] proved unsuitable for Canadian readers' is 'surely ... one strong mark of our inequality in the empire, and ought to go far to hush the mouths of those who talk about nationality' (5).

29  Lampman's personification of Winter as 'the slayer, / Slayer of loves, sweet world, slayer of dreams' who makes 'sad summer's arms grow cold,' and his concluding warning to Summer to make his 'bosom and ... sad lips ready / For the cold kisses of the folding snow' (62–3) anticipate the personifications and phrasing of such passages as the following from Part 2 of *Malcolm's Katie* (the Moon of Falling Leaves is speaking):

> 'Shame upon you, Moon of Evil Witches!
> 'Have you kill'd the happy, laughing Summer?
> 'Have you slain the mother of the flowers
> 'With your icy spells of might and magic?
> 'Have you laid her dead within my arms?' (2:109–13)

30  Probably 'Winter Evening' ('Westward the sun is waning slow ...') and 'Winter's Nap,' both of which date from early 1883 (see Early, 'Chronology' 77).

31  See Connor 66. Ritchie's 'May Time' appeared in the 30 April 1885 issue of the *Week*.

32  In his entry on Smith in the *Dictionary of Canadian Biography*, Ramsay Cook states flatly that from 1877 until 'the end of his life' Smith did not waver from his view that 'Canada could never become a genuine nation and that

its destiny lay in union with the United States' (973). See also the passage from Roberts's 'Goldwin Smith at the Grange' (1885) quoted in the opening paragraph of chapter 2 of the present study. The possibility should not be ignored that Roberts's departure from the *Week* was at least partly the result of the poor response in some quarters to the early issues of the periodical. 'We cannot conscientiously congratulate Mr. Roberts, the editor, upon having struck a vein which is likely to prove either popular or remunerative,' wrote the *Toronto Morning News* on 6 December 1883. 'A Canadian literary journal in order to have a reason for its existence should be instinct with the spirit of Democracy and Canadian nationalism ... [T]his is just where the *Week* conspicuously fails. With the exception of a few paragraphs, and a long and somewhat prosy article on international copyright [by Collins], there is nothing in the paper that would not be equally in place in an English or American publication. It is not distinctively Canadian, either in spirit or in standpoint, or in the class of subjects treated of ... If the *Week* does not fill the bill better in the future, than it has in its initial number, it will ... go the way of the *Nation*, the *Canadian Monthly*, and the rest' (2). Apparently, cosmopolitan nationalism did not satisfy such fervent advocates of Canadian Independence as the editor and proprietor of the *Toronto Morning News*, the erascible journalist and novelist Edmund Ernest Sheppard (1855–1924), who subsequently founded *Saturday Night* (1887–  ) and maintained a consistently sceptical and, at times, satirical 'standpoint' vis-à-vis Smith and the Confederation group (see, for example, the scathing depiction of Smith as 'the old-time high priest of Canadian literature' whose 'desire for the admiration of even the young and inexperienced' garnered a 'strange throng' at The Grange in the 4 March 1893 issue of *Saturday Night*, 1).

33 See, for example, the *Miramichi Advance* of October 30.

34 The fact that Roberts's review of literature in *The Dominion Annual Register and Review ... for 1883* (1884) refers to the *Week* as being under the 'editorship of Mr. Charles G.D. Roberts, the well-known poet' (218) indicates that it was written between September 1883 and the end of February 1884.

35 See also Adam's 'Literature, Nationality, and the Tariff' in the 27 December 1889 number of the *Week* for his slightly later views on the plight and prospects of Canadian literature and Canadian authors; and George L. Parker's *The Beginnings of the Book Trade in Canada* for discussions of the economic factors that adversely affected the Canadian publishing industry in the post-Confederation period and thus contributed to the exodus of writers such as Adams, most notably 'the failure of international copyright' to be implemented (178). In his excellent study of the 'Exodus,' Nick Mount 'reache[s] the very conservative estimate that between 1880 and 1900 upwards of two

hundred Canadian writers either quit their profession or quit their country' and observes that studies such as Marcus Lee Hansen's *The Mingling of the Canadian and American Peoples* and June Callwood's *The Naughty Nineties* estimate that 'Canadian emigration to the [United] States in the 1880s alone exceeded one million people' (5, 20).

36 In 'An Interregnum in Literature,' Adam indicates the economic reason for his movement from 'intellectual' culture (poetry, literary criticism, historical scholarship) to popular – that is, more saleable – culture when he notes that British and American publishers have observed a 'serious falling away, both in volume and character, of ... exports to Canada' and that 'native wholesale houses confirm ... [this] by the decay of the better-class booktrade' (439).

37 See the articles of this title by J.H.S. in the 8 May 1888 issue of the *Week*, 361.

38 Pomeroy identifies 'A Breathing Time,' which was first published in the *University Monthly* (Fredericton) in November 1882, as Roberts's 'first experiment with the difficult classical form which he was to make so peculiarly his own' (48) but incorrectly implies that it was written in the summer of 1883.

39 For a discussion of the appropriateness of alternating lines of dactylic hexameter and pentameter to the tidal movements and horizontal landscape of the Tantramar Marshes, see Bentley, 'The Poetics of Roberts' Tantramar Space,' 20–1 and 24–6 and *The Gay/Grey Moose*, 40.

40 It is clear from Roberts's ensuing remarks that he is responding specifically to the following passage by Graeme Mercer Adam in the 'Review of Literature, Science and Art' in *The Dominion Annual Register and Review for the Fourteenth and Fifteenth Years of the Canadian Union, 1880–1881* (1882): 'what our poetry most wants is that it should take its inspiration more largely from Canadian sources, treat more freely of the history and legends of the country, deck itself in the tints of our glorious land, and sing more of the songs of our woods and waters. This atmosphere of nationalism, indeed, is one that should more penetratively pervade all our literature than it does. If that literature is ever to fire the heart of the nation, and to create a distinguishing type of national character, it must cease to be imitative, and find the materials of its art and occupation at home. It may borrow the literary forms of the authorcraft of the Old World, but its themes must be those of the New. Let us import the high standards of old lands, by which to test our work, and to set a high ideal before our literary workmen; but, having these, let the rest be original and creative. If with half a continent to draw upon, we remain servile to Old World models we have inherited to little purpose the traditions of our race' (282). Adam's effective dismissal of poetry written on other than Canadian themes as lacking in originality and creativity serves to undercut somewhat his subsequent assessment of *Orion, and Other Poems*: '*Orion* [itself]

... is a vigorous example of the neo-classical poetry which came into fashion with Tennyson's "Œnone." Several of the minor poems in the volume, especially those in the "ballade" form, are of remarkable beauty, and deserve the place won for them in the pages of *Scribner's* Magazine and the *Canadian Monthly*' (288). Adam ranks *Orion, and Other Poems* with *The Coming of the Princess, and Other Poems* (1881), by Kate Seymour MacLean (18?–?), and *Lyrics, Songs and Sonnets* (1880), by Amos Henry Chandler and Charles Pelham Mulvaney, as volumes of 'far more permanent value' than others published by Canadian poets during 1880–1.

It is notable that, although Roberts rejects Adam's argument concerning Canadian themes in the epilogue to 'The Beginnings of a Canadian Literature,' his survey of that literature in the body of the essay is greatly indebted to Adam, particularly with regard to the work of Fréchette (whom Adam calls 'the genius of Canadian woods and waters' [287]). It is also notable that near the beginning of his review Adam calls for the establishment of a 'high-class literary weekly' and castigates Canadian universities for not doing enough to foster Canadian literature (280).

In the review of literature in *The Dominion Annual Register and Review for ... 1883* (1884), a piece almost certainly written by Roberts or Collins or both, the argument of the epilogue to 'The Beginnings of a Canadian Literature' is restated and, indeed, repeated. After commenting on the 'increase of genuine national feeling' that has been observable in Canada, quoting the 'uncompromising nationalist' Collins on the 'peril of falling into a narrow provincialism, both of subject and treatment,' in Canadian literature, and passing some dismissive remarks on American epics about Native peoples that 'smacked of the soil,' the review asserts that 'national individuality in our literature can not be procured by merely turning our pens to Canadian subject-matter; it must be the outcome of a potential national existence, and springing from such a source it will make itself visible in the production of our writers though they range time and space for subjects' (206) It then quotes the bulk of the epilogue of 'The Beginnings of a Canadian Literature' without naming Roberts as the author and describing him merely as 'one of our literary workers.' The review also compliments Smith and praises Collins's biography of Macdonald, quoting the laudatory review of it in the Saint John *Telegraph.*

41 For continuations of the debate in but one periodical, the *Week*, see James Wilberforce Longley (1849–1922), 'A Field for Canadian Achievement' (3 July 1884), 'Barry Dane' (John Edward Logan [1852–1915]) (21 August and 4 September 1884), Agnes Maule Machar ('Fidelis'), 'Patriotism versus Cosmopolitanism' (7 October 1886), Ethelbert F.H. Cross (1872–?), 'Genius and

Patriotism' (26 August 1892), and Pelham Edgar (1871–1948), 'Duncan Campbell Scott' (15 March 1895). During the winter of 1887–8, the newly launched Toronto *Empire* carried numerous reviews, articles, and letters centred on the question, as articulated in an article of 27 January 1888, by Edward Burrough Brownlow ('Sarepta') (1857–95), '"Has Canada a Native Literature or Not?"' Of particular issue in the debate was the merit of George Frederick Cameron's poems, which his brother and editor quoted Roberts as saying 'impressed [him] at once by their admirable force and beauty (15 March 1888, 8). 'There is no question but this is a *true and strong poet*,' Roberts is quoted as asserting; '*genuine inspiration, wide and fertile imagination, spontaneity, and a splendid lyric rush,* together with *artistic skill, conscientious craftsmanship,* all these I have found' in Cameron's poetry.

42 Collins thus describes Roberts's perspective on the Tantramar Marshes in *Canada under the Administration of Lord Lorne* (36) before proceeding to quote extensively from the description of them in 'The Rawdon's Luck' (1883).

43 See Bentley, *Mnemographia Canadensis,* 1: 357–8, for a discussion of the relationship between Roberts's preliminary description of the landscape and John Ruskin's definition of the picturesque in relation to Calais Church and its surroundings in the fourth volume of *Modern Painters.* Several elements of Roberts's preliminary description also appear in his 'observation from the cupola of the university' (2: 767) in Fredericton in his essay on New Brunswick in George Monro Grant's *Picturesque Canada; the Country As It Was and Is* (1882–4).

44 In *Canada under the Administration of Lord Lorne,* Collins describes 'the Tantramar marsh [as] the largest of the group' known as 'the Westmoreland Marshes,' noting that it 'extends over an area of about thirty miles square' of 'that vast expanse of fertile low-land' that is 'capable of producing abundant crops of luxurious grasses for nearly seventy years without showing any decrease of producing power' (34).

45 For an account of the inception, production, and reception of *Picturesque Canada,* see Bentley, 'Charles G.D. Roberts and William Wilfred Campbell As Canadian Tour Guides,' 80–3.

46 In a letter of 29 October 1881 to Grant, Roberts writes that 'with regard to Picturesque Canada' he will 'make [him]self thoroughly familiar' with 'whatever parts of N.B. [Grant] may wish described' and includes among the province's 'finest scenery' the area 'at the head of the Bay of Fundy,' adding that 'Fort Cumberland, on the isthmus, is picturesque and historically interesting' (*CL* 27). On Wednesday, 16 August 1882, the Chatham *World* reported that 'Mr. C.G.D. Roberts, and Mr. [F.B.] Schell ... were in town Monday, having come through the woods from Fredericton. Mr. Schell is making

sketches, and Mr. Roberts writing descriptions, of New Brunswick, for "Picturesque Canada." Mr. Roberts ... has a book full of notes and a head full of traditions, legends, and memories of men and things.' In his letter of 10 March 1883 to Carman, Roberts indicates, in addition to writing for the *Bystander*, he has 'a heap of work ahead ... on *Picturesque Canada*, and the Encaenal Oration [that is, "The Beginnings of a Canadian Literature"] to prepare' (*CL* 34).

47 Between 'The salt, raw scent of the margin ...' and '... Surging in ponderous lengths ...' the following line is omitted from the text of 'Tantramar Revisited' in Roberts's *Collected Poems*: 'While, with men at the windlass, groaned each reel, and the net,' (*SPCP* 53). In 'Roberts' Poetry of the Tantramar' (1895), Harry A. Woodworth quotes the description as the clearest indication of the 'poetic mind' in the poem and pronounces the metaphorical use of the word 'Winnowing' in 'Winnowing soft grey wings of marsh-owls' 'a speech-figure that alone entitles Roberts to a place in the front rank of poets' (3).

48 On the Tantramar area as Roberts's poetic or intellectual property as a consequence of the transformative imaginative labour of 'Tantramar Revisited' and other poems, see Bentley, *Mnemographia Canadensis,* 1: 303–13. In 'The Singer of Tantramar' in the January 1896 number of *Massey's Magazine* (Toronto), Pauline Johnson writes of the Tantramar Marshes as 'unheard of, unknown' until Roberts 'made the name' Tantramar 'familiar to the greater portion of the poetry-loving world ... And this is the spot that every lover of Canadian literature loves to see,' she continues; 'the marsh-lands are himself, the sea voices, the tides, the sands, the wet salt breath of the margin winds – all are Roberts, and all are his atmosphere ... For another to sing of Tantramar would be almost plagiarism ... The great Maritime marsh is not only his lyrical possession, it is *himself*...' (15, 17–18). According to a series of humorous articles in the Chatham *Star* during Collins's editorship and, very likely, from his pen, Roberts was preceded in his appropriation of the Tantramar area by George Chandler (18?–?), a doctor in Dorchester, NB whom the articles lampoon under such titles as the 'poet Laureate of Tantramar' and 'the Westmorland poet.' 'We have no doubt that "his songs will live" a long time,' runs a passage from 'The Bard of Tantramar' (4 December 1880), 'for books not read last a thousand years ... Dr. Chandler, the fact of the business is, ... is not understood and therefore is not appreciated. It was so with Shakespeare, so with Milton, so with Wordsworth; and so it is with the founder of the Tantramar school of poetry. These men were dead a long time before they were appreciated – and Dr. Chandler will also be dead a long time before he is appreciated.'

**2. Canadianism: 1885–1890**

1 As attested by 'Launcelot and the Four Queens' in *Orion, and Other Poems*, Roberts shared the enthusiasm for Arthurian material that was kindled for the Victorians by the work of Sir Walter Scott, Tennyson, and the second generation of Pre-Raphaelites. It is not beyond the bounds of possibility that Roberts himself perceived the parallel between the knights of the Round Table and the poets of the Confederation group. It is also quite possible to read Campbell's later Arthurian drama *Mordred* (1895) as, at least in part, a reflection of his place in the Confederation group, Arthur being Roberts and Campbell himself the ill-treated Mordred. I am grateful to Steven Artelle for this last suggestion.

2 In the course of the article, Roberts launches several barbs at Smith, some subtle ('... as his wife, whose bright hospitality gives [his house] its highest charm, is a Canadian woman, he has every right to regard himself as identified with Canada' [13]) and some much less so ('as I am writing for an American audience, it may not be irrelevant to say ... that, while Goldwin Smith is an ardent believer in and friend of the American people, he has at the same time but a tepid esteem for the chief part of American literature ... and is continually asking, privately, that America shall produce a book. As he has not, however, made this exorbitant demand as yet in printer's ink, and over his sign and seal, perhaps we may be permitted to regard it as no more than a mild British joke' [14]). Roberts must have relished the restraint and irony involved in his statement that the *Bystander* 'was written entirely' by Smith (13).

3 Roberts had an epistolary relationship with Reade that appears to have begun after Christmas 1879, when Reade sent him a copy of his *The Prophecy of Merlin and Other Poems* (1870). On 26 October 1885 Roberts wrote to Reade soliciting his help in getting Carman appointed as a correspondent of the *Montreal Gazette,* and on 28 May 1887 he refers by way of thanking Reade for his positive review of *In Divers Tones* in the same newspaper to 'the splendid generosity which [he has] always shown' (*CL* 26, 64). In view of his connections with both its author and place of publication, Roberts is almost certain to have known Reade's series of articles on 'Nation-Building' in the 23 June, 11 August, 25 August, 22 September, and 15 December, 1887 issues of the *Week.*

4 Despite its tributary nature, 'Mother of Nations' ends with the nationalistic assertion that Canada 'now in manhood shall not shame / The loins from whence it came' (*CP* 113).

5 See the essays in Eric Hobsbawm and Terence Ranger's *The Invention of Tradi-*

*tion*, particularly Hobsbawm's 'Mass-Producing Traditions, Europe, 1870–1914,' for the period prior to the First World War in the United States as well as Europe as the time in which such traditions as Bastille Day and American Thanksgiving were invented for the purposes of generating social cohesion.

6  In January and February 1890, Roberts published four anecdotes under the title 'Tales from the Lumber Camp' in the *Youth's Companion*, a Boston periodical for young people that was edited from 1891 to 1901 by the Canadian expatriate and close friend of Lampman, Edward William Thomson (1849–1924).

7  In addition to condensing and slightly altering the wording of the legend, Roberts changes the name of its hero from the Micmac Glooscap to the Melicite Clote Scaurp. (When he revised his poem on the legend for inclusion in his *Poems* [1901], its hero reverted from 'Clote Scarp' to 'Gluskâp.') 'How Glooscap, leaving the World, all the Animals mourned for him, and how, ere he departed, he gave Gifts to Man' (as Leland calls it [66]) is one of seven unattributed passages concerning Glooscap in *The Maritime Provinces*, which is clearly also the source of the Glooscap material in the Nova Scotia section of *Picturesque Canada* (see 1: 830, 842) – indeed, Murray and Simpson recount the same legend as Roberts, but do not attribute it to a Native or place it in quotation marks. The same source is directly or indirectly the basis of 'The Passing of Clote Scarp' (1899), by Agnes Maule Machar, a poem anthologized by Roberts in preference to his own rendition of the legend in *Poems of Wild Life* (1888) (63–6). For a further discussion of the sources and merits of the poems that Roberts based on (supposedly) Native materials, see D.M.R. Bentley, 'Charles G.D. Roberts's Use of "Indian Legend" in Four Poems of the Eighteen Eighties and 'Nineties.'

8  In 1888, 'Echoes of Acadia' were published together in *Canadian Leaves*, a 'Series of Papers' on 'History, Art, Literature, [and] Commerce' delivered at the Canadian Club of New York (founded 30 April 1885), probably during the winter of 1885–6 or possibly during the winter of 1886–7. The essays in the collection are bracketed by 'The Future of the Dominion of Canada,' by Collins, and 'The Advantages of Commercial Union to Canada and the United States,' by Erastus Wiman, and include contributions by Goldwin Smith and George Stewart, Jr.

9  For the proliferation of historical societies in the United States and Canada (especially Ontario) in the last two decades of the nineteenth century, see Carl Berger, 96–7. 'In keeping with their avowed purpose [of fostering the spirit of British Canadian identity],' observes Berger, the publications of Canadian historical societies 'were almost exclusively devoted to the hardship of the United Empire Loyalists and the incidents of the War of 1812'

(97). The centennial of the arrival of the Loyalists was widely celebrated in the Maritimes during 1883–4.

10   Writing on 8 February 1886 to Edmund Clarence Stedman to request a letter of recommendation for a new Chair of political science at the University of Toronto, Roberts characterizes political science as his '*secondary specialty*' and notes that 'as a student [he] graduated with honors in the subject' (*CL* 69). '[A]s a patriot, and one with high hopes for the future of my young country,' he adds, 'I have been always fitting myself to influence, if possible, [its] political development ... [T]he fact that I have been devoting myself to the study of Politics and History is not ... well known. Political Economy, however, is a subject attached to my present Chair at King's College' (70). In 1888, Roberts began formally to teach economics rather than French at King's College.

11   Both pictorially and formalistically, 'The Potato Harvest' recalls 'The Sower' (1886), the sonnet inspired by a reproduction of the painting of the same name by Jean-François Millet (1814–75), which Roberts first published in the *Manhattan* (New York) in July 1884 and subsequently included in *In Divers Tones* and in the sonnet series of *Songs of the Common Day.* In composing 'The Potato Harvest,' Roberts may have remembered the illustration of oxen and hay wagons entitled 'On the Tantramar Marshes' in the Nova Scotia section of *Picturesque Canada* (3: 845).

12   Both 'snake fence' and 'zigzag fence' are included in the *Gage Dictionary of Canadianisms on Historical Principles* (1967), the latter supported by quotations from Nathaniel Parker Willis's *Canadian Scenery* (1842) ('the large logs are ... rolled away for ... making ... zigzag log fences ...') and James Edward Alexander's *L'Acadie* (1849) ('our way led past small log or frame farm houses, separated from the road by the everywhere seen zigzag or snake fence').

13   'Shades of the prison-house begin to close / Upon the growing Boy, / But He / Beholds the light, and whence it flows ... At length the Man perceives it die away, / And fade into the light of common day' (4: 281).

14   Founded in 1884, the Imperial Federation League had as its principal aims 'the permanent unity of the Empire,' the formation of the colonies into 'one great Organization for purposes of defence and maintenance of common interests,' the unification of 'the scattered family of Great Britain,' and the 'increase of trade between Britain and the colonies' (quoted in Crowell 184).

15   Several articles in the Chatham *Star* are highly critical of Parkin; for example, on 15 December 1880, a piece bearing the hallmarks of Collins's wit expresses 'regret ... that the press has paid attention to Mr. Parkin's lecture on the Federation of the Empire' and on 12 and 15 January 1881 Parkin is

again the object of negative comments. For a full account of Parkin's career, ideas, and influence, see Willison's *George Parkin* and Terry Cook's 'Apostle of Empire: Sir George Parkin and Imperial Federation.'

16 The articles in question were to have been published together in the *Century Magazine* (New York), but in the event, Parkin's 'The Reorganization of the British Empire' appeared unaccompanied by a contribution from Roberts in the December 1888 number of the magazine (187–92).

17 In the remainder of his letter, Roberts records that James Wilberforce Longley, a one-time attorney-general of Nova Scotia who in 1888 was an editor of the Halifax *Chronicle,* has 'return[ed] to a right mind' on 'the Annexation question' and suggests that 'it was Goldwin Smith that misled him' (*CL* 100–1).

18 'Parkin is a splendid fellow – a man through and through,' Roberts told Richard Watson Gilder on 16 July 1888 (*CL* 86).

19 This is the definition of the term given by the Montreal journalist and novelist Watson Griffin (1860–1952) in 'A Canadian-American Liaison,' an anti-Annexation tract published in the *Magazine of American History* in February 1889. Since Roberts apparently came to know Griffin's work through Lighthall in the fall of 1888 (on October 6, he counts himself in on an unspecified scheme with Lighthall and 'the author of *TWOK*' [1887], Griffin's first novel, and on November 18, he thanks Lighthall for *An Irish Evolution* [circa 1888], Griffin's account of the history of Irish Home Rule), Griffin may have supplied him with the word 'Canadianism.' The first occurrence of the word cited by the *OED* is in 'Canada's Alternatives,' an article by Roswell Fisher in the November 1875 number of the *Canadian Monthly and National Review,* where it refers to a national 'feeling' that is 'not yet sufficiently strong to override all conflicting local feelings and interests' (429). It is worth observing that in 'A Canadian-American Liaison' Griffin regards 'Canadianism' as a stronger feeling than Canadian loyalty to Britain (138) and that in *An Irish Evolution* he discusses Thomas D'Arcy McGee's development from a belief in Irish separation in the days of Young Ireland to his conviction that 'union is strength' (4–5). It is also worth observing that in an article on 'Canadian Literature' in the 4 February 1888 number of *Saturday Night*, Edmund Ernest Sheppard or one of his staff responds to a new round of discussions about the nature of Canadian literature in the Toronto *Empire* (see also *Saturday Night* 3 March 1888, 3) by defining 'Canadianism' in terms reminiscent of Roberts's and Collins's arguments earlier in the decade: 'the best literature is not distinctively national. It does not emphasize race characteristics or flatter patriotic pride. Nobody would think of calling *Paradise Lost* an English, or *The Inferno* an Italian poem ... None of those who have written anything per-

manent strove and struggled to introduce distinctive national peculiarities or modes of thought. So far as these are apparent in these works they are spontaneous not assiduously cultivated. Really great writers appeal rather to universal humanity than to national instincts or tastes. True literature knows no boundary lines. We have reciprocity of thought, irrespective of treaties or commissions ... [T]he differences in national character between us and our neighbours are, after all, not so pronounced as to lead us to look for an obtrusive, irrepressible Canadianism as the natural feature of every literary product of a Canadian pen' (6).

20 In a letter of 31 October 1888, Roberts characterizes Sladen as 'a splendid fellow, head of the Australian singers, and popular in London' (*CL* 91). In the summer of the following year, Sladen was Roberts's guest at Windsor (see *Progress* 13 July 1889, 1) as part of a cross-Canada tour to gather material for his *On the Cars and Off: Being the Journal of a Pilgrimage ... from Halifax in Nova Scotia to Victoria in Vancouver's Island* (1895), which contains idyllic descriptions of the Windsor and Grand Pré areas and 'highly flattering descriptions of Carman and, especially, Roberts as '"the Canadian laureate" – Nova Scotia's link with the great world ... [whose] muscular exploits have instilled in the undergraduates a genuine regard for poetry' (!) and whose secluded life 'in the Arcadia of North America has given his poetry a certain aroma that one gets nowhere else in English verse' (6). At several points in the book, Sladen indicates his antipathy towards Annexation and its advocates and his admiration for Canadian Loyalism (see, for example, xii, 158, and 163).

21 The poetry selections are preceded by 'entry of the Minstrels' from *The Masque of the Minstrels* (1887), by Arthur John Lockhart ('Pastor Felix') (1850–1926), a Nova Scotia–born Methodist Episcopalian minister who, despite living in Maine, contributed a regular column to the Saint John *Progress* and was evidently sympathetic to the Canadianism and Imperialism of Roberts and Lighthall (see *CL* 93).

22 In the 'Biographical and Bibliographical Notes' in *Songs of the Great Dominion,* Lighthall lists *An Analysis of the Altruistic Act* (1885) as his first publication.

23 See Berger, 92–3 and 178–9, and Bentley, *Mimic Fires,* 225–47, for discussions of Kirby's (neo)loyalism. In his chapter on 'Thought and Literature' in the *Life and Times of the Right Hon. Sir John A. Macdonald,* Collins describes Kirby as a 'poor artist' while conceding that his 'imagination is rich' (448), and in the Introduction to *Songs of the Great Dominion,* Lighthall observes that the '*Chien d'Or* ... has remained the most popular of Canadian stories' while admitting that 'Kirby's strong point is his graphic descriptions' (xxviii).

24 The pseudonym under which Lighthall published the novel, 'Wilfred Chateauclair,' was obviously intended to serve the same reconciliatory purpose.

25 'I talk Canadianism all the time' to the Haliburton Society, Roberts told
Lighthall on 18 November 1888, 'we have a literary program, of Canadian
color, each night ...'

26 The reference is to the battle on 30 March 1814 at Lacolle, Quebec, in which
an American invading army was defeated by a force under the command of
Major R.B. Hancock.

27 François Bigot, the infamous intendant of New France from 1748 to the Con-
quest, looms large in Kirby's *Chien d'Or.*

28 Roberts's 'Liberty (*From the French of Louis Honore Fréchette*)' (1886), a stanza
of which he had quoted together with the French original in 'The Beginnings of a Canadian Literature,' may be construed as an earlier attempt to
build a bridge between English and French Canada, as may his 1881
'Rondeau / *To Louis Honore Fréchette*' and his 1891 'New Year's Eve (*After the
French of Fréchette*).'

29 'A Christmas-Eve Courtin',' a dialect poem first published in *Saturday Night*
(Toronto) in December 1889, contains a reference to '"High Church innovation"' (*CP* 124) that places it in a pre-Confederation context and marks it as
a rare attempt by Roberts to capture something of the spirit of early English
Canadians.

30 No doubt a factor contributing to Roberts's desire in and after January 1888
to obtain a Chair in Ontario was the fact that, as revealed by the minutes of
the board of governors of King's College, he and a fellow professor, William
Alexander Hammond (1861–1938), were accused at that time of conduct
involving women that '"ha[d] given cause for rumours injurious to the College"' (quoted in Henry Roper 55; and see Carol E. Martell *passim*). Both
men apparently admitted indiscretion but denied immoral conduct. Nevertheless, Hammond was 'informed that he would not be appointed the following year,' an outcome that Roberts attributed to one of his supporters in his
bid for a position at Toronto, Edmund Clarence Stedman, to his being 'an
*American*, and a *Presbyterian*, at a Church of England college' (*CL* 71). In his
February 19 letter to Stedman, Roberts states that 'a flimsy pretext was
found' to oust Hammond, hints at the likelihood of numerous resignations
from the College, and neglects to mention his own part in the scandal.

31 See the chapter 'The Appointment of W.J. Alexander' in Heather Murray's
*Working in English,* 17–45, for a full discussion of the issues and personalities
involved in the University of Toronto's appointment of its first Chair in
English.

32 An affiliate of the Royal Society of Canada, the Society of Canadian Litera-

ture was founded in January 1889 with John Reade as its first president. According to the 17 and 23 May 1889 issues of the Montreal *Gazette*, Roberts's paper was delivered on May 22 to an audience consisting of the two societies mentioned above and the Numismatic and Antiquarian Society (May 17, 3). On May 23, the *Gazette* reported Roberts's talk as follows: 'Mr. Roberts chose for his text a passage from Stedman expressive of the difficulty by which American idealism was retarded, and after introducing his subject, spoke first of neglect, and doubted if it had ever really pre-eminent talent. Apart from pecuniary neglect, Canadians did not suffer for lack of appreciation, for the first hint of special ability found a host of friends to herald it. The lack of pecuniary recognition was one of their "interdicts," and it was most felt by writers of fiction, who are dependent on the stimulus which a ready market affords. A limited population, books cheap and foreign, the unsatisfactory condition of the copyright law conspired against them. With poetry it was different; the failure to secure a money market for it was no discredit; but poets had to cultivate many practical qualities to live as well as sing, and they had no right to be unpractical or helpless. Every nation had to pass through a probationary period, but it could be expected that theirs would be shorter than that of the Americans and they might have a comforting augury from a remembrance of what has been accomplished by four heroic pioneers, Haliburton, Garneau, Heavysege, and Crémazie. The main obstacles the profession of letters in Canada had to contend with were the limitation of the market and the lack of international copyright and the comparative indifference of the non-literary population. Canadians had a motive and hope they could look back on a romantic past and forward to a future, full of mystery and radiant promise and immeasurable possibility. Dealing with the national life he did not commit himself to federation or independence, and he looked upon annexation as a quicksand, upon which if they were not vigilant some ignorant or unscrupulous pilot might steer the national ship. The literature of a people was shaped by their character and was the effect, not the cause, yet it influenced profoundly the direction of the nation's aims. It was the historians, the romancers and the poets that were singularly fortunate in the material ready to their hands. In concluding he spoke of the technique of poetry and urged what Swinburne calls "the splendid and imperishable excellence of sincerity and strength"' (3).

33 This is not to say that Roberts entirely neglected Canadian books and authors during this period. In a 'hasty notice' (*CL* 98) of *A Short History of the Canadian People* (1887), by George Bryce (1844–1931), in the April 1888 issue of the *Dial* (Chicago), Roberts begins and ends with references to Canada's 'young ... nationality' and Mair's *Tecumseh* ('that striking and imagina-

tive drama') (290, 292) and concentrates at some length on an incident that has loud nationalistic resonances: the capture during 'the embroilment between Maine and New Brunswick in 1839, known as the Aroostook War,' of an expedition from Maine by 'an irregular force of angry lumbermen' bent on avenging the Americans' ill-treatment of some of their comrades (291).

34 Roberts may also have had a hand in 'Children of Canada,' an article in the 26 January 1889 issue of *Progress* by Lockhart that begins by surveying Canadian poets past and present with pride and optimism (Canada's 'Roberts, her John Reade, are true to her, as were her Joseph Howe, and her Thomas D'Arcy McGee. We begin to look toward a Mair, a Lighthall, a Lesperance, a Weir, and Duvar,' and so on) and proceeds to offer a lengthy appreciation of *Among the Millet, and Other Poems* ('here is a book of song, in part unquestionably Canadian, and wholly powerful'), a brief discussion of *Poems* (1889), by Roberts's sister Jane Elizabeth Gostwycke Roberts (1864–1922), and a notice of Roberts's own *Poems of Wild Life* (1888) anthology. Writing to Campbell on 28 December 1888, Roberts informs him that his sister will be sending him a 'leaflet, or *booklet*, of poems printed for private circulation' and asks him: 'will you notice it for her, over y[ou]r name, in *Progress*?' (*CL* 100).

35 The fact that in a letter of 7 July 1888 to Lighthall, Roberts was not certain that Campbell was living in St Stephen, NB (see *CL* 85), supports the inference that the two were not in contact until the fall.

36 Campbell is followed by Cameron.

37 The most poems and pages (9 in both cases) in the Appendix are allotted to Arthur Wentworth Hamilton Eaton (1849–1937), a poet who, like Lockhart (see note 21, above) was born in Nova Scotia but worked as a minister in the United States. In 'To the Reader,' Sladen opines that 'Eaton ... has been the most happy of the Canadians in treating their national legends. There are few writers in the United States who can equal him in this respect. His [*Acadian Legends and Lyrics* (1889)], though only recently issued, is one of the best yet produced by a Canadian, with a fine Longfellow-like strain running through it' (li). From the selection of Eaton's poems in 'Younger Canadian Poets,' it would appear that Sladen was drawn to his use of ballad metres as well as by the 'Longfellow-like strain' of such poems as 'The Resettlement of Acadia.' Two poems in the selection, 'L'Ordre de Bon Temps' and 'The Legend of Glooscap,' work with material treated by Roberts, the former in 'The Order of the Good Times' in *Echoes from Old Acadia* and the latter in 'The Departing of Clote Scarp.'

38 Carman's letter is in the Lampman Papers at Simon Fraser University. His

review of *Among the Millet, and Other Poems* (if, indeed, he wrote one) has yet
to be located. In a letter of 19 January 1889 to Frank Dempster Sherman, an
American book collector, he described 'Lampman's ... book ... [as] well
worth looking into ... [and] far above the average first volume' (*L* 25; see also
Greig, 'Check List' 1:8)

39 It is surely not coincidental that in the extolment of the qualities and promise of Lampman and Carman with which he concludes 'The Poetic Outlook
in Canada,' Roberts describes the latter's 'genius' as 'autochthonous' –
'faithful to its source in atmosphere, color, and local setting [but] ... , nevertheless, free from our besetting fault of provincialism' (11). '[T]heir inspiration, for the most part,' Roberts says of both Carman and Lampman, 'is of
the soil and of the life about them.'

40 Although 'Autochthon' has suffered the same fate as 'Canada' and Roberts's
other patriotic poems, it is put at the head of the selection of his poems in
Carman and Lorne Pierce's *Our Canadian Literature* (1935) (51–2) for the
obvious reason that it spoke to and for both the mystical and the nationalistic strains of the Romantic-Victorian revival of the late 1920s and 1930s.

41 The column in which these comments appear is unsigned, but internal evidence such as references to Sharp, Sladen, and Phillips Stewart (1864–92),
whose *Poems* (1887) are lavishly praised in 'The Poetic Outlook in Canada'
(10–11) and whose achievements and premature death are the subject of a
later column by Roberts ('Modern Instances,' May 1892, 252–3), suggests
that it came from his pen.

42 This essay was probably written in the Summer of 1890, for in late July of that
year Roberts sent it to Carman for publication in the *Independent* (New York),
which Carman was then editing (see *CL* 121).

### 3. Aesthetics: Workmanship and Variety

1 As observed in the Introduction, Roberts expressed boundless admiration
for Keats in 1884. By September 1888, however, he was distancing himself
from what seemed to him, as to many Victorians, Keats's 'worship ... [of]
beauty' at the expense of concern for humanity (*CL* 40, 42, 87). In contrast,
Lampman, though he confessed in April 1894 that he had struggled for 'ten
years' to 'get ... quite clear' of Keats's 'influence,' never wavered from his
devotion to 'that marvellous person,' always referred to him in laudatory
terms in his letters and essays, and in the early 1890s wrote a monograph on
his 'Character and Poetry' (*AC* 19, and see *ER* 59–60, 128–34, 141–82).
'Keats has always had such a fascination for me and has so permeated *my*
whole mental outfit,' he told Edward William Thomson on 25 April 1894,

'that I have an idea that he has found a sort of faint reincarnation in me' (*AC* 119, and see Bentley, 'ReincarNations').

2 In his collected *Poems* (1905), thirty of Campbell's sonnets are grouped in one section (273–88), but several sonnets appear elsewhere in the book.

3 The letter, which is now in the Douglas Library at Queen's University, consists largely of a response to a sonnet entitled 'The Poet's Muse,' by Helen M. Merrill (18?–19?), who subsequently published several poems in the *Week*, a celebration in prose and poetry of *Picturesque Prince Edward County* (1892), and a small, privately printed chapbook entitled *Sandpipers and Other Poems* (1915). Scott's other comments regarding 'The Poet's Muse' are also valuable for what they reveal about his approach to the form: 'I remember reading a sonnet description of some Country house [the reference is apparently to another of Merrill's poems] which I recall the impression of and of which I would like a copy. It may be only my fancy but I think it was better even than this you have been kind enough to send me. But ... "The Poet's Muse" is excellent – there are some unimprovable lines in it such as the second. The concluding couplet is conclusive, and most couplets have a way of dangling down as if the sun had wilted them – that, in fact, is the difficult point of sonnets built on this plan ... My own opinions are: – The first eight lines should be rhymed 12211(x)2(x)21 or it is admissible to use two new rhymes in the second quatrain (xx) but I don't care for it. In the sestette you have greater liberty but the only prohibition is that you must never use a couplet to close, unless you are making an English or Shakespearean sonnett. In brief that is what I think the best sonnett. My model sonnett would be rhymed like this[:] may grace place day way race lace bay fair blow hills hair low fills or the sestette fair blow hair stow care grow.' – i.e., *abbaabba cdecde* or *cdcdcd*. The first of the two sonnets in Scott's 'The House of Dreams' rhymes *abbaabba cdcdcd*, and the second *abbaac(x)c(x)aefefef*. Like Roberts (as discussed later in the present chapter), Scott appears to have associated the sonnet with 'built' structures such as houses.

4 See, for example, the fourteen-line poems in 'The Green Oasis' and 'New England Scenes and Seasons' sections of Carman's *Poems* (1931) and in *Sanctuary: Sunshine House Sonnets* (1929). That Carman also associated the sonnet with built structures and, concomitantly, unrhymed 'sonnets' with freedom from such structures is suggested by 'Escape' (1929), the sestet of which reads:

No cabined luxury contents the soul,
Homesick for solace of its native air,
For healing of the wind among the pines,

> The stilling beauty of the clear new moon,
> The strength of hills, the joy of singing streams,
> Take any road at hand, to Out-of doors. (*PBC* 274)

A sense of Carman's attitude to the sonnet in the late 1880s and early 1890s can be gleaned from his correspondence with Lampman following the publication of *Among the Millet, and Other Poems*. Singling out 'The Truth,' he told Lampman in a letter of 28 December 1888 that he 'like[d] all the sonnets very much' but 'never could write a sonnet [him]self' (SFU). A little over two years later, two sonnets that Lampman had sent to Carman for publication in the *Independent*, 'In March' (1899) and 'Winter-Break' (1899), occasioned the following response from him in a letter of 9 February 1891: 'I like them very much; and I want to say that I think that the Shakespearian form is much better than the Italian for these transcripts from Nature that you and Roberts do so well. Roberts will not agree with me, b[ut] I dislike a landscape put in [other than (?)] Shakespearian form. "The Potato Harvest" e.g. has no possible wave beat of Emotion, no informing Surge of Spirit to justify the ... form that has been given it. The three quatrains and a couplet [of the Shakespearian sonnet] give so much more freedom. And in picturing Nature surely one must be free to select the right word, since *accuracy* is necessary. But in emotional work one may be as vagrant as he pleases at the bid of the Artistic Medium and the exigencies of rhyme and movement' (SFU). To this Lampman replied on 23 February 1891: 'I had never given much thought to the question of whether the Italian or the Shakespearean form was preferable for that kind of work, but I daresay you are right in your opinion, though as in everything else, one form or the other will immediately occur to the writer as applicable to the picture he has in mind, he can hardly define why' (quoted in Greig, 'A Checklist,' Part 1, 12). Carman's notion of a 'wave beat of Emotion' derives, of course, from Theodore Watts's 'wave theory' of the sonnet as expressed in his much-reprinted sonnet entitled 'The Sonnet's Voice: A Metrical Lesson by the Sea-Shore.' A discussion and refinement of the theory is provided by William Sharp in his Introduction to *Sonnets of This Century* (1886), lxi–lxiv, a volume that would almost certainly have been know to most if not all of the Confederation group (see also Maia Bhojwani, '"The Tides"').

5 See the editorial notes in Ross S. Kilpatrick's edition of *Orion, and Other Poems* for detailed discussions of the forms of the poems in the volume. The review of *Orion, and Other Poems* in the November 1880 number of the *Canadian Monthly* pronounces all Roberts's lyrics 'good, not one feeble or wanting in *verve*, and originality' and 'specially commend[s] those which revive ancient classical forms, those in *Sapphics* and *Choriambics*' (553).

6 See, for example, Roberts's letter to Carman of 25 October 1884, in which he encloses a 'a triolet – the first I have yet been delivered of,' adding: 'you see already the influence of one W.B.C.! ... [I]t is not perfect, but somewhat after the Carmanesque manner' (*CL* 43). The presence of a copy of the same triolet ('Pray you remember our day / In Quebec ...') together with a copy of Carman's 'On a Ball Programme,' both in Roberts's handwriting, in the Lampman Papers in the National Archives (MG 29 D59 vol. 3, 1560), indicates his desire to share his and his cousin's proficiency in the form with their fellow poet. Lampman does not appear to have tried his hand at the triolet, but the two ballades in *Among the Millet, and Other Poems* – 'Ballade of Summer's Sleep' and 'Ballade of Waiting' – were written in, respectively, October 1883 and May 1885.

7 This is A.J.M. Smith's definition of 'Light Verse' in *the Princeton Encyclopedia of Poetry and Poetics*, 447. Roberts's definition of *vers de société* as 'earnest song with a smile upon its lips' that excludes 'broad buffoonery,' 'the strong passions and the tragedies of life' ('Notes' 328) derives from that of F. Locker-Lampson in *Lyra Elegantiarum* (1867) as 'smoothly written verse, where a boudoir decorum is ... preserved; where sentiment never surges into passion, and where humour never overflows into boisterous merriment' (ix). In 'Oliver Wendell Holmes,' a commemorative poem published in the *Dial* (Chicago) and the *King's College Record* a year after Holmes's death on 7 October 1894, Roberts describes 'Humor's mild aristocrat' as the epitome of the 'gentlest breeding of the age' and characterizes the laughter engendered by his 'fun' as 'never long or loud' and frequently tinged with 'regret' and pathos (*CP* 200).

8 See Roberts's *Collected Letters*, 108, for his statement on 3 May 1889 that during a recent trip to Boston he spent 'a whole afternoon with Dr Holmes, who is good to me.'

9 On 22 March 1886, Roberts agrees with Carman's view that Fawcett is a 'fine, and a truly wonderful *artist*,' but adds that 'he is straitly limited, lacks *sustained* strength, and seems ... not always fresh and sincere. And he has little spontaneity ... He sings but rarely now-a-days – only some little highly wrought gem at rare intervals' (59); and see Roberts, 'American vers de société,' *Progress*, 5 May 1888, 6.

10 In the version of 'Edgar Fawcett' that appeared two days later, in the 28 June 1884 issue of *Current* (437–8), 'Sleep' is quoted in its entirety (437).

11 One of the earliest and most influential cries had come from Stedman in the final chapter ('The Outlook') of his *Poets of America* (1885): 'busying itself with intricacies of form and sound and imagery,' he observed in a statement that may have had a galvanic effect on Campbell, current poetry 'scarcely

deigns to reach the general heart' so that 'the people' say 'your skill is admirable ... and of interest to your own guild, but we ask that it be used to some purpose. Convey to us the intellect and passion wherewith poets are thought to be endowed, the gloom and glory of human life, the national aspiration, the pride of the past and vision of the future' (465, and see 455–65 and 465–76).

12 This remark is part of an extended commentary on form that deserves to be quoted at length, if only as an indication of the growing gulf between Collins and his old friends: 'I am still opposed to the use to which you [Lampman] and Roberts put the sonnet ... A descriptive sonnet may be beautiful but in my judgement there is no reason why a mere piece of description should be made fourteen lines any more than ten, twelve, sixteen, eighteen or one hundred. I know you will forgive me for taking the liberty of saying this when you reflect on our conversations on the subject years ago ... There is a reaction against mere form – and form and mannerism are ... about [all] that the modern school can display – and so ridiculous has the ordinary magazine poetry become in the eyes of discriminating people that it has become the stock subject for ... funny men all over the country and they are not fools and at *Harper's* and other prominent places they have practically ceased to buy verse because when most of it appears it is only made fun of. Now as I consider you all round the best poet that we have in Canada and I think without any superior living except among men of a half a century standing I put my views in this plain language. The more I write the more I learn that simplicity is essential to the highest art and the abominable vagaries of Italian verse are the very opposite of simplicity ... It is where you are simple that you are strong and that you have found the place that you occupy in our letters' (SFU).

13 The date of Lampman's essay on 'Style' is uncertain, but see the Introduction and Editorial Notes in his *Essays and Reviews,* xxvii and 260, for the evidence for situating it after 'The Modern School of Poetry in England' and before 'Two Canadian Poets: A Lecture,' probably between 12 December 1889 and 6 October 1892.

14 The 'attack' that occasioned the poem appeared in the 'Topics of the Week' section of the 7 February 1884 issue of the *Week* and reads in part: 'the death of Wendell Phillips has silenced perhaps the most eloquent voice on this Continent. It may be doubted whether any other man ever talked such nonsense in language so excellent and with a delivery so perfect ... Though he was the most intense of fanatics, there was nothing of the fanatic either in his diction or in his manner ... [His] manner was ... like that of a well-bred gentleman ..., while nobody out of Bedlam would have done the things which he

recommended for the reasons for which he recommended them. It was insanity calm and self-possessed ... It is impossible to doubt the sincerity of his philanthropy ... [b]ut there was in it a truculent, not to say sanguinary vein ... The atrocities of Fenianism were ... far too congenial to his temper.' The piece goes on to liken Phillips to Robespierre.

15 In a letter of 14 December 1892 to Wetherell, Roberts effectively agreed with Lampman's estimation of 'Canadian Streams': 'if you should wish that [for *Later Canadian Poems*], please *omit concluding stanza*, which is merely rhetoric, and poor rhetoric!' (*CL* 161). A copy of the Christmas 1892 issue of the *Dominion Illustrated* has yet to be located, but the version of 'Canadian Streams' published in the March 1895 number of the *University Monthly* contains a final stanza that can certainly be categorized as 'poor rhetoric':

> Sons of the North, to manhood grown,
> Be loyal, though ye stand alone.
>   Be true and strong, that men may know
> Canadian arms may guard their own! (*CP* 464)

Even without this stanza, 'Canadian Streams,' a stanzaic catalogue of eastern and central Canada's major rivers and their historical associations, is an orotundly bombastic product of Roberts's 'Canadianism' that may well have been intended to inspire a patriotic response to the Continental Union League, which in 1892 was attempting to rally support for Annexation in Congress. Another such product is the lyric entitled 'Canada' and beginning 'O strong hearts guarding the birthright of our glory ...,' which appeared in the April 1890 number of the *Anglo-Saxon*, an Ottawa journal 'devoted to the Interests of the Anglo-Saxon Race in Canada' and is not included in his *Collected Poems*.

16 Declaring that Aldrich is 'at his best in exquisitely delicate cameos,' Campbell proceeds to credit his poems with 'the Greek-like polish and repression of the artist' and to assert that 'he loves the well-kept lawns and parks and the cultural haunts of the old world too well to ever be a genuine American nature poet' (*MI* 160–1). 'Mr. Aldrich's verse structures are not human houses wherein men and women dwell, and suffer and enjoy like to those of Burns, Hood, and Wordsworth,' Campbell continues, 'but for the most part ... airy turrets carved with exquisite skill from gems' (see also notes 3 and 4 to the present chapter).

17 In the Introduction to his edition of *At the Mermaid Inn*, Barrie Davies argues that the phrase 'millet-like [*sic*] in its terse realism' is directed at Lampman (viii), but in a review of Davies' edition W.J. Keith points out that 'Campbell actually wrote "Millet-like" in reference to the French painter' (449). 'It

ought to be borne in mind,' adds Laurel Boone in her edition of Campbell's *Selected Poetry and Essays*, 'that Campbell may have borrowed the idea of "Millet-like" realism from W. Blackburn Harte, who (in "Some Canadian Writers of To-day" in the September 1890 number of the *New England Magazine* 21) compared poetry with the painting of Jean François Millet, reproductions of whose peasant scenes were ubiquitous; that ditties by the American versifier John Kendrick Bangs appeared regularly in important magazines such as *The Century*; that Charles G.D. Roberts's *Songs of the Common Day* ... had recently been published to wide acclaim; and that, according to Duncan Campbell Scott, despite "the constant watch that had to be kept upon [Campbell's] opinions," the column "was pretty well played out, simply because, situated as we were, there was not enough material available to keep the thing fresh"' (161, quoting Scott in McDougall, *The Poet and the Critic*, 56). It is also worth observing that, though Harte may well lie behind Campbell's 'Millet-like,' he was not alone in linking the landscape poems of Lampman and Roberts with the work of Millet and other painters of the so-called Barbizon school: see, for example, the review of *Among the Millet, and Other Poems* in the 9 February 1890 issue of the Boston *Sunday Herald*, in which Louise Chandler Moulton describes Lampman as 'above all, a landscape poet, as [Jean-Baptiste Camille] Corot was, above all, a landscape painter' and suggests that 'if Millet or Jules Breton had written their poems, instead of painting them, they would have read like these' (19).

18 As Lampman puts it in the opening paragraph of 'Style,' 'style ... might be defined as the habit or manner given to expression by the prevalence of a certain mental attitude peculiar to any individual or class of individuals or any age ... Style ... is not a quality peculiar to literature, but may be found in every sort of expression when carried to a certain point of culture, in action, in speech, in literature, and in all the arts. We know how noticeable the quality of style is in the conduct and bearing of many people who have a decided mental character and have mingled freely in the activities of the world ... In its finest development this style or manner ... is a revelation of character ... [P]erfec-tion of style ... [is] the expression of a certain poetic grace of nature' (*ER* 72).

19 For a further discussion of this equivalence, see Bentley, *The Gay]Grey Moose*, 28–30, 204–6, and 305n30.

20 See Kilpatrick's edition of *Orion, and Other Poems*, 104–5, for the description and illustration of Pozzuoli in Dana's *Manual* that probably inspired Roberts's sonnet.

21 See chapter 4 and Bentley, 'Roberts' Series of Sonnets' 398–401 for a discussion of the sexual aspect of these and related sonnets.

22 See *The Gay]Grey Moose,* 40, and Bentley, 'The Poetics of Roberts' Tantramar Space' 20–1 and 24–6.

23 Coleridge's distich is here quoted from Francis B. Gummere's *A Handbook of Poetics for Students of English Verse* (1885), 232. Although Gummere's *Handbook* was published after the composition of 'Tantramar Revisited' and Roberts's other poems in 'Ovidian elegiac metre' (see chapter 1), it is notable for being one of the texts presented for study in the third year of the 'Revised Course in English Literature,' which he began to teach at King's College in the fall of 1885 (see Roberts, 'The English Literature Course,' and letter to Carman on 22 March 1886 [*CL* 59]). In 'Roberts' Poetry of the Tantramar' (1895), Harry A. Woodworth, who appears to have lived in the Sackville area, quotes Coleridge's mimetic lines and segues to a lengthy quotation from 'Tantramar Revisited' with the comment that 'surely this is the measure that most fittingly tells the story of the rising and ebbing of the tides of Tantramar' (2).

24 To reflect Campbell's movement during the years surrounding the turn of the century from nationalism to imperialism, the dates given here are those of first publication as provided in Boone's edition of Campbell's *Selected Poetry and Essays* 211–21.

25 See Bentley, *The Gay]Grey Moose,* 4–6 and 15–16, for an elaboration of the consonances and equivalencies mentioned here and later in the paragraph.

26 See Bentley, 'Half Passion and Half Prayer.'

27 These remarks occur in the context of Roberts's assertion, perhaps partly in response to the nationalistic mood of the mid-1920s, that *The Book of the Native* was his 'first really significant volume' and that it 'contains more of the poems that [he] consider[ed] significant' than any of his other books' ('Interview' 74).

28 In the 'At the Mermaid Inn' column for 23 April 1892, Duncan Campbell Scott provides an assessment of Marston's work based on Louise Chandler Moulton's edition of his *A Last Harvest: Lyrics and Sonnets from the Book of Love* (1891) and expresses a strong preference for his 'garden fancies' (flower poems) over his sonnets, which he sees as too obviously derivative of those in Rossetti's *The House of Life* (1870, 1881) (59–60). Scott's comment in a letter of 12 April 1896 to J.E. Wetherell that 'for the most part the work' anthologized in his selection of *Later American Poems* (1896) 'lacks any spontaneity' (UT) indicates his agreement with Lampman, if not Campbell, that contemporary American poets were placing too much emphasis on workmanship and form.

29 See my Introduction to *The Story of an Affinity,* xix–xxii.

30 It is possible that Lampman's attention was drawn to the April 1884 number

of the *Manhattan* by a note in the 19 March 1884 issue of the *Toronto Evening News* that quotes the Irving passage with the comment that it 'applies as forcibly to Canada as to the Northern States.' It is also possible that this note was the sole source of his knowledge of the Irving passage.

31 In a letter of 19 May 1892 to Horace Elisher Scudder (1838–1902), a reader for both the *Atlantic Monthly* and the publishing house of Houghton, Mifflin, Lampman states that he 'know[s] quite well how difficult it is to induce a publisher to take up a volume of miscellaneous poems by an unknown writer,' and, in a letter of 4 December 1894 to the same correspondent, he remarks of 'A Century of Sonnets' that he 'could not make any selection from [his] work which would be more varied or more interesting ... Certainly these sonnets ... [deal] with a lot of subjects – and as regards workmanship [he] could do nothing better' (quoted in Greig, 'A Checklist,' Part 2, 13, 15).

32 See Carman's *Letters,* 52 and 59.

33 For example, the review in the 14 April 1894 issue of the *Athenaeum* (London) compliments Carman on the 'wise restraint' in collecting only poems 'in the same key' and concludes by expressing a preference for his 'spontaneous' lyricism over Aldrich's 'ornate finish': 'his form, with its fluctuating line, is much finer than the rigid angles and too careful decoration of ... others ... Mr. Carman writes blithely, and with the ease of the true artist' (473). The review in the 7 June 1894 issue of the *Nation* (New York) takes a somewhat different tack, complimenting Carman on his use of the 'local coloring' of the Maritimes and observing that 'he has that lyrical note and that power of imagination which lend to his poetry a haunting quality – a trait sure to secure a permanent charm beyond all wit and wisdom' (433). By comparison, 'Pharos' (Laura Bradshaw Durand), writing in the 10 March 1894 issue of the *Globe* was much more negative, judging the poems deficient in 'strength, ... dignity, and coherence' and finding in the title poem especially the baleful result of being 'delirious with the cadences of words' (6).

34 This information comes from Joe W. Kraus's *Messrs. Copeland & Day,* 131, and Sidney Kramer's *History of Stone and Kimball and Herbert S. Stone and Company,* 203. Initially, there were misgivings about the saleability of *Low Tide on Grand Pré,* at least in England, for, as H. Pearson Gundy notes in Carman's *Letters,* Carman's English publisher, the firm of David Nutt, 'agreed to import from Webster 250 copies of *Low Tide on Grand Pré* in sheets, to be followed by a second order if the book sold,' which the scion of the firm, Alfred Trubner Nutt, doubted because its '"art is too delicately personal ... [and its title] at once too long and too undistinctive"' (*L* 61).

35 Of the importance of Transcendentalism for Carman's thinking from at least the late 1880s onwards there can be no doubt. In 'The World of Books' column in *Progress* on 14 December 1889, he says of Emerson's *Essays* (1803–82) that 'there is perhaps no book that one would more gladly see put within the reach of a larger circle of readers' and confesses that 'when one has been a disciple [of Emerson] it is hard not to be an apostle also.' In assessing Emerson's message to an 'age dispirited and jaded ... by too long continued and curious thought,' Carman could almost be glossing 'Low Tide on Grand Pré': 'he had no fixed and inter-dependent scheme of philosophy. He himself says that if the fates were to offer him his choice of gifts he would say, "Give me continuity." He lives by intuition, takes the light as it comes to him. "Into every intelligence there is a door which is never closed, through which the Creator passes." This is the fundamental note of Emerson's faith, so that one may say that he has the first essential quality of the poet; he speaks from within. Logic and expediency are for all of us; we can draw our own conclusions "well enough, given the premises." But we look for higher wisdom than this from the poet. If he is not truly inspired, if he does not utter truths which we feel to be "beyond the reaches of our soul" and yet at once endorse as valid for ourselves ... then he is not truly a poet, but only a maker of rhymes, a juggler and a charlatan.'

**4. Natural Environments**

1 See also Hingston, 102–10, for a discussion of the actual and supposed effects of cold on the physical and mental faculties.
2 Carman also observed that two species of birds, the bluebird and the oriole, are present in New England but not New Brunswick and laments the absence in April in New Canaan, Connecticut of what 'Lampman so beautifully called "The hopeful, solemn, many-murmured night"' – that is, 'the sound of the brooks of melting snow pouring through the starry stillness' (*L* 174). Of course, bluebirds and orioles do visit Ontario, and 'brooks of melting snow' can be heard in other parts of New England.
3 Lampman's copy of *Birds and Poets, with Other Papers* is now in the collection of Michael Gnarowski in Kemptville, Ontario.
4 In *Fresh Fields* (1874), Burroughs, who visited England in 1871 and 1882, notes the absence of 'the voice of frog or toad' in that country (4: 194).
5 To judge by Roberts's 'I grieve for my poor frog' in a letter of 22 June 1887 to Richard Watson Gilder, and his notation 'Frog ret 6/16/87' on the letter (*CL* 66), he had composed a poem entitled 'Frog' (perhaps an early version of 'Frogs' [1893], which was first published in the *Dominion Illustrated Magazine*

in November 1888) before reading *Among the Millet, and Other Poems*, which he received some time between 16 November and 18 December 1888 (see *CL* 93, 97). 'When Milking-Time Is Done' (1893) was first published in the July 1889 number of the *Youth's Companion*. It is in a letter to Gilder on 14 August 1887 that Roberts first mentions that he is 'planning a series of sonnets of "The Common Day"' (*CL* 67).

6 Hingston refers to several 'members of the animal and vegetable kingdoms' in his discussion of spring but makes only passing mention of the 'harsh gutteral sounds' of the frog (46–7). He does, however, describe April as the month that 'divides the extremes [of cold and heat] equally' and 'the only month which may in truth be called a spring month' in Canada (44).

7 See Bentley, 'Watchful Dreams.' In his father's copy of C. Crispi Sallussii, *De Catellinae Conjuratione Belloque Jugurthmo Historiae*, which is now among the Lampman Papers in the National Archives (*MG* 29 D59 vol. 8), either Lampman or his father (who wrote poetry under the pseudonym 'Crowquill') draws attention to a note describing the four, fifteen-year 'stages' into which '"the most correct Roman writers"' divide human life: '*pueritia* was within fifteen; *adolescentia* within thirty; *juvenius* within forty-five; and *senectus* comprised the remaining period of life' (11–12n, endpaper). Lampman's conception of the relationship between the seasons and human activities may have been partly or even greatly affected by Keats's 'Four seasons ...' sonnet, where 'the mind of man' has its 'Spring, when fancy clear / Takes in all beauty with an easy span,' its 'Summer, when luxuriously / Spring's honey'd cud of youthful thought he loves / To ruminate, and by such dreaming high / Is nearest unto heaven,' its 'Autumn, when his wings / He furleth close; contented to look / On mists in idleness – to let fair things / Pass by unheeded,' and its 'Winter ... of pale misfeature' (423).

8 See especially *The Prelude*, 1:80–93, 250–4, 390–400, 425–63; 2:310–52; 3:177–90, 323–38, 370–87.

9 *Locusts and Wild Honey* includes Burroughs's account of his 1877 trip to Canada, during which, in addition to visiting the usual touristic sights on the St Lawrence ('a chain of Homeric sublimes from beginning to end') and the Saguenay (a river that 'suggest[s] something apocryphal and antemundane'), he visited a wilderness lake that he describes in terms that may have helped to shape Lampman's 'The Lake in the Forest' (1900): 'I was alone with the spirit of the forest-bound lake and felt its presence and magnetism ... [A] lake is the ear as well as the eye of the forest ... Nature ebbs and flows ... [There is] unity of movement in the two elements, air and water' (3: 192, 224, 210; and see *P* 313–16).

10 In the title essay in *Birds and Poets, with Other Papers*, Burroughs observes that

the 'golden-crowned thrush, or oven bird ... frequently sings on the wings up aloft after the manner of the lark. Starting from its low perch, it rises in a spiral flight far above the tallest trees, and breaks out in a clear, ringing, ecstatic song ... ceasing almost before you have noticed it' (6:16).

11 See note 7, above.

12 See also 'The Return of the Birds' in *Wake-Robin*, where Burroughs associates the robin with the 'universal awakening and rehabilitation of nature' in spring (1: 2).

13 A copy of Lampman's membership certificate from the Audubon Society is in the Lampman Papers at Simon Fraser University.

14 See also *MI*, 13, for Torrey's knowledge of the 'inner life and domestic characters of birds.'

15 Compare the opening sentences of the passage with the opening lines of Roberts's sonnet: 'With shy bright clamour the live brooks sparkle and run. / Freed flocks confer about the farmstead ways' (*CP* 120).

16 See also 'The Sower,' where the 'plodding churl' also 'treads the glebe' (*CP* 82).

17 See Bentley, 'Roberts' Series of Sonnets.'

18 In the final paragraph of 'Nature and Poets,' Burroughs gives verbal renditions of the song of several other birds and quotes an anonymous poem entitled 'A Masque of Poets' in which each of the three stanzas concludes with a four-line rendering of the robin's song (see 7: 109–11).

19 Although Arnold, whose phrase this of course is, and Burroughs may seem far apart, they had a mediator in the person of John Campbell Shairp (see Introduction and chapter 5), whose *On Poetic Interpretation of Nature* was advertised, interestingly enough, among the 'Out-Door Books' published by Houghton, Mifflin of New York (see, for example, the endpages of Leland's *The Algonquin Legends of New England*).

20 In fact, Burroughs frequently allows the partridge to drum in the spring: see, for example, 1:8, 11, 63–4, 2:101, and 6:109.

21 Admirer that he was of both Emerson and Burroughs, Carman would almost certainly have been aware that Emerson's death on 27 April 1882 called forth a eulogy from Burroughs in which he envisages his mentor in 'the bosom of the great Mother on this April day' and meditates at some length on the appropriateness of the month for his death: 'it was fit that he should pass in April, the month of Shakespeare's birth and death, the month that opens the door to the more genial season ... He was an April man, an awakener, full of light, full of prophecy, full of vernal freshness and curiosity' (quoted in Barrus 1:237).

22 See also Carman's letter of 30 April 1919, where he comments on the 'sick-

ness of heart' that he sometimes experiences in April and envisages camping and walking in the woods in May as a cure for 'regretful thoughts' (*L* 174).

23 When Burroughs did address such matters in such essays as 'Analogy' (1862) and 'Analogy – True and False' (1902), he shows himself to be a transcendentalist but not a believer in immortality, asserting in the former that 'material objects [are] ... symbols of the infinite' and in the latter that arguments for the 'survival of the soul' on the basis of natural processes are invalid (Westbrook 12, 116).

24 See Bentley, 'Threefold in Wonder: Bliss Carman's *Sappho: One Hundred Lyrics*.'

25 If the relationship between the following passages is not coincidental, then Carman's understanding of 'nature religion' was indebted to Müller:

> The changes of nature ... must have been considered [by the ancient Greeks] as typifying the changes in the lot of man ... [W]hen the goddess of inanimate nature had become the queen of the dead, it was a natural analogy which must have early suggested itself, that the return of Persephone to the world of light also denoted a renovation of life and a new birth to men. Hence the Mysteries of Demeter, and especially those celebrated at Elusis, ... inspired the most elevated and animating hopes with regard to the condition of the soul after death. (Müller 1:305–6)

> [The ancient Greeks and Britons] would grasp quickly at the poetic analogy between the life of man and the life of nature through the season's progress. Seeing all nature die down and revive, they would eagerly guess at a future for the soul, an eternal springtime supervening upon the autumn of mortality. (Carman, *The Friendship of Art* 258–9)

Other sources of Carman's knowledge of 'natural religion' might have included Andrew Lang's *Myth, Ritual and Religion* (1887) and the essay entitled 'The Myth of Demeter and Persephone' in Pater's *Greek Studies* (1895).

26 See also Lampman's heavily Wordsworthian 'Winter-Store' (1895) for spring and summer as the seasons for gathering and storing materials (memories) for later use (*P* 165–73).

27 This information is given in the 'Chit-Chat and Chuckles' column of the *Critic* (Halifax) on 25 January 1889 (3). In a letter of 9 April 1889 to Horace Elisher Scudder, Carman describes the poem as a 'trilogy' that would include 'six lyric interludes and preludes' (*L* 26).

28 No doubt, Roberts, whose essay 'Pastoral Elegies' was published in the *New Princeton Review* in May 1883, greatly aided Carman in his understanding of the components of the pastoral elegy.

29 Probably one reason for Carman's failure to complete 'Corydon' was the poor reception of 'Corydon: An Elegy' in England. As Muriel Miller puts it, '*The Spectator* (London) and *The Academy* (London) ... reviews' that followed 'in [the] train' of its publication in the *Universal Review* 'dashed Carman's spirit to the ground. *The Spectator*'s critic "pulled it to pieces ...," charging the author with every crime in the literary decalogue [and] ... in his review of it in ... [the] *Academy* [William] Sharp admitted that there was a certain "baleful obscurity" in the poem which the gifted young Canadian had not yet disciplined out of his work' (62).

30 'The first part is mournful merely, and pretends to offer no escape for emotion,' Carman told Scudder. 'Th[e] second part suggests satisfaction in the power of the spirit to mould itself with art, and the final return to nature – sleep, oblivion. It ends, however, ... with some slight desire for more than this' (*L* 26).

31 The terminology of the passages quoted is as complex as it is awkward: 'goldmouthed' is a translation of 'Chrysostom,' and an 'essoiner' is 'one who offers an excuse for the absence of another' in court (*OED*). Carman's reference to 'the High Court of Night' and his use of the term '*de servitio Regis*' in the lines surrounding 'essoiner' provide the word with the legal context that it requires. Among Carman's many occupations after his return to Fredericton in the summer of 1883 was a brief stint in the fall of 1884 as an articling student in a law firm (see *CL* 45).

32 These quotations are taken from trial sheets for the projected book in the Rufus Hathaway Collection at the University of New Brunswick.

33 See Westbrook, 17–19, for a discussion of the relationship between the thrushes of Burroughs and Whitman based on the fact that the two men became friends in 1863 and 'Whitman gave credit to Burroughs not only for the idea of using the thrush [in the elegy] but also for information about its habits and the quality of its song' (19).

34 In *The Rough Rider and Other Poems*, the final two lines of the poem read: 'Our minister here, entrenched in doctrine, may know no doubt upon Easter Eve. / And when it comes to the crucial question, Doctor, you skeptic, you too believe!' (36). In a letter of 30 January 1917, Carman told Odell Shepard that he considered '"On Ponus Ridge," "Resurgam," and "Easter Eve" in ... *The Rough Rider* ... the most definite presentations of what [he had] come to hold concerning the high (and dark) themes of man and nature and human fate. As poems, too, they are as good as any of the nature things, with the possible exception of some brief lyrics' (*L* 241–2). 'How do you like the new ending of 'Easter Eve'?' he asked Rufus Hathaway on 15 April 1922; 'I always disliked the old ending – too much in the familiar Vagabondia manner' (*L* 286).

35 Carman's letters of 1927–9 to Margaret Lawrence (1896–1973) provide a good window into his later ideas, which are briefly discussed in chapter 6 of the present study.

36 The name 'Marjorie,' 'Marjory,' or 'Margery,' which, 'in the eighteenth and nineteenth centuries, was used almost exclusively by poor country people' (Opie 298), was a favourite of both Carman and Roberts. In Carman's 'A Sea Child' (1897), it is attached to 'child Marjory,' who loses her 'lover' at sea and whose daughter 'Hath in her veins ... / The glad undomitable sea, / The strong white sun' (*Poems* 121); and in Roberts's 'The Tide of Tantramar' (1893) it is given to a woman who is killed with her lover when a dyke bursts (see *CP* 170–3). Miller notes that 'A Sea Child' is a compression of 'Marjory,' which Carman published as a broadsheet in 1889 (284n35).

37 The letter by 'W' is reprinted in the Addenda to the 1894 edition of Wicksteed's *Waifs in Verse and Prose* 302–3.

38 'The Night Express' was first published in the 6 October 1892 issue of the *Independent* (1).

39 Roberts, did, however, think that the poem had one 'serious' 'verbal blemish': 'Marjory's "perfect cheek" ... [T]hat line is just the one that the Philistines would delight to worry! There is no use giving them occasion to make merry, as the line does not seem to me to be in any way one of your inevitable ones' (*CL* 154).

40 On 31 October 1892 Roberts added that '"The Night Express" is a mighty fine and delightful new thing. Daring. I like every word of it save the last line, – which, it seems to me, needlessly asserts what has already been clearly indicated. But in this criticism I have no confidence ... "Night Express" ... will find many attempting imitators amongst thy disciples, who will be many' (*CL* 156). It is in the last line of the poem that the 'Driver' of the night express is named as 'God' (*Independent*, 6 October 1892, 1).

41 Lampman probably had in mind Carman's 'Olaf Hjörward,' a celebration of the physical and spiritual renovation produced by April in the European 'Norland,' which was published in the 31 March 1892 number of the *Independent* (1) and not included in any of the poet's collections. 'I like the "Olaf Hjörward" much,' he told Carman on 6 April 1892, 'especially some things in it, which are very solemnly beautiful' (Ware, ed. 'Letters' 61).

42 Roberts twice notes the debt of 'The Hermit-Thrush' to Carman (see *CL* 152, 154) but makes no mention of Burroughs or, indeed, Whitman.

## 5. Therapeutic Nature

1 See Parker, *Mind Cure in New England from the Civil War to World War I, passim*; Meyer, *The Positive Thinkers: Religion As Pop Psychology from Mary Baker Eddy,*

especially the early chapters; and Lears, *No Place of Grace: Antimodernism and the Transformation of American Culture, 1880–1920, passim*, but especially xiii–58. See also Horatio W. Dresser's *A History of the New Thought Movement;* Barbara Sicherman's *The Quest for Mental Health in America, 1880–1917;* and my own 'Carman and Mind Cure: Theory and Technique.'

2 Among the other contributors were J.W. Bengough (1851–1923), J.G. Bourinot, John Reade, George Stewart, Agnes Maule Machar, and Susan Frances Harrison – a veritable galaxy of the intellectual and literary stars of the day.

3 In 'Needless Noises – Effects of Noises on the Nervous System' in the January 1891 issue of the *Canada Health Journal,* a plea is made for efforts to 'suppress the many needless noises heard almost everywhere, not only in cities but in the smaller towns and villages' because of their effect on the 'nervous system.' 'Of "the new diseases that human life evolves in its progress," various forms of nervous irritability and weakness are distinctly traceable to noise,' continues the article (which may well be by Playter); '"the slow and almost insensible influence of noise on the nervous system tends to wear and break it down. Neuralgia, stimulant-craving, restlessness, and over-alertedness of a purposeless character commonly known as 'fidgets' are some of the evils directly caused by it." These evils are doubtless commonly intensified by inheritance in the next generation' (6). Among the other symptoms of 'American nervousness' that Beard identifies are 'dyspepsia,' 'insomnia,' indecisiveness, hopelessness, and numerous phobias, including a fear of 'open spaces,' 'closed spaces,' aloneness, 'society,' 'fears,' and, most alarmingly, 'everything' (*American Nervousness* 5–8).

4 The editor of the 1971 reprint edition of Beard's *A Practical Treatise on Nervous Exhaustion (Neurasthenia),* Marvin Sukov, notes that 'less than three months after [it] was published [in 1880] a second printing was required' and that 'altogether the book went through five editions, the last of which was enlarged and edited by Dr. A.P. Rockwell [in 1905] well after Beard's death in 1883' (2a). *American Nervousness* (1881) is a popularization of *A Practical Treatise,* and it too went through several printings. Mitchell's *Wear and Tear,* which is very likely the primary source of Oxley's 'Busy People' (see note 5, below), was reprinted eight times between 1871 and 1897, when a 'thoroughly revised' edition was issued. The rest-cure has of course been made infamous by feminist writings on 'The Yellow Wallpaper' (which was first published in the *New England Magazine* in 1891), by Charlotte Perkins Gilman.

5 It is possible, however, that the phrase 'overtaskèd brain' was suggested by a source other than Arnold – perhaps, indeed, *Wear and Tear,* where, although Mitchell is concerned primarily with 'men whose brains are engaged con-

stantly in the higher forms of mental labour' such as scientists, scholars, and poets, 'the difficulty of arresting at will the overtaskèd brain belongs more or less to every man who overuses this organ, and is the well-known initial symptom of numerous morbid states' (19). '[E]very sufferer has a remedy which he finds more or less available,' adds Mitchell, and 'this usually consists in some form of effort to throw the thoughts off the track upon which they are moving' (19–20).

6  'Wordsworth's poetry is great,' states Arnold in his Introduction to *Poems of Wordsworth* (1879), 'because of the extraordinary power with which [he] feels the joy offered to us in nature, the joy offered to us in the simple primary affections and duties; and because of the extraordinary power with which, in case after case, he shows us this joy, and renders it so as to make us share it' (*Complete Prose* 9:51).

7  It is not beyond the bounds of possibility that at least part of the program for 'Heat' was provided by Mitchell's account near the end of *Wear and Tear* of the symptoms and cure for 'nervous exhaustion': 'day after day ... work grows more trying ... At last come giddiness, dimness of sight [see stanza 1] ... and growing difficulty in the use of mental powers. So that to attempt a calculation, or any form of intellectual labor, is to insure a sense of distress in the head [see stanzas 2–4] ... [W]hile there are certain aids for [these and other] symptoms in the shape of drugs, there is only one real remedy ... [C]omplete and prolonged cessation from work is the one thing needful. Not a week, or a month, but probably a year or more of utter idleness may be absolutely essential ... We [Americans] probably idle less and play less than any other race, and [this] ... leaves the man of business with no inducement to abandon ... unceasing labor ...' (73–4). In his 'At the Mermaid Inn' column for 25 March 1893, Lampman may be drawing on Mitchell's argument that 'climatic peculiarities' in the North-eastern States are fundamentally responsible for the nervous ailments that he, like Beard, regarded as especially prevalent among Americans (see *Wear and Tear* 34–5) when he remarks that the 'superstitious value many people attach to hard work – mere sordid labour – ' is a 'monstrously puritanical notion' characteristic of 'northern lands' where 'the idea of recreation, of any period of idleness, is shocking' and 'to grant a holiday is almost to overturn the world' (281). The purpose of Lampman's column is to propose that 'whenever the weather rises to a certain grade of excellence ... all places of business should be closed and all workers permitted to go forth' (282). See Paul Fussell's chapter 'On the New Heliophily' in *Abroad: British Literary Traveling between the Wars*, 137–41, for a discussion of the emergence of twentieth-century heliotherapies from developments in the 1890s of which Whitman 'can be considered a precursor'

(138). For a superb analysis of the psychological movement and formalistic effects of 'Among the Timothy,' see Trehearne.

8  Given the religious cast of 'August Reverie,' it may owe a debt to another very popular mind-cure manual, *Mental Medicine* (1872; fifteen editions by 1885), by the Reverend W.F. Evans (1817–89), whose admixture of Christianity and Neoplatonism aims to cure 'the diseases of the present age' by 'impart[ing] a sanative spiritual virtue' and putting people in 'harmony and sympathy with external nature' and the 'grand symphony of [a] universe' pervaded by an 'ever-present spiritual life' (18, 19, 148, 135).

9  In *A Practical Treatise on Nervous Exhaustion (Neurasthenia)*, Beard uses the term 'neurasthenia' to subsume 'general debility,' 'nervous prostration,' 'nervous debility,' 'nervous asthenia,' and various other diagnoses, including 'nervous dyspepsia' (see note 3 and the discussion of Carman, above) (7). He also asserts in the same work that 'it cannot be denied that in America there are climatic and business and social environments to the influence of which the nervous system is peculiarly susceptible' and attributes the 'comparative rar[ity]' of 'nervous diseases' in Canada to less pronounced 'nervous development and activity' (256, 245).

10  Contributory and continuing causes of Roberts's depression were domestic problems and the unexpected death of his younger brother, Goodridge Bliss Roberts, on 4 Febrary 1892. For more details, see my 'Charles G.D. Roberts and William Wilfred Campbell,' 83–4.

11  The book was published in New York by Appleton, which had previously published a series of scenic books, including *Picturesque America; or, The Land We Live In* (1872–4), the model for *Picturesque Canada*. (For a brief history of the House of Appleton, see Tebbell 2:203–17.) It was also published in England by William Heinemann circa 1892 and thus secondarily directed towards a British audience.

12  Some examples may be found in Bentley, *Mimic Fires*, 25, 52, 174.

13  In her *History of the Dominion Atlantic Railway* (1936), Marguerite Woodworth places *The Land of Evangeline and the Gateways Thither* in the context of the amalgamation of the Windsor and Annapolis and the Yarmouth and Annapolis Railways as the Dominion Atlantic Railway in 1893 and the subsequent decision of the new company both to exploit the Boston-Yarmouth service of the Yarmouth Steamship Company and to purchase its own boats in order to further increase the lucrative 'tourist traffic': 'throughout 1895 and 1896 the DAR prepared the ground for the advent of their new boats. A New England Agency was installed ... [in] Boston ... , large sums were spent for newspaper publicity; supplies of literature, pamphlets, etc ... were printed in England and sent over for distribution; Charles G.D. Roberts ... was commissioned to

write a railway guide that would appeal to prospective tourists; the Maritime Express Co. was formed (April 1895) ... operating Halifax-Yarmouth-Boston-Saint John and connecting lines' (116). Woodworth also chronicles the 'phenomenal increase' in tourist traffic between New England and Nova Scotia in the early 1890s as a result of 'the co-operation between the province's railway companies and the introduction of steel steamers on the Boston-Yarmouth route' (115–16).

14 See chapter 3 for Roberts's earlier use of the word 'tonic' in regard to the climate of the Maritimes. The notice of *The Land of Evangeline and the Gateways Thither* in the 14 November 1895 number of the *Independent* describes Nova Scotia as 'that fascinating land of cool summers, mild winters and everlasting peace the whole year round' (20). The review of Roberts's *Songs of the Common Day and Ave: An Ode for the Shelley Centenary* (1893) in *Poet-Lore* ([Boston] 6 (1894): 370) concludes: 'the salt tides of the Northern seas fluctuate through these songs, breathing from them a spirit of health that heartens their melancholy; and two or three Indian legends, such as the Micmac tale of "The Succour of Gloskap," or a more rollicking country ballad, like "The Wood Frolic," add to the character of the whole.' The review also remarks on Roberts's 'praise for the Canadian mother country that should be proud of him' and on 'the series of homely bucolics that opens the volume,' calling such sonnets as 'The Sower' and 'The Cow Pasture' 'pictures that sensitively and truly mirror rustic scenes' and 'lyrics that rarely fail to sheathe a deeper thought.'

15 For a further discussion of ways in which Campbell's Imperialism and his therapeutic notions are reflected in his scenic guides, see my 'Charles G.D. Roberts and William Wilfred Campbell,' 90–4.

16 First published in 1878 as *The Queen of Bohemia: A Novel,* Joseph Hatton's somewhat racy work was reissued in 1882 as *The Queen of Bohemia: A Story of English Life and Manners.*

17 By 1891 (and under the abbreviated title *Delsarte System of Expression*), Stebbins's book had gone to four editions. It was joined in 1893 by Abbé Delaumosne's *Delsarte System of Oratory.* Two articles on 'Delsartean Physical Culture' by Agnes Crawford (18?–?) in the 22 August and 5 September 1891 numbers of *Saturday Night* gave Canadians succinct descriptions of the Delsarte system. See also the humorous poem entitled 'The Doings of Delsarte' by Eugene Field (18?–?) in the 26 March 1893 number of the same magazine (3).

18 The copyright pages of reprintings of *Last Songs from Vagabondia* give December 1900 as the date of the first edition of 1,000 copies (subsequent reprintings were in May 1901 [1,000], November 1903 [750], November 1905 [750], March 1908 [1,000], and September 1911 [350]). These and the simi-

lar figures for *Songs from Vagabondia* and *More Songs from Vagabondia* indicate that not all readers shared the reviewers' negative assessments of the *Vagabondia* volumes. The authorship of the poems in the second and third volumes is indicated in the table of contents.

19 See Ann Douglas, *The Feminization of American Culture.*

20 See my 'Threefold in Wonder' and 'Carman and Mind Cure' for discussions of the unitrinian and mind-cure aspects of *Sappho: One Hundred Lyrics.*

## 6: Supernaturalism

1 See Scott's 'At the Mermaid Inn' column for 9 July 1892 for a passing reference to his father's affiliation with the 'Wesleyan Church' (*MI* 107); and the letter to E.K. Brown quoted later in this chapter. Part of Scott's schooling was at the Wesleyan Academy in Stanstead Quebec.

2 One of Archibald Lampman Senior's poems, 'For Bella at Haverstraw on the Hudson,' is dated 'April 24th [1859?]' and preserved with a letter from him to Susanna Gesner dated 1859 in the Lampman Papers at Simon Fraser University (see Sommers 167–9). Other materials by Lampman's father, including a long poem entitled 'Mountain Point, Niagara T[ownshi]p,' which is signed 'Crowquill' and dated 'Toronto 10 July 1882,' are held by the National Archives.

3 *The Teetotaler's Hand-Book. In Four Parts. Being a Compilation of Valuable Information for the Use of All Classes* (1860); *Letters on Superior Education: In Its Relation to the Progress and Permanency of Wesleyan Methodism* (1860); *Report Relating to the Affairs of the Oka Indians Made to the Superintendent General of Indian Affairs* (1883); and *Hours with St. Paul and the Expositors of His First Epistle to the Corinthians, More Particularly Chapters III, IX, XIII* (1888).

4 As Carman puts it in 'Louise Imogen Guiney,' an essay on the American poet in the 15 November 1894 number of the *Chap-Book:* 'if the revelations of knowledge mean for [the artist in the turbulence of our days] the dissolution of old faiths and historic creeds, he must not despond; he must have merely so much faith the more, believing that what has come safely so far may be trusted to journey to the end without any anxiety of his. He must know that while dogma, which is only fossilized creed, can never be anything more than a curiosity, the need of worship is a craving of the human heart, a living desire neither to be ridiculed nor overthrown' (29). For a discussion of some of the aesthetic implications of agnosticism, see Bentley, 'From Allegory to Indeterminacy.'

5 This perception is drawn from the review of *Lake Lyrics and Other Poems* in the 21 December 1889 issue of *Saturday Night* by Andrew Stevenson (18?–?), who

had worked with Roberts on the *Week* and supported his bid for a professorship at the University of Toronto (see Heather Murray 25).

6 See Campbell's *Selected Poetry and Essays*, 163–5, for both the manuscript and the published versions of Campbell's rejoinder.

7 In *Selected Poetry and Essays*, Laurel Boone notes that in its 21 May 1900 issue the *Ottawa Evening Journal* included the information that 'The Lazarus of Empire' '"was written in the autumn of 1894, and prior to the great incidents that have happened since"' (212).

8 All three of these poems were published by Campbell in privately printed pamphlets in 1912 and 1913 (see *SPE* 222–4). Boone provides a valuable discussion of 'The Tragedy of Man' and its context in 'Evolution and Idealism' and has done an equally valuable service in printing large portions of the work in her edition of Campbell's *Selected Poetry and Essays*.

9 In the final stanzas of 'The Unsleeping,' which was published in the *Chap-Book* on 15 May 1894, Roberts envisages a time when 'Space, in the dim pre-destined hour, / Shall crumble like a ruined tower' and 'I only, with unfaltering eye, / Shall watch the dreams of God go by' (179), a statement that combines egoism and audacity in a way that his father must have found astonishing (though see E.M. Pomeroy 210 on his tolerance).

10 Quoted by John Robert Sorfleet in his Introduction to Carman's *Poems*, 6. Sorfleet's essays on the sources and development of Carman's thought, particularly his 'Transcendentalist, Mystic, and Evolutionary Idealist: Bliss Carman, 1886–1894,' are indispensible.

11 This is the original title of 'The Great Return' (1904), which, according to Muriel Miller, was written in 1890 and first published as a broadsheet in December 1891 (160).

12 The *Mahogany Tree* was published between January and July 1892. Its editors and contributors included both Day and Herbert Copeland, who together would form the publishing house of Copeland and Day (of which more above). Its statement of principles and purposes appeared in its inaugural issue, dated 2 January 1892.

13 The *Knight Errant*, which also numbered Copeland and Day among its progenitors, appeared between April 1892 and July 1893. Its moving spirit was the American architect and convert to Anglo-Catholicism Ralph Adams Cram (1827–1942), and it numbered among its contributors Ruskin's North American disciple Charles Eliot Norton (1827–1908), with whom Carman began to correspond on 7 March 1892 (see *L* 43 and Miller 69–70), and other 'Boston medievalists' (Lears 204), including Guiney and Bertram Grosvenor Goodhue (1869–1924), with whom Carman would travel to England and France in the spring and early summer of 1896 (see *L* 106–10

and Miller 150–2). The best discussion of the Boston renaissance of the *fin de siècle* remains Stephen Maxfield Parrish's 1954 Ph.D. thesis, 'Currents of the Nineties in Boston and London: Fred Holland Day, Louise Imogen Guiney, and Their Circle'; but see also Lears 203–6. In 'Louise Imogen Guiney,' Carman excerpts her poem 'The Knight Errant' and identifies 'two characteristics' that make 'her most worthy of distinction as a poet': a 'pagan quality of joy, which she must inherit from our New England saint, Emerson' and 'a rich and anything but modern quality of style entirely her own, yet one whose seeds must have been sown by those robust and individual poets of the Elizabethan times' (34–5).

14 It is possible that Roberts's interest in Lilith was also piqued by *The Soul of Lilith* (1892), a novel by 'Maria Corelli' (Mary Mackay) that uses the myth of Adam's first wife to explore the theme of life after death.

15 See also Robert's 1893 essay 'Pastoral Elegies,' 365–6.

16 For further discussion of the theological aspects of 'In the wide awe and wisdom of the night ...' and other sonnets in the context of the overall concerns and movement of the 'Songs of the Common Day' series, see Bentley, 'Roberts' Series of Sonnets,' 405–10.

17 'In the wide awe and wisdom of the night ...' was first published in the *Independent* on 11 December 1890 and reprinted in the *King's College Record* in November 1892.

18 See Pomeroy 85–6 for the 'psychic research' at Kingscroft. When Roberts, Carman, and Hovey published their joint composition 'Immanence' in the January 1894 number of the *King's College Record*, they left readers to determine from 'internal evidence alone' which poet had composed each of its stanzas, thus deflecting responsibility for any of them from Roberts:

> I come before the coming of the dawn,
> In the withdrawal I am not withdrawn,
> I am the spilth oblivion leaves behind
> And for my feet the strewings of death are strewn.
>
> Not only in the cataract and the thunder,
> Or in the deeps of Man's uncharted soul,
> But in the dew-star dwells alike the Wonder
> And in the whirling dust-mote the Control.
>
> Enthroned beyond the world although He is,
> Yet is the world in Him, and He in it.
> The self-same God in yonder sunset glows
> That kindled in the lords of holy writ. (quoted in Miller 110)

The presence of the second stanza of 'Immanence' in Roberts's *Selected Poems* (1936), 153, indicates that it is the one by Roberts (see also W.J. Keith, *Charles G.D. Roberts* 35–6, and August Leisner, *passim*).

19 For further discussion of the syncretic aspect of 'New York Nocturnes,' see Bentley, 'Half Passion and Half Prayer.' See also Roberts's '"My Religion": A Personal Confession of Religious Experiences and Convictions' for his reconciliation of Christianity with a theosophical belief in the 'evolution of the spirit through many earthly lives' and 'planes of perfection.'

20 Carman's correspondence collected in *Letters to Margaret Lawrence* provides many insights into his religious and spiritual development after the turn of the century, as, of course, do many of his other letters from that relatively uncharted period in H. Pearson Gundy's edition of his *Letters*.

21 Miller (148) quotes two positive reviews of *Behind the Arras* in English periodicals, one by Arthur Quiller-Couch. The review of the volume in the 11 January 1896 issue of *Globe* is so well informed about its symbolic technique and underlying assumptions as to suggest personal knowledge: '"A Book of the Unseen" [Mr. Carman calls it], but he has symbolized the subjective world with the objects which are its representation. His is a psychology which takes its greatest pains in forging the bond between humanity and the elemental forces. The predominant note of his work in the present instance is an exultant recognition of the unity of all things, a cheerful acquiescence in the higher pantheistic faith ... Phenomena impress him just in so far as they illustrate the action of the soul. Closely observant as he is, ... he seeks for an interpretation of the inner, the real, world by that which is without' (10). For a lengthy discussion of the strengths and weaknesses of *Behind the Arras*, see H.D.C. Lee, 111–27.

22 On 17 January 1896, he had confided to his sister Jean Murray (Muriel) Ganong (1863–1920), '... you know my iron faith that all art must be joyful ... "Out of the night that covers me" [by W.E. Henley] ... That's the creed' (*L* 104); and in 'A Spring Feeling' in the 4 April 1896 number of *Saturday Night,* he declares himself 'sick of all these Yellow Books, / And ... Bodley Heads ... all this Ibsen trash / And Maeterlinckian rot' ... 'For when you call it decadent, / It's rotten just the same' (14).

23 See Lampman's *Essays and Reviews,* 3–9 and 199–205.

24 See the Introduction to Lampman's *Fairy Tales,* xii–xiii.

25 See especially his essays 'The Modern School of Poetry in England' and 'The Poetry of Byron' in *Essays and Reviews,* 58–71 and 115–25.

26 Letter to Duncan Campbell Scott, 10 March 1943, Scott Papers, National Archives of Canada, MG 5473.

27 For further discussion of the presence of *News from Nowhere* in 'The Land of Pallas,' see Bentley, 'William Morris,' 35–9.

28 See Lampman's letters to his wife on 3 and 4 September 1892 (SFU) and to Thomson on 20 November 1891 (*AC* 24–26).

29 See also Campbell's final 'At the Mermaid Inn' column of 1 July 1893 (*MI* 343–4) for quotations from Harrison's 'The Decadence of Romance.'

30 An early version of the opening section of 'Winter-Store' appears under the title 'Vision' in Lampman's 'At the Mermaid Inn' column of 19 November 1892 (*MI* 191–2).

31 The three terms and definitions appear a few pages after a draft of 'Inter Vias' (1899; *P* 183–4) and among various personal poems in MG29. D59, vol. 2, of the Lampman Papers in the National Archives. On the same page (979) is a fragment that begins by asking, 'Do you hear the cry of the people?' and ends by asserting, 'There's enough in the old earth's granaries, / There's enough in her looms for all.'

32 The second and the third of Lampman's terms and definitions could have been gleaned from *A Working Glossary* as could his understanding of the 'astral plane' (see 5–6, 9, 26, 31, 48, 54, and elsewhere), but the absence of the first term from it suggests that he was drawing upon another source that has yet to be identified.

33 It may or may not be entirely fortuitous that Alcyone is a star favoured by theosophists (see Carman, *Letters to Margaret Lawrence* 3–4).

34 For an excellent discussion of Lampman's elegies, see L.R. Early, 'Poems of October.'

35 For an exploratory and very tentative discussion of Scott's possible knowledge and use of alchemical and hermetic texts, see Bentley, 'Alchemical Transmutation.' For Plato and for some occultists, the moon was the home of the soul after death.

36 A chapter of Smith's Ph.D. thesis on the Metaphysical poets is on Henry Vaughan, whose brother Thomas was an alchemist (again, see Bentley 'Alchemical Transmutation'). Both Scott and Smith wrote poems based on the work of Henry Vaughan, 'Variations on a Seventeenth-Century Theme' (1921) and 'To Henry Vaughan' (1962). See also Smith's 'Some Relations.'

37 An edition of Sutro's translation of *Le Trésor des humbles* (*The Treasure of the Humble*) was published in Toronto in 1908 by Musson, who also published editions of Maeterlinck's subsequent collections of essays.

## 7. International and National Recognition: 1889–1895

1 See, for example, the 3 February 1891 issue of the *Globe* (Toronto), where Theodore Harding Rand (1835–1900) is reported as concluding 'an informal and interesting talk' on Roberts's poems by 'recall[ing] the acceptance of [his] first pretentious poem, "Ariadne," by the *Century* after it had once

been refused because the amount of accepted poetry was already enormous. A day or two after the refusal Roberts received a check from the editor saying that after all he thought he must use it, as it was the best poetry he had seen for a year.' Of course, both Roberts himself and Collins assiduously reinforced the perception that he had achieved international recognition with *Orion, and Other Poems* (see chapter 1).

2 Although the program for 'Canadian Night at the Reform Club' that appeared in the 10 January 1889 issue of the *Globe* includes a 'reading ... from Charles G.D. Roberts,' no mention of such a reading appears either in the preliminary announcement of the event (*Globe*, January 5) or in the detailed account of its elements (*Globe*, January 15). This is all the more surprising in the light of Yeigh's statement in the paper on 'Our National Literature' with which he introduced the readings that until 'Canada ... shall become a free and independent nation ... the best that is in our people will not be developed in literature, in art, in goverment, or in any of the finer and higher pursuits that lie open to human endeavour and ambition.' In his paper, Yeigh twice mentions Roberts, first as a poet and then as an essayist (see 'Native Literature').

3 A useful definition of this influential term can be found in a letter by James Henry Morris (18?–?) that was first published in the Toronto *Sun* in 1875 and reprinted in the Toronto *Mail* on 16 July 1890: 'I mean by "the cultivation of a national sentiment" something more substantial and enduring than the ridiculous "hurrah for the union," which the Irish emigrant, two days after his arrival in New York, bellowed forth in a deafening key ... I mean ... the consideration of all those attributes of virtue which constitute [the nation's] brilliancy, and the building of our nationship thereupon. The foundation of a national sentiment should be respect for the memory of dead heroes' (8). Morris concludes the letter by disassociating '"cultivation of a national sentiment"' from the promotion of independence from Britain. See also 'Causes of the Canadian Exodus' in the 11 April 1890 issue of the *Week*, where K.L. Jones argues that the emigration of Canadians to the United States could only be prevented by the 'cultivation' of a 'national spirit. We want a national art, a national literature, national industries, and a national architecture' (293).

4 '[A] successful national literature will help to develop that pride in one's own country that is lacking to a certain extent with us,' continues the editorial, which also seems to envisage a movement towards Canadian independence that would be assisted by the existence of 'a strong Canadian spirit' (3).

5 Howells's 'self-satisfaction' may not have been entirely justified, however, for

several American magazines and newspapers had already 'discovered' Lampman. See, for example, the 30 March 1889 issue of the *Critic* (New York), where the reviewer quotes Lampman's 'Midsummer Night' (1888) 'to show that [the Canadian poet] is not an unworthy rival of his cousins over-seas' (155). The fact that Howells's sister Annie (1844–1938) was married to Fréchette's brother Achille (1847–1927) may help to explain his interest in Lampman.

6 'I think that both *Harper's* and the *Saturday* missed some of your chief distinctions, but they turned men's eyes to your work,' Roberts told Lampman on 10 November 1889. 'By the way, let me tell you how your work *wears* with me. *Among the Millet* is one of the vol[ume]s that lie on the table to my hand, for continual use. I find myself continually wanting it, and reading it in my brief moments. It never disappoints me, and I get lots of stimulus from it, and help for my own writing. Oh, would that *I* had done that "Between the Rapids." How I envy you that!' (*CL* 111). In a letter to Lampman on 24 April 1889, Edmund Charles Stedman remarked that 'no better poems of nature [than] "Heat" and "Among the Timothy" ha[d] appeared of late,' and in a letter to him on May 2, Hamlin Garland wrote expressing his desire to 'help a genuine man' and anticipating an imminent '*talk*' with Howells (SFU).

7 The other poets mentioned by Howells are 'John Boyle O'Reilly, G.P. Lathrop, R.W. Gilder, James Whitcomb Riley, H.H. Boyesen, J. Madison Cawein, ... H.C. Bunner, Edgar Fawcett, [and] Maurice Thompson' (646).

8 By 1890, McKenzie had published two volumes of poetry: *A Song of Trust and Other Thoughts in Verse* (1887) and *Voices and Undertones in Song and Poem* (1889). His subsequent volumes include *Songs of the Human* (1892), *Heartsease Hymns, and Other Verses* (1896), and *The Sower, and Other Poems* (1903).

9 Harte is probably refering to William Sharp's comment in his review of *Among the Millet, and Other Poems* in the 23 November 1889 number of the *Academy* that Carman is 'in some respects the most individual artist of the trio' consisting of Carman, Lampman, and Roberts (334).

10 'Does Milton's great indebtedness detract from him,' asks Lockhart, 'is Tennyson less, that he resolved Keats and Shelley, with others, in his spiritual alembic?' '[S]urely,' he adds, 'it is folly ..., as it seems unnecessary,' 'to allege ... that Mr. Lampman bears no such traces of the past' (4). Perhaps Roberts had Lockhart's defence in mind when he wrote in 'The Poetry of Nature,' which was first published in *Forum* (New York) in December 1897 and reprinted, with minor revisions, in the *Nature* volume of *The World's Best Poetry* (1904), that 'Nature becomes significant to man when she is passed through the

alembic of his heart' so that 'irrelevant and confusing details [are] ... purged away [and] what remains is single and vital' (*SPCP* 277).

11  The *Independent* also describes 'The Reed-Player' as 'a poem full of feeling and music, exquisitely modulated, and serene as a night in late spring' (23).

12  On 5 January 1889, the *Critic* (New York) contained a brief but positive notice of '*Sunbeams and Snowflakes* [*sic*]' as a collection of 'graceful poems' by an author already 'favourably known' for his publications in American periodicals (6).

13  I am deeply grateful to Frederick F. Foy for undertaking an exhaustive search of extant issues of the Chicago *Inter-Ocean* for materials by and about members of the Confederation group. For a partial list of reprintings of 'The Mother,' including two more in the *Globe* (18 January and 18 June 1892), see Laurel Boone's edition of Campbell's *Selected Poetry and Essays,* 210.

14  On April 25, both *Grip* and the *Globe* do little more than relay Sudduth's praise; however, on May 2, *Grip* used the enthusiasm of 'foreign critics' for 'The Mother' as a point of departure for calling attention to the poetry of John Imrie (1846–1902), whose *Songs and Miscellaneous Poems* (1891) had just appeared, observing that, though 'the reader who dotes on Browning will not find much use for this volume, because it requires no mental effort to understand Imrie's muse,' his poems 'will certainly secure for him a warm place in the affections of all right-minded readers.'

15  To date, this article has not been located.

16  On 6 October 1891, the *Globe* reported that Campbell had 'received some well deserved compliments in the House of Commons from Mr. Laurier and Mr. McNeill and added its own voice to the discussion: 'this clever young writer is now a clerk in the Department of Railways and Canals, with a salary of $1.50 a day. There are surely positions in which his services to the country would be worth more than this ... A few years ago *The Globe* had occasion to urge a similar claim on behalf of Mr. Archibald Lampman, who was in somewhat similar circumstances' (4).

17  On 3 August 1892, the *Globe* reported that Campbell had 'now received an appointment under the Secretary of State at a fair salary' and commended the Secretary of State for the appointment, adding that 'the Canadian people ... will ... be glad to know that a man who has charmed them and done credit to his country by his verses has received this little recognition of his services' (4).

18  Probably by Archibald McMechan.

19  See the *Globe,* 28 December 1892, 4.

20  'Canadian Literature,' *Globe,* 18 January 1892, 5.

21  For a further discussion of Johnson's conformity to the stereotype of the

tragic remnant of a dying race, see Bentley, *Mnemographia Canadensis* 1: 165–76.

22 The review certainly appears to be based on personal knowledge of the compositional circumstances of the poem: 'in its opening as well as its concluding stanzas ["Ave"] resembles certain parts of the "Elegy on the Death of Thomas Williams Parsons," by Richard Hovey, and published in *The Independent*, November 17th, 1892. Each of these odes begins with an address to marshlands, the tides and the sea, and each presently connects these with the memory of a dead poet. The two authors are personal friends; and we understand that their poems were at least partially written while working together as comrades in the Acadian country' (16). In a note to Carman on 8 October 1892, Roberts mentions that Hovey has just left Windsor (where he had been staying since early September), adding: 'he hath done a damn fine elegy here. I have done 80 lines of my Shelley poem' (*CL* 155). Like the *Independent*, the *Week* declared Roberts's 'ode ... a success' (30 December 1892, 112), but the *Athenaeum* disagreed, finding it 'far too long, too fluent, too rhetorical, too much what it professes to be – a centennial ode,' and faulting Roberts's association of the Tantramar marshes with Shelley: 'Mr. Roberts has before now done some charming and really individual work; indeed, after Bliss Carman he is the most poetical writer of verse that Canada has produced. But let him describe his rivers, which he can do admirably, and not attempt to find in Tantramar a symbol of Shelley' (15 April 1893, 471–2).

23 Wetherell's anthology was tardily but positively reviewed in the United States: for example, on 9 November 1893 the reviewer for the *Nation* (New York) hailed the anthology as the best existing showcase for 'recent Canadian poetry,' praised Wetherell for his 'taste and discretion,' and noted that he 'has verses by writers now well known in the United States – Roberts, Lampman, Cameron, Carman, and others' (352–3); and on November 23, a notice in the *Independent* described the anthology as 'a creditable showing' of 'real poets' from a country that 'seems to be just now unfolding her wings of imagination and opening her lips of song' (16).

24 Bok also refers in glowing terms to J. Macdonald Oxley ('older than the rest of the Ottawa group' and 'probably the most prolific and versatile writer in Canada') and to Parker ('personally charming; tells an excellent story; is fond of society, and is the best company in the world') (17). In his enormously useful *History of American Magazines*, the urbane Frank Luther Mott writes of Bok that he 'was a bachelor, devoted to his mother, but quite without an intimate understanding of women' (4:540).

25 In addition to the plaudits already discussed above, the article refers to

praise of Campbell's poems in the *Athenaeum* and the *Century Magazine* and suggests that only after Howells had praised 'Lazarus' (1889) in *Harper's* in 1892 did 'the Canadian people beg[i]n to conceive a sense of this poet's real range and power in dealing with human subjects' ('W.W. Campbell'). The article's aggrieved tone and copious biographical details indicate that it was written with Campbell's assistance.

26 '*Songs of the Common Day, and Ave: An Ode for the Shelley Centenary,* by Charles G.D. Roberts ..., really puts its author at the head of the ... young Canadian poets,' stated the *Nation* on 9 November 1893; 'it would be hard to find any one this side of the St. Lawrence who could surpass [his] fine imaginative touch' (353).

27 See chapter 3 for a discussion of the reception of *Low Tide on Grand Pré.*

28 In the 13 January 1894 number of the *Academy, The Magic House and Other Poems* is given a mixed review by Norman Gale ('Mr. Scott not seldom has the touch ... [but] he in carelessness has composed his book' [32]), and in the 3 March 1894 issue of the *Globe,* 'Pharos' (Laura B. Durand) uses the volume as a pretext for a meditation on 'the distinctive original quality of Canadian poetry': 'it seems at first to be but a development of the English Lake School. Yet, although the influence of Wordsworth may be as great on this side of the Atlantic as it has been in England, the chief inspiration and expression of Canadian poetry is to be sought for in the mind of this century rather than that of any particular school. In rhythmic voice, to speak with nature and behold the image of God falling as clearly on her tiniest flower as on her towering hills, and in this communion to feel the divine vitality within impelling them to strong and beautiful utterance and action – this is the striving of our poets. With such an unlimited object and subject, with such a universal impulse, they must proceed not as the poets of a certain group, but of all mankind' (6).

29 The other four volumes are *Songs of the Great Dominion, This Canada of Ours, and Other Poems* (1893), by James David Edgar (1841–99), *Songs of Life: A Collection of Poems,* by Edgar Hartley Dewart (1828–1903), and *Pine, Rose and Fleur de Lis* (1891), by Susan Frances Harrison.

30 Although Conant's articles prominently feature members of the Confederation group, they also accord extensive attention to Lighthall, Edgar, and other writers.

31 Between 18 May and 2 November 1894, Horning published a series of articles amounting to a history of Canadian literature in the *Week* (see Bentley and Wickens, *Checklist* 11).

32 The Society's *Proceedings and Transactions* for 1895 record that the following poets would be present at the 'symposium' either 'in person or in poems':

Machar, Wetherald, Lampman, Campbell, Duncan Campbell Scott, Frederick George Scott, Carman, Cornelius O'Brien (1843–1906), Davin, Edgar, Roberts, Reade, Harrison, and, last, but obviously not least, Johnson (vii). In the announcement of the 'poets' evening' in the 16 May 1895 issue of the *Globe*, however, Roberts is not mentioned (5).

33 The report of the evening in the May 25 issue of the *Globe* states that both Campbell and Lampman were asked for encores and that 'the latter made a local hit, so to speak, in his rendition of the '"Hull Ferry" [that is, "At the Ferry" (1895)], a word picture of the Ottawa River from that point'; and that Johnson, 'who wore her handsome Indian costume, made perhaps the most pronounced success of the evening, giving two numbers of her own' (9).

34 During the late 1880s and early 1890s, Clark, a professor at Trinity College, Toronto, published numerous articles on Dante, Coleridge, Tennyson, and others in the *Week* (see Bentley and Wickens, *Checklist* 5–6). His 'Canadian Poets' appeared in the 18 October 1895 issue of the same periodical.

35 Bourinot (1837–1902) was Clerk of the House of Commons from 1880 until his death, a charter member and president of the Royal Society of Canada, and 'an authority on constitutional history, law, and practice' (Story 91). He would be knighted in 1898.

36 Roberts has harsh criticism for two of Scott's poems, however: '... the whole method of ["Dion" (1894)] ... I think wrong. I think *no* poet could have made it a success along the lines you take. A long soliloquy delivered by one who is actually fighting his last fight is quite impossible methinks. Then the "Abbot" seems to me only a partial success ...' (*CL* 187).

37 Roberts may well have summoned up the energy to champion Scott's book, however, for the review, of it in the 4 January 1895 issue of the *Week* loudly echoes his views in the letter of December 15; for example, 'Samson,' 'In Via Mortis,' and 'The Frenzy of Prometheus' are accorded high praise in both the letter and the review, and 'Columbus,' 'number *I* of the three sonnets called "A Cyprus Wreath"' and 'one of the perfect sonnets ... of our language' according to the letter (*CL* 188), is described as a 'gem' in the review and quoted in full (136). After remarking in his letter on some verbal and metrical shortcomings in the book, Roberts says, 'But ... these are small blemishes, easy to be remedied.' The conclusion of the review reads: 'There are some slight faults in diction and versification that can easily be corrected in the author's next work.'

38 In fact, the quotation is from *Primitive Culture* (1871), by Edward Burnett Tylor, and was probably culled by Campbell from John Fiske's *Myths and Myth-Makers: Old Tales and Superstitions Interpreted by Comparative Mythology* (1886), 229–30, a source also for the solar imagery that runs through the

poem (see, for example, 'the red beams, slanting and bright,' and the unburyable 'red sunbeam' of the opening couplets).

39 See Burpee, 425, and *SPE*, 210.

40 In 'The Poems of William Wilfred Campbell,' a paper read before the Modern Language Club at the University of Toronto, James Alexander Tucker, identifies Campbell's 'genius ... [as] of almost precisely the same stamp as Edgar Al[l]an Poe's' and cites 'The Mother' as an instance of a similar 'love for the mystical and weird' and 'wealth of melodious expression and ... faculty of versification' (143).

41 For reasons similar to those that drew readers to 'Between the Rapids,' Scott's 'At the Cedars' (1893) was also frequently remarked and quoted; see, for example, *Progress*, 20 March 1890, where it is quoted in its entirety, and the *Nation*, June 7 1894, where it is described as 'a lumberman's tragedy' and as the product of 'an exceptional dramatic faculty' (433).

42 Burroughs describes such harsh birdcalls as the bittern's cry as 'the Richard Wagner music of the ornithological orchestra' (6: 4).

43 Only Scott is not honoured with a dedication in *The Magic House* volume. For further discussion of the figure of Pan in the poetry of the Confederation group, see Bentley, *The Gay/Grey Moose*, 235–50. By the late nineteenth century, Pan had been transformed by generations of writers on both sides of the Atlantic into an embodiment of the spirit of Nature.

45 See Bentley, *The Gay/Grey Moose*, 195–200, for a discussion of the American context of 'The City of the End of Things.' On 3 March 1894, Lampman told his sister that he thought the poem 'should attract some notice,' and on March 12 he received a letter from a friend of his college days who was now teaching at Bishop Ridley College (now Ridley College) in St Catharines, Ontario, expressing the view that it 'will ... do [him] good and add to [his] power' and the hope that '[he] will do more in [the same] line' (SFU).

46 See Brown's 'Memoir' in Scott's *Selected Poems* (1951), xviii–xix; and McDougall, *The Poet and the Critic*, 237–38.

47 See Bentley, 'Minor Poets of a Superior Order'; and Leon Surette, 'Ezra Pound.'

## 8. Disintegration

1 See note 40 in chapter 7 for the article in the May 1895 number of the *University of Toronto Quarterly* in which James Alexander Tucker identified Campbell's debts to Poe. Himself a promising poet (his *Poems* were posthumously published in 1904 with a 'Prefatory Memoir' by Arthur Stringer), Tucker nevertheless concludes that, while Campbell's 'characteristic work' is very

evidently indebted to Poe, he 'has done some work in an entirely different spirit ... "Pan the Fallen" ... cannot be said ... [to] resemble ... the work of the great southern singer' (144).

2 On learning that McArthur had resigned the editorship of *Truth*, Scott wrote on 29 July 1897 that the news caused him a 'selfish regret ... for [he] was always sure of friendly treatment' by the periodical (McGU).

3 Campbell is probably referring to Roberts's 'Mr. Bliss Carman's Poems' in the 15 June 1894 number of the *Chap-Book*, and Carman's 'Mr. Charles G.D. Roberts' in the 1 January 1895 number. In the former, a review of the second edition of *Low Tide on Grand Pré*, Roberts judges Carman 'a poet so significant and vital [that] it is worth while trying to trace his poetic lineage' (56). In the latter, a profile in a series on 'Contemporaries,' Carman names Roberts 'the acknowledged laureate' of Canada and places him with Lampman and Duncan Campbell Scott among 'poets of the first order' (163, 170).

4 Campbell's statement in a subsequent letter to the *Globe* that on 23 March 1890 Carman had written to him to apologize for 'the non-appearance of his [Campbell's] name in an article on Canadian poets which had just appeared' in the *Independent* (*War* 117) suggests that he may have been thinking here of 'Some Canadian Writers,' by George Stewart, Jr, in the 13 March 1890 number of the magazine. Roberts's 'Canada,' Carman's 'Low Tide on Grand Pré,' and Lampman's *Among the Millet, and Other Poems* are praised for their 'patriotic tone,' 'workmanship,' originality, and promise in Stewart's article, but no mention is made of Campbell (4).

5 Some of Morse's writings were later collected in *Apices Juris, and Other Legal Essays in Prose and Verse* (1906).

6 I am grateful to Tracy Ware for calling my attention to this letter in the Campbell Papers of the Lorne Pierce Collection in the Douglas Library at Queen's University.

7 In the 1895 edition of *Low Tide on Grand Pré*, Carman changed the line to 'With tiny multitudinous sound' (86). Evidently, McArthur drew Carman's attention to the appropriation soon after the appearance of the first edition of his book for on 26 February 1894 he responded to a letter from Lampman on the matter by writing: '... what a saint you are! [In your hearty letter about *Low Tide on Grand Pré*] you never m[entioned] my amazing theft of [a] line in "The Eavesdropper," from your "Heat." A friend of mine [McArthur] "called me down" on it, and I had to plead the same old extenuating circumstance, unconscious imitation. Of course I had remembered your line and then reproduced it quite innocently and unconsciously. The line will be changed at once ... for the first edition is almost exhausted' (SFU).

8  Between 1910 and 1936, Pollock published several novels, including *The Woods-Rider* (1922) and *Bitter Honey* (1935).

9  See note 4, above.

10  Waggishly, the reviewer also mentions the appearance of the expression '"laughs in his sleeve"' in the second act of *Hildebrand*, referring to it as 'a phrase of some notoriety' (*Globe*, 6 January 1895, 22) because Campbell had cited its appearance in Arnold's 'Empedocles and Etna' and in Carman's 'Wanderers' (1893) as an instance of the Canadian poet's 'stale expression' and 'audacious imitation' (*War* 40–1). In a response to Campbell's article a few days after its appearance, Miller suggests, probably ironically, that Carman 'should make an attempt to exonerate himself from having stolen' the phrase from Arnold (*War* 63).

11  Entitled 'The New Criticism,' the editorial traces the term 'The New Log-Rolling' to the 1893 reviews of English literature in the *Athenaeum*, 'which ... said the most marked feature [of the year's writing] was the touching unanimity and enthusiasm with which six or eight new geniuses had discovered each other' (159). A term derived from politics, 'log-rolling' also enjoyed wide currency in the late 1880s when it was appropriated by Andrew Lang's detractors to describe his practice of 'praising books by authors who were certain to review his own favorably' (Lanstaff 117). (Lang responded with 'The Log-Rolliad' [18].) Campbell may also have encountered the term in Graeme Mercer Adam's 'Native Literature and the Scoffing Spirit' in the 5 January 1888 issue of the *Week*, where the practice is seen as having some merit as an antidote to 'the cheap attitude of an essentially ignoble journalism [that] ... has not a single good word to say for the native author or his work' (86). 'Much harm ... may be done by overpraise,' concedes Adam, 'and, as a rule, only a sickly literature can come of coddling. No less pernicious is that pursuit of weak minds known by the modern phrase, "literary log-rolling," though not a little might be said in its favour in an overstocked book-market and among a people, in the main, indifferent to literature.'

12  Like so many other contestants in the 'War among the Poets,' Rogers was himself a creative writer: his *The Scraggville Bandits; or, The White Caps of Pepper Island, and Other Stories* was published in Ottawa in 1889, and two books of ballads, *Government Clerks* and *Ballads o' Barleycorn*, would follow in 1902 and 1925. His 'In the Streets Where I Live' was published in the 23 November 1893 number of the *Independent* (26).

13  Carman's poem is less interesting in itself than for the commentary that surrounds it, which begins as a meditation on the loss of a 'friend who withdraws himself from the circle of [one's] life' and proceeds to an analysis of Campbell's motives: 'I have lately been suffering from an acute attack of [my

late lamented friend's] literary egomania. So small a thing as a magazine article in which, naturally enough, he with his modesty came in for a smaller share of eulogy than a shameless and rampant egoist like myself, seems to have stirred his gall ... I wish I knew how to be reconciled with him; but I don't. I fear his ire is too hot to be cooled by words. There is really nothing left for me to do, but to write his *Hic jacet* ["here lies"], and let him depart into the limbo of false loves and broken idols' (225–6). In a 'Postscript added Aug. 8, 1895' to 'The Log-Rollers' (which is dated 'April 1895'), Campbell responds to 'Here lies little Willie . . .' by advising Carman 'to seek those hills you love to spout, / In your maudlin rhymes about ... Far from magazines and far / From self-boomers,' to 'Give no more facts to Miller, Bok, / Or others of the booming stock,' to 'cultivate a little shame [and] ... Forget that you were ever frantic, / To rise to heights of fame transcendent' (*World* [Toronto], 19 August 1895, 5). Not all the poems occasioned by the fracas were satirical; for example, 'To William Wilfrid [*sic*] Campbell' by Mary K. McQuoid (18?–?) in the 10 August 1895 issue of the *Globe*, enjoins the poet to 'kill [his] sense of wrong' by scorn and assures him that his 'fame will grow with years' (4).

14 In O'Hagan's essay, 'Mr. Wilfrid Campbell is declared to be one of the most original and bold among the younger Canadian poets,' observes Clark; 'he is said to have "a keen sense of colour and form," and "has, at times, a great deal of strength and resources of melody which might well be matched against the best music of Shelley and Swinburne." We may hope that this ungrudging testimony will be pleasing to Mr. Campbell's friends who thought him slighted in a recent article. It might be well if Mr. Campbell himself would meditate the kindly criticism of Mr. O'Hagan, which, however, need not be quoted here.' Clark judiciously allots more space to Campbell than to any other poet.

15 In R.E. Watters's invaluable *Checklist of Canadian Literature and Background Materials, 1628–1960* (1959, 1972), Stewart's poem is listed as a work of 'Scholarship,' a fact pointed out to me by Michael Gnarowski.

16 This is not to be confused with Lighthall's *Canadian Poems and Lays*, which was published in 1893 and, unfortunately, fails to fulfil the promise of its title.

17 This is just a small sampling of Stewart's invective, which at times combines wit and lampoon with memorable pungency, particularly when quoting the Confederation group and their admirers against themselves, as in the third 'object' in his Preface and in the following passage from Lighthall's Introduction: 'the foremost name in Canadian song at the present day is that of George Charles Douglas Roberts, poet, canoeist and Professor of Literature' (Stewart 74n).

18 On 6 February 1893, the *Globe* responded to Campbell's column in 'The Literary Calling' by chiding the poet for 'publish[ing] [his] woes' and expressing some scepticism about his assertions: 'it is difficult to believe that the grievances of which "C" speaks exist to such an extent as to have any perceptible influence on literature. It is possible that ... coteries are formed here and there who agree to admire intensely whatever any of its members puts forth, but, as literary work is not undertaken now for coteries, but for the many-minded general public, the ... mutual admiration to which "C" alludes must have a very microscopic influence on the great ocean of current literature' (4). Of course, several of Campbell's earlier contributions to 'At the Mermaid Inn' anticipated what was to come; see, for example, his columns of 1 October 1892 (on Aldrich), 12 November 1892 (on 'polish' or 'finish' in poetry), 3 December 1892 (on Lighthall's *Songs of the Great Dominion*), and 10 December 1892 (on 'cliques') (*MI* 160–2, 188–90, 203–4, 207–9).

19 The reference is probably to J.G. Bourinot, who received an honourary LL.D. from Queen's in 1887 (see Banks 106) and who was the subject of Collins's disdain in his biographies of Macdonald and the Marquis of Lorne and elsewhere. Collins also mentions, in closing, Harte's elevation 'high above his peers' of a writer who went to 'New York from a city like Toronto' but was unable to 'make his salt' and 'ha[d] to be sent home by friends,' a reference, perhaps, to Graeme Mercer Adam, who had made an unsuccessful foray from Toronto to New York in the late 1870s (see Mount 77–8) and is prominently featured in Harte's 'Some Canadian Writers of To-day' (see 32, 37).

**Aftermath**

1 William Francis Collier's definition of a 'school' of writers in *A History of English Literature, in a Series of Biographical Scetches* (1872) helps to explain why the Confederation group was considered as such by their contemporaries: 'a set of men whose works are founded on a certain known principle, which appears in all as a distinctive feature' (361–2). In his biographical note on Roberts in *A Victorian Anthology, 1837–1895* (1896), Edmund Clarence Stedman observes that his friend 'has now resigned his professorship to devote himself more freely to literature' and then makes a statement that accurately and economically characterizes the relationship of the six poets examined in the present study: '[Roberts] has been an influential leader of the new and promising group of writers' (762).

2 For a discussion of these components of Roberts's work, see Glennis Stephenson's 'The Bitter-Sweet Rose: The Conception of Woman in Roberts' *The Book of the Rose*,' Misao Dean's 'Political Science: Realism in Roberts's

Animal Stories,' and my own 'Half Passion and Half Prayer: The *New York Nocturnes*' and '"The Thing Is Found to Be Symbolic": *Symboliste* Elements in the Early Short Stories of Gilbert Parker, Charles G.D. Roberts, and Duncan Campbell Scott.'

3 For further discussions of these aspects of Carman's work, see my 'Threefold in Wonder: Bliss Carman's *Sappho: One Hundred Lyrics*' and 'Carman and Mind Cure: Theory and Technique.'

4 See Laurel Boone's Introduction to her edition of Campbell's *Selected Poetry and Essays*, 6–7, and my 'Charles G.D. Roberts and William Wilfred Campbell As Canadian Tour Guides.'

5 For the former, see my *Mnemographia Canadensis*, 1: 314 and 331n14; and for the latter my 'Alchemical Transmutation in Duncan Campbell Scott's "At Gull Lake: August, 1810" and Some Contingent Speculations' and 'Duncan Campbell Scott and Maurice Maeterlinck.'

6 See *Mnemographia Canadensis*, 1: 159, for a discussion of one of the poems that Carman wrote for the cause.

7 The prominence given to 'The Battle of Lundy's Lane' in *Lundy's Lane and Other Poems* (1916) was an attempt to make the volume relevant to the war effort, as is its front cover design of two British soldiers. A letter of 11 February 1916 from Scott to Pelham Edgar (VU) indicates that the idea for so naming (and, thus, rearranging) the book came from Edgar. Several letters written by and to Scott during the war are indicative of his interest in preserving the memory of Rupert Brooke, who had stayed with him in Ottawa in July 1913 (see, for example, the letter dated 1 May 1916 at DalU).

8 Nevertheless, see Don Conway, 'Roberts and Modernism: The Achievement of "The Squatter."'

9 For discussions of Canadian manifestations of anti-modernity, see R. Alexander Kizuk's *A Reassessment of Early Twentieth-Century Canadian Poetry in English*, several of the essays in Lynda Jessup's *Antimodernism and Artistic Experience*, and the chapter entitled '(Anti-)Modernity and Moving House(s)' in my *Mnemographia Canadensis* 1:333–54.

10 During the 1920s, Carman also made reading tours of the United States; see his *Letters to Margaret Lawrence, 1927–1929*, 29–86. Details of the Canadian reading tours of Carman and Roberts can be found in, Muriel Miller's *Bliss Carman* and E.M. Pomeroy's *Sir Charles G.D. Roberts*.

11 For contextualizations of these and related materials, see my *Mnemographia Canadensis* 1:313–17, and 'Bibliocritical Afterword.'

12 Between *New Poems* (1919) and *The Vagrant of Time* (1927), Roberts published an eight-page chapbook cloyingly entitled *The Sweet o' the Year and Other Poems*.

13 See Hathaway, 'Carman's Memorial Unveiling' and H.G. Wade, 'Bliss Carman's Shrine.' Not until 13 May 1954, however, was Carman granted his wish to have 'a scarlet maple / For the grave-tree at [his] head' (*PBC* 209, and see *Mnemographia Canadensis* 1:411–13).

14 The very titles of Daniells's chapters are telling: 'Lampman and Roberts,' 'Crawford, Carman and D.C. Scott.'

15 For the genesis and semiotics of the Lampman stamp, see *Mnemographia Canadensis* 1:326–8.

# Works Cited

Adam, Graeme Mercer. *The Canadian North-West: Its History and Its Troubles, from the Early Days of Fur Trade to the Era of the Railway and the Settler: With Incidents of Travel in the Region, and the Narrative of Three Insurrections.* Toronto: Rose, 1885.

– *Handbook of Commercial Union: A Collection of Papers Read before the Commercial Union Club, Toronto, with Speeches, Letters, and Other Documents in Favour of Unrestricted Reciprocity with the United States.* Introd. Goldwin Smith. Ed. G. Mercer Adam. Toronto: Hunter, Rose, 1888.

– 'An Interregnum in Literature.' *Week* [Toronto] 1 (12 June 1884): 438–9.

– 'Literature.' 'Review of Literature, Science and Art.' *The Dominion Annual Register and Review for the Fourteenth and Fifteenth Years of the Canadian Union, 1880–1881.* Ed. Henry J. Morgan. Montreal: John Lovell and Son, 1882. 279–98.

– 'Literature, Nationality, and the Tariff.' *Week* [Toronto] 7 (27 Dec. 1889): 59–60.

– *Muskoka Illustrated: With Descriptive Narrative of This Picturesque Region.* Toronto: W. Bryce, 1888.

– 'Native Literature and the Scoffing Spirit.' *Week* [Toronto] 5 (5 Jan. 1888): 85–6.

Adam, Graeme Mercer, and A. Ethelwyn Wetherald. *An Algonquin Maiden: A Romance of the Early Days of Upper Canada.* Montreal: J. Lovell; Toronto: Williamson, 1887.

Adams, James Eli. *Dandies and Desert Saints: Styles of Victorian Manhood.* Ithaca and London: Cornell UP, 1995.

Adams, John Coldwell. 'A Preliminary Bibliography.' *The Sir Charles G.D. Roberts Symposium.* Ed. Glenn Clever. Reappraisals: Canadian Writers 10. Ottawa: U of Ottawa P, 1984. 221–49.

– 'Roberts, Lampman, and Edmund Collins.' *The Sir Charles G.D. Roberts Sympo-*

*sium*. Ed. Glenn Clever. Reappraisals: Canadian Writers 10. Ottawa: U of Ottawa P, 1984. 5–13.

– *Sir Charles God Damn: The Life of Sir Charles G.D. Roberts*. Toronto: U of Toronto P, 1986.

Adams, Thomas. 'Frederick George Scott: A Review of His Poetry by the Principal of Bishop's College, Lennoxville.' *Canadian Magazine* [Toronto] 11.2 (June 1898): 160-4.

Anderson, Benedict. *Imagined Communities: Reflections on the Origin and Spread of Nationalism*. London: Verso and NLB, 1983.

Anderson, William S. 'The Theory and Practice of Poetic Arrangement from Vergil to Ovid.' *Poems in Their Place*. Ed. Neil Fraistat. Chapel Hill: U of North Carolina P, 1986. 44–65.

Arnold, Matthew. *Complete Prose Works*. Ed. R.H. Super. 11 vols. Ann Arbor: U of Michigan P, 1960–77.

– 'Literature and Science.' *Manhattan* [New York] 3 (April 1884): 323–31.

– *Poems*. 1965. Ed. Kenneth Allott. 2nd ed. Miriam Allott. Longman Annotated English Poets. London: Longman, 1979.

Ballstadt, Carl. 'Thomas D'Arcy McGee As a Father of Canadian Literature.' *Studies in Canadian Literature* 1 (1976): 85–95.

Banks, Margaret A. *Sir John George Bourinot, Victorian Canadian: His Life, Times, and Legacy*. Montreal and Kingston: McGill-Queen's UP, 2001.

Barrus, Clara. *Our Friend John Burroughs. Including Autobiographical Sketches by Mr. Burroughs*. Boston and New York: Houghton Mifflin, 1914.

Barry, Lilly E.F. 'Prominent Canadians—XXV: Archibald Lampman.' *Week* [Toronto] 8 (April 10 1891): 298–300.

Bator, Paul Adolphus. 'Edward Playter.' *Dictionary of Canadian Biography*. 13: 840.

Beard, George Miller. *American Nervousness, Its Causes and Consequences: A Supplement to Nervous Exhaustion (Neurasthenia)*. New York: G.P. Putnam's Sons, 1881.

– *A Practical Treatise on Nervous Exhaustion (Neurasthenia), Its Symptoms, Nature, Sequences, Treatment*. 1880. 5th ed. New York: E.B. Treat, 1905. Rpt. New York: Kraus Reprint, 1971.

Beckow, S.M. 'From the Watch-Towers of Patriotism: Theories of Literary Growth in English Canada, 1864–1914.' *Journal of Canadian Studies* 9.3 (1974): 3–14.

Bentley, D.M.R. 'Alchemical Transmutation in Duncan Campbell Scott's "At Gull Lake: August, 1810," and Some Contingent Speculations.' *Studies in Canadian Literature* 10 (1985): 1–23.

– 'American Meteorological Determinism and Post-Confederation Poetry.' *Informal Empire? Cultural Relations between Canada, the United States and Europe*. Ed. Peter Easingwood, Konrad Gross, and Harmut Lutz. Schriftenreihe des

Zentrums für Kanada-Studien an der Universität Trier 8. Kiel: l and f Verlag, 1998. 123–48.

– 'Bibliocritical Afterword.' *Early Long Poems on Canada*. Ed. D.M.R. Bentley. London: Canadian Poetry Press, 1993. 617–62.

– 'Carman and Mind Cure: Theory and Technique.' *Bliss Carman: A Reappraisal*. Ed. Gerald Lynch. Reappraisals: Canadian Writers 16. Ottawa: U of Ottawa P, 1990. 85–110.

– 'Charles G.D. Roberts and William Wilfred Campbell As Canadian Tour Guides.' *Writing and Culture in Nineteenth-Century Canada*. Ed. Michael Peterman. Special issue of *Journal of Canadian Studies* 32.2 (1997): 79–99.

– 'Charles G.D. Roberts's Use of "Indian Legend" in Four Poems of the Eighteen Eighties and 'Nineties.' *Canadian Poetry: Studies, Documents, Reviews* 51 (Fall/Winter 2002): 18-38.

– 'Duncan Campbell Scott and Maurice Maeterlinck.' *Studies in Canadian Literature* 21.2 (1996): 104–19.

– 'From Allegory to Indeterminacy: Dante Gabriel Rossetti's Positive Agnosticism.' *Dalhousie Review* 70 (Spring 1990): 70–106; 70 (Summer 1990): 146–68.

– *The Gay]Grey Moose: Essays on the Ecologies and Mythologies of Canadian Poetry, 1690–1990*. Ottawa: U of Ottawa P, 1992.

– 'Half Passion and Half Prayer: The *New York Nocturnes*.' *The Charles G.D. Roberts Symposium*. Ed. Glenn Clever. Reappraisals: Canadian Writers, 10. Ottawa: U of Ottawa P, 1984. 55–75.

– 'Introduction.' *Bliss Carman's Letters to Margaret Lawrence, 1927–1929*. Ed. D.M.R. Bentley. London: Canadian Poetry Press, 1995. ix–xxi.

– 'Introduction.' *Fairy Tales*, by Archibald Lampman. Ed. D.M.R. Bentley. London: Canadian Poetry Press, 1999. ix–xxviii.

– 'Introduction.' *Lyrics of Earth (1895)*, by Archibald Lampman. Ed. D.M.R. Bentley. Ottawa: Tecumseh, 1978. 1–20.

– 'Introduction.' *The Story of an Affinity*, by Archibald Lampman. Ed. D.M.R. Bentley. London: Canadian Poetry Press, 1986. xi–xxxi.

– 'Literary Sites and Cultural Properties.' *Writing Canadian Space*. Ed. John Clement Ball, Robert Viau, and Linda Warley. Special issue of *Studies in Canadian Literature* 23.1 (1998): 90–127.

– *Mimic Fires: Accounts of Early Long Poems on Canada*. Montreal: McGill–Queen's UP, 1994.

– 'Minor Poets of a Superior Order.' *Canadian Poetry: Studies, Documents, Reviews* 14 (Spring/Summer 1984): v–viii.

– *Mnemographia Canadensis: Essays on Memory, Community, and Environment in Canada, with Particular Reference to London, Ontario*. 2 vols. London: Canadian Poetry Press, 1999.

- 'Near the Rapids: Thomas Moore in Canada.' *Romantic Poetry*. Ed. Angela Esterhammer. A Comparative history of Literatures in European Languages 17. New York: John Benjamins, 2002. 355-71.
- 'Nervous ReincarNations: Keats, Scenery, and Mind Cure in Canada during the Post-Confederation Period, with Particular Reference to Archibald Lampman and Related Cases.' Forthcoming in *Nervous Reactions: Victorian Recollections of Romanticism*. Ed. Joel Faflak and Julia M. Wright. New York: State U of New York P, 2003.
- 'The Poetics of Roberts' Tantramar Space.' *Proceedings of the Sir Charles G.D. Roberts Symposium, Mount Allison University*. Ed. Carrie MacMillan. Anchorage Series 1. Sackville, NB: Centre for Canadian Studies, Mount Allison University; Halifax: Nimbus, 1984. 17-41.
- 'Roberts' Series of Sonnets in *Songs of the Common Day*.' *Dalhousie Review* 69 (1989): 393-412.
- '"The Thing Is Found to Be Symbolic": *Symboliste* Elements in the Early Short Stories of Gilbert Parker, Charles G.D. Roberts, and Duncan Campbell Scott.' *Dominant Impressions: Essays on the Canadian Short Story*. Ed. Gerald Lynch and Angela Arnold Robbeson. Reappraisals: Canadian Writers. Ottawa: U of Ottawa P, 1999. 27-51.
- 'Threefold in Wonder: Bliss Carman's *Sappho: One Hundred Lyrics*.' *Canadian Poetry: Studies, Documents, Reviews* 17 (Fall/Winter 1985): 29-58.
- 'Watchful Dreams and Sweet Unrest: An Essay on the Vision of Archibald Lampman.' *Studies in Canadian Literature* 6 (1981): 188-210; 7 (1982): 5-26.
- 'William Morris and the Poets of the Confederation.' *Scarlet Hunters: Pre-Raphaelitism in Canada*. Ed. David Latham. Toronto: Archives of Canadian Art and Design, 1998. 31-44.
Bentley, D.M.R., and MaryLynn Wickens. *A Checklist of Literary Materials in 'The Week' (Toronto, 1883-1896)*. Ottawa: Golden Dog, 1978.
Berger, Carl. *The Sense of Power: Studies in the Ideas of Canadian Imperialism, 1867-1913*. Toronto: U of Toronto P, 1970.
Bhojwani, Maia. 'A Northern Pantheism: Notes on the Confederation Poets and Contemporary Mythographers.' *Canadian Poetry: Studies, Documents, Reviews* 9 (Fall/Winter 1981): 34-49.
- '"The Tides": Roberts' Sonnet about the Sonnet.' *Journal of Canadian Poetry* 3.2 (1981): 14-21.
Birbalsingh, Frank. *Novels and the Nation: Essays in Canadian Literature*. Toronto: TSAR, 1995.
Boone, Laurel, ed. 'The Collected Poems of William Wilfred Campbell.' Diss., University of New Brunswick, 1981.
- 'Evolution and Idealism: Wilfred Campbell's "The Tragedy of Man" and Its

Place in Canadian Intellectual History.' *Studies in Canadian Literature* 8.1 (1983): 93–116.

Bourdieu, Pierre. *The Logic of Practice.* Trans. Richard Nice. Stanford: Stanford UP, 1990.

– 'The Production of Belief: Contribution to an Economy of Symbolic Goods.' *Media, Culture and Society* 2.3 (1980): 261–93.

Bourinot, John George. 'Canadian Materials for History, Poetry, and Romance.' *New Dominion Monthly* [Montreal] (April 1871): 193–204.

'Brief Literary Notes.' *Owl* [Ottawa] 3 (Feb. 1892): 307–8.

Brooke, Frances. *The History of Emily Montague.* 1769. Ed. Mary Jane Edwards. Ottawa: Carleton UP, 1985.

Brown, E.K. *On Canadian Poetry* 1943. Rev. ed. 1944. Ottawa: Tecumseh, 1973.

Brownlow, Edward Burrough ('Sarepta'). 'The Sonnet. – I' *Week* [Toronto] 6 (2 Aug. 1889): 552–3; 'Part II' (16 Aug. 1889): 584–5; 'Part III' (23 Aug. 1889): 601–2; 'Part IV' (30 Aug. 1889): 615–16; 'Part V' (20 Sept. 1889): 664–6; 'Part VI' (4 Oct. 1889): 695–6; 'Part VII' (18 Oct. 1889): 725–6; 'Part VIII' (1 Nov. 1889): 760–1; 'Part X' (22 Nov. 1889): 807–8; 'Part XI' 7 (6 Dec. 1889): 8–9.

Burpee, Lawrence J. 'A Canadian Poet: W.W. Campbell.' *Sewanee Review* 8 (Oct 1900): 425–36.

Burroughs, John. *Complete Writings.* Wake-Robin edition. 23 vols. New York: Wm. H. Wise, 1924.

Cameron, George Frederick. *Lyrics of Freedom, Love and Death.* Ed. Charles J. Cameron. Kingston: Lewis W. Shannon; Boston: Alexander Moore, 1887.

Campbell, Bruce F. *Ancient Wisdom Revived: A History of the Theosophical Movement.* Berkeley: U of California P, 1980.

Campbell, William Wilfred. *The Beauty, History, Romance, and Mystery of the Canadian Lake Region.* Toronto: Musson, 1910.

– *At the Mermaid Inn: Wilfred Campbell, Archibald Lampman, Duncan Campbell Scott in 'The Globe' 1892–93.* Ed. Barrie Davies. Literature of Canada: Poetry and Prose in Reprint. Toronto: U of Toronto P, 1979.

– *Mordred and Hildebrand. A Book of Tragedies.* Ottawa: J. Durie and Son, 1895.

– Papers. Lorne Pierce Collection. Douglas Library, Queen's University, Kingston, ON.

– *Poems.* Toronto: William Briggs, 1905.

– *Poetical Works.* Ed. W.J. Sykes. Toronto: Hodder and Stoughton, 1923.

– *Selected Poetry and Essays.* Ed. Laurel Boone. Waterloo: Wilfrid Laurier UP, 1987.

– *Snowflakes and Sunbeams.* 1888. Ed. Carl F. Klinck. Ottawa: Golden Dog, 1974.

'A Canadian Poet.' Rev. of *Among the Millet, and Other Poems,* by Archibald Lampman. *Spectator* [London], 12 Jan. 1889, 52–3.

Cappon, James. *Bliss Carman and the Literary Currents and Influences of the Times.* Toronto: Ryerson, 1930.

– *Charles G.D. Roberts and the Influence of His Time.* 1905. Ottawa: Tecumseh, 1975.

Carman, Bliss. 'An Apostle of Personal Harmonizing.' *Good Housekeeping* 52 (May 1911): 581–5.

– *Ballads of Lost Haven: A Book of the Sea.* Boston, New York, and London: Lamson, Wolff, 1897.

– 'Contemporaries – V. Mr. Charles G.D. Roberts.' *Chap-Book* [Chicago] 2.4 (1 Jan. 1895): 163–71.

– 'Corydon: An Elegy.' *Universal Review* [London] 5 (Nov. 1889): 425–37.

– 'Death in April.' *Atlantic Monthly* [Boston] 63 (April 1889): 458–62.

– *The Friendship of Art.* Boston: L.C. Page, 1904.

– *The Gate of Peace.* New York: The Village Press, 1906.

– *The Kinship of Nature.* Boston: L.C. Page, 1903.

– *Letters.* Ed. H. Pearson Gundy. Montreal: McGill-Queen's UP, 1981.

– *Letters to Margaret Lawrence, 1927–1929.* Ed. D.M.R. Bentley with the assistance of Margaret Maciejewski. Post-Confederation Poetry: Texts and Contexts. London: Canadian Poetry Press, 1995.

– 'Louise Imogen Guiney.' *Chap-Book* [Chicago] 2.1 (15 Nov. 1894): 27–36.

– 'Low Tide on Avon.' *King's College Record* [Windsor, NS] 78 (Oct. 1886): 5–6.

– *Low Tide on Grand Pré: A Book of Lyrics.* New York: Webster, 1893.

– *Low Tide on Grand Pré. A Book of Lyrics.* 3rd ed. Boston and New York: Lamson Wolffe, 1895.

– 'Mr. Charles G.D. Roberts.' *Chap-Book* [Chicago] 2 (15 Jan. 1895): 163–71.

– 'Mr. William Sharp's Poems.' *Chap-Book* [Chicago] 1 (Sept. 15 1894): 214–23.

– 'The Night Express.' *Independent* [New York] 44 (6 Oct. 1892): 1.

– *Pipes of Pan.* Toronto: Copp, Clark, 1906.

– *Poems.* Toronto: McClelland and Stewart, [1931].

– *The Poetry of Life.* Boston: L.C. Page, 1905.

– *The Rough Rider, and Other Poems.* New York: Kennerly, 1909.

– *Sappho: One Hundred Lyrics.* London: Chatto and Windus, 1903.

– 'The Vernal Ides.' *The Kinship of Nature.* Boston: L.C. Page, 1904. 61–9.

– 'Winter Sunshine.' Rev. of *Winter Sunshine,* by John Burroughs. *University Monthly* [Fredericton], May 1885, 123.

Carman, Bliss, and Lorne Pierce, eds. *Our Canadian Literature: Representative Verse, English and French.* Toronto: Ryerson, 1935.

Carman, Bliss, and Mary Perry King. *Daughters of Dawn: A Lyrical Pageant or Series of Historical Scenes for Presentation with Music and Dancing.* New York: Mitchell Kennerley, 1913.

– *Earth Deities and Other Rhythmic Masques*. New York: Mitchell Kennerley, 1914.

– *The Making of Personality*. Boston: L.C. Page, 1908.

Carman, Bliss, and Richard Hovey. *Last Songs from Vagabondia*. Boston: Small Maynard, 1901.

– *More Songs from Vagabondia*. Boston: Copeland and Day, 1896.

– *Songs from Vagabondia*. Boston: Copeland and Day, 1894.

– *Songs from Vagabondia*. 1894. Boston: Copeland and Day; London: Elkin Mathews, 1895.

Charlesworth, Hector. *More Candid Chronicles*. Toronto: Macmillan, 1928.

Clark, Edward B. 'Roosevelt on the Nature Fakirs.' *Everybody's Magazine* [New York] 16 (June 1907): 770–4.

Clark, William. 'Canadian Poets.' *Week* [Toronto] 12 (18 Oct. 1895): 1110.

Cogswell, Fred. 'Charles G.D. Roberts.' *Canadian Writers and Their Works*. Poetry Series. Vol. 2. Ed. Robert Lecker, Jack David, and Ellen Quigley. Downsview: ECW, 1983. 187–232.

– 'Introduction.' *Collected Letters*, by Charles G.D. Roberts. Ed. Laurel Boone. Fredericton: Goose Lane, 1989. 11–22.

Collier, William Francis. *A History of English Literature, in a Series of Biographical Sketches*. Toronto: James Campbell and Son, 1872.

Collins, Joseph Edmund. 'An Academy of Letters.' *Star* [Chatham, NB], 29 June 1881.

– 'The Bard of Tantramar.' *Star* [Chatham, NB], 4 Dec. 1880.

– *Canada under the Adminstration of Lord Lorne*. Toronto: Rose Publishing Company, 1884.

– 'Canadian Verse.' *Critic* [Halifax], special Jubilee number, June 1887, 21–2.

– 'Editorial Gleanings.' *Star* [Chatham, NB], 2 April 1881.

– 'English-Canadian Literature.' *Week* [Toronto] 1.39 (28 Aug. 1884): 614–15.

– 'The "Free Press" and Mr. Davin.' *Star* [Chatham, NB], 7 May 1881.

– 'The Future of Canada.' *Star* [Chatham, NB], 4 May 1881.

– 'The Future of Canada.' *Star* [Chatham, NB] 7 and 11 May 1881.

– 'The Future of the Dominion of Canada.' *Canadian Leaves: History, Art, Science, Literature, Commerce. A Series of New Papers Read before the Canadian Club of New York*. Ed. G.M. Fairchild, Jr. New York: Napoléon Thompson, 1887. 1–17.

– 'Honours for a Chatham Boy.' *Star* [Chatham, NB] 30 April 1881.

– 'International Copyright.' *Week* [Toronto] 1.1 (6 Dec. 1883): 5–6.

– *Life and Times of the Right Honourable Sir John A. Macdonald, K.C.B., D.C.L., &c., Premier of the Dominion of Canada*. Toronto: Rose, 1883.

– 'Literature.' In 'Review of Literature, Science and Art.' *The Dominion Annual Register and Review for the Eighteenth Year of the Canadian Union, 1884*. Ed. Henry J. Morgan. Toronto: Hunter, Rose, 1885. 168–83.

- 'Mr. Nicholas Flood Davin.' *Star* [Chatham, NB] 30 March 1881.
- 'Orion and Other Poems.' Rev. of *Orion, and Other Poems*, by Charles G.D. Roberts. *Rouge et Noir* [Toronto] 4 (Feb. 1883): 12–13.
- 'Sir Charles Duffy's Letter on the Land Bill.' Editorial. *Star* [Chatham, NB], 14 Sept. 1881.

Colum, Padraic. 'Prefatory Note.' *Sanctuary: Sunshine Sonnets*, by Bliss Carman. Toronto: McClelland and Stewart, 1929. v–viii.

Colvin, Sidney. *Keats*. 1887. English Men of Letters. London: Macmillan, 1913.

Conant, Thomas. 'Our Canadian Poets.' *Globe* [Toronto] 2 Dec. 1893, 1; 23 Dec. 1893, 7; 20 Jan. 1894, 3.

Connor, Carl Y. *Archibald Lampman: Canadian Poet of Nature*. Montreal: Louis Carrier, 1929.

Conway, Don. 'Roberts and Modernism: The Achievement of "The Squatter".' *The Charles G.D. Roberts Symposium*. Ed. Glenn Clever. Reappraisals: Canadian Writers, 10. Ottawa: U of Ottawa P, 1984. 77–88.

Cook, Ramsay. 'Goldwin Smith.' *Dictionary of Canadian Biography*. 13: 968–74.

Cook, Terry. 'Apostle of Empire: Sir George Parkin and Imperial Federation.' Diss., Queen's University, 1977.

Corse, Sarah M. *Nationalism and Literature: The Politics of Culture in Canada and the United States*. Cambridge: Cambridge UP, 1997.

Cox, George. *The Mythology of the Aryan Nations*. London: Longmans, Green, 1870.

Crawford, Agnes. 'Delsartean Physical Culture.' *Saturday Night* [Toronto] 4 (22 Aug. 1891): 6.
- 'Delsartean Physical Culture.' *Saturday Night* [Toronto] 4 (5 Sept. 1891): 7.

Crawford, Annie. 'Chautauqua.' *Dominion Illustrated* [Montreal], 21 Nov. 1891, 484–5.

Cross, Ethelbert F.H. 'Genius and Patriotism.' *Week* [Toronto] 9 (26 Aug. 1892): 618–19.

Crowell, Norton B. *Alfred Austin, Victorian*. London: Weidenfield and Nicolson, 1955.

Culler, A. Dwight, ed. *Poetry and Criticism of Matthew Arnold*. Boston: Houghton Mifflin, 1961.

Daniells, Roy. 'Lampman and Roberts.' *Literary History of Canada*. Ed. Carl F. Klinck. 1965. Toronto: U of Toronto P, 1973. 389–405.

Davies, Barrie. 'Introduction.' *At the Mermaid Inn: Wilfred Campbell, Archibald Lampman, Duncan Campbell Scott in 'The Globe,' 1892–93*. Ed. Barrie Davies. Literature of Canada: Poetry and Prose in Reprint. Toronto: U of Toronto P, 1979. vii–xxi.

Davin, Nicholas Flood. *British versus American Civilization: A Lecture Delivered in*

*Shaftesbury Hall, Toronto, 19th April, 1873.* National Papers 2. Toronto: Adam, Stevenson, 1873.

– *The Earl of Beaconsfield with Disraeli Anecdotes Never Before Published.* Toronto: Belford Bros, 1876.

– *Eos: An Epic of the Dawn, and Other Poems.* Regina: Leader Company, 1889.

– 'The Future of Canada.' *Rose-Belford's Canadian Monthly and National Review* [Toronto] NS 4 (May 1881): 490–8.

– 'Great Speeches.' *Rose Belford's Canadian Monthly and National Review* [Toronto] NS 4 (March 1881): 270–85.

Davis, Richard. *The Young Ireland Movement.* Dublin: Gill and Macmillan; Totowa, NJ: Barnes and Noble, 1987.

De Gaspé, Philippe Aubert. *Canadians of Old.* Trans. Charles G.D. Roberts. 1890. New Canadian Library. Toronto: McClelland and Stewart, 1974.

Deacon, William Arthur. *Dear Bill: The Correspondence of William Arthur Deacon.* Ed. John Lennox and Michele Lacombe. Toronto: U of Toronto P, 1988.

Dean, Misao. 'Political Science: Realism in Roberts's Animal Stories.' *Studies in Canadian Literature* 21.1 (1996): 1–16.

*Debates of the Senate of the Dominion of Canada. 1892. Second Session – Seventh Parliament.* Ottawa: Queen's Printer, 1892.

'The Decay of Imagination.' *Globe* [Toronto], 27 May 1889, 4.

Delaumosne, Abbé. *Delsarte System of Oratory.* New York: E.S. Werner, 1893.

Dewart, Edward Hartley. 'Introductory Essay on Canadian Poetry.' *Selections from Canadian Poets; with Occasional Critical and Biographical Notes, and an Introductory Essay on Canadian Poetry.* Ed. Edward Hartley Dewart. Montreal: John Lovell, 1864. ix–xix.

Dilke, Sir Charles Wentworth. *Greater Britain: A Record of Travel in English–Speaking Countries during 1866 and 1867.* New York: Harper and Brothers, 1869.

– *Problems of Greater Britain.* London: Macmillan, 1890.

Disraeli, Benjamin. *Sybil; or, The Two Nations.* 1845. Ed. Walter Sichel. London: Oxford UP, 1926.

Djwa, Sandra. 'Lampman's Fleeting Vision.' *Colony and Confederation: Early Canadian Poets and Their Background.* Ed. George Woodcock. Vancouver: U of British Columbia P, 1974. 124–41.

– *The Politics of the Imagination: A Life of F.R. Scott.* Toronto: U of Toronto P, 1987.

Douglas, Ann. *The Feminization of American Culture.* New York: Knopf, 1977.

Douglas, Mary. *Thought Styles: Critical Essays on Good Taste.* London: Sage, 1996.

Doyle, James. 'Archibald Lampman and Hamlin Garland.' *Canadian Poetry: Studies, Documents, Reviews* 16 (Spring/Summer 1985): 38–46.

– *The Fin de Siècle Spirit: Walter Blackburn Harte and the American/Canadian Literary Milieu of the 1890s.* Toronto: ECW, 1995.

Dragland, Stan. *Floating Voice: Duncan Campbell Scott and the Literature of Treaty 9.* Toronto: Anansi, 1994.

Dresser, Horatio W. *A History of the New Thought Movement.* New York: T.Y. Crowell, 1919.

Duffy, Sir Charles Gavan. *Four Years of Irish History, 1845–1849.* London: Cassell, Petter, Galpin, 1883.

– *Young Ireland: A Fragment of Irish History. 1840–1850.* 1881. New York: Da Capo Press, 1973.

Duncan, Sara Jeannette. *The Imperialist.* 1904. Ed. Thomas E. Tausky. Ottawa: Tecumseh, 1988.

Dussault, Gabriel. 'François-Xavier-Antoine Labelle.' *Dictionary of Canadian Biography.* 12: 500–3.

– *Le Curé Labelle: messianisme, utopic et colonisation au Québec, 1850–1900.* Montreal: Hurtubise HMH, 1983.

Early, L.R. *Archibald Lampman.* Twayne World Authors Series. Canadian Literature. 770. Boston: Twayne, 1986.

– 'A Chronology of Lampman's Poems.' *Canadian Poetry: Studies, Documents, Reviews* 14 (Spring/Summer 1984): 75–87.

– 'Lampman and Romantic Poetry.' Diss., York University, 1979.

– 'Poems of October: Lampman's Elegies'. *Canadian Poetry: Studies, Documents, Reviews* 45 (Fall/Winter 1999): 31-65.

– 'Roberts As Critic.' *The Sir Charles G.D. Roberts Symposium.* Ed. Glenn Clever. Reappraisals: Canadian Writers 10. Ottawa: U of Ottawa P, 1984. 173–89.

– ed. 'Twenty-Five Fugitive Poems by Archibald Lampman.' *Canadian Poetry: Studies, Documents, Reviews* 18 (Spring/Summer 1985): 46–70.

Edgar, James David. *The Commercial Independence of Canada: An Address Delivered 26th January, 1883 to the Reform Associations of Centre Toronto, on 'The Right of Canada to Make Her Own Commercial Treaties.'* Toronto: Grip, 1883.

Edgar, Pelham. 'Duncan Campbell Scott.' *Week* [Toronto] 12 (15 March 1895): 370–1.

Evans, Warren Felt. *Mental Medicine: A Theoretical and Practical Treatise on Medical Psychology.* 1874. 3rd ed. Boston: Carter and Pettee, 1874.

Faber, Richard. *Young England.* London: Faber and Faber, 1987.

Fawcett, Millicent Garrett. *Political Economy for Beginners.* London: Macmillian, 1884.

Fisher, Roswell. 'Canada's Alternatives.' *Canadian Monthly and National Review* [Toronto] 8 (Nov. 1875): 428-32.

Fiske, John. *Myths and Myth-Makers: Old Tales and Superstitions Interpreted by Comparative Mythology.* 1872. Boston: Houghton, Mifflin, 1886.

Forman, W[illia]m Henry. 'Jasper Francis Cropsey, N.A.' *Manhattan* [New York] 3 (April 1884): 372–81.

Foster, William Alexander. *Canada First: A Memorial of the Late William A. Foster, Q.C.* Introd. Goldwin Smith. Toronto: Hunter, Rose, 1890.

– *Canada First; or, Our New Nationality: An Address.* Toronto: Adam, Stevenson, 1871.

Fraistat, Neil. 'Introduction.' *Poems in Their Place: The Intertextuality and Order of Poetic Collections.* Ed. Neil Fraistat. Chapel Hill: U of North Carolina P, 1986. 3–17.

– ed. *Poems in Their Place: The Intertextuality and Order of Poetic Collections.* Chapel Hill: U of North Carolina P, 1986.

Fussell, Paul. *Abroad: British Literary Traveling between the Wars.* New York: Oxford UP, 1980.

Galt, Sir Alexander. *The Future of the Dominion of Canada.* [London: np, 1881.] Reprinted from *Proceedings of the Royal Colonial Institute.* Vol. 12, 1883. 88–109.

– *The Relations of the Colonies to the Empire.* London: McCorquodale, 1883.

Garvin, John W., ed. *Canadian Poets.* Toronto: McClelland and Stewart, 1926.

Geddes, Gary. 'Piper of Many Tunes: Duncan Campbell Scott.' *Duncan Campbell Scott: A Book of Criticism.* Ed. S.L. Dragland. Ottawa: Tecumseh, 1974. 165–77.

Gerson, Carole, and Gwendolyn Davies, eds. *Canadian Poetry: From the Beginnings through the First World War.* Toronto: McClelland and Stewart, 1994.

Gilmore, David D. *Manhood in the Making: Cultural Concepts of Masculinity.* London: Yale UP, 1990.

Gosse, Edmund. 'A Plea for Certain Exotic Forms of Verse.' *Cornhill Magazine* [London] 36 (1877): 53–71.

Grant, George Monro. 'Preface.' *Picturesque Canada; the Country As It Was and Is.* Ed. George Monro Grant. 2 vols. Toronto: Belden Bros, 1882. 1: i–ii.

Grayson, David. *Great Possessions: A New Series of Adventures.* New York: Doubleday, Page and Company, 1918.

Green, Roger Lancelyn. *Andrew Lang.* New York: Henry Z. Walck, 1962.

Greig, Peter E. 'A Check List of Lampman Manuscript Material in the Douglas Library Archives,' Part 1. *Douglas Library Notes* 15 (Winter 1967): 8–16. Part 2. *Douglas Library Notes* 16 (Autumn 1967): 12–27.

Griffin, Watson. 'A Canadian-American Liaison.' *Magazine of American History* 21 (Feb. 1889): 123–38.

– *An Irish Evolution: Home Rule from an American Standpoint.* Hamilton: Griffin and Kidner, n.d.

– *TWOK: a Novel.* Hamilton: Griffin and Kidner, 1887.

Groening, Laura. 'Duncan Campbell Scott: An Annotated Bibliography.' *The*

*Annotated Bibliography of Canada's Major Authors.* Ed. Robert Lecker and Jack David. Vol. 8. Toronto: ECW Press, 1994. 469-576.

Gross, A.H. 'The Emigration of Young Men to the United States – a Different View.' *Week* [Toronto] 1 (12 June 1884): 441.

Gundy, H. Pearson, ed. *Letters,* by Bliss Carman. Montreal: McGill-Queen's UP, 1981.

Haliburton, R.G. *The Men of the North and Their Place in History: A Lecture Delivered before the Montreal Literary Club, March 31st, 1869.* Montreal: John Lovell, 1869.

Haliburton, Thomas Chandler. *Nature and Human Nature.* 1855. London: Hurst and Blackett, 1859.

Hamilton, William B. *Place Names of Atlantic Canada.* Toronto: U of Toronto P, 1996.

Harte, Walter Blackburn. 'Canadian Journalists and Journalism.' *New England Magazine* NS 5.4 (Dec. 1891): 411–41.

– *Meditations in Motley: A Bundle of Papers Imbued with the Sobriety of Midnight.* Boston: Arena, 1894.

– 'Some Canadian Writers of To-day.' *New England Magazine* NS 3.1 (Sept. 1890): 21–40.

Hathaway, Rufus H. 'Carman's Memorial Unveiling.' *Canadian Bookman* [Toronto] 12 (Dec. 1930): 262–3.

– 'The Poetry of Bliss Carman.' *Sewanee Review* 33 (Oct. 1925): 467–83.

Hatton, Joseph. *The Queen of Bohemia: A Story of English Life and Manners.* 1878. New York: Harper and Brothers, 1882.

Haultain, Theodore Arnold. 'A "Canadian Literature."' *Lake Magazine* [Toronto] 1 (Aug. 1892): 17–20.

Headon, Christopher Fergus. 'George Whitaker.' *Dictionary of Canadian Biography.* 11: 916–18.

Herbin, John Frederic. *The Marshlands (Second Edition) and the Trail of the Tide.* Toronto: William Briggs, 1899.

Herder, Johann Gottfried. *Outlines of a Philosophy of the History of Man.* Trans. T. Churchill. London: J. Johnson, 1800.

Hingston, William H. *The Climate of Canada and Its Relations to Life and Health.* Montreal: Dawson Bros, 1884.

Hobsbawm, Eric. 'Mass-Producing Traditions: Europe, 1870–1914.' *The Invention of Tradition.* Ed. Eric Hobsbawn and Terence Ranger. Past and Present Publications. Cambridge: Cambridge UP, 1983. 263–307.

Hobsbawm, Eric, and Terence Ranger, eds. *The Invention of Tradition.* Past and Present Publications. Cambridge: Cambridge UP, 1983.

Holmgren, Michele J. 'Native Muses and National Poetry: Nineteenth-Century Irish Canadian Poets.' Diss., University of Western Ontario, 1997.

Hovey, Richard. 'Delsarte and Poetry.' *Independent* [New York] 43 (27 Aug. 1891): 3–4.

– 'The Elements of Poetic Technic.' Part 1. *Independent* [NewYork] 46 (27 Sept. 1894): 5–6; Part 2. 46 (4 Oct. 1894): 7–8.

– 'Modern Symbolism and Maurice Maeterlinck.' *Plays,* by Maurice Maeterlinck. Trans. Richard Hovey. 1894, 1896. New York: Herbert Stone, 1902. New York: Kraus Reprint, 1972.

– 'The Technic of Poetry.' Part 1. *Independent* [NewYork] 44 (7 April 1892): 9–10. Part 2. 44 (21 April 1892): 4.

– 'The Technic of Rhyme.' *Independent* [New York] 45 (19 Oct. 1893): 3–4.

Howells, William Dean. 'Editor's Study.' *Harper's New Monthly Magazine* [New York] 81 (Jan. 1892): 315–20.

– 'Editor's Study.' *Harper's New Monthly Magazine* [New York] 78 (April 1889): 820–5.

– 'Editor's Study.' *Harper's New Monthly Magazine* [New York] 79 (March 1890): 642–7.

Hurst, Alexandra J., ed. *The War among the Poets: Issues of Plagiarism and Patronage among the Confederation Poets.* Post-Confederation Poetry: Texts and Contexts. London: Canadian Poetry Press, 1994.

Jackel, David. 'The National Voice in Roberts' Poetry.' *The Proceedings of the Sir Charles G.D. Roberts Symposium.* Ed. Carrie MacMillan. Anchorage Series 1. Sackville, NB: Centre for Canadian Studies, Mount Allison University; Halifax: Nimbus, 1984. 43–51.

Jessup, Lynda, ed. *Antimodernism and Artistic Experience: Policing the Boundaries of Modernity.* Toronto: U of Toronto P, 2001.

Johnson, E. Pauline. 'The Singer of Tantramar.' *Massey's Magazine* [Toronto] 1.1 (Jan. 1869): 15–19.

Johnson, J.K. *The Canadian Directory of Parliament, 1867–1967.* Ottawa: Public Archives of Canada, 1968.

Jones, D.G. *Butterfly on Rock: A Study of Themes and Images in Canadian Literature.* Toronto: U of Toronto P, 1970.

Keats, John. *Poetical Works.* Ed. H.W. Garrod. 1956. Oxford: Oxford UP, 1973.

Keith, W.J. *Canadian Literature in English.* Longman Literature in English Series. New York: Longman, 1985.

– *Charles G.D. Roberts.* Studies in Canadian Literature. Toronto: Copp, Clark, 1969.

– 'Charles G.D. Roberts and the Poetic Tradition.' *The Proceedings of the Sir Charles G.D. Roberts Symposium, Mount Allison University.* Ed. Carrie MacMillan. Anchorage Series 1. Sackville: Centre for Canadian Studies, Mount Allison University; Halifax: Nimbus, 1984. 53–66.

- 'A Choice of Worlds: God, Man and Nature in Charles G.D. Roberts.' *Colony and Confederation.* Ed. George Woodcock. Vancouver: U of British Columbia P, 1974. 87–102.
- 'Introduction.' *Selected Poetry and Critical Prose,* by Charles G.D. Roberts. Ed. W.J. Keith. Literature of Canada: Poetry and Prose in Reprint. Toronto: U of Toronto P, 1974. xvi–xxxix.
- Rev. of *At the Mermaid Inn: Wilfred Campbell, Archibald Lampman, Duncan Campbell Scott in* 'The Globe' *1892–93,* ed. Barrie Davies. In 'Letters in Canada 1979.' *University of Toronto Quarterly.* 'Letters in Canada 1979.' 49 (Summer 1980): 447–52.

Kennedy, Margaret. 'Lampman and the Canadian Thermopylae: "At the Long Sault: May, 1660."' *Canadian Poetry: Studies, Documents, Reviews* 1 (Fall/Winter 1977): 54–9.

Kidd, Adam. *The Huron Chief.* Ed. D.M.R. Bentley. Early Canadian Long Poems. London: Canadian Poetry Press, 1987.

Kilpatrick, Ross S. 'Introduction.' *Orion, and Other Poems,* by Charles G.D. Roberts. Ed. Ross S. Kilpatrick. Post-Confederation Poetry: Texts and Contexts. London: Canadian Poetry Press, 1999. ix–xxxii.

Kizuk, R. Alexander. *A Reassessment of Early Twentieth-Century Canadian Poetry in English.* Canadian Studies, 24. Lewiston, NY: Edwin Mellen, 2000.

Klinck, Carl F. 'A Complete Bibliography of William Wilfred Campbell (1858–1918).' D.B. Weldon Library, University of Western Ontario.

- *Wilfred Campbell: A Study in Late Provincial Victorianism.* Toronto: Ryerson, 1942.

Koester, Charles Beverley. 'The Parliamentary Career of Nicholas Flood Davin, 1887–1900.' Diss., University of Saskatchewan, 1964.

Kramer, Sidney. *A History of Stone and Kimball and Herbert S. Stone and Co., with a Bibliography of Their Publications.* Chicago: U of Chicago P, 1940.

Kraus, Joe W. *Messrs. Copeland & Day, 69 Cornhill, Boston, 1893–1899.* Philadelphia: George S. MacManus, 1979.

Kuhn, Alvin Boyd. *Theosophy: A Modern Revival of Ancient Wisdom.* New York: H. Holt, 1930.

Lampman, Archibald. *An Annotated Edition of the Correspondence between Archibald Lampman and Edward William Thomson (1890–1898).* Ed. Helen Lynn. Ottawa: Tecumseh, 1980.

- *Essays and Reviews.* Ed. D.M.R. Bentley. Post-Confederation Poetry: Texts and Contexts. London: Canadian Poetry Press, 1996.
- *Fairy Tales.* Ed. D.M.R. Bentley. Post-Confederation Poetry: Texts and Contexts. London: Canadian Poetry Press, 1999.
- *At the Mermaid Inn: Wilfred Campbell, Archibald Lampman, Duncan Campbell Scott*

in '*The Globe,*' *1892–93.* Ed. Barrie Davies. Literature of Canada: Poetry and Prose in Reprint. Toronto: U of Toronto P, 1979.

– Papers. National Archives of Canada, Ottawa, ON.

– Papers. W.A.C. Bennett Library, Simon Fraser University, Burnaby, BC

– *Poems.* Ed. Duncan Campbell Scott. Toronto: George N. Morang, 1900.

– *Selected Poetry.* Ed. Michael Gnarowski. Ottawa: Tecumseh, 1987.

– *The Story of an Affinity.* Ed. D.M.R. Bentley. Early Canadian Long Poems. London: Canadian Poetry Press, 1986.

Lanstaff, Eleanor de Selms. *Andrew Lang.* Twayne's English Authors Series 241. Boston: Twayne, 1978.

Leacock, Stephen. *My Recollection of Chicago and the Doctrine of 'Laissez Faire.'* Ed. Carl Spadoni. Toronto: U of Toronto P, 1998.

Lears, T.J. Jackson. *No Place of Grace: Antimodernism and the Transformation of American Culture, 1880–1920.* New York: Pantheon, 1981.

Lee, H.D.C. *Bliss Carman: A Study in Canadian Poetry.* Np: Buxton, 1912.

Lehmann-Haupt, Hellmut. *The Book in America: A History of the Making and Selling of Books in the United States.* New York: R.R. Bowker Company, 1952.

Leisner, August. 'Charles G.D. Roberts: Mystical Poet.' Ed. Laurel Boone. *Studies in Canadian Literature* 9.2 (1984): 267–93.

Leland, Charles G. *The Algonquin Legends of New England; or, Myths and Folk Lore of the Micmac, Passamaquoddy, and Penobscot Tribes.* Boston: Houghton, Mifflin, 1884.

Levesque, Robert, and Robert Migner. *Le Curé Labelle: le colonisateur, le politicien, la legende.* Montreal: La Presse, 1979.

Lewis, Wyndham. *Blasting and Bombardiering.* 1937. London: Calder; New York: Riverrun, 1982.

Lighthall, William Douw. *Adjustable Federation.* Np: np, [Sept. 1885].

– *Canada, a Modern Nation.* Montreal: Witness, 1904.

– 'Canadian Literature.' Rev. *The Soul's Quest, and Other Poems,* by Frederick George Scott. *Week* [Toronto] 6 (28 Dec. 1888): 56–7.

– *Old Measures: Collected Verse.* Montreal: A.T. Chapman; Toronto: Musson, 1922.

– *Spiritualized Happiness-Theory; or, New Utilitarianism: A Lecture before the Farmington School of Philosophy, June, 1890.* Montreal: 'Witness,' 1890.

– *Thoughts, Moods and Ideals: Crimes of Leisure.* Montreal: 'Witness' Printing House, 1887.

– *The Young Seigneur; or, Nation-Making.* Montreal: Wm. Drysdale, 1888.

– ed. *Songs of the Great Dominion: Voices from the Forests and Waters, the Settlements and Cities of Canada.* London: Walter Scott, 1889.

Lloyd, J.A.T. 'Onomatopoeia and Mr. Bliss Carman.' *Week* [Toronto] 9 (7 Oct. 1892): 709.

Locker-Lampson, Frederick. 'Preface.' *Lyra Elegantiarum: A Collection of Some of the Best Social and Occasional Verse, by Deceased English Authors.* London: Ward, Lock, 1891.

Logan, J.D., and Donald G. French. *Highways of Canadian Literature: a Synoptic Introduction to the Literary History of Canada (English) from 1760 to 1924.* 1924. 2nd ed. Toronto: McClelland and Stewart, 1928.

Logan, John Edward ('Barry Dane'). 'National Literature.' *Week* [Toronto] 1 (21 Aug. 1884): 600–1; 1 (4 Sept. 1884): 632–3.

Longley, James Wilberforce. 'A Field for Canadian Achievements.' *Week* [Toronto] 1 (3 July 1884): 485–6.

Lutts, Ralph. *The Nature Fakers: Wildlife, Science, and Sentiment.* Golden, CO: Fulcrum, 1990.

MacFarlane, W.G. 'The Canadian Goldsmith.' *Lake Magazine* [Toronto] 1 (Dec. 1892): 285–9.

– 'New Brunswick Authorship.' *Dominion Illustrated* [Montreal] 7 (24 Oct. 1891): 401–3; 7 (31 Oct. 1891): 425–6; 7 (7 Nov. 1891): 437–8; 7 (21 Nov. 1891): 494–5.

Machar, Agnes Maule ('Fidelis'). 'Patriotism versus Cosmopolitanism.' *Week* [Toronto] 3 (7 Oct. 1886): 716.

– 'Some Recent Canadian Poems.' Rev. of *Among the Millet, and Other Poems*, by Archibald Lampman. *Week* [Toronto] 6 (22 March 1889): 251–2.

MacMechan, Archibald. *Head-Waters of Canadian Literature.* Toronto: McClelland and Stewart, 1924.

Madison, Charles A. *Book Publishing in America.* New York: MacGraw-Hill, 1966.

Magoon, E.L. 'Scenery and Mind.' *The Home Book of the Picturesque; or, American Scenery, Art, and Literature.* 1852. Gainsville, FL: Scholars Facsimiles and Reprints, 1967. 1–48.

Mair, Charles. *Dreamland and Other Poems; Tecumseh: A Drama.* Introd. Norman Shrive. Literature of Canada: Poetry and Prose in Reprint. Toronto: U of Toronto P, 1974.

– 'The New Canada: Its Resources and Productions.' *Canadian Monthly and National Review* [Toronto] 8 (July 1875): 2–8; 8 (Aug. 1875): 156–64.

Malloch, Faith L. 'An Intimate Picture of Wilfred Campbell.' [Canada]: np, nd

Mangan, J.A., and James Malvin, eds. *Manliness and Morality: Middle-Class Masculinity in Britain and America, 1800–1940.* Manchester: Manchester UP, 1987.

Marquis, T.G. 'Roberts' *Canadian Magazine* [Toronto] 1 (Sept. 1893): 572-5.

Martell, Carol E. 'Sir Charles G.D. Roberts: The King's College Years.' Thesis. Mount Allison University, 1978.

McDougall, Robert L. 'D.C. Scott: The Dating of the Poems.' *Canadian Poetry: Studies, Documents, Reviews* 2 (Spring/Summer 1978): 13–27.

– *Totems: Essays on the Cultural History of Canada.* Ottawa: Tecumseh, 1990.

– ed. *The Poet and the Critic: A Literary Correspondence between D.C. Scott and E.K. Brown.* Ottawa: Carleton UP, 1983.

McGee, Thomas D'Arcy. *Canadian Ballads, and Occasional Verses.* Montreal: J. Lovell; Toronto: W.C.F. Caverhill, 1858.

– 'The Mental Outfit of the New Dominion' (From the *Montreal Gazette,* 5 Nov, 1867). Np: np, nd.

– 'Protection for Canadian Literature.' *New Era* [Montreal] (24 April 1858), 2.

McLeod, Les. 'Canadian Post-Romanticism: The Context of Late Nineteenth-Century Canadian Poetry.' *Canadian Poetry: Studies, Documents, Reviews* 14 (Spring/Summer 1984): 1–37.

Merrill, Helen M. *Picturesque Prince Edward County.* Picton, ON: Gazette, 1892.

– *Sandpipers, and Other Poems.* Toronto: np, 1915.

Meyer, Donald. *The Positive Thinkers: Religion As Pop Psychology from Mary Baker Eddy.* 1965. 2nd ed. New York: Pantheon, 1980.

Miller, Muriel. *Bliss Carman: Quest and Revolt.* St John's: Jesperson, 1985.

Milton, John. *Complete Poems and Major Prose.* Ed. Merritt Y. Hughes. New York: Odyssey, 1957.

Mitchell, S. Weir. *Wear and Tear; or, Hints for the Overworked.* 1871. 8th ed. Philadelphia: J.P. Lippincott, 1897.

Moir, John S. *Character and Circumstance.* Toronto: Macmillan, 1970.

Moore, Thomas. *Poetical Works.* Ed. A.D. Godley. London: Oxford UP, 1915.

Morgan, Henry J. *Bibliotheca Canadensis; or, A Manual of Canadian Literature.* Ottawa: G.E. Desbarats, 1867.

Morse, Charles. *Apices Juris, and Other Legal Essays in Prose and Verse.* Toronto: Canada Law Book Co., 1906.

Mott, Frank Luther. *A History of American Magazines, 1741–1850.* 5 vols. 1930. Cambridge: Harvard UP, 1966.

Mount, Nick. 'Exodus: When Canadian Literature Moved to New York.' Diss., Dalhousie University, 2001.

Muddiman, Bernard. 'Duncan Campbell Scott.' *Duncan Campbell Scott: A Book of Criticism.* Ed. S.L. Dragland. Ottawa: Tecumseh, 1974. 31–40.

Müller, Karl Otfried. *History of the Literature of Ancient Greece.* Trans. Sir George Cornewall Lewis. Continued after [Müller's] death by John William Donaldson. 2 vols. London: Longmans, Green, [1858].

Murray, Heather. *Working in English: History, Institution, Resources.* Toronto: U of Toronto P, 1996.

Murray, R., and A. Simpson. 'Nova Scotia.' *Picturesque Canada; the Country As It Was and Is.* Ed. George Monro Grant. 2 vols. Toronto: Belden Bros, 1882. 2: 789–852.

Myers, Frederic W.H. *Collected Poems, with Autobiographical and Critical Fragments.* Ed. Eveleen Myers. London: Macmillan, 1921.

'Native Literature.' *Globe* [Toronto], 15 Jan. 1889, 3.

Neatby, Hilda. 'Thomas D'Arcy McGee.' *Dictionary of Canadian Biography.* 9: 489–94.

'Needless Noises – Effects of Noises on the Nervous System.' *Canada Health Journal* [Ottawa] 13 (Jan 1891): 2.

New, W.H. *A History of Canadian Literature.* Macmillan History of Literature. Basingstoke: Macmillan Education, 1989.

'The New Criticism.' *Nation* [New York] 28 (Feb. 1895): 159–60.

Newcomb, Simon. *Principles of Political Economy.* New York: Harper, 1886.

O'Brien, Kevin. *Oscar Wilde in Canada: An Apostle for the Arts.* Toronto: Personal Library, 1982.

O'Donnell, Kathleen M. 'Thomas D'Arcy McGee's Irish and Canadian Ballads.' M.A. thesis, University of Western Ontario, 1956.

*Official Report of the Debates of the House of Commons of the Dominion of Canada. First Session – Seventh Parliament. 54–55 Victoriae, 1891.* Vol. 33. Ottawa: Brown Chamberlin, 1891.

*Official Report of the Debates of the House of Commons of the Dominion of Canada. Fourth Session – Sixth Parliament 53ᵈ Victoriae, 1890.* Vol. 30. Ottawa: Brown Chamberlin, 1890.

O'Hagan, Thomas. *Canadian Essays, Critical and Historical.* Toronto: William Briggs, 1901.

– 'Canadian Poets and Poetry.' *Catholic World* 69 (Sept. 1895): 783–801.

Olmsted, Frederick Law. *Mount Royal, Montreal.* New York: G.P. Putnam's Sons, 1881.

O'Neill, Patrick. *Ireland and Germany: A Study in Literary Relations.* Canadian Studies in German Language and Literature. New York: Peter Lang, 1985.

Opie, Iona, and Peter Opie, eds. *Oxford Dictionary of Nursery Rhymes.* Oxford: Clarendon, 1951.

'Orion and Other Poems.' Rev. of *Orion, and Other Poems,* by Charles G.D. Roberts. *Rose-Belford's Canadian Monthly Magazine and Literary Review* [Toronto] 5 (Nov. 1880): 552–3.

Oxley, J. Macdonald. 'Busy People.' *Man: A Canadian Home Magazine* [Ottawa] 1 (Dec. 1885): 55–7.

– *Up among the Ice Floes.* Philadelphia: American Baptist Pub. Society, 1890.

Pacey, Desmond. 'Introduction.' *Selected Poems,* by Charles G.D. Roberts. Ed. Desmond Pacey. 1955. Ottawa: Tecumseh, 1980. xi–xxv.

– *Ten Canadian Poets: A Group of Biographical and Critical Essays.* 1958. Toronto: Ryerson, 1969.

Parker, Gail Thain. *Mind Cure in New England from the Civil War to World War I.* Hanover, NH: UP of New England, 1973.

Parker, George Leo. *The Beginnings of the Book Trade in Canada.* Toronto: U of Toronto P, 1985.

Parkin, George R. 'The Reorganization of the British Empire.' *Century Magazine* [New York] 37. 2 (Dec. 1888): 187–92.

Parkman, Francis. *The Old Regime in Canada.* Boston: Little, Brown, 1874.

Parrish, Stephen Maxfield. *Currents of the Nineties in Boston and London: Fred Holland Day, Louise Imogen Guiney, and Their Circle.* New York: Garland, 1987.

Pascoe, C.F. *Two Hundred Years of the S.P.G.: An Historical Account of the Society for the Propagation of the Gospel in Foreign Parts, 1701–1900.* London: S.P.G., 1901.

Payne, William Morton. 'Recent American Poetry.' *Dial* [Chicago] 18 (1 Feb. 1895): 82–6.

– 'Recent American Poetry.' *Dial* [Chicago] 25 (1 Sept. 1898): 132–6.

– 'Recent Books of Poetry.' *Dial* [Chicago] 9 (April 1889): 323–8.

– 'Recent Poetry.' *Dial* [Chicago] 8 (May 1887): 15–19.

Pearson, Charles H. *National Life and Character: A Forecast.* 1893. London: Macmillan, 1913.

Perkins, David. *A History of Modern Poetry: From the 1890s to the High Modernist Mode.* Cambridge: Harvard UP, 1976.

Pierce, Lorne. *An Outline of Canadian Literature (French and English).* Toronto: Ryerson, 1927.

– 'Lorne Pierce's 1927 Interview with Charles G.D. Roberts (as Reported by Margaret Lawrence).' Ed. Terry Whalen. *Canadian Poetry: Studies, Documents, Reviews* 21 (Fall/Winter 1987): 59–76.

Pomeroy, E.M. *Sir Charles G.D. Roberts: A Biography.* Toronto: Ryerson, 1943.

Pound, Ezra. *Selected Poems.* New York: New Directions, 1957.

*Proceedings and Transactions of the Royal Society of Canada.* 2nd ser. Vol 1. *Meeting of May, 1895.* Ottawa: John Durie, 1895.

*Proceedings and Transactions of the Royal Society of Canada for the Year 1894.* Vol 12. Ottawa: John Durie and Son, 1895.

Reade, John. 'Literature.' In 'Review of Literature, Science and Art.' *Dominion Annual Register and Reviews for the Twentieth Year of the Canadian Union, 1886.* Ed. Henry James Morgan. Montreal: Eusébe Senécal et Fils, 1887. 210–30.

– *The Prophecy of Merlin and Other Poems.* Montreal: Dawson, 1870.

– 'Thomas D'Arcy McGee – the Poet.' *New Dominion Monthly* [Montreal] (Feb. 1870): 12–21.

'Recent Canadian Literature.' *Bystander* [Toronto] NS 1 (Jan. 1883): 67–8.

Reed, T.A., ed. *A History of Trinity College Toronto, 1852–1952.* Toronto: U of Toronto P, 1952.

Roberts, Charles G.D. 'Authors at Home. XII. Goldwin Smith at the Grange.'
    *Critic* [New York] 4 (11 July 1885):13–14.

– 'Canada' ['O strong hearts guarding the birthright of our glory ...']. *Anglo-Saxon* [Ottawa] (April 1890): 2.

– *The Canadian Guide-Book: The Tourist's and Sportsman's Guide to Eastern Canada and Newfoundland.* London: William Heinemann, 1892.

– 'Canadian Literature.' *Bystander* [Toronto] NS 3 (July 1883): 212.

– 'Canadian Literature.' *Bystander* [Toronto] NS 4 (Oct. 1883): 328–30.

– 'Canadian Poetry in Its Relation to the Poetry of England and America.' Ed. D.M.R. Bentley. *Canadian Poetry: Studies, Documents, Reviews* 3 (Fall/Winter 1978): 76–86.

– 'The Change in Government in N.B.' *Bystander* [Toronto] NS 2 (April 1883): 92–95.

– 'Charles G.D. Roberts' Review of *Among the Millet.*' Ed. Tracy Ware. *Canadian Poetry: Studies, Documents, Reviews* 29 (1991): 38–45.

– *Collected Letters.* Ed. Laurel Boone. Fredericton: Goose Lane, 1989.

– *Collected Poems.* Ed. Desmond Pacey. Wolfville: Wombat, 1985.

– 'Defends Nature Stories.' *New York Times*, 14 June 1907, 6.

– *Earth's Enigmas.* Boston: L.C. Page, 1903.

– *Earth's Enigmas: A Book of Animal and Nature Life.* Boston: Lamson, Wolffe, 1896.

– 'Echoes from Old Acadia.' *Canadian Leaves: History, Art, Science, Literature, Commerce: A Series of New Papers Read before the Canadian Club of New York.* Ed. G.M. Fairchild, Jr. New York: Napoléon Thompson, 1887. 145–73.

– 'Edgar Fawcett.' *Week* [Toronto] 1.30 (26 June 1884): 437–38.

– 'The English Literature Course.' *King's College Record* [Windsor, NS] 8 (Nov. 1885): 19.

– 'The Future of Canada.' Rev. *of Canada and the Canadian Question*, by Goldwin Smith. *Dial* [Chicago] 13 (16 Dec. 1892): 385–7.

– *A History of Canada for High Schools and Academies.* 1897. Rev. ed. Toronto: Morang Educational, 1909.

– 'Imperial Relations.' *Bystander* [Toronto] NS 3 (July 1883): 195–6.

– *In Divers Tones.* Boston: Lothrop, 1889.

– 'Introduction.' *The Canadians of Old*, by Philippe Aubert de Gaspé. Trans. Charles G.D. Roberts. 1890. New Canadian Library. Toronto: McClelland and Stewart, 1974. 5–9.

– 'Introduction.' *Poems of Wild Life.* Ed. Charles G.D. Roberts. London: Walter Scott, 1888. ix–xviii.

– *The Kindred of the Wild; A Book of Animal Life.* 1902. Boston: L.C. Page, 1935.

– *The Land of Evangeline and the Gateways Thither.* Kentville, NS: Dominion Atlantic Railway Company, 1895.
– 'Literature.' In 'Review of Literature, Science and Art.' *The Dominion Annual Register and Review for the Seventeenth Year of the Canadian Union, 1883.* Ed. Henry J. Morgan. Toronto: Hunter, Rose, 1884. 206–19.
– 'Literature and Politics.' *Canada* [Benton, NB] 1 (May 1891): 51–2.
– 'Lorne Pierce's Interview with Charles G.D. Roberts (As Reported by Margaret Lawrence).' Ed. Terry Whalen. *Canadian Poetry: Studies, Documents, Reviews* 21 (Fall/Winter 1987): 59–76.
– 'Modern Instances.' *Dominion Illustrated* [Montreal] NS 1 (May 1892): 251–3.
– 'Mr. Bliss Carman's Poems.' Rev. of *Low Tide on Grand Pré,* by Bliss Carman. *Chap-Book* [Chicago] 1.3 (15 June 1894): 53–7.
– '"My Religion": A Personal Confession of Religious Experiences and Convictions.' *Manitoba Free Press* [Winnipeg] 5 June 1926, 29.
– 'New Brunswick.' *Picturesque Canada; the Country As It Was and Is.* Ed. George Monro Grant. 2 vols. Toronto: Belden Bros, 1882. 2: 741–88.
– 'Notes on Some of the Younger American Poets.' *Week* [Toronto] 1.21 (24 April 1884): 328–9.
– *Orion, and Other Poems.* 1880. Ed. Ross S. Kilpatrick. Post-Confederation Poetry: Texts and Contexts. London: Canadian Poetry Press, 1999.
– 'Pastoral Elegies.' *New Princeton Review* 5. 3 (May 1888): 360–70.
– 'The Poetic Outlook in Canada.' *Critic* [Halifax], Jubilee number (June 1887): 10–11.
– Rev. of *A Short History of the Canadian People,* by George Bryce. *Dial* [Chicago] 8 (April 1888): 290–2.
– 'The Savour of the Soil.' In 'Modern Instances.' *Dominion Illustrated* [Montreal] NS 1 (May 1892): 251–2.
– *Selected Poems.* Toronto: Ryerson, 1936.
– *A Sister to Evangeline: Being the Story of Yvonne de Lamourie, and How She Went into Exile with the Villagers of Grand Pré.* Boston: Lamson, Wolffe, 1898.
– 'The Teaching of English.' *King's College Record* [Windsor, NS] (Nov. 1888): 13–16. Reprinted from *Christian Union* 37 (19 April 1888): 488–9.
– 'The Work of the English Department.' *King's College Record* [Windsor, NS] 9 (Nov. 1886): 18.
– ed. *Poems of Wild Life.* London: Walter Scott, 1888.
– trans. *The Canadians of Old,* by Philippe Aubert de Gaspé. 1890. New Canadian Library. Toronto: McClelland and Stewart, 1974.
Roberts, Goodridge Bliss. 'Younger Canadian Poets.' *Younger American Poets, 1830–1890.* Ed. Douglas Sladen. New York: Cassell, 1891. 517–633.

Roper, Gordon. 'New Forces: New Fiction, 1880–1920.' *Literary History of Canada*. Gen. ed. Carl F. Klinck. 1965. Toronto: U of Toronto P, 1973. 260–83.

Roper, Henry. 'A "High Anglican Pagan" and His Pupil: Charles G.D. Roberts, Robert Norwood and the Development of a Nova Scotian Literary Tradition, 1885–1892.' *Dalhousie Review* 75 (Spring 1995): 51–73.

Rosenberg, Charles. 'Sexuality, Class, and Role in Nineteenth-Century America.' *The American Man.* Ed. Elizabeth H. Pleck and Joseph H. Pleck. Englewood Cliffs, NJ: Prentice-Hall, 1979. 219-54.

Ross, Malcolm. 'Introduction.' *Poets of the Confederation.* Ed. Malcolm Ross. New Canadian Library, 1. Toronto: McClelland and Stewart, 1960. ix–xiv.

– '"A Strange Aesthetic Ferment."' *Canadian Literature* 68–9 (Spring/Summer 1976): 13–25.

Rossetti, Dante Gabriel. *Works.* Ed. William M. Rossetti. London: Ellis, 1911.

Rotundo, E. Anthony. 'Learning about Manhood: Gender Ideals and the Middle-Class Family in Nineteenth-Century America.' *Manliness and Morality: Middle-Class Masculinity in Britain and America, 1800–1940.* Ed. J.A. Mangan and James Malvin. Manchester: Manchester UP, 1987. 35–51.

Russell, Henrietta. *Yawning.* The Delsarte Series 1. New York: United States Book Company, 1891.

Sacks, Peter M. *The English Elegy: Studies in Genre from Spenser to Yeats.* Baltimore: Johns Hopkin UP, 1985.

Sangster, Charles. *The St. Lawrence and the Saguenay.* Ed. D.M.R. Bentley. Early Canadian Long Poems. London: Canadian Poetry Press, 1990.

Schwarz, Michiel, and Michael Thompson. *Divided We Stand: Redefining Politics, Technology and Social Choice.* New York: Harvester Wheatsheaf, 1990.

Scott, Duncan Campbell. *Addresses, Essays, and Reviews.* Ed. Leslie Ritchie. 2 vols. Post-Confederation Poetry: Texts and Contexts. London: Canadian Poetry Press, 2000.

– *At the Mermaid Inn: Wilfred Campbell, Archibald Lampman, Duncan Campbell Scott in 'The Globe' 1892–93.* Ed. Barrie Davies. Literature of Canada: Poetry and Prose in Reprint. Toronto: U of Toronto P, 1979.

– *The Magic House and Other Poems.* Boston: Copeland and Day, 1895.

– *More Letters.* 2nd ser. Ed. Arthur S. Bourinot. Ottawa: The Editor, 1960.

– Papers. National Archives of Canada, Ottawa, ON.

– *Selected Poems.* Ed. Edward Killoran Brown. Toronto: Ryerson, 1951.

– *Some Letters of Duncan Campbell Scott to Archibald Lampman and Others.* Ed. Arthur S. Bourinot. Ottawa: Bourinot, 1959.

Scott, Frederick George. *Collected Poems.* Vancouver: Clarke and Stuart, 1934.

– *A Hymn of Empire and Other Poems.* Toronto: William Briggs, 1906.

– *My Lattice and Other Poems.* Toronto: William Briggs, 1894.

– Papers. McCord Museum, Montreal, QC.

– *Poems: Old and New.* Toronto: William Briggs, 1900.

– *The Soul's Quest, and Other Poems.* London: Kegan Paul, Trench, 1888.

– *The Unnamed Lake, and Other Poems.* Toronto: William Briggs, 1897.

Scott, F.R. *Collected Poems.* Toronto: McClelland and Stewart, 1981.

Scott, William. *Hours with St. Paul and the Expositors of His First Epistle to the Corinthians, More Particularly Chapters III, IX, XIII.* Ottawa: J. Durie, 1888.

– *In the Battle Silences: Poems Written at the Front.* Toronto: Musson; London: Constable, [1915].

– *Letters on Superior Education: In Its Relation to the Progress and Permanency of Wesleyan Methodism.* Toronto: Wesleyan Book Room, 1860.

– *Report Relating to the Affairs of the Oka Indians Made to the Superintendent of Indian Affairs.* Ottawa: MacLean, Roger, 1883.

– *The Teetotaler's Hand-Book, in Four Parts Being a Compilation of Valuable Information for the Use of All Classes.* Toronto: Dredge, 1860.

Seeley, Sir J.R. *The Expansion of England: Two Courses of Lectures.* 1883. London: Macmillan, 1895.

Seneca. *Ad Lucilium Epistulae Morales.* Trans. Richard M. Gummere. 3 vols. Loeb Classical Library. London: William Heinemann; Cambridge: Harvard UP, 1917.

Shairp, John Campbell. *Aspects of Poetry, Being Lectures Delivered at Oxford.* 1881. Freeport, NY: Books for Libraries Press, 1972.

– *On Poetic Interpretation of Nature.* Boston: Houghton Mifflin, 1877.

Sharp, William. Rev. of *Among the Millet, and Other Poems,* by Archibald Lampman, and *La Légende d'un peuple,* by Louis Honoré Fréchette. *Academy* [London] 36 (23 Nov. 1889): 334–5.

– Rev. of *Low Tide on Grand Pré: A Book of Lyrics,* by Bliss Carman. *Academy* [London] 45 (6 Jan. 1894): 7–8.

– Rev. of *Songs of the Common Day, and Ave: An Ode for the Shelley Centenary,* by Charles G.D. Roberts. *Academy* [London] 44 (21 Oct. 1893): 534–5.

– ed. *Sonnets of This Century.* London: Walter Scott, 1887.

Shepard, Odell. *Bliss Carman.* Toronto: McClelland and Stewart, 1923.

Shrive, Norman. *The Voice of the Burdash: Charles Mair and the Divided Mind in Canadian Literature.* Post-Confederation Poetry: Texts and Contexts. London: Canadian Poetry Press, 1995.

Sicherman, Barbara. *The Quest for Mental Health in America, 1880–1917.* New York: Arno, 1980.

Sisson, C.J. *Shakespeare's Tragic Justice.* London: Lowe and Brydone, 1965.

Sladen, Douglas. *On the Cars and Off: Being the Journal of a Pilgrimage along the Queen's Highway to the East, from Halifax in Nova Scotia to Victoria in Vancouver's Island.* London: Ward, Lock and Bowden, 1895.

- 'To the Reader.' *Younger American Poets, 1830–1890.* Ed. Douglas Sladen. New York: Cassell, 1891. xxv–lii.
- ed. *Younger American Poets, 1830–1890.* New York: Cassell, 1891.

Slonim, Leon. 'A Critical Edition of the Poems of Duncan Campbell Scott.' Diss., University of Toronto, 1978.

Smith, Adam. *An Inquiry into the Nature and Causes of the Wealth of Nations.* Ed. J.E. Thorold Rogers. 2 vols. Oxford: Clarendon, 1869.

Smith, A.J.M. 'Introduction.' *The Oxford Book of Canadian Verse.* Ed. A.J.M. Smith. Toronto: Oxford UP, 1960. xxii–li.
- 'Light Verse.' *Princeton Encyclopedia of Poetry and Poetics.* Ed. Alex Preminger. 1965. Enlarged ed. Princeton: Princeton UP, 1974. 446–8.
- 'The Poetry of Duncan Campbell Scott.' *Duncan Campbell Scott: A Book of Criticism.* Ed. S.L. Dragland. Ottawa: Tecumseh, 1974. 115–34.
- 'Some Relations between Henry Vaughan and Thomas Vaughan.' *Papers of the Michigan Academy of Science, Arts and Letters* 18 (1933): 551–61.

Smith, Goldwin. 'The Ascendancy of Gambetta.' *Bystander* [Toronto] 1 (June 1880): 377–8.
- 'The Book Duty.' *Bystander* [Toronto] NS 3 (July 1883): 169–70.
- 'Consequences of the Death of Gambetta.' *Bystander* [Toronto] NS 2 (April 1883): 130–5.
- 'Editorial.' *Bystander* [Toronto] NS 1 (Jan. 1883): 1.
- 'Mackenzie's Life of George Brown.' *Bystander* [Toronto] NS 1 (Jan. 1883): 70–8.
- 'Mr. Romanes on Evolution.' *Bystander* [Toronto] NS 2 (April 1883): 139–40.
- 'The New Governor General.' *Bystander* [Toronto] NS 3 (July 1883): 186–8.
- 'Positivism on the Death of Gambetta.' *Bystander* [Toronto] NS 2 (April 1883): 136–9.
- 'The Royal Society.' *Bystander* [Toronto] NS 3 (July 1883): 212–13.
- 'Third Parties.' *Bystander* [Toronto] NS 1 (Jan. 1883): 25.

Sommers, Carol Marie. 'The Letters of Archibald Lampman in the Simon Fraser University Library.' M.A. thesis, Simon Fraser University, 1979.

Sorfleet, John Robert, 'Transcendentalist, Mystic, Evolutionary Idealist: Bliss Carman, 1886–1894.' *Colony and Confederation: Early Canadian Poets and Their Background.* Ed. George Woodcock. Vancouver: U of British Columbia P, 1974. 189–210.
- ed. *Poems,* by Bliss Carman. New Canadian Library Original 9. Toronto: McClelland and Stewart, 1976.

*Speeches Delivered at the Public Meeting Held under the Auspices of the Toronto Branch of the Imperial Federation League in Canada on Saturday, 24th March, 1888.* Toronto: Ellis, Moore and Bangs, 1888.

Stebbins, Geneviève. *Delsarte System of Dramatic Expression.* New York: E.S. Werner, 1886.

– *Delsarte System of Expression.* 4th ed. New York: E.S. Werner, 1891.

Stedman, Edmund Clarence. *Poets of America.* 1885. New York: Johnson Reprint, 1970.

– ed. *A Victorian Anthology, 1837–1895: Selections Illustrating the Editor's Critical Review of British Poetry in the Reign of Victoria.* Boston: Houghton Mifflin, 1896.

Stephen, A.M. 'The Poetry of Charles G.D. Roberts.' *Queen's Quarterly* 36 (Winter 1929): 48–64.

Stephenson, Glennis. 'The Bitter-Sweet Rose: The Conception of Woman in Roberts' *The Book of the Rose.*' *Canadian Poetry: Studies, Documents, Reviews* 14 (Spring/Summer 1984): 53–63.

Stevens, Paul. 'Sir James David Edgar.' *Dictionary of Canadian Biography.* 12: 291–4.

Stevenson, Andrew. 'Lake Lyrics and Other Poems.' Rev. of *Lake Lyrics and Other Poems,* by William Wilfred Campbell. *Saturday Night* [Toronto] 3 (21 Dec. 1889): 6.

Stewart, A.C. *The Poetical Review: A Brief Notice of Canadian Poets and Poetry.* 1896. Ed. D.M.R. Bentley. *Canadian Poetry: Studies, Documents, Reviews* 1 (Fall/Winter 1977): 66–88.

Stewart, George, Jr. 'Some Canadian Writers.' *Independent* [New York] 42 (13 March 1890): 4–5.

Story, Nora. *The Oxford Companion to Canadian History and Literature.* Toronto: Oxford UP, 1967.

Stringer, Arthur. 'The Poet in Everyday Life.' *Addresses Delivered at the Dedication of the Archibald Lampman Memorial Cairn at Morpeth, Ontario.* London: Western Ontario Branch of the Canadian Authors' Association, 1930. 9–11.

Strong, William. 'Charles G.D. Roberts' "Tantramar Revisited."' *Canadian Poetry: Studies, Documents, Reviews* 3 (Fall/Winter 1978): 26–37.

[Sudduth, T.H.] Rev. of 'The Mother,' by William Wilfred Campbell. *Inter-Ocean* [Chicago] 20 (5 April 1891): 4.

Sukov, Martin. 'Introduction.' *A Practical Treatise on Nervous Exhaustion (Neurasthenia), Its Symptoms, Nature, Sequences, Treatment,* by George Miller Beard. 1880. 5th ed. New York: E.B. Treat, 1905. Rpt. New York: Kraus Reprint, 1971. 2a–2e.

Surette, Leon. 'Ezra Pound, Bliss Carman, and Richard Hovey.' *Canadian Poetry: Studies, Documents, Reviews* 43 (Fall/Winter 1998): 44–69.

Sweetser, M.F., ed. *The Maritime Provinces: A Handbook for Travellers.* Boston: James R. Osgood, 1875.

Swinburne, Algernon Charles. *Collected Poetical Works*. 2 vols. London: William Heinemann, 1924.

Symons, Arthur. 'Arthur Symons' Reviews of Bliss Carman.' Ed. Tracy Ware. *Canadian Poetry: Studies, Documents, Reviews* 37 (1995): 100–13.

– 'Two Unpublished Letters from Arthur Symons to Bliss Carman.' Ed. Tracy Ware. *English Language Notes* 28 (1991): 42–6.

T., J.G. 'A Canadian Poet.' *Anglia: Zeitschrift für Englische Philologie Suplement* 2 (1891–2): 315–19.

Taine, Hippolyte Adolphus. *Lectures on Art*. Trans. John Durand. 1875. New York: Henry Holt, 1889.

Taylor, Bayard. *Studies in German Literature*. New York: G.P. Putnam's Sons, 1879.

Taylor, M. Brook. 'Joseph Edmund Collins.' *Dictionary of Canadian Biography*. 12: 204–6.

Tebbell, John. *A History of Book Publishing in the United States*. 3 vols. New York: R.R. Bowker, 1973.

Tennyson, Alfred. *Poems*. Ed. Christopher Ricks. Longman's Annotated English Poets. London: Longmans, Green, 1969.

*Theocritus, Bion, and Moschus*. Ed. A. Lang. New York: Macmillan, 1896.

Thomas, Clara. 'Introduction.' *Canadians of Old*, by Philippe Aubert de Gaspé. Trans. Charles G.D. Roberts. 1890. New Canadian Library. Toronto: McClelland and Stewart, 1974. vii–xii.

Thompson, John Herd. 'Nicholas Flood Davin.' *Dictionary of Canadian Biography*. 13: 248–53.

Thomson, Edward William. 'Among the Millet.' Rev. of *Among the Millet, and Other Poems*, by Archibald Lampman. *Globe* [Toronto] 10 Aug. 1889, 4.

– 'Concerning Archibald Lampman and Sir John Macdonald.' Editorial. *Globe* [Toronto] 12 March 1890, 4.

Trehearne, Brian. 'Style and Mind in Lampman's "Among the Timothy."' *Canadian Poetry: Studies, Documents, Reviews* 45 (Fall/Winter 1999): 66–98.

Tucker, James A. 'The Poems of William Wilfred Campbell.' *University of Toronto Quarterly* 1 (May 1895): 140–5.

Van Steen, Marcus. *Pauline Johnson: Her Life and Work*. Toronto: Musson, 1965.

Vincent, Thomas. 'Bliss Carman's "Low Tides."' *Canadian Literature* 129 (Summer 1991): 130–37.

Wade, H.G. 'Bliss Carman's Shrine.' *Western Home Monthly* [Winnipeg] 32 (Feb. 1931): 28

Wagner, Charles. *The Simple Life*. Toronto: William Briggs, 1904.

Wakefield, Edward Gibbon. *England and America: A Comparison of the Social and Political State of Both Nations*. 1834. Reprints of Economic Classics. New York: Augustus M. Kelly, 1967.

Waldron, Gordon. 'Canadian Poetry: A Criticism.' *Canadian Magazine* [Toronto] 8 (Dec. 1896): 101–8.

Walkley, A.B. 'Introduction.' *The Treasure of the Humble*, by Maurice Maeterlinck. Trans. Alfred Sutro. New York: Dodd, Mead; London: George Allen, 1897.

Wallace, W. Stewart. *Macmillan Dictionary of Canadian Biography*. Toronto: Macmillan, 1945.

Ward, Thomas Humphry, ed. *The English Poets: Selections in the Critical Introductions*. 1880. 4 vols. 1885. Rpt. New York: Books for Libraries, 1971.

Ware, Tracy. 'The Beginnings of Duncan Campbell Scott's Poetic Career.' *English Studies in Canada* 16 (1990): 215–31.

– 'Bringing "Gladness out of Sorrow": *By the Aurelian Wall*.' *Bliss Carman: A Reappraisal*. Ed. Gerald Lynch. Reappraisals: Canadian Writers. Ottawa: U of Ottawa P, 1990. 111–27.

– 'Charles G.D. Roberts and the Elegiac Tradition.' *The Sir Charles G.D. Roberts Symposium*. Ed. Glenn Clever. Reappraisals: Canadian Writers. Ottawa: U of Ottawa P, 1984. 39–53.

– 'D.C. Scott's "The Height of Land" and the Greater Romantic Lyric.' *Canadian Literature* 111 (1986): 10–25.

– 'A Generic Approach to Confederation Romanticism.' Diss. University of Western Ontario, 1984.

– 'The Integrity of Bliss Carman's *Low Tide on Grand Pré*.' *Canadian Poetry: Studies, Documents, Reviews* 14 (1984): 38–52.

– 'Notes on D.C. Scott's "Ode for the Keats Centenary."' *Canadian Literature* 126 (1990): 646–8.

– 'Remembering It All Well: "Tantramar Revisited."' *Studies in Canadian Literature* 8 (1983): 221–37.

– ed. 'Letters to Bliss Carman, 1890–92, from Campbell, Lampman, and Scott.' *Canadian Poetry: Studies, Documents, Reviews* 27 (1990): 46–66.

– *A Northern Romanticism: Poets of the Confederation*. Canadian Critical Editions. Ottawa: Tecumseh, 2000.

Westbrook, Perry P. *John Burroughs*. Twayne's United States Authors Series 227. Boston: Twayne, 1974.

Wetherell, J.E. 'Preface.' *Later Canadian Poems*. Ed. J.E. Wetherell. Toronto: Copp, Clark, 1903.

– ed. *Poems of Wordsworth (from Arnold's Selections)*. Toronto: Gage, 1892.

– *Later American Poems*. Toronto: Copp Clark, 1896.

Wicksteed, Gustavus William. *Waifs in Verse and Prose*. Ottawa: Bureau, 1894.

Wiebe, Robert H. *The Search for Order, 1877–1920*. New York: Hill and Wang, 1967.

Willison, Sir John. *Sir George Parkin: A Biography*. London: Macmillan, 1929.

Woodcock, George. 'Introduction.' *Canadian Writers and Their Works.* Poetry
    Series. Vol. 2. Ed. Robert Lecker, Jack David, and Ellen Quigley. Downsview:
    ECW, 1983. 7–24.

Woodworth, Harry A. 'Roberts' Poetry of the Tantramar.' Anniversary Number.
    *Chignecto Post and Borderer* [Sackville, NB], Sept. 1895, 1–7.

Woodworth, Marguerite. *History of the Dominion Atlantic Railway.* Kentville, NS:
    Kentville Publishing for Dominion Atlantic Railway, 1936.

Wordsworth, William. *Poetical Works.* Ed. E. de Selincourt. 1940. 5 vols. Oxford:
    Clarendon, 1963.

*Working Glossary for the Use of Students of Theosophical Literature.* 1st ed. New York:
    The Path, 1892.

# Index

Aberdeen, Lord, 261

Acklom, George M., 276, 286, 288

Adam, Graeme Mercer, 55, 56, 89, 92, 358n11, 360n19

Adams, James Eli, 303n25

Adams, John Coldwell, 24, 33, 34, 54, 192, 194

Adams, Thomas, 205

Addison, Joseph, 26

aesthetic-decadent movement, 22, 222

Aldrich, Thomas Bailey, 50, 117, 123, 331n33

Alexander, James Ellis, 320n12

Alexander, William John, 100, 323n31

Alexandra, Queen of England, 272

Alighieri, Dante, 216, 321n19

Amiel, Henri-Frédérick, 235

Anderson, Benedict, 88

Anderson, George, 29, 306n9

Anderson, William S., 132

Anglicanism. *See* religion and spirituality

annexationism, 16, 26, 29, 49, 50, 70, 88, 89, 92, 321nn17, 19, 322n20, 324n32, 331n15

anti-modernity, 214, 293, 294, 361n9

Appleton, 343n11

Arndt, Ernst Moritz, 109

Arnold, Matthew, 19, 20, 44, 58, 86n, 93n, 125, 135, 136, 141, 165, 166, 173, 183, 184, 189, 206, 213, 224, 274, 276, 337n19, 341n5, 342n6, 358n10

Aroostock War, 325n33

Artelle, Steven, 318n1

arts and crafts movement, 214

Ashley, William James, 261

'At the Mermaid Inn' column, 12, 13, 54, 122, 123, 256, 257; Campbell in, 12, 13, 123, 124, 125, 128, 148, 188, 208, 287, 290, 301n10, 331n17, 349n29, 360n18; Carman in, 174; demise of, 13, 125; Lampman in, 54, 122, 125, 148, 149, 155, 172, 228, 235, 257, 342n7, 349n30; Duncan Campbell Scott in, 172, 174, 201, 235, 333n28, 345n1

Aubert de Gaspé, Phillipe-Joseph, 98, 99

Audubon Society, 156, 337n13

Aylen, Elise, 232

Bacon, Francis, 95

Baker, Lorin Ellis, 192

Ballstadt, Carl, 41

Barbizon School, 332n17

Baring-Gould, Sabine, 216

Barron, Frederick William, 247

Barron, John Augustus, 247

Barrus, Clara, 163

Barry, Lilly E.F., 118

Bator, Paul Adolphus, 178

Baxter, J.B.M., 295

Beard, George Miller, 183, 189, 190,
    341nn3, 4, 343n9

Beckow, S.M., 41

Bengough, John Wilson, 282, 431n2

Berger, Carl, 41, 49, 91, 210, 301n16,
    319n9, 322n23

Bhojwani, Maia, 271, 328n4

Bigot, François, 98, 323n27

Birbalsingh, Frank, 301n16

Bismarck, Otto, Prince von, 109

Bjørnson, Bjørnstjerne, 189

Blake, William, 214, 222

Blavatsky, Helen, 207

Blewett, Jean, 299n3

Bliss, Donald, 204

Bok, Edward William, 259, 353n24

Boone, Laurel, 210, 299n1, 332n17,
    333n24, 346nn7, 8, 352n13, 361n4

Botsford, Belle Warner, 237n

Bourdieu, Pierre, 16, 83, 206

Bourinot, John George, 39, 106, 262,
    290, 341n2, 355n35, 360n19

Boyesen, H.H., 351n7

Breton, Jules, 332n17

Brock, Isaac, 91, 97

Brockett, L.P., 309n14

Brooke, Frances, 146

Brooke, Rupert, 361n7

Brown, E.K., 131, 231, 233, 295, 296,
    356n46

Brown, John Henry, 274

Browning, Robert, 19, 162, 173,
    306n8, 352n14

Brownlow, Edward Burrough
    ('Sarepta'), 121, 316n41

Bryant, William Cullen, 103

Bryce, George, 324n30

Bunner, H.C., 351n7

Burns, Robert, 331n16

Burpee, Lawrence J., 267

Burroughs, John, 20, 59, 145–76, 189,
    227, 269, 275, 335n4, 336nn9, 10,
    337nn12, 18–21, 339n33, 340n42,
    356n42

Byron, Lord, 36, 224, 302n20

'Bystander,' 45, 49

Cabot, John, 9,15

Cabot, Sebastian, 38

Callimachus, 132

Callwood, June, 314n35

Cameron, George Frederick, 10, 11,
    101–2, 118, 121, 134, 242, 259,
    316n41

Cameron, Mrs John, 254

Campbell, Archibald, 226

Campbell, Bruce F., 228

Campbell, William Wilfred, 3; and
    imperialism, 14, 130–1, 210, 291,
    292, 333n24, 344n15; and 'log-roll-
    ing,' 280–1, 284–90, 358n13,
    359n14; and nationalism, 130,
    333n24; and natural environment,
    187–9; and plagiarism, 21, 176,
    197, 263, 274, 275, 280; and poetic
    form and technique,113, 123–5,
    128–31; and politics, 210; psychol-
    ogy of, 288; and religion, 204, 207–
    12, 212n; reputation of, 241, 249,
    250–4, 255, 257, 259–60, 261, 262,

272, 273, 274, 283–5, 295; and Roberts, 102, 103, 104, 107, 128, 133; and therapeutic culture, 187–9, 191, 192; *Works:* 'At Even,' 124; 'An August Reverie,' 187, 188, 343n8; 'Autumn,' 262; 'Bereavement of the Fields,' 272; 'Canadian Folk Song,' 252; *The Canadian Lake Region,* 192; 'Crowning of Empire,' 130; 'December in the Lake Region,' 252;'The Discoverers,' 130; 'The Divine Origin,' 20; *The Dread Voyage: Poems,* 8, 102, 209, 260, 262, 274; 'Dusk,' 257; 'An Empire's Greeting,' 272; 'England,' 130; 'Hildebrand,' 358n10; 'How One Winter Came to the Lake Region,' 252; 'Immortality,' 210, 212; 'In Autumn,' 262; 'In the Strength of the Morning,' 187, 188, 209; 'In the Winter Woods,' 252; 'Keziah,' 104; 'Lake Huron,' 250; *Lake Lyrics and Other Poems,* 8, 104, 128, 208, 260, 288, 345n5; 'A Lake Memory,' 104, 128; 'Lazarus,' 354n25; 'The Lazarus of Empire,' 210, 346n7; 'Maguire's Nan,' 253; 'Manitou,' 104; *Mordred and Hildebrand: A Book of Tragedies,* 279, 280, 283, 318n1; 'The Mother,' 252–3, 254, 255, 257, 258, 263, 265, 266, 274, 281, 284, 352n13, 356n40; 'National Thanksgiving Chant,' 130; 'Ode to Canada,' 130; 'Our Heritage,' 130, 131; 'Pan the Fallen,' 252, 271, 357n1; 'Pitching Hay,' 124; *Poems!,* 300n8; 'Poetry and Piracy,' 142, 275; 'Sebastian Cabot,' 130; *Snowflakes and Sunbeams,* 6, 102, 103, 104, 108, 128,

133, 282, 352n12; 'The Tragedy of Man,' 210, 211, 346n8; 'Vapor and Blue,' 252; 'Victoria,' 130; 'When the Birds Fly Home,' 282

'Canada First' movement, 16, 26, 32, 33, 39, 49

Canadian Authors' Association, 3, 294–5

Canadian literature evenings, 28, 39, 242, 246, 255, 256

Canadian Pacific Railway, 16

Canadianism, 68, 72–110, 120, 210, 321n19, 322n21, 323n25

Cappon, James, 21, 57, 62, 66, 100, 293

Carlyle, Thomas, 19, 224, 227, 278, 311n27

Carman, Bliss, 3; and Acadia, 87–8; and April, 147–8, 162–5, 337nn21–2, 340n41; and influences and plagiarism, 13, 21, 132, 142, 176, 197, 275, 278–80, 337n21, 357n7, 358n10, 358–9n13; and Lampman, 105; legal studies, 339n31; 'log-rolling,' 284, 290; memorial, 295; and modernism, 292; and nationalism, 87–8; and natural environment, 147–8, 161–9, 171–2, 280; and poetic form and technique, 132, 138, 139, 141–4, 327n4; psychological and physical health of, 200, 214, 343n9; reading tours, 293, 295, 361n10; and religion and spirituality, 166–9, 204, 213–23, 291, 348n20; relocation to New York, 13–14, 52; reputation of, 139, 245, 249, 250, 254, 259, 260, 261, 271–5, 283–5, 293–6; and Roberts, 48, 50, 52, 53, 87, 90, 111, 115, 116, 118, 140; and therapeutic culture, 193,

195–201; and unitrinianism, 193,
196, 197, 200–1, 212, 218, 223; and
Vigilantes, 292; and Young Canada,
52; *Works: April Airs: A Book of New
England Lyrics*, 163; 'April Weather,'
163; 'At Michaelmas,' 279; *Ballads
and Lyrics*, 294; 'Behind the Arras,'
222, 348n21; *Behind the Arras*, 220–
2, 234, 282; 'La Belle Canadienne,'
46; 'Beyond the Gamut,' 221, 222;
'Clarion,' 90; 'Corydon: An Elegy'
('Death in April'), 165–7, 339n29;
'Easter Eve,'163, 164, 165, 167, 168,
339n34; 'Easter Hymn,' 204; 'The
Eavesdropper,' 198, 278, 357n7;
'The Friendship of Art,' 200,
338n25; 'The Great Return,'
346n11; 'Immanence,' 347n18; 'In
the Wings,' 222; 'The Juggler,' 222;
*The Kinship of Nature*, 162, 163, 199,
200, 207; *Later Poems*, 168; 'The
Lodger,' 222; 'Low Tide on Grand
Pré,' 87–8, 93n, 141–4, 213, 275,
335n35, 357n4; *Low Tide on Grand
Pré: A Book of Lyrics*, 9, 111, 138, 140,
141, 190, 222, 260–2, 293, 294,
334n34, 335n35, 357n3; 'Marjorie
Darrow,' 160, 171–5, 275; 'Mar-
jory,' 340n36; 'Mr. Charles G.D.
Roberts,' 357n3; 'The Night
Express,' 173,174, 222, 340nn38,
40; 'Olaf Hjörward,' 340n41; 'On a
Ball Programme,' 329n6; 'On
Ponus Ridge,' 339n34; 'A Pagan's
Prayer,' 213; *Pipes of Pan*, 15, 163,
201, 222; *Poems*, 294; *Poems* (1931),
327n4; *The Poetry of Life*, 199, 200;
'Pulvis et Umbra,' 278; 'The Reed
Player,' 271; 'Resurgam,' 167, 168,
339n34; *The Rough Rider and Other
Poems*, 167, 201, 339n34; *Sanctuary:
Sunshine House Sonnets*, 327n4; *Sap-
pho: One Hundred Lyrics*, 15, 88n,
164, 201, 345n20, 361n3; 'A Sea
Child,' 340n36; 'Shamballah,' 219;
*Songs of the Sea Children*, 219–20; 'A
Spring Feeling,' 348n22; 'Spring
Song,' 163, 164, 213; 'Sweetheart of
the Sea,' 294; 'The Vernal Ides,'
162, 165; 'Wanderers,' 358n10;
'Wild Geese,' 294; 'The Yule
Guest,' 271

Carman, Bliss, and Lorne Pierce, *Our
Canadian Literature*, 326n40

Carman, Bliss, and Mary Perry King,
*Daughters of Dawn: A Lyrical Pageant
or Series of Historical Scenes for Presentation with Music and Dancing*, 200;
*Earth Deities and Other Rhythmic Mas-
ques*, 200; *The Making of Personality*,
200, 223; *The Man of the Marne and
Other Poems*, 200

Carman, Bliss, and Richard Hovey,
Vagabondia series, 199, 223, 283,
339n34, 344n18, 345n18; 'The
Adventurers,' 199; 'At the End of
the Day,' 199; 'Comrades,' 199;
'Jongleurs,' 199; 'Holiday,' 199;
'Vagabondia,' 199

Cartier, Jacques, 38, 74

Caverhill, W.C.F., 38

Cawein, J. Madison, 351n7

Chamberlain, Joseph Edgar, 272

Champlain, Samuel de, 74

Chandler, Amos Henry, 305n5,
315n40

Chandler, George, 317n48

*Chap-Book*, 140, 208, 281, 302n22,
345n4, 346n9, 357n3

Charlesworth, Hector W., 253, 306n6

Chateauguay, Battle of, 74, 76, 97

Chaucer, Geoffrey, 162

Chautauqua (Canadian), 294

Christian natural theology. *See* religion and spirituality

Christianity. *See* religion and spirituality

Chrysler's Farm, Battle of, 74, 75, 76

Clark, Edward B., 161

Clark, Maud ('Queen of Bohemia'), 160, 193

Clark, William, 261, 282, 355n34, 359n14

Clarke, William, 29, 306n9

climate. *See* natural environment

Clote Scarp (or Scaurp). *See* Glooscap

Clough, Arthur Hugh, 243

Cogswell, Fred, 57

Coleman, Helena, 8, 9, 300n6

Coleridge, Samuel Taylor, 128, 135, 333n23

Collier, William Francis, 360n1

Collins, Joseph Edmund, 17, 24, 42–7, 49, 53–5, 56, 59, 61, 99, 102, 121, 128, 178–9, 180, 214, 290, 305nn3, 5, 306n6, 307n10, 308n13, 309n17, 310n22, 312n28, 313n32, 315n40, 316nn42, 44, 319n8, 320n15, 321n19, 322n23, 330n12, 360n19; biographical sketch of, 304n2; early influence on Lampman, 33; early influence on Roberts, 24–7; historical romances, 24, 53

Colvin, Sidney, 302n21

Conant, Thomas, 260, 354n30

Connor, Carl Y., 33, 34, 35, 45, 47, 48, 52, 155, 156, 226, 247, 294, 308n13, 309n16, 312n31

Conway, Don, 361n8

Cook, Ramsay, 312n32

Cook, Terry, 321n15

Copeland and Day, 138, 140, 220, 237n, 334n34, 346nn12, 13

copyright, 46, 47, 56, 324n32

Corot, Jean-Baptiste Camille, 332n17

Corse, Sarah M., 301n16

cosmopolitanism (universality, internationalism), 3, 17, 22, 48, 59, 60, 61, 62, 63, 67, 68, 93, 94, 101, 102, 112, 114, 175, 248, 286, 288, 313n32, 315nn40–1

Courthope, W.J., 135

Cram, Ralph Adams, 346n13

Crawford, Agnes, 344n17

Crawford, Annie, 194

Crawford, Isabella Valancy, 11, 46, 108, 285, 296, 312n29

Crémazie, Octave, 324n32

Crofton, Frances Blake, 101

Cropsey, Jasper Francis, 136

Cross, Ethelbert F.H., 315n41

Crowell, Norton B., 320n14

Culler, A. Dwight, 19

Dana, James, 126, 332n20

Daniells, Roy, 9, 296, 362n14

Darwin, Charles, 34, 210, 311n26

Daulac, Adam. *See* Dollard des Ormeaux

David, Richard, 38, 39

David Nutt (publishing house), 334n34

Davies, Barrie, 331n17

Davies, Gwendolyn, 71

Davin, Nicholas Flood, 26, 27, 28, 29, 30, 31, 32, 39, 42, 59n, 247, 305n5, 306nn6, 8, 307nn10–11, 308n12, 310n19, 355n32

Dawson, Edward, 258–9

Dawson, Sir William, 179

Day, Frederick Holland, 214, 215, 220
de Béranger, Pierre-Jean, 310n18
De Mille, James, 174
Deacon, William Arthur, 295
Dean, Misao, 360n2
decorum, 116, 125–6
Delaumosne, Abbé, 344n17
Delsarte, François, 192, 193–4, 195, 196, 200, 212, 223
Denison, George Taylor, 75, 88, 89, 90, 91, 105
Dewart, Edward Hartley, 41, 242, 354n29
*Dial* (Chicago), 10, 85, 196, 221, 324n33, 329n7
Dilke, Sir Charles Wentworth, 72
Disraeli, Benjamin, 40, 310n19
Djwa, Sandra, 58, 205, 206
Dollard des Ormeaux (Adam Daulac), 87, 97
Douglas, Ann, 345n19
Douglas, Mary, 286
Doyle, James, 183, 248
Dragland, Stan, 296
Dresser, Horatio W., 341n1
Drummond, William Henry, 300n5
Dufferin, Lord, 146
Duffy, Sir Charles Gavan, 37, 39, 41, 310n17
Duncan, Sara Jeannette, 11, 16, 301n10
Durand, Laura Bradshaw ('Pharos'), 262, 334n33, 354n28
Durham, Lord, 301n15

Early, L.R., 18–19, 35, 149, 203, 302nn19, 22, 309n14, 312n30, 329n9, 349n34
Eaton, Arthur Wentworth Hamilton, 325n37

Eaton, Timothy, 17
'eclectic detachment,' 176
Edgar, James David, 311n26, 354n29
Edgar, Pelham, 131, 238, 316n7, 355n32
elasticity, 79, 111, 113, 122, 136, 137
Eleusinian mysteries, 88n, 164, 212, 338n25
Eliot, T.S., 293
Ellis, Edwin J., 215
Emerson, Ralph Waldo, 20, 102, 103, 116, 148, 157, 162, 183, 184, 214, 227, 335n35, 337n21, 347n13
environmental determinism, 28, 33, 51, 59, 60–1, 67–9, 79–80, 136, 137, 145–6, 148–50, 175, 306nn6, 8, 306–7n10, 322n20, 335n1
Evans, Rev. W.F., 343n8
'Exodus' (brain drain), 16, 57, 77, 255–6, 258, 261, 313n35, 350n3

Faber, Richard, 40,
Fawcett, Edgar, 116, 117, 122, 133, 329n9, 351n7
Fawcett, Millicent Garrett, 83
Fenianism, 331n14
Fichte, Johann Gottlieb, 109
Field, Eugene, 344n17
First World War, 18, 200, 238, 268–9, 270, 292–3, 361n7
Fisher, Roswell, 321n19
Fiske, John, 207, 208, 355n38
Flaubert, Gustave, 18, 235
formalism. *See* poetic form and genre
Forman, William Henry, 136
Foster, William Alexander, 39, 146
Foy, Frederick F., 352n13
'fraternalism,' 8, 12, 13, 14, 31, 286. *See also* masculinity
Fréchette, Achille, 351n5

Fréchette, Louis-Honoré, 27–8, 42, 45, 47, 54, 59, 133, 246, 306n8, 315n40, 323n28
Frederic, Harold, 222
French, Donald G., 4, 299n3
Frost, Robert, 272
Fussell, Paul, 342n7

Gale, Norman, 354n28
Galt, Sir Alexander, 311n26
Gambetta, Léon, 227, 302n20, 311–12n27
Ganong, Jean Murray (Muriel), 348n22
Garland, Hamlin, 183, 226, 351n6
Garneau, François-Xavier, 324n32
Geddes, Gary, 238
Genesis, 210
Gerson, Carole, 71
Gibbon, Edward, 268
Gilder, Richard Watson, 11, 50, 89, 98n, 116, 263, 289, 321n18, 335–6n5, 351n7
Gilman, Charlotte Perkins, 341n4
Gilmore, David D., 303n25
Gladstone, William Ewart, 37
Globe (Toronto), 12, 25, 190, 242, 243, 244, 252, 253, 254, 255, 256, 259, 260, 261, 262, 275, 276, 277, 278, 279, 280, 282, 286, 334n33, 349n1, 350n2, 352nn13–14, 16–17, 19–20, 354n28, 355nn32–3, 357n4, 358n10
Glooscap (Gluskâp, Clote Scarp, Clote Scaurp), 81, 82, 86, 190, 319n7, 325n37
Gnarowski, Michael, 303n24, 335n3, 359n15
Goethe, Johann Wolfgang von, 48, 109, 133, 244

Golden Dawn, Order of the, 230
Goldsmith, Oliver, 122
Goodhue, Grosvenor, 346n13
Gordon, Arthur Hamilton, 81
Gordon, Charles William ('Ralph Connor'), 299n3
Gordon, General Charles George, 76
Gosse, Edmund, 112, 113, 222
Grant, George Monro, 65, 75, 89, 91, 316nn43, 46
Green, Thomas Hill, 95–7, 226
Greig, Peter E., 326n38, 328n4, 333n31
Griffin, Watson, 321n19
Griffith, William, 162
Grove, Frederick Philip, 296
Guiney, Louise Imogen, 214, 215, 223, 345n4, 346–7n13
Gummere, Francis B., 333n23
Gundy, H. Pearson, 165, 334n34
Gustafson, Ralph, 77
Guthrie, Norman, 294

Haight, Canniff, 242,
Haliburton, R.G., 146
Haliburton, Thomas Chandler, 15, 101, 324n32
Haliburton Society, 96, 101, 107, 174, 323n25
Hamilton, William B., 64
Hammond, Melvin Ormand, 148
Hammond, William Alexander, 323n30
Hansen, Marcus Lee, 314n35
Harrison, Frederic, 227, 312n27, 349n29
Harrison, Susan Frances ('Seranus'), 11, 299n3, 301n10, 341n2, 354n29, 355n32
Harte, Walter Blackburn, 12, 248–51,

253, 259, 286, 289, 301n11,
332n17, 351n9, 360n19
Hathaway, Rufus H., 293, 339n34,
362n13
Hatton, Joseph, 344n16
Haultain, Theodore Arnold, 118n,
241
Hawthorne, Nathaniel, 17, 227
Hayes, William, 309n13
Headon, Christopher Fergus, 205
Heavysege, Charles, 17, 114, 118,
324n32
Heine, Heinrich, 303n23
Hellenism, 58, 168, 226
Henley, W.E., 348n22
Herbin, John Frederic, 58
Herder, Johann Gottfried, 40, 41, 79,
145, 146, 148
High Church movement. See religion
and spirituality
Hilts, Joseph Henry, 242
Hingston, William H., 146, 335n1,
336n6
Hobsbawm, Eric, 318n5
Holmes, Oliver Wendell, 103, 116,
329nn7, 8
Holmgren, Michele J., 41, 303n1
Homer, 199, 252, 310n18, 336n9
Hood, Thomas, 331n16
Horace, 132, 303n26
Horning, Lewis Emerson, 261, 287,
354n31
Hovey, Richard, 13, 14, 22, 139, 142,
192, 193, 195–7, 199, 200, 213, 216,
218, 220–2, 235, 236, 347n18,
353n22. See also Carman, Bliss
Howe, Joseph, 308n12, 325n43
Howells, Annie, 351n5
Howells, William Dean, 244–7, 249,
263, 273, 281, 288, 289

Hudson, Henry, 38
Hunter-Duvar, John, 101–2, 114,
325n34
Hurst, Alexandra J., 276, 286
Huxley, T.H., 34, 206

Ibsen, Henrik, 235
imperialism, 14, 16, 29, 30, 70, 86,
88–92, 94, 141, 210, 291, 301n16,
311n26, 320n14, 321nn15–16,
322n21, 324n32
Imrie, John, 352n14
independence (Canadian), 16, 25,
43, 45, 47, 49, 50, 70–2, 88, 90, 94,
313n32, 324n32, 350n4
Independent (New York), 13, 214, 216,
250–2, 257, 260, 263, 279, 289,
326n42, 328n4, 340nn38, 40–1,
347n17
'Indian' subjects. See Native peoples,
myths, legends
Ingersoll, William Ernest, 190
Irving, Washington, 80, 136, 137, 145,
147, 149, 150, 189, 334n30

Jackel, David, 57, 71
Jessup, Lynda, 361n9
Johnson, E. Pauline, 4, 8, 9, 10, 11,
12, 14, 119, 255, 256, 259, 261, 274,
282, 285, 301n10, 317n48, 352–
3n21, 355nn32, 33
Johnson, Helen M., 242
Jones, D.G., 57
Jones, K.L., 350n3

Kappeler, Jessie, 219
Keats, John, 18, 19, 20, 102, 112, 114,
135, 144, 151, 187, 257, 302n21,
326n1, 336n7, 351n10
Keble, John, 205

Keith, W.J., 5, 57, 62n, 84, 331n17

Kennedy, Howard Angus, 300n5

Kidd, Adam, 22, 303n28

Kilpatrick, Ross S., 126, 328n5, 332n20

King, Mary Perry, 200, 223. *See also* Carman, Bliss

Kipling, Rudyard, 162, 210, 275

Kirby, William, 75, 95, 98, 322n23, 323n27

Kizuk, R. Alexander, 361n9

Klein, A.M., 296

Klinck, Carl F., 13, 20, 280, 295–6

Koester, Charles Beverley, 306n6

Kraus, Joe W., 220, 334n34

Lacolle Mill, Battle of, 97, 326n26

Lampman, Archibald, 3; and Joseph Edmund Collins, 24, 33, 35, 44, 47, 54–5; and influences and plagiarism, 18–20, 58, 86, 136, 147, 148, 326n1, 351n10; memorial cairn, 294, 295; and nationalism, 33–6, 40; and natural environment, 145–57, 181; and poetic form and technique, 113, 114, 118, 119, 121, 123, 126, 128, 134, 135, 137, 138, 145; psychological and physical health of, 52, 178, 203; and religion, 204, 223–31; reputation of, 241, 243–51, 254, 259, 260–1, 272–4, 282, 283, 285, 294–6; and Roberts, 48, 51, 104–5, 111, 114–16, 119–20, 133, 134; and therapeutic culture, 52, 178–87, 198, 202–3; *Works:* 'After Mist in Winter,' 257; 'Alcyone,' 231; *Alcyone,* 135, 137, 152, 204, 230, 231; 'Among the Millet,' 86, 102, 182; *Among the Millet, and Other Poems,* 8, 86, 102–5, 116,

118, 120, 125, 133, 135, 137, 139, 152, 187, 189, 197, 224, 243, 249, 260, 261, 325n34, 326n38, 328n4, 332n17, 336n5, 351n6, 357n4; 'Among the Timothy,' 20, 52, 153, 182–8, 197, 202, 243, 244, 343n7, 351n6; 'April,' 52, 151, 152, 182, 183; 'April in the Hills,' 149, 154; 'At the Ferry,' 355n33; 'At the Long Sault: May 1660,' 87, 98n; 'At the Railway Station,' 174; 'An Athenian Reverie,' 224; 'The Autumn Waste,' 153; 'Ballade of Summer's Sleep,' 329n6; 'Ballade of Waiting,' 329n6; 'The Better Day,' 226; 'Between the Rapids,' 86, 243, 244, 263–6, 351n6, 356n41; 'The Character and Poetry of Keats,' 19, 326n1; 'The City of the End of Things,' 260, 272, 356n45; 'The Clearer Self,' 231; 'The Comfort of the Fields,' 154, 198; 'The Coming of Winter,' 46; 'Derelict,' 115; 'The Dog,' 126, 244; 'Easter Eve,' 224; 'The Fairy Fountain,' 52; *Fairy Tales,* 302n20; 'A Fantasy,' 54; 'The Favorites of Pan,' 23, 58, 226, 271; 'The Frogs,' 137, 151, 181, 183, 245; 'German Patriotic Poetry,' 34, 36, 310n21; 'Godspeed to the Snow,' 154; 'The Growth of Love,' 52; 'Hans Fingerhut's Frog Lesson,' 52, 179–80; 'Happiness,' 224; 'Heat,' 52, 124, 153–4, 181, 183, 184, 187, 188, 197, 202, 245, 278, 342n7, 351n6, 357n7; 'An Impression,' 181; 'In March,' 152, 328n4; 'In November,' 126, 155; 'In October,' 52, 124, 156, 225; 'In the Pine Grove,' 156; 'Indian Summer,' 152;

'Inter Vias,' 349n31; 'An Invitation to the Woods,' 202–3; 'An Invocation,' 250; 'The Lake in the Forest,' 15, 87, 231, 336n9; 'The Land of Pallas,' 20, 226, 227, 231, 348n27; 'The Largest Life,' 231; 'The Last Sortie,' 35, 115; 'The Loons,' 86; *Lyrics of Earth*, 9, 137, 138, 154, 198, 226, 283; 'Manitou,' 87; 'The Martyrs,' 224; 'Midsummer Night,' 351n5; 'The Modern School of Poetry in England,' 134, 137, 184, 330n13, 348n25; 'The Monition,' 46–7; 'The Monk,' 224; 'Nesting Time,' 156; 'An October Sunset,' 152; 'An Old Lesson from the Fields,' 126; 'On the Companionship with Nature,' 156–7; 'The Organist,' 224; 'Peccavi Domine,' 229; *Poems*, (1900) 230, 294; 'Poetic Interpretation,' 135, 184; 'The Poetry of Byron,' 302n20, 348n25; 'The Poets,' 271; 'The Poet's Song,' 279; 'The Return of the Year,' 154; 'The Revolt of Islam,' 303n20; 'The Robin,' 156; 'Sirius,' 257; *The Story of an Affinity*, 48, 225, 333n29; 'Style,' 184, 330n13, 332n18; 'The Sun Cup,' 154; 'The Sweetness of Life,' 226; 'Temagami,' 15; 'Three Flower Petals,' 54; 'The Three Pilgrims,' 224; 'To a Millionaire,' 226; 'To My Wife,' 182; 'To the Warbling Vireo,' 156; 'The Truth,' 126, 245, 328n4; 'Two Canadian Poets: A Lecture,' 10, 80, 111, 118, 121, 122, 134, 136, 137, 145, 149, 175, 330n13; 'A Vision of Twilight,' 231; 'Vivia Perpetua,' 231; 'We Too Shall Weep,' 231; 'What Do Poets Want with Gold?,' 244; 'White Pansies,' 231; 'Winter,' 244; 'Winter-Break,' 328n4; 'Winter Evening,' 312n30; 'Winter Hues Recalled,' 152, 243, 244; 'Winter Store,' 154, 212, 228, 338n26, 349n30; 'Winter's Nap,' 312n30; 'The Woodcutter's Hut,' 23; 'Xenophanes,' 226

Lampman, Archibald, Senior ('Crowquill'), 204, 205, 336n6, 345n2

Lamson, Wolffe, 140, 220

Lang, Andrew, 105, 266, 336n25, 358n11

Lanier, Sidney, 52, 116, 142

Lathrop, G.P., 351n7

Laurier, Sir Wilfrid, 247–8, 253, 352n16

Lawrence, Margaret, 223, 340n35

Le Gallienne, Richard, 14, 223

Le Sueur, W.D., 92

Lears, T.J. Jackson, 178, 214, 267, 341n1, 346n13

Lee, H.D.C., 348n21

Lefebvre, Henri, 63

Leisner, August, 347n18, 348n19

Leland, Charles G., 81, 82, 319n7

Lesperance, John (Jean Talon), 94, 325n34

Lewes, George Henry, 227

Lewis, Wyndham, 293

Lighthall, William Douw ('Wilfred Chateauclair'), 4, 8, 9, 12, 17, 79, 82, 89, 92–8, 107, 120, 226, 227, 242, 249, 284, 300n5, 307n10, 321n19, 322nn21–3, 323nn23–4, 325nn34–5, 359n16

Lloyd, J.A.T., 172, 173

Locke, John, 145–6

Locker-Lampson, F., 329n7

Lockhart, Arthur John ('Pastor Felix'), 173, 175, 251, 322n21, 325nn34, 37, 351n10
'log-rolling,' 263, 280, 282, 358n11, 359nn12–13
Logan, John Daniel, 4, 119, 299n3
Logan, John Edward ('Barry Dane'), 315n41
London, Jack, 161
Longfellow, Henry Wadsworth, 21, 48, 81–5, 87, 103, 116, 190, 191, 250–2, 262, 274, 306n8, 325n37
Longley, James Wilberforce, 315n41, 321n17
Lorne, Marquis of, 26, 66, 360n19
Louise, Princess, 66
Lovell, John, 38
Lowell, James Russell, 54, 183
Loyalists, 75, 80, 83, 204, 319n9
Lundy's Lane, Battle of, 75, 238, 361n7
Lynn, Helen, 156

Macdonald, Sir John A., 16, 17, 26, 33, 49–50, 89, 246, 305n3, 306n6, 360n19
MacFarlane, W.G., 122n, 134, 254
Machar, Agnes Maule ('Fidelis'), 11, 118, 244, 259, 265, 301n10, 307n10, 315n41, 319n7, 341n2, 355n32
MacKay, Isabel Ecclestone, 299n3
Mackay, Mary ('Maria Corelli'), 347n14
Mackaye, Steele, 193
Macoun, John, 226
Maeterlinck, Maurice, 22, 220, 221n, 235, 236, 238, 239, 361n5
magazine verse, 12, 124, 274, 284, 287, 330n12

Magoon, C.L., 79
Mair, Charles, 32, 33, 91, 92, 102, 242, 307n10, 324n33, 325n34
Malloch, Faith L., 299n1
Malvin, James, 303n25
Mangan, Clarence, 37
Mangan, J.A., 303n25
Marquis, Thomas Guthrie, 26, 32, 40, 77, 119, 257, 262, 307–8n12
Marston, Philip Bourke, 135–7, 333n28
Martell, Carol E., 323n30, 348n18
masculinity, 8, 12, 13, 14, 20, 31, 43, 53, 54, 73, 92, 122, 201, 251, 259, 303n25. See also fraternalism
Masefield, John, 236, 272, 295
McArthur, Peter, 10, 276, 286, 299n3, 357nn2, 7
McDougall, Robert L., 232, 295, 332n17
McGee, Thomas D'Arcy, 24, 38, 39, 41, 146, 285, 303n1, 306nn6, 8, 308n12, 310n18, 321n34
Mckeggie, May, 52
Mckenzie, William Patrick, 249, 351n9
McLachlan, Alexander, 17, 242, 285
McLean, Kate Seymour, 114, 315n40
McLeod, Les, 18–19, 302n19
McMechan, Archibald, 4, 8, 11, 12, 300n7, 352n18
McNeill, Alexander, 253, 352n16
McQuoid, Mary, 359n13
Mercier, Alan, 234
Meredith, George, 235
Merrill, Helen E., 254
Meteyard, Thomas, 220
Methodism. See religion and spirituality
Meyer, Donald, 178, 340n1

Miles, Alfred Henry, 104
Miller, Joachim, 116
Miller, Joseph Dana, 273–6, 278, 279, 281, 288, 301n13, 358n10
Miller, Muriel, 213, 221, 223, 339n29, 346n13, 347n18, 361n10
Millet, Jean-François, 118, 125, 320n11, 331n17
Milnes, Richard Monckton, Lord Houghton, 302n21
Milton, John, 211, 212, 216, 252, 267, 317n48, 321n19, 351n10
mind-cure. *See* therapeutic techniques, culture, and writing
Mirabeau, Honoré Gabriel Riqueti, Comte de, 312n27
Mitchell, S. Weir, 183, 341nn4, 5, 7
modernism, 3, 18, 22, 55, 173, 270, 295, 296, 299n2, 361n8
Montcalm de Saint-Servan, Marquis de, 74, 75
Montesquieu, Charles-Louis de Secondat, 79, 148
Montreal Society for Historical Studies, 100
Moore, Charles Leonard, 50, 71, 78, 116
Moore, Thomas, 86, 265, 310n18
More, Sir Thomas, 95
Morgan, Henry J., 39
Morgan, Mary, 101–2
Morris, James Henry, 350n3
Morris, William, 20, 36, 113, 135, 172, 219, 227, 235, 303n26
Morse, Charles, 277, 357n5
Mott, Frank Luther, 282, 353n24
Moulton, Louise Chandler, 332n17, 333n28
Mount, Nick, 313n35
Muddiman, Bernard, 236

Müller, Karl Otfried, 164, 338n25
Müller, Max, 207
Mulvaney, Charles Pelham, 27, 305n5, 315n40
Murray, Heather, 323n31, 346n5
Murray, R., 65, 319n7
Myers, F.W.H., 30n
mysticism. *See* religion and spirituality
mythology and folklore. *See* religion and spirituality

nationalism and nationalistic movements: Canadian (Young Canada) 24–69, 78–9, 101, 109, 141, 175, 242, 249, 255, 291, 293, 310n18, 325n33, 350n4, 357n4 (*see also* 'Canada First' movement, Canadianism, and Young Canada); English (Young England), 39, 40, 42, 310n19; German, 34, 40–2, 309n16; Irish (Young Ireland), 24, 27, 28, 36–40, 42, 68, 146, 303n1, 306n6, 321n19; literary, 25, 306n6, 312n28; Romantic, 16, 24, 34–5, 40. *See also* patriotic poetry
Native peoples, myths, legends, 80–2, 94, 175, 231, 256; Campbell and, 208; Lampman and, 87; Roberts's treatment of, 319n7; Duncan Campbell Scott's treatment of, 292; Frederick George Scott's treatment of, 108
natural environment: climate and landscape, 5, 21, 43, 67, 84, 136, 190; flora and fauna, 148, 150, 153, 294, 335n2, 336n6, 337nn10, 20, 339n33, 356n42. *See also* environmental determinism; religion and spirituality

'Nature Fakir' controversy, 161
nature worship. *See* religion and spirituality
nature writing, 5, 20, 218, 332n17
Neatby, Hilda, 38
neo-platonism. *See* religion and spirituality
New, W.H., 299n4
New Criticism, 57, 296
New Woman, 11
Newcomb, Simon, 83
Nietzsche, Friedrich Wilhelm, 206
Noel, Roden, 19, 302n20
Norse culture, 175
North West Rebellion, 16
Norton, Charles Eliot, 346n13
Nutt, Alfred Trubner, 334n34

O'Brien, Cornelius, 355n32
O'Brien, Kevin, 302n18
occultism. *See* religion and spirituality
O'Connell, Daniel, 306n6
O'Donnell, Kathleen M., 303n1
O'Hagan, Thomas, 28, 68, 72, 253, 254, 282, 285, 306n8, 359n14
Olmstead, Frederick Law, 177–8, 180, 183, 184, 198
O'Neill, Patrick, 310n20
Opie, Iona and Peter, 340n36
O'Reilly, John Boyle, 351n7
Orphic mysteries, 164, 166
Ottawa Literary and Scientific Society, 121, 137, 303n23
Ovid, 132
Oxley, James MacDonald, 180, 341n4, 353n24

Pacey, Desmond, 57, 84, 219, 296
Pan, 58–9, 212, 226, 252, 269, 271, 356n43

pantheism. *See* religion and spirituality
Parker, Gail Thain, 178, 340n1
Parker, George L., 313n35
Parker, Gilbert, 4, 5, 8, 9, 220n, 258, 285, 353n24
Parkin, George Robert, 20, 89–91, 303n26, 320n15, 321nn16, 18
Parkman, Francis, 75, 98n
Parnell, Charles Stewart, 37
Parrish, Stephen Maxfield, 214, 347n13
Pater, Walter, 235, 338n25
patriotic poetry, 34, 71, 121
Payne, William Morton, 85, 139, 189, 196, 221, 222
Pearson, Charles H., 257
Perkins, David, 272
Phillips, Wendell, 122, 330n14
picturesque, the, 80, 84, 126–9, 136, 254, 316n43; *Picturesque Canada*, 65, 66, 75, 81, 89, 190, 316nn43, 46
Pierce, Lorne, 4, 66, 132, 308n13
Plato, 95, 219, 235, 349n35
Playter, Dr Edward, 178, 341n3
Playter, Maud, 52, 178
Plotinus, 238
Poe, Edgar Allan, 21, 102, 103, 116, 138, 252, 267, 274, 275, 356n40, 357n1
poetic form and genre, 12, 58, 114, 115, 119, 121, 129–31, 196–7, 262, 266, 283, 314nn38–40, 330n12, 331n16, 355n37; ballad, 42, ballade, 103, 113, 114, 119–21, 126, 133, 137, 315n40, 329n6; chant royal, 113; choriambic, 58, 114, 328n5; epyllion, 82, 87; ode, 114; ovidian elegiac metre (dactylic hexameter and pentameter), 58, 62,

128, 333n23; rondeau, 113–15, 119, 126, 133; rondel, 113, 115; Sapphic, 58, 114, 328n5; sonnet, 84–6, 113, 114, 116–21, 124–7, 130–1, 134, 137, 138, 141, 156, 172, 287, 327nn3–4, 328n4, 330n12, 333n28, 355n37; and technique, 119, 195, 197; triolet, 103, 113, 115, 120, 126, 329n6; *vers de société* ('society verse'), 116–17, 133, 329n7; versification, 175, 283; villanelle, 103, 113, 120

politics, 16, 25, 43, 45, 47, 49, 50, 70–2, 88, 90, 94, 313n32, 324n32. *See also* annexationism; imperialism; independence; nationalism; social liberalism; socialism; Young Canada; Young England; Young Ireland

Pollock, Francis Lillie, 279–81, 358n8

Pomeroy, E.M., 25, 40, 46, 48–51, 57, 58, 71, 72, 78, 117, 161, 194, 205, 213, 219, 272, 294, 295, 308n13, 361n10

Pope, Alexander, 284, 308n12

positivism, 227, 312n27

Pound, Ezra, 18, 272

Pratt, E.J., 295, 296

Pre-Raphaelites and Pre-Raphaelitism, 20, 132, 133, 135, 172, 214, 224, 303n26, 318n1. *See also* Morris, William; Rossetti, Dante Gabriel; Swinburne, Algernon Charles

Propertius, 132

Pusey, E.B., 205

Queenston Heights, Battle of, 74, 75

Quiller-Couch, Arthur, 348n21

'racy of the soil,' 28, 68, 69, 146

Rand, Theodore Harding, 349n1

Ranger, Terence, 318n5

Reade, John, 37, 71, 72, 91, 94, 134, 305n5, 307n10, 318n3, 324n32, 325n34, 341n2, 355n32

realism, 84–5, 157, 161, 173–4 291, 360n2

Red River Rebellion, 16

Reed, T.A., 205

regionalism, 5, 15, 16, 59, 63, 68, 78–86, 245, 259, 278

religion and spirituality: Anglicanism, 204, 205, 206, 207, 213, 216, 217, 225, 292; Christian Natural Theology, 216; Christianity, 15, 22, 76–7, 97, 163, 164, 167, 169, 204–11, 216–18, 223–30, 239, 267–8, 271, 323n30, 343n8, 345n1, 348nn19–20; High Church Movement, 205; Methodism, 204, 205, 232; mysticism, 213, 235; mythology and folklore, 206, 208, 210, 216; natural religion, 164, 166, 169, 209, 212, 338n25; nature worship, 22, 212; neo-platonism, 22, 212, 215, 219, 238, 343n8; occultism, 22, 207, 212, 230, 235, 349nn35–6; pantheism, 22, 212, 213, 216–18; Rosicrucianism, 215, 230; spiritualism, 168, 207; Theosophy, 22, 168, 207, 210, 212, 215, 219, 227–9, 232, 238, 349nn32–3; transcendentalism, 20, 212, 214, 219, 227–8, 238, 335n35; unitrianism, 193, 196, 197, 200, 201, 212, 218–23. *See also* entries under individual poets

Rhys, Ernest, 92, 93

Riel rebellion, 73, 77, 108

Riley, James Whitcomb, 123, 351n7

Ritchie, J.A., 34, 47, 52, 312n31

Ritchie, Leslie, 303n23

Roberts, Charles G.D., 3; academic career of, 12, 14, 32, 59, 77–8, 100, 101, 320n10, 323n30, 333n23; and Acadia, 64, 78, 82–5; and the animal story, 291; assault charge against, 309n13; as critic, 17, 102, 254, 302n22, 329n9; and French Canada, 75–6, 78, 98, 99; and 'Indian Legend,' 80–2; influences, 18, 19, 20, 324n32; 326n1; and Joseph Edmund Collins, 24–8, 31–5, 37, 42–6, 49, 53–6, 59, 60–2; as leader, 5, 14, 15, 36, 42, 103, 107, 115, 118, 242, 245, 251, 257, 259, 263, 276, 278, 285, 286, 291, 318n1; and 'log-rolling,' 280; and modernism, 292–3; and nationalism (Canadianism, Young Canada), 24, 25, 31–6, 39–40, 49, 59, 70–86, 88–94, 96–107, 109–10, 321n19, 323n25; and natural environment, 145–8, 157–61; physical and psychological health of, 12, 13, 14, 52, 70, 189, 190, 193, 194, 214, 263, 301n12, 343n10; and poetic form and technique, 111–23, 125–8, 131, 132, 314nn38, 39; and politics, 24, 31–3, 36, 45, 70, 324n32; promotion of other poets, 17, 105, 107, 263, 326n39; reading tours, 293, 295; and religion, 204, 212–13, 216–19, 348n19; reputation of, 28, 43, 241–2, 245, 249–51, 254, 257–61, 272, 274, 283–5, 293, 295; and therapeutic culture, 178, 189–94, 344n14; *Works:* 'Actaeon,' 58; 'American Vers de Société,' 329n9; 'Ariadne,' 349n1; 'Around the Campfire,' 283; 'At Pozzuoli,' 126; 'Authors at Home. XII. Goldwin Smith at the Grange,' 70, 313n32; 'Autochthon,' 105–7, 212, 213, 326n40; 'Ave: An Ode for the Shelley Centenary,' 9, 120, 123, 216, 257–8, 260, 284, 352n22; 'The Ballad of Crossing the Brook,' 23, 194; 'Beausejour,' 98; 'The Beginnings of a Canadian Literature,' 59, 61, 67, 75–6, 79, 111–12, 114, 315n40, 317n46, 323n28; 'La Belle Tromboniste,' 117; 'Birch and Paddle,' 53, 94, 294; *The Book of the Native*, 131, 161, 217–18, 283, 333n27; *The Book of the Rose*, 14, 161, 219; 'A Breathing Time,' 58; 'Burnt Lands,' 94; *Bystander*, contributions to, 45–6, 49; 'Canada,' 11, 31, 71–8, 93, 94, 98n, 100, 107, 133, 212, 326n40, 357n4; 'Canadian Poetry in Its Relation to the Poetry of England and America,' 20, 212, 213; 'Canadian Streams,' 123, 331n15; 'Canadians Are We,' 71; *The Canadians of Old (Cameron of Lochiel)*, 98–9; ' A Child's Prayer at Evening,' 217; 'A Christmas Eve Courtin',' 323n29; 'Collect for Dominion Day,' 71, 73, 77, 94, 133; 'The Cow Pasture,' 157, 344n14; 'The Departing of Clote Scarp' ('The Departing of Gluskâp'), 82, 86, 94, 133, 190, 325n37; 'Drowsihood,' 241; 'Earth's Complines,' 218; *Earth's Enigmas: A Book of Animal and Nature Life*, 161, 221n, 283; *Echoes from Old Acadia*, 82, 319n8, 325n37; 'Edgar Fawcett,' 52, 116–18, 329n7; 'The Flight of the Geese,' 152, 294; 'Frogs,' 94, 151, 335n5; 'The Furrow,' 124, 127, 128,

158, 159; 'The Future of Canada,'
90; *The Haunters of the Silences: A
Book of Animal Life*, 161; 'The Hermit Thrush,' 159–60, 340n42; *A
History of Canada*, 75, 90; 'How the
Mohawks Set Out for Medoctec,'
98; 'The Iceberg,' 57; *The Iceberg
and Other Poems*, 293; 'Immanence,'
347–8n18; *In Divers Tones*, 8, 54, 65,
82, 85, 86, 108, 119, 133, 260,
318n3, 320n11; 'In the Night
Watches,' 294; 'In Nôtre Dame,'
52; 'In September,' 126; 'In the
Wide Awe and Wisdom of the
Night,' 216, 347nn16, 17; 'Introduction,' *Haliburton: The Man and
the Writer*, by Francis Blake Crofton,
101; 'Iterumne?' 126; 'The Keepers
of the Pass,' 98; *The Kindred of the
Wild: A Book of Animal Life*, 161,
189, 195; 'Kinship,' 195, 213; *The
Land of Evangeline and the Gateways
Thither*, 83, 191; 'Launcelot and the
Four Queens,' 318n1; 'Liberty
(From the French of Louis-Honoré
Fréchette),' 323n28; 'Literature
and Politics,' 109; 'The Marvellous
Work,' 117; 'Memnon,' 58, 241;
'Miriam,' 58; 'Mother of Nations,'
318n4; 'Mr. Bliss Carman's Poems,'
357n3; 'New Brunswick,' 65, 81,
316n43; *New Poems*, 361n12; 'New
Year's Eve (*After the French of
Fréchette*),' 323n28; 'New York Nocturnes,' 219, 348n19; *New York Nocturnes and Other Poems*, 14, 132, 161,
218–19; 'A Nocturne of Consecration,' 219, 272; 'Notes on Some of
the Younger American Poets,' 52,
116, 117; 'An Ode for the Canadian Confederacy,' 71–3, 77, 79,
106; 'Off Pelorus,' 26; 'Oliver Wendell Holmes,' 329n7; 'On the Night
Trail,' 161; 'Origins,' 213, 218;
'Orion,' 58, 113, 114; *Orion, and
Other Poems*, 4, 8, 25, 27, 32, 33, 42–
4, 54, 60, 61, 113, 114, 116, 118,
119, 121, 126, 132, 133, 139, 204,
212, 241, 242, 310n22, 311n25,
314n40, 328n5, 332n20; 'Out of
Pompeii,' 178; 'The Outlook for
Literature: Acadia's Field for
Poetry, History, and Romance,' 78–
84, 86, 87; 'Pastoral Elegies,' 100,
338n28, 347n15; 'The Pipes of Pan,'
23, 57–9, 61, 122, 133, 189, 211,
271; *Poems*, 294; 'Poems of Wildlife,' 189, 325n34; 'The Poet Is Bidden to Manhattan Island,' 50, 133;
'The Poetic Outlook in Canada,'
92, 326n41; 'The Poetry of Nature,'
218, 219; 'The Potato Harvest,' 84–
5, 133, 320n11, 328n4; 'The Quelling of the Moose,' 82, 133; 'The
Quest of the Arbutus,' 194; *The
Raid from Beauséjour, and How the
Carter Boys Lifted the Mortgage: Two
Stories of Acadie*, 98–9; 'The Rawdon's Luck,' 64, 316n42; 'Reckoning,' 123; 'Renewal,' 194;
'Reporting in New York,' 52; 'Res-
urrection,' 194; 'Rondeau / *To
Louis Honoré Fréchette*,' 323n28;
'The Savour of the Soil,' 146; *A Sister
for Evangeline: Being the Story of
Yvonne de Lamourie*, 161, 218; 'The
Slave Woman,' 52; 'The Solitary
Woodsman,' 23; 'Songs of the Com-
mon Day,' 93, 126, 332n17, 347n16;
*Songs of the Common Day and Ave: An*

*Ode for the Shelley Centenary*, 9, 93n, 99, 151, 152, 157–61, 219, 257, 260–2, 282, 320n11, 336n5, 344n14, 354n26; 'The Sower,' 50, 117, 125–7, 320n11, 337n16, 344n14; 'Spring Breaks in Foam,' 294; 'The Squatter,' 361n8; *The Sweet o' the Year and Other Poems*, 361n12; 'Tales from the Lumber Camp,' 319n6; 'Tantramar Revisited,' 46, 57–9, 61–8, 77, 79, 82, 83, 93, 94, 122, 128, 133, 206, 265; 'The Teaching of English Literature,' 100; 'The Tide of Tantramar,' 340n36; 'To Fredericton in May-Time,' 126; 'To the Memory of Sidney Lanier,' 52; 'To Winter,' 94; 'The Unsleeping,' 213, 346n9; *The Vagrant of Time*, 294, 361n12; 'The Vengeance of Gluskap' ('Menagwes'), 190; 'The Waking Earth,' 120, 158; 'When Milking-Time Is Done,' 151, 336n5; 'Whitewaters,' 216; 'The Wood Frolic,' 344n14; 'The Work of the English Department,' 147; *The Young Acadian: or, The Raid from Beauséjour*, 98–9; 'The Young Ravens That Call upon Him,' 22, 220n

Roberts, George Goodridge, 204, 205

Roberts, Goodridge Bliss, 96, 104, 107, 214

Roberts, Jane Elizabeth Gostwycke, 325n34

Roberts, Theodore Goodridge, 205

Robinson, Edwin Arlington, 272

Rockwell, A.P., 341n4

Rogers, Charles Gordon, 281, 355n12

Romanticism, 18–19, 20, 23, 62, 148, 157, 173, 270, 299–300n4

Romantic-Victorian tradition, 3, 173, 265, 326n40

Roosevelt, Theodore, 161, 201

Roper, Henry, 323n30

Rosicruceanism. *See* religion and spirituality

Ross, Malcolm, x, 4, 33, 205

Rossetti, Christina, 112

Rossetti, Dante Gabriel, 20, 86n, 113, 118, 138, 142, 160, 172, 214, 216, 219, 233, 235, 265, 275, 303n26, 333n28

*Rouge et Noir* (Toronto), 34, 35, 44, 227, 310n22, 311n25, 27

Royal Society of Canada, 26, 61, 273, 292, 293, 323n32, 354n32, 355n35

Royce, Josiah, 213, 219

Runeberg, Johan Ludwig, 48

Ruskin, John, 132, 303n26, 316n43, 346n13

Russell, George ('A.E.'), 300n6

Russell, Henrietta, 192–6, 200, 223

Sallussii, C. Crispi, 336n7

Sangster, Charles, 17–18, 75, 242

Saunders, Margaret Marshall, 299n3

Scandinavia, 48, 137, 145, 175

Schell, F.B., 316n46

Schiller, Johann Christoph Friedrich von, 109

Schlegel, Friedrich von, 40

Schopenhauer, Arthur, 206

Schwarz, Michiel, 286

Scott, Duncan Campbell, 3; health of, 203; influences, 175, 303n23; and modernism, 293; and Native peoples, 15, 131; and natural environment, 169–71; and poetic form and technique, 111, 113, 131, 327n3; and religion, 204, 231–9,

292; reputation of, 249, 251, 255, 256, 259, 272, 274, 282, 285, 295–6; and *symbolisme,* 173, 233; and therapeutic culture, 201–2; *Works:* 'At Gull Lake: August, 1810,' 131, 361n5; 'At the Cedars,' 356n41; 'The Battle of Lundy's Lane,' 361n7; 'Chiostro Verde,' 238; *The Circle of Affection and Other Pieces in Prose and Verse,* 15; 'Compline,' 238; 'The End of the Day,' 169, 170; 'The Fifteenth of April,' 169, 170; 'The Forsaken,' 131; *The Green Cloister: Later Poems,* 238, 293; 'The Height of Land,' 238, 239, 270, 292; 'In the Country Churchyard,' 262; 'In May,' 169; *In the Village of Viger,* 201, 232–3, 237n, 283; *Labor and the Angel,* 169, 201, 236, 237n; 'Lines Written in Memory of Edmund Morris,' 238; *Lundy's Lane and Other Poems,* 238, 361n7; 'The Magic House,' 233; *The Magic House and Other Poems,* 8, 111, 169, 210, 233, 234, 237n, 251, 260–2, 271, 354n28; 'March,' 169, 170; 'Meditation at Perugia,' 238; *New World Lyrics and Ballads,* 15, 170, 236; 'On the Way to the Mission,' 131; 'The Onondaga Madonna,' 131; 'The Piper of Arll,' 174, 236, 237, 270–2, 276; *Poems,* 294; 'Rain and the Robin,' 169; 'Reality,' 238; 'The Reed Player,' 251, 255, 263, 264, 269–71, 352n11; 'A Scene at Lake Manitou,' 131; 'The Sea by the Wood,' 236; 'September,' 169, 170; 'The Sleeper,' 234; 'Song' ('I have done...'), 108; 'To a Canadian Aviator Who Died for His

Country in France,' 292; 'Veronica,' 255; 'Watkwenies,' 131; 'The Wood by the Sea,' 236

Scott, Frederick George, 4; and natural environment, 169; and poetic form and technique, 113, 115, 116, 300n7; and religion, 169, 204, 205, 255, 267–9, 271, 292; reputation of, 254–5, 259, 262–4, 272, 274, 285, 294, 296; *Works:* 'Aestheticism,' 108; *Alton Hazlewood: A Memoir, by His Friend,* 254; 'Catholicism,' 108; 'Columbus,' 355n37; 'Dion,' 264, 355n36; 'Evolution,' 107; The Frenzy of Prometheus,' 268, 355n37; 'In Memoriam: Those Killed in the Canadian North-West 1885,' 108; 'In the Winter Woods,' 169; 'Justin,' 107; *Justin and Other Poems,* 300n8; *My Lattice and Other Poems,* 9, 14, 254, 260–3, 268, 282; 'Requiescant,' 272, 292; 'Samson,' 254–5, 263, 264, 267–9, 355n37; 'Shakespeare,' 113; 'A Song of Triumph,' 255; 'The Soul's Quest,' 107; *The Soul's Quest, and Other Poems,* 8, 107, 108, 205, 242; 'Via Mortis,' 264, 274, 355n37; 'Wahonomin,' 108

Scott, F.R., 3, 293
Scott, Sir Walter, 26, 310n18, 318n1
Scott, William, 204
Scudder, Horace Elisher, 334n31, 338n27, 339n30
Seeley, Sir J.R., 130
Seneca, 61
Shairp, John Campbell, 19, 20, 135, 184–5, 249, 302n22, 337n19
Shakespeare, William, 135, 317n48

Sharp, William ('Fiona McLeod'), 92–3, 93n, 245–6, 328n4, 339n29, 351n9

Shaw, George Bernard, 227

Shelley, Percy Bysshe, 18, 27, 34, 36, 77, 100, 114, 123, 224, 252, 257, 302n20, 351n10, 353n22

Shepard, Odell, 139, 204, 223, 293, 339n34

Sheppard, Edmund Ernest, 313n32, 321n19

Sherman, Francis, 205, 299n3

Sherwood, William Albert, 242

Shrive, Norman, 91, 92

Sicherman, Barbara, 341n1

Sidney, Sir Philip, 141

Simpson, A., 65, 319n7

Sladen, Douglas, 92, 104, 134, 213, 281, 322n20, 325n37, 326n41

Small, Maynard, 140

Smith, A.J.M., 5, 77, 176, 235, 291, 329n7, 349n36

Smith, Adam, 83, 84

Smith, Goldwin, 16, 45, 48–50, 59n, 70, 71, 89, 90, 253, 311n27, 313n32, 318n27, 319n8, 321n17

Smith, Mary Barry, 94

Smith, William Wye, 94

Smythe, Albert E., 8, 276, 299n3, 300n6

social liberalism, 95–7, 226

socialism, 97, 226–7

Society for the Propagation of the Gospel, 204

Society of Canadian Literature, 100, 323n32

Solas, Frank, 81

Sorfleet, John Robert, 167, 204, 213, 294, 346n10

Spenser, Edmund, 272

spiritualism. See religion and spirituality

spontaneity, 112, 118–19, 121, 134, 136, 333n28, 334n33

Stebbins, Genevieve, 193, 344n17

Stedman, Edmund Clarence, 11, 42, 93n, 117, 147, 157, 263, 323n30, 329n11, 351n6, 360n1

Steele, Sir Richard, 26

Stephen, A.M., 293

Stephenson, Glennis, 360n2

Stevens, Paul, 311n26

Stevens, Wallace, 272

Stevenson, Andrew, 345n5

Stevenson, Robert Louis, 275

Stewart, A.C., 8, 284–5, 359n17

Stewart, George, Jr, 319n8, 341n2, 357n4

Stewart, Phillips, 326n41

Stoddard, Richard Henry, 272

Stone and Kimball, 139–40, 334n34

Story, Norah, 33

Stringer, Arthur, 294–5, 299n3, 356n1

Strong, William, 57

sublime, the, 128–9, 130, 131, 136, 141, 147

Sudduth, T.H., 252, 253

Sukov, Marvin, 341n4

Sutro, Alfred, 238, 349n37

Sweetser, M.F., 81

Swinburne, Algernon Charles, 20, 36, 44n, 53–4, 62, 102, 113, 114, 128, 135, 138, 210, 212, 219, 249, 251, 303n26

Sylvester, J.J., 142

Symbolism (symbolisme), 22, 173, 174, 220–2, 234, 236, 237

Symonds, John Addington, 19, 302n20

Symons, Arthur, 222

Taine, Hippolyte Adolphus, 146, 148

Taylor, Bayard, 26

Taylor, M. Brook, 24, 33, 53, 54

Tebbell, John, 343n11

Tennyson, Alfred, Lord, 15, 19, 82, 94n, 107, 113, 114, 124, 128, 133, 135, 209, 212, 249, 251, 258, 273, 280, 285, 303n26, 306n8, 315n40, 318n1, 351n10

Theosophy. See religion and spirituality

therapeutic techniques, culture, and writing, 52–3, 80, 183, 341n3, 344n14; neurasthenia, 183, 189, 190, 191, 341n4, 343n9

Thompson, John Herd, 305n3

Thompson, Maurice, 351n7

Thompson, Michael, 286

Thomson, Edward William, 138, 154, 156, 203, 225, 229, 246–7, 249, 272, 281, 285, 319n6, 326n1

Thomson, James, 170

Thoreau, Henry David, 23, 155, 157, 162, 214, 227

Tibullus, Albius, 132

Tilley, Sir Leonard, 51

Torrey, Bradford, 155–7

tourism, 189–93, 316n45, 343nn11, 13, 361n4

transcendentalism. See religion and spirituality

Trehearne, Brian, 343n7

Tucker, James Alexander, 356n40, 356n1

Tylor, Edward Burnett, 266, 355n38

unitrianism. See religion and spirituality

Van Steen, Marcus, 14

variety, 111–13, 132–8, 141

Vaughn, Henry, 349n36

Vaughn, Thomas, 349n36

Victoria, Queen of England, 73

Victorianism, 20, 62, 173

Vincent, Thomas, 88

Virgil, 132, 303n26

Voorhis, Isabel, 187

Wade, H.G., 362n13

Wadell, Kate, 224

Wakefield, Edward Gibbon, 301n15

Waldron, Gordon, 283, 284

Walkley, A.B., 238

Wallace, W. Stewart, 285

'War among the Poets,' 13, 21, 123, 124, 142n, 263, 271, 273, 285, 291, 300n6, 301n13

War of 1812, 38, 64, 75, 98n, 319n9

Ward, T.H., 19

Ware, Tracy, 18–19, 302n19, 340n41, 357n6

Watters, R.E., 359n15

Watts, Theodore, 328n4

Webb, Sidney, 227

Week (Toronto) 45, 46, 47, 48, 52–5, 57, 58, 67, 70, 92, 107, 111, 116, 118, 119, 121, 122, 133, 172–4, 244, 253–5, 258, 271, 282, 283, 287, 308n13, 312n31, 313nn32, 34, 35, 315n41, 318n3, 330n14, 355n34, 358n11; Roberts's resignation from, 48–9, 52

Weir, Arthur, 101–2, 109, 325n34

Westbrook, Perry P., 148, 149, 160, 338n23

Wetherald, Agnes Ethelwyn, 11, 56, 254, 282, 299n3, 301n10, 355n32

Wetherell, J.E., 9–12, 189, 300n9, 331n15, 333n28; Later Canadian

*Poems*, 6–7 (photographs), 13, 107, 258–9, 353n23

Whitaker, Rev. George, 205

Whitman, Walt, 21, 116, 138, 148, 167, 172, 255, 275, 339n33, 340n42, 342n7

Whittier, John Greenleaf, 26, 262

Wickens, MaryLynn, 355n34

Wicksteed, G.W. ('W'), 172, 175

Wilde, Oscar, 17, 116, 302n18

Willis, Nathaniel Parker, 320n12

Willison, Sir John, 321n15

Willison, John Stephen, 242

Wilson, Sir Daniel, 249

Wiman, Erastus, 89

Winthrow, Henry, 56

Williams, Richard D'Alton, 37

Wolfe, General James, 74, 75

Woodcock, George, 57

Woodworth, Harry A., 333n23

Woodworth, Marguerite, 343n13

Wordsworth, William, 18, 62, 67, 86, 106, 128, 129, 135, 144, 152, 157, 165, 183–5, 187, 227, 228, 243, 244, 249, 259, 265, 317n48, 320n13, 331n16, 336n8, 338n26, 342n6, 354n28

word painting, 84, 123, 124, 126, 128, 138, 250, 252, 253, 320n11, 331n17, 344n14, 355n33

workmanship, 5, 12, 17, 34, 60, 62, 103, 104, 111–32, 134, 144, 256, 259, 264, 286, 288, 289, 334n31, 357n4, 360n18

World War I. *See* First World War

Yeats, William Butler, 207, 212, 215, 222, 230, 235, 238

Yeigh, Frank, 39, 242, 255–6, 306n7, 350n2

Young Canada, 24–69, 71, 97–8, 178

Young England. *See* nationalism

Young Ireland. *See* nationalism

*Youth's Companion* (Boston), 156, 202, 319n6, 336n5